# Selecting the President

# Selecting the President

From 1789 to 1996

 CONGRESSIONAL QUARTERLY INC.
WASHINGTON, D.C.

Book design and production by Kachergis Book Design,
Pittsboro, North Carolina

Printed and bound in the United States of America

The paper used in this publication meets the minimum requirements of the American National Standard for Information Science—Permanence of Paper for Printed Library Materials, ANSI Z 39.48-1984.

Cover illustration credits (clockwise from top right): Susan Biddle, White House; Library of Congress; New York Public Library; courtesy of Dwight D. Eisenhower Library; National Archives; Library of Congress.

Illustration credits and acknowledgments appear on page 227, which is to be considered an extension of the copyright page.

LIBRARY OF CONGRESS CATALOGING-IN-PUBLICATION DATA
Selecting the president: from 1789 to 1996.
        p.      cm.
        Includes bibliographical references and index.
        ISBN: 1-56802-312-x (alk. paper)
        1. Presidents—United States—Election—History.    2. Presidents—United States—Nomination.    3. Campaign finance—United States.
        I. Congressional Quarterly, Inc.
        JK524.S45  1997
        324.6'3'0973—dc21                                                           97-6398

# Table of Contents

# Preface

In 1789 when george washington was first elected president, there were no political parties, no primaries, no national conventions, no campaign financing, no poll taking, no presidential debates. From that first presidential election to the most recent in 1996, the process of selecting the president has changed dramatically. Nothing has changed so markedly over the years as the electorate. The expansion of the right to vote has steadily opened participation in what is arguably the most influential event in U.S. politics to all men, to all races, to all women, and to virtually all citizens of eighteen years or older.

The process for electing the president not only has shifted political power from the few to the many, but it also has become longer and more complicated. A presidential campaign must direct itself toward fund-raising, state primaries and caucuses, national conventions, televised debates, and the vote of electoral college. Complex national and state campaign laws must be closely followed. A vast array of people and organizations interlock in a campaign to elect one person president. And not least among these diverse elements are the candidates themselves who must address the substantive and symbolic issues of the day.

*Selecting the President: From 1789 to 1996* covers all aspects of presidential elections from the organizing of a presidential bid and a political party's nominating process to the general election campaign and the inauguration. Chapter 1, The Electoral Process, begins with a look at how the political process of electing the president has evolved from 1789 to the present day. This chapter then examines the modern nominating process, focusing on the decision to compete, campaign fund-raising, primaries and caucuses, national party conventions, and proposals for reform. This chapter also explores the general election campaign in terms of strategy considerations; the role of the media, campaign staff, political parties, and interest groups; the personal campaigning of the candidates; and the electoral college.

Chapter 2, Taking Office, discusses the period between the election day and the oath of office, during which presidents-elect put together their White House staffs. The organizational decisions and presidential appointments made during this transition period can be crucial to the success of the future administration. This chapter also takes a look at the pageantry of the inauguration: the ceremony itself, inaugural addresses, and the accompanying festivities.

Throughout U.S. history presidential politics have moved in cycles of conservatism and liberalism, activism and consolidation, elitism and populism, isolationism and internationalism. Presidential elections have been at the center of national discussions involving federalism, banking, tariffs and taxation, economic prosperity, corporate and union power, foreign affairs and wars, social welfare programs, and the size and scope of government. Chapter 3, Chronology of Presidential Elections, provides the history of the major events and issues of every presidential election from 1789 to 1996.

Tables and figures of historical data supplement the discussions in the *Selecting the President: From 1789 to 1996*. Each chapter concludes with a note section and a selected bibliography for further reading. A comprehensive index is also provided.

## Acknowledgments

The discussion of the 1996 election in Chapter 3 was written by Mark J. Rozell, associate professor of political science at American University.

# Contributors

CHARLES C. EUCHNER is assistant professor of political science at Holy Cross College. He has written several books, including *Extraordinary Politics: How Protest and Dissent Are Changing American Democracies* (1996).

JOHN ANTHONY MALTESE is associate professor of political science at the University of Georgia. His book *The Selling of Supreme Court Nominees* (1995) won the C. Herman Pritchett Award for best book in judicial politics from the American Political Science Association. He is also the author of *Spin Control: The White House Office of Communications and the Management of Presidential News*, second revised edition (1994).

CHAPTER 1

# The Electoral Process

BY CHARLES C. EUCHNER AND JOHN ANTHONY MALTESE

AGAINST a contemporary backdrop, the early days of presidential politics seem quaint. The early system aspired to be a *republic,* in which sovereign power resided in the electorate and was exercised by elected representatives of the people. *Democracy,* in the sense of *direct* rule by the people, was considered a pejorative term. The Founders premised their insulated system on the ability of an "electoral college" of the nation's most virtuous and learned men to rise above petty factions and select leaders with national vision.

Since the election of the first president, George Washington in 1789, the franchise, or right to vote, in U.S. presidential elections has expanded numerically and by class, sex, and race. In the 1824 presidential election, the first for which reliable statistics are available, only 3.8 percent of the population voted. By 1856, after states eased tax-paying and property qualifications, voter participation reached 16.7 percent. By 1920, after women had won the franchise, the figure rose to 25.1 percent. In 1928 participation of the voting age population topped 50 percent for the first time in a presidential election. Participation continued to rise to reach a high of 63 percent in 1960. By 1996, despite the "motor-voter" law that expanded the ease of registering to vote, participation had fallen to 49 percent.[1]

In the nation's early elections, only the upper economic classes could participate. Over the years, however, as different political factions sought national leadership, the electoral process opened up. By 1971 virtually every adult citizen at least eighteen years of age was eligible to vote. The presidential campaigns of Andrew Jackson, Abraham Lincoln, William Jennings Bryan, Theodore Roosevelt, Woodrow Wilson, Franklin D. Roosevelt, and Lyndon B. Johnson all appealed, in different ways, to an expanding electorate. In 1828, for example, Jackson's populist approach gave the growing number of voters hopes of landing jobs with the expanding federal government.

The process for electing the president not only has shifted political power from the few to the many but also has become longer and more complex, and more subject to the unintended consequences of reform and the changing technologies of business and everyday life. Indeed, elections never have been so simple as candidates making appeals to greater and greater numbers of citizens. Today, every campaign organization mediates the relations between the candidate and the voter. It may seem at times as if the candidate is speaking directly to a voter, but every move has been influenced by campaign workers, the media, consultants, and public attitudes.

In fact, overall, a vast array of interlocking elements now makes up the campaign to elect one person president. People involved in a campaign include the candidate and his or her family, a running mate, political allies, campaign strategists, lawyers and accountants, television producers and consultants, schedulers and advance people, advertising experts, issues experts, fund-raisers, pollsters, computer analysts, and sometimes the incumbent president. Organizations affecting the campaign include corporations, labor unions, interest groups, political action committees, the national party, and state parties. Constitutional requirements for candidates and complex national and state campaign laws establish rules for the campaign. The campaign must direct itself toward state primaries and caucuses, conventions, televised debates, and the vote of the electoral college (and possibly Congress). And not least among these diverse elements are the substantive and symbolic issues of the day.

## History of Presidential Elections

Presidential elections are perhaps the most influential events in national politics, giving shape to dominant issues, the makeup of national parties and interest groups, regional economic and political alignments, and the way citizens understand and talk about society.

Campaigns for the White House have shaped U.S. politics in several stages and cycles. For example, as the franchise has expanded and the electronic media have exercised greater influence over public thinking, presidential politics has become more broad-based and concerned about the way government can address the needs and demands of innumerable groups. Historically, presidential elections have been at the center of political controversies involving federalism, banking, tariffs and other taxes, economic change, corporate power, unions, international affairs, social welfare programs, moral values, consumer issues, and disputes among the branches of government. Meanwhile, presidential politics has moved in cycles of conservatism and liberalism, activism and consolidation, elitism and populism, isolationism and internationalism. Overall, presidential elections have articulated the changing moods of the nation since the very first election.

### ORIGINAL CONSTITUTIONAL PROVISIONS

The method of choosing the president proved to be but one of many vexing problems for the fifty-five men who assembled in Philadelphia in May 1787 to draft the Constitution. The Articles of Confederation, which the Constitution would replace, were riddled with weaknesses. Adopted in 1781, the Articles established an impotent federal government consisting of a weak Congress and no single executive (although there was a "Committee of States" with no significant power that sat when the Congress was not in session). By the time the Constitutional Convention convened, the confederation was but a "cobweb."[2]

From the start of the convention, it was clear that the federal government would be strengthened and that there would be some sort of executive branch. The convention was split, however, between those who wanted a strong executive (the "presidentialists") and those who were wary of executive authority and wanted to increase the power of the national legislature instead (the "congressionalists").[3]

There also was the question of whether the "national executive" should consist of several persons or just one. Congressionalists wanted a plural executive with minimal power. Presidentialists wanted a strong executive with power vested in the hands of one individual. Debate over this point was extremely heated.

As it became clear that the executive power would be singular, the tension between the two camps shifted to the question of presidential selection. Congressionalists, intent on having the executive remain subservient to the legislature, wanted the president to be elected by Congress. Presidentialists, however, did not want Congress to exercise that power.

This issue remained unresolved for most of the summer. By the end of August, there still was no consensus on how to select the president. Therefore, that issue—along with other "questions not settled"—was sent to the Committee on Postponed Matters for resolution. Since the committee was dominated by presidentialists, it pushed for a proposal that would avoid legislative appointment. The result was a compromise that was reported to the convention on September 4, 1787, and that served, with little alteration, as the basis for the actual constitutional provision.

The compromise, as finally approved, provided for indirect election of the president by what later would be known as the electoral college.[4] This system allowed each state to appoint (in the manner directed by its legislature) the same number of electors as it had senators and representatives in Congress. (Virginia, for example, had two senators and ten representatives in Congress and so could choose twelve electors.) Those electors would then meet in their respective states and vote by ballot for two persons (at least one of whom must be from a state other than that inhabited by the elector). When the ballots of all the electors from all the states were tallied, the candidate with the greatest number of votes would become president (assuming it was a majority), and the second-place candidate would become vice president. In case of a tie, or if no candidate received a majority, the House of Representatives would decide.[5]

The compromise won the support of the convention because it placated all parties concerned. First, it provided for the president to be selected by electors. This satisfied the presidentialists who were opposed to appointment by Congress. It also satisfied those who were wary of direct election by the masses. Electors, it was thought, would infuse an element of reason into the selection process, thereby stabilizing the whims of mass opinion.

Second, individual state legislatures were allowed to determine how electors would be chosen in their respective states. The language of the clause left open a wide range of options for that process. As a result, the convention did not have to agree on one method of appointing electors for all the states.

Third, if no candidate received a majority, the outcome of the election would be decided by the House of Representatives. Since it was widely assumed that no candidate after George Washington would receive a majority of votes from the electors, many thought that selection by the House would become the norm. Thus congressionalists could argue that they had lost the battle but won the war. From their perspective, electors usually would nominate candidates, and the House would select the winner.

Finally, since each elector voted for two persons—one of whom could not be from the elector's state—"favorite-son" candidates would tend to cancel one another out. This helped to dispel the fear that large states would consistently elect their own favorite sons. Nevertheless, since the number of electors from each state would equal the state's total number of senators and representatives in Congress, the relative weight of more populous states would not be discounted.

Despite the Framers' good intentions, numerous flaws emerged in the electoral system in the nation's early years. A constitutional crisis developed in 1800, for example, when both the presidential and vice-presidential candidates claimed to win the presidency. As a result, the Twelfth Amendment soon was adopted to prevent a repeat of that crisis. But however flawed the early electoral system, it met the needs of the moment. The electoral process was an acceptable compromise of the diverse positions both within the Constitutional Convention and among the states that would ratify it. Later other problems developed, but they reflected the different conceptions of political parties and suffrage that dominated American politics when the Framers designed the process of presidential selection.

### The Framers' Views of Parties

Whatever the particular motivations of the Framers, it is clear that they were proponents of moderation. It also is clear that they held a quite different understanding of the presidential selection process than that generally accepted today. Most notably, the Framers envisaged a nonpartisan process. Political parties (or "factions") were viewed as a political evil. The goal of the selection process was to promote men of civic virtue who would be able to exercise unfettered judgment.

The Framers' views of political parties were a natural outgrowth of the Anglo-American tradition. Opposition parties are now considered an essential part of representative democracy, but the Framers believed they would cause tumult and discord. Historian Richard Hofstadter has argued that in eighteenth-century British political thought there were three archetypal views of party that could have influenced the Framers.[6]

The first, which he called "the Hamiltonian view" (since it was a position associated with Alexander Hamilton), was based on the antiparty doctrine of Bolingbroke, an English statesman who wrote two important pamphlets on politics in the 1730s. For Bolingbroke, the best sort of state would be led by a "patriot king"—a benign monarch who would subdue factions by good statecraft. To him, parties were by definition antithetical to the common good. Nevertheless, he conceived of instances when a uniting "country party," speaking for the nation as a whole rather than particular interests, could be used to restore stability in a state.

The second view, which Hofstadter termed "Madisonian" after James Madison, was based on the writings of the eighteenth-century Scottish philosopher David Hume. Like Bolingbroke, Hume thought that parties were evil, but unlike Bolingbroke he thought that their existence was inevitable in a free state. Champions of liberty could check and limit the excesses of parties, but they could not abolish them. Madison expressed this view in *Federalist* No. 10, concluding that the only satisfactory method of "curing the mischiefs of faction" was to control their effects. To remove their cause would be to destroy liberty.

Finally, Hofstadter pointed to the views of British statesman Edmund Burke, who felt that parties were not only inevitable but—for the most part—good. But Burke's writing, published in 1770, came too late to influence the Framers at the Constitutional Convention. Instead, both the Federalists and Anti-Federalists condemned parties. Each side hoped to eliminate the other, thereby forming a united nonpartisan state. From their perspective, the common good would triumph over the petty rivalries and selfish interests that political parties would produce.

Thus the Framers adhered to one or the other of Hofstadter's first two archetypes. The resulting doctrine of nonpartisanship allowed for the original vice-presidential selection process. But, because the Framers did not contemplate partisan contests among candidates, they did not foresee a problem with having the second-place candidate become vice president.

### Voting Requirements

The electorate of the eighteenth century was quite different from the electorate of today. The Constitution left it up to the states to determine who would vote, and all states agreed on one requirement: only men could cast a ballot. In many states, property ownership also was a prerequisite for the right to vote. Indeed, property qualifications had existed in all the colonies and went on to endure in many of the states, although the exact qualifications differed among states. Colonial restrictions tended to be harsher than those adopted by the states and often were based on a measure of real estate ownership. Some colonies, such as Massachusetts, even had religious qualifications for voting.[7]

In Virginia—the home of some of the most important members of the Constitutional Convention and four of the first five presidents—property possession had been a prerequisite for voting since 1677. From 1705 until 1736, the laws were quite liberal: any male tenant who rented or owned land for life (his own or that of another person such as his wife or child) was considered a "freeholder" and could vote. In other words, as a qualification to vote, leasing property for the duration of one's lifetime or for that of a family member was the equivalent of owning property. From 1736 onward, the definition of *freeholder* was more restrictive. To vote, a man living in the country had to hold twenty-five acres of cultivated land with a house, or one hundred acres (changed to fifty in 1762) of uncleared land. A man living in town had to hold a house with a lot.[8] By the standards of the time, those requirements were not excessive.[9]

The American Revolution brought no suffrage reform to Virginia, although it did to other states. The Virginia constitution of 1776 stated that voting requirements "shall remain as exercised at present."[10] Thus even those who paid taxes or fought in the militia could not vote unless they held the requisite amount of land. By 1800 Virginia was one of five states that retained real estate property qualifications. (At the other extreme, four states had established universal suffrage by 1800.) While various other states allowed the ownership of personal property or the payment of taxes to substitute for holding real estate, Virginia held on to its old property qualifications until 1830. By that time, it was the only state to retain freehold suffrage. But even the reform of 1830 brought little change. Householders were added to the franchise—a very modest step toward universal manhood suffrage.[11]

Property requirements of one kind or another were not abandoned by all the states until 1856. It is not clear how much of the electorate was excluded by property requirements; historians differ on this point, sometimes quite markedly.[12] But the effect of property qualifications—while certainly restrictive—can be overstated. Because the United States was predominantly a middle-class society with fairly widespread ownership of property, such qualifications were not so significant a limit as they may first have appeared.

### EARLY EXPERIENCE, 1789–1828

The years 1789–1828 saw a tremendous change in many of the concepts and institutions that the Framers had envisaged. Nonpartisan elections did not last even a decade. Deadlock in the election of 1800 forced the young nation to change the method of choosing the vice president. Restrictions on the right to vote were eased. A system of nominating presidential candidates by congressional caucus was developed, then overturned. And the original understanding of the function of electors was significantly altered.

### Role of the Electoral College and the Selection of Electors

The Constitution provided that each state appoint electors "in such manner as the legislature thereof may direct." As a result, diverse methods for choosing electors were used throughout the country. In some states, the legislature appointed the

A war hero from Virginia and presiding officer of the Constitutional Convention, George Washington, more than six feet tall, was the very symbol of legitimacy for the new republic.

electors, either by joint ballot (both houses voting together) or a concurrent vote (both houses voting separately). Others used popular election on a statewide general ticket; still others, popular election by districts. There also were mixed systems in which electors were chosen partly by the people in districts and partly by the state legislature, or by the legislature from nominees voted by the people, or by the legislature from among the top candidates if there was no majority in the popular vote.[13] It was even suggested during the Constitutional Convention that electors be chosen by lot, although no state adopted that method.[14]

The first group of presidential electors was chosen on the first Wednesday of January 1789. Only four states (Delaware, Maryland, Pennsylvania, and Virginia) used direct popular election. New Hampshire also called for popular election but required that an elector receive a majority vote to win. When a majority was not forthcoming, the election was thrown to the legislature. Likewise, Massachusetts preferred a mixed system. Five states (Connecticut, Georgia, New Jersey, New York, and South Carolina) used legislative appointment to choose electors, but New York—deadlocked between its Federalist Senate and its Anti-Federalist House—could not agree and chose no electors. The twelfth and thirteenth states, North Carolina and Rhode Island, had not yet ratified the Constitution and therefore did not participate.

Members of Congress apparently had assumed that state legislatures would appoint the electors, at least for the first election, because they allowed less than four months (from September 13, 1788, to the first Wednesday in January 1789) for the electoral system to be implemented—not much time given the slowness of communication and the amount of work to be done. Distant states would not learn of Congress's directive for two weeks or more. The states then had to call their legislatures into session (itself time-consuming), pass laws providing for the selection of electors (which often entailed lengthy and acrimonious debate), canvass and choose the electors, and arrange for the electors to meet and vote. In some cases, there was not enough time to prepare for popular election, even if that were the preferred method of selection.[15]

The appointment of electors by state legislatures continued to be the norm in the election of 1792; nine states—Connecticut, Delaware, Georgia, New Jersey, New York, North Carolina, Rhode Island, South Carolina, and Vermont—used that method. Electors were chosen by popular election on a general ticket in Maryland and Pennsylvania, and by popular election within districts in Virginia and Kentucky. Massachusetts also called for popular election within districts but required a majority to win. In five districts, majorities were achieved; in the nine others, the General Court (the Massachusetts legislative body) chose the electors. New Hampshire had a mixed system in which both the people and the legislature chose the electors.[16]

By 1792 Congress had changed the dates for elections. Electors were required to cast their votes on the first Wednesday in December, with electors to be chosen in each state within the thirty-four days preceding that date.[17] This change caused a problem for North Carolina, which had undergone reapportionment after the 1790 census. The reapportionment became law on April 13, 1792, but North Carolina's legislature was out of session and was not scheduled to meet again until November 15. Since electors had to be chosen by December 5, there was not enough time to provide for popular election. To respond to the situation, the state government divided the state into four districts. Members of the state legislature residing in each district then met on November 25 and chose three electors. That unusual arrangement, however, was never used again by any state. Before adjourning, the North Carolina legislature made a provision for electors to be chosen by popular election in districts in future years.[18]

After the first three presidential elections (1789, 1792, and 1796), popular vote increasingly became the preferred method of choosing electors. By 1824 only six of twenty-four states—Delaware, Georgia, Louisiana, New York, South Carolina, and Vermont—still used legislative appointment.[19] From 1832 until 1860, all states except South Carolina chose electors by popular vote. Since 1860, only Florida in 1868 and Colorado in 1876 have used legislative appointment.[20]

After 1832 the statewide "winner-take-all" popular vote largely prevailed—that is, electors were chosen by the people of the state at large (as opposed to in districts). In addition, under the so-called unit rule, electors for each party were grouped together on a general ticket for each party and were elected as a bloc. In this way, a vote for one elector on a general ticket was equivalent to a vote for all the electors of that ticket. Often electors' names did not even appear on the ballot; rather, people voted for the ticket of a particular party, and the general ticket with a plurality of votes won. The winning ticket, then, consisted of all the electors representing the state—the concept of "winner take all." Electors were not divided in proportion to the popular vote.[21]

Because under the general ticket system voters selected a party rather than individual electors, general tickets were closely associated with the rise of partisan contests. As a result, the nature of the electoral college changed. The Framers of the Constitution had expected electors to act as free agents, exercising individual (that is, nonpartisan) judgments in their selection of the president. Instead, the electoral college was transformed into a contingent of party proxies. As Supreme Court Justice Robert Jackson wrote in *Ray v. Blair* in 1952: "Electors, although often personally eminent, independent, and respectable, officially became voluntary party lackeys and intellectual nonentities. . . . As an institution the electoral college suffered atrophy almost indistinguishable from *rigor mortis*."[22]

In addition to increasing the power of political parties, the general ticket system allowed states to maximize their influence in the election. Instead of scattering a state's electors among many candidates, the system consolidated each state's electors behind the candidate who received the most votes.

In 1801 former Treasury secretary Alexander Hamilton had drafted a constitutional amendment that would have prohibited the selection of electors by general ticket or by state legislatures, but it had been rejected.[23] Years later, the selection of electors by general ticket had become so much the norm that when Michigan passed a law in 1891 providing for the election of presidential electors by congressional districts instead of by general ticket, the law was contested and ultimately made its way to the Supreme Court. In the case, *McPherson v. Blacker* (1892), the Court stated that the Constitution had clearly provided state legislatures with plenary, or full, power to prescribe the method of choosing electors; the fact that states had come to adopt a uniform method of selection did not in any way reduce that power.[24] Since then, only Maine (as of 1972) has used the district system; all other states (including Michigan, which quickly returned to its former system) have chosen their electors by general ticket.

### Emergence of Parties

Although the early electoral system was undemocratic by modern standards, Washington's unanimous election as president in 1789 and 1792 has been described as "a triumph of popular will."[25] Over six feet tall, Washington was, at the age of fifty-five, the very symbol of legitimacy: a hero who held the confidence of virtually all the people. As the presiding officer of the Constitutional Convention he had lent credence, if not dis-

A civilian and former minister to France and Great Britain, John Adams was considered an excellent complement to Washington in 1789. The short, stocky, bald New Englander soon came to be regarded as the candidate for the vice presidency.

course, to the enterprise. (Yet during the entire span of the convention he had spoken only once in debate, and then on a minor issue.[26]) Now he would lend credence to the new government.

For the election of 1789, there is no record of any elector expressing opposition to the election of Washington. Each elector had to vote for two persons, however, with the candidate having the second highest number of votes becoming vice president. In the days before the electors met, it was the "talk about town" that the vice president should be a person who complemented Washington: he should be from a northern state and be a civilian. It also was suggested that he should not have to vacate an office in which his services were needed. John Adams—a short, stocky, bald New Englander—fit all of those qualifications, and he soon came to be regarded as the candidate for vice president.

Adams, however, was a proud man who saw himself as on an equal footing with Washington: technically they were, after all, both candidates for the presidency. There was no separate ballot for the office of vice president; whoever came in second in the presidential election would fill that post. As a result, some electors began to worry: if Adams came to be regarded as the vice-presidential candidate, he could conceivably get the same number of votes as Washington. At best, such a situation would be an embarrassment; at worst, it could degenerate into a divisive power struggle.

## WHEN AND WHY DID PARTIES BEGIN?

Although there is no precise date for the beginning of parties, both Alexander Hamilton (a Federalist) and Thomas Jefferson (a Democratic-Republican) referred to the existence of a Jeffersonian republican "faction" in Congress as early as 1792.

The two competing parties developed as a result of public sentiment for and against adoption of the Constitution. The Federalist Party—a loose coalition of merchants, shippers, financiers, and other business interests—favored the strong central government provided by the Constitution. Their opponents were intent on preservation of state sovereignty. Underlying the controversy was the Federalists' desire to create a government with power to guarantee the value of the currency (and thus protect the position of creditors) and the desire of the Democratic-Republican agrarians and frontier settlers to maintain easy credit conditions. The Democratic-Republicans also wanted to protect state legislatures against encroachments by a remote federal government.

Although party organization became more formalized in the 1790s and early 1800s, the Federalists never considered themselves a political party but rather a gentlemanly coalition of interests representing respectable society. What party management there was, they kept clandestine, a reflection of their own fundamental suspicion of parties. The Jeffersonians achieved a high degree of organization but never acquired a nationally accepted name. They most commonly referred to themselves as "Republicans." (In his conciliatory inaugural address of 1801, Jefferson said, "We are all Republicans, we are all Federalists.") Their opponents labeled them "Anti-Federalists," "disorganizers," "Jacobins," and "Democrats"—the latter an unflattering term in the early years of the Republic. To many Americans in the late eighteenth century, a democrat was considered a supporter of mob rule and revolution and often ideologically identified with the bloody French Revolution.

The designation "Democrat-Republican" was used by the Jeffersonians in several states but was never widely accepted as a party label. Historians often refer to the Jeffersonians as the "Democratic-Republicans," however, to avoid confusion with the later and unrelated Republican Party founded in 1854.

Although the early American political leaders acknowledged the development of parties, they did not foresee the emergence of a two-party system. Rather, they often justified the existence of their own party as a reaction to an unacceptable opposition. Jefferson defended his party involvement as a struggle between good and evil: "[When] the principle of difference is as substantial and as strongly pronounced as between the republicans and the Monocrats of our country, I hold it as honorable to take a firm and decided part, and as immoral to pursue a middle line, as between the parties of Honest men, and Rogues, into which every country is divided."

To avoid this situation, Hamilton maneuvered to siphon votes away from Adams. In doing so, he earned Adams's ire, creating a political split that would prove critical in the coming years. In the end, all the electors cast one of their votes for Washington, giving him a total electoral count of sixty-nine. Adams received thirty-four electoral votes, and the thirty-five other votes were divided among ten other candidates.[27]

Washington expressed no particular taste for politics, and after two terms in office he decided not to run for reelection, even though no constitutional or statutory law would have blocked him. Much has been made of Washington's precedent of serving only two terms, but his decision to retire seemed mainly personal. Indications were that he would have preferred to retire after one term had he felt able to do so without adversely affecting the young nation.[28] He informed his closest associates of his decision early in 1796, and by autumn it was public knowledge. The first two presidential elections had been nonpartisan; in each, the will of the people had been clear. Neither would be the case again.

Students of the American electoral system disagree about just when and why political parties really emerged.[29] For his part, Washington was avowedly nonpartisan, yet he did not appoint staunch Anti-Federalists (or Democratic-Republicans, as they also were known) to positions in his administration because to do so, he thought, would put the Constitution at risk. *(See box, When and Why Did Parties Begin? left.)*

Nonetheless, splits developed within the new government. For example, when Secretary of the Treasury Hamilton lobbied Congress for passage of such administration programs as an excise tax and the establishment of a national bank, opposition arose from James Madison, then a member of the House of Representatives, and others. In the cabinet, Hamilton and Jefferson often disagreed. Federalists, such as Hamilton, believed in a strong central government led by a vigorous executive; Democratic-Republicans, such as Jefferson and Madison, were more concerned with states' rights and the will of the people as expressed through the legislature.

Newspapers both reflected and widened those splits. In 1789 Hamilton established the *Gazette of the United States* to serve as the official mouthpiece of the administration and, not coincidentally, of the Federalist position.[30] In return, the newspaper was awarded government patronage in the form of printing orders from the Treasury Department and, for a time, a contract to print the laws.[31]

In 1791 Jefferson was instrumental in establishing a rival newspaper—the *National Gazette*—to serve as the voice of the Democratic-Republican position. When Jefferson left Washington's cabinet in 1793, his *Gazette* was replaced by the rabidly pro–Democratic-Republican *Aurora*. The polarized positions of the rival papers and their exchanges of editorial attacks attracted attention throughout the country. Such exchanges went to extremes in both personal and policy-oriented attacks. The *Aurora,* for example, deemed most of President Washington's acts unconstitutional, accused the president of overdrawing his salary, and labeled him "a frail mortal, whose passions and weaknesses are like those of other men, a spoiled child, a despot, an anemic imitation of the English kings."[32] On another occasion, the *Aurora* proclaimed: "If ever a nation was debauched by a man, the American nation has been debauched by Washington. If ever a nation has suffered from the improper influence of a man, the American nation has suffered from the influence of Washington. If ever a nation was deceived by a man, the American nation has been deceived by Washington."[33]

Events abroad served only to widen the splits in the government. The French Revolution was under way, and in 1793 France declared war on England. Although the United States remained officially neutral, passions ran high and American political thought was affected by the conflict on the other side of the Atlantic. Likening them to the Jacobins of the French uprising, Federalists denounced the Democratic-Republicans as populist radicals who wanted to undermine the authority of the executive through a powerful legislature. Democratic-Republicans condemned the Federalists as being a pseudo-British party of aristocratic monarchists.[34]

*The 1796 Election.* Although there was no formal party machinery, the election of 1796 was a de facto contest between the Federalists and the Democratic-Republicans. The Democratic-Republicans had formed a congressional caucus, but it was not convened to choose candidates. That Jefferson would be chosen as the presidential nominee was obvious, and although there was no clear agreement on a vice-presidential candidate, the problem was not considered important enough to call the caucus into session.[35] An informal meeting on the choice of a running mate ended with the issue unresolved. By the time the campaign was in full swing, however, it was understood that the Democratic-Republicans' vice-presidential candidate would be Aaron Burr of New York.

Federalist members of Congress appear to have discussed their choice of candidates in the summer of 1796. Hamilton was considered but rejected because he had made many enemies during the Washington administration. John Jay also was rejected, primarily because he had negotiated a controversial treaty with England. The Federalists finally placed their support behind Vice President Adams. Thomas Pinckney of South Carolina was the Federalists' choice for vice president because it was thought that he would take votes away from Jefferson (a Virginian) in the South.

In September 1796 Washington wrote his famous Farewell Address. The address, written with Madison's and Hamilton's help, warned against the dangers of parties. While the address was largely a response to the divisiveness of recent events, it is likely that his denunciation of parties was a veiled attack on the Democratic-Republicans.[36] He cited "the common and continual mischiefs of the spirit of Party" and said that this was "sufficient to make it the interest and the duty of wise people to discourage and restrain it." Elaborating on the spirit of parties and its baneful effects, Washington wrote:

It serves always to distract the public councils and enfeeble the public administration. It agitates the community with ill founded jealousies and false alarms, kindles the animosity of one part against another, foments occasionally riot and insurrection. It opens the door to foreign influence and corruption, which find a facilitated access to the government itself through the channels of party passions. . . . A fire not to be quenched; it demands a uniform vigilance to prevent its bursting into flame, lest instead of warming it should consume.[37]

Yet despite Washington's warning, the election of 1796 quickly became an intensely partisan contest. Newspapers fanned the flames as the Federalist press attacked Jefferson and the pro–Democratic-Republican *Aurora* attacked Adams.[38]

When the electors met to choose the winners, the weakness of the selection process became apparent. As designed, the system did not take into account partisan contests—that is, no provision had been made for candidates from the same party to be elected as a team. Although Pennsylvania, for example, chose electors by party tickets, party organization was largely ephemeral. In South Carolina, the electors did not follow party lines in their choice; they voted for an all-southern ticket with the Democratic-Republican Jefferson and the Federalist Pinckney splitting the votes equally. In the North, electors did not give equal support to Adams and Pinckney because they feared that Pinckney's vote might exceed that of Adams. Apparently, Hamilton, who urged northern electors to give equal support to the two Federalist candidates, hoped that Pinckney would upset Adams.

Because there still was no separate ballot for vice president, the candidate with the second highest number of electoral votes was assigned that office. Thus Adams was elected president with seventy-one electoral votes, and his rival from the Democratic-Republican Party, Jefferson, was named his vice president with sixty-eight electoral votes. Pinckney came in third with fifty-nine electoral votes, and Burr trailed a distant fourth with thirty.

*The 1800 Election.* The election of 1796 had served as a portent of the problems of the existing presidential selection process. The election of 1800 proved them. In the spring of 1800, Adams and Gen. Charles Cotesworth Pinckney of South Carolina were nominated as the Federalist candidates by a caucus of Federalist senators and representatives. About the same time, a caucus of forty-three Democratic-Republican senators and representatives convened. Once again there was no question that Jefferson would be the candidate for president. Rather, the caucus met to designate a candidate for vice president and unanimously nominated Burr.[39]

When the electors voted in December 1800, the two Democratic-Republican candidates, Jefferson and Burr, tied for first place. As specified in the Constitution, the election was thrown into the House of Representatives (which was dominated by Federalists) and a majority of states was required to elect a president. Although it was common knowledge that Jefferson was the presidential candidate and Burr was the vice-presidential candidate, some Federalists considered Burr the lesser evil and plotted to elect him president. Hamilton, cognizant of the new nation's delicate balance, roundly discouraged the idea. In a letter to New York senator Gouverneur Morris he wrote: "I trust the Federalists will not finally be so mad as to vote for Burr. . . . His elevation can only promote the purposes of the desperate and profligate. If there be a man in the world I ought to hate, it is Jefferson. With Burr I have always been personally well. But the public good must be paramount to every private consideration."[40] Nevertheless, many Federalists continued to support Burr.

On Wednesday, February 11, 1801, the House met to vote. On the first ballot, Jefferson received the votes of eight states and Burr the votes of six. Two states were divided. There was no majority. The House balloted eighteen more times that day with no change in the outcome. Balloting continued through Saturday, February 14, and resumed on Monday. In all, there were thirty-six ballots. The tide finally turned on Tuesday, February 17. Jefferson received a majority, with the votes of ten states. On March 4 there was a peaceful transfer of power.

*The Twelfth Amendment*

It was evident from the problems of 1796 and 1800 that the constitutional provision for presidential selection was flawed. Even before the election of 1800, Vermont had adopted a resolution calling for a constitutional amendment. Similar resolutions were introduced in Congress in 1802, but they were defeated. When the Eighth Congress convened in October 1803, the matter of a constitutional amendment was considered at great length. After much debate, the resolution for an amendment was passed December 8, 1803. The amendment was ratified by the states with unusual speed. It was officially adopted as the Twelfth Amendment to the Constitution on September 25, 1804. Thirteen states voted for ratification; three (Connecticut, Delaware, and Massachusetts) dissented.[41]

The Twelfth Amendment called for electors to vote for president and vice president on separate ballots. If none of the candidates for president had a majority, the House of Representatives would choose the winner from no more than the top three candidates. As before, a majority of the states in the House was needed to elect. If none of the candidates for vice president had a majority, the winner would be chosen from the top two vice-presidential candidates by a majority of the whole number of senators. The vice presidency, then, was no longer awarded to the runner-up (in theory, the second-most-qualified person to be president).

*Congressional Caucus Nominating System*

By 1804 caucuses in Congress were nominating presidential candidates. To some degree, this approximated what the congressionalists had wanted at the Constitutional Convention: selection of the executive by the legislature. The Democratic-Republican caucus nominated Jefferson in 1800 and 1804, although the real purpose of the caucus in those two years was to select a candidate for vice president. In 1808 the Democratic-Republican caucus nominated James Madison for president and George Clinton of New York (already vice president under Jefferson) as his running mate. Madison was renominated by a near unanimous vote of the caucus in 1812. Initially, John Langdon of New Hampshire was chosen as his running mate, but he declined the nomination because of his age. (He turned seventy-one in 1812.) At a second caucus, Massachusetts governor Elbridge Gerry was nominated for vice president. In 1816 Secretary of War James Monroe was nominated by a vote of 65–54 over Secretary of War William H. Crawford of Georgia. New York governor Daniel D. Tompkins was nominated as Monroe's running mate.

By 1820 the Federalist Party was virtually dead. The Federalists had performed dismally in presidential elections since their narrow loss in 1800 and had been discredited by their opposition to the War of 1812. There is no record of how they selected their candidates in 1804. In 1808 and 1812, their candidates were chosen by secret meetings of Federalist leaders in New York. By 1816 they had given up nominating candidates for president. According to historian Edward Stanwood, "Nothing whatever was done to nominate candidates in opposition to Monroe and Tompkins. On December 3, the day before the electors were to vote, the *Boston Daily Advertiser,* published in one of the three states that had chosen Federalist electors, remarked: 'We do not know, nor is it very material, for whom the Federal electors will vote.'"[42] (They voted for New York senator Rufus King.) In 1820 Democratic-Republican Monroe ran unopposed. With virtual one-party rule, nomination by the Democratic-Republicans' "King Caucus" was tantamount to election.

In 1824, however, King Caucus was dethroned. There had been objections to the caucus system from the start. In 1808, when Sen. Stephen Bradley of Vermont had conveyed notice to the Democratic-Republican members of the House and Senate that the caucus would meet, a representative from Virginia published a response that said, in part: "I cannot . . . countenance, by my presence, the midnight intrigues of any set of men who may arrogate to themselves the right, which belongs only to the people, of selecting proper persons to fill the important offices of president and vice president."[43]

After Madison's nomination by the caucus in 1808, seventeen Democratic-Republican members of Congress signed a protest against the system. (Even Vice President Clinton, who was nominated by the caucus, expressed disapproval of it.) They did so because they felt the caucus system was undemocratic. Citizens had no direct say in the nomination, and those states and districts not represented by the party in Congress were effectively disenfranchised.

At the Democratic-Republican caucus in 1824, only 66 of 261 members of Congress were present (three-quarters of whom were from only four states). By the time the caucus met, five serious candidates had emerged—all with roughly equal strength: Secretary of State John Quincy Adams of Massachusetts, Secretary of War John C. Calhoun of South Carolina, House Speaker Henry Clay of Kentucky, Secretary of the Treasury William Crawford, and Sen. Andrew Jackson of Tennessee. Crawford won the caucus nomination, and Albert Gallatin of Pennsylvania was chosen as his running mate. The other candidates, however, refused to follow the decision of the caucus. In his home state of Tennessee, Jackson was nominated by the state legislature, which also passed a resolution condemning the caucus system. Kentucky did the same for Clay. Among the candidates, Calhoun was the only one to withdraw.

At the polls, Jackson got the most popular votes. He also got the most electoral votes—ninety-nine electoral votes to Adams's eighty-four—but not the necessary majority. Crawford came in third with forty-one votes. His running mate had withdrawn from the race in October. Clay came in fourth with thirty-seven. Thus the race was thrown into the House of Representatives where Adams—despite Jackson's dominance of the popular and initial electoral vote—was elected.

Ironically, the Democratic-Republican caucus died when the party was at its zenith, largely because other candidates within the party would not acquiesce to the choice of the caucus. But the demise of the caucus also reflected the growing democratization of the political system. By 1824 only six states were still choosing electors by legislative appointment; all the other states were doing so by popular election. Mass participation in presidential elections was increasing dramatically. Furthermore, there was a trend toward expansion of suffrage. As early as 1791,

Vermont had instituted universal manhood suffrage. Kentucky and New Hampshire followed suit in 1792, as did Indiana in 1816. By 1824 most states had dropped property restrictions on voting, although several still retained tax-paying restrictions. Mississippi, which entered the Union in 1817, was the last state to institute tax-paying restrictions, and these were dropped in 1832.[44] The caucus system was a holdover from an age that distrusted mass democratic sentiments. That age was dying.

But it was the caucus's selection of the staid Crawford over the frontier hero Jackson—and the subsequent House election in 1824 of Adams—that was the kiss of death for the caucus system. It also hastened the decline of the Democratic-Republican Party.

## MAJOR ELECTORAL DEVELOPMENTS, 1828–1996

After the election of 1828, party alignments crystallized, and the United States began to develop what would become the stablest two-party system in the world. Party conventions were held regularly beginning in 1831, and presidential primaries took their place in party politics shortly after the turn of the century. Throughout the nineteenth and twentieth centuries, the electorate continued to expand as African Americans, women, and other groups in U.S. society won the right to vote.

Andrew Jackson was greeted by enthusiastic crowds as he traveled from Tennessee to Washington for his inauguration in 1829. Capturing the spirit of America's expanding frontier, "Old Hickory" established the age of popular politics.

The Whigs nominated two military heroes for president: William Henry Harrison in 1840, left, and Zachary Taylor in 1848, right. The party picked such charismatic figures for leadership to compensate for deep schisms and poor organization.

### The Two-Party System

In 1828 Andrew Jackson swept into the presidency as the head of the newly formed Democratic Party. The Democratic-Republicans had split earlier in the decade over an issue that would divide U.S. politics to the present day—the protective tariff. Under the "American system" of Henry Clay, the United States would use high tariffs both to protect nascent domestic industries and to fund internal improvements. After his election as president in 1824, Adams adopted much of Clay's program. But agrarian interests resisted the high tariffs because of the higher costs for finished products and the investment bias given to the North and West, and Jackson emerged as the agrarian hero. Under Jackson, the geographic and economic expansion of the nation and the development of a broader-based national party organization reached a peak.

*The Democrats and the Whigs.* Jackson, who inaugurated an age of popular politics, was an activist president from the beginning of his two terms. His programs for internal improvements, decentralization of the assets of the Bank of the United States, and control of the federal bureaucracy were landmarks in U.S. history.

In reaction to Jackson's populism, a collection of aggrieved interests pulled together under the Whig Party label. The Whigs aimed to restore moderate policies and end what they considered to be an era of "mob rule" that gave the president excessive authority. Two military heroes, William Henry Harrison (1840)

and Zachary Taylor (1848), won presidential elections under the Whig banner. But the Whigs suffered two ills: the lack of a sophisticated national organization and contradictions within the party that could not be overcome—such as the diverse geographic, economic, and cultural backgrounds of its members. The rise of industrialism and a religious-based abolition movement in the North made Whig Party unity impossible at mid-century.

In the 1836 election, the Whigs fielded a set of regional candidates against Jackson's vice president, Democrat Martin Van Buren. By running several regional candidates rather than one national candidate, the Whigs hoped to send the election to the House. Van Buren easily won, however. The fact that their later presidential victories (Harrison and Taylor) came with the nomination of military heroes pointed to the organizational weakness of the Whigs. Only strong leadership could temporarily overcome growing Whig schisms and the lack of organization.

Slavery split the Whigs badly. As the abolitionist movement grew in northern states, the Whigs had difficulty appealing to southerners. By 1856 the Whigs had been replaced by the Republican Party. The founding of the Republican Party stemmed from public anger over the Kansas-Nebraska Act of 1854, which allowed new territories to decide whether to enter the Union as either slave states or as free states. In the debate over the act, the Republicans emerged as a collection of groups antagonized by

the major parties. Many Whigs were abolitionists, but even more Whigs simply opposed the extension of slavery into new territories. By supporting the extension of slavery into the new territories and opposing high tariffs, the Democrats lost any hope of building an alliance with northern industrialists who were becoming a greater force in U.S. politics. The Republicans were able to overcome the divisions that the slavery issue had created in the 1840s and 1850s.

The Republicans ran their first national campaign in 1856, when John Charles Fremont ran against Democrat James Buchanan. They lost that year but won the White House in 1860 when a former Whig, Abraham Lincoln, defeated the divided Democratic Party. The Republicans dominated U.S. politics for most of the next seven decades.

*Republican Dominance.* Over the seventy years after the Union won the Civil War, the Republicans largely dominated U.S. politics. Between 1860 and 1932, the Democrats won the presidency only in 1884 and 1892 (with Grover Cleveland on the ticket) and 1912 and 1916 (with Woodrow Wilson).

The electoral bargain that settled the election of 1876—in which Republican Rutherford B. Hayes won the presidency even though Democrat Samuel Tilden won the popular vote—created an electoral crisis that eventually led to a new party alignment. After long negotiations between Republicans and Democrats, Hayes was declared the winner. But as part of the election deal the Republicans agreed to pull federal troops out of the South and increase federal funding for internal improvements. As soon as the troops left the old Confederacy, the Democrats took over and disenfranchised blacks through an elaborate set of racially discriminatory, or "Jim Crow," laws. The Republicans, however, maintained national hegemony by vigorously pursuing a national economic policy. The federal government aided economic expansion with a high-tariff system, funding of exploration and transportation, limitations on labor unions, and tight-money policies. When the Democrats won the presidency under Cleveland, the nation continued to follow conservative policies. Especially in the areas of labor relations and monetary policy—the most important issues of the time—Cleveland pursued basically Republican policies.

The Democrats became particularly vulnerable toward the end of the century when discontent among the nation's farmers reached an almost revolutionary pitch. Farmers were hurt by the high-tariff and tight-money policies that Republicans promoted, which depressed farm prices and inflated the costs of the manufactured and imported goods that farmers needed, such as plows and other farm implements. One solution to the problem was unlimited coinage of silver to expand the money supply.

The Democratic Party not only confronted splits caused by the populist uprising in western states but also faced a Republican Party with better financing and organization. The 1896 election, in which Republican William McKinley defeated Democrat William Jennings Bryan for the presidency, solidified Republican dominance of U.S. politics.

Woodrow Wilson, a former political scientist at Princeton University who became a reform governor of New Jersey, was the only Democrat to win the White House in the thirty-six years that passed after the McKinley-Bryan showdown in 1896. Elected to the first of two terms in 1912, Wilson helped the Democrats to take control of Congress and produced a unique period of party-government activism. Wilson's reforms covered antitrust laws, labor relations, banking regulations, women's suffrage, and international law.

But the Democrats' ascendance in national politics was short-lived, largely because of the bitterness that accompanied the end of World War I. President Wilson's failed attempt to get Senate approval of the Versailles treaty, which would have brought the United States into the League of Nations, shattered his career and split the party badly. Able to exploit the national mood of cynicism about liberal activism abroad and at home, the Republicans won the presidency in the elections of 1920, 1924, and 1928.

*The Age of the New Deal.* Republican dominance ended with the stock market crash of October 29, 1929, when Herbert C. Hoover occupied the White House. Hoover reluctantly took a number of measures to provide relief for victims of the nation's greatest economic catastrophe, but his lack of empathy for those victims and his failure to understand the fundamental nature of the crisis made him into a political scapegoat. For most of his four-year term, many Americans viewed Hoover as an object of enmity. Any Democrat promoting change in 1932 was practically guaranteed victory.

Democrat Franklin D. Roosevelt, governor of New York and former assistant secretary of the navy, not only won the presidency in 1932 but also changed the face of U.S. politics. Supported by coalition that Roosevelt built, the Democrats dominated national politics for the next three decades. The New Deal coalition included international business leaders, bankers, southerners, blacks, organized labor, urbanites, Catholics, and Jews. The Democrats won seven of the next nine presidential elections. The only Republican winner between 1932 and 1964 was Dwight D. Eisenhower (in 1952 and 1956), who originally was wooed by the Democrats.

The issue of race and a variety of economic developments began to pull the Democratic Party apart in the years after World War II. When the party adopted a strong civil rights platform in 1948, a group of southerners led by Gov. J. Strom Thurmond of South Carolina bolted the national nominating convention and formed their own party. *(See "Third Parties," p. 116.)* With the defection the same year of the liberal former vice president Henry Wallace, the Democrats and President Harry S. Truman retained the middle-of-the-road vote and the White House. But the party's once-strong hold on the South was gone. In 1948 Thurmond won more than 22 percent of the popular vote in the South, as well as the electoral votes of Alabama, Louisiana, Mississippi, and South Carolina (and one "faithless elector" from Tennessee).

Organizers of the civil rights rally in Washington, D.C., lead the march on the National Mall on August 28, 1963.

Republicans suffered splits of their own during this period. The party's isolationist, high-tariff wing was still strong under the leadership of Sen. Robert A. Taft of Ohio. But other party leaders, such as Eisenhower, New York governor Thomas E. Dewey, former State Department official Nelson A. Rockefeller, and Rep. Richard Nixon of California, propounded an American role as a bulwark against the Soviet Union in world politics and economic expansion at home and abroad. The more traditional GOP wing remained strong until the late 1960s, however.

*The Postwar Party System.* In the years after World War II, two major economic changes and the race issue shifted the balance of power in U.S. politics. First, the locus of economic activity in the United States shifted from the urban Northeast to the suburbs and the South and the West. The loosening of economic ties led to the loosening of social and political ties. Second, the United States faced growing competition in world markets from the countries rebuilding after the war's devastation. By the late 1960s, the U.S. share in world markets had been cut in half, the position of the dollar in international finance was in decline, and inflation was posing a threat to domestic prosperity. An explosion in social spending created resentment among some middle- and upper-class groups. The American economic "pie" was not growing fast enough to satisfy all the elements of the Democratic coalition, which began to compete with one another.[45]

A number of social movements helped to undermine the stable party system in the post–World War II years. One of the most dramatic, the civil rights movement, shook up the Demo-

cratic Party's dominance of the South. President Lyndon Johnson ruefully remarked that when he signed major civil rights legislation he was delivering the South to the Republican Party. Other liberal movements—feminism, environmentalism, bilingualism, gay rights—also initiated basic changes in public policy. But by doing so, these movements upset a wide range of relationships that had been the foundation for permanent political alliances. At the same time, conservative movements challenged government policies on taxes, busing, gay rights, abortion rights, and secularism in schools. The Democratic Party was especially torn by the new factionalism of the 1970s and 1980s.[46]

The Democratic coalition split not only over race and economic issues but also over the proper U.S. role in international affairs. The Vietnam War divided the party into "hawk" and "dove" factions. Other developments fragmenting the party in the 1960s and 1970s included the emergence of a post-colonial Africa and Latin America, revelations about certain notorious activities of the Central Intelligence Agency, a thaw in relations with the Soviet Union and the People's Republic of China, and the emergence of the Organization of Petroleum Exporting Countries.

The Republicans won control (albeit slim) of Congress during some of the Truman and Eisenhower years and of the Senate for six years of the Reagan administration. The party regained control of both chambers of Congress, by healthy margins, in the 1994 midterm elections during the administration of Bill Clinton. Nevertheless, by the end of 1995 polls showed that a majority of Americans still considered themselves Democrats and that many were disillusioned with the GOP "Contract with America"—a list of ten promises that Republicans pledged in 1994 to keep if they took over Congress. The contract, which helped to end forty years of Democratic rule in the House, promised reforms to cut spending and reduce the federal budget's massive annual deficits. Among the first targets were Medicare, Medicaid, and other social programs enacted by Democratic Congresses since the 1960s. Republicans contended that the actions were needed to save the programs from bankruptcy, but Democrats charged that the reductions would hurt the poor and elderly and benefit those better off, who were promised a tax cut under the Contract with America.

Democratic skill in responding to constituency demands also helped the party in local politics. Beginning with the Roosevelt revolution, Democrats dominated governorships and state legislatures in most elections until 1994, when the Republicans' sweep also gave them a majority of governorships for the first time since 1970. Democrats still controlled most state legislatures, but Republicans held almost as many for the first time since 1968.[47]

Although the Republicans usually were outperformed in congressional and gubernatorial races, contests for the White House were another story. The GOP won five of the six presidential elections from 1968 to 1988, four by landslides, before the Democrats won in 1992 and 1996. The only Democrat to win the once-solid Democratic South during this period was the Georgian Jimmy Carter in 1976. The Republicans had a strong hold on the West and made strong inroads into the blue-collar and northeastern suburban votes. The Republican Party became competitive in the South below the presidential level for the first time since Reconstruction, even though Democrats controlled most state governments. After the 1990 census, the eleven states of the old Confederacy held almost one-third of all House seats (136 seats) and more than half of an electoral college majority (147 electoral votes). Some political observers predicted that the "Sunbelt," which boomed with suburbanization and the rise of the defense and space industries, would hold the balance of power in U.S. politics for the next generation.

Although southern resistance to the increasingly liberal policies of the Democrats created an opening for the GOP, the Democrats still had strong natural bases. After 1964, for example, no Democratic presidential candidate had won less than 84 percent of the African American vote. In the 1986 Democratic takeover of the U.S. Senate, the black vote was crucial in five southern states that went Democratic. Populist appeals on economic issues also produced Democratic victories in the South.

Democrat Clinton's victories in 1992 and 1996 suggested that the Democratic Party could bring parts of the South back into its coalition. For both elections Arkansan Clinton and running mate Albert Gore Jr. of Tennessee built a border state base with Arkansas and Tennessee safely in their camp. Appealing to other states with traditions of moderation and recent economic growth and social change, the ticket twice won the nearby border states of Missouri and Kentucky, and the southern state of Louisiana.

The race in Georgia was close for both elections: Clinton won the state in 1992 but lost it in 1996. Clinton more than made up for the lost of Georgia in 1996 by winning Florida—the first time that state went for a Democratic candidate since 1976.

The key to party alignments in the 1990s could be the way different social and economic groups cluster geographically. Urban-suburban segmentation and the redrawing of legislative district lines after the 1990 census could affect the way coalitions are created or maintained. If social groups are segregated by geographic boundaries, it could be difficult to build a broad political coalition in which diverse groups see common interests. Lack of real competition in congressional and local races could undermine party balance and affect presidential politics.

Experts were uncertain about whether new patterns of dominance and competition would develop by the early twenty-first century. Political scientists in the 1970s and 1980s were reluctant to proclaim a "realignment" of political forces. They were more comfortable with the term "dealignment," which suggested a breakup of traditional alliances without an obvious set of new alliances. Until 1994 the Democrats were too strong in the states and in Congress to suggest that they were a minority party. But even after 1994, political scientists were still arguing about whether the Republican takeover of Congress signaled a realignment or merely a temporary lapse of Democratic loyalties. Clearly, the Democrats had lost much of the financial backing on which they had relied for four decades, and many groups in the New Deal coalition were lukewarm in their support. Especially because of unprecedented numbers of independent voters, a new party alignment could take a long time to develop.

## The Development of Party Nominating Conventions

Perhaps because the Framers resisted the idea of partisan contests for the presidency, they did not outline any procedures for party selection of candidates. Under "King Caucus," the nation's first system for selecting nominees, congressional caucuses, or meetings of top party leaders, were used to select candidates. In 1824, however, a popular reaction against the closed nature of the caucus system paved the way for the birth of the national convention system, in 1831.

Since the adoption of nomination reforms by both parties, nominating conventions of party leaders from all states have been held to choose their presidential and vice-presidential candidates. Conventions also produce platforms, or statements of party principles. Present-day national conventions are more media events than deliberative bodies.

The Anti-Masonic Party held the first party convention in September 1831. Delegates from thirteen states nominated William Wirt of Maryland as president. The National Republican, or Whig, Party held a convention in December 1831 and nominated Henry Clay as president. The next May, the Democrats convened to nominate Andrew Jackson.

Although they were a repudiation of the Framers' dislike for partisanship, conventions were in tune with the nation's federal ideals: states could decide for themselves how they wished to se-

In September 1831 the Anti-Masonic Party held the first national nominating convention in U.S. history. Delegates from thirteen states nominated William Wirt for president. Wirt lost the 1832 election to Democrat Andrew Jackson.

When conventions were still deliberative events, the Democrats, in the summer of 1924, went through seventeen days, 103 ballots, and sixteen candidates before choosing John W. Davis as the presidential nominee. Davis lost to Republican Calvin Coolidge.

lect delegates, but once a state's delegates met with other states' representatives, they had to bargain and consider more than parochial concerns. The convention system strengthened state party organizations because each state selected its own delegates.

Early nominating conventions were open and deliberative. Party leaders often met without any idea which candidates would head the national ticket or how the party would stand on major issues. Those matters were subject to debate and bargaining. In fact, conventions were so open to deliberation that several "dark-horse" candidates were allowed to emerge. James K. Polk, who won the Democratic nomination in 1844, is considered the first true "outsider" candidate to lead a party. At the extreme, some conventions were so badly divided that party leaders were forced to stay in session longer than planned or even reconvene. The Democrats, split by the slavery issue, needed a second convention in 1860 to nominate Stephen A. Douglas, and then a rival faction ran its own ticket in the fall election. The 1924 Democratic convention went through seventeen days, 103 ballots, and sixteen candidates in New York's sweltering Madison Square Garden before nominating John W. Davis. Republican donnybrooks have included the 1880 rejection of Ulysses S. Grant's bid for a third term and the 1940 emergence of Wendell L. Willkie despite his lack of any political experience.

At early conventions it was common practice to arrange "drafts" of candidates before the convention—that is, the political party asks a person to accept a candidacy. Horatio Seymour's 1868 Democratic draft was genuine, but others have been scripted by political operatives. Franklin Roosevelt was disappointed that his 1940 draft for a third term did not work out as he had planned because other Democratic candidates sought the nomination. In more recent years, only one candidate has been "drafted" for the race by enthusiastic supporters. In 1964 young conservative supporters of Barry Goldwater worked behind the scenes for two years to "take over" state and local party organizations, particularly in southern states. Goldwater sometimes dismissed their efforts but ultimately was persuaded to run in 1964. He won the Republican nomination but lost the election to President Lyndon Johnson in a landslide.[48]

With the onset of state presidential primary elections at the beginning of the twentieth century, conventions became more representative of the electorate. Party leaders increasingly referred to the importance of public opinion rather than their duty to use their independent political judgment. To use the terminology of political science, conventioneers became less like "trustees" and more like "delegates."[49]

By the end of World War II, conventions were losing control over the nominating process. In 1952 the convention battle between Dwight Eisenhower and Sen. Robert A. Taft of Ohio was important, but the outcome was shaped by results from Republican primaries. The last open bargaining for the national ticket was the jockeying for the Democratic vice-presidential nomination in 1956. Since then, nomination front-runners have had to hold on to the coalition they built before the convention rather than continue building at the convention. The nomination victories of Democrats John Kennedy (1960), George McGovern (1972), and Jimmy Carter (1980) and Republican Gerald R. Ford (1976) were secured when they, as front-runners, avoided an erosion of support in key early convention votes.

Today, conventions are perceived by many observers to be simply gatherings held to ratify the choice of the voters in the states—their votes are held to be more legitimate than convention bargaining. In fact, almost all states now offer party members the opportunity to select the candidates in primaries and caucuses. The candidate with enough delegates to win the nomination usually is determined before the convention. Gov. Mario Cuomo of New York, considered a draft candidate in 1988, said it would be "immoral" to win the nomination without entering primaries.

One factor working against open conventions is the majority vote rule used by both parties. Before the rule was adopted by the Democratic Party in 1936, candidates needed the support of two-thirds of all convention delegates to win the nomination, a difficult feat usually achieved by bargaining with opponents within the party. President Franklin Roosevelt insisted on the abolishment of the two-thirds rule in 1936, but in 1940 his rivals tried to restore it as a way to block a third Roosevelt term.

The rise of choreographed conventions also is explained by the growth of media politics and the use of proportional representation for delegate allocation in primaries and caucuses. Media politics undermines the legitimacy of political "deals" made among elites at conventions. Proportional representation prevents long-shot candidates from winning big chunks of delegate support with narrow primary and caucus wins.

Attempts to reopen the nominating conventions to deliberation have failed. Former California governor Ronald Reagan struck out in his 1976 attempt to establish a requirement that candidates name a running mate before the convention; if he had succeeded, delegates would have been free to reassess their allegiance based on the vice-presidential candidate. Sen. Edward M. Kennedy of Massachusetts led the unsuccessful movement for an "open convention" in 1980.

Battles over the credentials of convention delegates have been among the livelier aspects of modern conventions. In 1912 Theodore Roosevelt unsuccessfully contested the seating of delegates for William Howard Taft. Forty years later, Taft's son, Ohio senator Robert Taft, lost an important credentials dispute and the nomination to Eisenhower. The Democrats endured divisive credentials disputes in 1968 and 1972.

And not to be forgotten, the way the party frames controversial issues during a convention can have a dramatic effect on debate during the fall campaign. Democratic platforms set the debate in 1888 (tariffs), 1896 (currency), 1948 (civil rights), and 1992 ("change"). GOP platforms set the debate in 1860 (preservation of the Union), 1952 (the Korean War and economic controls), 1964 (Goldwater conservatism), and 1980 (taxes and foreign policy).

### History of the Primary System

One of the progressive movement's greatest contributions to presidential politics was its introduction of the primary election to the nominating process at the turn of the century. Progressives persistently complained about the undemocratic way in which urban and state political machines chose leaders. Their solution was to put the selection of high officials in the hands of the electorate. Similarly, a purer democracy was the rationale behind reforms such as the Seventeenth Amendment (which provides for direct election of U.S. senators, previously selected by state legislatures), provisions for referendums and recall votes in state constitutions, and voter initiatives (which are similar to referendums but are instigated by citizen petitions rather than legislative action).

The logical extension of pure democracy to presidential politics was the direct primary. The idea was to bypass completely the vested interests that controlled nominations and thereby limited the people's choices in the general election. Some proponents of the primary wanted to abolish completely the deal making that had been characteristic of the nominating process throughout U.S. history. Primaries would provide for the direct election of delegates, or an election in which voters expressed their preferences for the presidential candidates themselves, or some combination of the two.

*Early Days.*  Florida passed the first presidential primary law in 1901, but the primary got its biggest impetus when the 1904 Republican convention refused seating to the backers of Progressive Party leader Robert M. La Follette. As a result, in 1905 La Follette successfully promoted legislation in Wisconsin that provided for primary election of delegates to national party conventions. Likewise, in 1906 Pennsylvania established a primary.

In 1910 Oregon established the first "beauty contest," a primary election in which voters expressed a preference for the candidates themselves. Convention delegates were legally bound to vote for candidates according to the results of the beauty contest. Oregon voters, appropriately enough, approved the plan in a referendum.

By 1916 twenty-five states had passed laws for presidential primaries. The greatest surge of support for primaries, and the primary system's greatest disappointment, came with the 1912 Republican nomination struggle. Former president Theodore Roosevelt used the primaries to battle his handpicked successor, President Taft, for the nomination. But despite his nine primary victories, compared with La Follette's two and Taft's one, Roosevelt lost the nomination to Taft. After declaring that Taft had "stolen" the nomination, Roosevelt ran on his own "Bull Moose" ticket and called for national primaries to decide nominations.[50]

In 1912 former president Theodore Roosevelt won nine out of twelve GOP primaries but was outmaneuvered by William Howard Taft at the Republican convention. In reaction, Roosevelt ran on his own "Bull Moose" ticket, calling for national primaries to decide the nomination.

But resistance to primaries persisted for years. Even as the states enthusiastically moved toward direct voter selection of presidential nominees in the years before World War I, conservatives in state legislatures, courts, and local election boards worked against the new system.

Time, however, accomplished what opponents of primaries could not manage. The arrival of World War I, the political apathy of the 1920s, and the struggle for economic survival during the Great Depression brought about the collapse of the primary system. The high costs of primaries, the low voter turnout, and the avoidance of the primaries by candidates turned them into irrelevant vestiges of the progressive movement.

Eight of the twenty-five states that had adopted primaries during the progressive surge had abolished them by 1935. Only a three-way Republican race in 1920 created any local interest or candidate activity in primaries—and even then the biggest vote-getter, Hiram Johnson, was denied the nomination. The disaster that befell Republican Wendell Willkie in 1944 when he tried to use the Wisconsin primary as a springboard to a second nomination—he won only 4.6 percent of the vote—seemed to indicate that primaries offered great risk and little potential for gain.

But a comeback for primaries was not far away. Former Minnesota governor Harold E. Stassen almost captured the Republican nomination in 1948 when he won the Wisconsin, Nebraska, and Pennsylvania primaries. But Stassen saw his chance for the nomination slip away when he took on Sen. Robert Taft in the

latter's home state of Ohio and lost. New York governor Thomas Dewey, the eventual nominee, then beat Stassen in the critical Oregon primary after campaigning there for three weeks.

After the dramatic events of 1948, interest in primary selection surged. A number of states—such as Indiana, Minnesota, and Montana—reinstated primaries in time for the 1952 election, and voter participation in primaries jumped from 4.8 million in 1948 to 12.7 million in 1952. Thus, although enthusiasm did not run as high as it had during the Progressive Era, and some states even repealed primary laws during the 1950s, primaries had found an important niche. *(See Table 1-1, p. 17.)*

*The Mixed System.* Presidential nomination politics evolved into a "mixed system" in the 1950s and 1960s. Under a mixed system, candidates could restrict their public campaigns to a few primaries that would supplement other strengths, such as fundraising ability, endorsements, control of state and local machines, regional and ideological distinctiveness, and skill in negotiations with other political forces. In many cases, the nomination was settled only during negotiations at the summer convention.

The major function of primaries under the mixed system was to allow the candidate to demonstrate an ability to campaign and to appeal to voters. Primaries served to supplement—not replace—other strengths such as ties to the party leadership, to organized labor, or to the business community. Primaries were a rough test of "electability." In 1960 John Kennedy used

**TABLE 1–1** Votes Cast and Delegates Selected in Presidential Primaries, 1912–1996

| Year | Democratic Party | | | Republican Party | | | Total | |
|------|------------------|------|------------------------------------------|------------------|------|------------------------------------------|------------|------------------------------------------|
| | No. of primaries | Votes cast | Delegates selected through primaries (%) | No. of primaries | Votes cast | Delegates selected through primaries (%) | Votes cast | Delegates selected through primaries (%) |
| 1912 | 12 | 974,775 | 32.9 | 13 | 2,261,240 | 41.7 | 3,236,015 | 37.3 |
| 1916 | 20 | 1,187,691 | 53.5 | 20 | 1,923,374 | 58.9 | 3,111,065 | 56.2 |
| 1920 | 16 | 571,671 | 44.6 | 20 | 3,186,248 | 57.8 | 3,757,919 | 51.2 |
| 1924 | 14 | 763,858 | 35.5 | 17 | 3,525,185 | 45.3 | 4,289,043 | 40.4 |
| 1928 | 16 | 1,264,220 | 42.2 | 15 | 4,110,288 | 44.9 | 5,374,508 | 43.5 |
| 1932 | 16 | 2,952,933 | 40.0 | 14 | 2,346,996 | 37.7 | 5,299,929 | 38.8 |
| 1936 | 14 | 5,181,808 | 36.5 | 12 | 3,319,810 | 37.5 | 8,501,618 | 37.0 |
| 1940 | 13 | 4,468,631 | 35.8 | 13 | 3,227,875 | 38.8 | 7,696,506 | 37.3 |
| 1944 | 14 | 1,867,609 | 36.7 | 13 | 2,271,605 | 38.7 | 4,139,214 | 37.7 |
| 1948 | 14 | 2,151,865 | 36.3 | 12 | 2,653,255 | 36.0 | 4,805,120 | 36.1 |
| 1952 | 16 | 4,928,006 | 38.7 | 13 | 7,801,413 | 39.0 | 12,729,419 | 38.8 |
| 1956 | 19 | 5,832,592 | 42.7 | 19 | 5,828,272 | 44.8 | 11,660,864 | 43.7 |
| 1960 | 16 | 5,686,664 | 38.3 | 15 | 5,537,967 | 38.6 | 11,224,631 | 38.5 |
| 1964 | 16 | 6,247,435 | 45.7 | 16 | 5,935,339 | 45.6 | 12,182,774 | 45.6 |
| 1968 | 15 | 7,535,069 | 40.2 | 15 | 4,473,551 | 38.1 | 12,008,620 | 39.1 |
| 1972 | 21 | 15,993,965 | 65.3 | 20 | 6,188,281 | 56.8 | 22,182,246 | 61.0 |
| 1976 | 27 | 16,052,652 | 76.0 | 26 | 10,374,125 | 71.0 | 26,426,777 | 73.5 |
| 1980 | 35 | 18,747,825 | 71.8 | 35 | 12,690,451 | 76.0 | 31,438,276 | 73.7 |
| 1984 | 30 | 18,009,217 | 52.4 | 25 | 6,575,651 | 71.0 | 24,584,868 | 59.6 |
| 1988 | 37 | 22,961,936 | 66.6 | 37 | 12,165,115 | 76.9 | 35,127,051 | 70.2 |
| 1992 | 40 | 20,239,385 | 66.9 | 39 | 12,696,547 | 83.9 | 32,935,932 | 72.7 |
| 1996 | 36 | 10,963,044 | 65.3 | 43 | 15,301,688 | 84.6 | 26,264,732 | 69.2 |

SOURCES: *Guide to U.S. Elections*, 3d ed. (Washington, D.C.: Congressional Quarterly, 1994). The percentages of delegates selected by party for the years 1912–1976 were computed by F. Christopher Arterton and are contained in Arterton, "Campaign Organizations Confront the Media-Political Environment," in *Race for the Presidency*, ed. James David Barber (New York: The American Assembly, 1978), 7. For 1980, *Congressional Quarterly Weekly Report*, June 5, 1980, 1870–1873; for 1984, calculations by CQ staff from data supplied by the Democratic National Committee, and *Congressional Quarterly Weekly Report*, August 25, 1984, 2128; for 1988, *Congressional Quarterly Weekly Report*, February 27, 1988, 532; July 9, 1988, 1894; August 13, 1988, 2254; for 1992, Richard M. Scammon and Alice V. McGillivray, *America Votes 20* (Washington, D.C.: Congressional Quarterly, 1993), and *Congressional Quarterly Weekly Report*; for 1996, Federal Election Commission and *Congressional Quarterly Weekly Report*.

West Virginia's Democratic primary to demonstrate to skeptical party leaders that he could overcome resistance to a Catholic candidacy. Kennedy's earlier victory in Wisconsin's primary had demonstrated an ability to appeal to the more liberal elements of the party. Later, in 1968, Richard Nixon used a string of primary victories to demonstrate that he was not a "loser" with the voters, despite losses in the 1960 presidential and 1962 California gubernatorial campaigns.

Except for candidates whose vote-getting ability was viewed skeptically, the primary under the mixed system was considered a risk. Performing below expectations could be fatal to a campaign, as Lyndon Johnson learned in 1968. Good primary showings, moreover, did not ensure a nomination, as Estes Kefauver learned in 1952.

Primaries always have been vehicles for dark-horse candidates. Eugene J. McCarthy's second-place finish to President Johnson in the 1968 New Hampshire primary established him as a serious candidate. Other dark-horse candidates who became instant contenders after important primary showings included Estes Kefauver (1952), George S. McGovern (1972), Jimmy Carter (1976), George Bush (1980), and Gary Hart (1984).

Under the mixed system, a candidate who dominated the primaries could lose the nomination if enough state party organizations rallied behind other candidates—a highly unlikely event today. For example, Kefauver lost the 1952 Democratic race to Adlai E. Stevenson despite attracting 64.5 percent of the total primary vote to Stevenson's 1.6 percent. In 1968 McCarthy had 38.7 percent of the total primary vote, yet Vice President Hubert H. Humphrey, closely associated with the Vietnam War, won the nomination even though he did not enter any primaries.

The candidacies of Lyndon Johnson in 1960 and Barry Goldwater in 1964 illustrate the possibilities for conducting a candidacy under the mixed system without depending on the primaries. Although Johnson did not announce his candidacy formally until just before the Democratic convention—stating that his duties as Senate majority leader had been too pressing—he had managed to build a strong base of support in the months leading up to the convention. By delivering a series of weekend speeches before state conventions, attending fund-raisers, and appearing before other party groups, Johnson won high visibility for his "noncandidacy" and gained the support of some four hundred southern and Rocky Mountain delegates. But LBJ was painted by rivals as a regional candidate, and his strength going into the convention was limited to a possible vice-presidential nomination to "balance" the national ticket.

Before the primary season began, Goldwater lined up enough delegates to make himself the front-runner for the 1964 Republican nomination. To gain the support of state party organizations, however, he needed some primary wins to persuade party leaders of his popular appeal. The California victory dissipated the chances for a late entry by Pennsylvania governor William Scranton.

Selective participation in primaries no longer appears to be a viable option for a presidential campaign. Humphrey hoped that the Democratic Party would turn to him in a deadlocked convention in the 1970s, but McGovern in 1972 and Carter in 1976 controlled the process before the convention. Humphrey entered most Democratic primaries in 1972 and narrowly outpolled McGovern. Four years later, he participated in few primaries after Carter won in New Hampshire. Gov. Edmund G. "Jerry" Brown Jr. of California was considered a "stalking horse" in 1976 by many Humphrey backers, but he always insisted that he was running for himself. Brown's run was the last serious mixed strategy for a candidate on the sidelines. The last nominee who took part in only a limited number of primaries was Nixon in 1968. Humphrey won the Democratic nomination that year without running in any primaries.

*Recent Years.* Since 1968, primaries, which almost tripled between 1968 and 1996, have been at the center of the nominating process. *(See box, How Primaries Work, p. 19.)* Today, early contests such as the Iowa caucus and New Hampshire primary are vital to any campaign since the media and campaign professionals use those tests to determine a "front-runner."

Candidates now routinely campaign for two years before the first electoral test. Early contests eliminate all but a few candidates, and the survivors battle until one wins enough delegates for a first-ballot nomination at the convention. In recent years, the eventual nominee has emerged well before the convention. Not since Walter Mondale and Gary Hart battled for the Democratic nomination in 1984 has either party had a contest that continued into the final week of the primary season.[51]

*Caucuses.* Since the passage of Democratic reforms after the 1968 election, the nominating process has been dominated by open primaries and caucuses. Caucuses represent a middle ground between primary elections, dominated by the voters, and state conventions, dominated by the party professionals. Before the 1970s, state conventions had been the center of nomination battles. *(See box, How Caucuses Work, p. 20.)*

Caucuses are neighborhood or precinct meetings at which party members debate the merits of the candidates before voting for them; backers of candidates try to persuade other caucus-goers to change sides. At the end of as much as three hours of debate and deal making, each precinct meeting votes on which delegates it will send to county, congressional district, and state conventions. The often sparsely attended caucus meetings covered by the national media, then, are just the first step in allocating delegates to the national party convention. Bargaining continues as a select few party members move from the precinct to the county, congressional district, and state conventions. Because the whole process often takes months, the winner of the early rounds does not always succeed at higher levels.

The media usually cover the outcomes of early caucus maneuverings as if they were straightforward primary balloting. The Iowa caucuses and the New Hampshire primary receive more media attention than other nomination contests. The public nature of today's preelection-year activities stems, in part, from the realization that today's early efforts are unambiguous tests of strength. More sophisticated, open tallying and reporting techniques enable the media to report hundreds of precinct caucuses and conventions quickly. This gives early organizing maneuvers the appearance of being conclusive tests of voter appeal.

## The Franchise and the Electorate

The history of U.S. elections has been the story of efforts to break down legal barriers to voting and expand the size of the electorate. *(See Table 1-2.)* (But in fact the counterpoint to that history was a wide range of practices intended to exclude certain groups from voting.) For example, of the seventeen new amendments added to the Constitution since passage of the Bill of Rights, nine address the way citizens participate in elections.[52] The Supreme Court also has been active in this area. In *Smith v. Allwright* (1944), the Court held that where parties are the chief organizing institution of democracy, all-white primaries are unconstitutional. *Harman v. Forssenius* (1965) struck down the poll tax for federal elections, and *Harper v. Virginia State Board of Elections* (1966) found the poll tax unconstitutional for state and

**TABLE 1–2**    Growing Franchise in the United States, 1932–1996

| Presidential election year | Estimated population of voting age | Vote cast for presidential electors | |
|---|---|---|---|
| | | Number | Percent |
| 1932 | 75,768,000 | 39,758,759 | 52.5 |
| 1936 | 80,174,000 | 45,654,763 | 56.9 |
| 1940 | 84,728,000 | 49,900,418 | 58.9 |
| 1944 | 85,654,000 | 47,976,670 | 56.0 |
| 1948 | 95,573,000 | 48,793,826 | 51.1 |
| 1952 | 99,929,000 | 61,550,918 | 61.6 |
| 1956 | 104,515,000 | 62,026,908 | 59.3 |
| 1960 | 109,672,000 | 68,838,219 | 62.8 |
| 1964 | 114,090,000 | 70,644,592 | 61.9 |
| 1968 | 120,285,000 | 73,211,875 | 60.9 |
| 1972 | 140,777,000 | 77,718,554 | 55.2 |
| 1976 | 152,308,000 | 81,555,889 | 53.5 |
| 1980 | 164,595,000 | 86,515,221 | 52.6 |
| 1984 | 174,468,000 | 92,652,842 | 53.1 |
| 1988 | 182,779,000 | 91,594,809 | 50.1 |
| 1992 | 189,044,000 | 104,405,155 | 55.2 |
| 1996 | 196,509,000 | 96,397,564 | 49.1 |

SOURCES: Bureau of the Census, *Statistical Abstract of the United States 1993* *(Washington, D.C.: Government Printing Office, 1993);* Federal Election Commission.

## HOW PRIMARIES WORK

Presidential primaries fall into two categories. In the presidential preference primary, the first category, voters vote directly for the person they wish to be nominated for president. In the second, voters elect delegates to the national nominating conventions.

States use various combinations of these methods:

• A state may have a preference vote but choose delegates at party conventions. The preference vote may or may not be binding on the delegates. Idaho, Montana, North Dakota, and Vermont have this system for one or both parties. Their preference votes are nonbinding.

• A state may combine the preference and delegate-selection primaries by electing delegates pledged or favorable to a candidate named on the ballot. Under this system, however, state party organizations may run unpledged slates of delegates. Most states use this system or a variation of it.

• A state may have an advisory preference vote and a separate delegate-selection vote in which delegates may be listed as pledged to a candidate, favorable to a candidate, or unpledged.

• A state may have a mandatory preference vote with a separate delegate-selection vote. In these cases, the delegates are required to reflect the preference primary vote. Colorado and Oregon use this system. For 1996, Oregon was the first state to organize a presidential primary conducted by mail.

For those primaries in which the preference vote is binding on the delegates, state laws may vary as to the number of ballots through which delegates at the convention must remain committed.

Most primary states hold presidential preference votes, in which voters choose among the candidates who have qualified for the ballot in their states. Although preference votes may be binding or nonbinding, in most states the vote is binding on the delegates, who either elected in the primary itself or are chosen outside of it by a caucus process, by a state committee, or by the candidates who have qualified to win delegates.

Delegates may be bound for as short a time as one ballot or as long as a candidate remains in the race. National Democratic rules in effect in 1980 required delegates to be bound for one ballot unless released by the candidate they were elected to support. The rule was repealed for 1984.

Until 1980 when it was repealed, the Republicans had a rule requiring delegates bound to a specific candidate by state law in primary states to vote for that candidate at the convention regardless of their personal presidential preferences.

Delegates from primary states are allocated to candidates in various ways. Most of the methods are based on the preference vote—proportional representation, statewide winner-take-all (in which the candidate winning the most votes statewide wins all the delegates), congressional district and statewide winner-take-all (in which the high vote-getter in a district wins that district's delegates and the high vote-getter statewide wins all the at-large delegates), or some combination of the three. States using proportional representation include Colorado, Kansas, Michigan, New Hampshire, and Oregon. Some fifteen states allocate delegates on a statewide or district winner-take-all basis, or a combination of the two. They include California, Florida, Massachusetts, Ohio, and Wisconsin. Still another method is the selection of individual delegates in a "loophole," or direct election, primary. Then the preference vote is either nonbinding or there is no preference vote at all. Among states choosing delegates this way are Illinois, New Jersey, New York, and Pennsylvania.

In the proportional representation system, the qualifying threshold for candidates to win delegates can vary. After a decade of intensive debate, Democratic leaders voted to require proportional representation in all primary and caucus states in 1980. But by 1984, after more rules changes, states were given the right to retain proportional representation only if they wished, awarding delegates to any candidate who drew a minimum of roughly 20 percent of the vote. This threshold was changed for the 1988 election to 15 percent of the vote.

The Republicans allow the primary states to set their own thresholds, which in many states were lower than the Democrats'. In Massachusetts, for example, a GOP candidate in 1980 had to receive only 2.4 percent of the vote to win a delegate.

In nearly half the primary states, major candidates are placed on the ballot by the secretary of state or a special nominating committee. The consent of the candidate is required in only three states: Kentucky, Michigan, and North Carolina. Elsewhere, candidates must take the initiative to get on the ballot. The filing requirements range from sending a letter of candidacy to elections officials (the case in Puerto Rico) to filing petitions signed by a specified number of registered voters and paying a filing fee (the case in Alabama).

On many primary ballots, voters have the opportunity to mark a line labeled "uncommitted" if they do not prefer any of the candidates.

local elections as well.[53] On the legislative front, some of the nation's most storied legislative battles have been fought over the regulation of elections. Voting rights have been a continual source of contention in U.S. politics for the nation as a whole as well as for the individual states.

Almost every U.S. citizen at least eighteen years old is now entitled to vote, subject no longer to restrictions based on wealth and property, sex, and race. Only convicted felons and the insane are denied the vote. Limits on electoral participation are based on registration requirements and the drawing of jurisdictional lines.

The Framers of the Constitution left the regulation of voting rights in the hands of the states. These rights have been expanded at two levels. First, many states have moved to liberalize voting requirements. Second, the federal government has intervened to prohibit the states from excluding certain classes of

History teaches military leaders not to "fight the last war." A strategy that is effective in one conflict might not be so effective in the next—in part because the opposition anticipates the strategy, and in part because battlefield conditions change.

The same lessons apply to a presidential campaign strategy, especially regarding how much emphasis to put on contesting party nominating caucuses. In some years, winning caucuses can be the key to the nomination; in other years, caucuses are simply unimportant to the process. Caucuses were important in the 1960s, unimportant in 1972, and then made a dramatic comeback with the elections of 1976, 1980, and 1984. But the influence of caucuses waned in 1988 and 1992, and campaign strategists were uncertain whether their importance will increase or decline in 1996.

## COMPLEX METHOD

Compared to a primary, the caucus system is complicated. Instead of focusing on a single primary election ballot, the caucus is a multitiered system that involves meetings scheduled over several weeks, sometimes even months. Mass participation occurs at the first level only, with meetings often lasting several hours and, in most of them, attracting only the most enthusiastic and dedicated party members.

Caucuses are operated differently from state to state, and each party has its own set of rules. Most begin with precinct caucuses or some other type of local mass meeting open to all party voters. Participants, often publicly declaring their votes, elect delegates to the next stage in the process.

In smaller states such as Delaware and Hawaii, delegates are elected directly to a state convention, where the national convention delegates are chosen. In larger states such as Iowa, there is at least one more step. Most frequently, delegates are elected at the precinct caucuses to county conventions, where the national convention delegates are chosen.

Voter participation, even at the first level of the caucus process, is much lower than in the primaries. Caucus participants usually are local party leaders and activists. Many rank-and-file voters find a caucus complex, confusing, burdensome, or intimidating.

In a caucus state the focus is on one-on-one campaigning. Thus time, not money, is the most valuable resource for a candidate, as well as an early start, which is far more crucial in a caucus state than in most primaries. Because only a small segment of the electorate is targeted in most caucus states, candidates usually use media advertising sparingly.

Although the basic steps in the caucus process are the same for both parties, the rules that govern them are vastly different. Democratic rules have been revamped substantially since 1968, establishing national standards for grassroots participation. Republican rules have remained largely unchanged, with the states given wide latitude in the selection of delegates. Most Democratic caucuses are open to Democrats only. Republicans generally allow crossovers where state law permits, creating a wide range of variations in caucuses that are closed to members of other parties, open regardless of party, or partially open to independents or voters willing to switch parties. The first step of the Democratic caucus process must be open, well-publicized mass meetings. In most states Republicans do the same. Generally, voters participate only in the election of local party officials, who then meet to begin the caucus process.

## MODERN INFLUENCE

Caucuses in Iowa have dramatically changed the dynamics of presidential nominating campaigns in the modern era.

An obscure former governor of Georgia, Jimmy Carter, spent months wooing the voters of Iowa—and gained national attention with his victory in that state's Democratic caucuses, the nation's first formal balloting. The favorable publicity Carter received for his Iowa upset helped him to win the New Hampshire primary and march to the party nomination.

During the 1960s, a candidate sought to run well in primary states mainly to have a bargaining chip with powerful leaders in the caucus states. Republicans Barry Goldwater in 1964 and Richard Nixon in 1968 and Democrat Hubert Humphrey in 1968 all built up solid majorities among caucus state delegates that carried them to their parties' nominations. Humphrey did not even enter a primary in 1968.

More recently, candidates have placed their principal emphasis on primaries. In 1972 Democrat George McGovern and in 1976 Republican president Gerald Ford and Democratic challenger Jimmy Carter won nomination by securing large majorities of the primary state delegates. Neither McGovern nor Ford won a majority of the caucus state delegates. Carter was able to win a majority only after his opponents' campaigns collapsed.

Carter's victory in the Iowa caucuses transformed caucuses into means of attracting national publicity. Later dark-horse candidates—Republicans George Bush in 1980 and Marion G. "Pat" Robertson in 1988, and Democrats Gary Hart in 1984 and Richard Gephardt in 1988—attracted national attention because of their wins or surprisingly strong showings in the Iowa contests.

But caucuses became controversial in 1984 as they gained in popularity at the expense of presidential primaries. A strong showing in the caucuses by Walter Mondale led many Democrats—and not only supporters of his chief rivals—to conclude that caucuses were inherently unfair.

Mondale's caucus victories could have been termed the revenge of the insiders. More so than primaries, the often complex, low-visibility world of caucuses is open to takeover. The mainstream Democratic coalition of party activists, labor union members, and teachers was primed to dominate the caucuses in Mondale's behalf.

## RECENT CONTESTS

Iowa's influence on the nominating process declined in 1988 and 1992 because of the presence of native-son or near-native-son candidates who easily outdistanced their rivals. In 1988 Richard Gephardt and Paul Simon from the neighboring states of Missouri and Illinois finished a close first and second in the first round of the Democratic caucuses. Neighboring son Robert J. Dole of Kansas took the Republican caucuses in 1988. In 1992 Iowan Thomas Harkin easily defeated the rest of the Democratic field, winning 76 percent of the precinct delegate votes.

Because the winners came from Iowa or thereabouts, pundits dismissed the victories as unimportant signs of provincialism rather than presidential vote-getting ability. Iowans used to exercising exaggerated influence in presidential selection looked forward to 1996, when the Republicans had a wide-open field for their party's nomination for the first time since 1980. Dole again prevailed in Iowa in 1996, but he took only 26.3% of the vote.

The first African American to serve in Congress was Republican Hiram R. Revels of Mississippi, left, who served in the Senate from 1870 to 1871. In 1874 Mississippi Republican Blanche K. Bruce, right, was elected to the Senate. He was the first black member to serve a full term in that chamber.

voters. Over the years, the "nationalization" of economic and political life has been accompanied by the nationalization of election laws. In the first few decades after the United States won independence from Great Britain, the thirteen states allowed only male property-holders or taxpayers to vote. Seven of those states required ownership of land; the others required a certain value of possessions or evidence of having paid taxes. This being the case, about half of all white males were qualified to vote in the Republic's early days. Religious restrictions on voting, prevalent in the colonial period, no longer were the norm. Still, in 1790 women, blacks, Indians, and indentured servants could not vote. Tax-paying requirements gradually replaced property requirements, but by 1850 most states had eliminated the tax-paying restriction as well.[54]

*African Americans and the Right to Vote.* The group facing the most persistent discrimination has been African Americans. The Constitution sanctioned slavery, and in the infamous 1857 *Dred Scott* case the Supreme Court held that slaves are property. The constitutional provision that declares a black to be three-fifths of a person, for census considerations, is perhaps the most convoluted expression of early American disregard for blacks.

Because blacks were at first considered indentured servants who eventually would gain citizenship, blacks in all but three southern states enjoyed some voting rights in the early 1800s. But the extension of slave status to the blacks' entire lifetime steadily reduced the number of potential black voters. By the outbreak of the Civil War, all but six of the thirty-three states

barred blacks from voting at any time, solely because of their race.

The Civil War was not fought primarily over the morality of slavery, as romantic versions of U.S. history assert, but over the issue of states' rights and the regional balance of power in U.S. national politics. The war led, however, to the extension of the vote to blacks. President Abraham Lincoln issued the Emancipation Proclamation on New Year's Day 1863. The proclamation—which had questionable legal status and was derived at least partly from a desire to enlist blacks as soldiers for the Union—granted freedom to slaves in states fighting the Union. Lincoln expressed a desire in writings and public and private talks to move slowly to include blacks in the democratic process. He wished to give priority to "very intelligent" blacks and to blacks who fought for the Union.

In response to the passage of "black codes" in many southern states, which barred blacks from voting and holding office, the Radical Republicans, who controlled Congress after the Civil War, passed a number of measures to bring blacks into U.S. political life. The most important was the Reconstruction Act of 1867, which set up military governments in the Confederate states and tied readmission to the Union to passage of the Fourteenth Amendment, which that year failed to win ratification.

The Fourteenth Amendment is probably the most important constitutional addition besides the Bill of Rights. The amendment—particularly after more expansive readings by the Supreme Court in the twentieth century—bans states from limiting the "privileges and immunities" of U.S. citizens. It orders states to respect all citizens' rights to "due process" and the more general "equal protection of the laws." The amendment also reduces the representation of states that deny the franchise to any male over twenty-one years of age. It passed in 1868. The Fifteenth Amendment, which grants the franchise to all adult males regardless of race or "previous condition of servitude," passed in 1869.

The addition of blacks to the electorate was crucial in Ulysses S. Grant's slim 300,000-vote margin of victory over Horatio Seymour in the 1868 presidential election. Also in that year, blacks for the first time won election to state and federal offices. Between 1870 and 1900, twenty-two southern blacks won election to Congress. Two blacks, Mississippi Republicans Hiram R. Revels and Blanche K. Bruce, served in the U.S. Senate. Federal troops with ties to the Republican Party enforced voting rights.

Federal resolve to guarantee civil rights to blacks died during the maneuvering over the 1876 presidential election results. As part of a deal that gave the disputed election to Republican Rutherford B. Hayes, the Republicans agreed to pull federal troops out of the South and to allow southern states to pass laws restricting blacks' ability to participate in politics and economic and social life.

The old Confederacy kept blacks from the polls with a variety of racially discriminatory measures known as "Jim Crow" laws: poll taxes, literacy tests, "grandfather clauses" (which exempted poor whites from the measures by guaranteeing the franchise to citizens whose ancestors voted or served in the state militia), property requirements, tests of "morality," and the "white primary" (which banned blacks from the Democratic Party with the legal reasoning that the party was a private organization not subject to the Fourteenth Amendment). When these legal means did not block black political activity, violence and threats did. By the turn of the century, southern politics was solely a white man's vocation.

In response to the wide range of voter registration requirements that restricted ballot access to blacks and vulnerable groups of whites, such as illiterates and voters who could be intimidated, the total vote in southern states fell by as much as 60 percent between 1884 and 1904.[55] Ballot restriction during this period was aimed at white agrarian radicals who backed the 1896 presidential campaign of Democrat William Jennings Bryan, but it had the effect of tightening exclusion of blacks.

Shortly after the turn of the century, Congress and the federal courts began to chip away at voting discrimination against African Americans. In 1915 the Supreme Court struck down the use of grandfather clauses, and it banned all-white primaries in 1944 and poll taxes in 1966.[56]

The Civil Rights Act of 1957 established the Civil Rights Commission, which was empowered to study voter discrimination, and expanded the attorney general's authority to bring federal lawsuits against anyone restricting blacks' right to vote. A 1960 law empowered the attorney general to bring further action in suits that disclosed patterns of discrimination and au-

thorized the appointment of federal officials to monitor elections. The Civil Rights Act of 1964 required states to adopt uniform election procedures for all citizens, required states to show sufficient cause for rejecting voters who had completed the sixth grade or demonstrated an equivalent level of intellectual competence, and eased procedures for federal consideration of voting rights cases.

Constitutional revisions further advanced voting rights. The Twenty-fourth Amendment (1964) banned the use of poll taxes in federal elections. Congressional action was crucial to enforcing the constitutional provisions.

The sweeping Voting Rights Act of 1965 suspended literacy tests in seven southern states and parts of another. It also required federal supervision of voter registration in states and counties that on November 1, 1964, still had literacy tests or other qualifying tests and where less than 50 percent of all voting-age citizens had voted in the 1964 presidential election. Jurisdictions under federal supervision needed to receive federal approval for any changes in election procedures. This act led to the addition of one million blacks to the voting rolls.

A 1970 amendment to the Voting Rights Act suspended for five years all literacy tests, whether they were discriminatory or not. In 1970 the Supreme Court upheld that law's constitutionality, and the tests were banned by law permanently in 1975. The "trigger" for federal involvement was applied to additional states and jurisdictions by amendments passed in 1970, 1975, and 1982. The 1982 law extended for twenty-five years the provisions requiring nine states and parts of thirteen others to get Justice Department approval for election law changes. The law also included: "bail-out" procedures for states that had demonstrated a clean ten-year record on voting rights; tests for discrimination based on results rather than intent; and bilingual ballot provisions. For cases involving voting requirements, district lines, and nominating processes, the federal courts consistently have backed up the federal laws extending suffrage to African Americans who had been "locked out" of the system.

*Women and the Vote.* Women won the right to vote with passage of the Nineteenth Amendment in 1920. But the battle for suffrage lasted more than a century, with victories accumulating in the new states in the West, which led the way in complete women's suffrage, before a movement developed nationwide. As in Great Britain and other nations, the women's suffrage question involved not just the right to vote but also bitter protests such as calls for single-issue voting and hunger strikes.

Several states granted women the vote in school board elections in the nineteenth century, but the push for suffrage for women did not end there. The Women's Rights Convention in Seneca Falls, New York, in 1848 marked the unofficial beginning of the feminist movement in the United States. In the late nineteenth century, Susan B. Anthony of Massachusetts led a suffragist movement that claimed the right to vote under the Fourteenth Amendment and sought a constitutional suffrage amendment. But in 1887 Congress defeated the proposal of such an amendment.

Supporters of the Nineteenth Amendment—giving women the right to vote—picket the White House in 1916.

The movement for women's suffrage peaked in 1914 when a more militant group led a campaign against congressional candidates who opposed the amendments. President Woodrow Wilson initially opposed a constitutional amendment, arguing that state action was more appropriate. But when protests escalated to hunger strikes, Wilson announced in 1918 his support for the amendment. As noted, the western states formed the foundation of the suffrage movement and helped to secure quick ratification of the Nineteenth Amendment once Congress sent the amendment to the states in 1919—on its third try in three years. Full voting rights were granted women in Wyoming in 1890; Colorado in 1893; Utah and Idaho in 1896; Washington in 1910; California in 1911; Arizona, Kansas, and Oregon in 1912; Montana and Nevada in 1914; and New York in 1917.

Debate over women's suffrage was not always enlightened. Assertions that women's suffrage would usher in a utopian era of open political action and respect among all citizens were countered with the argument that the amendment would wipe away all distinctions between the sexes.[57] In its push for the vote, the movement did not link up with the civil rights movement; in fact, some suffragists argued that the women's vote would be a bulwark against black demands because women presumably would be more regular and conservative voters.

*Other Issues Related to Voting and Voting Rights.* Residency laws have long posed difficulties for millions of mobile citizens. Many states have required residency in the state of two years, and shorter periods for residency in the county and election district. The 1970 voting rights legislation guaranteed the vote in presidential elections if the citizen had lived in the voting district at least thirty days before the election. This measure made an additional five million people eligible to vote in the 1972 election.

In 1973 the Supreme Court ruled in *Marston v. Lewis* that states could not deny the full franchise to people who had not lived in a state for a year and in a county for three months.[58] By 1980 seventeen states had no residency requirement, and all but one had requirements of thirty days or less.

Congress passed legislation in 1976 guaranteeing the vote to Americans living overseas. Absentee ballots now go to overseas citizens according to their last U.S. address.

The most recent constitutional change affecting the right to vote was the lowering of the voting age to eighteen. Before World War II no state allowed citizens to vote before age twenty-one. Led by Georgia's change in the voting age to eighteen in 1943, after a campaign marked by the slogan "Fight at 18, Vote at 18," several states passed the more liberal requirement. President Dwight Eisenhower proposed a constitutional amendment in 1954, but it died in a Senate committee. The Voting Rights Act of 1970 set a minimum voting age of eighteen for all federal, state, and local elections, but the act was declared unconstitutional for state and local elections. The Court said Congress exceeded its authority because some state constitutions set the voting age at twenty-one. In 1971, however, the voting age was approved under the Twenty-sixth Amendment for all elections.

Low voter participation in the United States has been an ongoing source of concern among democratic theorists and leaders of movements for poor people. No state or federal laws ban any significant class from voting, but only slightly more than half of all eligible citizens vote in presidential elections, and only about a third vote in congressional elections. Explanations for the disappointing turnout range from a lack of meaningful choice to a contentedness with the current policies of the government. The highest percentage of voter participation in recent years was in 1960, when 63 percent of all eligible citizens voted in the presidential race. By 1996 the participation rate had fallen to 49 percent, the lowest point since the 1920s. *(See Figure 1-1, p. 24.)*

The United States and the Western nations with high turnout—such as Great Britain, Germany, Canada, and Australia—differ in how they register citizens to vote. The United

FIGURE 1–1   Percentage of Voting-Age Population that Voted for President, 1920–1996

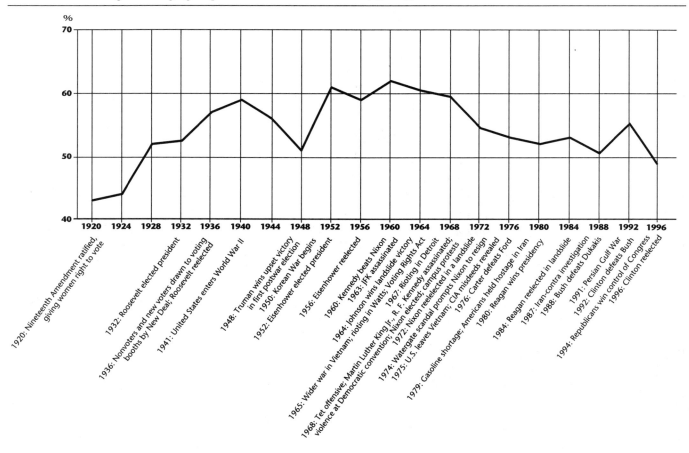

Sources: *Elections '88* (Washington, D.C.: Congressional Quarterly, 1988), 141; *Presidential Elections, 1789–1992* (Washington, D.C.: Congressional Quarterly, 1995), 5.

States is the only nation that places the burden of qualifying for electoral participation on the citizen. In other nations, government agencies sign up voters. Registration is inconvenient in many U.S. jurisdictions (but much less than in the past).

For years, political activists have tried to simplify the process for registering to vote. President Carter backed bills to allow voters to register on election day. By the late 1980s, the majority of U.S. citizens lived in states that allowed postcard registration. Oregon and Wisconsin allow registration on the day of the election, which may explain why the participation rate in those states is about 10 percentage points higher than the national rate.

In 1993 President Clinton signed the "motor-voter" bill into law. The measure requires all states to provide voter registration forms in government offices such as motor vehicle bureaus and public assistance agencies. It also requires states to allow voters to send in registration forms by mail. From 1993 to 1996, a record numbers of new voters—10 million—were registered. Much to the consternation of motor-voter supporters, however, this increase in voter registration did not translate into an increase in voters. In 1996 only 49 percent of the electorate turned out to vote, a decrease of 6 percent from 1992.

In presidential politics, many primaries and caucuses use congressional districts as geographic units. Candidates who win

a congressional district get delegate bonuses. At a lower level, state legislative and local voting districts also hold importance for presidential elections. These smaller, grassroots districts are the basic grounds for participation in all forms of politics, and voters can be encouraged or discouraged to participate because of the competitiveness of local races. Uncompetitive races can undermine the legitimacy of politics.

But the ways in which state legislatures have drawn lines for legislative districts have been an ongoing source of voting rights controversy. The Supreme Court has approved city annexation programs, even if annexation diluted black representation, yet it also has conditionally approved redistricting that created "safe" racial districts. According to the Court, consideration of race is sometimes appropriate in drawing district lines, as long as it does not result in contorted districts intended solely to segregate voters on the basis of race.

The 1982 amendments to the Voting Rights Act of 1965 allow states to create minority legislative districts by concentrating blacks and Hispanic voters. The Republican Party and the National Association for the Advancement of Colored People (NAACP) found themselves unlikely allies on this measure. The NAACP favored creation of guaranteed minority seats, and the GOP favored separating black voting power from nearby districts. Proponents of "stacking" voters point out that minorities are underrepresented in Congress and state legislatures because whites tend to vote against minority candidates. But in the 1993 *Shaw v. Reno* decision, the Supreme Court ruled that such districts could be so "bizarre" that they could be considered unconstitutional racial gerrymandering.[59] Striking down three districts in Texas and one in North Carolina as unconstitutional in 1996, the Court ruled that the districts were drawn with race as the overwhelming factor. The question as to how states were to draw up districts that provided for the equal treatment of all races according to the Voting Rights Act promised to remain clouded until the Court set clear guidelines on redistricting.

### Campaign Practices and Technology

In the early days of partisan politics, newspapers conveyed most campaign messages—and they were unabashedly biased. In the tradition of the Federalist and Anti-Federalist newspaper arguments, leading politicians and interest groups created newspapers specifically for campaigns. Alexander Hamilton started the *Gazette of the United States,* and his rival Thomas Jefferson founded the *National Gazette.* As popular participation in presidential selection grew in the early nineteenth century, parties began to organize partisan appeals and get-out-the-vote drives. Concurrently, they were building the party structures needed to carry out their campaign activities. The two major parties at the time, the Democrats and Whigs, developed hierarchical party organizations. One Whig supporter described a prevalent model:

The fundamental idea is borrowed from the religious organizations of the day. The model of my primary local association is the Christian Church. The officers, the exercises, the exhortations, the singing, the weekly meetings (on Wednesday night), the enrollment of members, the contributions, and all are to be on the primitive apostolic model. . . . These little unit associations are to be mutually fraternized and affiliated to County, District—and state central associations, with regular and definite means of communication. . . .[60]

Tammany Hall, the most famous party organization in U.S. politics, began as a fraternal society in New York City in the late 1700s. Tammany came to typify the party organizations of the nation's states and cities. These "machines" were marked by a pyramidal organization with top-down control, door-to-door recruitment, demands of loyalty, extensive use of patronage, exacting vote-counting, aggressive poll tactics, close relations with businesses and utilities seeking government protection, recreational activities, and parochial concerns. As sociologist Robert Merton has argued, party organizations gained hegemony not only because of their discipline but also because they fulfilled many social needs that governments did not address.[61] In fact, state and local party organizations were central to U.S. politics for more than a century.

After the advent of the New Deal in the 1930s, government at all levels assumed a vast number of functions and specific interest groups began to bear the burden of making demands on the political establishment. As a result, instead of going to a party leader for action, citizens began to approach government agencies and interest groups, as well as legislative representatives. In addition, organizations loyal to specific candidates rather than the parties began to take over the presidential selection process.

The importance of money and patronage in presidential campaigns grew along with the size of the electorate. By 1896 political strategist Mark Hanna had raised as much as $16 million for the presidential campaign of William McKinley. Richard Nixon's reelection campaign in 1972 cost more than $60 million. The total cost of elections at all levels in 1988 was $2.7 billion. In 1992 it was $3.2 billion.[62]

It was not until the late 1800s and early 1900s that candidates were impelled to tour the country making speeches in their own behalf. Not all candidates took to the campaign trail, however; in some campaigns the candidates assumed at least the appearance of a nonpartisan stance. These candidates often were content to stay at home and occasionally issue statements or answer questions while the party organizations mobilized voters. In 1920, for example, Republican Warren Harding spent most of the fall campaigning from his front porch in Marion, Ohio. Even as late as 1932, when Franklin Roosevelt sought the White House, candidates were striking disinterested, nonpartisan poses during the nominating process.

As the public philosophy of "democracy" replaced the more elitist "republicanism" in the 1800s, and as political messages began to be delivered through the mass media, candidates dropped their reluctance to "barnstorm" the country to give a series of speeches. The harbinger of future campaign practices was the 1896 underdog campaign of William Jennings Bryan. Bryan traveled eighteen thousand miles and delivered some six hundred speeches to approximately five million people. The development of the state primary election in the first decade of the twentieth century, and of advanced transportation and communications systems later on, contributed to the tendency of candidates to set out on the hustings.

Primaries demanded that candidates make public appeals for support. Theodore Roosevelt's participation in the 1912 Republican primaries against his handpicked successor as president from four years earlier, William Howard Taft, set the standard for political barnstorming that continues to this day. The primary and Roosevelt institutionalized the kind of public campaign that Bryan inaugurated.

Before the 1960s, primaries were just part of the presidential nominating process. But since a series of Democratic Party reforms were put in place before the 1972 election, primaries have dominated the nominating process. *(See "History of the Primary System," p. 15.)* Today, a candidate cannot win the nomination without undertaking a long public campaign.

The rise of the mass media contributed to the need to make public appeals. Some cities at the turn of the century had as many as a dozen newspapers and many more radio stations. In addition, dozens of mass-circulation magazines helped to shape political debate. Meanwhile citizens had begun to demand more information about the candidates' personal backgrounds and demeanors as well as policy positions. Franklin Roosevelt excelled in making mass media appeals. His campaign talks and "fireside chats" on radio set a new standard for political communication.

The acquisition of television by middle-class American families in the years after World War II ushered in a new age of political discourse. The first presidential candidate to use television advertising was Dwight Eisenhower in 1952. By the 1960s television advertising was an integral element in political campaigning. Virtually every aspect of today's presidential campaign is shaped by considerations of television coverage. The simplicity and visual impact of television messages shape the way candidates are able to present themselves and the way experts judge the strength of a campaign.

The sophisticated polling methods developed after World War II were based on computer analysis and telephone sampling techniques. A Princeton University professor's assessment of consumer demands and shortages during World War II was among the first polls to move beyond simple "snapshots" of candidate strength.[63] Today, media, campaign staffs, and contributors use polls to determine the "viability" of campaign strategies. Privately held polls have become central to the internal strategy of the candidates by helping them to understand the importance of issues and voters' attitudes. In 1952 Eisenhower used polling data to develop themes for television advertising and to target specific socioeconomic voter blocs for appeals. And John Kennedy used polling extensively in his 1960 campaign. Kennedy's strategy for dealing with public resistance to his Catholicism was developed partly with such data.

Today's candidates demand information about how voting groups with specific economic, ethnic, religious, geographic, educational, occupational, and residential characteristics approach issues. Polling data were crucial to the political victories of George McGovern in 1972, Jimmy Carter in 1976, Ronald Reagan in 1980, and Bill Clinton in 1996.

In 1984 campaigns began to use instant polling procedures to determine the effects of specific candidate performances. Selected voters watch candidates in debates and other appearances and register their feelings at intervals of several seconds by adjusting knobs on a handheld computer device. The knobs indicated whether they were feeling positive or negative toward the candidate's specific statements or actions.

More recent campaigns have used videotapes, faxes, electronic mail, telephone calling technology, and targeted radio and cable television appeals to get their messages to the voters. Candidates employ videotapes to promote their own causes and attack their opponents. An "attack video" that depicted Democrat Joseph Biden's plagiarism of a speech by British Labor Party leader Neil Kinnock helped to drive Biden out of the 1988 race. In 1992 the Bush and Clinton campaigns "mass-faxed" attacks and responses to major news outlets. New telephone technology in 1992 allowed automatic dialing and sophisticated routing of calls.

Some democratic theorists have expressed concern about the effects of some technologies—such as sophisticated polling techniques—and media-related tactics. These critics contend that the new technologies are instituting a pervasive process of manipulation. Others maintain that technology offers new possibilities for involving citizens in key electoral and governmental decisions.

### Rules Changes in the Democratic Party

Since 1968 many efforts have been made to reform the presidential nominating process. The most notable of these took place within the Democratic Party, although once the Democrats made changes, the Republicans followed suit. *(See Tables 1-3 and 1-4, p. 27.)* The roots of such reform can be traced in part to the tumultuous political climate of 1968, a year of widespread public disillusionment with politics.[64] In 1968 protests against the Vietnam War reached a new height, and Martin Luther King Jr. and Robert F. Kennedy were assassinated. There were race riots in major cities, student uprisings throughout the country, and bitter confrontations between demonstrators and police. In Washington, President Lyndon Johnson was forced to call out federal troops to protect the White House.

The Tet offensive, launched by North Vietnam against South Vietnam in January 1968, brought massive U.S. casualties and provoked renewed opposition to the Vietnam War. In preparation for the New Hampshire Democratic primary, held March 12, Sen. Eugene McCarthy of Minnesota campaigned against the Vietnam policies of President Johnson. In response, Democratic Party regulars waged a last-minute write-in campaign for the president. They managed to beat McCarthy by 49.6 to 41.9 percent, but the media—impressed by McCarthy's showing against the president in a conservative state—portrayed Johnson as the big loser.

McCarthy's "victory" underscored the lack of popular support for Johnson's policies and prompted Sen. Robert Kennedy of New York to enter the race against the president on March 16. Two weeks later, on March 31, with a McCarthy victory predicted in the Wisconsin primary, Johnson withdrew his candidacy. Nevertheless, divisiveness within the Democratic Party continued. Vice President Hubert Humphrey entered the race as Johnson's heir apparent on April 27, having purposely delayed his formal entry into the campaign to avoid participating in the Democratic primaries. With the support of party regulars (who commanded delegate votes), Humphrey banked on a victory at the Democratic national convention. That victory was ensured when Robert Kennedy was assassinated on June 5. But it was a hollow one, won at a bitterly divided convention that was shaken by violent protests and ugly confrontations between the police and demonstrators. Humphrey, who had campaigned on the theme of the "politics of joy," accepted the nomination amid the politics of anger.

But the anger was felt not merely on the streets. Beyond the rancor of the antiwar demonstrators, the hurling of rocks and debris in the streets, and the clubbings and gassing by the police, there was anger on the convention floor. State delegations who opposed the nomination of Humphrey felt excluded from the

**TABLE 1-3**  Democratic Party's Reform Commissions on Presidential Selection

| Known as | Formal name | Years in operation | Chair | Size | Mandating body | Major recommendations | Distinctive features | Principal report |
|---|---|---|---|---|---|---|---|---|
| McGovern-Fraser Commission | Commission on Party Structure and Delegate Selection | 1969–1972 | Sen. George McGovern (S.D.), 1969–1970; Rep. Donald M. Fraser (Minn.), 1971–1972[a] | 28 | 1968 national convention | "Quotas"; rules for opening delegate selection to 1972 national convention | First, most ambitious, and most important of reform groups. Completely rewrote rules for presidential selection; made them mandatory for state parties and state practices; changed power distribution within Democratic Party; set model other reform commissions attempted to follow. | *Mandate for Change* (1970) |
| Mikulski Commission | Commission on Delegate Selection and Party Structure | 1972–1973 | Barbara A. Mikulski, Baltimore city councilwoman | 81 | 1972 national convention | Modified McGovern-Fraser rules; revised quotas; provided for proportional representation of presidential candidates' strength; increased role of party regulars in delegate selection | Commission had a stormy, if brief, life. Its principal recommendations were intended to placate regulars and modify most controversial aspects of McGovern-Fraser rules. Its major achievement, however, was in *not* seriously revising the McGovern-Fraser provisions. With the work of this commission, the assumption underlying the reforms became generally accepted within the party. | *Democrats All* (1973) |
| Winograd Commission | Commission on Presidential Nomination and Party Structure | 1975–1976 1976–1980[b] | Morley Winograd, former chairman of Michigan Democratic Party | 58 | 1976 national convention | 10% "add-on" delegates for party officials; steps to close system at top | Vehicle of party regulars and Carter administration to tighten system, increase role of party regulars, and adopt rules expected to help Carter's renomination. Developed complicated procedures that are heavily dependent on national party interpretation. | *Openness, Participation and Party Building: Reforms for a Stronger Democratic Party* (1978) |
| Hunt Commission | Commission on Presidential Nomination | 1980–1982 | Gov. James B. Hunt Jr. of North Carolina | 70 | 1980 national convention | 25% quota for party officials | Expanded role of party and elected officials in national conventions. | *Report of the Commission on Presidential Nomination* (1982) |
| Fairness Commission | Fairness Commission | 1984–1986 | Donald Fowler, chairman of South Carolina Democratic Party | 53 | 1984 national convention | Loosened restrictions on "open primaries"; lowered the threshold for "fair representation" to 15%; increased number of "superdelegates." | Tried to satisfy both wings of the party by simultaneously increasing the power of party leaders (by increasing the number of superdelegates) and by lowering the threshold for fair representation. | No formal report. |

SOURCE: Reprinted by permission from William J. Crotty, *Party Reform* (New York: Longman, 1983), 40–43. Updated by the authors.
NOTES: a. Fraser assumed chair January 7, 1971.  b. The original Winograd Commission was not authorized by the national convention. It was created by the national chairman, Robert Strauss. The post-1976 committee membership was expanded.

**TABLE 1-4**  Republican Party's Reform Committees on Presidential Selection

| Known as | Formal name | Years in operation | Chair | Size | Mandating body | Major recommendations | Distinctive features | Principal report |
|---|---|---|---|---|---|---|---|---|
| DO Committee | Committee on Delegates and Organization | 1969–1971 | Rosemary Ginn, member, Republican National Committee, from Missouri | 16 | 1968 national convention | Proposals for increasing participation in delegate selection process. | The committee's recommendations were not binding; designed "to implement the Republican Party's Open Door policy." | No formal report. |
| Rule 29 Committee | Rule 29 Committee | 1973–1975 | Rep. William A. Steiger (Wis.) | 57 | 1972 national convention | Implement "positive action" to open delegate selection process; institute RNC review of such actions. | Most ambitious reform effort by the Republican Party. The committee's major recommendations, however, were rejected by the RNC and by the 1976 national convention. | No formal report. |

SOURCE: Compiled by the authors.

process, and they let their bitterness be known. Supporters of McCarthy were particularly angry. During the campaign, they had formed the ad hoc Commission on the Democratic Selection of Presidential Nominees, chaired by Iowa governor Harold Hughes. Just before the start of the convention the commission had issued its report, which told of unfair representation of McCarthy during the delegate-selection process and of manipulation by party leaders. In fact, the nominating process allowed for relatively little influence by rank-and-file Democrats. Nearly one-third of the convention delegates already had been chosen by the time McCarthy announced his candidacy.[65] As political scientist William Crotty has written: "Presidential selection [in the Democratic Party] was controlled from the top down. The rules governing the process, to the extent that they existed, were made and enforced by those in power, the party regulars in charge of party operations. Such things as primary victories and popular support among grassroots party elements had little effect on the choice of a presidential nominee."[66] In short, the Hughes Commission report concluded that the Democratic Party's delegate-selection process displayed "considerably less fidelity to basic democratic principles than a nation which claims to govern itself can safely tolerate."[67]

*The McGovern-Fraser Commission.* At the 1968 Democratic convention, examples of perceived abuses received widespread attention and served to increase animosity toward Humphrey and the party regulars. In the wake of Humphrey's nomination, many elements of the Democratic Party were determined to change the rules of the game. The report of the convention's Credentials Committee echoed that sentiment. The report alleged unfair and exclusionary practices in the delegate-selection process and proposed the establishment of a committee to examine the problem and offer recommendations. As a result, in February 1969 the party established the Commission on Party Structure and Delegate Selection, chaired by Sen. George McGovern of South Dakota and, later, by Rep. Donald M. Fraser of Minnesota. (The commission came to be known as the McGovern-Fraser Commission.) Its report, issued a little more than a year later, set forth eighteen detailed "guidelines" for the state delegate-selection processes.

The commission's guidelines were designed to counteract rules and practices that either inhibited access to the processes or diluted the influence of those who had access. They condemned discrimination because of race, color, creed, sex, or age and required that affirmative steps be taken to give delegate representation to minorities, women, and young people in proportion to their population in each state. The guidelines further required that restrictive fees (defined as those exceeding $10) and petition requirements for delegate candidates be eliminated and "urged" that undue restrictions on voter registration (such as literacy tests, lengthy residency requirements, and untimely registration periods) be eliminated. To help prevent dilution of individual delegates' influence, the guidelines banned the "unit rule" (whereby a majority of delegates bound the rest to their will) and "proxy voting" (which allowed votes to be cast for

someone who was absent from a meeting) at every level of the delegate-selection process; set minimum quorum provisions for party committees; and disallowed ex officio delegates (who were automatically appointed because of their public or party position). In addition, the guidelines limited the influence of party committees in the selection of delegates, required written rules for governing the process, demanded adequate public notice of all meetings pertaining to delegate selection, and called for standardized apportionment.

Stressing that its guidelines were mandatory, the McGovern-Fraser Commission finished its work early. Thus by the time the 1972 Democratic national convention met, the commission was able to claim that virtually all the states were in at least substantial compliance with the guidelines, that only 1.1 percent of the convention delegates were still elected by state party committees, and that the percentages of black, females, and young delegates had increased three to four times over their percentages in 1968.[68]

The guideline's effects were considerable. On the one hand, compliance substantially democratized the system by opening avenues for citizen participation. On the other hand, it greatly reduced the power of party leaders, prompting some observers to say that the reforms had "dismantled" the party.[69] In the process, delegate-selection systems were fundamentally altered. For example, "party caucuses" and "delegate primaries" were abolished in favor of "participatory conventions" and "candidate primaries." In the party caucus system, national convention delegates had been chosen by delegates who had been chosen by low-level party officers. In the participatory convention, selection of the intermediary delegates was not limited to party officers but was open to any party member. In the delegate-primary system, the names of delegates to the national convention (rather than the names of presidential candidates) had appeared on the ballot. The candidate primary required that the names of presidential candidates, instead of just the names of their potential delegates, be listed on the ballot.[70]

The McGovern-Fraser guidelines also urged a move toward the proportional representation—or what they called fair representation—commonly found in European electoral systems but unusual in the United States. Under proportional representation, delegates were assigned in proportion to the percentage of the total that each candidate received. (The usual alternative was a "winner-take-all" system, in which the candidate who won a plurality of the popular vote received all of the delegate votes in the electoral district.) Furthermore, the guidelines were interpreted as requiring mandatory "quotas" for the representation of minority groups in proportion to their share of the population.

Although states were in substantial compliance with the guidelines by the 1972 Democratic convention, there was considerable resistance to the reforms. More than 40 percent of the convention's membership and more than half of the states challenged some aspect of the guidelines.[71] But complete compliance was achieved because a state's delegation at the convention could not be seated unless the state had followed the guidelines.

Criticism of the reforms increased after the Democratic Party's debacle in the 1972 election. Some observers argued that the new rules contributed to McGovern's overwhelming loss to Nixon. They argued that a demographically balanced slate of delegates was not necessarily representative of the constituency of the Democratic Party. More to the point, the rules had produced a slate of delegates that was significantly more liberal than the party's rank and file. Political scientist Jeane J. Kirkpatrick, for example, found that in 1972 the policy preferences of the average Democrat were better represented by Republican delegates than by Democratic delegates.[72] While it was not clear that the reforms themselves were responsible for the situation in 1972, as some critics have contended,[73] there was no denying the magnitude of the Democrats' loss.

*The Mikulski Commission.* The 1972 Democratic convention called for the establishment of another delegate-selection commission. The call was largely in response to the controversy over some of the McGovern-Fraser reforms. By the time it was actually appointed, the new Commission on Delegate Selection and Party Structure (chaired by Baltimore city councilwoman Barbara Mikulski) was facing a Democratic Party even more badly split than in 1968 between those who wanted a return to traditional procedures and those advocating further reforms. The commission responded by trying, at least rhetorically, to appease both sides.[74]

Since the strongest reaction against the McGovern-Fraser Commission had been over quotas, the Mikulski Commission sought to placate critics by making it clear that quotas were not required, although they were permitted. (Indeed, the McGovern-Fraser Commission had not originally intended for them to be mandatory.) The Mikulski Commission dictated, however, that "affirmative action programs" be adopted to expand the participation of women and minority groups in party affairs.[75] As further concessions to the critics of McGovern-Fraser, the Mikulski Commission allowed party regulars to appoint up to 25 (instead of 10) percent of a state's delegation; partly removed the ban on proxy voting and eased quorum requirements; extended convention privileges (not including voting rights) to public officials and party regulars (although it retained the ban on ex officio delegates); and loosened the formula for apportioning delegates within states.

Nevertheless, advocates of reform won a major victory in the decision of the Mikulski Commission to require proportional representation of all candidates receiving a minimum of 10 percent of the vote (later changed to "from 10 to 15 percent," to be decided by individual state parties)—something that McGovern-Fraser had "urged" but not required. In short, the Mikulski Commission advanced, to the extent that it could, the goals of the McGovern-Fraser Commission. To the degree that it loosened earlier requirements, it did so not to emasculate them but to make the reforms more palatable to those within the Democratic Party who had opposed the reforms established by the earlier commission.[76]

In the wake of the Democratic Party's reforms, the number of presidential primaries mushroomed. Between 1968 and 1976 they nearly doubled (increasing from seventeen to thirty). Most state party leaders felt that the adoption of a presidential primary was the easiest way to conform to the rules and thereby prevent a challenge to their delegates at the next national convention. Party regulars also feared that reformed caucuses would bring activists into wide-ranging party decision making—a consequence that they felt was worse than turning to a primary system.

Members of the McGovern-Fraser Commission had not intended for there to be such an increase in primaries. As Austin Ranney, a distinguished political scientist and member of the commission, has written:

I well remember that the first thing we members of the [commission] agreed on—and about the only thing on which we approached unanimity—was that we did not want a national presidential primary or any great increase in the number of state primaries. Indeed, we hoped to prevent any such development by reforming the delegate-selection rules so that the party's nonprimary processes would be open and fair, participation in them would greatly increase, and consequently the demand for more primaries would fade away. . . .

But we got a rude shock. After our guidelines were promulgated in 1969 no fewer than eight states newly adopted presidential primaries, and by 1972 well over two-thirds of all the delegates were chosen or bound by them. . . . So here was a case in which we had a clear objective in mind; we designed our new rules to achieve it; we got them fully accepted and enforced; and we achieved the opposite of what we intended.[77]

*The Winograd Commission.* Whether or not it was caused directly by the McGovern-Fraser reforms,[78] the proliferation of presidential primaries was disturbing to party regulars because primary elections tend to weaken the role of state political parties in selecting candidates. The result was the formation of yet another Democratic Party commission in 1975: the Commission on the Role and Future of Presidential Primaries (later changed to the Commission on Presidential Nomination and Party Structure), headed by former Michigan Democratic chairman Morley Winograd. Despite its original purpose, the Winograd Commission ultimately skirted the question of primaries. With the election of Jimmy Carter in 1976, the commission was recast to reflect at least partially the interests of President Carter (which included protecting the incumbent). When it produced its final report, the commission stated that it could not reach a consensus on the issue of primaries, and it offered no recommendations in that area.

Unlike its earlier counterparts, the Winograd Commission worked without the fanfare of publicity—the media had largely lost interest in the reform process. Political scientist William Crotty suggested that this lack of publicity played into the hands of the White House and a number of the commission's recommendations seemed to bear that out.[79] First, the nominating season was shortened to three months, from the second Tuesday in March to the second Tuesday in June (although exemptions to go earlier were given later to several states, including Iowa and New Hampshire). This change tended to favor the incumbent president because in a tightened time frame, the effect of early primaries and caucuses (where long shots can be thrust onto center stage) would have been diminished, and there would have been less time for unknown candidates to gain name recognition and money.

Second, the Winograd Commission proposed that filing deadlines for a candidate to enter a primary or a caucus be at least fifty-five days before the selection of delegates. This, too, favored an incumbent by discouraging last-minute challengers. The Democratic National Committee (DNC) later amended the proposal and allowed deadlines to fall within a more flexible thirty- to ninety-day range, according to each state.

Third, the commission proposed that the threshold for a candidate to be eligible for a proportional share of delegates be based on an increasing scale of from 15 to 25 percent as the nominating season progressed. Although it was argued that this system would give a fair chance to long shots in the early phase of the campaign, the proposal made it extremely difficult for a candidate to wage a successful challenge to a front-runner or incumbent over the entire course of the season. Again, the DNC overruled the proposal and set a threshold range of from 15 to 20 percent.

Finally, the commission proposed the "bound-delegate" rule, which required that a delegate who was elected in behalf of a particular candidate be bound to vote for that candidate at the national convention. This became a major point of contention at the 1980 Democratic convention when Sen. Edward Kennedy of Massachusetts—hoping to upset the renomination of Carter—forced a floor fight over the rule. Kennedy's argument was that the bound-delegate rule prevented delegates from taking into account events since their selection (such as the entry of a new candidate into the field). This rule also was problematic because it weakened the role of the national convention (and thus, arguably, party regulars) by allowing delegates no discretion on early ballots, while ostensibly promoting the grassroots participatory ethos of earlier reforms.

In ultimately altering a number of these proposals, the Democratic National Committee made them less favorable to the White House. Indeed, the influence of the White House on the commission can be overstated. Some of the proposals were adopted because of considerations other than simply protecting an incumbent. Many reformers saw the shortening of the primary season, for example, as a way of "reducing the fragmentation" of the nominating process—of cutting costs and streamlining a process they felt was unnecessarily long.[80]

Other proposals of the Winograd Commission included a ban on open primaries (meaning that a registered Republican could no longer vote in a Democratic primary); a suggestion that state party committees be able to appoint an additional 10 percent of the delegates to the national convention; continued support of affirmative action programs to represent women and minorities; and a rejection of the idea that state delegations should be equally divided between men and women because

such a recommendation too closely resembled quotas. The Democratic National Committee later overturned this last point in its call to the 1980 convention.

Finally, the commission eliminated so-called loophole primaries, which had served to undermine proportional representation. In such primaries, citizens voted directly for individual delegates (rather than the delegates being distributed in proportion to the relative vote tallies of the presidential candidates). The individual delegates receiving pluralities won. Since such primaries generally produced winner-take-all results, they were a "loophole" to the proportional representation requirement of the party rules.[81]

*The Hunt Commission.* By 1980 the establishment of commissions on party rules at the Democratic national convention had become a tradition. That year the party created the Commission on Presidential Nomination, chaired by North Carolina governor James B. Hunt Jr. The express purpose of the Hunt Commission was to strengthen the party.

One of its most important recommendations was to increase the number of delegate slots reserved for party leaders and elected officials (since known as superdelegates). The Hunt Commission went beyond the 10 percent "add-on" of the Winograd Commission to one of approximately 25 percent. Negotiations for the add-on had been complicated. The final proposal called for two delegate slots from each state for the chair and vice chair of its Democratic Party; one hundred additional slots to be distributed among the states in proportion to the size of their base delegations; and a guarantee that every state would have enough slots to accommodate its "core" Democratic officials (governor, members of Congress, and mayors of cities with populations of more than 250,000). Although the 10 percent add-on provided by the Winograd Commission had consisted of delegates entirely pledged to candidates, the scheme adopted by the Hunt Commission allowed for a relatively large increment (almost twice the number of the original 10 percent) that would not be pledged.[82]

Another important move by the Hunt Commission was its decision to cut back on the trend toward proportional representation. Most notably, it rescinded the Winograd Commission's ban on loophole primaries. Furthermore, the threshold for receiving proportional representation was raised to 20 percent in caucus states and to 25 percent in primary states, and states were allowed to give "bonus delegates" to the winner of the primary to better reflect that candidate's strength (the "winner-take-more" option).

In addition, the Hunt Commission repealed the bound-delegate rule that had caused controversy at the 1980 convention. This action returned delegates to the pre–Winograd Commission "good conscience" standard. Finally, the Hunt Commission retained the affirmative action rule; maintained the policy that delegations be equally divided between men and women (the "equal division" rule); continued to allow candidates to approve their delegates; and reaffirmed the Winograd Commission's shortening of the nominating season to three months. (The commission gave specific exemptions—notably to Iowa and New Hampshire—but with strict limits as to how much earlier than the other states they could be.)

*The Fairness Commission.* The most recent of the long-standing series of reform efforts within the Democratic Party, the Fairness Commission, was headed by Donald Fowler, chairman of the Democratic Party in South Carolina. In its report, adopted by the DNC on March 8, 1986, the commission reiterated many of the recommendations of earlier commissions. Most notably it provided an opportunity for some states (such as Wisconsin and Montana) to hold open primaries. The rule, however, was tightly worded so that states that traditionally had restricted participation to Democrats could not move to open systems.

The Fairness Commission also eased the mechanism for loophole primaries, but it lowered the threshold for "fair" (proportional) representation to 15 percent. In addition, it further increased the number of delegate slots that were reserved for unpledged superdelegates. In 1988, two years after the commission finished its work, Jesse Jackson won primaries in ten states plus the District of Columbia, Puerto Rico, and the Virgin Islands. At the Democratic national convention, however, Jackson won only two states (South Carolina and Mississippi), the District of Columbia, and the Virgin Islands because of the votes of superdelegates.[83] As a concession to Jackson, the Rules Committee recommended at the convention that the number of superdelegates be reduced in 1992. Instead, the Democrats added more superdelegates, raising the total to 18 percent of the delegates in 1992 and 1996.

*Effects of Democratic Reforms.* The combined effects of the Democratic Party's quadrennial reform efforts have been significant. For example, the codification of rules that were binding on state parties has led to a centralization of power within the national Democratic Party and a loss of autonomy of state party leaders. At the same time, the reforms have greatly increased the participation of rank-and-file members, leading to the rise of a more "plebiscitary" system (that is, a system based on the vote of the people). The proliferation of primaries that accompanied the reforms also has bolstered the rise of direct democracy. And not least, the reforms have transformed the national party convention. Although many observers had thought that the rise of proportional representation would increase the role of the convention by creating a situation in which there were many candidates and no front-runners, this has not happened. Instead, the convention has become a rubber stamp—formally adopting a decision already made by the popular vote of the rank and file. Indeed, no major party presidential nomination has required more than a single vote since the Democrats nominated Adlai Stevenson on the third ballot in 1952.

### Rules Changes in the Republican Party

Although the proliferation of primaries that accompanied the reforms of the Democratic Party also affected the Republicans, they did not experience the same kind of internal pressures to reform that the Democrats did.[84] While liberal insurgents within the Democratic Party found the party's rules to be a barrier to their participation, prompting them to push for reform in 1968, the Republicans faced no such problem. To a large degree, this was because the Republicans were a smaller, more ideologically cohesive party than the Democrats. The Republicans also had far fewer minority members, which meant that from within its ranks there was less demand for equal representation.

To the extent that ideological factions did exist within the Republican Party, they did not find the rules problematic. Indeed, conservative insurgents had been quite successful in 1964. In short, a grassroots movement promoting specific policy goals (an "amateur" movement, to use the terminology of James Q. Wilson) was apparently more feasible among the Republicans than among the Democrats. It was the failure of a similar "amateur" movement against party "professionals" within the Democratic ranks that helped to spawn that party's reform.[85]

There also were differences in the structures of the two parties. Republican rules were strictly codified and could be changed only with the approval of the national convention, whereas the Democrats' rules were very loose and not codified, and changes did not have to be approved by the national convention. The ad hoc (or "common law") tradition of the Democratic rules at the national level thus made changes easy and invited reform.

Finally, the Republicans already had achieved several reforms sought by Democrats. Use of the unit rule at the Republican national conventions had been banned since the mid-nineteenth century. A similar ban on proxy voting at the national convention had long been in force. Leaders of the Republican Party were quick to point out that the reforms the Democrats were getting around to in 1968 had been accomplished by their party years before.

But clearly the Democrats' reforms went beyond the existing rules of the Republican Party. Nevertheless, rank-and-file Republicans were not overly anxious to keep up the pace. The Democrats were more amenable to the centralization of national party control, and a number of the Democrats' farther-reaching efforts—such as quotas or strictly enforced affirmative action programs—were discouraged by the conservative ideology of the Republican Party. Indeed, after the initial reforms of the Democrats, the Republicans warned against the effects that "McGovernizing" their party could bring about.

Nonetheless, the Republicans did institute some reforms in the post-1968 era, often along the same lines as the Democrats. *(See Table 1-4, p. 27.)* David Price, a political scientist and U.S. representative from North Carolina who served as staff director of the Hunt Commission, has written that the Republicans' efforts were partly "imitative," often "reactive," and to a degree "defensive."[86]

The reforms were *imitative* in the sense that the Republicans were eager to garner some of the publicity that the Democrats had engendered from their early reforms. The Republicans also were eager to reduce discrimination and to broaden their demographic base—especially among young voters who had recently been enfranchised by the Twenty-sixth Amendment in 1971.

Republican reforms were *reactive* in that Republicans did not want to adopt what they perceived to be the debilitating aspects of the Democrats' reforms—this is what they feared when they warned against "McGovernizing." The Republican national convention amended its rules in 1976 so that a subcommittee of the Republican National Committee (RNC) would undertake all future rules review—an effort to prevent "run-away" commissions.

Finally, the Republican Party reforms were *defensive* in the sense that reforms by the Democratic Party often prompted changes in state laws that also affected the Republicans. As a result, Republicans had to accommodate those changes—whatever their own rules may have been. More recently, Republicans have tried to anticipate Democratic rules changes that would affect them.

In 1968 the Republican national convention called for the establishment of a committee to consider party rules changes. All sixteen members of the Committee on Delegates and Organization (DO Committee), chaired by Rosemary Ginn of Missouri, came from the Republican National Committee. Unlike the recommendations of the McGovern-Fraser Commission, the DO Committee's recommendations were not binding. Indeed, the report contained no enforcement or compliance mechanism at all, which reflected the states' rights orientation of the Republican Party.

Among the DO Committee's recommendations were proposals to ban ex officio delegates, to eliminate proxy voting in meetings on delegate selection, and to "attempt" to have an equal number of men and women in each state's delegation to the national convention. The 1972 national convention later approved these recommendations but rejected a DO Committee proposal that delegations try to include youths under the age of twenty-five in proportion to their population in each state. Nevertheless, the convention strengthened the rule to end discrimination and increase participation. It also established a new reform committee under Rule 29 of its bylaws.

The Rule 29 Committee was chaired by Rep. William A. Steiger of Wisconsin. Its fifty-eight members included not only members of the RNC but also state party leaders, governors, members of Congress, young people, and other representatives of the Republican Party. Among its recommendations was a proposal that state parties be required to take "positive action" to broaden participation and, most important, that state action be reviewed by the RNC. Although no sanctions were attached to the review procedure, and quotas were not a part of the recommendation, the RNC objected to the proposal on the grounds that it interfered with the states' rights outlook of the party. The 1976 national convention rejected the establishment of any compliance procedures.

Since 1976, subcommittees of the RNC have undertaken all rules reviews. To date, such subcommittees have not brought about any significant changes affecting the delegate-selection process.

### Constitutional Change

After Franklin Roosevelt won four terms to the White House, Republicans in Congress succeeded in initiating a constitutional amendment that would limit future presidents to two terms. By 1951 the Twenty-second Amendment, barring third terms, was part of the Constitution. The incumbent president, Harry Truman, was exempted from the limit, which took effect with the election of Dwight Eisenhower in 1952.

The Twenty-second Amendment has changed the dynamics of national elections. To the extent that a president derives bargaining strength by appealing to possible future electoral tests, a second-term president is less powerful.

The two-term limit had been followed as a matter of tradition before FDR. Thus the precedent George Washington unintentionally set when he refused to seek a third term held until 1940. An effort to pass a two-term amendment in 1876, to prevent President Ulysses Grant from seeking a third term, failed. (He was denied renomination by his party.) Other presidents, such as Woodrow Wilson, indicated that they would like a third term, but they did not receive the nomination again. Even if a third term was in practice not probable, the mere possibility that a president always could seek reelection affected the power maneuverings between the president and Congress.

Franklin Roosevelt was the only president to run for a third term. Members of the administration who had become candidates on their own—such as Vice President John Nance Garner and Postmaster General James Farley—found themselves undercut by the maneuvers of their boss. After months of speculation about whom the president might tap as his successor, Roosevelt willingly accepted a "draft" for the Democratic nomination in 1940.

Since the amendment's passage, prominent figures including Eisenhower and Ronald Reagan have questioned the wisdom of the two-term limit. In 1984, with President Reagan's popularity at an all-time high and no other Republicans developing a similarly loyal following, a brief movement to repeal the Twenty-second Amendment developed. But the movement probably never had a chance because Reagan was by far the oldest president in history. The movement died when Reagan became embroiled in a controversy over the arms-for-hostages deal with Iran and the secret use of profits from the arms sales to support Nicaraguan rebels.

### Turning Points in the Alignment of the Electorate

Several elections since 1828 have fundamentally altered the population's voting habits and the discourse of U.S. politics. Scholars differ over the proper definition of terms such as *critical election* and *realignment*. Nevertheless, a number of elections stand out as turning points. *(See Chapter 3, Chronology of Presidential Elections.)*

*The Rise of Andrew Jackson: 1828.* The hold of the so-called Virginia dynasty on U.S. politics was routed by the ascendance of Andrew Jackson, a hero of the War of 1812. The rough-hewn Tennessean lost the 1824 election to John Quincy Adams after the electoral college deadlocked and sent the contest to the House of Representatives. Jackson asserted that Adams stole the election by making a deal with Henry Clay, and Jackson plotted revenge. In 1828 Jackson won easily with his broad appeal among farmers and common laborers, especially in the West. As the nation expanded economically and geographically, Jackson's appeal for democratic processes to replace elite maneuverings was bound to get a sympathetic hearing.

Under the tutelage of Vice President Martin Van Buren of New York, Jackson developed a strong national Democratic Party based on patronage. Strict party organization soon became a prerequisite for competition in national politics. The Whigs' 1836 presidential campaign was the last in which a party eschewed a unified national ticket (that year the Whigs backed three presidential nominees and two vice-presidential nominees). Van Buren easily defeated the Whigs in 1836.

*Preservation of the Union: 1860 and 1864.* After passage of the Kansas-Nebraska Act in 1854, which reopened the slavery question by allowing several new territories to decide the issue by popular sovereignty, the nation became irreparably divided over whether slavery should be extended into new territories. The legislation undermined the delicate balance of power between slave and nonslave states and aroused dissension over a wide variety of sectional issues such as internal improvements, protective tariffs, economic regulation, and the currency.

In the 1860 presidential race, Abraham Lincoln of Illinois defeated two candidates from the divided Democratic Party and one from the Constitutional Unionist Party on a platform of containment of slavery. After Lincoln's election in November 1860, the Southern states seceded and in February 1861 formed the Confederate States of America. For the next four years, the Union and the Confederacy fought the Civil War.

Lincoln won reelection in 1864 under the banner of the Republican Party. As for the war, it was the most technologically sophisticated and, at the time, the bloodiest in U.S. history. In the end, however, the Confederacy was restored to the Union.

*Radical Reconstruction: 1868.* Northern Republicans were bent on revenge in 1868, particularly because the stubborn Southern Democrat Andrew Johnson had succeeded to the presidency after Lincoln's assassination in April 1865. The Republicans nominated Gen. Ulysses Grant of Illinois, who narrowly defeated New York Democrat Horatio Seymour. With the Republicans in control of Congress, the South came under a set of retributive policies. The Republicans controlled the South through military governors and proceeded with industrial expansion in the North and West aided by high tariffs. Grant's administration is considered to be one of the most corrupt in history. Republican Reconstruction policies—motivated in part by humanitarian concern for the recently freed slaves and in part by a desire for revenge—embittered the South perhaps as much

as the war. Once Reconstruction was over, the Democrats dominated the old Confederacy for years to come.

*Electoral Legitimacy and the Rise of Jim Crow: 1876.* Disputed election results in the 1876 contest between Republican Rutherford B. Hayes of Ohio and Democrat Samuel Tilden of New York created a constitutional crisis and brought fears that another civil war was imminent. The crisis was solved, however, through backroom bargaining that gave the Republicans the presidency in exchange for a pledge to pull federal troops out of the Confederacy and commit federal money to internal improvements in the South. The deal essentially left southern politics in the hands of many of the same figures who had led the Confederacy. In the years that followed, Democrats took control of the political apparatus and passed a series of racially discriminatory measures—known as "Jim Crow" laws—that disfranchised African Americans.

*Defeat of Populism: 1896.* After decades of falling agricultural prices, debt, and bankruptcy, farmers took over the Democratic Party and in 1896 nominated one of their own, William Jennings Bryan of Nebraska, as president. Bryan called for unlimited coinage of silver to expand the money supply and to lighten the financial burden of farmers. But his opponent, Republican William McKinley, spent ten times as much as Bryan and won the election, which saw voter turnout at an all-time high. As it turned out, Bryan had failed to bring labor into his "common man" coalition, probably because his criticism of high tariffs threatened the jobs of protected U.S. industries.

In the aftermath of the election, the competitive two-party system that existed in most parts of the United States shifted to stronger Republican domination in the North and continued Democratic domination in the South. Less-competitive, one-party politics developed in nearly all regions of the country as sectional rhetoric undermined populist appeals for a more class-oriented politics.

*The Republicans Self-destruct: 1912.* Between 1860 and 1932 only two Democrats won the presidency—Grover Cleveland in 1884 and 1892 and Woodrow Wilson in 1912 and 1916.

In Wilson, a former university professor and governor of New Jersey, the Democrats nominated a real liberal. But Wilson probably would not have won the general election without a bitter battle in the Republican Party that pitted the incumbent, William Howard Taft, against the popular former president Theodore Roosevelt. When all was said and done, Wilson left a lasting legacy not only in domestic and foreign affairs, but also in the style of presidential leadership.

The Taft-Roosevelt feud stemmed largely from Roosevelt's feeling that Taft had betrayed the trust-busting, environmental, and foreign policies that Roosevelt had pursued between 1901 and 1908. (Some historians actually give Taft credit for being more vigorous than Roosevelt in these areas, but Roosevelt grew increasingly critical of Taft because of the deliberative way in which Taft approached those policies.) Roosevelt was a proud advocate of the presidential "bully pulpit," and Taft was ill suited to much of the rough-and-tumble of public controversies.

While Roosevelt challenged Taft in the GOP primaries—the first exhibition of a popular campaign for the nomination—Wilson plodded to the Democratic nomination. He finally managed to win the nomination on the forty-sixth ballot at the convention in Baltimore, after unsuccessful maneuvering by William Jennings Bryan, House Speaker Champ Clark, antiprotectionist Oscar Underwood, and a cast of governors, favorite sons, and party leaders.

Wilson took to the hustings in the fall campaign, urging Americans to seek a moral awakening and to approve a program of liberal reforms involving labor relations, regulation of corporations and financial institutions, agriculture, and relations with other nations.

Wilson won the November election when Roosevelt bolted the Republican Party to run his own Progressive ("Bull Moose") Party campaign. The politically inexperienced Wilson won the presidency with 41.8 percent of the vote, while the upstart Roosevelt finished second with 27.4 percent and the incumbent, Taft, brought up the rear with 23.2 percent (less than half of his winning percentage of 51.6 percent in 1908). It was the most unusual of U.S. presidential election results, with a newly created third party outpolling the incumbent and both losing to a candidate with little political experience.

*Dawn of the New Deal: 1932.* After three years of Republican Herbert Hoover's uncertain leadership following the stock market crash of 1929, Democrat Franklin Roosevelt won the presidency in 1932 and oversaw one of the greatest shifts in political alignments in U.S. history. The diverse Democratic coalition included urbanites, blacks, Jews, Catholics, laborers, farmers, and southerners. The New Deal, by involving for the first time the federal government in almost every aspect of economic and social life, changed the scope and concept of American government forever. By Roosevelt's third term, Republicans did not oppose the basic structure of the New Deal, only the Democrats' implementation of its programs. The United States also adopted an activist role in international affairs.

*Mandate for the Great Society: 1964.* After John Kennedy's assassination in 1963, his successor, Lyndon Johnson, moved to enact Kennedy's unfinished agenda. In 1964 Johnson needed a landslide not only to enact that agenda but also to move out from under Kennedy's shadow. And indeed Johnson got his landslide and oversaw one of the most prolific sessions of Congress in history. The Eighty-ninth Congress passed ambitious programs affecting civil rights, medical care, education, welfare, urban development, and housing. But some of those programs created a "backlash" against social planning, especially after riots in Los Angeles in 1965 and other cities in 1968. Meanwhile, Johnson increased U.S. involvement in the Vietnam War, which eventually gave rise to a widespread protest movement. As a result, some of the traditional groups of the Democratic coalition—blue-collar workers, pacifists, young voters—broke away from the party and in 1968 elected Richard Nixon president.

*The Reagan Revolution: 1980 and 1984.* Ronald Reagan, a former movie star and television personality, won the hearts of America's conservatives with a televised speech for Barry Goldwater in 1964. For a quarter century, Reagan delivered a standard speech that attacked government involvement in the U.S. economy and called for an aggressive foreign policy toward the Soviet Union and other communist countries. After serving two terms as California governor, Reagan almost defeated a sitting Republican president, Gerald Ford, for the party nomination in 1976.

In 1980 and 1984, Reagan won landslide elections over President Jimmy Carter and former vice president Walter F. Mondale. He shepherded dramatic cuts in taxes and the domestic budget through Congress in 1981 and promoted the largest military buildup ever in peacetime. Reagan put a conservative stamp on a wide range of issues: the environment, federalism, welfare, education, intervention in civil wars from Afghanistan to Nicaragua, civil rights, and energy. He also filled more than half of the federal judiciary, mostly with relatively young conservatives. Overall, Reagan helped to rekindle American awe of the presidency; scholars had wondered whether anyone could handle the pressures of the modern office. At the end of Reagan's second term, however, it was still doubtful whether the Reagan era constituted a political realignment, since Americans expressed steady support in the polls for some of the very programs Reagan attacked.

*End of the Cold War: 1989–1996.* By the time Reagan left office in 1989 the world had begun to change and so had America's political landscape. With the gradual collapse of communism and the fizzling-out of the cold war, the United States was left as the lone superpower and voters' concerns had shifted from the threat of nuclear attack to the economy, crime, pollution, and other serious problems at home. In this changed atmosphere the battle to succeed Reagan produced a contest between moderates of the two parties—Republican George Bush and Democrat Michael S. Dukakis. Bush's forty-state electoral victory did not ratify a clear direction for either foreign or domestic policy. The campaign was dominated by symbolic appeals and attacks on Dukakis, not a plan of action.[87]

Once in office, Bush became deadlocked with Congress on virtually every major domestic issue—civil rights, taxes, the budget, the environment, regulation, economic and trade strategy, abortion, religion and the arts, and voter registration. But Bush dominated foreign affairs, especially during the Persian Gulf crisis of 1990–1991. He did not, however, produce the vision for the "new world order" that he had promised after the fall of the Soviet Union and its empire from 1989 to late 1991.

Bill Clinton defeated Bush in 1992 by focusing on "the economy, stupid," as a sign in Clinton headquarters exhorted staffers. Clinton charged that Bush was inattentive to the long-term economic decline of the United States. A founder of the Democratic Leadership Council, which sought to push the Democratic Party toward the right, Clinton appealed to both the visionary and the pragmatic in the American public. As a result, he was able to put together a coalition that was diverse enough to beat Bush and independent candidate Ross Perot.

Clinton's administration, though ambitious, was marked by centrism and compromise. Clinton's early incremental approach produced a strong legislative record but did not unsettle the entrenched Washington establishment. Even his health care proposal comprised a collection of compromises with such interest groups as doctors and insurance companies. Ultimately, the reform proved too complicated to rally adequate support. Faced with a Republican Congress in 1995, Clinton fought successfully to maintain his budget priorities. Reaching for the center ground in 1996, he signed welfare reform—perhaps the most sweeping legislation of his first term—despite opposition from the liberal wing of his party.

During his first four years in office, Clinton slowly reoriented the nation's tax and budgetary policies, courts, regulatory policies, and social programs. But the era's restraints—budget deficits, tax resistance, slow economic growth, public cynicism—did not allow him to give the country an ambitious social legacy like that of Franklin Roosevelt or Lyndon Johnson. Yet the public approved of the course he had set and gave him a convincing reelection in 1996.

## The Campaign Finance System

The Beatles sang in the 1960s that "money can't buy you love." Money cannot buy electoral success either—but it can help. Just how much money contributes to political campaigns always has been a matter of debate. From the first national elections, dominated by the "Virginia dynasty," until the most recent ones, dominated by federal funding and interest group donations, citizens have debated whether money strengthens or undermines democracy.

To say that money matters to campaigns is an understatement. The total cost of general election campaigns for the four presidential candidates in 1948 was $4.86 million. By 1992 the three top contenders were spending $170 million in the general election. The amount of money spent per voter has doubled in real terms over the last half-century. The cost per voter in 1948 was 42 cents in constant 1982–1984 dollars; by 1988 it was 85 cents.[88] These figures do not include money spent on vote-getting efforts independent of the official campaign organizations.

In modern elections, money is essential to successful campaigns. As the "universal equivalent" commodity, it can be converted quickly into other resources, such as polls, media, computer-generated direct-mail operations, and even "machine" party organizations.[89] Thus a campaign with ample funds can develop a wide range of strategies. Furthermore, loopholes in the election laws make it possible for some sources and uses of money to be concealed from the public.

Money has been called both the ultimate corrupter and a major source of vigorous competition. "The kind of person who might enter national politics is changing," wrote journalist Elizabeth Drew. "Politicians who . . . do not have great wealth of their own to spend, are signed up on a systematic basis by interests who wish to enjoy influence over their official conduct. Un-

'Your honor, my client believes that campaign spending limitations are a curb on free speech because everybody knows money talks!'

til the problem of money is dealt with, it is unrealistic to expect the political process to improve in any other respect."[90]

Taking a different point of view, another journalist, Robert J. Samuelson, wrote of proposals for campaign finance reform: "Groups need to feel they can express themselves and participate without colliding with obtuse rules intended to shut them out. Our politics is open and freewheeling. Its occasional excesses are preferable to arbitrary restraints."[91]

Much of the debate about money in politics can be traced to the explosion in campaign spending after World War II. But all along, Congress has attempted to control the influence of private donors on the political process. In the early 1970s Congress passed major reform legislation—the Federal Election Campaign Act (FECA)—and then amendments to that act. Reform has been limited, however, by the institutional interests of Congress. For example, on the major issue of political action committees (PACs) formed by business, labor, and other special interest groups, Congress has moved slowly, arguably because PAC contributions go to incumbents over challengers by a margin of almost four to one. PACs have grown in importance because FECA permits them to receive $5,000 a year from each contributor, while individual candidates may receive no more than $1,000 per election from any one source.[92]

The campaign finance debate turns on the extent to which private money affects a candidate's behavior both before and after the election and on whether electoral competition is stifled by private money. Money was arguably the difference in the 1968 election of Nixon and a factor in the 1980 election of Reagan. With estimated expenditures of $25.4 million, Nixon spent more than twice as much as Hubert Humphrey to win the presidency in 1968. In 1980, even with the FECA limitations in place, $191.3 million was spent in behalf of Reagan and other Republican presidential candidates, compared with $107.8 million for the defeated Democratic incumbent, Carter.[93]

The quixotic presidential campaign of Texas business executive Ross Perot in 1992 was a testament to the possibilities of money. Perot spent $68.3 million of his own fortune in his 1992 independent bid. The money enabled Perot to bypass reporters and deliver his message directly to the American public. Perot's strongest surge of support in the fall campaign came when he delivered a series of half-hour "infomercials" that attracted large television audiences.

Perot's 1992 bid may have been the inspiration for Maurice "Maury" Taylor and Malcolm S. "Steve" Forbes Jr., two conservative business owners who ran self-financed campaigns for the 1996 Republican nomination. Magazine publisher Forbes generated the most interest, especially with his call for a "flat" income tax. He spent about $30 million of his own money during the six months he spent trying to topple front-runner Bob Dole. Although unsuccessful, Forbes won the Arizona and Delaware primaries, seventy delegates, and much national attention.

Understanding the link between contributions and the positions candidates take on issues can be difficult because of the circularity and subtlety of candidate-donor relations. Contributors usually eschew a "hard sell" and insist only that their views on relevant issues be heard. But if their concerns are rejected frequently, contributors probably will abandon a politician—a prospect likely to enter the calculations of election-conscious officials.

Sen. Dale Bumpers of Arkansas has argued that fund raising affects the entire governmental process: "You can't have a sensible debate about how much is enough for defense when those PACs representing defense contractors are contributing so much. The decisions aren't based on what the likely mission of the Pentagon is going to be."[94] Perot, campaigning against "special interests" in his 1992 independent campaign, criticized Bush and Clinton for accepting federal money to conduct their campaigns. However, as the Reform Party candidate in 1996, Perot reversed his stance and accepted federal campaign money.

Supporters of unlimited campaign spending maintain that even if "elites"—the wealthiest and most influential groups and individuals—contribute the most money, so many factions exist among elites that they tend to check the influence of one another. To use the language of economist John Kenneth Galbraith, the goals of one interest will serve as a "countervailing force" against the goals of another interest.[95]

Many studies of campaign finance explain U.S. politics in economic terms: the U.S. political system is an "economy" of public views with a "demand" side and a "supply" side. By forming interest groups to express their concerns and by casting a ballot on election day, voters send "signals" to politicians. These signals are the demand side of the political economy. They force the suppliers of political goods—the politicians—to be respon-

sive to the wishes of the electorate. These studies emphasize the voters' abilities to shape the political environment by making independent choices: that is, demand is presumed to shape the supply of political goods. A look at the political science literature analyzing the ways in which groups attach themselves to the two major parties and the ways in which various coalitions shape the political debate reveals that coalitions display great consistency in what they demand from the political system.[96]

Political scientists Thomas Ferguson and Joel Rogers take a different view, however. They have argued that the American citizenry is disorganized and fragmented and that it therefore does not exert anywhere near the amount of control over the system that the traditional studies of campaign finance in U.S. politics suggest. Instead, the authors have contended, the system is dominated by elites who "invest" in the system: "The real market for political parties is defined by major 'investors'—groups of business firms, industrial sectors, or, in some (rare) cases, groups of voters organized collectively."[97] In short, Ferguson and Rogers argue that campaign contributions constitute a form of political participation that is more important than voting.

Campaign donors can coordinate their actions, and their actions shape the choices offered to voters. The concerted action of independent oil producers in the 1980 election, for example, did much to shape debate about taxes and business regulation. Low voter participation—slightly over half of the electorate votes for president and about a third in midterm elections for members of Congress—is just one indication that most Americans are not sufficiently organized as voters to press their political demands. The upper-class bias of interest groups underscores the difficulties that many groups have in organizing to make their views known.[98]

In the 1960s, economist Mancur Olson analyzed the difficulties encountered in forming groups to press broad social demands. Large groups of individuals, he argued, often do not pull together to promote common concerns because the possible benefits of group membership seem too distant or indirect to potential group members. Only direct incentives or compulsion enable large groups to form and stay together.[99]

While businesses and professional associations have the resources and unity to form effective interest groups, ordinary people usually have neither. For that reason, the federal government has played an increasing role in helping groups to organize. Some 30.9 percent of all groups in a 1985 survey reported getting funds from the government. The government not only offered start-up funds but also provided contacts with important agencies. Groups receiving government support included citizens' groups, employees of nonprofit institutions, and associations in social welfare, transportation, health, and other fields affecting wide segments of the population. Examples include the National Governors' Association, the U.S. Conference of Mayors, and the National Bureau of Economic Research. Foundation grants provided funds for about one-fifth of all citizen groups.[100]

The U.S. labor movement traditionally has been the cornerstone of the Democratic Party alliance. The movement peaked during the Great Depression when the economic crisis—which produced wholesale pay and benefit cuts—aroused workers in hundreds of spontaneous protests and strikes. Later, New Deal legislation such as the National Industrial Recovery Act and the Wagner Act encouraged workers to form unions. Since the 1950s, however, the labor movement has declined. Unions represent barely 15 percent of the private labor force, and they have lost important battles in Congress ranging from legislation to restore powers to strike to the North American Free Trade Agreement. Labor still exerts power in Rustbelt states and Democratic primaries, but nationally it is at its lowest ebb since the early days of the Great Depression.[101]

### HISTORY OF CAMPAIGN FINANCE

The extensive role of money in politics can be traced to the requirements of the American party system. When Federalist John Adams was elected president in 1796, Thomas Jefferson formed newspapers to promote Democratic-Republican opposition views. Only with expansion of the electorate between 1824 and 1828, when all but two states voted directly for presidential candidates, did money become a central element in campaigns. Reaching an expanded pool of voters required mass propaganda, which, in turn, required money.

#### Campaign Finance in the Nineteenth Century

In 1828 Andrew Jackson challenged John Quincy Adams in the fiercest battle for the presidency in the forty-year history of that office. Jackson decried the "corrupt bargain" of the previous election, in which the House of Representatives decided the deadlocked election. Adams's supporters, meanwhile, spread gossip about Jackson's character, and they urged Adams to use patronage to support newspapers critical of Jackson. Adams recalled the dilemma:

To pay money [in an election] directly or indirectly, was in my opinion incorrect in principle. This was my first and decisive reason for declining such a contribution. A second reason was that I could not command such a sum as $5,000 without involving myself in debt for it; and the third was, that if I once departed from my principle and gave money, there was no rule, either of expediency or of morality, which would enable me to limit the amount of expenditure which I ought to incur.[102]

When Jackson defeated Adams in 1828, the age of mass popular politics began. Money, from that time on, would be crucial in reaching an expanding electorate.

Henry Clay, who took up the opposition to Jackson, did not share Adams's reservations about money's corrupting influence. President Jackson's opposition to the Bank of the United States stirred urban financiers to action; between 1830 and 1832, the bank spent $42,000 on pamphleteering. Clay wrote: "It seems to me that our friends who have ability should contribute a fund for aiding the cause; and if that be deemed advisable, the appeal should be made in the large cities where alone the Capital is to be found."[103]

Mining magnate and financier Mark Hanna (standing at the far right between President and Mrs. McKinley) raised millions of dollars for McKinley's 1896 and 1900 campaigns. His fund-raising practices sparked the first major effort toward campaign finance reform.

The parties attracted large donors long before the Civil War. Whig sponsors included the Weed and du Pont families, and Democratic sponsors included the Rothschild family, August Belmont, and Samuel Tilden. The parties attempted to build systems to extract regular contributions from members at all levels.

By the time of Abraham Lincoln's election in 1860, a presidential campaign required $100,000. Money, it had been learned, could make or break a campaign: Stephen Douglas's losing 1860 campaign suffered from poor fund raising; Salmon P. Chase's failed 1864 race for the GOP nomination was made possible by the largesse of financier Jay Cooke and a few others. Cooke also contributed $1,000 to Lincoln in the 1864 race—one of the first recorded instances of private interests contributing to both contestants to ensure access to the eventual winner.

Industrialism fed the campaign cost spiral. Wealthy entrepreneurs who donated money to Ulysses Grant in the 1868 election included Cooke, Cornelius Vanderbilt, A. T. Stewart, Henry Hilton, and John Astor. One historian wrote: "Never before was a candidate placed under such great obligation to men of wealth as was Grant."[104] Expenses grew to $16 million—mostly because of advertising and travel costs—for William McKinley's winning effort in 1896.[105]

The first major effort toward campaign finance reform

stemmed from concern about the power of trusts and the role of campaign professionals such as Mark Hanna. Hanna, an Ohio mining magnate and a key strategist for McKinley, raised money for the Republican Party through a systematic assessment of banks and corporations. He used the money to make McKinley financially solvent, to influence possible delegates, and to pay for the kind of mass propaganda campaign that would change the face of national politics forever.[106]

McKinley's successor, Theodore Roosevelt, accepted large gifts in his 1904 campaign. Roosevelt was ambiguous about the role of money in politics. He refused to return major contributions, arguing that "the wrong lies not in receiving the contribution" but in exercising improper pressure or making promises to get it.[107]

### Campaign Finance in the Twentieth Century

After revelations by "muckraking" journalists about campaign finances and agitation by the Progressive Party leader Sen. Robert La Follette of Wisconsin, Congress in 1907 passed the Tillman Act, which banned bank and corporate gifts to candidates seeking federal office. The legislation, however, was ineffective because it contained no formal mechanism for monitoring the far-flung activities of various campaigns.

The earliest campaign finance acts dealt with congressional campaigns, but they helped to pave the way for future attempts to regulate the raising and spending of money for presidential races. The Federal Corrupt Practices Act of 1910 set disclosure requirements for candidates for the House of Representatives. The law required committees and individuals "which shall in two or more states . . . attempt to influence the result" of House races to provide a complete record of campaign transactions. The record was to include the names and addresses of donors giving $100 or more and all candidates receiving $10 or more. The law did not enable voters to use the information before the election; disclosure did not take place until after the election.

The next year, Congress extended the requirements to Senate campaign contributors. The 1911 law also required House and Senate candidates to submit campaign expense reports. The legislation contained a provision that would be controversial throughout the rest of the century: a limitation on spending by candidates. Senate candidates could spend no more than $10,000, and House candidates were limited to $5,000. Congressional candidates also were subject to any restriction that might be imposed by state laws.

The Federal Corrupt Practices Act of 1925 was the most important finance legislation until 1971. It continued contribution bans and required campaigns to report receipts and expenditures. But neither the 1910 nor the 1925 legislation contained enforcement mechanisms to monitor the activities and connections of political campaigns. Thus spending limits were avoided by breaking up party and campaign committees into smaller units and by selling advertising in party publications, then selling copies of the publications at inflated prices.

The Hatch Act, passed in 1939, all but eliminated the last vestiges of the federal patronage system that was once prominent in U.S. elections. The law stemmed from a series of newspaper reports that Franklin Roosevelt's administration was improperly using the Works Progress Administration to bolster the reelection campaign of a Senate ally. Democratic senator Carl Hatch of New Mexico led a coalition of Republican and anti–New Deal Democrats to pass the act.

The act barred federal employees from taking part in organized national political activity. It also banned solicitation from anyone receiving any federal relief funds. President Roosevelt considered a veto but instead signed the bill and led a successful effort the next year to extend the restrictions to employees in state agencies receiving federal funds.

Amendments to the Hatch Act, which passed in 1940, banned federal contractors from contributing to campaigns of candidates for federal office, asserted the authority of Congress to regulate the nominating process, limited contributions to a federal candidate or committee to $5,000 a year (contributions to a "state or local committee" were exempt), and limited the spending of committees operating in two or more states to $3 million. The last provision underscored the toothlessness of the law. Single political forces could evade the spending limits by simply breaking up into many legally distinct but coordinated committees.

The Hatch Act continued a long process of removing the executive establishment from campaign politics. Since passage of the Pendleton Act in 1883, the federal government has been filled with greater numbers of civil servants. Indeed, political appointees in the civil service declined from 90 percent in 1882 to 50 percent in 1896 to 20 percent in 1932.[108] Political appointees now make up less than 1 percent of the civil service.

In 1942 Congress passed the War Labor Disputes Act, which included labor unions along with national banks and corporations in the 1907 ban on contributions to political campaigns. That provision was made permanent in the Taft-Hartley Labor-Management Relations Act of 1947.

By the campaign of 1952, both parties were well financed. In the race for the Republican nomination, opponents of California governor Earl Warren spent between $500,000 and $1 million in the California primary while Warren backers spent between $50,000 and $100,000. Supporters of Sen. Robert Taft spent $58,000 in Ohio; Dwight Eisenhower spent $65,000 to Taft's $50,000 in New Hampshire; and Eisenhower outspent Taft in South Dakota $44,000 to $40,000. Eisenhower, the 1952 Republican nominee, was the first presidential candidate to make television commercials a central part of his campaign. He spent $500,000 on television; his Democratic rival, Adlai Stevenson, spent $77,000.[109]

Allegations of personal "slush funds" were made during the campaign in 1952 and were capped by the tearful denial of Republican vice-presidential candidate Richard Nixon—in the now-famous "Checkers" speech—that he had improperly received contributions.[110]

Vice-presidential candidate Richard Nixon, seen here as he appeared to millions on television September 23, 1952, denied allegations of personal "slush funds" in his famous "Checkers" speech.

From 1952 to 1968, campaign spending steadily climbed with the rise of television advertising, professional campaign consultants, polling, and more public barnstorming by candidates. Concern about campaign spending rose alongside such developments as John Kennedy's extensive use of family money to win the 1960 Democratic nomination, Barry Goldwater's need to use many small donors in 1964, and Richard Nixon's two-to-one spending advantage over rival Hubert Humphrey in 1968.

Congress considered several election finance reform initiatives in the 1950s and 1960s but passed none. In 1962 President Kennedy's Commission on Campaign Costs issued its report and made a number of recommendations, including tax credits for campaign donors, the removal of limits on interstate political committees, reporting requirements for presidential campaigns, government funding of transitions, and establishment of a federal agency to enforce campaign regulations. In May 1962 Kennedy proposed five bills pertaining to election finance reform, but none passed.

### The 1971 Legislation

At long last, Congress passed two major reform laws: the Federal Election Campaign Act of 1971 and the Revenue Act of 1971. President Nixon signed the 1971 legislation only after congressional leaders agreed to delay its provisions until after Nixon's reelection campaign in 1972.

*The Federal Election Campaign Act of 1971.* The FECA was the most important piece of campaign finance legislation since the 1925 Federal Corrupt Practices Act. The law attacked the growing influence of the media and private contributors with blunt instruments: a limit on the amount of money that could be spent on media campaigns (repealed in 1974), per-voter spending limits on the nominating process, and a requirement for periodic disclosure of campaign spending and of funds provided by private sources.

The legislation was passed by a bipartisan majority, with both parties concerned about protecting their sources of financial support but also limiting private influence. Republicans were determined to protect their business support, and Democrats were determined to maintain an effective electoral alliance with labor unions.

The idea behind the legislation was to reduce what was seen as the insidious influences of private money by bringing it into the light of day. Like many "sunshine" ordinances of the era, the FECA logic was that illicit influence thrives in secret and healthy contests for influence thrive in public view.

Media spending limits would be based on a formula of 10 cents per voter and pegged to the inflation rate. *Media* was defined as newspaper, magazine, television, and radio advertising. Of total media spending, only 60 percent could be earmarked for television and radio.

For presidential candidates, the overall media limit for 1976, the first year of such limits, was $14.3 million per candidate, of which no more than $8.5 million could be used for television and radio. In the 1968 election, Nixon had spent $12.6 million of his general election treasury of $24.9 million on media broadcasting; Humphrey had spent $6.1 million of his $10.3 million for broadcasting.[111] The legislation also contained a requirement that broadcasters charge the candidates the same unit cost that other advertisers would be charged for the same advertising time.

The FECA disclosure provisions called for federal candidates to file quarterly reports on spending and receipts. For the receipts, candidates had to list the names, businesses, and addresses of donors who contributed $100 or more. Candidates were required to file additional reports fifteen and five days before election day. Donations of $5,000 and more had to be disclosed publicly within forty-eight hours of receipt.

Congress required that the disclosure be made during primary, caucus, convention, and runoff periods as well as during the general election. Any political committee with assets greater than $1,000 had to make public disclosures—partly closing a loophole in which campaigns hid expenses by creating separate campaign organizations that were technically independent of the main campaign committee.

But the law still had enforcement difficulties. One notable loophole, for example, made it possible for the wealthy to coordinate donations made by family members and friends in amounts of less than $100 in order to keep the source of gifts secret.

Even more limiting were the difficulties faced in making use of the information provided by candidates. True disclosure required a thorough examination and dissemination of the information, but listings of contributions were often so bulky and complex that no group could adequately determine the sources of influence. Moreover, a flood of contributions late in a campaign could not be examined before the election. Newspapers generally reported on the top donors to the campaigns and listed other donors. But finance stories usually lasted only a day or two; disclosure and the effects of the donations were rarely explored.

According to campaign finance experts David W. Adamany and George E. Agree,

The effectiveness of disclosure depends entirely on the transmission of campaign finance information to the voters. The media may simply find this too burdensome, or they may cover it in ways consistent with editorial preferences. Nor can candidates be relied on to transmit campaign finance information. When candidates are well funded both are likely to count big givers and interest groups among their contributors; neither has an interest in raising the political finance issue.[112]

*The Income Tax Checkoff.* Congress passed the Revenue Act of 1971 after a long and bitter partisan struggle between congressional Democrats and the Nixon administration. The legislation, now a centerpiece of the government financing of presidential elections, created the Presidential Election Campaign Fund for federal financing of both the nomination and general election campaigns. The act specified that the amount of money that candidates would receive during the nominating process would be determined by a per-voter spending formula. A candidate would qualify for matching federal funds by raising at least $100,000 in twenty or more states, with at least $5,000 from each state in individual contributions of $250 or less.

Candidates accepting federal funds would not be allowed to accept private contributions for their general election campaigns. The act's sponsors hoped federal campaign funding would "level the playing field" for candidates who qualified for the matching funds. In the 1968 election, Nixon had outspent Humphrey more than two-to-one.

Presidential candidates of minor parties could receive partial funding based on votes received in the general election. Major parties were defined as those that received 25 percent or more of the vote in the previous election. Minor parties were those receiving between 5 and 25 percent. Candidates of new parties could obtain funding retroactively if they received 5 percent or more of the vote. No provision was made for independent candidates, but in 1980 Federal Election Commission (FEC) ruling enabled John Anderson of Illinois to receive partial funding after his independent candidacy drew 6.6 percent of the presidential vote.

The federal campaign money was to be raised through a "checkoff" option for taxpayers. When filling out tax forms, taxpayers could designate that $1 of their tax payment be put into a presidential election campaign fund. Couples filing joint returns could designate $2 to go into the fund. Because the campaign fund faced a shortage of money in the early 1990s, in 1993 Congress authorized an increase in the taxpayer checkoff from $1 to $3. The number of Americans opting to earmark tax money for the fund fell from a high of 29 percent in 1980 to a low of 14.5 percent in 1993.[113]

The Democrats, long the debt-ridden party, contended that the legislation was needed to control the amount of influence that the wealthy could exert in a presidential campaign. Republicans, looking forward to a bountiful presidential election in 1972 with an incumbent president of their own seeking reelection, opposed the measure. The legislation passed but with the 1972 election exempted.

Despite the public's lukewarm attitude toward the checkoff, the two parties now accept its role in the electoral process. Part of their acceptance of the mechanism stems from the loopholes that allow independent groups to spend unlimited amounts of money in behalf of favorite candidates. The tax checkoff has not ended private influence. But the expansion of public financing into the nominating process has allowed numerous candidates to compete, at least in the early stages of the campaign.

### The Watergate Election

The last completely privately financed election was the 1972 race. Although spending on broadcasting fell, overall campaign costs soared. President Nixon's campaign organization spent $61.4 million, while the Democratic campaign of George McGovern spent $21.2 million.

The Committee to Re-elect the President (or "CREEP," as it became known) relied mostly on large contributions. Nixon's chief fund-raiser, Maurice Stans, got the campaign off to a fast start by raising $20 million before April 7, the date after which, under the FECA, contributions were required to be made public. Some $5 million came into the Nixon coffers on April 5 and 6 alone. Leading contributors included insurance magnate W. Clement Stone, who gave $2 million, and Richard Scaife, an heir to the Mellon oil and banking fortune, who gave $1 million.[114] The Nixon campaign troubled outsiders because of some large donors' apparent expectation that they would receive government favors in return for their generosity. Stans reportedly informed wealthy individuals and corporations that they had to contribute 1 percent of their net worth or gross annual sales to the campaign if they wished to have a good working relationship with the White House.[115]

Perhaps the most blatant single example of influence buying was the offer from International Telephone and Telegraph (ITT) to provide $400,000 in services at the Republican national convention scheduled to be held in San Diego—ITT later had an important antitrust case settled by the Justice Department. Eventually the Nixon campaign turned down the offer from ITT and even asked that the convention be moved to Miami Beach to avoid the further appearance of impropriety.[116] Other large contributors with an interest in influencing government policy included Robert Vesco, under investigation by the Securities and Exchange Commission; Dwayne Andreas, seeking a federal bank charter; the dairy industry, seeking higher milk price supports; and the Seafarers International Union, seeking a Justice Department dismissal of an indictment.[117]

Besides access to key administration officials, the rewards for hefty donations apparently included positions in the administration. Nine of Nixon's appointees as ambassadors or heads of foreign missions contributed more than $20,000 to the 1972

## CURRENT LAWS FOR CAMPAIGN FINANCE

Since Congress started legislating the financing of national elections, a number of provisions have come and gone. The provisions no longer in effect have been either superseded by congressional action or declared unconstitutional by the Supreme Court.

The following provisions regulating presidential campaigns, listed in order of the progress of the nominating and general election campaigns, are still on the books. The provisions are followed by a reference to the appropriate legislation or ruling. When one year's amendments superseded previous law, both citations are listed.

• Federal regulation. The Federal Election Commission (FEC) is the federal agency responsible for enforcing campaign laws (Federal Election Campaign Act of 1971 [FECA], 1976 amendments).

• Disclosure. Presidential candidates must file regular reports listing campaign contributions and expenditures (1971). Donors of $200 or more must be listed in the reports (1971, 1979 amendments), which go to the FEC (1974, 1976 amendments). Any organization spending more than $5,000 on campaigns must establish formal political committees (FECA 1971, 1979). Candidates must establish a single organization for their campaigns (1974). The name of the candidate must be listed on campaign materials (1979).

Certain expenses of local party organizations—such as get-out-the-vote drives and voter education activities—do not have to be reported (1979). Up to $1,000 in voluntary services, such as lending a home for meetings and lodging, do not have to be reported as contributions (1979).

Independent spending of $250 or more must be reported to the FEC (1971, 1979). Organizations without formal ties to campaign organizations do not have to adhere to spending limitations (1974).

• "Lowest-unit" rule. Broadcasters can charge campaigns only as much as they charge other advertising clients for spot commercials (1971).

• Political action committees (PACs). Corporations and labor unions may establish separate units to promote political ends and not be in violation of federal prohibitions on direct contributions (1971).

• Equal time. Broadcasters selling or giving time to a federal candidate must provide equal time opportunities to the candidate's campaign opponents (section 315 of the Federal Communications Act). Typically, this law gives spokespersons for both parties a chance to respond to the remarks of the other. After a State of the Union address, for example, a representative of the other party delivers a statement. Hollywood movies and television programs featuring Ronald Reagan were not permitted to be aired on television during his 1976, 1980, and 1984 campaigns because of this provision.

• Taxpayer checkoff. Citizens may indicate on their tax forms that they would like $3 ($6 for joint filings) of their tax money to be put into the Presidential Election Campaign Fund. This fund has been used to help finance nominating and general election campaigns (1971, 1993).

• Matching funds during primaries. Candidates may receive federal "matching funds" if they raise at least $100,000 in twenty or more states. Each of those states must contribute a total of $5,000 to the candidate in individual donations of $250 or less (1974).

• Limits on contributions. Citizens may contribute only $1,000 to each primary or general election campaign, a total of $25,000 to federal candidates overall, and $20,000 to committees of national parties (1976).

Candidates may spend only $50,000 of their own or their family's money on their campaigns if they accept federal funding (1971, 1976).

Multicandidate committees—most commonly PACs—may contribute only $5,000 per candidate and $15,000 to committees of the national parties (1976).

• Federal funding of national conventions. The parties receive $3 million each for their quadrennial conventions (1974, 1979).

• Spending limits. Presidential candidates receiving federal matching funds may spend limited amounts during the nomination season and other limited amounts in each of the states (state limits are determined by population). The limit in 1976, the first year, was $10 million; the limit has been adjusted to account for inflation.

• Federal funding of general election campaigns. The federal government offers the nominees of the major parties equal sums of money for the general election campaign. Candidates who accept the money may not raise or use additional campaign funds. In 1976 each candidate received $17 million for the general election campaign; in 1992, with adjustments for inflation, each candidate received $55.2 million (1974).

---

campaign. Fifteen of Nixon's thirty-four noncareer appointees as heads of foreign missions contributed a total of $252,000 to the 1968 campaign.[118]

The Nixon campaign did not rely solely on large donors. It also continued the party's 1964 efforts to raise money from small donors. The Committee to Re-elect the President spent $4 million on direct-mail appeals. Later legislation, which provided candidates seeking a presidential nomination with matching funds for small amounts collected in at least twenty states, institutionalized the system of massive small-donor appeals.

*Post-Watergate Finance Laws*

Congress passed the most sweeping campaign finance legislation ever amid the climate of electoral reform produced by the public outcry in reaction to the Watergate scandal. Gerald Ford, who rose to the presidency with the resignation of Nixon, reluctantly signed into law the Federal Election Campaign Act amendments in October 1974. *(See box, Current Laws for Campaign Finance, above.)*

Congress was not the only body to get involved in campaign finance reform. By the time Nixon had been driven from the

White House because of his campaign's electoral scandals, some seventeen states had imposed limitations on the amount of money that individuals could donate to campaigns. New Jersey's limit of $600, which was eligible for state matching funds, was the lowest in the nation.[119]

The federal law was most important for presidential politics. Technically just an amendment to the 1971 law, the post-Watergate statute superseded some of the previous law's provisions and expanded others. The Federal Election Campaign Act amendments contained provisions for the following:

• Establishment of a federal election commission. The make-up of the commission was later found unconstitutional because the method of members' appointment (some by the president and some by Congress) violated the separation of powers doctrine. The Federal Election Commission later was reconstituted as a body with members appointed by the president and confirmed by the Senate.

• A limit of $1,000 per election on an individual's annual donation to a candidate for a federal (presidential and congressional) office. The presidential nominating contest was considered a separate election. Gifts made in nonelection years would be counted toward the gifts for the election year.

• A limit of $25,000 on total individual contributions for all federal offices.

• Spending limits of $10 million for the presidential nominating process and $20 million for the general election. Spending in the nominating process also would be limited in each state according to the size of the state's voting-age population. In future elections, these sums would rise according to the inflation rate. In 1992 the limits for each presidential candidate (except Perot) in the nominating and general election phases were $27.6 million and $55.2 million, respectively.

• A system of matching funds for presidential candidates in nominating campaigns. Candidates who raised $100,000 on their own initiative—$5,000 in each of twenty states in denominations of $250 or less—could collect up to $5 million in federal matching funds.

• A limit of $5,000 per election (presidential and congressional) on the contributions of independent political committees (usually PACs). To qualify as an independent committee, a group must register six months before making the donation, receive contributions from at least fifty persons, and make gifts to five or more candidates for federal office. Any group not qualifying would be bound by the $1,000 individual contribution limit. Under this provision, an organization with legally independent federal, state, and local branches could give three gifts of $5,000 to a single candidate.

• Inclusion of indirect donations in tallies of donations. Gifts made to ancillary committees that end up in the campaign's treasury would be considered a direct contribution to the campaign.

• A requirement that gifts greater than $100 be made by check. Any combination of cash gifts exceeding $100 would be illegal. This provision was intended help track donations and make "laundering" of money difficult.

• A limit of $50,000 on candidates' contributions to their own presidential campaign and a limit of $1,000 per person on contributions from members of the candidates' family. The Supreme Court later struck down the limitation on candidates' use of their own money.

• A federal grant of $2 million to each major party for staging the national summer conventions. That amount would be increased in later elections according to the inflation rate. Each party received $11 million in 1992 and about $12 million each was earmarked for 1996.

• A ban on contributions by foreign nationals. This provision was designed to prevent laundering of money.

• A requirement that candidates establish a single organization through which all campaign spending would flow and which would submit regular reports.

## Court Cases and Constitutional Issues

The 1974 FECA amendments faced an important federal court challenge, *Buckley v. Valeo*, soon after they took effect.[120] The Supreme Court's final 1976 ruling reduced congressional authority over campaign activity.

A broad ideological coalition challenged the 1974 law on a wide range of constitutional grounds. The main argument was that restrictions on campaign contributions amounted to restrictions on political expression and association. Another argument: the financial disclosure requirement violated the right to privacy. The coalition also argued that the law posed unreasonable barriers to minor political parties and violated the separation of powers. In all, the plaintiffs said, the law violated the First, Fourth, Fifth, Sixth, and Ninth Amendments to the Constitution. The coalition opposing the law included James Buckley, conservative Republican senator from New York; former Democratic senator Eugene McCarthy of Minnesota, a prospective third party presidential candidate; the New York Civil Liberties Union; the American Conservative Union; and *Human Events*, a conservative periodical.

Many analysts were concerned that the law would quell third party candidacies and "maverick" movements within the two major parties. Such dissident movements have been a crucial element in forcing major parties to respond to the changing demands of the electorate. The "threshold" provision, which required a party to receive at least 5 percent of the vote in the previous election in order to receive federal funding, effectively ended the life of George Wallace's 1968 American Independent Party. Limitations on legal donations could have crippled McGovern's 1972 run since it depended in its early stages on large donations from figures such as General Motors heir Stewart Mott.

When the U.S. Court of Appeals for the District of Columbia upheld the law on August 14, 1975, the coalition appealed the decision to the Supreme Court. On January 30, 1976, the high court issued a 137-page unsigned opinion in *Buckley v. Valeo* that upheld some of the law's provisions and struck down others. In five separate opinions, the justices concurred and dissented with various parts of the main ruling. Congress responded to the Court's ruling the same year with amendments that answered many of the decision's objections, but Congress was unable to restore all of the law's tough provisions.

The Court approved limitations on how much individuals and organizations could contribute to national candidates as well as the disclosure provisions. The Court also approved the federal financing of presidential nominating campaigns and general election campaigns. But one of the most controversial elements of the reform—limits on spending by individuals—was overturned. The Court agreed with the plaintiffs' First Amendment argument that restrictions on spending amounted to abridgment of free speech. The Court ruled, however, that campaign organizations could be required to honor spending limits if they accepted federal money. The Court stated:

A restriction on the amount of money a person or group can spend on political communication during a campaign necessarily reduces the quantity of expression by restricting the number of issues discussed, the depth of their exploration, and the size of the audience reached. This is because every means of communicating ideas in today's mass society requires the expenditure of money.

Only Justice Byron White rejected the reasoning. White noted the "many expensive campaign activities that are not themselves communicative or remotely related to speech."[121]

An important Supreme Court ruling, overlooked at the time, was that the $25,000 limitation on personal donations to federal candidates could not be extended to political action committees. This opened the way for PACs to spend as much as they could gather in behalf of a candidate so long as they did not have a formal connection with the candidate. Later legislation allowing donations of $5,000 to PACs, compared with $1,000 to candidate committees, also promoted PAC growth.

The Court struck down the FECA limit of $50,000 on how much presidential candidates could spend of their own money on their own campaigns if they received federal funds. The Court, however, accepted limits on outside contributions. The rationale for the apparent double standard was that allowing candidates to spend unlimited amounts in their own behalf would free them from the same outside influences that limits on outside contributions were intended to curb. The majority opinion read: "The use of personal funds reduces the candidate's dependence on outside contributions and thereby counteracts the coercive pressures and attendant risks of abuse to which the act's contribution limits are directed." Justice Thurgood Marshall, in a dissenting opinion, wrote: "It would appear to follow that the candidate with a substantial personal fortune at his disposal is off to a significant 'head start.'" Marshall added that the Court's reasoning on this issue could have the effect of encouraging wealthy candidates more than others to enter the political process.[122]

The Court also struck down the provision for creation of a federal election commission because the makeup of the panel would violate the separation of powers and appointment provisions of the Constitution. In its *Buckley v. Valeo* decision, the Court maintained that members of the commission appointed by Congress should not be permitted to exercise executive authority. The 1976 amendments to FECA reconstituted the Federal Election Commission as a presidential commission and dropped the provision that the clerk of the House and secretary of the Senate serve as ex officio members of the commission.

*More FECA Amendments*

Congress was unable to reconstitute the section of the legislation pertaining to a federal election commission within the Court's thirty-day stay of the decision. But rather than simply rework the legislation to fit the Court's dictates about the separation of powers, Congress in 1976 passed a completely new set of FECA amendments. President Ford had wanted only some minor tinkering with the commission to satisfy the Court.[123]

The Federal Election Commission of the 1976 law was a six-member panel appointed by the president and confirmed by the Senate. Commission members were not permitted to take part in any outside business activities. The commission was given the authority to prosecute civil violations of campaign finance law and jurisdiction over violations formerly covered only in the criminal code.

Also in response to the Court ruling, Congress passed an amendment limiting independent spending. The Court had declared unconstitutional the 1974 law's limitations on independent political expenditures. In 1976 Congress required individuals and committees making independent expenditures over $100 to swear that the expenditures were not made in collusion with the candidate or the candidate's agent.

The 1976 amendments set new contribution limits. An individual could give no more than $5,000 to an independent committee and $20,000 to the national committees of a political party. The new amendments also set a total limit of $50,000 on donations from the families of candidates who were receiving federal funds.

In 1979 Congress passed new FECA amendments designed to strengthen state and local parties and reduce red tape. The legislation did not involve any major partisan controversies. President Jimmy Carter signed the legislation in 1980.

The legislation's most important provisions addressed complaints that federal regulation strangled state and local party organizations. The bill allowed unlimited spending by state and local organizations on voter registration and get-out-the-vote drives. Those organizations also were permitted to buy unlimited campaign materials for volunteer activities. The items included buttons, bumper stickers, yard signs, posters, and hand bills. Mentioning a presidential candidate in local campaign literature no longer counted as a contribution under the 1979 amendments. Determining the value of such mention had been the source of bookkeeping nightmares.

Volunteer activities were encouraged by doubling to $1,000 the amount of money a person could spend on housing, food, or personal travel in behalf of a candidate without reporting the amounts to the FEC. A person could spend $2,000 for such things in behalf of a party.

The amendments reduced the number of reports required of federal candidates from twenty-four to nine in the two-year election cycles, reduced the amount of detail required in financial disclosure reports, and eliminated disclosure requirements for candidates spending less than $5,000.

### Reform Efforts in the 1990s

Complaints about the influence of money on presidential campaigns continued into the 1990s. But a "Catch 22" undermined reform efforts. Members of Congress rely on interest groups for campaign contributions, but interest groups are the major force against reform.

Reform proposals have foundered whenever Republicans and Democrats have feared losing fund-raising advantages. During the Bush administration, Republicans favored proposals to eliminate campaign contributions from political action committees—major Democratic donors. Democrats favored proposals that targeted independent money—a key Republican source of support. Rep. Richard Cheney of Wyoming summed up the reform stalemate: "If you think this Congress, or any other, is going to set up a system where someone can run against them on equal terms at government expense, you're smoking something that you can't buy at the corner drugstore."[124]

As for the Federal Election Commission and its watchdog function, its joint control by three Democratic and three Republican members undermines its ability to take decisive action. Rep. Robert L. Livingston of Louisiana has called the FEC "a worthless, toothless organization."[125] Mark Braden, former counsel for the Republican National Committee, said: "If we had an efficient commission, then we might have them having an impact on elections, which I don't think, at least from my perspective . . . I would be really happy with. In some ways I sort of like the snail's pace that you have now, so that they never get anything done, so it does not affect any election."[126] But Herbert E. Alexander, a leading scholar of funding elections, concluded in 1989 that the reforms had improved the American political system. "The present campaign finance system has flaws, and some of them are quite serious. Nevertheless, for all its shortcomings, the current system represents a notable improvement over the system in effect only a decade ago."[127]

With lawmakers reluctant to change the way their campaigns are financed, only a major public uprising against the system will put enough pressure on Congress to enact reform. In 1996, allegations of illegal foreign contributions to the Democratic Party and record donations by interest groups to both parties brought campaign finance reform once again into the national spotlight. Newly reelected President Clinton and members of Congress promised to take up the issue of campaign finance reform during the 105th Congress.

## MONEY IN PRESIDENTIAL PRIMARIES

The pursuit of a presidential nomination always has been expensive. In 1920 Gen. Leonard Wood spent $1.8 million in thirteen primaries in his unsuccessful campaign for the Republican nomination. Other big spenders in the nominating process have included Herbert Hoover, Franklin Roosevelt, Robert Taft, John Kennedy, and Robert J. Dole.

From 1928 to 1948, the average cost of taking part in a single contested primary rose from $50,000 to $100,000. The costs increased much faster in the postwar years. By 1960 the average cost of a single contested primary had risen to $200,000; in 1964 the figure was $400,000. Costs of primaries in later presidential elections have varied so much that an "average" is not meaningful. But it is clear that costs have soared. In 1972, for example, Democrat George McGovern spent $316,000 in Massachusetts; $182,000 in Pennsylvania; $231,000 in Ohio; $159,000 in Oregon; and $4.2 million in California—more than a third of what he spent on his entire nominating drive. By contrast, Hubert Humphrey, McGovern's top rival, spent only $500,000 in California.[128]

In the nominating phase of the 1992 presidential race the thirteen candidates (not including Ross Perot, who did not seek a party nomination or accept federal funds) spent a total of about $153 million. (See Table 1-5, p. 45) Most of that money—$117.6 million—was direct spending on such expenses as staff, advertising, polling, and travel. Other major spending categories included spending by labor PACs ($20 million), the costs of compliance with federal election laws ($8 million), and spending by minor parties and independent groups ($1.2 million). The two major parties spent an additional $33.1 million before the conventions.[129]

In 1992, of the $126.45 million in total receipts for the major party candidates and several other fringe candidates, $82.55 million came from individual contributions, $42.67 million from federal matching funds, and $920,976 from PACs. Small contributors gave more to Bill Clinton than to George Bush in their respective campaigns for their party's nomination. Clinton did the best in contributions of less than $500—$14 million, compared with Bush's total of $5.3 million. In contributions totaling $500–$750, Clinton ($3.8 million) and Bush ($2.6 million) were closer. But Bush's $19.8 million in contributions of $750–$1,000 was far greater than Clinton's total of $7.6 million.

FEC figures for 1992 indicate that primary candidates spent almost all of the $126.45 million received. Their total expenditures were $120.79 million. (Receipts or expenditures of Perot were not included because he did not participate in the public funding program administered by the FEC.)

President Bush's prenomination spending of $37.94 million exceeded Clinton's $33.90 million. Both far outspent their rivals for the nominations they eventually won.

Clinton, governor of a small and generally poor state, seemed like an unlikely fund-raiser when he launched his campaign in 1991. But Clinton's home state of Arkansas included

TABLE 1-5 1992 Prenomination Campaign Receipts, by Candidate
(millions of dollars)

| Party/candidate | Federal matching funds | Individual contributions minus refunds | Adjusted total receipts |
|---|---|---|---|
| **DEMOCRATS** | | | |
| Larry Agran | 0.27 | 0.33 | 0.61 |
| Jerry Brown | 4.24 | 5.18 | 9.42 |
| Bill Clinton | 12.52 | 25.11 | 37.64 |
| Tom Harkin | 2.10 | 3.07 | 5.68 |
| Bob Kerrey | 2.12 | 3.91 | 6.47 |
| Lyndon La Rouche | 0 | 1.57 | 1.57 |
| Paul Tsongas | 2.99 | 4.94 | 7.97 |
| Doug Wilder | 0.29 | 0.51 | 0.80 |
| TOTAL DEMOCRATS | 24.60 | 44.62 | 70.16 |
| **REPUBLICANS** | | | |
| Patrick Buchanan | 5.00 | 7.15 | 12.18 |
| George Bush | 10.56 | 27.09 | 37.91 |
| David Duke | 0 | 0.22 | 0.27 |
| TOTAL REPUBLICANS | 15.58 | 34.46 | 50.36 |
| **OTHER PARTY** | | | |
| Andre Marrou | 0 | 0.56 | 0.58 |
| Lenora Fulani | 1.94 | 2.20 | 4.14 |
| TOTAL OTHER PARTY | 1.94 | 2.76 | 4.72 |
| GRAND TOTAL | 42.10 | 81.84 | 125.24 |

SOURCE: Federal Election Commission, "Adjusted Receipts" (Through March 31, 1993).

some big businesses of its own—Wal-Mart, the nationwide discount store chain; Arkla, a *Fortune* 500 natural gas company run by a boyhood friend; Tyson Foods, the nation's leading producer of poultry; and a number of banks and savings and loan institutions. In his roles as a member of the Democratic Leadership Council and National Governors Association, Clinton developed a national network of sympathetic followers. Clinton told friends that he would not run unless he had $1 million in contributions by the time of his announcement. Clinton also attracted leading party fund-raisers such as Robert Farmer of Massachusetts, who had raised money for Michael Dukakis in 1988.

Money, however, does not ensure success. The record for futile big spending belongs to former Texas governor John B. Connally, who spent $12.6 million, raised mostly from the business community, in the 1980 Republican primaries and won just one delegate. The same year, President Jimmy Carter outspent Sen. Edward Kennedy $722,000 to $215,000 in the Pennsylvania primary but lost badly. Four years earlier, in 1976, Sen. Henry M. Jackson of Washington spent $2.4 million in his losing two-month effort.

Congress first encouraged small political donations with the Revenue Act of 1971, which allowed an income tax credit or a deduction for political contributions in primaries and general elections. (The tax break was eliminated in 1986.) The 1974 Federal Election Campaign Act then offered matching funds to contenders for party nominations who raised a minimum of $100,000 on their own with at least $5,000 coming from each of twenty states in donations of $250 or less. Partial federal funding encourages campaigns to seek small donations. (Before passage of the 1974 FECA, a small number of "sugar daddies" underwrote major nomination expenses. General Motors heir Stewart Mott, for example, gave liberals Eugene McCarthy $300,000 in 1968 and George McGovern $400,000 in 1972. Mott also made a practice of making large loans to candidates—such as $200,000 to McGovern in 1972.) Matching funds have accounted for about 40 percent of the total nominating campaign expenditures since 1976. Some $31.3 million in federal money was disbursed to candidates meeting matching-fund requirements in 1980, $30.9 million in 1984, $66.7 million in 1988, and $42.1 million in 1992.[130]

The FECA limited the money that candidates could spend in primaries. In 1976, the first year of the law's operation, no candidate could spend more than 16 cents per voting-age person in a state. That figure is adjusted for inflation each election year.[131]

Presidential hopefuls traditionally followed an unwritten rule against public campaigns early in the election cycle. In recent years, however, the need to raise money in small sums has spurred candidates to conduct formal fund-raising drives early. By February 1975, a year before the first primary test, five Democrats had announced their candidacies. Republican Bush met matching-fund requirements in January 1979, a full year before the 1980 race began. Many candidates began their efforts just as early in previous elections, but the efforts were not so public.

Early fund raising can be crucial to a campaign because of the high costs of organization and the need to demonstrate viability. Two key rules of fund raising are to "find some fat cats, quick" and "go where the money is." Because of individual donor limits, a presidential campaign must have access to fundraisers with "lots of rich friends." The best states for fund raising have been California, New York, Florida, and Texas, which supply about one-half of all campaign donations. As one observer has put it: "A modern presidential campaign is designed to suck money out of New York and California and spend it in Iowa and New Hampshire."[132]

Fund-raisers target their appeals even more narrowly than states. In the 1991–1992 election cycle, the 10021 ZIP code—which includes the upper east side of Manhattan—donated $6.59 million to federal campaigns. Residents of the ZIP code 10022, just south of 10021, contributed about $4 million. The celebrated 90210 ZIP code zone in Beverly Hills, California, contributed $3.11 million to those campaigns.[133]

Candidates often have a special fund-raising entree with particular social groups. Dukakis raised millions in 1988 from Greek Americans proud to see one of their own seek the White House. In 1984 and 1988 Jesse Jackson had the support of African Americans and other minority groups across the country. Clinton's forthright stance on gay rights spurred activists such as David Mixner to raise more than $2 million for the Arkansas governor in 1992. Clinton also enjoyed his access to Hollywood figures who have become prominent fund-raisers in both parties in recent years.

Because matching funds are limited to candidates who receive at least 10 percent of the vote in at least one of the last two succeeding primaries they enter, candidates seeking delegates face a dilemma: risk missing out on the delegate hunt or risk losing matching-fund eligibility. The matching funds "threshold" is a crucial factor in the campaign's high dropout rate after the first three or four primaries. Poor primary performances—and the fund-raising drought and loss of federal matching funds that result—forced all but Clinton and Jerry Brown out of the Democratic race early in 1992. Sen. Robert Kerrey of Nebraska dropped out on March 5, Sen. Thomas R. Harkin of Iowa withdrew March 9, and former senator Paul E. Tsongas of Massachusetts suspended his effort March 19. For the Republican nomination in 1996, the only two major contenders remaining by the middle of March were Bob Dole and Pat Buchanan. In previous years, candidates had stayed in the race much longer. The first dropout in the 1972 presidential race was Mayor John V. Lindsay of New York, in April.

Candidates with strong voter appeal have found their prospects damaged because they failed to meet the threshold in two consecutive primaries. Sen. Al Gore of Tennessee ended his 1988 campaign after failing to meet the threshold in the New York primary, which cut off his federal matching funds. Rep. Morris K. Udall of Arizona did not receive federal matching funds for nine weeks in 1976, partly because the implementation of federal regulations in their maiden year of operation was uncertain.

Spending limits do not apply to candidates who decline federal assistance, as did John Connally in 1980, Ross Perot in 1992, and Steve Forbes in 1996. Ronald Reagan briefly considered declining the federal money in his 1980 campaign, as did Pat Robertson in 1988.

The spending restrictions and expansion of the primary schedule have created a problem: candidates must compete in as many primaries as possible using as little money as possible. The conventional wisdom after Maine senator Edmund Muskie's ill-fated Democratic 1972 drive was that he had squandered money by entering too many primaries. But in 1976, Carter, who was more adept at trimming costs and taking advantage of free media exposure, won the nomination by winning seventeen primaries.

An important element of campaign "momentum" is fund-raising ability. Carter's early fund raising and electoral tests in 1976 enabled him to increase total monthly receipts from $125,000 in January to $400,000 in February, $612,000 in March, and $732,000 in April. Just as previous candidates relied on a few wealthy donors, Carter depended on a strong base of regional pride: almost half of his $900,000 primary treasury came from his home state of Georgia.[134] As noted, Dukakis benefited from the contributions of fellow Greek Americans and businesses associated with his state's government.

Insurgent campaigns always have depended on small contributions from loyal followers. Goldwater in 1964, McCarthy in 1968, and McGovern in 1972 all relied on small donors. It now appears that even establishment candidates need a broad base of small contributors.

Spending is much heavier in the early stages of the nominating campaign. Reports on recent presidential races found that in the early primary states, campaigns spent about 85 percent of their state limits but that in the March primary states spending dropped to 30–40 percent, and in April to 25–30 percent.[135] (Each state contest has its own limit according to population.) In the 1976, 1980, and 1984 campaigns, candidates spent more than 50 percent of the limits only 5 percent of the time; more than half the time, they spent less than 5 percent of the spending limits.[136] So few candidates have reached the individual primary and caucus spending limits that in 1994 reformers proposed eliminating them altogether.[137]

But early spending is not always wise spending. Gary Hart's 1984 campaign spent most of its reserves in the campaign's early stages, neglecting costly organizing in later states that could have earned him more than one hundred additional delegates. The major 1976 candidates displayed the same inability to save their money for the important battles. For the 1976 race, eleven Democratic and Republican candidates spent in 1975 $13 million of the $13.3 million they had raised that year. In contrast, a frugal Carter paid his 1976 campaign staffers one-third the salaries of staffers working for Sen. Henry Jackson, ensuring that the Carter campaign never faced a cash-flow crisis.[138] In 1980 Sen. Kennedy "spen[t] himself virtually out of existence" on high staff salaries, first-class travel, and extravagant headquarters—$2.4 million in two months compared with the Carter campaign's expenses of $2.8 million in ten months.[139]

An election's unpredictability can create enormous difficulties in making financial choices because candidates make spending decisions based on their strategy for winning nomination. Adhering to an "early knockout" strategy in 1984, the Mondale campaign used most of its funds in the early primary states. When Hart surprised Mondale with strong showings in Iowa, New Hampshire, and the South, Mondale had to scramble to win New York, Illinois, Pennsylvania, and Ohio—with less money than Hart.

Campaigns have been ingenious in getting around the state limits, especially in the early contests. In New Hampshire, for example, campaign workers sometimes rent cars and set up lodging in neighboring Massachusetts. They also list headquarters expenses as the cost of complying with federal regulations, which are exempt from the spending limits.

The 1984 Mondale campaign deliberately violated state limits. Mondale spent $2.85 million in the New Hampshire primary (and lost), despite a legal limit of $404,000; he later accepted a $400,000 fine. "It [the fine] wasn't a lot, and that's the whole point," said Mondale aide Robert Beckel. "The FEC is not one of the great enforcement agencies of modern politics."[140]

One harmful effect of the spending limits is that campaigns are forced to shut down their headquarters in a state right after the caucus or primary takes place. Efforts to continue to organize staffs and educate voters are dropped until the general election. If the headquarters could remain in operation, the state organizations could build strong links between state and na-

## CRITIQUES OF THE CAMPAIGN FINANCE SYSTEM

The system of financing presidential and congressional campaigns in the United States does not stem from any coherent design but rather the haphazard development of vague laws passed during crisis periods in U.S. electoral history. The result, critics say, is a system in which some campaigns are overfinanced and others are underfinanced. Instead of creating elections in which the candidates have an equal opportunity to present themselves to voters, the system leads to a situation in which a few leading candidates for party nominations dominate fund raising.

Almost anyone exposed to presidential campaigns agrees that the time required for fund raising is a distraction that binds prospective candidates to special interests.

Limits on campaign contributions also damage the strength of the two-party system, other critics say. The $1,000 individual limit on donations to campaigns pales in comparison with the $5,000 limit on donations to political action committees (PACs). The different limits encourage big donors to give to PACs, which usually concentrate on a small number of issues rather than on the coalition building of parties.

Many critics, eyeing the threefold increase in real campaign expenditures since 1960, maintain that too much money is in circulation. Heavily financed campaigns, according to this view, are dangerous because of the superficial media images they produce. Of greater importance, perhaps, is the amount of influence expensive campaigns give to the special interests that make contributions. Of these critiques, that by journalist Elizabeth Drew, *Politics and Money,* is the most prominent.[1]

David Adamany and George Agree, longtime experts on campaign finance, argue that any limits on campaign spending or donations might work against education of voters. They point out that spending on campaigns is slight compared with spending by the rest of the advertising industry. Since most Americans are ill-informed about the presidential candidates, what is needed is more, not less, spending.[2] Some have proposed allocating free television time for the candidates to talk about issues.

The requirements for disclosure of campaign receipts and spending are often criticized as being "too little, too late." Critics argue that the information is so voluminous and newspaper reports so skimpy that voters do not get much useful information when they are making their decisions.

The Working Group on Electoral Democracy proposed reforms that would reduce the importance of incumbency and large donors. The proposal could work for both presidential and congressional campaigns. Candidates would get federal financing for their campaigns, as well as discounts for mailings and broadcast commercials. Broadcasters would be required to offer the candidates free air time during prime time in exchange for the use of public airwaves.

To qualify, a candidate would have to raise "seed money" with a high number of $5 or $10 contributions. Parties who reached a threshold of support in the last election—say, 5 to 20 percent of the vote—would qualify for public funding automatically. Public funding would depend on the acceptance of certain formats for advertising, such as requiring candidates to appear in 50 percent of the spot to reduce the slick "Madison Avenue" production of emotional appeals. Candidates also would be required to participate in a series of debates with their opponents. Compliance would be ensured by requiring campaigns to pay their expenses only with a special credit card, which would be monitored by the Federal Election Commission (FEC).

The proposal also would rein in independent spending. Any group that wants to support a candidate financially would be required to tell the FEC which candidate it is seeking to benefit. The FEC would then provide a line of credit for that amount to the other candidates.

Proponents of the reform estimate its costs to be $500 million at the most, or $5 per eligible voter: "Compared to the billions of dollars that moneyed interests take from the treasury in the form of corporate bailouts, tax breaks, subsidies, and regulatory favors, $5 a year is a small price to pay for fair and honest elections."[3]

To exact such a sweeping reform, the Working Group suggests a grassroots movement, styled on the movements that extended suffrage to women and African Americans. Others have suggested that only limitations on the number of terms served by members of Congress could produce serious reform.[4] Congress, however, is unlikely to enact reforms that would undermine its own reelection prospects.[5]

Other reformers advocate opening up the system to more private money. Norman Ornstein of the American Enterprise Institute suggested raising the amount that individuals can contribute to candidates "sharply" from the current $1,000 and reducing the $5,000 contributions allowed to political action committees. Ornstein opposes limits on "soft" money on the grounds that it would weaken party organizations at all levels. He also advocates public financing of all federal elections.[6]

1. Elizabeth Drew, *Politics and Money: The New Road to Corruption* (New York: Macmillan, 1983).
2. David Adamany and George Agree, *Political Money: A Strategy for Campaign Financing in America* (Baltimore: Johns Hopkins University Press, 1975).
3. Marty Jezer and Randy Kehler, "Let's Have Real Campaign Reform," *The Nation,* November 2, 1992, 497.
4. George F. Will, *Restoration: Congress, Term Limits, and the Recovery of Deliberative Democracy* (New York: Free Press, 1993).
5. "Freshmen Got to Washington with the Help of PAC Funds," *Congressional Quarterly Weekly Report,* March 27, 1993, 723–727.
6. Norman Ornstein, *Current,* October 1992, 10–14.

tional party officials and keep the campaign atmosphere alive all year. *(See box, Critiques of the Campaign Finance System, above.)*

Even though campaigns pump millions of dollars into television and radio outlets, the stations often are wary of doing business with them. Campaign spending is minor compared with the overall advertising budgets of the stations, and campaigns provide only a short burst of business that may endanger the standing of regular clients. Furthermore, the ad hoc nature of many campaigns makes doing business with them difficult. Broadcast outlets therefore set stringent standards for campaign advertising. Candidates often must contract for broadcast spots weeks ahead of time, and they must pay in advance to comply with FEC standards.

The mood and content of a campaign can change dramatically in a matter of days, which makes the broadcast spending decisions even more difficult. It is not always possible to pull advertising spots off the air, as the Hart campaign discovered when it failed to halt a television commercial during the 1984 Illinois primary that was critical of the Chicago Democratic machine.

## MONEY IN THE GENERAL CAMPAIGN

Between the conventions and election day, no presidential nominee must spend precious campaign time seeking money. Under the Federal Election Campaign Act, the campaigns of the major party nominees for president are financed entirely by the federal government. Participants say the federal provision of campaign funds has improved the process. But private money and nominally independent organizations have continued to play an important role in the general election.

The first campaign underwritten by public money was the 1976 race. In that year, each candidate was given $22 million. Funding rose in later years because of automatic inflation adjustments—to $29 million in 1980, $40 million in 1984, $46 million in 1988, and $55.2 million in 1992. The federal funding goes directly to the presidential candidates' campaign organizations. Direct support reduces the role of the two parties in the daily operations of the fall campaign.[141]

Despite federal funding of the major parties' general election campaigns, President Bush outspent Governor Clinton in 1992 by a margin of $179.5 million to $155.9 million. In addition to the $55.2 million each candidate received from the federal government for his campaign, the party presidential committees spent another $10.3 million apiece for them. Bush also benefited from $110 million in "soft money"—independent efforts made in his behalf but not under his campaign umbrella—while Clinton benefited from $86 million in soft spending.[142] As noted, independent candidate Perot avoided spending limits by paying for his own campaign in 1992, largely with money from his personal fortune of $4 billion. Perot spent $68.3 million, mostly on television and radio commercials.

Federal financing was supposed to free presidential candidates from the time-consuming and corrupting process of fund raising. But candidates have found enough loopholes in the laws that they can raise millions and legally spend it to supplement the federal grants. Indeed, federal funding has not served so much to eliminate private interests from the election as to redirect their money into independent committee efforts. In 1980 committees independent of the campaign organizations spent $13.7 million on the presidential election and another $2.3 million on congressional elections. Some $12.2 million of the independent presidential campaign spending supported Republican Reagan. Four years later, independent expenditures rose to $18.5 million, with $15.5 million spent for Reagan and only $160,000

against Reagan. (The remainder was spent for Mondale and other efforts such as interest group appeals and general civic messages that cannot be called either pro-Reagan or pro-Mondale.) Groups supporting Reagan tended to be large operations. Five conservative organizations, for example, spent more than $14.5 million. Mondale's largest supporter was the Senior Political Action Committee, which spent $218,000.

Many of the independent expenditures went for direct-mail operations. An aide to Reagan estimated that fund-raisers brought in $4 for every $1 in direct-mail expenses; officials from other campaigns said the ratio was smaller for their candidates.[143] But the value of direct mail extends far beyond the money raised. Appeals for contributions advertise and make an argument as well. The appeals also provide a campaign with important feedback (information passed along informally or published in direct-mail newsletters) that some of the most sophisticated survey techniques cannot match.

Federal funds are supplemented by funds from the treasuries of the national committees of each major party—an area in which the Republicans have had a strong advantage. (See Table 1-6.) In 1981, for example, the Republicans spent $6 million to support selected party candidates for the 1982 elections. Some $2.8 million went for communications systems, $2.3 million to promote President Reagan's tax-cutting policies, and $800,000 to national and state polling operations. These expenditures do much to complement the party's efforts in presidential campaigns.[144] Similar ends are served with donations to party organizations in states that do not have restrictions on fund raising. The money is used for "party-building" activities such as voter registration efforts, polling, and advertising.

The Democratic ticket in 1988 countered the Republican advantage in outside spending with heavy spending in the Texas Senate race. Lloyd Bentsen, the vice-presidential candidate, spent $8 million on his reelection campaign against a weak opponent, Rep. Beau Boulter. Bentsen ran both for vice president and for reelection to his Senate seat under a 1959 state law designed for Lyndon Johnson. In 1959 Johnson, the Senate majority leader, was planning a presidential race, but he did not want to forfeit his Senate seat if he did not make it to the White House. When Johnson won the vice presidency in 1960 on a

TABLE 1–6 Funds Raised by Democratic and Republican National Committees, 1983–1992 *(millions of dollars)*

| Election cycle | Democratic Party | Republican Party |
| --- | --- | --- |
| 1983–1984 | 84.4 | 289.0 |
| 1985–1986 | 57.0 | 255.2 |
| 1987–1988 | 116.1 | 257.5 |
| 1989–1990 | 76.9 | 206.4 |
| 1991–1992 | 162.2 | 254.8 |

SOURCE: Harold W. Stanley and Richard G. Niemi, *Vital Statistics on American Politics*, 5th ed. (Washington, D.C.: CQ Press, 1995), 141.

ticket with Kennedy, as well as reelection to the Senate, he re-signed his Senate seat.

In his well-financed Texas campaign, Bentsen almost never mentioned his race for the Senate. Republicans charged that the Dukakis-Bentsen campaign was violating the spirit if not the letter of federal campaign finance legislation, which gives both presidential tickets equal amounts for the fall campaign. Thus the GOP asked the Federal Election Commission to count some of Bentsen's Senate money toward the Dukakis campaign limit of $46 million. The FEC and federal courts rejected the requests.

## MAJOR DONORS IN U.S. POLITICS

Perpetual fund raising is the electoral equivalent of an arms race. Candidates are so concerned with survival that they spend more and more time and use more and more sophisticated technology to gain an advantage over rivals. Candidates raise money not according to objective standards of need but out of a fear of falling behind their rivals. The arms race mentality, said Elizabeth Drew, affects every aspect of politics. "It is not relevant whether every candidate who spends more than his opponent wins. What matters is what the chasing of money does to the candidates, and to the victors' subsequent behavior. The point is what raising money, not simply spending it, does to the political process."[145] Hubert Humphrey, who sought the presidency in 1960, 1968, and 1972, described the ways that fund-raising affects the tenor of the campaign:

Campaign financing is a curse. It's the most disgusting, demeaning, disenchanting, debilitating experience of a politician's life. It's stinky, it's lousy. I just can't tell you how much I hate it. I've had to break off in the middle of trying to make a decent, honorable campaign and go up to somebody's parlor or to a room and say, 'Gentlemen, and ladies, I'm desperate. You've got to help me.' . . . And you see the people there—a lot of them you don't want to see. And they look at you, and you sit there and you talk to them and tell them what you're for and you need help and, out of the twenty-five who have gathered, four will contribute. And most likely one of them is in trouble and is someone you shouldn't have had a contribution from.[146]

The major financial supporters of the Democratic and Republican parties have remained basically the same for much of the twentieth century. Republicans are backed by a relatively unified and wealthy business coalition, but they also have been much more successful than the Democrats at raising money from small contributors. Democrats are backed by an uneasy alliance of business, labor, and liberal groups. The different make-ups of the parties produce different public images: the Republicans have a single coherent message, while the Democrats more often are beset by conflicting internal demands.

Fund raising varies according to the condition of the economy, the existence of salient issues, and the prospects for a competitive election. In 1988, when both parties held open contests for the nomination, candidates had raised a total of $90 million by February. At the same point in 1992, with a strong incumbent president, candidates in both parties had raised a total of $20 million.[147]

Fund-raisers are torn about whether to seek money from large or small donors. Both parties have been drawn to big donors because of the quicker returns on fund-raising efforts. But critics of the large-donor approach point out that the party risks being perceived as beholden to big donors.

Small contributors—once dismissed as piddling by former Democratic Party chairman Robert Strauss—played a major role in the 1992 presidential campaign. Former California governor Jerry Brown based his Democratic primary campaign on donations of $100 or less. In fact, Brown led all candidates in April 1992 with $1.64 million in contributions from 32,686 donors.[148] Democrat Tom Harkin of Iowa, with strong ties to organized labor and farm interests, established a strong direct-mail fund-raising operation.

A campaign dependent on small donations is not necessarily a modest "people's" insurgency. To the contrary, both parties have developed sophisticated—and expensive—telephone and direct-mail operations for getting thousands of small donors. Independent Perot set up sophisticated computer systems at his Dallas headquarters to parlay telephone calls into fund-raising data that might be used to get other donations. The telephone numbers of incoming calls were recorded and sent to a computer system for analysis, thereby revealing which communities seemed to be fertile territory for Perot's fund raising.

### Democratic Donors

The Democratic coalition since the New Deal has been built around the notion of a growth economy that allows the party to attract the less economically fortunate members of society with a variety of social programs. Big financial backers have included multinational corporations, real estate developers, and elements of the communications and entertainment industries. The manufacturing concerns that ally with the Democrats have tended to be capital-intensive companies, seeking new markets abroad as a way of spurring growth. (Capital-intensive businesses are those that rely more on machinery in mass production than on cheap labor.) Historically, the Democratic commitment to "international liberalism" has come in the form of low tariffs, an international monetary system dominated by the dollar and U.S. banks, and international development programs.

The U.S. economy was so strong after World War II that the demands of the less well-off groups—farmers, organized labor, blacks, the elderly, and the poor—did not antagonize the party's more conservative members of the business establishment. There was room in the party for both the masses of people seeking government protection and the large financial supporters. Ferguson and Rogers noted: "Because they were capital-intensive, firms in the bloc were less threatened by labor turbulence and organization. They could thus 'afford' a coalition with labor. Because [these companies] were world, as well as U.S., pacesetters, they stood to gain from global free trade."[149]

The New Deal coalition included large, growing corporations such as General Electric, International Business Machines, and R. J. Reynolds, as well as big oil concerns and commercial and investment banks. Until the post-Watergate era of campaign reform and the Carter administration's windfall profits tax and emphasis on conservation, the oil industry favored many Democrats.

The importance of growth to the Democratic coalition is underscored by prominent party fund-raisers. Two of Mondale's top fund-raisers in 1984 were real estate developers Nathan Landow of Maryland and Thomas Rosenberg of Chicago. Rosenberg had based his career on subsidized housing projects and said bluntly, "My business would be a lot better if the Democrats were in power."[150]

The alliance of the "haves" and the "have nots" was strained in the 1970s and 1980s by slower economic growth. After World War II, U.S. companies controlled 60 percent of all manufacturing production in the West and 40 percent of the total goods and services. But the U.S. share of manufactured goods dropped from 26 to 18 percent between 1960 and 1980. Likewise, the U.S. share of the world's gross national product dropped from 40 percent in 1950 to 22 percent in 1980. In 1956 forty-two of the world's largest corporations were American; by 1980 only twenty-three were.[151]

Since it entered a precarious age in the 1970s, U.S. business has been less willing to accommodate liberal causes. Business concerns increasingly rely on the Republican Party to represent their interests. Nevertheless, business issues and support remain an important element of the Democrats' strategy because business provides about half of all Democratic campaign contributions.

Since the administration of Franklin Roosevelt, the labor movement has been an integral element of the Democratic Party. Critics of contribution limits argue that the Democrats' labor support neutralizes any advantage that Republicans may enjoy from corporate support. Because union workers often are organized as campaign volunteers, Democrats enjoy nonfinancial benefits that are as influential as the straight cash contributions to the GOP. Furthermore, unions can spend unlimited funds on internal communications that aid their mobilization efforts.

Despite their declining membership (down to 15.8 percent of the U.S. workforce in 1993),[152] unions remain an important money source for the Democratic Party. Labor-connected PACs contributed $39.9 million to Democratic congressional candidates in 1993–1994, against $1.7 million to Republican candidates.[153]

Relations between labor and the Democratic Party have been strained since the late 1960s. Democratic support for labor initiatives—such as the unsuccessful drive to repeal a provision of the 1947 Taft-Hartley Act that impedes union organizing efforts, import protection for vulnerable labor-intensive industries such as textiles, and minimum-wage and training bills—has not been unanimous as was Democratic support for previous prolabor measures. In fact, many Democratic presidential candidates have criticized labor's demands. Meanwhile, during the cold war much of the labor movement has criticized the party's dovish foreign policy stances.

*Republican Donors*

The Republican Party traditionally has been the bastion of domestic businesses. Of these, the labor-intensive businesses have demanded that protectionist and antilabor policies survive, and the GOP has responded. The party began the twentieth century as the champion of protective tariffs to spur industrialization. And as time went on, the Republicans continued to support policies that would protect industry from floods of cheap imports from countries with lower labor costs. Supporters of Republican presidential candidate Barry Goldwater in 1964 included George Humphrey of National Steel, Roger Milliken of the textile company Deering Milliken, and independent oil producers John Pew and Henry Salvatori.[154] Goldwater's platform included a strong plank in favor of protectionist legislation.

The financial bases of the two parties evolved with the emergence of new issues in the 1960s and 1970s: the ascendance of Japanese and Western European economies, expanded relations with the Soviet Union and the People's Republic of China, oil shortages, political unrest in Africa and Latin America, the "internationalization" of the economic system, environmentalism, soaring budget deficits, imbalances in trade relations with other countries, and the combination of high inflation and high unemployment rates, or "stagflation."

As the economy stagnated in the 1970s, business became more involved in the political process. Groups that had been hostile to one another coalesced. Large and small oil producers, for example, moved fully into the Republican camp in the period of price increases after the oil crises of 1973 and 1979. Worldwide increases in oil prices were spurring the growth of independent producers. When President Carter in 1979 pushed a windfall profits tax, those interests moved to the GOP. In the 1981–1982 election cycle, some 26 percent of the individual contributions to the Republican National Committee came from Texas, Louisiana, and Oklahoma—the nation's leading oil states.[155] In 1980 independent oil producers contributed $25.7 million to the Republican Party, the Reagan campaign, and non–oil state Republican candidates.[156]

Over the years, the Republicans also have established an impressive list of small contributors. The party receives an average donation of $25 from people responding to direct-mail initiatives, according to 1982 figures.[157] The names come from lists provided by the Carte Blanche credit card, the *Wall Street Journal*, McGraw-Hill business publications, and stock and investment firms. As *Washington Post* reporter Thomas Byrne Edsall has noted, "Those willing to give $25 a year to a political party come overwhelmingly from an economic elite."[158] In 1964 Goldwater had raised some $5.8 million from 651,000 such donors—that is, an "elite" comprising not simply wealthy individuals but also middle-class and upper-middle-class persons with more disposable income than the average American.

President Nixon's 1972 campaign drew on the Goldwater initiative, seeking more contributions from small donors and building up mass-mailing lists. Republicans expanded their mailing lists and relied almost entirely on smaller contributors in 1976. Republican committees received 58 percent of their funds from donors of less than $100. By 1980, 73 percent of GOP funds came from small contributors.[159]

The Democrats have been forced to play "catch-up" in the direct-mail fund-raising game. George McGovern developed a mailing list with 600,000 names from various liberal causes in his 1972 campaign, but Democratic chairman Robert Strauss dumped the lists four years later and stressed fund raising from large donors, telethons, and special events.[160] Only 20 percent of the Democratic National Committee's receipts came from small contributors in the 1979–1980 election cycle.

## POLITICAL ACTION COMMITTEES

Political action committees have been the source of great controversy in recent years because of their explosive growth, negative campaign tactics, special-interest messages, and limited accountability. Potential presidential candidates often form their own PACs to make political contacts and explore the viability of a campaign. But once a campaign begins, and public funding prevents presidential candidates from accepting PAC money, PAC influence is usually limited to the fallout from congressional and state campaigns. PACs account for only about 2 percent of all spending in presidential elections.

A PAC is a committee designed to raise and distribute money for political purposes. Many PACs are affiliated with corporations, trade and professional associations, or labor unions. Many are independent. Between 1974 and 1996 the number of PACs grew from 608 to 4,079. *(See Figure 1-2.)* PAC contributions to or independent spending for federal candidates grew even faster—from about $14.2 million in 1972 to $394.1 million in 1991–1992. Of the latter, $178.4 million went to congressional candidates and $215.7 million to presidential candidates.

Business and labor PACs provided the most money to candidates in 1992. The leading donor was the Democratic Republican Voter Education Committee of the American Federation of Labor-Congress of Industrial Organizations (AFL-CIO), with $11.8 million in overall spending and contributions. Other big donors included PACs for the American Medical Association ($6.3 million), National Education Association ($5.8 million), National Rifle Association ($5.7 million), and the Realtors Political Action Committee ($4.9 million). Insurance and health care interests donated a total of $41.4 million. Eight labor PACs gave more than $2 million each, and seven corporate PACs gave more than $1 million each.[161]

Independent PAC spending was an important element in Ronald Reagan's 1984 victory. In the general election campaign, political action committees favorable to Reagan spent $7.2 million, while those favorable to Democratic challenger Walter Mondale spent only $657,000.[162]

Legal limits on campaign and PAC contributions are, for all practical purposes, unenforceable. Wealthy political activists can work around limits on individual donations by persuading their

FIGURE 1-2 Growth of PACS, 1974–1996

Number of PACs

■ Corporate    ■ Nonconnected

■ Labor    ☐ Other

▥ Trade/membership/health

**Source:** Federal Election Commission.
   **Note:** Membership PACs are mostly the PACs of professional associations such as trial lawyers, real estate, and medical and academic organizations. Nonconnected PACs do not have any connection with a specific business firm, union, party, or candidate. The "Other" category consists of PACs formed by corporations without capital stock and incorporated cooperatives. For the years 1974–1976, numbers are not available for nonconnected PACs or PACs in the "Other" category.

families and friends to give money to a number of PACs and campaigns. Once donors run up against limits to national campaign contributions, they can start giving "soft money"—that is, donations to unregulated state party organizations. One indication of the importance of soft money was Reagan's 1980 campaign in Texas, one of the most important states in the nation because of its large bloc of electoral votes.[163] The Reagan campaign spent virtually no money in that state because the Texas Republican organizations spent so much in his behalf.

From 1995 to 1996 the Republican Party raised $141.2 million and the Democrats raised $122.3 million in soft money. This money paid for printing and distributing literature, telephone banks for get-out-the-vote drives, and other party-building activities that directly helped the parties' presidential campaigns.[164]

The proliferation of PACs can be traced to the provision in federal law allowing larger donations to independent committees (up to $5,000 a year) than to the candidates' own campaign organizations ($1,000 one time). The five-to-one donation advantage encourages prospective donors to give to the multicandidate PACs more than to parties or candidates.

Another factor behind PAC growth is organized labor's 1972 request for "clarification" of a federal law on independent spending. Concerned that the Nixon administration would attempt to bar independent spending by unions, the AFL-CIO solicited the clearance for unlimited PAC spending. The resulting 1972 amendment stated that a ban on direct campaign contributions by unions and corporations did not also imply a ban on creation of independent organizations by unions and corporations to advertise and conduct political campaigns for whatever cause they wished. The amendment also held that union and corporate money could be used for get-out-the-vote drives and internal communications such as meetings, newsletters, and surveys. When Congress passed the 1972 amendment to the previous year's Federal Election Campaign Act sanctioning political action committees, few organizations had PACs.[165] In the two decades after the amendment's passage, business PACs grew in number eleven times as fast as labor PACs.[166]

Perhaps more important than the PAC spending during a campaign are the PACs that candidates create before the election year. The PACs ostensibly are designed to promote a wide range of congressional and state campaigns across the country; by law, PACs must make donations to at least five candidates. But, in reality, most of these PAC dollars are used to support the presidential aspirations of the PAC founders. Because PACs do not have the formal status of campaign organizations, they escape many of the spending and reporting requirements of formal campaign structures.

Among the advantages of presidential PACs over presidential campaign organizations, donors may contribute $5,000 annually to a multicandidate PAC but only $1,000 to a presidential campaign, and PACs are not subject to the campaign spending ceilings and other regulations that formal campaign organizations must heed.

As recently as 1976, none of the prospective candidates set up their own PACs. But before the 1980 election, four of the ten candidates set up PACs and five of nine did so before the 1984 election. By the 1988 election, nine of fourteen candidates had set up PACs and three others had set up similar organizations.

Political scientist Anthony Corrado argues that the preelection-year PAC "fosters inequities" by favoring potential candidates with an ability to raise money early in the election cycle. In this way, candidates with sophisticated fund-raising operations can become prohibitive favorites for the nomination, leaving behind long-shot candidates. Two examples of the latter, McGovern and Carter, might not have had the chance to win the nomination if their well-heeled opponents had established PACs early in the election cycle. This being the case, candidates with demonstrated government abilities do not succeed as often as candidates with fund-raising and other campaign advantages. Corrado writes:

The race for the presidency has come to display more of the characteristics of an endurance contest than an electoral one. . . . Individuals considered a presidential candidate have begun campaigning at least two or three years in advance of an election in order to remain competitive or at least to not concede a substantial head start to a prospective opponent. The system, therefore, is not necessarily conducive to the best or most qualified candidates. . . . Instead, it favors candidates who have the desire, time, and stamina to endure at least two or three years of virtually nonstop fundraising, travel, and politicking.[167]

Missouri representative Richard Gephardt's PAC, the Effective Government Committee, spent more than $1 million in 1985 and 1986, but only $65,597 on campaigns for fellow Democrats. The rest of the money paid for Gephardt's travel to early caucus and primary states and for the salaries and expenses of many campaign workers. More than a third of the money for other campaigns went to candidates from Iowa and New Hampshire.[168] Most people involved with Gephardt's PAC made no serious attempt to hide its status as an arm of Gephardt's presidential bid.[169]

Gephardt was not the only presidential aspirant to establish a nominally independent PAC. In 1985 and 1986, PACs associated with Republican presidential candidates George Bush, Bob Dole, and Jack Kemp raised $10.4 million and distributed only $1.2 million to Republican congressional candidates. Democrats Gary Hart, Joseph Biden, and Bruce Babbitt collected $577,000 for their PACs during the same period.[170]

Candidates can evade spending limits—illegally—by creating several PACs or "independent committees." The 1984 Democratic campaigns of Walter Mondale and his chief challenger, Gary Hart, did not accept any PAC money during the primaries. But Mondale allowed the creation of a number of nominally independent state committees that accepted PAC money and spent it to promote his candidacy. More than one hundred "delegate committees" solicited PAC money and enabled Mondale to avoid limits on total primary spending. After weeks of Hart's hectoring—"Give the money back!"—Mondale agreed to return the contributions from business and labor committees. But rather than give the money back, Mondale made a financial settlement with the Federal Election Commission.[171]

The delegate committee expenditures were crucial. Because Mondale's "early knockout" strategy failed, his campaign nearly ran out of money during the middle stages of the primary season. Delegate committee spending enabled Mondale to stay alive during a period when Hart appeared to have enough momentum to win the nomination.

PACs have a middle- and upper-class bias. Business, banking, real estate, and communications are among the largest PAC interests. Middle-class interests also are central to fund raising around the issue of Social Security, the most lucrative liberal, direct-mail appeal. Environmentalism, human rights, and abortion are other liberal causes dominated by middle-class constituencies. Even unions, the most class-conscious of donors, have a middle-class bias. Labor appeals stress the needs of workers already enjoying wage and workplace protection. Because of its interest in economic growth, labor often adopts probusiness stances.

Kansas senator Bob Dole, who unsuccessfully sought the presidency in 1980, 1988, and 1996, and who served as national chair of the Republican Party from 1971 to 1973, rejects the argument that PAC dollars balance each other and allow all major positions to be heard on issues: "There aren't any Poor PACs or Food Stamp PACs or Nutrition PACs or Medicare PACs."[172]

Although PACs must be independent of campaigns for their expenditures to be exempt from the legal limits on campaign spending, the independence is often a facade. PACs with common interests find ways to plot strategy together and receive signals from campaign organizations. Leaking the results of polls—an expensive and strategic part of any campaign—is common. The leaks help coordinate the efforts of the various groups working for a candidate. "Social" visits—such as receptions or fund-raisers where people with common political goals gather—are enough for PACs to know how to direct their efforts. Coordination can be completely unstated. Said Georgetown University professor Roy Schotland: "Any dummy can figure out where it will help the candidate to spend money. And the candidate is going to observe that money is being spent. No communication is necessary."[173]

Public appeals by PACs and campaign organizations—on issues such as Social Security, tax policy, and defense policy—often dovetail with presidential and congressional ads. PAC commercials even attack specific candidates. In 1980 the National Conservative Political Action Committee sponsored a campaign of broadcast commercials attacking Democratic senators George McGovern, Frank Church, Birch Bayh, and John Culver. This "negative campaigning" was considered instrumental in the senators' defeat and in Ronald Reagan's overall campaign against the Washington establishment.

Some PACs depend on direct-mail solicitation. One of them, the conservative National Congressional Club, was ninth largest among PACs in 1991–1992 in terms of overall spending ($3.9

million) in behalf of candidates.[174] In the 1980s and 1990s, with the conservative movement exhausting itself, a number of direct-mail operations declined.[175] But with the return of the Democrats to the White House in 1992, conservative groups revived their efforts with anti-Clinton appeals. The strategy paid off. Record fund raising by Republican candidates, much of it through direct mail, helped them to take control of Congress in 1994 after years of Democratic dominance. Individual donors gave $219.4 million to GOP candidates, $55.2 million more than in the 1991–1992 election cycle. Democratic candidates received $180.7 million from individuals. Democrats led in receipts from PACs, $111.8 million, but the Republican figure of $66.7 million from PACs was higher than in the past.[176]

## TRENDS IN CAMPAIGN SPENDING

Concern about money in politics has increased as spending at all levels of electoral politics has increased. Total costs for presidential campaigns jumped from $30 million in 1960 to $160 million in 1976 and approximately $550 million in 1992.[177] (See Table 1-7.) Because the formal campaigns of the major party candidates are federally funded, their costs have not risen as dramatically as the costs of the nominating process, which have exploded in recent years. The New Hampshire primary alone costs millions of dollars. Even with federal funding of general elections and matching funds for primaries, private donors have continued to influence the process through their contributions to the national parties and to political action committees.[178]

Expenses for the primary and general election campaigns can be broken down into four main categories:

• Advertising. About half of a campaign's funds are spent on the media—the researchers and producers who design the advertising spots and the television and radio stations that air the spots. The campaigns must be careful to save enough money for an advertising blitz just before the election when the voters are most attentive.

TABLE 1-7 Presidential Spending, 1960–1992
(millions of dollars)

| Year | Actual spending | Adjusted spending |
|---|---|---|
| 1960 | 30.0 | 30.0 |
| 1964 | 60.0 | 57.3 |
| 1968 | 100.0 | 85.1 |
| 1972 | 138.0 | 97.7 |
| 1976 | 160.0 | 83.2 |
| 1980 | 275.0 | 98.9 |
| 1984 | 325.0 | 96.3 |
| 1988 | 500.0 | 126.5 |
| 1992 | 550.0 | 117.8 |

SOURCES: Herbert E. Alexander and Brian A. Haggerty, *Financing the 1984 Election* (Lexington, Mass.: Lexington Books, 1987), 84; Citizen's Research Foundation; and Herbert E. Alexander and Anthony Corrado, *Financing the 1992 Election* (Armonk, N.Y.: Sharpe, 1995), 21.

• Staff salaries. In 1984 the Reagan campaign employed three hundred full-time staff members; Mondale employed half as many. Salaries range from highs of around $100,000 annually for key strategists to lows of around $125 a week for clerical workers. Strategists, pollsters, fund-raisers, and speechwriters occupy the most visible positions in the campaign and usually have a direct relationship with the candidate. But the campaign depends on a variety of other staffers who the candidate might not get to know, such as "advance" experts, issues researchers and analysts, bookkeepers, experts on state delegate selection and allocation rules, office managers, secretaries, and receptionists.

Because of complex federal regulations, most campaigns hire a phalanx of lawyers and accountants. The 1992 Bush-Quayle campaign employed forty-nine staff members to keep track of financial matters—donations, bills, and federal regulations. The staffers included five full-time lawyers and four computer specialists. The organization claimed an error rate of around 1 percent for its financial records.[179]

• Polling and other professional services. The cost of polling has increased as pollsters have adopted more sophisticated techniques. These include "longitudinal" (long-term) analyses of selected groups of voters; "multivariate" studies of smaller population segments, which examine many variables in different combinations; and focus group studies, which involve intense interviews with small groups of voters. The complexity and expense of surveys today are mind-boggling compared with the sorting of postcards relied on just a half-century ago. The Clinton campaign spent $1.6 million on polling in the fall 1992 campaign.

• Travel and headquarters expenses. National campaigns today do not have any choice but to travel all over the country by chartered airplane. Candidates often must appear in three or four states in a single day, bringing with them key staffers. In addition to the cost of planes, the campaign also must pay for room and board for staff on the road. The Mondale campaign spent $10.9 million on travel expenses in the fall 1984 campaign.

Rental of campaign headquarters—usually located in the high-priced real estate market of Washington, D.C.—costs several thousand dollars a month. And the costs of business furniture, office supplies, and computer and communications services are astronomical.

The inflation of campaign costs stems from several factors: increased radio and television advertising, the rise of interest groups operating on a national scale, the decline of state and local party organizations, the shift of many campaign operations to paid political consultants, more public tests of candidate strength such as primaries and caucuses, and greater geographic dispersal of voters.

Compared with other democracies, however, the United States spends little per voter on elections, especially considering the fragmentation inherent in its federal system. The 1983 West German parliamentary elections cost about $3.20 per voter, and the 1981 Irish parliamentary elections cost about $3.93 per voter.

In addition, in both of these countries the government pays for broadcast expenses. In the United States, the 1980 congressional elections cost about $1.51 per voter.[180]

Increases in campaign expenses have exceeded the national inflation rate. The Consumer Price Index—and with it, the spending limits in presidential nominating and general election campaigns—increased 40 percent between 1976 and 1980. But the major expenses of campaigns increased much faster. Price increases for mass mailings (50 percent), television commercials (100 percent), and air travel (300 percent) all exceeded the increases in spending limits.[181]

For losers, the curse of campaign financing lingers long past the election. Most candidates for party nominations incur debts that must be paid off over the next several years. Some campaigns renegotiate debts with their lenders so they only pay a fraction of their obligations. Hart's 1984 campaign, however, never paid back all of its creditors for loans in the critical Iowa caucuses, prompting businesses there to require up-front payment from future candidates. Often, party organizations help losing candidates pay debts. For example, the Democrats helped to pay off the debts from the 1968 campaigns of Robert Kennedy and Hubert Humphrey. Candidates with plans to run for office in the future feel greater urgency to settle their financial affairs. Candidates with a lingering debt can expect hectoring from opponents about their fiscal ineptitude.

Critics of interest group influence contend that the major problem of U.S. elections is that candidates do not have enough money to deliver their message. Any limitation on private donors, they say, must be accompanied by a significantly larger contribution to elections by the government. Only massive public financing will both reduce the influence of special interests and provide enough money for competitive campaigns.[182]

Because broadcast expenses have been the major element in the inflation of campaign costs, many experts have suggested that Congress arrange with television and radio stations, which are under the jurisdiction of the Federal Communications Commission, to provide free air time to major candidates so they can deliver their messages without undue private influence. One proposal, modeled after the French system, would require television networks to give presidential candidates free air time during which they would speak in front of a simple backdrop for five minutes to an hour—that is, the candidates would not be permitted to use the time to present slick commercials. The emphasis would be on presentation of issues rather than on marketing.[183]

## Comparative Party Strength

The parties' financial strength always has been unequal, but the disparity has grown in recent years even though since 1976 presidential nominees have accepted equal amounts of campaign funds from the federal government. In every presidential election since World War II, the Republican Party has outspent the Democratic Party. With the exception of President Lyndon Johnson's 1964 landslide, the Republicans have received more money in large donations than the Democrats.[184] The efforts of the national party organizations, state and congressional candidates, and independent committees have combined to give the Republican candidate a strong financial advantage, which might have been decisive in some elections.[185]

In 1968 Nixon spent more than twice as much money as Humphrey—$24.9 million to $10.3 million—in winning one of the closest elections in history. Humphrey was unable to afford television advertising during several weeks of the fall campaign. In 1980 Reagan benefited from a lopsided spending advantage by the national party organization and by PACs. Total fund-raising by the two major parties grew dramatically during the 1996 election cycle. The Republican Party reported $416.5 million in federal receipts (excluding soft money), an increase of 57 percent over the 1992 election cycle. The Democrats raised $221.6 million, an increase of 36 percent over 1992.[186]

### Regulations and Experts

More expensive electioneering, complex federal regulation, and the rise of public primary campaigns have combined to give finance experts a central role in campaigns. Because candidates need to reach voters in a more public way, and because federal regulations are tight, the most effective professionals are those who can meet legal requirements and find loopholes in federal and state election laws. Accountants, lawyers, and other staff members responsible for compliance with election laws also play an important role in planning the campaign.[187]

The Federal Election Campaign Act requires candidates to submit reports quarterly until the late stages of the campaign, when the reports must be submitted more frequently. Campaigns employ several full-time staffers just to fill out forms. Five percent of a presidential campaign's expenses can be tied to compliance with a plethora of often conflicting legal structures and disclosure requirements, according to campaign finance expert Herbert Alexander. The 1980 campaigns of Carter and Reagan, for example, spent some $3.5 million on legal counsel for financial issues. Former FEC attorney Benjamin Vandergrift says no candidate for national office can be isolated from legal problems: "Very few decisions at any level can be made by politicians without consulting their attorneys because money is always involved, and you've got to be so careful."[188]

The FEC's incremental decision-making process makes compliance difficult. The FEC outlines its standards through case decisions; the law's interpretation, therefore, is often in flux. The complexity is further aggravated because FEC members are political appointees with ties to politicians having national ambitions.

Even more complexity arises from changing campaign technology and interest group activity. Some technological innovations, such as videocassettes distributed to individuals and groups, raise questions about whether they should be regulated as media or other tools of the campaign. The short lifespan of political campaigns also makes compliance with the rules difficult. Institutional memory is impossible for a campaign staff to achieve, despite the elite group of campaign professionals who work over several election years.

Often the best that campaign officials can do is to make decisions about spending practices after examining the cases the FEC has addressed. Because of time pressures, however, many campaigns proceed with questionable actions without carefully resolving their legality. The effect is to delay the consequences of the questionable practices until the campaign is over. Mondale's 1984 campaign, for example, delayed the consequences of its one hundred illegal "delegate committees" until the primary season was over. Mondale had to pay a penalty to the FEC, but only long after the campaign had benefited from his excessive spending during the close race against Colorado senator Gary Hart. The Mondale campaign considered the $400,000 fine just one of the costs of nationwide organization.

The time and expense of bookkeeping have become such a burden that the FEC allows campaigns to exempt the costs of compliance with federal regulations from their spending limits. But the exemption has become a loophole. Campaigns list many expenses—including rent, telephone charges, and staff salaries —as compliance costs in order to exempt them from spending limits.

Campaign finance regulation has contributed to the nationalization of the two parties. But whether the regulations have strengthened or weakened the party system as a whole is a subject of debate. The parties have become more centralized organizations mainly because of the complexity of complying with federal and state campaign finance regulations. Before finance reform, party committees at all levels operated independently and therefore had more leverage in dealing with the national party. Now presidential campaigns must account for the activities of state and local organizations. Election efforts in earlier years relied on coordination of state and local fund-raising machines, but they are now barred from donating funds directly to presidential campaigns.

## HOW OTHER CAMPAIGNS AFFECT THE PRESIDENTIAL RACE

Debate about the financing of congressional and state elections has been more intense than debate about financing presidential elections. Those contests rely entirely on private money and are more difficult to monitor and control because hundreds take place every two years.

Even though presidential and congressional elections are separate—in contrast to the parliamentary systems of Great Britain and France—the finance system of nonpresidential elections has a profound effect on presidential politics. The system in the United States depends on campaigns at all levels for its political education and energy. Spending at lower levels is an important supplement to the presidential campaign.

Nonpresidential campaigns can reinforce presidential campaign themes and activities. Candidates for lower offices often adopt the campaign themes of the standard-bearer, so any spending in these contests augments spending for the presidential race. Economic conditions and foreign affairs regularly become important campaign issues for congressional candidates as well as presidential candidates. Perhaps more significant, many activities important to national politics, such as voter registration, can be undertaken by local party organizations.

Local contests have become "nationalized" as interest groups with national organizations such as antiabortion and senior citizen activists have become involved in these contests. Congressional races, then, are shaped by many of the same interest groups that are active in presidential politics. Local races still have a parochial quality, but the way those parochial interests find expression increasingly is influenced by nationally based interest groups.[189]

Two-thirds of the contributions made by political action committees go to incumbents, according to the public interest group Common Cause. The bias in campaign contributions fosters a high reelection rate for incumbents in Congress. Low congressional turnover, in turn, helps to determine the shape of presidential politics.[190]

Presidential candidates have to piece together states to win election. They therefore must make some parochial appeals, especially in swing states. In 1988, for example, Michael Dukakis made a concerted effort to appeal to southerners with campaign trips stressing crime, national defense, and the oil industry. The terms of debate in the states—influenced by contributions to Senate and House candidates—are therefore important for presidential appeals.

Even when parochial interests are not shaped by national interest groups, they can influence the national debate. Especially when they cluster together at the regional level, parochial concerns create boundaries for political debate. Candidates seeking votes in states dominated by agriculture, military spending, manufacturing, or the elderly must work within the confines of those dominant interests. The electoral college system—which encourages national candidates to assemble a coalition of states rather than attract a simple national majority—gives weight to clusters of regional and local concerns.[191]

## The Nominating Process

In the United States, voters exercise choice at two stages of the electoral process. In the first stage, the voters select nominees for the two major parties. In the second stage, the voters choose between those two candidates (and possibly one or more third party or independent candidates) in the general election.

The nominating process for most political offices—including that of president—attracts less attention than the general election. But, in many ways, nominations represent the more important phase of the democratic process. As observers since James Madison have noted, controlling people's choices is more important than influencing how people respond to those choices. Political scientist E. E. Schattschneider also has noted that a small minority of the public determines the candidates and is-

sues. The rest of the system—the citizens themselves—can respond in only a limited way: "The people are a sovereign whose vocabulary is limited to 'yes' and 'no.' This sovereign, moreover, can speak only when spoken to."[192]

In U.S. presidential politics, the vast majority of voters have a chance to say "yes" or "no" at two points—the nominating process and the general election. But less than a third of the eligible electorate participates in the nominating process, and in some states as little as 4 percent. The nomination contest is "biased" not only by this low participation but also by the structure of the process—that is, it all comes down to a narrow yes-or-no choice in the general election.

The ability of the most active political participants to include or exclude other participants, issues, and even elements of political language goes a long way toward determining a nominating system's bias. Schattschneider illustrated this point with the example of the schoolyard fight, the outcome of which depends on the combatants pulling spectators into the fight.[193] By determining the national candidates and a party platform, the Democratic and Republican Parties include some concerns and exclude others.

With its two-party system, the American electoral process has usually proved to be a consensual, moderating, incremental method for generating electoral options. The system's candidate-centered nature, length, expense, complexity, media saturation, and tedium create choices—that is, candidates—that are uniquely American.

### ELIGIBILITY

Prospective presidential candidates must meet certain constitutional requirements, but just as important are a number of unwritten, informal requirements. The American political culture demands that its chief executive meet standards of political and managerial expertise as well as moral and social standing.

#### Constitutional Requirements

Article II of the Constitution stipulates that all presidents be "natural born citizen[s]" who have "been 14 years a Resident within the United States" and are at least thirty-five years old. Under the Twelfth Amendment, those requirements also apply to the vice president. The requirements were intended to ensure that candidates have absolute fidelity to the nation and (in the case of the age requirement) maturity. The Founders were wary of the new nation coming under foreign influence.[194]

The presidency's most important requirement—the Article I ban on serving simultaneously as president and as a member of Congress—stems from the Framers' concern with separation of powers in the federal government. Having such a ban in place, the United States will never be governed by a parliamentary system like that found in Great Britain; such a ban also can break down party solidarity and prevent swift congressional action on the president's agenda. The Twenty-second Amendment, which forbids a president to serve more than two full terms, also

---

## PRESIDENTIAL NOMINATING PROCESS

| BEFORE 1968 | SINCE 1968 |
|---|---|
| **Party-dominated** | **Candidate-dominated** |
| The nomination decision is largely in the hands of party leaders. Candidates win by enlisting support of state and local party machines. | Campaigns are independent of party establishments. Endorsements by party leaders have little effect on nomination choice. |
| **Few Primaries** | **Many Primaries** |
| Most delegates are selected by state party establishments, with little or no public participation. Some primaries are held, but their results do not necessarily determine nominee. Primaries are used to indicate candidate's "electability." | Most delegates are selected by popular primaries and caucuses. Nominations are determined largely by voters' decisions at these contests. |
| **Short Campaigns** | **Long Campaigns** |
| Candidates usually begin their public campaign early in the election year. | Candidates begin laying groundwork for campaigns three or four years before the election. Candidates who are not well organized at least eighteen months before the election may have little chance of winning. |
| **Easy Money** | **Difficult Fund Raising** |
| Candidates frequently raise large amounts of money quickly by tapping a handful of wealthy contributors. No federal limits on spending by candidates. | Campaign contributions are limited to $1,000 per person, so candidates must work endlessly to raise money from thousands of small contributors. PAC contributions are important in primaries. Campaign spending is limited by law, both nationally and for individual states. |
| **Limited Media Coverage** | **Media-focused** |
| Campaigns are followed by print journalists and, in later years, by television. But press coverage of campaigns is not intensive and generally does not play a major role in influencing the process. | Campaigns are covered intensively by the media, particularly television. Media treatment of candidates plays crucial role in determining the nominee. |
| **Late Decisions** | **"Front-loaded"** |
| Events early in the campaign year, such as the New Hampshire primary, are not decisive. States that pick delegates late in the year, such as California, frequently are important in selecting nominee. Many states enter convention without making final decisions about candidates. | Early events, such as the Iowa caucuses and New Hampshire primary, are important. The nomination may be decided even before many major states vote. Early victories attract great media attention, which gives winners free publicity and greater fund-raising ability. |
| **Open Conventions** | **Closed Conventions** |
| National party conventions sometimes begin with nomination still undecided. Outcome determined by maneuvering and negotiations among party factions, often stretching over multiple ballots. | Nominee is determined before convention, which does little more than ratify decision made in primaries and caucuses. Convention activities focus on creating favorable media image of candidate for general election campaign. |

---

affects the president's relations with Congress since much of the president's leverage is based on public appeals for support.[195]

The Constitution does not have property or class qualifications. The Framers were wary of duplicating the aristocratic bent of British government, which made high social class a prerequisite for membership in the House of Lords and property a requirement for voting and thus inclusion in the House of Commons. State property qualifications for voting privileges and political candidacy were eliminated by 1856.

### Unwritten Requirements

More important for screening potential presidential candidates are cultural norms. Political scientist Clinton Rossiter's classic study of the American presidency describes a limited pool of candidates: middle-aged, white, Protestant males who embody small-town family values, have legal and state government experience, and come from large northern states.[196] Since Rossiter's study, however, three southerners (Lyndon Johnson in 1964, Jimmy Carter in 1976, and Bill Clinton in 1992 and 1996),

Celebrity status often assists presidential ambition. Former astronaut and Ohio senator John Glenn ran unsuccessfully for the Democratic nomination for president in 1988.

one man more than sixty-five years old (Ronald Reagan in 1980 and 1984) and another less than forty-five (John Kennedy in 1960), one Catholic (Kennedy), and four who were not lawyers (Johnson, Carter, Reagan, and Bush) have been elected president.

Celebrity status can overcome a lack of the traditional qualifications. Celebrity presidential hopefuls—former actors (Reagan), athletes (Jack Kemp), astronauts (John Glenn), media personalities (Pat Buchanan, Pat Robertson), heirs (Edward Kennedy, Pierre Du Pont), military heroes (Bob Dole, Robert Kerrey), and business executives (Ross Perot and Steve Forbes) —have the critical advantage of name recognition.[197] Politicians without celebrity status must make names for themselves through the drudgery of years of campaigning in primary and caucus states to obtain visibility. "The barriers have changed," journalist Alan Ehrenhalt has argued. "The primary obstacle to nomination is no longer an elite [passing judgment on people who wanted to hold political office]. The obstacle now is a physical one, a personal one. The aspiring candidate no longer needs to worry much about what important people think of him. He needs to worry whether he has the stamina and desire to make it through the grueling work that lies ahead."[198] Presidents must look imposing, but they do not need to conform to Rossiter's list of qualifications.

Geraldine Ferraro's Democratic vice-presidential nomination in 1984 broke the exclusion of women from serious consideration for high offices. Ferraro's nomination followed a long period of public lobbying by organizations such as the National Organization for Women.[199] Democratic representative Patricia Schroeder of Colorado and Republican Jeane Kirkpatrick, Reagan's first United Nations ambassador, each considered a 1988 campaign. The percentage of the electorate professing a willingness to vote for a woman jumped from 52 percent in 1958 to 80 percent in 1983. The number of women holding elective office has grown dramatically in recent years, increasing the pool of women who might pursue more ambitious political goals.[200]

Jesse Jackson's pursuit of the Democratic nomination in 1984 and 1988 might have weakened the race barrier. Jackson, leader of the civil rights group Operation PUSH, attracted 18 percent of the vote in the 1984 primaries. In 1988 Jackson won the near-unanimous support of African American leaders—many of whom had been wary of him four years earlier—and made small inroads into white farm and industrial votes.[201] That year Jackson finished second out of the eight Democratic candidates who began the primary and caucus season. At the end of the nomination contest, Jackson was the only surviving candidate besides the eventual nominee, Gov. Michael Dukakis of Massachusetts.

Rossiter's portrait of a president may be obsolete, but it still captures the desire of Americans for a leader who combines the often contradictory qualities of political involvement and nonpartisanship, majesty and simplicity, experience and freshness, morality and toughness, friendliness and detachment. The electorate seeks candidates who can fill the symbolic functions of the head of state as well as the policy-oriented functions of the executive.[202]

*Moral Values and Character.* Americans look for moral leadership in their presidents. Lacking a royal family to symbolize the nation, Americans also look for a president who will personify the nation's values and spirit.

Thanks in part to Geraldine Ferraro's Democratic vice-presidential nomination in 1984, women have won consideration as serious candidates for high offices.

Former governors William McKinley, left, and Theodore Roosevelt, right, were the first two twentieth-century presidents. Six other twentieth-century presidents also held governorships before becoming president.

Bill Clinton struggled against charges of "character flaws" throughout his 1992 campaign. Charges of draft-dodging and adultery dogged Clinton from the earliest phases of the campaign. Eventually, Clinton's compelling personal story—son of a widow, popular small-town boy, Rhodes scholar, energetic reform governor—helped him to overcome these charge. In 1996 Republican challenger Bob Dole, down in the polls, attempted to exploit White House ethical questions by raising the character issue again. Dole's attacks cut Clinton's lead but did not prevent Clinton's reelection.

"Toughness" is another character trait sought by the electorate and the media. Gov. George Romney of Michigan, a strong contender for the 1968 Republican nomination, dropped out early when he said that he had been "brainwashed" by generals about the U.S. role in the Vietnam War. Sen. Edmund S. Muskie's 1972 Democratic campaign faltered when he appeared to cry as he lashed out against the attacks being made against his campaign and his wife by the *Manchester Union Leader.*[203]

*Wealth.* Wealth often is viewed as a positive trait simply because the candidate is presumed free of a selfish interest in government, just as Plato's ideal *polis* separates the "guardians" from pecuniary motives. The "Virginia dynasty" that ruled the nation in its early years embodied this principle. But since the administration of Andrew Jackson, a down-to-earth image has been important to a candidate's success. Lyndon Johnson, Richard Nixon, Jimmy Carter, Ronald Reagan, and George Bush were millionaires when they won the presidency, but each presented himself as an ordinary citizen.

*Political Experience.* The political experience of presidential nominees has undergone three distinct phases in the twentieth century. Until 1960, governors were predominant among the nominees, and state organizations led by governors dominated party conventions. William McKinley, Theodore Roosevelt, Woodrow Wilson, James Cox, Calvin Coolidge, Alfred E. Smith,

Franklin Roosevelt, Alfred M. Landon, Thomas E. Dewey, and Adlai Stevenson all were former governors. *(See box, Governors Who Became President, p. 60.)* Other candidates included members of Congress, judges, cabinet members, a business leader, and a military hero.

From 1960 to 1972, the nominees were all former senators: John Kennedy, Nixon, Johnson, Goldwater, Humphrey, and McGovern. *(See box, Members of Congress Who Became President, p. 60.)* In this period, the electorate was preoccupied with national concerns, such as the civil rights movement, the Vietnam War, the welfare state, environmentalism, and the "space race."

From 1976 to 1992, governors again dominated the nominating process. Lengthy, media-centered campaigns and an anti-Washington mood brought nomination victories to governors or former governors Carter, Reagan, Dukakis, and Clinton.

When experience in elective politics has not been enough to persuade voters of their qualifications, candidates have boasted other experience. Wendell Willkie and Dwight Eisenhower, the Republican nominees in 1940 and 1952, respectively, claimed executive experience as a business leader (Willkie) and a general (Eisenhower). Democrat Carter in 1976 augmented his short political résumé—two years as a state legislator and four years as governor of Georgia—with entries of nuclear engineer, farmer, and businessman. Reagan often mentioned his term as the head of the Screen Actors Guild to augment his political experience as California governor. In his campaigns, Democrat Jesse Jackson stressed his civil rights activities and leadership of Operation PUSH. Republican Pat Robertson, an evangelist, introduced himself as a businessman and lawyer in 1988. Lawyers dominate the ranks of politicians at all levels, but a number of presidential candidates—including Eisenhower, Johnson, McGovern, Carter, Reagan, and Bush—were not lawyers.

*Foreign Policy Experience.* Voters regularly list foreign policy experience as an important electoral consideration. Members of

## GOVERNORS WHO BECAME PRESIDENT

When Bill Clinton was first elected president in 1992, he continued the recent trend of governors advancing to the White House. Between 1976 and 1996, former governors won five out of six presidential elections. In 1992 Clinton was the first sitting governor to be elected president since Franklin Roosevelt in 1932. Over the course of U.S. history, sixteen presidents have served previously as state governors.

Following is a list of these presidents and the states in which they served. Thomas Jefferson's term of governor of Virginia was during the Revolutionary War. Two other presidents served as governors of territories: Andrew Jackson was the territorial governor of Florida and William Henry Harrison was the territorial governor of Indiana.

| President | State |
| --- | --- |
| Thomas Jefferson | Virginia |
| James Monroe | Virginia |
| Martin Van Buren | New York |
| John Tyler | Virginia |
| James K. Polk | Tennessee |
| Andrew Johnson | Tennessee |
| Rutherford B. Hayes | Ohio |
| Grover Cleveland | New York |
| William McKinley | Ohio |
| Theodore Roosevelt | New York |
| Woodrow Wilson | New Jersey |
| Calvin Coolidge | Massachusetts |
| Franklin D. Roosevelt | New York |
| Jimmy Carter | Georgia |
| Ronald Reagan | California |
| Bill Clinton | Arkansas |

SOURCE: *American Leaders 1789–1994* (Washington, D.C.: Congressional Quarterly, 1994).

## MEMBERS OF CONGRESS WHO BECAME PRESIDENT

From James Madison to George Bush, twenty-four presidents have served previously in the House of Representatives, or the Senate, or both.

Following is a list of these presidents and the chambers in which they served. Three other presidents—George Washington, John Adams, and Thomas Jefferson—had served in the Continental Congress, as had James Madison and James Monroe.

James A. Garfield was elected to the Senate in January 1880 for a term beginning March 4, 1881, but declined to accept in December 1880 because he had been elected president. John Quincy Adams served in the House for seventeen years after his term as president, and Andrew Johnson returned to the Senate five months before he died.

| House Only | Both Chambers |
| --- | --- |
| James Madison | Andrew Jackson |
| James K. Polk | William Henry Harrison |
| Millard Fillmore | John Tyler |
| Abraham Lincoln | Franklin Pierce |
| Rutherford B. Hayes | James Buchanan |
| James A. Garfield | Andrew Johnson |
| William McKinley | John F. Kennedy |
| Gerald R. Ford | Lyndon B. Johnson |
| George Bush | Richard Nixon |

*Senate Only*

James Monroe
John Quincy Adams
Martin Van Buren
Benjamin Harrison
Warren G. Harding
Harry S. Truman

SOURCE: *Biographical Directory of the United States Congress, 1774–1989* (Washington, D.C.: Government Printing Office, 1989); *American Leaders 1789–1994* (Washington, D.C.: Congressional Quarterly, 1994).

Congress who seek the White House regularly invoke their experience in issues such as arms control, the North Atlantic Treaty Organization, international trade, military oversight, and intelligence activities as reasons they should be elected.

In the nuclear age, a perceived inability to manage foreign affairs could cripple a campaign. Goldwater, Carter, Reagan, Dukakis, and Clinton all faced criticism of their relatively light foreign policy experience. In 1988 Representative Schroeder tried to overcome doubts about a woman's candidacy by stressing her experience on the House Armed Services Committee: "Every year I have been on the committee, I have submitted an alternative defense budget." Referring to the Reagan administration's inability to find the proper type of ships for military maneuvers in the Persian Gulf, Schroeder said, "[My defense budgets] have always included mine sweepers."[204]

Clinton had no foreign policy experience in 1992, but he compensated for this shortcoming by showcasing members of the foreign policy establishment who supported his candidacy. The former chairman of the Joint Chiefs of Staff, Adm. William J. Crowe Jr., was Clinton's most visible military backer. Vice-presidential candidate Al Gore, a Vietnam veteran and an expert on defense policy, shored up his credentials as well. Clinton also took bold foreign policy positions that outflanked President Bush. On the former Yugoslavia, Iraq, the former Soviet Union, the Middle East, and Haiti, Clinton rhetorically "out-toughed" the Republican White House. But more important than any of his foreign policy signals, Clinton appealed to the yearning of Americans to refocus attention on domestic concerns.

In recent years, several candidates with negligible foreign policy experience have been elected president. As experience, Carter, Reagan, and Clinton had only their efforts to attract foreign trade as governors and, for Carter, membership in organizations such as the Trilateral Commission. Inexperience was countered by emotional vows to shift the foreign policy goals of the nation. In 1976 and 1980, Reagan punctuated his campaigns with bitter denunciations of the Soviet Union, arms-control initiatives, treaty negotiations with Panama, and "abandonment" of Taiwan, a longtime U.S. ally.

*Age.* A candidate's age has on occasion been an issue, but it has not deterred the candidacies of some old and some young men. John Kennedy—who asked headline writers to call him "JFK" rather than the youthful-sounding "Jack"—was the youngest elected president in 1960 at age forty-three. His opponent, Nixon, was forty-seven. Jerry Brown and Al Gore ran for the presidency when they were still in their thirties. Reagan was elected in 1980 at the age of sixty-nine. His vigorous campaigning in the primaries eliminated questions about his ability to meet the job's physical demands. In 1984, when asked about his age in a debate, Reagan deflected the question with a quip; he did not, he said, intend to exploit his opponent's "youth and inexperience."

*Party Identification.* Close party identification has declined in recent years. In fact, since the early 1960s some candidates have found it useful to switch parties. Reagan was a Democrat for much of his adult life and, as a television personality, headed a "Democrats for Nixon" effort in 1960. But he switched parties before the Republican convention of 1964. Republicans John Connally and Pat Robertson, candidates in 1980 and 1988, also were former Democrats, as was Phil Gramm, a candidate in 1996. The Republican mayor of New York, John V. Lindsay, switched parties and sought the Democratic presidential nomination in 1972. Many candidates have downplayed the party label after winning the nomination. Campaign paraphernalia has stressed the candidate rather than the party.

Clinton overcame voters' distrust of parties by depicting himself as a reformer of the Democratic Party—a "new Democrat." Clinton's leadership of the Democratic Leadership Council (DLC) enhanced his image as a critic of the old "liberal" policies of the Democrats. Clinton and the DLC co-opted many popular Republican positions on crime, affirmative action, welfare, defense spending, and economic policy.

However cynically voters view parties, they offer candidates a way to gain nationwide networks of support. Ford, who served in Congress for twenty-four years, used party ties to withstand a nomination challenge from Reagan in 1976. Two major candidates in recent years, Vice President Bush and Senate leader Dole, had chaired the Republican National Committee. Those positions enabled Bush and Dole to develop a national identity, work with a wide variety of office seekers, and make important financial contacts.

## THE DECISION TO COMPETE

The decision to seek the presidency is among the most mysterious and difficult in American politics. In one respect, it is highly logical, even scientific. The decision involves complicated calculations about financial and time requirements; the tangle

Since the early 1960s, candidates have downplayed their party label. Campaign buttons usually stress the candidate rather than the party.

of party and state rules and the states' electoral makeups; and the need to master a complex set of policy issues, to attract endorsements, to recruit a competent and enthusiastic staff, and to develop an "image" suitable for media presentation. The prospective candidate also must consider the effect a national campaign will have on his or her family, the demands of the office, and possible revelations about personal "skeletons" that might hinder a campaign.

In other ways, the decision is as idiosyncratic as the psychological makeups of the potential candidates. Some candidates, such as the sons of former ambassador to Great Britain Joseph P. Kennedy, are instilled with high political ambition from their youth. Others are groomed from childhood for great deeds; John Quincy Adams, Benjamin Harrison, and both Roosevelts were such presidents. When his son was inaugurated as vice president in 1993, former senator Albert Gore Sr. said he had groomed his son for the White House since he was a boy. Bill Clinton recalled that he was inspired to pursue a political career when he shook President Kennedy's hand at a White House ceremony in 1963. Others acquire the ambition late in life. Reagan did not run for political office until he was fifty-five.

Some presidents come to the White House driven by ambition that many consider unhealthy and maybe even psychologically dangerous. Woodrow Wilson, Richard Nixon, and Lyndon Johnson are examples.[205]

Still others seem to be uninterested in the presidency until it comes to them. Calvin Coolidge was the little-known governor of Massachusetts when he was selected for vice president; he moved to the White House when President Warren Harding died. Rep. Gerald Ford of Michigan never aspired to any office above House Speaker until President Nixon appointed him vice president after major administration scandals. Successful business executives Wendell Willkie and Ross Perot ran in 1940 and 1992 in response to strong public calls for them to become candidates. Neither had held political office.

Prospective candidates gradually develop confidence that they can handle the office's demands. Carter decided to run for president soon after being elected governor of Georgia. Carter says he first considered the idea after meeting several past presidential candidates who, he said, did not impress him as possessing any more raw intelligence or energy than he had.[206]

Occasionally, candidates in the presidential race will shift their hopes to the vice-presidential nomination. Presidential candidates who received the vice-presidential nomination instead include Estes Kefauver, Lyndon Johnson, Walter Mondale, and George Bush.

Some presidential campaigns have been undertaken as symbolic crusades, designed not to win the White House but to publicize certain issues. For these candidates, campaign calculations are reduced to a question of visibility.

Many observers considered Barry Goldwater's 1964 campaign to be at least partly symbolic because Goldwater did not appear to have any chance of defeating President Johnson. In his primary battles with New York governor Nelson Rockefeller, Goldwater stressed the party's need to change its ideology rather than to field a candidate capable of defeating Johnson. Goldwater's campaign is credited with moving the party in a conservative direction and thus enabling Reagan to be elected president in 1980.

Sen. George McGovern's brief 1968 campaign was a symbolic effort designed to help the Democratic Party heal the wounds it had developed during the tumultuous nomination struggle. McGovern stood in for the assassinated senator Robert Kennedy.

Ellen McCormack's 1976 Democratic campaign focused on a single issue: banning abortion. McCormack did not attract more than 4 percent of the vote in any primary, but her campaign forced other candidates to address the divisive issue.

Jesse Jackson's 1984 Democratic campaign followed months of deliberation among black leaders about how to counter the perceived rightward drift of U.S. politics. But many black leaders opposed his candidacy and backed instead former vice president Mondale. The Jackson candidacy, with its religious fervor and cries of "Our time has come," was seen as strictly symbolic from the start. Partly because he did not expect to win, Jackson was not forced to moderate his positions. If Mondale had not won enough delegates to secure the nomination before the convention, Jackson could have played a pivotal role in a brokered convention.

The Republican campaigns of Pat Robertson in 1988 and Patrick Buchanan in 1992 offered a way to rally the party's "cultural conservatives."[207]

## INCUMBENCY AND ITS IMPLICATIONS

Despite the real advantages of incumbency for a presidential campaign, recent years have shown that renomination is not inevitable. Truman, Johnson, Ford, Carter, and Bush all faced strong challenges when they sought a new four-year lease on the White House. Vice-presidential candidates have been even more vulnerable when they have sought to succeed their bosses as president. Bush is a good example. As vice president in 1988, he faced five major contenders for the Republican nomination. As president in 1992, he had to beat back the challenges of only two.

If the incumbent appears at all vulnerable, another candidate likely will emerge to contend for the nomination. The decline of party solidarity and the rise of candidate-centered campaigns and organized interest groups means that an incumbent could be vulnerable if economic or foreign policy crises develop. Since World War II, presidents have not had a political anchor that strongly ties their fortunes to those of the rest of the party.

Although challenges are more likely today, the president still has a powerful command of media attention, budgetary and regulatory operations, and foreign policy initiatives—an advantage that helps to defeat rivals. In addition, the prestige of the office is so great that most party members are reluctant to reject an incumbent. Fears that a prolonged intraparty battle could cripple the eventual nominee in the fall campaign are a major consideration. No president has lost a renomination effort at a party convention since 1884. Even then, whether President Chester A. Arthur actually wanted the nomination is a matter of dispute among historians.[208]

When President Carter confronted the challenges of Massachusetts senator Edward Kennedy and California governor Jerry Brown for the 1980 nomination, the unemployment and inflation rates were both high, and the country had experienced foreign policy crises with Iran and the Soviet Union. The administration's relations with the Democratic Congress also were bad. Brown had long planned to oppose Carter, and Kennedy entered the race when polls showed him leading Carter by a margin of more than two-to-one.

But President Carter defeated Brown and Kennedy by using the powers of incumbency. His chief advantage was his Rose Garden strategy. Instead of campaigning and directly countering the criticism of his administration, Carter displayed a preoccupation with governmental affairs by staying at the White House. When Kennedy and others criticized his performance in the Iranian hostage crisis, Carter intimated that they were being unpatriotic.

After public and private posturing failed to dissuade Kennedy from making a run, Carter's campaign manager, Hamilton Jordan, developed a strategy that unabashedly used the powers of the White House. (Jordan argued that Ford had lost the presidency in 1976 because he failed to take full advantage of his incumbency.) On the morning of the Wisconsin primary, for example, Carter announced an imminent breakthrough in the hostage crisis; the breakthrough fizzled, but he won the primary.

Carter operatives also were able to manipulate the primary schedule, pushing southern primaries to the early part of the schedule and mingling likely Carter states with likely Kennedy states.

Drawing further on the power of the office, Carter enticed voters with promises of federal funds. But he was by no means the first to use this advantage of incumbency. In 1976, for example, while campaigning against challenger Reagan in the Florida primary, President Ford promised a Veterans Administration hospital in St. Petersburg, an interstate highway in Fort Myers, and an aerospace plant contract and mass transit funds in Miami. Referring to the president's campaign promises, Reagan quipped to a crowd of supporters in North Carolina, "If he comes here with the same bag of goodies to hand out that he's been giving away elsewhere, the band won't know whether to play 'Hail to the Chief' or 'Santa Claus Is Coming to Town.'"[209]

One built-in advantage of incumbency is a reluctance of voters to jettison a known commodity for a newcomer. The campaign slogans of incumbents usually stress the stability that re-election of the president will bring; the Carter-Mondale slogan in 1980 was "A Tested and Trustworthy Team."

## THE EXPLORATORY STAGE

Candidates always have maneuvered for position long before the election year. In the past, however, the maneuvering took place behind the scenes and was designed to impress party leaders across the nation rather than gain a high public profile. Kennedy's 1956 convention bid for the vice-presidential nomination and his 1958 polling of many primary states, for example, helped him to establish credibility for a run for the presidency in 1960. Sen. Goldwater's organization of conservative activists at the local level in October 1961 was a crucial element in his "insurgency" strategy for the 1964 Republican nomination struggle.

Some of the most important victories of the nomination struggle occur even before any primaries or caucuses. In the year before the campaign, reporters and campaign professionals watch a number of events to see which candidates are likely to be viable. In the so-called "invisible primaries" of 1992, Arkansas governor Clinton performed well. He gave well-received addresses at Georgetown University and to the Democratic National Committee's executive committee and the Association of Democratic State Chairs. He also won media praise for his interviews, established a strong campaign staff, and raised more money than other candidates. Most important, other Democrats with stronger national followings decided to stay out of the race.

Contenders traditionally delayed announcing their candidacy until late in the year before the election. Even when they knew they would run, the candidates wanted to avoid the disadvantages of candidacy, such as legal spending limits and strong public scrutiny. In recent years, however, politicians have not considered an early announcement the sign of a weak candidacy. Carter's surprise election in 1976, after a two-year public

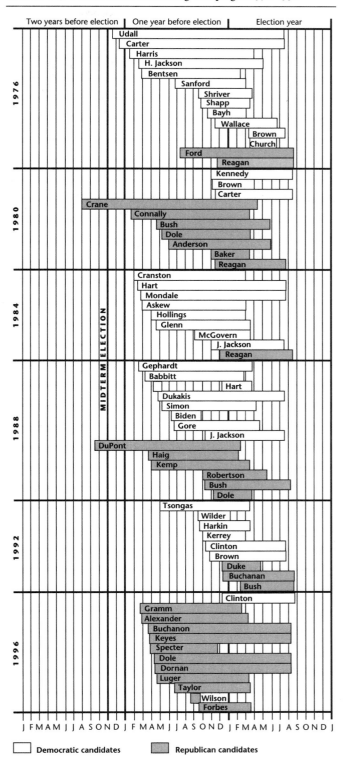

FIGURE 1–3 Presidential Nominating Campaigns, 1976–1996

Source: *Guide to U.S. Elections* (Washington, D.C.: Congressional Quarterly, 1994), 562.

campaign, caused Republican candidates in the 1980 election to get started right after the 1978 congressional elections.[210] *(See Figure 1-3.)*

Just a year into the Clinton administration, Republican senators Bob Dole and Phil Gramm, as well as the former Republican governor of Tennessee Lamar Alexander, were visiting the sites of early primary and caucus contests and raising money for possible presidential campaigns. Alexander took an eight-thousand-mile trip across the country in 1994 to test campaign themes and seek support from political and campaign professionals.

But in fact the exploratory stage really begins before the end of the previous campaign. In 1988 Republicans meeting for the convention in Houston started to round up support for potential 1992 candidates. A number of polls of delegates provided the first clues about which candidates might have a chance at the nomination next time around. Keynote addresses often serve as showcases for up-and-coming political figures. For example, New York governor Mario Cuomo stirred talk of a possible future run with his oratory at the 1984 Democratic convention.

## Political Action Committees

It has been customary in recent years for politicians to create political action committees to broaden their visibility from state and local politics to national politics and to test their appeal and fund-raising ability. Many politicians form PACs with little chance that they will run for president. PACs enable a prospective candidate to raise money, to assess strength with interest groups and geographic regions, to undertake polling and other marketing operations, to recruit political professionals, and to travel around the country.

PACs also allow the candidate to pick up important political IOUs. Since Nixon's successful barnstorming in behalf of Republican state and congressional candidates in the 1966 midterm election, when the GOP made major gains in congressional races, presidential hopefuls have built their base of support by making campaign appearances for other politicians. Mondale's 1984 Democratic nomination can be attributed partly to the endorsements he garnered after extensive travel in behalf of other candidates. Mondale held a particularly strong edge in support from "superdelegates"—that is, Democratic party officials who made up almost 15 percent of the party convention.

Reagan was one of the first major political figures to organize his national candidacy around a PAC. In 1977, after losing his 1976 bid for the Republican presidential nomination, Reagan used $1.6 million in leftover funds to form Citizens for the Republic in preparation for his eventual 1980 run. By 1986 PACs created by several candidates were paying for the early travel and office expenses of the 1988 campaign. Democrats Richard Gephardt, Gary Hart, Joseph Biden, and Jesse Jackson, and Republicans George Bush, Jack Kemp, and Bob Dole all got off to an early start with their PACs.[211]

## Fund Raising

Because of the lack of competition in the preelection-year maneuvering, fund raising is one of the few tangible ways to assess a candidate's early strength. For some, fund-raising success is the most important element of campaign decisions because without adequate funds, it is impossible to become a contender.

In 1987 Colorado representative Schroeder announced that she needed to raise $2 million in five months to make a run. When she raised less than $1 million, she decided not to run.

## Public Opinion Polls

Candidates use public opinion polling extensively to help them determine their chances. Modern polling techniques indicate the candidate's potential on a number of issues and with a number of groups. Besides polling broad demographic groups, campaigns also intensively interview smaller groups of people from selected demographic groups.

## Exploratory Committees

When prospective candidates form an "exploratory committee," they are in effect announcing their presidential ambitions. While PACs are crucial in giving a candidate a base for a national campaign, the exploratory committee undertakes a sober analysis of the candidate's prospects for a presidential run. The members of the committee consider possible campaign themes and strategies, write speeches and position papers, line up major endorsements, recruit professionals and volunteers, assemble campaign organizations in key primary and caucus states (such as Iowa and New Hampshire), hire pollsters and campaign consultants, and develop media appeals.

The model for detailed organization in the exploratory stage is the 1984 Mondale campaign. More than any other candidate, Mondale understood the changes in party rules and was prepared to take advantage of them. He was able to parlay his long Senate career into a bevy of congressional endorsements, especially helpful under the superdelegate system of elite party representation. Mondale beat out other Democrats for a number of union endorsements, raised more money than any other candidate, and hired an experienced campaign staff.

## Straw Polls

Candidates' primary and caucus successes often are presaged by skirmishes at the exploratory stages of the campaign. Straw polls—informal tallies of candidate preference at gatherings of party activists—provide the first statistical measures of candidate support. If they attract media coverage or impress campaign professionals, these mock elections can influence the early stages of the nominating process. Straw polls seem to be held at earlier and earlier dates in the campaign cycle. The first straw poll of the 1996 campaign was held in Iowa in June 1994; Sen. Bob Dole of Kansas won in absentia.

Long shots try to use straw polls to increase their visibility. In October 1975 Carter gained national press attention by winning 23 percent of the vote in a straw poll conducted at the annual Jefferson-Jackson Day dinner in Iowa. Supporters of both President Carter and Senator Kennedy spent $1 million on a Florida straw poll in November 1979 (Carter won handily). Sen. Howard H. Baker Jr. of Tennessee damaged his Republican presidential prospects in November 1979 with a poor performance at a similar contest in Maine.[212] In 1987 Pat Robertson made headlines with his displays of organizational strength in the Michigan and Iowa skirmishes.

Michigan officials have used a complex, many-tiered delegate-selection process to gain national attention even before election year. Florida's "straw votes" also provide hints about the candidates' strengths before the formal nomination competition begins.

### THE PRIMARY AND CAUCUS SCHEDULE

The sequence of electoral tests provides the basic strategic setting for the nominating contests. Primaries and caucuses early in the year have a greater impact than contests later in the year because they "weed out" the weaker candidates and increase the early winners' visibility and fund-raising strength.

Concerns about the length and divisiveness of campaigns prompted the Democratic Party to shorten the campaign schedule and push many contests to the early part of the calendar in 1980. Party reformers hoped to limit the campaign to three months to sustain voter interest, to attract candidates with nationwide support, and to reduce party infighting. The Democratic National Committee adopted a rule restricting delegate selection to the period from the second Tuesday in March until the second Tuesday in June. But the "window" exempted Iowa and New Hampshire, which conduct the nation's first caucuses and primary, respectively. By law and tradition, New Hampshire initiates the primary season and attracts any candidate seeking the nomination. Since 1976, the Iowa caucuses also have influenced the nominating process by showing the organizational strength of the candidates.

Even though New Hampshire and Iowa have a secure hold on the first binding nominating contests, other states (Alaska, Hawaii, and Louisiana) recently set earlier dates for their contests. "Front-loading"—concentrating nominating contests at the beginning of the calendar—has resulted from the jockeying of states for national media attention, the manipulations of candidates seeking to establish name recognition, and a more general concern for controlling the length of the campaign. *(See box, Delegate Selection Calendar for 1996, p. 66.)*

Before party reforms expanded the number of primaries in 1972, the spacing of primaries was fairly even. Few states held contests in March, and the bulk of the contests took place in April and May. By 1984 seventeen states were scheduling primaries or caucuses in the first twenty-two days of the season. In 1988 more than half of the delegates were selected at the conclusion of the twenty primaries and caucuses that states scheduled on Super Tuesday, March 8.

Front-loading the primacy calendar accelerated in 1996 with thirty primaries held by the end of March. In race for the Republican nomination, 352 delegates were selected in eleven primaries held from March 2–7, an event known as "Junior Tuesday Week." Bob Dole's strong performance in all states gave him one-third of the delegates needed to clinch the nomination. Dole's momentum carried him into the following week's Super Tuesday, where he won 349 out of 362 delegates in seven southern primaries. In the following week's "Big Ten" Tuesday, he captured 196 out of 219 delegates from four midwestern states.

The biggest change in 1996 was the shift of the California primary from June to late March. The change increased the importance of early fund raising because of the need to conduct a mass-media campaign in the nation's most populous state. However, the move was nearly anticlimactic in 1996. Although Dole did not clinched the GOP nomination until he won the California primary on March 26, most of his major competitors had already dropped out of the race.

After reviewing the 1996 primaries, the Republican Party, concerned that early-voting states had too much sway in the nomination process, took some steps to move primaries back for the nomination in 2000. One step was to give states that delay their primaries more delegates to the national convention. But whatever the order of the nominating contests, only about one-third of eligible voters participate in them. In 1996, 15.3 million Republican voters participated in forty-three primaries, while 11 million Democrats participated in thirty-six.[213]

### The Early Contests

The early stages of the campaign for the presidency have become important because the nominating process has shifted its emphasis from the old smoke-filled-room system of candidate selection by party bosses to rank-and-file participation in primaries and caucuses that indicate their presidential preferences. Especially when the campaign does not have an obvious front-runner, early contests determine a possible leader.

After several early tests, the field of candidates shrinks. Within a month and a half after the New Hampshire primary in 1972, four major candidates had left the Democratic field.[214] Four years later, all the original Democratic candidates except Carter and Morris Udall withdrew within nine weeks.[215] The "winnowing" process was most evident in the Democratic contest of 1984, when five candidates withdrew less than three weeks after the New Hampshire primary. Within a slightly longer period, all but two candidates had quit the 1980 Republican race. In 1988 most Republican candidates lost their public profile after New Hampshire and were soon out of the race.

The media pay far more attention to Iowa and New Hampshire than to other states with larger, more representative populations. An analysis of 1984 media coverage found that the New Hampshire primary received 19.2 percent of the total nomination coverage, and the Iowa caucus received 12.8 percent, although together the states make up only 2.9 percent of the U.S. population.[216] One reason for the attention to New Hampshire, however, may be that—except for Clinton—no one has ever been elected president without winning the New Hampshire primary. Larger states such as California and Pennsylvania receive extensive coverage in early spring, but by then the winnowing of candidates has largely taken place. "To put matters in perspective," wrote William Adams, professor of public administration at George Washington University, "if one-third of all European media coverage were about Luxembourg and Portu-

## DELEGATE SELECTION CALENDAR FOR 1996

This calendar lists 1996 presidential primary and first-round caucus dates. The Republicans sent 1,990 delegates to the 1996 GOP convention (1,684, or 84.6 percent, selected in primaries; 275, or 13.8 percent, selected in caucuses; and Kansas's 31 delegates selected by state committee). Democrats sent 4,290 delegates to their national party convention (2,802, or 65.3 percent, selected in primaries; 719, or 16.8 percent, selected in caucuses). The remaining 769 Democratic delegates (17.9 percent) were sent as superdelegates by virtue of their elected or party position. Democrats in Texas and Republicans in Louisiana and Washington used both a primary and caucus process to elect delegates. The Democratic primaries in Michigan and North Dakota were nonbinding and did not elect delegates. The Democratic primaries in Connecticut, Florida, New York, and Puerto Rico were not held as Bill Clinton was the only candidate to qualify for the ballot in those states. States that selected Democratic and Republican delegates on different dates in 1996 are designated by a "D" or an "R." States listed in normal type held caucuses; states listed in **bold** type held primaries.

| | |
|---|---|
| January 25–31 | Hawaii (R) |
| January 27–29 | Alaska (R) |
| February 6 | Louisiana (R) |
| February 10 | Guam (R) |
| February 12 | Iowa |
| February 20 | **New Hampshire** |
| February 24 | **Delaware** |
| February 27 | **Arizona (R)** |
| | **North Dakota** |
| | **South Dakota (R)** |
| March | Virginia (R) |
| March 2 | **South Carolina (R)** |
| | **Wyoming (R)** |
| March 3 | **Puerto Rico (R)** |
| March 5 | **Colorado** |
| | **Connecticut (R)** |
| | **Georgia** |
| | **Maine** |
| | **Maryland** |
| | **Massachusetts** |
| | Minnesota |
| | **Rhode Island** |
| | South Carolina (D) |
| | **Vermont** |
| | Washington |
| | American Samoa (D) |
| March 7 | Missouri (D) |
| | **New York (R)** |
| March 9 | Alaska (D) |
| | **Arizona (D)** |
| | Missouri (R) |
| | South Dakota (D) |
| March 9–11 | Democrats Abroad (D) |
| March 10 | Nevada (D) |
| March 12 | **Florida (R)** |
| | Hawaii (D) |
| | **Louisiana** |

| | |
|---|---|
| March 12 | **Mississippi** |
| | **Oklahoma** |
| | **Oregon** |
| | **Tennessee** |
| | **Texas** |
| | Texas (D) |
| March 16 | Michigan (D) |
| March 19 | **Illinois** |
| | **Michigan** |
| | **Ohio** |
| | **Wisconsin** |
| March 23 | Wyoming (D) |
| March 25 | Utah |
| March 26 | **California** |
| | **Nevada (R)** |
| | **Washington** |
| March 29 | North Dakota (D) |
| March 30 | Virgin Islands (D) |
| April | Kansas (D) |
| April 13, 15 | Virginia (D) |
| April 23 | **Pennsylvania** |
| May 4 | Guam (D) |
| May 7 | **District of Columbia** |
| | **Indiana** |
| | **North Carolina** |
| May 14 | **Nebraska** |
| | **West Virginia** |
| May 21 | **Arkansas** |
| May 28 | **Idaho** |
| | **Kentucky** |
| June 4 | **Alabama** |
| | **Montana** |
| | **New Jersey** |
| | **New Mexico** |
| August 12–15 | Republican national convention in San Diego |
| August 26–29 | Democratic national convention in Chicago |

SOURCE: *Congressional Quarterly Weekly Report*, various 1996 issues; Federal Elections Commission.

Vice President George Bush, GOP presidential candidate, appears before supporters after winning the New Hampshire presidential primary in 1988.

gal, it would be small consolation that the balance of the coverage were apportioned more sensibly."[217]

The early primaries and caucuses also are important because they indicate to financial contributors which candidates have a chance for the nomination. Since making a contribution is in many ways an investment in the next administration, it makes greater sense to give money to someone with a good chance of heading that administration than to someone unlikely to win. Money flows to some candidates but not to others once the contributors are able to identify the "viable" candidates.

Many experts have criticized the role of New Hampshire and Iowa in the nominating process. Both states are predominantly rural with largely white, Anglo-Saxon, Protestant populations. Iowa's economy is dominated by agriculture, and New Hampshire boasts a burgeoning electronics industry; candidates therefore pay almost no attention to major problems such as the decline of U.S. heavy industry and the cities. Activists in both states pull the political debate to the outside margins of the parties' mainstreams. The antiwar movement dominated the 1968 and 1972 New Hampshire campaigns, for example, and the controversial Seabrook nuclear power plant dominated later contests.

Critics complain that the priority given those states leads to the selection of bad candidates. Professor William Mayer said: "Why in the world would we want to give an unknown, inexperienced person a good chance to be president in the first place? Given that the presidency is one of the most difficult and important jobs in the world it seems absurd to me to argue that we want to confer it on a person who has temporarily caught the fancy of a few New Hampshire voters."[218]

Not everyone, however, finds fault with the disproportionate influence of the Iowa and New Hampshire contests. Several observers have lauded the old-fashioned American values of industry, family, and community that seem to exist in those two rural states. In 1987 Sen. Al Gore, a 1988 Democratic aspirant, told an Iowa gathering: "All of us who have come to your state

have noticed the approach you take. You are almost worried you might make a mistake and choose the wrong candidate, because you have such an impact." *Washington Post* columnist David Broder wrote of the event: "If there was a winner, democracy was its name."[219]

For several weeks after the Iowa caucuses and the New Hampshire primary, the goal of the remaining candidates is to attract media attention by winning, or performing "better than expected," in the subsequent contests. Especially with proportional representation rules, the number of delegates at stake in the first contests does not matter as much as the media attention those states receive.

Ultimately, candidates seek to develop enough momentum to carry them to the nomination. One important cause of momentum is the voters' belief that a candidate has the best chance to win the fall election, and voters often flock to the winners of early contests. In 1988 Bush and Dukakis benefited from the perception among primary voters that they had the best chance to win in the fall. Political scientist Alan I. Abramowitz argues that Bush's margin of support in Republican primaries and caucuses "would have been substantially smaller" without the perception that Bush had a better chance to beat a Democrat in the fall.[220] Some primary voters, then, are thinking about the long-term consequences of their actions in the voting booth. They want to vote for a winner—not just of primaries but of the whole election process.

In 1984 Democrats Mondale and Hart competed hard for the Super Tuesday electoral marathon, paying less attention to delegate counts than to their ability to show momentum and broad vote-getting ability. Hart won more states, but Mondale was able to portray his performance as a comeback from his upset loss in New Hampshire. Mondale's campaign arranged to push forward in the calendar primaries in favorable states such as Rhode Island, Massachusetts, and Michigan.

Carter's 1976 campaign turned on scheduling changes that

Carter himself initiated. Winning a southern state over Alabama governor George Wallace was central to Carter's strategy, and Florida was probably Carter's best bet. With the help of Gov. Reubin Askew, Carter had the Florida primary scheduled ahead of the primaries in other southern states. Carter beat Wallace and swept the South.

Carter continued his "sequence as strategy" approach in 1980 when he arranged to move up southern primaries and to mix states favorable to his rival, Senator Kennedy, with states that were favorable to him. In 1992 Clinton gained momentum when he finished second in New Hampshire and won a decisive primary in Georgia the following week. Clinton performed so well in the next week's "Super Tuesday" set of eleven primaries and caucuses that the nomination was "his to lose." In 1996 Dole had wrapped up the GOP nomination by the end of March.

### The Late Contests

After most of the primaries have been held, attention turns to the question of which candidate leads in the delegate race and how many delegates are needed for a first-ballot convention victory. Candidates try not so much to win later primaries and caucuses as to accumulate the delegates allocated by various systems of proportional representation.

The candidates also woo the delegates of candidates who have dropped out, delegates pledged to "favorite-son" candidates, and, for Democrats, the bloc of superdelegates (elected and party officials) that constitute 15–20 percent of the party's conventions.

In 1976 Carter managed to accumulate enough delegates for a first-ballot Democratic nomination by finishing in second or third place in many late primaries. Carter had a commanding delegate lead that enabled proportional delegate allocations to clinch the nomination.[221] Mondale, the eventual 1984 Democratic nominee, followed a similar strategy, but he also dominated the superdelegate competition.[222]

In 1992 Democrat Clinton eliminated most of his competition early but still faced taunts from his rival, former California governor Brown, until the convention. Brown's shoestring campaign was not dependent on money, so he could afford to stay in the race. Clinton could not afford to get complacent in case Brown appealed to restless voters in the later primary and caucus states. Clinton's main job in the later contests, however, was to rebut Brown's charges of character flaws and corruption. Had some of Brown's charges stuck, the Democrats might have searched for an alternative to Clinton.

### CAMPAIGN STRATEGIES

All presidential aspirants must have a detailed strategy for attracting voter support and delegates before announcing their candidacy. Such a plan incorporates analyses of the candidate and the nominating environment, and it attempts to forecast likely high and low points of the campaign. The strategy is often so detailed that the candidate will know at prescribed points whether the campaign continues to be viable.

Patrick J. Buchanan, from the conservative wing of the Republican Party, mounted a serious challenge of incumbent George Bush in 1992 and GOP front-runner Robert J. Dole in 1996.

### Types of Strategy

The approaches a candidate may pursue are: the insider strategy, the outsider strategy, the early knockout, trench warfare, the slow buildup, and the wait-and-see strategy.

• Insider strategy. Heavily dependent on the endorsements and resources of major party and government figures, this approach was dominant in the period before the party reforms of 1968. Franklin Roosevelt (1932, 1936, 1940, 1944), Harry Truman (1948), Robert A. Taft (1952), John Kennedy (1960), Richard Nixon (1960), and Hubert Humphrey and Nixon (1968) all used this approach. George Bush's 1988 and 1992 campaigns called for continuance of the status quo and were backed by powerful GOP elites. Bill Clinton voiced the outsider rhetoric of "change" in 1992 but otherwise ran an insider campaign. Clinton's courting of key party leaders, interest groups, and journalists helped him to overcome voter hesitation about giving the nomination to the governor of a small state.

• Outsider strategy. The candidate presents a "fresh face" to voters weary of current politics and then stages an insurgent "takeover" of the system. Barry Goldwater in 1964, Eugene McCarthy and Robert Kennedy in 1968, Jimmy Carter in 1976, and Ronald Reagan in 1976 and 1980 based their campaigns on moralistic rhetoric critical of the Washington establishment. Jesse Jackson in 1984 and 1988 and Jerry Brown in 1992 and Pat Buchanan in 1992 and 1996 gave voice to disaffected outsiders but never posed a real threat to the front-runners.

• Early knockout. Front-runners hope to parlay their early strength in polls, fund raising, and endorsements into decisive primary victories at the beginning of the primary season. The hope is that the candidate will build such an impressive early lead that the competition will quickly drop out. Nixon in 1968 and Reagan in 1980 both won their nominations early. Mondale in 1984 planned an early knockout but was forced to adopt a more gradual approach with the emergence of Gary Hart. George Bush's 1988 and 1992 campaigns won swift victories.

• Trench warfare. No candidate's favorite strategy, this approach requires candidates to struggle through the primaries with the hope of barely outpacing opponents. The danger lies in sapping the party's resources to the extent that the eventual nominee is handicapped in the general election. The races between McCarthy, Kennedy, and Humphrey in 1968; McGovern, Humphrey, and Wallace in 1972; Ford and Reagan in 1976; Carter and Kennedy in 1980; and Mondale and Hart in 1984 were examples of trench warfare. In 1988 Michael Dukakis won the Democratic nomination with a deliberate, plodding strategy designed to outlast seven rivals. Dukakis never made a spectacular breakthrough but managed to accumulate enough delegates to win the nomination.

• Slow buildup. The idea here is to build support for the campaign slowly so that the candidate can avoid early traps and criticism and gain the aura of party savior when other candidates look weak. New York senator Robert Kennedy entered the 1968 campaign late and appeared to have a chance for the nomination when he won the winner-take-all California primary to cap the season. In 1976 Sen. Henry Jackson of Washington hoped to win the nomination with victories in the states holding primaries late in the schedule. This strategy might be obsolete today since early losses are considered almost fatal.

• Wait and see. Even though all nominations but one since 1960 have been decided largely by results of primaries and caucuses, a number of politicians have tried to sit on the sidelines and eventually emerge as the consensus candidate after an indecisive primary season. Humphrey won the 1968 Democratic nomination after a divisive primary season without entering a single contest, and he hoped to win the same way in 1976. In 1980 New York governor Hugh Carey joined a movement to free delegates from obligations to vote for a particular candidate with the hope that another candidate might emerge in a deadlocked convention. In 1988 another New York governor, Mario Cuomo, refused to enter the primaries but said he would accept a convention draft.

Carter's 1976 victory was the product of a classic outsider strategy. In an astute 1972 memo, Carter aide Hamilton Jordan had urged the candidate to travel extensively to build up foreign policy "experience," to get involved in national party politics, and to stress innovative programs of his governorship to supplement his "good guy brand of populism." Jordan wrote: "It will take more than the hand-shaking and the projection of the 'I understand the problems of the average man' image to put Carter over. This is still his greatest asset and it must still be projected but he will also have to convince the press, public, and politicians that he knows how to run a government."[223] Carter conducted an anti-Washington campaign based on his reputation as a leader of the "New South" and his appeals for the na-

tion to heal the wounds of the Watergate scandal and the Vietnam War. By the time the media began exploring his record in Georgia, Carter had become a strong front-runner. The party's new proportional representation system meant that Carter needed to win just ten of the last twenty-one primaries to secure enough delegates for the nomination.

In contrast, Carter's 1980 nomination campaign followed a classic insider strategy. Carter consciously used the advantages of incumbency to line up the support of party and business elites. He also successfully manipulated the primary and caucus calendar to his advantage. Carter staffers arranged for three southern states where Carter was strong—Alabama, Florida, and Georgia—to hold their primaries together on March 11, which ensured a big sweep for Carter. They also arranged to switch the date of Connecticut's primary from March 4 to March 25 to avoid a possible Kennedy sweep on March 4, the day Massachusetts—Kennedy's home state—was holding its primary.

### Strategy Considerations

The campaign strategy selected will depend on a wide variety of considerations. These include the nature of the competition, the primary schedule, the candidate's fund-raising ability and endorsements, media requirements, and the tenor of the electorate.

*Size and Makeup of the Competition.* Different strategies work for different candidates. A candidate successful in a one-on-one contest may have difficulty playing a number of other candidates off each other. A liberal candidate might deal well with a conservative opponent but struggle against another liberal or moderate.

Going into the 1976 Democratic primaries, most experts rated Indiana senator Birch Bayh and Arizona representative Mo Udall top prospects for the nomination because they had strong liberal backing. The candidates' combined 37.9 percent (Udall, 22.7 percent; Bayh, 15.2 percent) share of the New Hampshire primary vote was an impressive start, but former Georgia governor Jimmy Carter's 28.4 percent was enough to win the primary. Udall, Bayh, former Oklahoma senator Fred R. Harris, former Peace Corps director Sargent Shriver, Idaho senator Frank Church, and Jerry Brown split the liberal vote throughout the primaries. Carter received only 39 percent of the total primary vote, but he won the nomination because his opposition was fragmented.

If Carter had faced a single politician with national experience, he might have lost. A poll of Democrats before the Pennsylvania primary showed Minnesota senator Hubert Humphrey, perhaps the most prominent liberal in the party, with a commanding lead over all rivals including Carter. But with Humphrey not in the race, Carter was a strong winner.[224]

In 1980 California governor Brown planned to run against Carter on a platform stressing economic and environmental limits—a campaign that would address directly the national discontent that came with the energy crisis of 1979. When Sen. Edward Kennedy joined the race, however, Brown's voice was drowned out.

Bill Clinton became the prohibitive favorite for the 1992 Democratic nomination when better-known candidates decided to stay out of the race. President George Bush's high approval ratings discouraged nationally known figures such as New York governor Mario Cuomo and senators Bill Bradley and John D. Rockefeller IV from entering the race. Even Clinton considered his campaign to be a "trial heat" for a later race.

*The Stage of the Campaign.* Candidates must compete in the early stages of the campaign to gain the national visibility they need to survive the whole campaign. Colorado senator Gary Hart's nearly successful 1984 bid for the Democratic nomination was an example of a campaign sustained in later stages by the burst of success at the beginning. But to actually win the nomination, a candidate must stay in the race long enough, despite any early defeats, to participate in the primaries and caucuses of "friendly" states. It is a fact, though, that after the Iowa caucus and the New Hampshire primary, the attention given by the media to state contests varies greatly, and candidates differ widely on which of the later contests they would like to see highlighted in the press.

Whatever strategy a candidate pursues, early primary contests have a disproportionate influence. Success in Iowa and New Hampshire can transform a candidate from dark horse to front-runner in a matter of weeks in poll standings, delegate counts, endorsements, financial backing, and media play. If a leading candidate fails in these contests, the candidate's campaign faces a crisis. Most candidates drop out early in the campaign, often before testing, and possibly displaying, their strength on friendly political turf.

In recent years all but two or three candidates have dropped out after a few early contests because they could not finance a sustained drive. Gov. George Romney in 1968, Sen. Henry Jackson in 1976, and Sen. Ernest Hollings in 1980 did not have the opportunity to bring the campaign to favorable turf because of early losses. Speculation about a possible late bid by New York governor Cuomo in 1988 turned on whether he could remain viable until the New York and California primaries.

Once the nomination struggle eliminates most candidates, the delegate count becomes the major focus of attention. States such as Pennsylvania, Ohio, New Jersey, and California—which hold their primaries late in the campaign—arguably deserve more media attention as indicators of the political leanings of the U.S. electorate than the small delegate-count states. But by the time they hold their primaries, the large states are viewed simply as stepping-stones—and often critical ones—in the candidates' tedious quest for a majority of delegates. If a delegate race is deadlocked in the late stages of a campaign, victories in the large states can help "tip the balance." For example, a victory by Hart in New Jersey as well as California on June 5, 1984, might have enabled him to wrest the Democratic nomination from Mondale. A big victory also can breathe new life into a moribund campaign, as Reagan's 1976 North Carolina victory

over President Ford and Kennedy's 1980 Pennsylvania and New York victories over President Carter attest. It is the delegate race that ultimately is important, however. Especially in an age of proportional representation, late surges of support are unlikely to undo the mathematics of delegate counts.

*Fund-raising Ability and Spending Strategies.* One of the few measures of candidate strength in the preprimary stage is fund raising. Financial disclosure reports to the Federal Election Commission are reported in the media as indications of campaign strength.

Candidates face important decisions about how to allocate money—whether to spend most funds early in the hope of making an electoral "breakthrough," which could bring a windfall of contributions, or to spend frugally and extend the time for making their case to the primary voters.

Generally, established candidates can afford to husband their resources for later primaries and caucuses. But newcomers to national politics must gain credibility with good showings in early contests, and so they invest most of their resources in the small-state contests that dominate the early stages of the nomination drive. Candidates do not even think about getting delegates for the national convention until they have established themselves with the media and financial contributors. Fred Harris, a long shot for the Democratic nomination in 1976, said: "If we could raise the money and we could do well in those early contests, then the delegates would take care of themselves as we got into the later contests. . . . Then you're going for delegates; the first [contests] you're not, you're just going for staying in it."[225]

Because of spending limitations, important decisions are forced on the candidates. Long-shot candidates, like Harris, usually must spend most of their money on early contests to spur greater contributions. If long shots bide their time, they risk missing fund-raising opportunities completely. The Iowa and New Hampshire contests usually produce two or three early favorites who will dominate donations until the convention.

Fund-raising success stories, like endorsements, have their risks, however. One is a false sense of security. Senator Kennedy's 1980 campaign was marked by profligate staff spending and poor planning that undercut the early momentum built around the fame of the Kennedy family. Spending mistakes early in the race reduced the amount of money the campaign was legally permitted to use in the later stages.

Another risk is getting tagged as the candidate of special interests. In 1980 the lavish spending of former Treasury secretary John Connally in the Republican primaries aggravated uneasiness among voters about his honesty.[226] In 1988 Dukakis led other Democratic candidates in contributions by as much as eight to one; his opponents quickly dubbed him the candidate of "moneyed interests."

Jerry Brown, the son of an old-style Democratic politician and himself a former state party chair, freed himself from fundraising pressures in 1992 by deciding on a "shoestring" operation. Declaring that special interests had taken over both parties, Brown set a contribution limit of $100. He asked voters to call a toll-free telephone number to offer contributions to his quixotic quest for the nomination. Brown's rejection of large contributions enabled him to avoid dependence on unstable contributors—and gave him a populist message that resonated with a core of disaffected voters.

*Economic and Political Makeup of the States.* Candidates are famous for donning the popular garb and eating the foods typical of the region in which they campaign. But more important is the way the candidates fashion their rhetoric to each region.

Candidates, it is guaranteed, will discuss farm problems, energy costs, and trade issues in distinctive ways in Iowa and New Hampshire. But the prevalence of farm and "small-town" concerns in those two states may alienate the rest of the electorate. Some observers have attributed nationwide voter apathy in the early stages of the contest to the emphasis on the smaller states.[227]

Attention later turns to industrial concerns in northern Rustbelt states and to defense and social issues in the southern states. Senator Kennedy's populist rhetoric on unemployment in New York and Pennsylvania produced important primary victories during his troubled 1980 bid for the Democratic nomination.[228]

Jimmy Carter achieved a bond with voters of Iowa and New Hampshire in 1976 partly because of the background they shared as farmers and rural dwellers. In contrast, then-Tennessee senator Al Gore developed problems in the 1988 New York primary when he became embroiled in the bitter racial politics of New York City. Gore was embraced by Mayor Edward I. Koch, who offended many voters with his attacks on African American candidate Jesse Jackson.

*Media Requirements.* When Democratic senator Paul Simon of Illinois began his 1988 presidential campaign, analysts argued that his chances were minimal not only because he was an old-fashioned "New Deal liberal" but also because of his "frumpy" appearance. The small man with the horn-rimmed glasses and bow tie, it was said, was not what the "new generation" of media-saturated voters in the Democratic Party were seeking.[229]

The conventional wisdom of contemporary presidential politics stresses cosmetic requirements in the media age. With references to John Kennedy, some pundits argue that good looks are required for a candidate to have widespread appeal. Others reason that a candidate must simply appear to be "presidential"—calm, sincere, knowledgeable, tough, gentle, and commanding.

Some analysts assert that Kennedy prevailed over Vice President Nixon in 1960 solely because of his appearance in the first presidential debate. On the black and white television screens of the time, Nixon appeared pale and ill at ease, while Kennedy looked tan and calm. Polls showed that many people who heard the debate on radio thought that Nixon had "won." After President Reagan's landslide victory in the 1984 election, Democratic candidate Mondale complained that television required candidates to be masters of "the 20-second snip, the angle, the shtick, whatever it is."[230]

Complaints aside, however, to compete in the primary process candidates must make appeals to what political scientist Nelson Polsby has called "mass publics"—and, to make those appeals, the candidates need access to the media. Carter's foresight in being available in New York City for morning television programs after his 1976 Iowa caucus victory was a good example of candidate recognition of the importance of the media in modern politics. Spending on television commercials is the main reason for the tremendous increase in campaign costs in recent years.[231]

*Strength of State Parties and Other Institutions.* Until 1968 state party organizations held hegemony over the presidential nominating system. But in recent years the state parties have been overshadowed by candidate organizations and state and national interest groups.

The leaders of state parties tend to be political executives—usually the governor or a mayor. Executives have control over the patronage and contracts that are the glue of parties. Political parties tend to be organized hierarchically, with state leaders playing important roles in the national organization.

Because of the media saturation of campaigns, the rise of interest groups, and changes in the rules for selecting presidential candidates, in recent years state party organizations have lost much of their influence on national politics.

More generally, parties at all levels have lost influence because of a growing cynicism about politics among the populace. The share of the electorate declaring themselves members of national parties declined from 80 percent to a low of 67 percent between 1940 and 1976, and the share of independents increased from 20 to 33 percent.[232] *(See Table 1-8.)* At the same time, ticket splitting and issue voting increased.[233] Most analysts trace the disillusionment to the tumultuous events of the 1960s and 1970s: assassinations; the Vietnam War; urban riots and increases in crime; and scandals involving the Nixon administration,

TABLE 1–8  Party Identification, 1940–1995 *(percent)*

| Year | Republican | Democratic | Other |
|---|---|---|---|
| 1940 | 38 | 42 | 20 |
| 1950 | 33 | 45 | 22 |
| 1960 | 30 | 47 | 23 |
| 1964 | 25 | 53 | 22 |
| 1968 | 27 | 46 | 27 |
| 1972 | 28 | 43 | 29 |
| 1976 | 22 | 45 | 33 |
| 1980 | 26 | 43 | 31 |
| 1984 | 31 | 40 | 29 |
| 1988 | 29 | 43 | 28 |
| 1995 | 32 | 32 | 36 |

SOURCE: Gallup polling organization; Harold W. Stanley and Richard G. Niemi. *Vital Statistics on American Politics*, 5th ed. (Washington, D.C.: CQ Press, 1995), 149.

Congress, the Federal Bureau of Investigation, and the Central Intelligence Agency.

State parties still play major roles in recruiting people for political activity, in organizing elections and governmental institutions, in providing "cues" for voters, and in mediating some important policy issues. Because its main goal is to win election for its slate of candidates, the party is likely to compromise on specific issues and to occupy the center of the ideological spectrum. State parties also are concerned about the "coattail" effects of national campaigns. A strong national candidate could add as much as 5 percent to the vote of statewide candidates.[234]

Presidential candidates must know the relative strengths of state party organizations. States with strong, hierarchical organizations have provided reliable, if sometimes limited, bases for support. These organizations tend to be more pragmatic and compromising in their approach to issues, especially divisive issues that might alienate important elements of the party coalition. States with weak top-down control allow candidates to make more direct appeals to voters.

In 1964 Goldwater recruited loyalists to join local and state party organizations and "take over" the organizations. Nelson Polsby and Aaron Wildavsky wrote: "The absence of central leadership on a state-by-state basis meant that delegates were freer to follow their personal preferences and also free to weigh ideological considerations more heavily than if they had been responsible to a leader who would suffer badly if Republicans were defeated for state offices. Similar considerations have affected Democrats in recent years. . . ."[235]

Interest groups by their very definition—organizations designed to further a specific cause by donating money to campaigns—are less likely than parties to be concerned about a wide range of issues. Most interest groups are geared to specialized areas of national policy and lobbying before legislatures and agencies.[236]

*Endorsements.* Voters often judge candidates by the company they keep. Endorsements by prominent politicians, business and labor leaders, and citizens organizations can give credibility to a presidential candidate. But endorsements also can cause trouble if they make the candidate appear beholden to special interests.

The campaigns of Walter Mondale in 1984 and Richard Gephardt in 1988 underscore the plusses and minuses of endorsement-based candidacies. Before the campaign even started, Mondale won endorsements from labor organizations, women's groups, and civil rights organizations.[237] The endorsements—and the volunteers and fund-raising capabilities that they offered—gave Mondale front-runner status and sustained him in a difficult race against Gary Hart. Even though other Democrats sought the same endorsements, Mondale was tagged as the candidate of the "special interests."

Gephardt built his early viability in 1988 on his insider ties. He appeared on the steps of Capitol Hill to accept the endorsements of dozens of fellow lawmakers. He also lined up support from interest groups. Gephardt's rivals and the media called him a creature of "the system" who was beholden to special interests. After a victory in the Iowa caucuses, his campaign faltered.

"Covert endorsements" also can affect the nominating campaign. Candidates from the opposite party sometimes try to promote the candidate that they deem the easiest opponent. President Herbert Hoover maneuvered behind the scenes in 1932 to promote the Democratic candidacy of Franklin Roosevelt, whom he considered unprincipled and politically weak. But Hoover's calculation turned out to be spectacularly wrong.[238] Forty years later, President Nixon ordered "dirty tricks" to damage Edmund Muskie's campaign and boost George McGovern's effort. Nixon's strategy helped to produce the desired effect: Muskie was driven out of the race early and McGovern won and proved a weak opponent to Nixon.

*Grassroots Organizations.* In early 1975 Carter gained an advantage on the competition for the Democratic nomination by visiting Iowa almost a year before the caucuses. His surprise Iowa victory gave him the credibility he needed to win a string of primaries.

Organizing in Iowa did not work in 1988. A dozen presidential candidates concentrated early on the Iowa caucuses, spending more than eight hundred days in the state. Democratic representative Richard Gephardt of Missouri typified the candidates' concern with Iowa: he actually rented an apartment in the state and kept his family there to campaign when he was not able to be on hand.

The organizational demands of both Iowa and New Hampshire are based on the likelihood that voter turnout will be light. Thus candidates concentrate their resources on getting their supporters to the caucus meetings in Iowa and the voting booths in New Hampshire. Pat Robertson bussed his supporters to key "straw votes."[239]

The early tests entail more than get-out-the-vote drives, however. The candidates need state political operatives who know the political makeup of the localities and local fund-raising experts, in addition to the usual office staffers, speechwriters, and issues experts. When Gary Hart and Joseph Biden dropped out of the Democratic race in 1987, other candidates scrambled for the backing of their local organizations.

For the later states, which are dominated by media appeals, other aspects of grassroots organizing become important. It is still essential to get voters to the polls, but the candidates also must recruit slates of delegates and develop ties to newspaper and broadcast journalists. The move from intimate, grassroots politicking to states large in area and population requires a campaign organization to prepare the stage for the state-hopping candidate and to target appeals and polling information to large blocs of voters, such as residents of nursing homes, religious organizations, and veterans groups.

*The Tenor of the Electorate.* A number of scholars have asserted that U.S. history follows distinct "cycles" and that candidates must fashion messages that parallel the dominant mood of the electorate.

Political scientist Stephen Skowronek has presented his no-

On the campaign trail in 1948, Republican presidential candidate Thomas Dewey lets himself be "kidnapped" by members of the Oregon Cavemen Club.

tion of "political time" in a sophisticated cyclical theory. Skowronek argues that presidential politics moves through three stages: from "order-creating" to "order-affirming" to "order-shattering." Each stage contains the makings of the next stage. All presidents, then, must respond to the durable policies and ideas that their predecessors established and tailor their initiatives to respond to what went before. In modern times, presidents have had more freedom to innovate. The fast pace of politics constantly reshapes the political environment, freeing the president from previous patterns. In 1995, for example, President Clinton's diplomatic successes in Northern Ireland and Bosnia freed him—at least temporarily—from the "inexperienced in foreign affairs" label.[240]

Another cyclical theorist is historian Arthur M. Schlesinger Jr., who has argued that politics swing from periods of activism to periods of preoccupation with private interests. Intervals of minimalist government include the late nineteenth century, the 1920s, the 1950s, and the years beginning with Nixon's election in 1968. Periods of activism include the Progressive Era of the early twentieth century, the New Deal Era, and the Kennedy and Johnson years.[241] Schlesinger's prediction that the 1990s would be an age of liberalism appeared to be refuted by massive distrust of government. One 1994 survey found that only 2 percent of the public trusted the federal government.[242]

Erwin C. Hargrove and Michael Nelson have argued that political cycles move according to the stage of policy development and implementation.[243] Government activism waxes and wanes depending on the cycles of policy preparation, achievement, and consolidation.

Presidents of achievement included Woodrow Wilson, Franklin Roosevelt, Lyndon Johnson, and Ronald Reagan. Their activist administrations oversaw major changes in domestic legislation, regulation, tax policy, and defense and foreign policies.

The Wilson, Roosevelt, Johnson, and Reagan presidencies also stood in the middle of major shifts in electoral politics. The only lasting realignment was Roosevelt's New Deal Era. Wilson temporarily moved the national government to the Democrats, and Johnson helped to strengthen Democratic dominance. Scholars question whether Reagan produced a "realignment" of the parties, but they agree that he was central to a growing conservatism that dominated U.S. politics in the late 1970s and 1980s. Under Reagan, the Republicans held the U.S. Senate for six years (for the first time since the 1950s) and developed national strength.

The presidents of achievement exploit the groundwork of the presidents of preparation. During these administrations, policy proposals that have been percolating in the bureaucracy and in academic and media circles are raised to the top of the national political agenda by the president. The nation is not yet ready for broad-based initiatives but is preparing for an era of activism. Preparation presidents included Theodore Roosevelt, John Kennedy, and Jimmy Carter.

Presidents of consolidation make previous innovations part of the norm of government. Even presidents who have opposed programs for philosophical reasons will work to implement the programs well. The Republican presidents of the 1920s along with Dwight Eisenhower and Richard Nixon were in this category.

In addition to the cycles of history, some scholars have argued that modern candidates must deal with a "sullen" political mood that is a byproduct of the age of media politics. They contend that the decline of parties and fixed ideologies in recent years has created a political climate in which candidate personalities have taken on greater importance than ever before.

James MacGregor Burns has argued that "lacking the moorings of party or the anchors of ideology . . . a profound, perverse, almost revolutionary change" in national politics has occurred since the rise of the welfare state and of active government regulation of the economy (especially since the 1960s when growth was fastest).[244] The rise of interest groups with cross-cutting purposes—in which alliances last only as long as a particular issue is under public consideration—has undermined the "cues" that voters traditionally have used to orient themselves to national campaigns. The result, Burns and others say, is a politics dominated by media attention to many personal and trivial aspects of the candidates' lives. Before even the first caucus or primary of the 1988 race, for example, the media concentrated on the perceived personality disorders of candidates Gary Hart, Joseph Biden, Michael Dukakis, Jesse Jackson, Pat Robertson, and George Bush.

*Past Electoral Performances and "Electability."* More than ever, candidates must demonstrate widespread voter appeal whether they are considered front-runners or underdogs. Candidates with little national exposure need to perform better than others just to receive serious consideration by politicians, campaign professionals, and financial donors.

In 1968 Nixon needed a series of primary victories to shed the "loser" image he had developed in his unsuccessful 1960 presidential and 1962 California gubernatorial campaigns. Because he had been out of elective office for almost eight years, there were doubts about his "electability." Nixon eliminated those concerns with victories in the New Hampshire, Wisconsin, Pennsylvania, Oregon, and New Jersey primaries. Other strong contenders with questionable past performances have included Walter Mondale (who dropped out of the 1976 campaign early) in 1984 and George Bush and Bob Dole in 1988.

Hubert Humphrey's strong 1968 presidential campaign gave his 1972 bid more credibility. Reagan's string of primary victories in 1976 established him as a proven vote-getter in 1980.

Dole's disastrous experience as President Ford's running mate in 1976 created doubts that he could be an effective presidential candidate. Unsuccessful in 1980 and 1988, Dole on his third attempt was poised to attain the Republican nomination for president by spring 1996. Jerry Brown, once a legitimate presidential contender, was considered too inconsistent to win in 1992. Since his two terms as governor ended in 1982, Brown had lost a race for the U.S. Senate, dropped out of politics, and

served one tumultuous year as California's Democratic Party leader. Pat Buchanan's lack of experience in electoral politics undermined his claim to Reagan's right-wing legacy.

Numerous studies have indicated that some voters are so concerned about "wasting" a vote that "electability" is a major aspect of their decision making. Assertions about which candidate has the best chance of winning in November reverberate throughout the nominating process. The electability issue is most prominent toward the end of the primary season. The candidates try to show the public, the media, and political professionals that they would do best against the likely nominee of the other party.

President Ford used the electability issue effectively against Reagan in 1976, and President Carter used it well against Senator Kennedy in 1980. Those candidates stressed polls that showed them leading the other party's possible nominees. They also argued that their party would suffer if it denied the nomination to a sitting president.

## THE COMPLEXITY OF PRIMARY AND CAUCUS RULES

The states have a wide variety of rules for ballot qualifications and allocation of delegates. When Colorado representative Patricia Schroeder announced that she would not seek the Democratic nomination in 1988, she cited the complexity of state rules as a major consideration. Because of such rules, a late-starting campaign is practically impossible, even for longtime national figures. Candidates not only must follow legal requirements to qualify for state contests, but they also must adapt their campaign strategies to the state's imperatives.

The state rules differ on many aspects of the contest, including eligibility of nonparty members to vote in the primary or caucus, filing requirements and entry deadlines, allocation of delegates, stages in the selection of delegates, timing of the contests, and the choice of superdelegates.

### Eligibility of Nonparty Members

Most states limit participation in primary and caucus voting to registered party members, but many welcome independents and members of the other party. When nonparty members participate, they usually sign a form stating that they would like to join the party.

"Open" primaries can have an important effect on the campaign. John Kennedy won the 1960 Democratic primary in Wisconsin largely on the basis of crossover Catholic Republican voters, dealing his opponent, Sen. Hubert Humphrey of Minnesota, a severe defeat in his home region. Alabama governor George Wallace won the 1972 Wisconsin Democratic primary with as many Republican as Democratic votes. Four years later, Reagan gained a North Carolina primary victory over President Ford with the help of Democratic "crossover" voters. Open primary victories often are termed "illegitimate" by the losers because of the involvement of nonparty members. Humphrey complained that Kennedy's 1960 Wisconsin victory was unimportant for that reason. The winners' response is that a broad base of support is essential to victory in the general election.

### Filing Requirements and Deadlines

The first step in the competition for delegates is to get on the ballot. Most states require petitions (at either the state or local level), filing fees, or both to get on the primary ballot. Other states leave the makeup of the ballot to state or party officials and committees.

South Dakota requires only that the candidate file a letter of intent to run. Louisiana requires proof that the candidate has appeared on the ballot in two other states or a petition or a filing fee. North Carolina automatically lists candidates who have qualified for federal matching funds. Most states require a minimal test of strength statewide, but some also require proof of backing in each of the state's congressional districts.

The range of legal requirements that candidates must meet to put delegates on the ballot at the congressional district and state levels requires extensive planning. In 1984 Hart neglected to recruit delegate candidates in all states; consequently, he received few delegates in later Democratic primaries in which he polled well. Hart's failure to field full slates of delegates was partly intentional. His strategy called for allocating resources to the early stages of the campaign since it would have been foolish for him to spend time and energy on the later primaries if he was not assured of surviving until then.

### Allocation of Delegates

The diverse ways in which states allocate delegates for the national convention constitute a major organizational concern for candidates. Systems for determining the number of delegates that a candidate wins in a primary or caucus are complicated and, if neglected, could deal major setbacks to a strong candidate. Moreover, understanding the different systems is crucial to allocating scarce campaign time and resources. If a candidate spends a lot of time in a state with a delegate-allocation system more favorable to a competitor, the results can be disastrous.

Party members in "binding presidential preference" states vote directly for candidates, and delegates are allocated to the candidates in a number of ways. "Beauty contest" states use the vote simply as a rough measure of popular preference for the candidates; binding selection of delegates takes place later. The results of beauty contests might not have any effect on delegate selection. A candidate with good contacts among party activists in the state but little widespread popular support could win the majority of delegates after losing the primary. Voters in "delegate selection" states choose delegates without indicating which candidate the delegates will support.

Delegates are allocated at different levels. Some states require candidates to recruit delegates to run in each congressional district; other states allow delegates to be recruited from anywhere in the state.

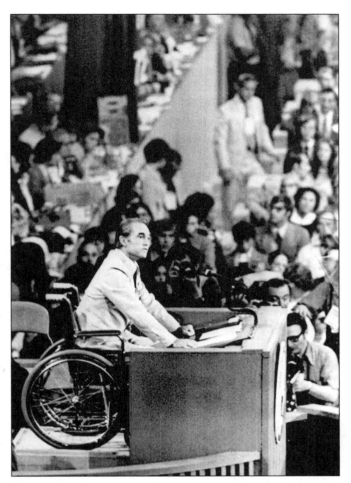

Alabama governor George Wallace explains his views of the Democratic platform to the party's delegates at the 1972 national convention.

In some states, delegates are allocated proportionally ("proportional representation"). In 1976, 80 percent of Idaho's delegates were allocated proportionally to the candidates receiving at least 5 percent of the vote. In Kentucky, only the top four finishers with at least 15 percent of the vote receive proportional allocation of delegates.[245] A number of other states use "bonus proportional representation" systems in which candidates receive delegate bonuses for winning congressional districts, in addition to an allocation based on their overall share of the vote.

Because of the "thresholds" required by proportional primaries, an allocation bias favors the top candidates. Carter received 5.1 percent more delegates than his vote totals would have suggested in the fourteen proportional Democratic primaries of 1976. President Ford was overrepresented by 2.1 percent in proportional Republican states.[246]

Winner-take-all primaries are now largely obsolete. Reformist Democrats were the first to do away with this system. Republicans eventually were compelled to drop winner-take-all contests because they fell under the jurisdiction of Democrat-dominated state legislatures. Winner-take-all contests had provided big boosts. For example, Reagan's 1976 campaign against Ford was boosted by winner-take-all victories in his home state of California and in Georgia, Montana, and Texas.[247] McGovern was boosted by a winner-take-all primary victory in California in 1972.

Candidates in Illinois, New Jersey, Pennsylvania, and West Virginia operate at the congressional district level under a "loophole" winner-take-all system—so called because it avoids the bans on statewide winner-take-all contests. In these states, a candidate may win a bare plurality in every congressional district and end up winning all of the delegates in the state. It also is conceivable that candidates finishing in second or third place statewide win an overwhelming majority of delegates.

In some states—such as Illinois, New Jersey, Pennsylvania, Vermont, and West Virginia—voters are required to make two decisions. First, voters cast a presidential preference ballot for the candidate of their choice; they then vote for the slate of delegates, which may or may not be listed as supporters of particular candidates.

### Stages of the Delegate-Selection Process

Many states select their delegates in several stages. Although the media sometimes convey the impression that party members automatically select delegates when they vote, the public balloting often is just the start of the process.

Caucuses are the starkest example of multistage delegate selection. In some caucus systems, party members meet several times before making final decisions on the presidential candidates. This explains why candidates who appear to do well on the major caucus day sometimes end up with a smaller number of delegates than was first projected.

The multistage system is more sensitive to fluctuations in candidate strength throughout the process. In the 1988 Iowa precinct caucuses, for example, Rep. Richard Gephardt of Missouri and Sen. Paul Simon of Illinois led a Democratic field of seven candidates. But as the delegate-selection process moved up to the county, congressional district, and state levels, Gephardt and Simon dropped out of the race. Massachusetts governor Michael Dukakis, who had finished third, took most of the Iowa delegates.

### Timing of State Electoral Contests

States follow various practices for scheduling state and presidential electoral contests. Some states schedule primaries for gubernatorial, congressional, and mayoral contests to coincide with the presidential contest. Depending on the strength of state and local politics, such a move could tilt presidential contests toward parochial concerns. The candidate's grasp of state politics becomes more important when the presidential and state contests coincide.

Holding presidential and state primaries on the same day can cause trouble for some state politicians. Because the national conventions are held in the summer, a state's presidential primary or caucus must take place in the spring. Many state officials, however, favor a September primary for state offices in order to open up the process for challenges. Other states assiduously separate their statewide and local contests from the presidential primaries. The effect of the separation usually is to keep voter turnout to a minimum in both selection processes.

About two-thirds of the states do not have important statewide elections in a presidential election year, although every two years a third of the states have senatorial races. Governors are selected in off-years in, for example, Maryland, Massachusetts, New York, and Tennessee.

### Superdelegates

In 1984 the Democratic Party adopted a rule requiring it to apportion a bloc of superdelegates—delegate positions reserved for elected officials and party officials. The purpose of the rule was to create a stronger link between the concerns of the government and the presidential selection process. Superdelegates were intended to give the selection process more stability.

The rule came about because party members had complained that the selection process was biased in favor of primary voters who were susceptible to "image" politics and caucus participants promoting ideological or single-issue politics. Low voter turnout and the domination of the process by ideological extremists also were said to be a reason for the rule. Discontent over former president Carter's inability to establish good relations with Congress was an additional factor. With some superdelegate seats reserved for senators and representatives, members of Congress felt that they would partially regain the status they had lost under Carter.

The superdelegates were integral to former vice president Mondale's strategy in 1984. Mondale won 450 of the 568 superdelegates—about 80 percent—compared with Hart's total of 62.[248] Mondale and his delegate-tracking team spent hours on the telephone courting the superdelegates. Without any of them, Mondale would have fallen short of a majority.

### WHO VOTES IN PRIMARIES?

Under the American electoral system, the size of the electorate has continually increased in response to the demands of different factions for a greater role in politics. The widening "scope of conflict" has given more groups access to the system.[249] Yet this apparently open system suffers from low turnout in both the nominating process and the general election. Only a third of all party members typically vote in primaries; a mere tenth, or less, participate in caucuses. In the general election, just over half of the electorate actually vote.

Austin Ranney found in a study of competitive presidential primaries between 1948 and 1968 that the mean voting turnout was 39 percent. Ranney defined "competitive" primaries as those with two or more candidates in which no candidate got more than 80 percent of the vote. The mean turnout in such states was 28 percent in 1976—an eleven-point drop. The decline in primary participation was larger than the drop in the general election turnout from its high of 62.8 percent in 1960 to 53.5 percent in the 1976 general election.[250]

Only in Oregon and Wisconsin has the participation rate come close to half of all eligible party members. The crucial New Hampshire primary usually attracts about a third of the voters. Delegates awarded in the California primary—the most of any state—are allocated by less than 40 percent of eligible party members.[251]

Low turnout rates for nominating contests give the process a bias toward well-organized and well-staffed campaigns. Especially in caucuses—which are more demanding on party members than the simple voting requirements of the primary—the ability to get supporters to the polls takes on great importance. With a low overall turnout, control over certain blocs of voters could be tantamount to control over a large part of the overall voting population.

The "wild card" aspect that low turnouts give primaries and caucuses can undo the best-laid plans. Bad weather in Iowa and New Hampshire, for example, can undermine the efforts of candidates to get elderly supporters to the polls. An especially salient issue such as Social Security or farm policy can spur certain groups to show up at polling places more than others. The controversy over the Vietnam War—exacerbated by the Tet offensive in early 1968—spurred students to become more active than ever in the nomination.

The primary system is unrepresentative because of a class bias in turnout. Studies of voting behavior have found that the citizens most likely to vote are "plugged into" party organizations and feel they can effect change. Level of education also is crucial to a citizen's level of activity. Finally, sometimes onerous registration requirements work against a high degree of participation by people of lower socioeconomic status.[252]

Groups making up the Republican coalition tend to have higher voter turnout than Democratic groups. In the 1992 general election, for example, groups associated with the GOP coalition had some of the highest voter participation rates: older voters (over forty-five), 70.0 percent; midwesterners, 67.2 percent; whites, 63.6 percent; and college educated, 81.0 percent. Young people, southerners, blacks, people with little education, and the unemployed, groups traditionally associated with the Democratic coalition, had considerably lower turnout rates in 1992.[253]

Political scientist James Q. Wilson's study of the amateur club movement of the 1950s suggests the kinds of party members that presidential contenders must attract. The "amateur" is a party activist devoted to the public pursuit of issue-oriented, "clean" politics. Modern-day examples of amateurs include environmental groups, antiwar and civil rights activists of the 1960s, and supporters of the Proposition 13 tax-reduction movement in California in the 1970s. "Professionals" are party members less concerned with ideological and policy matters than with maintaining the party's long-term viability.[254]

The tug-of-war between amateurs and professionals could be a key indicator of a presidential candidate's most favorable strategy. The strong performances of Barry Goldwater (1964),

Eugene McCarthy (1968), George McGovern (1972), Jimmy Carter (1976), and Ronald Reagan (1976 and 1980) can be attributed to their appeal to the amateurs. The strong performances of Hubert Humphrey (1968), Gerald Ford (1976), Carter (1980), Walter Mondale (1984), and Bob Dole (1996) might be attributed to their appeal to professionals.

Political scientists have argued that preconvention participants tend to be "activists" with more of an ideological bent than the rest of the party and electorate. To win the nomination, candidates must package their messages so they are acceptable to the more rigid, issue-oriented parts of the electorate. In recent years, for example, the Democratic Party has adopted liberal positions on arms control, world human rights, civil rights, abortion, and the environment in order to satisfy party activists. Republicans have taken conservative positions on taxes, military spending, domestic spending, and U.S.–Soviet relations. Candidates who deviated from these basic requirements, such as Republican John Anderson in 1980 and Democrat Reubin Askew in 1984, failed.

Besides appealing to the activists, candidates often stake out fringe positions to distinguish themselves from the competition. Democratic Alabama governor George Wallace, who complained that there was not "a dime's worth of difference" between Democrats and Republicans, articulated right-wing populist positions in 1968 and 1972. Tennessee senator Al Gore attempted to assume a more activist military stance than his Democratic rivals in 1988.

Centrists, however, often have enjoyed better success in primary contests. In 1976 Carter won the nomination when liberal candidates split the vote among themselves. Also that year, President Ford withstood a strong challenge from former California governor Reagan to win the nomination. Reagan's campaign was based on highly charged, conservative complaints about détente with the Soviet Union and the negotiation of a treaty to cede control of the Panama Canal to Panama. Bush emerged as the main competition to Reagan in the 1980 Republican primaries on the basis of his being a "moderate" alternative to Reagan. Hart established himself as an alternative to Mondale's traditional liberalism.

## THE STATE OF STATE PARTY ORGANIZATIONS

Although state party organizations have assumed a secondary role in presidential politics, they still can be decisive in nominating campaigns. For example, state parties play a crucial role in writing the rules of primaries and caucuses. Moreover, they have extensive lists of political activists and technical know-how on matters ranging from polling to media.

Yet state parties overall appear to be in decline. Political scientist Kay Lawson has argued that state parties have withered because they have not been able to control their own affairs. The imposition of primaries by state legislatures, she says, is "a form of legalized theft." Primaries take control of the parties away from those who work to build the organization and give it to those who take only occasional interest in politics. State governments also have weakened party strength by imposing campaign finance regulations, which encourage contributions to political action committees and interest groups rather than parties, and by banning straight-ticket voting, which reduces party identification. The decline of parties is perhaps most stark in Florida and California, which are not allowed by state law to endorse candidates before the primary.[255]

State legislatures are not the only factor behind the decline in state parties. The rise of organized interest groups also has reduced the roles of state parties in political education and mobilization. Citizen allegiance to political causes usually does not take the form of party membership—where different interests would have to accommodate one another—but of specialized interest groups.

## NOMINATING CAMPAIGN ISSUES, POLLS, AND ORGANIZATIONS

Modern presidential nominating campaigns are built on a three-legged stool of issues, polls, and organizations. Issues are what set the candidates apart. Polls help a candidate to define the issues and identify the groups of voters most interested in issues on which the candidate is willing and able to take a position that will appeal to those voters. And organizations hold the campaign together and give continuity to the candidate's efforts to gather the most votes by addressing the issues and adjusting strategy as the polls indicate.

### Issues

The "spatial model" of politics perhaps best explains the way presidential candidates approach issues. Economist Anthony Downs and others have argued that the nominating process pulls candidates away from the national ideological center and toward the ideological extremes; the general election battle between the two parties then pulls the candidates back to the center.

According to this model, candidates search for the party's ideological midpoint during the nominating contest. The party's midpoint is off-center from that of the entire electorate, however—to the right for Republicans, to the left for Democrats. In the general election, then, candidates have to move away from party orthodoxy and toward the national center to attract wide support. Presumably, the candidates will retain the support of the more extreme party members when moving to the center since the party members have no better place to go.[256]

In 1976 Jimmy Carter originally positioned himself as a moderate to set himself apart from the liberal candidates such as Morris Udall and Birch Bayh. To stave off late challenges by Frank Church and Jerry Brown, and a possible draft of Hubert Humphrey, Carter moved to the left. Carter's proposals for cuts in the defense budget, a national health system, and full employment allayed suspicions of the party's left. But once the fall campaign had begun, Carter shifted to conservative themes, such as

family issues, government reorganization, and federal deficits. Even so, Democrats stood behind Carter because he was more compatible than the conservative incumbent president, Gerald Ford.

Ronald Reagan moderated many of his emphases in the 1980 campaign after winning the Republican nomination. Reagan rebutted President Carter's charges that he would dismantle important social welfare programs such as Social Security and Medicare. He also shifted the focus of his call for a military buildup, saying that it would make arms negotiations more productive rather than enable the United States simply to be more aggressive in world affairs.

The spatial model, however, obscures a number of elements of the campaign dynamic. Often it is more important to appeal to activists in the party than to abandon them for the center. In 1960, for example, the efforts of Massachusetts senator John Kennedy in behalf of jailed civil rights leader Martin Luther King Jr. not only solidified African American and liberal support but also provided an example of the vigorous leadership that Kennedy promised the electorate. In 1980 Republican Reagan found he was able to broaden his overall support by making strongly conservative statements. "New Right" groups such as the Moral Majority—which called for a constitutional ban on abortion, reinstatement of prayer in public schools, and policies to restore "traditional" family structure—actively worked for his election by sponsoring advertising and bringing to the polls people who had never voted. The effort did not alienate Republican centrists who were more concerned about the economy and foreign policy.[257] Bill Clinton's appeal to social conservatives in 1992 on issues such as the death penalty, race, and welfare undermined President Bush's hold on those voters who had voted Republican in the past three or more elections.

Third party candidates who appeal to one of the extreme reaches of the ideological spectrum can upset the normal shifts of presidential campaigns. For example, a Republican uncertain of the support of hard-right voters might not be able to move to the center in the general election campaign. Moderate third party candidates also can send the major party candidates scampering to the extremes of the ideological spectrum. Ross Perot's 1992 bid confused both Republican and Democratic strategists, who shied away from strong ideological appeals.

Candidates tailor their pitches to appeal to the mainstream of the particular state in which they are campaigning. Granted, a candidate's overall message must have some consistency, but the emphasis of political arguments can vary greatly from state to state. The disadvantage of this practice is its potential effect on the president's ability to govern. President Carter experienced difficulties building coalitions for energy and welfare reform proposals, and President Reagan was limited by his separate promises to Social Security recipients, military weapons producers, and business leaders. Reagan's political appointments often were threatened by some of his own allies on the right.

U.S. politicians always have been able to pull together dis-

Pollster Patrick Caddell, left, worked closely with Carter in campaigns and in the White House.

parate factions to build electoral and governing coalitions. What is different now, according to many analysts, is that parties no longer serve as a cohesive political force. With the decline of party discipline and the increase in organized factions, party and public officials have less "bargaining" authority and must respond to the discrete and contradictory signals of the factions. Furthermore, voters' signals become unclear when they cannot be directed at a comprehensive party program.[258]

Whenever possible, a candidate will try to appeal both to party activists and to the general public with "fuzzy" statements. Clinton's stance on abortion in 1992—he personally opposed abortion but believed it should be "safe, legal, and rare"—was designed to appeal to all sides of the divisive issue. Carter's 1976 promise to offer pardons, not amnesty, to Vietnam War draft resisters was a gesture both to liberals who wanted to end punishment and to conservatives who wanted a statement that draft resistance is wrong. Patrick Caddell, Carter's pollster, wrote in a memorandum to the candidate: "We have passed the point when we can simply avoid at least the semblance of substance. This does not mean the need to outline minute, exact details. We all agree that such a course could be disastrous. However, the appearance of substance does not require this. It requires a few broad, specific examples that support a point."[259]

### Polls

Polling data are used extensively during the nominating campaign, even though they are not always helpful. Media, campaign staffs, and contributors use polls to determine the "viabil-ity" of various campaigns. Privately held polls have become central to the internal strategies of candidates—helping them to understand which issues are important to voters and the electorate's complex psychological makeup.

Scientific polls have been a regular part of campaigns since the 1936 election, when the accuracy of George Gallup's forecasts provided a stark contrast to a *Literary Digest* mail survey that predicted Republican Alfred Landon would defeat President Franklin Roosevelt.

Until 1952, however, campaign polling remained restricted to simple "snapshots" of the strength of the candidates. Republican presidential candidate Dwight Eisenhower used polling data to develop themes for television advertising and to target specific socioeconomic voter blocs for appeals. When he ran for reelection to the Senate in 1958, John Kennedy of Massachusetts hired Louis Harris to conduct polls of several important 1960 presidential primary states to prepare for a possible national candidacy. Kennedy's concern that his Catholicism could be a political liability and his selection of mostly Protestant West Virginia as an important primary test state both stemmed from the Harris polls.

President Lyndon Johnson and several other candidates in 1964 used extensive "image" polling and determined that Sen. Barry Goldwater's chief liability was a widespread perception that he was an ideologue with a dangerous tendency to act "without thinking." Both New York governor Nelson Rockefeller and Johnson hammered away at the issue in their primary and general election battles against Goldwater.

In more recent years, polling has moved beyond broad-brush portraits of the electorate to sophisticated geographic, ethnic, and issue breakdowns. Polling is one of the most expensive elements of a modern campaign because campaigns now receive information on the specific economic, ethnic, religious, geographic, educational, occupational, and residential characteristics of many groups and how those characteristics affect attitudes about a wide range of policy issues.

In his surprising second-place finish in the 1972 New Hampshire primary, George McGovern had followed pollster Patrick Caddell's advice and concentrated his campaign on university towns, blue-collar workers, and the young professionals living near the southern border of the state. Similarly, in 1976 Jimmy Carter concentrated on the southern and middle parts of Florida in his important primary win over George Wallace.

In the 1984 election, campaigns began using a process pioneered by the advertising industry: instant polling procedures to determine the effect on voters of specific candidate performances. Selected groups of voters watching candidate debates registered their feelings throughout the debates by adjusting knobs on a handheld computer device. The knobs indicated whether their response was "positive" or "negative" toward a candidate's specific statements or actions. Campaign analysts could then tabulate and analyze the reactions of whole groups.

### Nominating Campaign Organizations

The modern campaign is dominated by professional, technically oriented staffs with loyalty to the candidate rather than to the party as a whole. Presidential candidates, able to appeal to activist voters in primaries and caucuses, no longer need to rely on state party leaders. The primary campaign, especially, turns on how successfully candidates fashion and transmit their messages to blocs of likely voters and how well the candidates' staffs get those voters to the polls and caucus meetings. Party machinery frequently is ignored in these tasks.

Perhaps the most important stage of any campaign is recruitment of campaign professionals, such as fund-raisers, strategists, pollsters, speechwriters, media advisers, issues experts, delegate rules experts, and volunteers. Newspaper reporters and other students of presidential selection closely watch the shaping of the candidate's staff as the first indication of the campaign's viability.

Clinton became a viable contender for the 1992 Democratic nomination when he attracted fund-raiser Robert Farmer and strategists such as James Carville, Paul Begala, George Stephanopoulos, and Stanley Greenberg. Having worked in several national campaigns, they offered technical prowess, as well as a "populist" orientation in a year when voter dissatisfaction with Washington was boiling over. Carville had run the 1991 Senate race of Harris Wofford of Pennsylvania, which had helped to raise the issue of health care to national prominence.

An example of the extent to which campaigns turn on their professional help is the 1988 Democratic campaign. Gary Hart recruited many of the top campaign professionals but dropped out of the race in spring 1987. Although Hart later reentered the race, he was unable to attract his former professional supporters. Sen. Joseph Biden picked up many of Hart's aides and was considered a top contender, but then he quit the campaign in fall 1987. At that point, Sen. Paul Simon hired many of Biden's top Iowa operatives—and zoomed to the top of state polls. Simon then ran a strong campaign in the Iowa caucuses, but his third-place finish in New Hampshire was considered inadequate to expand his base significantly.

Almost every aspect of a campaign is now scripted by professionals. Aides determine the "theme of the day" for the nonstop campaign and brief the candidate between stops about the day's events and issues. Not since Adlai Stevenson in 1956 have major candidates written their own speeches.[260]

Campaign professionals make up a well-defined, if transient, lot. Most rise to the top by working in congressional or gubernatorial elections and then, after a period of "candidate shopping," hitching up with a presidential effort. William Henkel, the head of President Reagan's advance team in 1984, had done similar work for Nixon and Ford. Howard Druckman, the head of Mondale's 1984 advance team, began campaign work with Edmund Muskie's 1972 effort.

Many campaign experts have become legendary figures because of their ability to shape a campaign. Among the more prominent campaign strategists of recent years are John Sears (Nixon, 1968), Gary Hart (McGovern, 1972), Hamilton Jordan (Carter, 1976), Patrick Caddell (McGovern, 1972; Carter, 1976), Oliver Henkel (Hart, 1984), Edward Rollins (Reagan, 1984), Lee Atwater (Bush, 1988), James Carville (Clinton, 1992), and Dick Morris (Clinton, 1996). Less well-known figures are, nevertheless, famous within the world of campaign staffers.

Because modern candidates run in all regions, they must delegate much of the campaign authority to other people. The way candidates manage their organizations can be a double-edged sword. On the one hand, management of the campaign can present a good indication of the candidate's executive ability. On the other hand, missteps within an organization of strangers often can have a profound effect on the shape of the campaign. For example, the 1988 campaign of Gov. Michael Dukakis stumbled after revelations that two top aides had secretly prepared a videotape critical of Biden.

The importance of campaign professionals is underscored by the campaigns that fail to organize delegate pursuits adequately. After victories in Florida and Michigan, Governor Wallace was ineligible to compete in the 1972 winner-take-all California primary because he had missed the state filing deadline. Four years later, Rep. Mo Udall was left off the Indiana Democratic ballot because he fell fifteen signatures short of the petition requirement in one congressional district. In 1984 Hart did not receive all the delegates that his electoral performance would allow in several states because he had failed to recruit slates of delegates.

The development of formal training programs is an indication of the professionalization of campaigns—and of their separation from state party structures. In 1987 Rutgers University

The 1984 Democratic presidential candidates pose for a picture before their debate at Dartmouth College in Hanover, N.H. From left to right: John Glenn, Alan Cranston, Ernest Hollings, George McGovern, Gary Hart, Walter Mondale, Jesse Jackson, and Reubin Askew.

announced the creation of a graduate program in campaign management. The program provides technical training for the major phases of campaign work—polling, strategy, canvassing, fund raising, speech writing, office management, and advance work. Designed for people from all parts of the political spectrum, the program has been criticized for not stressing the moral dilemmas of the democratic process.

## CANDIDATE DEBATES

Debates among candidates have become a prominent part of the nominating process. When the chairs of the Democratic and Republican Parties in 1987 committed their nominees to a series of debates in the general election campaign, the effect may have been to increase the importance of debates during the nominating process. Indeed, in recent years debates have become commonplace during the drive for the nomination.

Given the now central importance of primaries to the nominating process, and the increasing tendency of the parties to have large fields of contenders, voters and political pundits have come to rely on debates to sort out and get to know the candidates. Especially in the early stages of a campaign, debates are important because they offer the only large event at which candidates can be judged.

Debates among party contenders have been significant parts of all of the nominating campaigns since 1980. That year, debates in Iowa and New Hampshire were considered crucial turning points in the Republican nominating season. Reagan became vulnerable in Iowa when he refused to debate his opponents: he fell from 50 percent to 26 percent in the preference polls between December and the day after the January 5 debate. Trivial as it may seem, Reagan's posturing in the 1980 Nashua, New Hampshire, debate gave his campaign an important lift. Reagan invited other GOP candidates to join a one-on-one debate he had scheduled with Bush. When Bush resisted the inclu-

sion of the others and debate moderator Jon Breen ordered Reagan's microphone cut off, Reagan, misstating Breen's name, declared angrily: "I paid for this microphone, Mr. Green." The righteous declaration won applause for Reagan and made Bush appear stiff and uncompromising.

The 1984 Democratic debates first chipped away at Mondale's status as front-runner, then dealt a devastating blow to Hart's candidacy. Mondale's mocking of Hart's "new ideas" campaign with an allusion to a popular television commercial—"Where's the beef?"—left Hart on the defensive in a major Atlanta debate. Hart also stumbled when asked if U.S. military pilots could distinguish between military and civilian aircraft intruding on U.S. air space; he said they could tell the difference by looking into the plane to see if its occupants were wearing uniforms. Throughout the 1984 and 1988 campaigns, Jackson used the debates to portray himself as a mediator of party disputes. In 1992 Clinton showed his mastery of policy minutiae in his debate appearances. Clinton's face-to-face debate with Brown on the *Donahue* television show, which was not moderated, was considered one of the most illuminating moments of the year. By taming the maverick former governor of California, and a formidable opponent for the nomination, Clinton helped to dispel the notion that his experience as a small-state governor did not qualify him to be president.

The intramural debates started earlier than ever in the 1988 campaign. In the summer of 1987, a group of Democrats gathered for a debate under the auspices of the television program *Firing Line*. The Republicans debated on the same program in the fall. The 1988 campaign also included one-on-one matchups, such as the trade debate between Democrats Gephardt and Dukakis and the debate between Republican Pete du Pont and Democrat Bruce Babbitt. The ten major candidates for the Republican 1996 nomination met in a televised "news conference" debate in New Hampshire in November 1995.

## NATIONAL PARTY CONVENTIONS

The establishment in 1831 of national conventions for the purpose of nominating presidential candidates marked the formalization of political parties in the United States. The Framers had neither anticipated nor wanted partisan elections. Certainly, they had made no provision for the nomination of candidates by political parties. Instead, that process emerged incrementally.

The early elections followed the selection process set out in the Constitution. They were nonpartisan, and the electoral college made the choice of candidates without prior nomination. The practice of nominating candidates by congressional caucus emerged with the rise of the partisanship that followed Washington's administration. It reflected the desire of competing factions to have candidates that would represent their political positions.

Associated with the rise of partisanship was a fundamental change in the nature of the electoral college. Instead of exercising their own individual judgments in electing presidents, electors became instructed agents of political parties. Thus the choice of particular electors was tantamount to a choice for a particular candidate.

When two-party competition between the Federalists and the Democratic-Republicans gave way to single-party Democratic-Republican rule during the "Era of Good Feeling" (a phrase used to describe the presidency of James Monroe, 1817–1825), nomination by "King Caucus," as it was called by its detractors, virtually guaranteed one's election. With no opposition party to challenge its candidate, the congressional caucus was sovereign. The caucus system came under attack and was finally dismantled by the election of 1824.

In the transitional phase between King Caucus and the national convention system, a variety of methods were used to nominate candidates. These included nomination by state legislative caucuses, by state party conventions, by "mixed" state conventions (consisting of both party members of the state legislature and elected delegates from those sections of the state not represented by that party in the legislature), and by mass meetings of rank-and-file voters. All of these, however, were decentralized systems that did not generate the degree of mass support that the national convention system later would.

The first national party nominating convention was held by the Anti-Masons (a short-lived splinter party) in Baltimore, Maryland, in September 1831. *(See "Third Parties," p. 116.)* With 116 delegates from thirteen states, the convention nominated William Wirt for president and Amos Ellmaker for vice president. Within the next eight months, two other parties followed suit. In December the National Republicans held a convention where they nominated Henry Clay and John Sergeant, and in May 1832 the Democrats convened to nominate Andrew Jackson and Martin Van Buren. With that, the convention system was born and has remained intact ever since.

### Convention Sites

Baltimore proved to be a popular spot for the first conventions. From 1831 to 1852, ten conventions (including the Democratic Party's first six) were held there. To a large degree, the choice of Baltimore was a matter of convenience. Transportation was slow, and a central location was desirable. Most other sites (such as Pennsylvania cities Harrisburg, Philadelphia, and Pittsburgh) conformed to that rule, although Buffalo, New York, hosted the northern-based Liberty Party in 1843 and the Free Soilers in 1848.

The choice of convention sites after 1856 reflected the country's expansion westward. Since then, Chicago has been the most popular choice (having hosted twenty-five major party conventions by 1996). Cincinnati and St. Louis were two other popular sites in the latter 1800s. Until recently, the South seldom was the site of a convention. In 1860 the Democrats held a tumultuous one in Charleston, South Carolina, that ultimately deadlocked, forcing a second convention to be held in Baltimore. The Democrats did not hold another southern convention until 1928, when Houston, Texas, was chosen (largely in an effort to appease southerners, who, party leaders knew, would be unhappy with the nomination of Al Smith, a Catholic from New York). The Republicans did not hold a southern convention until 1968. In 1988, however, both parties chose to hold their conventions in the South—the Democrats in Atlanta, the Republicans in New Orleans.

At some point, the criterion of a central location gave way to a more pressing one: money. For a time, the major consideration in choosing a convention site was the amount of money that the city in question would donate to the national party committee in cash and services. By 1968 contributions from cities were approaching $1 million. Local economies get a significant boost from the influx of thousands of conventioneers and journalists into their cities. Illinois officials estimated that the 1996 Democratic convention in Chicago would provide a $100 million boost to the local economy. Chicago won the right to host the event with a package worth $32 million for the use of facilities and services.[261] Aside from that, a convention offers a city tremendous exposure in the form of media attention.

Corporate underwriting of national conventions ended in 1972 when it was discovered that an antitrust suit against International Telephone and Telegraph (ITT) was settled in ITT's favor by the Justice Department of the Nixon administration shortly after Sheraton (an ITT subsidiary) offered to supply $400,000 worth of services to the Republicans if they would locate their 1972 convention in San Diego. (The revelation forced the GOP to move its convention to Miami Beach. In 1996 the GOP finally held a convention in San Diego.) Campaign finance legislation passed in the wake of the Nixon administration's Watergate scandal prohibited corporate contributions and free services and provided for each national party to receive $2.2 million from the government to finance its convention. Although that amount has since increased to reflect inflation ($12 million

At the Republican convention in Chicago in May 1860, Abraham Lincoln won the nomination and went on to become the first Republican president. From 1856 to 1996 Chicago hosted twenty-five conventions, the most of any city. The Democrats hosted their 1996 convention in Chicago.

each in 1996), it is still far less than that needed to fund conventions. As a result, the Federal Election Commission loosened its restrictions to allow private businesses to offer services (such as free hotel accommodations) as long as the other party receives comparable benefits. It also allowed state and local governments to offer a number of services free of charge (such as security and the use of a convention hall). Thus the 1976 Democratic national convention received $3.63 million in direct subsidies from New York City.[262] In 1988 the Republican national convention received $5.50 million in subsidies from New Orleans.

The choice of a convention site also depends on the facilities that are available. Conventions require 20,000 or more hotel and motel rooms to house delegates, party officials, members of the press, television crews, and the candidates' advisers and staff. Lack of hotel space prevented Philadelphia from hosting the Democrats in 1968. The city also needs a convention hall large enough to seat delegates and accommodate the media—including space for overhead booths for the television networks.

In 1988 the Omni Coliseum in Atlanta proved to be a tight fit for the Democrats. The stage alone—a huge structure that soared eighty-five feet into the air and included two large screens, space for an orchestra, and a podium that could be adjusted by hydraulic lifts to make everyone appear to be the same height—took up space for 7,200 seats. As a result, the Omni provided fewer than 10,000 seats and a maximum capacity of 12,500 people. That capacity was inadequate for the 5,373 delegates and alternates, 12,000 members of the press, and thousands of other guests.[263] On several occasions, the fire marshal

blocked entry to the building because of overcrowding. During Jesse Jackson's speech to the convention, hundreds were stranded outside, including Martin Luther King III.

In contrast, the New Orleans Superdome proved to be too big for the 1988 Republican convention. The building, which can seat more than 97,000 people, was divided by a curtain that rose nine stories high and weighed three tons. Behind the curtain were twenty-seven trailers that served as offices. The rest of the building was used to accommodate the convention itself. A side effect of the cavernous interior was that many of those in the hall could not hear the proceedings. It seemed that the vast open space of the Superdome (some twenty-four stories high) simply swallowed the sound. In 1996 some Republican delegates grumbled that the San Diego Convention Center was too small—especially because the height of the main hall did not allow a spectacular "balloon drop."

Security considerations play a major role in the choice of a convention site. New York hosted three Democratic conventions (1976, 1980, 1992) only after state and city officials offered extraordinary security measures. President Nixon approved Miami Beach for the Republican convention in 1972 when he was assured that antiwar protesters would be kept at bay.

National image and political strategy are other important factors. Republicans portrayed the 1984 Democratic convention in San Francisco as a radical and un-American spectacle. San Francisco's liberal social environment, said UN Ambassador Jeane Kirkpatrick, a Republican, was emblematic of the "blame America first" mentality of the Democratic Party. Democrats selected Atlanta as their site in 1988 as part of a strategy to appeal to moderate voters and get away from the image of San Francisco. In 1992 the GOP selected Houston as an appeal for the state's cache of thirty-two electoral votes and as a tribute to its adopted son President George Bush. The Democrats selected Chicago for the 1996 convention partly to secure the party's base in the industrial heartland. The selection also was intended to exorcise memories of the party's disastrous 1968 convention.

The choice of a site often serves as a gesture to a particular part of the country or reflects the personal preferences of an incumbent president running for another term. Ronald Reagan, for example, wanted to have Dallas selected as the site of the 1984 Republican convention because of the support he had received from Texas conservatives in 1976 and 1980. When the race for the party nomination is considered wide open, according to an unwritten rule, states with candidates cannot host the convention.

Choice of a site may be symbolic of a theme that the party wishes to convey. The Republicans met in Detroit in 1980 to counteract the party's image as antiblack and antiurban. The selection also was intended to depict Detroit as "a back-from-trouble renaissance city, much as the GOP sees itself as a party restored to health."[264]

A site is usually chosen more than a year before the convention by a committee of a dozen or so party members appointed by the party's national chair. The national party committee then officially announces the convention's date and site, allocates convention delegates to each state, and appoints its officers and committees. An occasional suggestion that a permanent national convention center be built for use by both parties never has generated much enthusiasm.

*Delegates*

Setting the number of votes that each state delegation will have at the national convention is one of the most important parts of the formal call to the convention. This distribution of votes (known as *apportionment*) originally coincided with the number of votes each state had in the electoral college (which, in turn, was determined by the size of the state's congressional delegation). From the beginning, however, states often sent more representatives than the number of their electoral votes. In 1848 the Democrats tried (without success) to limit the actual voting power of a state delegation to its electoral college vote, regardless of the actual number of delegates from the state. In an effort to deal with the problem of extra delegates, the Democrats passed a rule in 1852 giving every state twice as many delegates as it had electoral votes (with each delegate receiving a half vote). To do away with fractional votes, the number of votes was doubled in 1872, giving each delegate a whole vote.[265]

From its beginning in 1856, the Republican Party also followed a system of apportionment that was roughly analogous to the electoral college. It gave each state six delegates at large, plus three delegates for each congressional district. This was changed in 1860 to four at-large delegates, plus two delegates for each congressional district.

Both parties, then, followed a system that allocated convention delegates mainly according to population rather than their voting strength in a given state. That system of apportionment came under attack after the Civil War with the rise of "one-party" states. In such states, a minority party (such as the Republicans in the post-Reconstruction South) would be overrepresented at their convention. The term *rotten borough* was often used to describe districts that were so represented.

Since overrepresentation was more of a problem for the Republicans than the Democrats, Republican apportionment has been more complicated. Although the problem has been addressed by the party since 1880, the Republicans did not change their method of apportionment until after their disastrous loss in the presidential election of 1912.

Beginning in 1916, the Republicans adopted a system of "bonus delegates," which were apportioned according to Republican voting strength in that state. Initially, the system called for each state to receive four at-large delegates, one delegate for each congressional district, and one bonus delegate for each congressional district that had cast at least 7,500 Republican votes in the presidential race in 1908 or in the congressional race in 1914. In 1924 the number of votes necessary for bonus delegates was raised to 10,000. In addition, the Republicans instituted a new system for awarding bonus delegates that gave three at-large delegates (instead of individual delegates to particular congressional districts) to each state that the party carried in the last presidential election.

Over the years, the Republicans have increased the number of bonus delegates that they award and have made it easier to receive those delegates.[266] Since 1972 the Republicans have followed a complicated formula that gives each state six at-large delegates, three delegates for each congressional district, four-and-a-half bonus delegates (plus 60 percent of its electoral vote total, rounded up) if the state carried the Republican ticket in the last presidential election, one bonus delegate for each Republican senator, one bonus delegate for a House delegation that is at least one-half Republican, and one bonus delegate for states with a Republican governor. In addition, fourteen at-large delegates are awarded to the District of Columbia, eight to Puerto Rico, and four each to Guam and the Virgin Islands. The rule also ensures states that they will receive at least the number of votes that they had in the previous election.[267]

The Democrats did not institute a "bonus" system until 1944. At that point they simply awarded two bonus delegates to each state that the Democrats carried in the last presidential election. The number of bonus delegates was increased to four in 1948. Since then, various delegate allocation formulas have been used. Beginning in 1972, the Democrats used an apportionment formula that based nearly half of a state's convention voting strength on its Democratic vote in the last three presidential elections. The remaining strength was based on the state's electoral college votes.[268]

The number of delegates attending national conventions has increased dramatically through the years. The first convention, held by the Anti-Masons in 1831, boasted 116 delegates. The

Democratic convention the next year had 283. In 1856 the first Republican convention was attended by 567 delegates. By the early 1900s, both parties had approximately 1,000 delegates. That number remained fairly stable until the 1950s, when the Democratic Party began its efforts to increase participation in the national convention.

In 1956 the Democrats allowed states to send delegates on a "half-vote" basis. Under that system, states could send twice as many delegates while maintaining the same voting power. Between 1952 and 1956, the number of Democratic delegates increased from 1,642 to 2,477. At the same time, the number of delegate votes was increasing as well. This increase initially reflected the use of bonus delegates but was later spurred by the greater democratization of its conventions (brought about by the party's post-1968 reforms). Thus the number of delegate votes at Democratic conventions increased from 1,230 in 1952 to 3,331 in 1980. In 1988, 3,531 regular delegates and 672 superdelegates (elected officials and party leaders who have automatic seats at the convention) were able to cast total and partial votes adding up to 4,162—even though their total ranks equaled 4,203.[269] In 1996 there were 3,521 regular delegates and 769 superdelegates for a total of 4,290.[270]

The size of Republican conventions has not increased quite so dramatically. Nevertheless, party reform in the early 1970s provided for a 60 percent increase in delegate strength. As a result, the number of delegates at the Republican convention increased from 1,348 in 1972 to 2,259 in 1976.[271] In 1988 there were 2,277 Republican delegates. The number dropped to 1,990 in 1996.

Delegates, however, make up only part of the attendance at modern-day national conventions. During the 1976 Democratic convention, for example, 26,594 "official" credentials were distributed each day, although the actual number of credentials topped 30,000 each day. Credentials were collected not only by the 3,353 delegates and their 2,086 alternates, but also by 5,200 members of the media; 869 officeholders and members of the Democratic National Committee; 1,500 security officials; and more than 10,000 "guests," or observers. For that convention, credentials tags were printed on specially laminated layers of paper with blue on the interior. This allowed security personnel to detect counterfeits by tearing a corner of the tag.[272]

The reforms that helped to increase the size of conventions also formalized the method of choosing delegates. In the nineteenth century, delegates usually were chosen by "closed" caucus meetings of state or local party regulars, or they were appointed by the governor or another state party leader. In the early part of the twentieth century, primaries evolved in which delegates were chosen by direct popular vote (usually restricted to party members). By 1968 the two dominant forms of delegate selection were the caucus and primary systems.

Since 1968, reforms instituted by Democrats (and to a lesser extent, Republicans) have set specific criteria for delegate selection. (See "Rules Changes in the Democratic Party," p. 26.) The re-sult has been the democratization of the selection process—the demise of "closed" caucuses and the rise of grassroots participation through primaries and "participatory" caucuses that are open to every voter in the party. The reforms also altered the characteristics of the delegates themselves by decreasing the number of party professionals and public officeholders and increasing the number of rank-and-file members (especially women, minorities, and young people).

### Preconvention Committees

Even though conventions have become largely symbolic affairs, struggles over the quadrennial meetings and platforms are long and difficult. Losing factions get to work right away to shape the party in their image. Soon after the Republicans lost the 1992 election, for example, moderates began an effort to eliminate the party's platform support for a constitutional amendment banning abortion.

Three major committees carry out the work of the national convention: credentials, rules, and platform. These committees traditionally have met before the start of the national convention—usually in the week before it begins. More recently, the Democrats have begun holding committee sessions several weeks before the convention.

The Credentials Committee reviews all disputes arising over delegates to the convention. Before the start of the convention, the committee receives a list of the delegates from each state. It then holds hearings on any challenges to those delegates (usually based on the procedures by which they were chosen) and makes its recommendation to the convention, which makes the final decision on the matter. Such disputes usually involve rival delegations for the same seats. If the challenge is found valid, the committee may seat the competing delegation. When there is a close presidential nominating contest, the Credentials Committee can significantly influence who is nominated. A notable instance was the 1912 Republican convention when President William Howard Taft was locked in a bitter nomination battle with former president Theodore Roosevelt. In the four states holding primaries, Roosevelt was the overwhelming winner. Taft, however, controlled the party machinery, so in caucus states he had the advantage. In particular, that control all but guaranteed that the Republicans' rotten boroughs in the South would go for Taft. Ironically, Roosevelt had hand-picked Taft as his successor in 1908, using that very machinery to guarantee Taft's success.[273]

The preconvention fight between Taft and Roosevelt was one of the most bitter on record. Roosevelt forces contested 254 pro-Taft delegates, but the Credentials Committee recommended that all but 19 of them be seated. The convention upheld that recommendation, virtually guaranteeing Taft's renomination. The problems caused by rotten boroughs in 1912 were decisive in bringing about reform of the delegate apportionment process.

A similar battle brewed in 1952 in the fight between Dwight Eisenhower and Ohio senator Robert A. Taft (son of William Howard Taft) for the Republican nomination. Like his father in

Vice President Hubert H. Humphrey, campaigning here in front of a union crowd, had the firm support of labor during his campaign for president in 1968.

1912, Taft controlled the party machinery. At the convention, sixty-eight pro-Taft delegates from Georgia, Louisiana, and Texas were contested. The Credentials Committee recommended that they be seated, but after a series of emotional speeches in support of Eisenhower stressing the theme "Thou shalt not steal," the convention overturned the recommendation. Eisenhower went on to win the nomination and election.

The credentials challenge with the greatest long-term impact occurred at the 1964 Democratic gathering in Atlantic City. The Mississippi Freedom Democratic Party (MFDP)—a contingent that formed a new, racially integrated party when blacks were not allowed to vote in the state's presidential primary—demanded to be seated at the convention. MFDP delegates were selected in a state convention open to all Mississippians. Civil rights leaders Martin Luther King Jr. and James Farmer, among others, testified in behalf of the insurgents in nationally televised hearings. After nervous negotiations involving President Johnson, Minnesota senator Hubert Humphrey, civil rights lawyer Joseph Rauh, and MFDP members, convention officials agreed to give the MFDP two "at-large" seats and integrate Mississippi delegations in the future. The MFDP contingent rejected the compromise and went home. The drama, which enlivened an otherwise boring convention paying homage to President Johnson, attract-

ed nationwide attention to the growing civil rights revolution. By the time of the 1972 convention, the party had opened its delegations to African Americans, students, and women.

Humphrey, then the vice president, figured in another Democratic credentials dispute four years later, when Minnesota senator Eugene McCarthy was challenging Humphrey for the nomination to succeed Johnson. The Credentials Committee dealt with seventeen different challenges from fifteen states—an unprecedented number for the Democrats. Humphrey forces (who controlled the party machinery) won all of the contested seats.

Many of the credentials disputes at the 1972 Democratic convention centered on whether or not states had complied with the guidelines of the McGovern-Fraser Commission, but there also were bitter skirmishes between George McGovern and the opposing "ABM" ("Anybody But McGovern") forces. Over eighty challenges involving more than 1,300 delegates were brought before the committee.[274] Since 1972, both parties have reformed their rules to help to ensure fair decisions by their Credentials Committees.

The Rules Committee is responsible for proposing the operating rules of the convention. Until 1972 the Democrats did not have a formal set of rules that were retained from convention to convention. Instead, the rules evolved in an ad hoc fashion, although many rules from the previous convention were readopted. In contrast, Republican rules were strictly codified.

Among the most controversial rules used by the Democrats were the "two-thirds" rule and the "unit" rule. The two-thirds rule required that any nominee for president or vice president receive not just a simple majority but a full two-thirds of the convention vote. Because the two-thirds rule made it more difficult to receive the nomination, protracted balloting was commonplace. While the Republican Party (which nominates by simple majority of more than 50 percent) has had just one convention in its entire history that required more than 10 ballots (36 in 1880), the Democratic Party has had seven (requiring 49 ballots in 1852, 17 in 1856, 59—spread over two conventions—in 1860, 22 in 1868, 46 in 1912, 43 in 1920, and 103 in 1924).

Proposals were introduced to abolish the two-thirds rule in the wake of the 1924 marathon convention and again in 1932 by supporters of Franklin Roosevelt who feared that he might not be able to gather the votes necessary to win the nomination. Despite considerable opposition, the Democrats finally eliminated the two-thirds rule at the 1936 convention. The South, in particular, objected to its elimination because the two-thirds rule had allowed that region to have a virtual veto over any nominee. To make up for that loss, the South received more votes at later conventions.

The unit rule allowed the majority of a delegation (if so authorized by its state party) to cast all of the votes of that delegation as a "unit" for the candidate or position supported by a majority of the state's delegation. Again, this rule was never used by the Republicans. Proponents of the unit rule argued that it muted conflict within the party (since dissident minorities would be overridden) and therefore strengthened state party organiza-

With a national party's presidential nominee determined by primaries, modern conventions have become carefully choreographed television productions aimed at the successful marketing of the presidential ticket.

tions. Opponents argued that the rule was undemocratic. Conceivably, a candidate with a minority of the delegates could win the nomination under the rule by simply controlling the votes of a dozen or so of the largest state delegations. Furthermore, it was argued that the unit rule undermined the notion of participatory democracy by ignoring the popular sentiments of minority factions. As used in the Democratic Party, the unit rule largely served to consolidate the voting strength of the South.[275] In 1968 the Democratic Rules Committee recommended that the unit rule be repealed. That action was later ratified by the 1968 convention and has been supported by subsequent reforms.

Actions by the Rules Committee can influence the outcome of a convention. In 1976 Reagan—who had announced his intention to nominate Pennsylvania senator Richard Schweiker as his running mate if he won the Republican presidential nomination—proposed a rules change to force his opponent, Ford, to name his own choice. Reagan, with a 110-delegate vote deficit, hoped he might be able to win over enough delegates alienated by Ford's choice to secure the nomination. But Ford forces voted down the rules change, and Ford went on to become the Republican nominee.

The so-called "bound delegate" rule (which required delegates to vote according to their pledge at the time of their selection) was the subject of a major rules fight at the 1980 Democratic convention. President Carter was in favor of the rule because it bound the majority of delegates to vote for him. Carter's rival, Senator Kennedy, fought to overturn the rule in the hope that some of those delegates would transfer their support to him. The Carter forces won the rules fight, and Carter went on to win the nomination.

The Platform Committee is responsible for preparing a statement of party principles (a *platform*) for presentation to the convention for its approval. Because party leaders want to mute

conflict within the party and appeal to as wide a base as possible, platforms seldom have much punch. Wendell Willkie (the Republican nominee in 1940) called them "fusions of ambiguity." Nevertheless, their adoption sometimes causes bitter fights. The passage of a strong civil rights plank in the 1948 Democratic platform provoked opposition from southern states and prompted the walkout of the entire Mississippi delegation and thirteen members of the Alabama delegation. Some of the disgruntled southerners then formed their own party—the States' Rights Democratic Party, or the Dixiecrats—who held their own convention in Birmingham, Alabama, and nominated South Carolina governor J. Strom Thurmond for president and Mississippi governor Fielding L. Wright for vice president.

Party platforms offer interest groups a welcome opportunity to influence the direction of the parties; about 150 groups appear before each party's platform-writing committee. Most groups appeal to the party that offers "greater access" and a "friendly ear." These appeals are directed to the party's "power center"—the party's likely nominee—except in some circumstances when working with the underdog candidate enables them to make a splash at the convention. About one-fifth of all groups active in the process take the "even money approach" and appeal to both parties.[276]

Since 1852, most conventions have adopted their platform before nominating their candidates. As a result, platform fights can serve as yet another indicator of the relative strength of rival candidates, especially when those candidates hold different ideological positions. Platform fights also can signal splits within the party that may prove fatal in the general election. Such was the case for the Republicans in 1964 and the Democrats in 1968. In contrast, consideration of the platform at the 1988 Democratic convention was more a debate than a fight. The approved platform was the party's shortest in fifty years and was filled with generalizations rather than specific promises. Its aim was to promote unity. Republicans assailed the Democrats for vagueness. Their platform was six times longer than the Democrats' (more than thirty thousand words) and reflected a strong conservative stance.

In 1992 Republicans faced a platform fight on abortion that was over before it began. Abortion rights advocates needed six delegations to challenge the platform committee's conservative right-to-life plank, but they could muster only four delegations in opposition. Besides supporting an antiabortion amendment to the U.S. Constitution, the platform as adopted stated: "We oppose using public revenues for abortion and will not fund organizations that advocate it. . . ." The platform overall was even more conservative than the 1988 version.

For many years, each party's Committee on Permanent Organization confirmed the national chair's choice of permanent officers for the convention and then recommended that slate to the convention itself. Since the post-1968 reforms, the Democrats have had no such committee. Rather, their choice of permanent officers has been made by the Rules Committee.[277] The Republicans have retained their Committee on Permanent Organization.

### Convention Officers

National party conventions are called to order by the national committee chair, who presides until a temporary convention chair is appointed. The temporary chair then presides until the convention acts on the recommended slate of candidates for permanent officers. For the first half of the twentieth century, the temporary chair usually served as the "keynote" speaker at the convention. Also it was a tradition that the temporary chair be a U.S. senator. Since 1952, when Gen. Douglas MacArthur delivered the keynote address at the Republican convention, the keynote speaker usually has been someone other than the temporary chair. And in recent years, the tradition of appointing a senator to be temporary chair has been less frequently observed.

Usually the temporary chair does not hold great power at a convention and the appointment is routine, but there have been exceptions. In the feverish fight between Taft and Roosevelt at the 1912 Republican convention, maneuvering in the early part of the convention was essential to victory. The permanent chair was not chosen until credentials contests had been decided (as is standard practice).[278] Because contested delegates were seated until the convention acted on the recommendations of the Credentials Committee, and because the temporary chair ruled on motions brought from the floor and generally controlled the proceedings, the temporary chair was in a position to exert considerable influence in 1912. The Roosevelt forces supported Wisconsin governor Francis E. McGovern, but Sen. Elihu Root of New York—the favorite of the Taft supporters—won the post of temporary chair.

The choice of Root played an important role in Taft's eventual nomination because, thanks to his maneuvers, the Taft forces won the credentials fight. Many accused Root of "steamroller" tactics, and in the galleries, pro-Roosevelt forces rubbed sand-paper and blew horns to imitate the sound of a steamroller. Dissension on the floor was rampant. Police squads stood ready to uphold the rulings of the temporary chair should he meet with violent resistance. Indeed, party officials were taking no chances. Even the decorations around the rostrum were used to conceal barbed wire should violence erupt.

The permanent chair usually is appointed on the second day of the convention, but the national committee's choice for the post is announced before the convention begins. It is usually approved by the convention itself with no contest. The permanent chair presides during the adoption of the platform and during the actual nominating procedure. Thus the permanent chair also is in a position to exercise strategic rulings that can help or hinder particular candidates. Indeed, the permanent chair is often described as the most important officer of the convention.[279]

In the late 1800s and early 1900s, prominent leaders in state and local politics usually filled the post of permanent chair. Since the 1930s, however, it has been the custom for the party leader in the House of Representatives to serve as permanent chair of the national convention. In 1972 the Democrats began to require that the position alternate every four years between men and women.

### Prenomination Oratory and Films

H. L. Mencken once wrote that convention orators are "plainly on furlough from some home for extinct volcanoes."[280] Indeed, oratory—and lots of it—plays a major role at national party conventions. During much of the behind-the-scenes maneuvering and unfinished committee work in the early phase of the convention, speeches are a way of marking time. They also are a means of staking out positions over important rules or platform fights, rallying support for candidates, or reestablishing unity at the end of a bitter convention.

The first major speech of the convention is the keynote address, usually heard on the first day. This address is preceded and followed by many other words: the call to order; the invocation; addresses by party notables, former presidents, and presidential candidates; the reading of committee reports; entertainment; nominating speeches; roll calls; and acceptance speeches.

Keynote speakers typically are chosen for their oratorical skills since they are there to whip up enthusiasm among the delegates. And, indeed, that is a charge most keynoters have taken very seriously. Before the age of television, keynote addresses often lasted well over an hour.

Until the 1950s, the temporary chair of the convention customarily delivered the address, but in more recent years that honor has fallen to someone else. In both parties, current or former governors have been popular choices as keynoters (Reubin Askew, Evan Bayh, Frank Clement, Mario Cuomo, Paul Dever, Daniel Evans, Thomas Kean, Zell Miller, Harold Stassen, Earl Warren). Others have been current or former senators (Howard Baker, Bill Bradley, Frank Church, Phil Gramm, Mark Hatfield, Daniel Inouye, John Pastore), military and space heroes (John Glenn, Douglas MacArthur), and women (Anne Armstrong,

Barbara Jordan twice, Susan Molinari, Katherine Ortega, Ann Richards). Besides having the necessary oratorical skills, modern keynote speakers appear to have been chosen as credible persons to address the issues of the day.

Keynotes offer well-known political figures an opportunity to set the tone for the upcoming campaign—and for emerging political figures an opportunity to distinguish themselves. Ann Richards, the Texas state treasurer, delivered a memorable keynote at the 1988 Democratic convention. "For eight straight years George Bush hasn't displayed the slightest interest in anything we care about. And now that he's after a job that he can't get appointed to, he's like Christopher Columbus discovering America. He's found child care. He's found education," Richards thundered in a twangy Texan accent. "Poor George, he can't help it. He was born with a silver foot in his mouth."[281] The delegates roared approval at her mockery of Bush's elite background. Two years later, Richards won election as Texas governor. But in 1994 the Bush family had the last laugh. Bush's son, George W. Bush, defeated Richards in her bid for reelection.

Much convention oratory is neither riveting nor profound. More often than not, scant attention is paid to the speakers, and their words are quickly forgotten. But in the millions of words that have poured forth from national conventions, a few have struck a chord and galvanized a convention. Often the phrases live on: Franklin Roosevelt's promise of a "new deal" in his 1932 acceptance speech; the coinage of the term "G.I. Joe" by Clare Booth Luce in an address to the Republicans in 1944; and the invocation of the phrase "Our time has come!" by Jesse Jackson in his speech to the 1984 Democratic convention.

Perhaps the greatest convention speech of all occurred in 1896 when William Jennings Bryan—a young leader of the Nebraska delegation—stunned the Democratic national convention with what has become known as his "Cross of Gold" speech. By the end of the convention he was that party's nominee for president. The speech evolved out of the platform fight over the currency issue (whether the United States should maintain the gold standard or allow the unlimited coinage of silver). The Democratic National Committee favored the gold standard, but prosilver forces had much support at the convention. Bryan's speech was instrumental in leading the convention to a prosilver stance. Throughout the speech, delivered before the days of microphones, Bryan held some twenty thousand spectators spellbound. He later recalled that the vast crowd would "rise and sit down as one man" as it responded to his oratory.[282]

Couching his appeal for free silver as a fight for "the struggling masses," Bryan intoned: "We have petitioned, and our petitions have been scorned. We have entreated, and our entreaties have been disregarded. We have begged, and they mocked when our calamity came. We beg no longer, we entreat no more, we petition no more. We defy them." And from the wellspring of the convention hall, the thousands echoed: "We defy them." In the hush that fell back over the hall as Bryan spoke, he concluded, ". . . we will answer their demand for a gold standard by saying to them: You shall not press down upon the brow of labor

this crown of thorns, you shall not crucify mankind upon a cross of gold."[283]

In more recent times, New York governor Mario Cuomo was catapulted into the public eye by his memorable keynote address at the 1984 Democratic convention. Had he delivered such a speech in an earlier age, he might have found himself nominated for president practically on the spot. Playing off President Reagan's use of the phrase "a shining city on a hill" to describe the United States, Cuomo responded: "The president is right. In many ways we are 'a shining city on a hill.' . . . But there's another part of that city, the part where some people can't pay their mortgages and most young people can't afford one, where students can't afford the education they need and middle-class parents watch the dreams they hold for their children evaporate. . . . There is despair, Mr. President, in faces you never see, in the places you never visit in your shining city." Invoking the image of family and community, Cuomo called for the new president of the United States to be "a Democrat born not to the blood of kings but to the blood of pioneers and immigrants."[284]

In recent years, both parties have complemented convention oratory by showing films largely devoted to introducing the candidates to the public—and extolling their achievements in carefully produced packages of propaganda. Like other aspects of modern campaigns, the films have become more artistic and professional in recent years.

A film on President Nixon at the 1972 Republican convention chronicled his accomplishments in Peking, Moscow, and Washington. It brought hushed attention even from the three thousand reporters in the press gallery—people who were usually inattentive at such presentations.[285] In 1976 the Democrats showed a fourteen-minute film about Carter: a "Lincolnesque story of a determined barefoot boy from the peanut fields of Plains, Georgia, working his way to a presidential nomination."[286] The 1980 film for Ronald Reagan tried to broaden his appeal, stressing his early ties with labor unions when he was president of the Screen Actors' Guild.[287]

The biographical films of Bush in 1988 and Clinton in 1992 spun tales of the American dream. Bush's film highlighted his World War II heroism, independent oil business in Texas, humble early years, and marriage to Barbara. Clinton's film, put together by television producers Harry Thomason and Linda Bloodworth-Thomason, told the familiar American story of a man's rise from humble origins to national service. Clinton's story stressed his mother's sacrifice after the death of his father, his popularity as a boy growing up in Hot Springs, and his growth as a young politician. The film also showed footage suggesting that the torch was handed from Kennedy to Clinton when the young Bill Clinton met his hero. As a member of a youth organization, Clinton had gone to the White House and shook President Kennedy's hand. The film showed the encounter in slow motion.

Films also are used to celebrate party greats from the past. In 1980 the Republicans showed a film tribute to their one-time presidential nominee Alfred M. Landon. In 1968 the Democrats

As a high school youth and member of Boys Nation, Bill Clinton shakes President John F. Kennedy's hand at the Rose Garden ceremony in 1963.

screened a film memorial to Robert Kennedy, followed by a mass singing of "The Battle Hymn of the Republic."

The great appeal of films is that they are virtual campaign commercials beamed free of charge across network television. Such films can reach more than fifty million Americans. Convention organizers are careful to plan the films for the prime-time viewing hours, often scheduling them just before the nominee's acceptance speech. In the days when there was gavel-to-gavel coverage of the conventions, networks were especially bound to carry the films. Because house lights were shut off during their showing, television was unable to cover other events from the floor. But since 1980 the networks have been more restrictive in their coverage. They balked, for example, at airing a film on Ronald Reagan prepared for the Republican convention in 1984. Ultimately, only CBS refused to carry it—a practice the network continued for both conventions in 1988. That year, the Republican film introducing Bush again caused problems. NBC, for example, aired the short, six- to seven-minute films introducing Michael Dukakis and Jesse Jackson at the Democratic convention but said that the Republican film—lasting twenty minutes—was too long. NBC agreed to show it only after Bush aides desperately trimmed it down to seven minutes and seven seconds.[288]

### Presidential Nomination

Recent reforms have helped to transform national conventions into mere ratifying assemblies. Since 1952 all candidates of the two major parties have been nominated on the first ballot. Candidates use the conventions as a form of extended advertising, a way to introduce themselves and their themes to millions watching the proceedings on television.

Several factors account for the decline of conventions as deliberative assemblies. The abolition of the unit rule and the two-thirds rule by the Democrats helped to reduce the protracted balloting that was common in that party. Even more important was the changing nature of the political landscape: the rise of primaries (which bind delegates to candidates before the convention), the increased cost of campaigning (which has added to the "winnowing" process of candidates because losers in early primaries quickly find themselves without contributors), and the televising of conventions (in which the appearance of party unity is of utmost concern).

The democratization of the selection process makes an old-style "brokered" convention, where party bosses choose the nominee behind closed doors, all but impossible. In recent years, political enthusiasts have developed a number of scenarios for drafts of candidates that would restore the suspense of old-time conventions. But for such an event to happen, the primaries and caucuses would have to end in stalemates—a highly unlikely occurrence.

To corral votes at the convention, campaign managers and strategists keep in close contact with the state delegations. Candidates have floor leaders and "whips" to direct voting on the floor and to deal with any problems that may arise among state delegations. In addition, "floaters" wander around the floor in search of trouble. Today, all such people have access to virtually instant communication with their candidate's command post via walkie-talkies, direct phone lines, television monitors, and the like. Floor leaders, whips, and floaters often wear specially colored clothing or caps so they can be spotted easily.[289] Candidates go to these lengths at the convention because they are eager to please the delegates and to ensure their support. In 1976

Carter met and shook hands with each of the more than 1,800 delegates pledged to him.[290]

Nominating speeches mark the beginning of the formal selection process. The convention of the National Republican Party (which met in Baltimore in December 1831, three months after the Anti-Masons held the first national party convention) is said to have had the first nominating speech.[291] In the early years, such speeches were short. In 1860 Abraham Lincoln's name was placed into nomination with only twenty-seven words; the name of his chief rival for the nomination, William H. Seward of New York, was put forward with only twenty-six.[292] Over the years, the length of nominating speeches increased. It also became the tradition to schedule a series of shorter seconding speeches after the nominating speech. The seconding speeches were interspersed with floor demonstrations to show candidate support.

Television, however, has reshaped nominating and seconding speeches, just as it has reshaped so much of the activity at national conventions. Anxious that coverage of the event be streamlined and entertaining to viewers, convention managers have encouraged a return to shorter nominating speeches and have seen to it that there are fewer seconding speeches (in 1936 Franklin Roosevelt was seconded fifty-six times), but things can still go awry. At the 1988 Democratic convention, Arkansas governor Bill Clinton was allotted fifteen minutes to nominate Michael Dukakis, and seconding speeches were eliminated altogether. To the dismay of Dukakis organizers, Clinton spoke for more than half an hour, despite constant signals to stop. Dukakis later joked that Clinton was available "to do the same fine job at the Republican convention as he did for me at the Democratic convention."[293]

The best nominating speeches underscore common themes that unify the party. Gov. Mario Cuomo of New York nominated Clinton at the 1992 Democratic convention in New York. Cuomo talked of the United States as a "family," a metaphor he used in his successful 1984 keynote address, and extolled Clinton's embrace of "the politics of inclusion, the solemn obligation to create opportunity for all our people. Not just the fit and the fortunate."[294]

Sometimes the persons who nominate candidates or second them are strategically chosen to display party unity. Thus New York governor Nelson Rockefeller—a longtime foe of Richard Nixon—was chosen to nominate Nixon in 1972. Similarly, after an unsuccessful effort by Harold Stassen to "dump" Vice President Nixon and replace him with Massachusetts governor Christian Herter in 1956, Nixon was renominated for vice president by Herter and seconded by Stassen. In 1968 Maryland governor Spiro Agnew was nominated for vice president by another frequently mentioned contender for the nomination, New York mayor John Lindsay.

Those who nominate the candidates also can be chosen for other strategic reasons. In 1988 George Bush was nominated by his daughter-in-law as part of an effort by the Republicans to stress the importance of family.

Once the nominating and seconding speeches are over, the roll call begins. When the name of each state is called, the chair of the state's delegation rises and gives the vote of that delegation.[295] At early conventions, the order of the roll call was determined partly by geographical location and partly by the order in which states had entered the Union. Since the latter part of the 1800s, however, both parties have called the roll in alphabetical order, except in 1972. That year, the Democrats determined the order of the roll call by lottery, thereby giving states that came early in the alphabet the chance to be called later to have the honor of pushing the nominee "over the top." Thus the roll call in 1972 started with California and ended with Oklahoma. Yet despite these good intentions, the change brought disaster because delegation chairs were not familiar with the new order and seldom were ready to announce their delegations' votes when called on.

In 1988 computer terminals were installed for each delegation at the Democratic convention, allowing virtually simultaneous electronic voting. Only the roll calls for the nomination of the presidential and vice-presidential candidates were done the "old fashioned way"—by voice vote in alphabetical order.[296] Still, Dukakis organizers tinkered with the process to ensure that California, the state where Dukakis clinched the nomination in its June 7 primary, also would officially clinch the nomination for him at the convention. To do this, California and several other strategically chosen state delegations passed when called

Cartoonist Rube Goldberg's view of convention speeches reflects the popular opinion.

on to vote. According to plan, the alphabetical rotation began a second time. California then voted and pushed Dukakis to victory.[297]

Before the post–World War II era, many ballots often were required to nominate candidates. Of the deadlocked Democratic conventions, those of 1860 and 1924 were the most famous. The 1860 convention in Charleston, South Carolina, was turbulent from the start because of major splits between northern and southern delegates. When the convention adopted a platform plank that took a northern "moderate" stance on slavery, forty-five delegates from nine states, including the majority of six southern delegations, walked out. The convention's chairman, Caleb Cushing of Massachusetts, then ruled that the nominees would require two-thirds of the total number of delegates originally allocated rather than two-thirds of the delegates still in attendance. As a result, it was almost impossible for any candidate to receive the nomination. After fifty-seven ballots, the convention disbanded and reconvened in Baltimore the next month. Stephen A. Douglas of Illinois then won the nomination on the second—or fifty-ninth—ballot.

The 1924 Democratic convention at New York's Madison Square Garden spawned 103 roll calls and crawled on for an unprecedented seventeen days. At that convention, the split was between urban and rural delegates. The leading contenders were New York governor Alfred E. Smith and William Gibbs McAdoo of California, but fourteen others also were on the ballot. With so many candidates, the two-thirds rule prevented anyone from being nominated. Balloting went on and on. During the 38th ballot, William Jennings Bryan, who was serving as a delegate from Florida, stood and spoke in opposition to Smith. Unlike his triumphant "Cross of Gold" speech twenty-eight years before, Bryan's last convention speech was drowned out in a chorus of boos from urban delegates.

As balloting continued, McAdoo consistently came out ahead. After the 82d ballot, a resolution was passed that released all delegates from their commitments to candidates. On the 86th ballot, Smith topped McAdoo, but without the two-thirds majority necessary for the nomination. It eventually became obvious that neither of the two major candidates could garner the support necessary for nomination. On the ninth day of balloting and the 103d ballot, the Democrats nominated John W. Davis of New York for president. That was the first Democratic convention to be broadcast live on radio, and listeners got an earful.

The most notable deadlock in the Republican Party came in 1880, when former president Ulysses S. Grant sought the nomination for a third term. After thirty-six ballots, James A. Garfield was nominated for president.

More recently, Thomas Dewey entered the 1940 Republican convention the clear front-runner, with Ohio senator Robert Taft close behind. But there was growing support at the convention for Wendell Willkie, a Wall Street lawyer and former Democrat. On the first ballot, Dewey received 360 votes against 189 for Taft, 105 for Willkie, and 76 for Sen. Arthur Vandenberg of Michigan. As the balloting proceeded, Willkie worked his way up. In the galleries there were chants of "We want Willkie," and an outpouring of public sentiment for Willkie came in the form of thousands of letters and telegrams urging his nomination. On the sixth ballot, Willkie won and the convention went wild. As Newsweek magazine reported: "Nothing exactly like it has ever happened before in American politics. Willkie had never held public office or even sought it. Virtually a neophyte in politics, he had entered no primaries, made no deals, organized no campaign."[298] The "amateur" movement had succeeded in nominating a candidate—although there was help from big-business backers who had very effectively publicized his campaign.

A genuine draft of a reluctant candidate at a convention is very rare. The first was New York governor Horatio Seymour who was nominated by the Democrats in 1868. Again, it was a convention with protracted balloting. The chief contenders for the nomination were President Andrew Johnson, George H. Pendleton of Ohio, and Gen. Winfield Scott Hancock of Pennsylvania. On the fourth ballot, North Carolina voted for Seymour, who promptly let it be known that he did not want the nomination: "I must not be nominated by this convention. I could not accept the nomination if tendered, which I do not expect."

The Johnson and Pendleton candidacies eventually collapsed, leaving General Hancock the front-runner. Opponents of Hancock introduced a new opponent, Sen. Thomas A. Hendricks of Indiana. Determined that an eastern candidate be nominated, the Ohio delegation voted for Seymour on the twenty-second ballot, and suddenly the tide turned toward him. Seymour rushed to the rostrum shouting, ". . . your candidate I cannot be!" Friends pulled him from the platform and hustled him to the Manhattan Club, where he later learned of his nomination. His response, with tears streaming down his face, was "Pity me! Pity me!"[299] Since then there have been two other drafts of reluctant candidates: the selection of Supreme Court Justice Charles Evans Hughes by the Republicans in 1916 and the selection of Illinois governor Adlai Stevenson by the Democrats in 1952.

In the age of brokered conventions, nominations were often decided by powerful party bosses in "smoke-filled rooms." Mark Hanna—who was instrumental in achieving the nomination of William McKinley by the Republicans in 1896—was one of the most famous of those bosses. The reforms instituted by the parties after 1968 were largely an effort to reduce the influence of such people and increase rank-and-file participation in a democratization of the selection process.

For many years, a good deal of convention time was taken up by the nomination of favorite-son candidates put forth by their own state's delegation. Such nominations were seldom taken seriously by the convention as a whole. Since 1972, the Democrats have required that every name placed into nomination have the written support of at least fifty delegates from three or more delegations and that no more than twenty signatures come from one delegation. That action streamlined the proceedings and effectively ended favorite-son nominations.[300]

In 1868 New York governor Horatio Seymour did not want the Democratic presidential nomination, declaring "Your candidate I cannot be!" He was drafted anyway.

Tradition used to dictate that the new party nominee stay away from the convention until the appointed hour for the acceptance speech. In 1992 two Hollywood producers scripted a dramatic departure from this norm. After his nomination at the New York City convention, Bill Clinton walked with his wife and daughter from Macy's department store, where he had attended a party with fellow Arkansans, to Madison Square Garden. The Clintons were cheered on the way to the convention site, where they briefly thanked enthusiastic delegates.

### Vice-Presidential Nominee and Party Chair

After the nomination of the presidential candidate, the convention chooses a vice-presidential candidate. Until relatively recently, presidential candidates had little success in selecting their running mate. The 1920 Republican convention ignored Warren G. Harding's choice of Sen. Irwin L. Lenroot and chose Massachusetts governor Calvin Coolidge instead. Sometimes presidential candidates (such as William McKinley and William Jennings Bryan in 1900) did not even bother to indicate a preference for their running mate. Such a choice had become the prerogative of the party leaders.

This practice changed in 1940 when Franklin Roosevelt threatened not to run unless the convention accepted his vice-presidential choice: Secretary of Agriculture Henry A. Wallace. The convention acquiesced, but Wallace was persuaded not to deliver an acceptance speech.[301]

The method of nominating the vice-presidential candidate mirrors the procedure for presidential nominations: nominating and seconding speeches, demonstrations, and balloting. In recent years, likely nominees have selected their running mates before the convention begins. In 1976 Reagan, who finished second to Ford in the primaries, chose Pennsylvania senator Richard Schweiker in a futile effort to expand his appeal. Democrats Mondale in 1984 and Dukakis in 1988 chose their running mates early to clear the convention agenda for shows of unity.

The actual choice of the vice-presidential candidate often is motivated by geographical considerations in an effort to "balance the ticket." For years, a balanced ticket was one that boasted an easterner and a midwesterner. More recently, the balance has shifted so that it is more often between a northerner and a southerner. Ideological considerations also play a part in the balance. Thus a liberal presidential candidate may be paired with a more conservative running mate to attract a broader base of votes. Finally, the choice of the vice-presidential candidate may be used to appease factions of the party who are unhappy with the presidential candidate. With the increasing number of vice presidents who go on to be president, greater attention is being given to the abilities of the person who is chosen (and more prominent figures are willing to accept the nomination).[302] In 1972 the Democrats' vice-presidential nominee, Missouri senator Thomas F. Eagleton, was forced to withdraw from the ticket when it was disclosed that he had been hospitalized for "nervous exhaustion and fatigue" three times during the 1960s. The Democratic National Committee subsequently chose R. Sargent Shriver of Maryland to replace him.

As for vice-presidential nomination "firsts," in 1980 Reagan gave brief but apparently serious consideration to nominating former president Ford as his vice president with expanded powers. But this plan for what observers termed a "co-presidency" fell apart, and Reagan went on to nominate his former rival, George Bush. In 1984 Democrat Geraldine Ferraro of New York became the first woman to be nominated for vice president.

Candidates seldom campaign openly for the vice-presidential nomination, but Jesse Jackson made it clear in the days before the 1988 Democratic convention that he wanted the number-two spot. Dukakis ultimately chose conservative Texas senator Lloyd Bentsen as his running mate in an effort to offer a Democratic ticket with a balance of ideology, experience, and regional background and to evoke images of the Massachusetts-Texas team of John Kennedy and Lyndon Johnson in 1960.

At the 1988 Republican convention, sixty-four-year-old Vice President Bush chose forty-one-year-old conservative Indiana senator Dan Quayle to bring the ticket an image of youth. Quayle was the first presidential or vice-presidential candidate to be born after World War II. Almost immediately, reports surfaced that Quayle's wealthy family had helped to secure him a spot in the National Guard in 1969 to prevent him from serving combat duty in Vietnam. The allegations embarrassed the Republicans, who took pride in asserting their patriotism and military service.

In 1992 Clinton selected Al Gore to be his running mate, which was considered unconventional because Clinton and Gore were from the neighboring states of Arkansas and Tennessee. But Gore helped Clinton to compensate for his lack of Washington and foreign policy experience, avoidance of military service during the Vietnam War, and low environmental credentials.

Bob Dole boldly chose former New York representative and HUD secretary Jack Kemp as his running mate in 1996. Kemp and Dole had long been antagonistic rivals—Kemp had endorsed Forbes earlier in the year. Yet the voluble and energetic Kemp was seen as broadening the ticket's appeal among younger conservatives and minority groups.

Once the candidates have been chosen, it is the prerogative of the presidential nominee to select the national party chair. The nominee does so by informing the national committee of the choice. The committee then convenes to elect the individual formally. This power to appoint carries over into the nominee's term in office if the candidate succeeds in winning the White House. Since the average tenure of party chairs is two years, presidential candidates have an opportunity to influence significantly the workings of their party.[303]

### Acceptance Speeches

In recent times, the acceptance speeches of the candidates for vice president and president have been the climax of the convention. Acceptance speeches were not a part of conventions, however, until 1932, when Franklin Roosevelt broke precedent. Eager to show that his physical disability would not hinder his activities, Roosevelt made a dramatic flight from Albany to Chicago to address the Democratic national convention that had nominated him for president. To mark a turning point for the nation in the grip of the Great Depression, Roosevelt triumphantly entered the convention hall as a band played "Happy Days Are Here Again." Noting that he was the first candidate ever to deliver an acceptance speech to a national convention, Roosevelt said: "I am here to thank you for the honor [of nominating me]. Let it be symbolic that in so doing, I broke traditions. Let it be from now on the task of our party to break foolish traditions."[304] In 1944 New York governor Thomas Dewey became the first presidential nominee to deliver an acceptance speech at a Republican convention.

The drafting of acceptance speeches is now a major endeavor, often involving the work of many writers. Strategic lines are inserted to satisfy specific voting blocs and interest groups, and the overall structure and delivery of the speech are designed to capture the interest of the millions of viewers. Even light touches are added by comedy writers. Two such writers, Jack Kaplan and John Barrett, sent Carter a memorandum suggesting an opening for his acceptance speech to the 1976 Democratic convention. Although their lines were not included in advance texts of the speech, Carter took their advice. Their memo, including parenthetical directions, suggested the following: "(After thank yous, Jimmy turns to the audience and says:) Hello, I'm Jimmy Carter. (Laugh) And I'm running for president of the United States. (Applause)." Carter's use of his line from the days when he was an unknown candidate became one of the most famous passages in his acceptance speech.[305]

### Television and Other Press Coverage

National party conventions are media events par excellence. The most powerful leaders of a political party and hundreds of other notables are all to be found in one spot—a flamboyant setting with cheering crowds and mob demonstrations, passionate speakers and poignant appearances by party elders, and limitless opportunities for on-the-spot interviews and human-interest stories. Of course, there are times when conventions are hard on both "the cerebral centers and the *gluteus maximus*,"[306] as H. L. Mencken said. But, on the whole, conventions are the breeding ground of drama, and drama is the grist for news.

The convention system originated in an age before the telegraph or telephone, when newspapers were highly partisan mouthpieces of political parties. Communication and transportation were slow, so conventions took place with relative anonymity. Today, all that has changed. Thousands of reporters attend conventions, and millions of Americans are privy to the action via television and radio.

The 1924 conventions were the first to be broadcast on the radio. The 1940 Republican convention was televised on an experimental basis, but it was seen by only a tiny audience. Likewise, the televised 1948 Democratic convention reached an audience of only about 400,000 along the eastern seaboard. The Democrats also used television that year so that an overflow crowd of some 6,000 could watch the proceedings in an auditorium adjacent to the convention hall.[307]

The advent of this new age has had a tremendous effect on national party conventions. Television brought the 1952 conventions—the first to be nationally televised—into the living rooms of an estimated seventy million Americans. All three networks carried gavel-to-gavel coverage of the conventions themselves, as well as considerable coverage of Credentials Committee hearings that took place before the conventions convened and while they were in recess.[308] It soon became clear that under the close scrutiny of the television eye, the use of "unfair" tactics against the opposition could have disastrous consequences.

Credentials fights between the Taft and Eisenhower forces at the Republican convention were played out for all the world to see. Eisenhower forces introduced their now-famous "Fair Play" amendment and won their fight after emotional "Thou shalt not steal" speeches by Eisenhower's floor leaders. As ABC commentator Elmer Davis said, it was "no longer possible to commit grand larceny in broad daylight."[309] Steamroller tactics such as blatantly unfair rulings by the convention chair, or forced recesses during roll calls to deflate enthusiasm for a candidate or mobilize opposition support, are largely things of the past.

The 1952 conventions were the first to be broadcast to a coast-to-coast television audience. Republican nominees Dwight D. Eisenhower and Richard Nixon were seen by approximately seventy million television viewers.

Since the key to electronic media is "image," conventions are now choreographed for television. Convention planners are careful to prevent boring lulls in the action, to keep potentially divisive rules or platform fights out of prime-time viewing hours, and to orchestrate "spontaneous" demonstrations and telegenic events such as the release of hundreds of colorful balloons on the convention floor. Consultants coach speakers on makeup, wardrobe, and how to read the TelePrompTer. The party leader warns state delegations about how to act. Even the convention chair is coached on how many times to bang the gavel. Eric Lieber, a television consultant for the Democrats in 1976, said that gavel banging was a sign of disorder. Subsequently, use of the gavel was restricted to three times a session—regardless of what was happening on the floor.[310] Individual speakers often are astute as well. When Mary Anne Krupsak, the lieutenant governor of New York, mounted the podium to give a five-minute speech to the Democrats in 1976—an opportunity often taken to cut away for commercials or commentary—the networks stayed with her because she used a sign-language interpreter (now a standard procedure).[311]

But attempts at image control do not always succeed. The 1968 Chicago convention was a disaster for the Democrats. Bloody confrontations between antiwar demonstrators and helmeted police outside the hall and anger and divisiveness among participants inside the hall set the tone for television coverage. In 1972 George McGovern, the Democratic nominee for president, had the ignominious distinction of delivering his acceptance speech at almost three o'clock in the morning (eastern standard time) because of a long string of symbolic vice-presidential nominations brought about by the "open politics" of the new Democratic Party rules. On the first day of their 1976 convention in New York's Madison Square Garden, Democrats were aghast to see television cameras pointing to some three thousand empty seats. Harried convention aides were instructed to hand out credentials passes along Seventh Avenue to anyone who walked by.

The media age has changed conventions substantively as well. Lengthy Credentials and Rules Committee sessions now precede the opening of the convention to cut down on the delays while the convention awaits their reports. The Democrats have passed rules that effectively eliminate lengthy favorite-son nominations. Limits have been set on the number and length of seconding speeches. Roll calls have been streamlined, and the old practice of state chairs delivering a short speech in behalf of their state and candidate is gone.[312]

Those covering the convention also are concerned with image. Officials of the television networks are anxious about winning higher ratings than their competitors, and they assign their most important reporters to cover the event. Anchors and analysts cover the convention from overhead booths, while scores of reporters roam the floor in search of fast-breaking stories. The networks also hire "spotters" to scan the floor for possibly interesting interviews. So that the anchor can talk intelligently about everything that is going on at the convention at any given time, "gophers" scramble through reference books or call researchers for background about persons the camera might focus on, and researchers stand by to explain what is happening on the podium or on the floor.[313]

Television often produces images just as misleading as those the media consultants conjure up for the political parties. In particular, television cultivates an illusion of action to maintain viewer interest. This is accomplished by covering at the same time activities taking place at various locations and by switching cameras back and forth between events. As a result, television sometimes exaggerates or creates a false sense of confusion and disorder at conventions.[314] As Theodore H. White observed, television "displays events, action, motion, arrival, departure; it cannot show thought, silence, mood or decision. And so [television catches] the carnival outer husk of the convention in all its pageantry. . . ."[315]

Major networks spend enormous sums of money on coverage of national party conventions. In 1980 one network executive indicated that such coverage cost approximately $10 million.[316] Perhaps that is why since 1980 television networks have pulled away from gavel-to-gavel coverage of conventions. In 1996 the three major networks scheduled live coverage for only one to two prime-time hours a day. After the Republican convention, where everything—including the vice-presidential choice—was wrapped up before the convention even convened, some commentators questioned the utility of even that much live coverage.[317]

Although the networks cut back their coverage of conventions from 1988 to 1996, overall coverage expanded. Cable television stations, syndicated talk shows, and radio programs all increased their coverage. By appearing on broadcast outlets that "narrowcast" news to specific social and demographic groups, the nominees could tailor their messages for those groups. In addition, outlets such as MTV and *Comedy Central* offered untraditional coverage.

Whatever the format, both parties treat their conventions as four-day television commercials. Recognizing this, networks frequently cut away from the proceedings themselves to offer commentary or interviews. In 1988 Republican efforts to shape the television image of the convention were thwarted by network coverage that was dominated by the vice-presidential selection process. Coverage of the first two days centered on speculation over who would be selected. Coverage of the last two days centered on controversy surrounding the choice of the young Indiana senator Dan Quayle as George Bush's running mate.[318]

To attract larger audiences, the Democrats considered shifting their 1996 convention to include the weekend. Because weekday audiences for the network coverage have steadily declined, it was thought that a weekend extravaganza with a different format might draw a broader—and more alert—audience. They abandoned the idea, however.

### Other Functions of National Party Conventions

In serving as a forum for officially selecting candidates and determining party policy and rules, national party conventions help to make the actions of the party legitimate. Furthermore, because conventions bring together all factions of the party, they serve as a place for bargaining and compromise.[319]

The ultimate aim of a national convention is to foster party unity by closing ranks behind the nominee—even though divisiveness before the nomination may have been bitter. This process of consensus-building is aided by the fact that most factions are, in the end, loyal to the party. Moreover, bitterness is diffused because any given group has several opportunities to score success. If it is unsuccessful in nominating a presidential candidate, it may succeed in winning a key platform plank or

gaining a favorable vice-presidential nominee. Furthermore, there always is the possibility of future victories if its party wins the general election campaign, such as political appointments and the passage of legislation that the group espouses.

On a more basic level, the elaborate populist rituals offered by conventions legitimize the actual selection process. They aim toward conciliation and unity while allowing for the expression of disparate viewpoints. Particularly because today's conventions tend merely to ratify the choice voters expressed in the primaries, they serve as a means of wedding the candidate and the party and provide a basis for mass support of the ticket during the general election campaign.

Ideally, the convention introduces the ticket to the public so positively that voters from both parties will seriously consider supporting it. Polls showed that Clinton in 1992, Reagan in 1980, Carter in 1976 and 1980, and Nixon in 1968 got double-digit "bounces" in support from convention coverage. The average bounce of all conventions from 1964 to 1988 was 6.3 points, but Republican bounces (7.9 points) were better than the Democratic ones (4.8 points). The biggest bounce can come from a convention in which warring factions come together as a unified party for the fall campaign. The key for the candidates is to follow up the convention with events that reinforce whatever positive impressions the convention has produced. The convention bounce is not always temporary, but it can be if the convention message is not reinforced. In 1988, for example, Dukakis gained 5.9 percentage points in opinion polls, but then he suspended his public campaign while Republican Bush attacked him.[320]

### Death or Resignation of the Convention Nominee

If a nominee dies or resigns from the ticket before election day, Democratic and Republican rules call for the national party committee to meet and choose a replacement. Thus in 1972 the Democratic National Committee chose Sargent Shriver as the party's vice-presidential nominee when Thomas Eagleton resigned from the ticket.

## PROPOSALS TO REFORM THE NOMINATING PROCESS

Does the existing nominating process lead to the selection of the "best" candidates—those who are most qualified or who are most likely to win in the general election? Does it weaken the power of political parties? Does it give too much influence to particular states or regions of the country? Is it "deliberative" enough? Is it responsive to voter preferences? Is it too long? Too fragmented? Too oriented to the media?

These are some of the questions raised by observers of the nominating process. Many are unhappy with the current system and have suggested various changes, depending on what they think the process should achieve.[321]

The post-1968 reforms served to open the system, making it more responsive to the rank and file and less responsive to party elites. For many, this was good. Indeed, reformers wanted to produce a more participatory system. But others argue that the reforms went too far. The antireform group wants to increase the influence and involvement of party elites in the selection process. Such critics argue that the post-1968 reforms explicitly weakened the parties. Nonetheless, as political scientist Michael Nelson has pointed out, the parties were already in a state of decline in the 1950s and 1960s. Indeed, he has argued that the decline has been halted, and in many cases reversed, since the mid-1970s—partly by the reforms themselves because they helped the parties adapt "to the changed social and political environment that underlay their decline."[322]

Those who want to strengthen the power of party elites adhere to an "organizational" (or "party regular") model of presidential selection. Those favoring a more open system adhere to a "participatory" (or "reform") model.[323] There are, of course, a range of positions between the two extremes. Most proposals to increase the power of party elites have been far from radical. Usually such proposals have called for increased participation by party officials at the national convention through the reservation of delegate slots for them and for increased power of state parties to design their delegate selection systems.[324] Both of these proposals were incorporated in the recommendations of the Democratic Party's Hunt Commission. *(See "The Hunt Commission," p. 30.)* More radical proposals, such as the suggestion that Congress require that nominating conventions consist only of party leaders and elected officials (with the total elimination of primaries) are seldom taken seriously. As political scientist Thomas E. Mann has written, most proposals "move in the direction of increasing or channeling, not eliminating, participation by rank-and-file party identifiers."[325]

## The National Primary

If democracy on a small scale is good, then democracy on a large scale is even better. So goes the logic of the frequent call to expand the scope of nomination-preference voting from the state to the national level.

A national primary was proposed in Congress as early as 1911, quickly winning the endorsement of President Woodrow Wilson.[326] Since then, numerous versions of such a system have been presented. One of the best known of these would allow each party a single national primary on a designated day. To appear on the ballot, each candidate would have to file a petition containing signatures equivalent to 1 percent of the votes cast in the previous presidential election, or more than one million names based on the 1992 election. This primary (with a runoff election, if necessary) would determine the presidential nominee, although a convention could still be held to choose a vice-presidential nominee, adopt a platform, and conduct other party business. A variation would have the national primary select two-thirds of the delegates to a national convention. The other third would consist of party elites. When a national primary was not decisive, this system would allow for a deliberative convention rather than a runoff election.[327]

Another proposal would create a national convention to develop a party platform and select several candidates who would later compete in a national primary. This proposal aims to combine the best of elite and populist approaches. Elite convention delegates, dominated by professional politicians at the national, state, and local levels, would select candidates based on governmental abilities. Party members would then have a chance to pass judgment on the elites' suggestions.[328]

Those who support a national primary argue that it would simplify the process by having one uniform system of candidate selection. They further argue that it would make the system more democratic: votes would count equally, the candidate would be representative of the rank and file, and voter participation might even increase. In the process, the campaign season would be shortened, particular states would no longer be accorded special weight, issues of national concern would be addressed, and the effect of the media's interpretation of early primaries and caucuses would be eliminated.[329]

Opponents argue that a national primary would severely weaken—if not destroy—the party system and would all but eliminate grassroots campaigning. They further argue that it would increase candidates' use of the media and allow for no "winnowing" of candidates through the campaign season.[330] Finally, they contend that the system would be biased against little-known candidates (who, in the existing system, can make a name for themselves in the early primaries) and could lead to the selection of a candidate with ephemeral or even demogogic appeal. This would be so, they argue, since candidates would not have to survive a string of contests and continually prove themselves over a long primary season.[331]

A change to a national primary would itself be quite complicated. It would require, at the least, national legislation, and possibly even a constitutional amendment. There is no doubt that it would be bitterly contested by many factions including party regulars and those who favor a states' rights approach to the election process.[332]

## The Regional Primary

Another frequently mentioned suggestion to reform the nominating process is the idea of regional primaries. Proposals for such a system were introduced by two men no longer in the Senate, Democrat Walter Mondale of Minnesota and Republican Bob Packwood of Oregon. Under both proposals, the country would be divided into regions (six in Mondale's proposal; five in Packwood's). Each state within that region would be required to hold its primary or caucuses on the date assigned that region. These dates would fall at intervals of two weeks (Mondale) or one month (Packwood). The order of the regional primaries would be chosen by lot, and therefore the order would change from one election year to the next.[333] Under both plans, state primaries would be optional. Others have suggested that the primaries be mandatory.[334] Such primaries would be used to select delegates to a national nominating convention.

The regional primary plan is an attempt to correct a system that critics say is too fragmented. By requiring that all states within a particular region hold their primary on a set day, the undue influence of individual states that hold early primaries (such as New Hampshire) would be eliminated. That advantage would be transferred to a region as a whole, but the shifting order of the primaries would prevent any one region from enjoying an advantage for long. As political scientists William Crotty and John S. Jackson III have written, such plans attempt "to resolve some of the difficulties of the current system of scattered primaries, while retaining the strengths both of the party system and of reform era democratization."[335]

Critics say that regional primaries would severely weaken the role of the states in the presidential selection process. Not only would the process be nationalized under a uniform system, but candidates would focus less attention on the needs of individual states. In short, they see such plans as merely a modified version of national primary plans. Like the national primary, they say, regional primaries would undermine the need for grassroots campaigning, be biased against obscure candidates, and increase the candidates' use of media. In 1988 Super Tuesday served as a de facto regional primary for the South. A variant of the regional primary plan, introduced by Arizona representative Mo Udall, would require states that hold primaries to do so on one of four dates. Under this plan, the grouping of states would be voluntarily chosen rather than set by region.[336]

As reformers continually discover, proposals for change often bring unanticipated consequences. Thus, it is difficult to say with full assurance what would happen if any of the reform proposals were instituted. Michael Nelson, for one, has suggested that we stick with our current system. Even though strong cases can be made for certain reforms, he has argued that continued tampering with the process lends instability to the system since continued rules rewriting is not only distracting, but also subversive of the system's legitimacy.[337]

## General Election Campaign

Once they have won their party's nomination, presidential candidates focus their attention on winning the general election. They must choose the strategy they think will propel them to victory and interact with a complex political environment that includes scrutinizing news media, the opposition party, and interest groups. Not least among their problems is that of organizing their own staffs—pollsters, media consultants, and other senior advisers—and coordinating their campaign activities with those of the state and national organizations of their own party.

### TYPES OF STRATEGY

Presidential politics in the United States is like a game. And as in all games, its strategies are endlessly debated and studied. Despite all the debates, however, candidates often base their strategies on the lessons learned during the most recent campaigns.

The whole process of making strategy begins with the candi-

date's personal characteristics. Other factors include the early standing of the candidate in the polls, the source of the candidate's core support (for example, regional or national, partisan or personal, ideological or consensual), the strength of the parties, the mood of the electorate, the expected voter turnout, and the chances of winning the election in November.[338]

Most strategies also entail geographic considerations. Democratic candidates usually are strongest in large industrial states; Republicans, in the Midwest and western states. Until recently, the South was a Democratic stronghold, but conservatives there increasingly have been so attracted to Republicans in presidential elections that pundits have pronounced the region a "lock" for the GOP. (See Figure 1-4, p. 99.)

To appeal to a large geographic constituency, most tickets include presidential and vice-presidential candidates from different parts of the country—one element of "ticket balancing" (which also includes such considerations as ideology). (See "The Vice-Presidential Campaign," p. 109.) When Walter Mondale chose Geraldine Ferraro as his running mate in 1984, Ronald Reagan's strategist, Lee Atwater, was elated. He predicted that the Democrats' choice of a "North-North" ticket would give the South to the Republicans and guarantee victory for Reagan.[339] In 1992 Bill Clinton of Arkansas formed a "South-South" ticket by choosing Al Gore of Tennessee as his running mate. It became the first successful all-southern ticket since Andrew Jackson (Tennessee) and John C. Calhoun (South Carolina) in 1828.

Regional strength does not tell all, however. Since states do not count equally in the electoral college, candidates often concentrate their efforts on certain key states with large electoral vote counts. Indeed, after the 1990 census the electoral votes of twelve states—California, New York, Texas, Pennsylvania, Illinois, Ohio, Florida, Michigan, New Jersey, North Carolina, Massachusetts, and either Georgia, Virginia, or Indiana—were enough to secure victory in the general election. With those victories, votes in the thirty-eight other states would not matter.

To concentrate time and attention on all the states can be a waste of resources. Richard Nixon promised to visit each of the fifty states when he ran for president in 1960, but he later regretted that decision when he was forced to waste valuable time visiting states with almost no influence, while his rival, John Kennedy, was targeting key states. This point was driven home on the last weekend before the election when Nixon had to fly to Alaska to fulfill his promise, while Kennedy visited important northeastern states including New York, New Jersey, and Massachusetts. When Nixon ran again in 1968 he was careful to target particular states. For example, he did not visit Kansas that year. As Robert Ellsworth, a Republican campaign aide from that state, said: "If you have to worry about Kansas, you don't have a campaign anyway."[340]

Aside from deciding what kind of geographic strategy to pursue, candidates are faced with other strategic choices. Should they stress their party affiliation or their individual merit?

FIGURE 1-4  Party Strength in Presidential Elections, by State, 1960–1996, and Electoral Votes, 1996

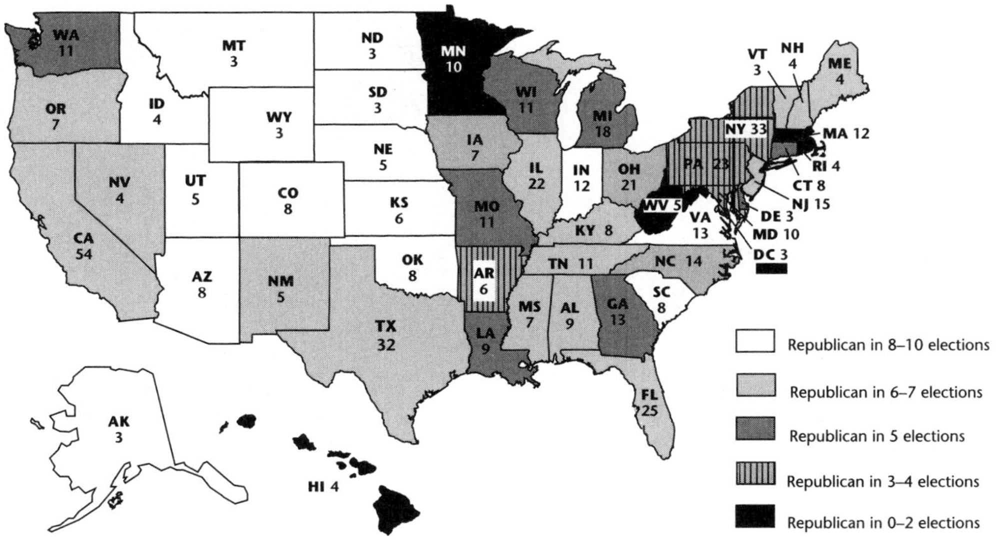

Source: *Presidential Elections, 1789–1992* (Washington, D.C.: Congressional Quarterly, 1995); Rhodes Cook, "Clinton's Easy Second-Term Win Riddles GOP Electoral Map," *Congressional Quarterly Weekly Report,* November 9, 1996, 3190.
Note: Of the ten presidential elections from 1960 to 1996, the Republican Party has won five (1968, 1972, 1980, 1984, and 1988), the Democratic Party has won five (1960, 1964, 1976, 1992, and 1996). In 1968 the American Independent Party carried Alabama, Georgia, Louisiana, and Mississippi. Alaska and Hawaii first voted for president in 1960; the District of Columbia in 1964.

Should they run an ideological campaign or emphasize conciliation and consensus? Should they concentrate on style or on substance?

Since the New Deal, the Democrats consistently have had more registered voters than the Republicans. As a result, it is more advantageous for the Democrats to follow a strictly partisan campaign than it is for the Republicans. It also behooves the Democrats to encourage a large voter turnout. This can be done either through "neutral" efforts stressing the civic obligation to vote, or through more specific efforts, such as providing baby sitters and transportation to the polls.[341] Efforts of both types appear to have secured victory for Kennedy in 1960.[342] In recent years, Democrats have appeared nervous about expanding the pool of voters. Candidates Walter Mondale and Michael Dukakis rejected proposals to use party funds for registration drives in core constituency areas because they were afraid, critics said, of alienating moderate voters.

Republicans can be hurt by a large voter turnout or by running an intensely partisan campaign. While maintaining their base of support, they also must reach out to independents and Democrats with weak party ties.[343] To do this, Republican candidates sometimes de-emphasize their party. In 1976 Gerald Ford's official campaign poster featured his picture but gave no indication of his party affiliation—something that might have reminded voters of the Watergate debacle that drove Richard Nixon from office in 1974.[344] Likewise, Nixon's campaign organization in 1972—the Committee to Re-elect the President—was a blatant attempt to bypass the Republican Party. Earlier, the nomination of the World War II hero, Gen. Dwight Eisenhower, had successfully de-emphasized partisanship.

Despite a decline in importance, party labels are still important cues to voters. Nelson Polsby and Aaron Wildavsky have argued that even independents have party preferences: "About two-thirds of all independents have leanings; scratch an independent and underneath you are likely to find an almost-Republican or a near-Democrat, and those who are left are least likely to turn out."[345]

Unlike partisan campaigns, which stress party loyalty, ideological campaigns stress a strict adherence to a particular political ideology. In so doing, ideological campaigns can alienate those who are opposed to the ideological stance of the candidate (including members of the candidate's own party). This alienation solidifies the opposition, prompts defection, and decreases the likelihood of broad-based support.[346]

Yet another strategy is a "consensual" campaign, which makes broad appeals beyond the confines of either partisanship or ideology. Republican Barry Goldwater in 1964 and Democrat George McGovern in 1972 headed two ideological campaigns that failed. Their opponents, Lyndon Johnson and Nixon, respectively, both waged successful consensual campaigns. George Bush's failed 1992 reelection bid suffered when the Republican convention in Houston struck many observers as extreme— particularly in its antiabortion platform plank and the strident attacks on liberals by speakers from the religious right.

Bill Clinton, in contrast, stressed themes in 1992 designed to appeal to moderate Republicans as well as traditional Democrats. His self-designation as a "new Democrat" was calculated to distance himself from the more ideological candidates of the past. As the candidate with the most delegates, Clinton had controlled the writing of the platform adopted at the Democratic

Unlike most candidates, Adlai Stevenson crafted new speeches for every occasion—a tactic that ultimately hurt him. By not repeating a well-worn text, his delivery suffered, and he was accused of speaking over people's heads.

convention. It stated: "We reject both the do-nothing government of the last twelve years and the big government theory that says we can hamstring business and tax and spend our way to prosperity." Instead the platform offered "a third way" stressing economic growth, family vitality, personal responsibility, and law and order—all themes espoused by Republican candidates. Clinton reprised this strategy of occupying the center of the political spectrum in his successful 1996 campaign.

Candidates also must decide how specific they will be on the issues. Fearful of antagonizing portions of the electorate, many candidates couch their positions in generalities. The same phrases are repeated in speech after speech, and candidates are careful to tell their audiences what they want to hear. A few candidates, such as Adlai Stevenson in 1952, took pride in crafting new speeches for every occasion, but this is not the norm. In fact, the tactic ultimately hurt Stevenson. Since he was not repeating a well-worn text, his delivery suffered. Furthermore, Stevenson often was accused of speaking "over people's heads" and of not being sure that his speeches were tailored to his audiences.[347]

In 1984 Democrat Walter Mondale tried to appear honest and straightforward by taking specific stands on controversial issues. He promised, for example, to raise taxes. He also lost. Most candidates from both parties are cautious and repetitive. They strive for short "extractables" or "sound-bites" that can be lifted from their speeches and included in fifteen- or thirty-second segments on the evening news. Thus Reagan saying "There you go again!" to Carter in 1980 and Clinton's repetition of rhetoric about "change" in 1992 and "bridge to the twenty-first century" in 1996 were more memorable than the substance that surrounded those lines.

## ADVANTAGES AND DISADVANTAGES OF INCUMBENCY

Deciding whether to participate in televised debates is but one of many tactical decisions facing candidates. Candidates also must decide whether potential voters should be targeted primarily through the mass media, personal campaigning, party organization, or independent political action committees. Techniques used through these various avenues include spot commercials on television, door-to-door canvassing, direct mail, and endorsements by such groups as the American Association of Retired Persons that can turn out a large number of votes.[348]

Presidential incumbents have access to a broader set of strategic options than their opponents, many of which stem from the simple fact that they already are in an office that lends them credibility, respect, and visibility. More important, they are in a position to influence events and benefit key constituencies. In adopting the so-called Rose Garden strategy, presidents avoid active campaigning, make official appearances in carefully controlled settings (such as greeting heads of state and signing legislation), and act "presidential" by wrapping themselves in the symbols and backdrop of the office. This strategy isolates presidents from the press (while not diminishing their visibility), reduces the likelihood of their committing a costly blunder, saves money, and appears to put the president above petty politics. Such a strategy was used most effectively by Nixon in 1972 and by Reagan in 1984.[349]

Both the Rose Garden strategy and incumbency itself can have their drawbacks, however. Presidents are blamed for failures as well as remembered for successes. Even events over which presidents have little control may be blamed on them. Oil shortages, regional conflicts abroad, and adverse economic con-

Behind in the polls, President Gerald R. Ford chose a campaign strategy that included televised debates with former Georgia governor Jimmy Carter.

ditions may arise through no particular fault of the incumbent president. Indeed, adopting a Rose Garden strategy in times of trouble can lead to the accusation that the president is hiding in the White House rather than attending to official duties. Carter was accused of this in 1980, when there was widespread public displeasure over his handling of the Iranian hostage crisis and he was facing a serious challenge for his own party's presidential nomination from Sen. Edward Kennedy of Massachusetts.

In 1976 Ford's Rose Garden strategy included challenging his opponent, Carter, to a series of televised debates. The plan was suggested in a memorandum from two White House staffers to Richard B. Cheney, Ford's White House chief of staff, in June of that year.[350] As Cheney later observed, the debate option was "part of a 'no campaign' campaign strategy," with the debates serving as "a means of deemphasizing traditional campaigning, maximizing the advantages of incumbency, and forcing Governor Carter to deal substantively with the issues."[351] Journalist Martin Schram noted that the debates also were "a chance for the President to dispel the notions that he was not intelligent and not capable of running the country. . . . The debates would be a chance for the President to demonstrate competence and poise."[352]

Ford chose the debate strategy largely because he was very far behind in the polls. He generally was perceived to be poor on the stump but well prepared for debates. Ford and his advisers calculated that he had little to lose and much to gain in a debate. There had been no debates of the kind since 1960, and they were bound to be a decisive element in the campaign.

As a rule, however, incumbents stand more to lose than their opponents in face-to-face debates. Such debates allow opponents to prove their mettle. They are put on an equal footing with the president and given the opportunity to demonstrate

that they too can deal with substantive issues. Because the incumbents are tied to their records and their policies, they easily are placed on the defensive.

President Bush obviously was reluctant to debate Clinton and Ross Perot in 1992. When a heckler dressed as a chicken started to attend Bush rallies, Bush finally agreed to "get it on" with his foes. By most accounts, Bush performed poorly in the debates. His misunderstanding of a question about the recession reinforced his image of being out of touch. Clinton and Perot, meanwhile, were comfortable with the informal debate formats and performed well.

Once the general election campaign is under way, the two major party nominees are in many ways equals. For example, since 1976 they have received identical grants from the federal government to finance their campaigns. The media dispatch teams to cover the two candidates on a roughly equal basis. Even when third party or independent candidates—such as George Wallace in 1968, John Anderson in 1980, or Perot in 1992—run for the presidency, the spotlight usually stays trained on the Democratic and Republican nominees.

When a sitting president is running for reelection, however, the balance of power can tilt. The incumbent not only already has the stature of the presidency but is able to influence media coverage with official presidential actions and to use pork-barrel politics to appeal to specific constituencies. Announcements of favorable government statistics on the economy or of well-timed plans for domestic initiatives also can help the incumbent, and, not least, the president benefits from the public's reluctance to reject a tested national leader for an unknown quantity.

The emotional bond of the people with the president is an important, if unquantifiable, factor in a president's reelection advantages. Perhaps the greatest examples in recent years are Lyndon Johnson's 1964 reelection, which benefited from the nation's deep desire for continuity in the wake of the assassination of President Kennedy, and President Reagan's evocation of patriotic themes in his 1984 campaign for reelection.

Managing foreign relations probably provides the greatest opportunity for an incumbent to enhance the chances for reelection. In 1972 President Nixon orchestrated a number of major foreign policy initiatives that guaranteed him continued media coverage. Indeed, he co-opted many Democratic calls for greater efforts to negotiate solutions to difficult world problems. He visited both the Soviet Union and the People's Republic of China and oversaw the negotiation of a cease-fire treaty in the long and bitter Vietnam War. The China trip was especially dramatic: it was the first time a U.S. president had visited that nation since before the 1949 revolution.

As the campaign neared its end, the Nixon administration expressed greater confidence about the prospects of a settlement of the Vietnam War. In late October, Secretary of State Henry Kissinger announced that "peace is at hand." The public pronouncements on Vietnam undercut the antiwar campaign of Nixon's Democratic rival, Sen. McGovern of South Dakota.

Even foreign policy difficulties can be an advantage for an incumbent. Vice President Hubert Humphrey's 1968 campaign got a late boost when President Lyndon Johnson announced a halt in bombing of Vietnam. Initially at least, Carter got a temporary boost from the November 1979 Soviet invasion of Afghanistan and the continued holding of U.S. citizens as hostages in Iran. After the tragic truck-bombing of U.S. Marine barracks in Lebanon in 1983—a policy disaster since Reagan had been explicitly warned about the dangers of such an attack—Reagan benefited politically from the nation's willingness to "rally 'round the flag." Two days after the Lebanon attack, Reagan stirred up more feelings of patriotism with the invasion of the tiny Caribbean island of Grenada.

In times of economic or foreign policy crisis, the president's prominence also can have a negative effect on the campaign. President Carter's bid for reelection in 1980 was doomed by "stagflation"—a combination of high unemployment and high inflation rates—and Iran's refusal to release U.S. citizens being held as hostages in Iran. Carter's credibility on foreign policy was damaged by his apparent surprise at the Soviet invasion of Afghanistan and his retaliatory actions against the Soviets (an embargo of grain sales to the Soviets and a U.S. boycott of the 1980 Moscow Olympics), which were resented by many groups.

Despite his reputation as a foreign policy expert, President Bush struggled in his 1992 reelection campaign. Bush's leadership in the United States–led victory in the Persian Gulf War actually undermined his campaign because the aftermath of the war did not produce the "new world order" that Bush had promised. Bush's 1992 visit to Japan also undermined his foreign affairs mystique because he appeared to be begging his hosts for trade concessions.

On the economic front, most first-term presidents seem intent on managing the economy so that the inevitable cyclical slump occurs early in the administration. The hope is that by the time the reelection campaign begins, the economy will have rebounded and voters will have gained confidence in the administration's economic management. President Reagan presided over the highest unemployment rate since the Great Depression early in his first term, but by the time he sought reelection in 1984 both the unemployment and inflation rates had declined significantly. President Bush presided over economic recovery during his 1992 reelection effort, but persistent budget deficits and low job growth undermined his claims of prosperity. With continued high levels of unemployment, the majority of Americans still believed the economy was getting worse and were pessimistic about the future.[353] In contrast, Clinton's 1996 reelection effort was boosted by a slowly growing economy with low inflation and unemployment.

As the defeats of Presidents Ford, Carter, and Bush demonstrate, the incumbent's advantages do not guarantee victory. The existence of negative symbolic issues—such as Ford's pardon of the disgraced president Nixon and Carter's handling of economic and foreign policy crises—can doom an incumbent. Factors such as heavy campaign expenditures by political opponents—also one of Carter's problems in 1980—can badly damage the sitting president. Both Ford and Carter suffered from bitter struggles for their party nominations.

## ROLE OF THE CAMPAIGN STAFF AND ADVISERS

Presidential elections in the media age are elaborate, multimillion-dollar operations. Within these operations, important tactical decisions are made by the professional campaign consultants—a complex organization of pollsters, media producers, accountants, advertising executives, and other advisers. Consultants usually are engaged in highly specialized tasks such as public opinion sampling, data processing, policy formulation, fund raising, and the production of television commercials. The rise of professional campaign consultants is, in part, an attempt to provide the expertise needed (or perceived to be needed) to run the increasingly complex modern election. Such consultants also help to fill the void left by the now weaker party organizations that once coordinated campaigns.[354]

### Pollsters

Candidates always have relied on advisers to guide them through the campaign. But technological advances—most notably, in telecommunications and information management—have spawned a new breed of consultants. Among them, pollsters have risen to the top of presidential campaigns because of their ability to gather and decipher strategic information.

Historians disagree about the first use of polls in American politics. Some cite the election of 1908 when the *Literary Digest* started surveying its readers. Others argue that formal polling did not begin until the 1930s, when advances in communications and sampling techniques made polls more reliable. But the beginning of formal surveys really dates back more than a century and a half. In 1824, for example, the *Harrisburg Pennsylvanian* published a survey of the presidential preferences of the voters of Wilmington, Delaware.[355] Newspaper surveys that year were unsophisticated and were published primarily as a form of "entertainment."

What now would be called "straw polls" also were conducted in 1824. In view of the dramatic expansion of suffrage and the fall of the King Caucus system of presidential nominations, politicians needed reliable ways to measure public sentiment and how it would affect the presidential race. At state conventions, meetings of militia, grand juries, holiday celebrations, and tax gatherings, participants were asked to express their preferences for candidates, and newspapers kept regular tallies of the opinion samplings. Although these straw polls were flawed, like modern polls they attempted to quantify sentiment so that campaign operatives and ordinary citizens could make better political decisions.

Today, polls tell the candidates where their bases of support lie, what the electorate thinks of them personally, and what issues are important to the electorate.[356] Thus polls can be used by candidates to decide whether or not to run, to improve name recognition and image, to target opposition weakness, to formulate mass media advertising, to allocate resources, and to build coalitions.[357] Candidates also find polls helpful in deciding how to use the media to cultivate their images and to target specific voting blocs.

Pollster Louis Harris maintains that the use of polls can change the outcome of an election by as much as 4 percent if candidates use the data to target their resources most efficiently.[358] Since 1960, when John Kennedy hired Harris, every presidential candidate has made extensive use of polls. Presidents also have kept close tabs on survey data once they are in office. For example, Jimmy Carter's close association with pollster Patrick Caddell strongly influenced his decisions both on the campaign trail and in the White House.[359] Recent candidates have spent millions for polling and other voter surveys.[360]

Polling played a central role in Bill Clinton's winning 1992 and 1996 campaigns. In 1992 pollster Stanley B. Greenberg conducted surveys that helped candidate Clinton develop his almost instant responses to charges made by his opponents, Bush and Perot. Polls were especially important—and volatile—because of the presence of a strong independent candidate. The two major parties struggled to navigate the political waters roiled by the maverick candidate Perot, who was cutting into President Bush's conservative and suburban constituencies and also challenging Clinton for the reform vote. Polls were just as important in Clinton's 1996 reelection effort. Campaign strategist Dick Morris used polls to identify popular initiatives at the center of the political spectrum. Clinton embraced a number of popular conservative measures, such as welfare reform, a television program rating system, teenage curfews, and a balanced budget, while he backed popular Democratic ones, such as tuition tax credits, environmental safeguards, and no cutbacks in Medicare.

Polls, however, are not infallible; there is room for error both in polls themselves and in their interpretation.[361] The most famous example is from 1948, when virtually all pollsters predicted that Republican Thomas Dewey would beat the Democratic incumbent, Harry Truman. For a variety of reasons—including poor sampling techniques, the fact that polling stopped too early in the campaign, and mistaken assumptions about how the uncommitted would vote—the pollsters were wrong. Many pollsters also substantially underestimated the size of Ronald Reagan's victory in 1980.[362]

According to sociologists James R. Beniger and Robert J. Giuffra Jr., polls that forecast the actual outcome of elections are only one of many types of polls used by candidates. Preliminary *benchmark* or *baseline surveys* provide basic information about candidate strength and the political mood of the nation. These can be useful to candidates in deciding whether to run. *Follow-up surveys* are used to gather more in-depth data about particular concerns raised in initial benchmark surveys. These often are conducted state by state and are used in planning campaign strategy.

*Panel surveys* are used to refine strategy further by reinterviewing previous respondents to determine opinion shifts on specific issues within various demographic categories. These surveys are supplemented by continual tracking polls, which measure fluctuations in general voter support for the candidate across time.

Finally, continuing developments in computer technology have allowed the establishment of new techniques, such as the geodemographic targeting system in which census data and specially programmed voter registration lists pinpoint swing voters.[363] Used together, all these surveys are a source of information that candidates feel they cannot do without.

### Media and Other Consultants

Image building has become especially important since the development of television. Urging symbolic actions that would play well on television (such as holding folksy town meetings and carrying one's own luggage), pollster Caddell warned Carter in 1976 that "too many good people have been beaten because they tried to substitute substance for style."[364] Increasingly, candidates are turning to media consultants for help in cultivating a style. With the help of polls and survey data, such consultants "market" their candidate.

Media savvy was a vital part of Clinton's winning 1992 campaign. Political strategists James Carville and Mandy Grunwald, among others, helped the Arkansas governor to keep his campaign focused. The famed "War Room"—a crisis-control center at the Clinton headquarters in Little Rock—coordinated rapid responses to Bush campaign charges. The campaign's bus tours of small towns helped foster a populist image. Clinton, vice-presidential nominee Gore, and their wives basked in large crowds at all hours of day and night.

Bush's two presidential campaigns were case studies in both effective and ineffective media presentation. In 1988, guided by

Political strategist James Carville, left, managed Bill Clinton's 1992 campaign for president from the "War Room" in Little Rock, Arkansas.

media gurus Roger Ailes and Lee Atwater, Bush developed a tough but folksy persona. His unrelenting attacks on Michael Dukakis not only tarred the Democratic nominee, but also helped Bush to overcome the "wimp" label that had dogged him as Reagan's loyal vice president. In 1992 Bush's media experts were less focused and his campaign suffered. Campaign officials regularly lamented the loss of Atwater, who died before the campaign.

Dwight Eisenhower was the first presidential candidate to make extensive use of television commercials and an advertising agency when he ran as the Republican nominee in 1952. Nixon shunned the use of an advertising agency and most modern media techniques in the 1960 campaign. Even his participation in televised debates with Kennedy was marred by his poor make-up, haggard appearance, and lack of attention to his wardrobe. Nixon lost the election. His subsequent campaign for president in 1968 was a paradigm for campaigning via marketing techniques.[365] Since then, media consultants have become an integral part of presidential campaigns, coordinating everything from the personal appearance of the candidates to the color of their bumper stickers.

Media consultants also have fine-tuned the production and use of television advertisements. For example, Nixon's foreign policy experience was stressed in 1968 after polls showed that viewers thought such experience was important. After Vietnam and Watergate, Carter's commercials stressed that he was an honest, folksy candidate—"a leader, for a change." Even the color of his campaign literature (green) stressed his difference from mainstream politicians, who usually used red, white, and blue.[366]

Technological advances also have led to the use of direct mail. Using computers, campaign organizations send "personalized" mailings to "targeted" individuals whose names are culled from lists of contributors to the candidate's party or to related causes, from the mailing lists of magazines that indicate an ideological preference, and from membership lists of various organizations, among other sources. Names and addresses of individuals also can be bought from list brokers in any major city.

Direct mail is used primarily as a fund-raising device. It was first employed in 1952 by Eisenhower, who compiled a donor list with the aid of *Reader's Digest* publisher DeWitt Wallace. But it was not until the 1970s that vigorous use of direct mail was spurred by campaign finance legislation that limited individual contributions to $1,000 per candidate. In such a climate, direct mail served as a grassroots approach to reaching a wide base of small contributors. Through a well-coordinated program that contacts both potential contributors ("prospective mailings") and those who have given money in the past ("in-house" or "contributor mailings"), a relatively small investment can reap a tremendous profit.[367]

The goal of such mailings is to establish a degree of intimacy that will encourage the recipient to make a donation. In 1980 mailings for Bush included reprints of newspaper articles with "personal notes" laser-printed in the margin: "To [recipient's name]—I thought you might be interested in these recent clippings—G.B."[368] The facade of intimacy, coupled with careful packaging and emotional pleas, is designed to draw the recipient into the campaign by giving money.

Perhaps the most famous direct-mail consultant is conservative activist Richard Viguerie. Viguerie came to prominence in

1976 when he managed a highly successful direct-mail operation for George Wallace, who was seeking the Democratic nomination for president. Four years later, Viguerie helped the Republican Party broaden its financial base and usher in the presidency of Reagan and the first Republican Senate since 1955. By 1982 the Viguerie Company was employing more than three hundred people and directing several subsidiaries, including American Mailing Lists Corporation, American Telecommunications Corporation, Diversified Mailing Services, and the Viguerie Communication Corporation (which published *Conservative Digest* and the *Right Report*).[369] Viguerie himself maintained that his operation had amassed an "in-house list of eleven million proven contributors."[370]

In addition to direct mail, candidates use telephone banks to recruit volunteers and to target potential voters. Contacting households by phone is quick and easy—a way to reach many more voters with less effort than door-to-door canvassing.[371] Likewise, telephones are used in conjunction with fund-raising drives. In an effort to generate impulsive contributions, some media ads encourage voters to call a toll-free number and pledge money on credit cards.[372]

Recognizing that presidential campaigns are increasingly shaped by the mass media, campaign strategists attempt to develop memorable appeals. Between 30 and 50 percent of all advertising in political campaigns is negative. Cognitive studies have shown that voters process negative information more deeply than positive information. Jill Buckley, a Democratic consultant, explained: "People say they hate negative advertising, but it works. They hate it and remember it at the same time. . . . With negative [advertising], the poll numbers will move in three or four days."

The effect of media consultants on the outcome of political campaigns is debatable. Their effect on the process itself, however, is clear. Professionals drive up the costs of competing, weaken the link between candidates and parties, and make the importance of style and image more glaring.[373] The danger, as political scientist Larry Sabato has concluded, lies not so much in the techniques—Sabato points out that they could be used to strengthen the party system—but in the danger that candidates and voters will confuse the style of campaigning with the substance of policy making.[374] Candidates may be well suited to win elections but ill equipped to handle the rigors of governing.

## ROLES OF PARTIES AND INTEREST GROUPS

Winning elections, fundamentally, is a matter of giving voters the reason and the wherewithal to show up and vote. Traditionally, state party organizations have organized party appeals, but since World War II interest groups have played a greater role in this activity. The media have played an important part as well in spurring voters to action.

### State Party Organizations

The proportion of citizens claiming party membership has declined from about three-fourths to two-thirds since the 1950s. But despite their diminished role in national politics, state and local party organizations can be an important supplement to the efforts of the national campaign.

In recent years, parties have become better at recruiting and training candidates, more sophisticated at using modern campaign technology, stronger at raising money, and better at coordinating their activities with national party organizations and officials. State parties also undertake grassroots efforts to register likely supporters and get them to the polls on election day. Party organizations own extensive lists of supporters and "leaners." As election day approaches, the organization sends these voters letters and cards urging them to vote, and volunteers phone them to reinforce the message.

Coordination of a party's national, state, and local campaign efforts is informal. The national campaign's receipt of federal funds requires it to limit spending, so the efforts of other groups must be formally separate. By setting campaign priorities, the national campaign organization gives important cues to its allies.

Under the 1979 amendments to the Federal Election Campaign Act, state and local organizations may spend unlimited amounts of money on get-out-the-vote drives and political paraphernalia such as bumper stickers, buttons, and lawn signs. The organizations also can produce and distribute media appeals that promote the whole party—appeals that usually follow the national campaign theme set by the presidential candidate.

State parties are loose coalitions of the state's many distinctive social and economic groups. Many of these organizations still have influence over patronage, construction and service contracts, and routine political operations. Many also control the mechanics of the electoral process. Ohio law, for example, requires that registration officials be approved by county party leaders. In addition, twenty-one states allow single-ticket voting (where voters cast their ballot for all candidates of a party by pulling a single lever or using one ballot), which, by creating strong party competition in all races simultaneously, increases the importance of intraparty cooperation. Many political struggles are fought within the party structure.

Activists have become more involved in many state parties in recent years. In Iowa, for example, the Christian right is playing a growing role in Republican politics. The evangelist Pat Robertson finished second in the state's 1988 caucuses; since then, his supporters have become even more influential. In New York and other states, consumer and civil rights activists play an important role in Democratic politics.

State and local party positions on a variety of political issues often provide the starting point of political debate. It is true that single-issue interest groups have increased in importance, but party cohesion is still possible. The unity of congressional delegations in such states as California and New York, dominated by

Because voter turnout often is low, state and local organizations work to register voters and get them to the polls on election day.

one party, frames a wide variety of policy concerns. New York City's Democratic delegation, for example, was unified enough in 1976 to press successfully both presidential candidates for aid to the fiscally distressed city.

Political scientist Kay Lawson argues that national party rules and state legislation have undermined the organizational integrity of state parties. But even if parties do not enjoy the autonomy they once did, they still play a permanent and independent role in state and national politics.[375]

### National Party Organizations

In addition to their important organizing function in presidential campaigns, committees of the national parties raise large sums of money and develop long-range strategies. The efforts of party chairs, such as Republican William E. Brock and Democrats Charles T. Manatt and Paul G. Kirk Jr., have been instrumental to presidential politics. During the 1970s and 1980s, the three chairs developed wide-ranging strategies for coordinating presidential campaigns and reaching out to important political groups. Brock was central in developing the GOP as a broad-based party after the disaster of Watergate. Manatt developed ties to influential business leaders neglected by the Democrats, and Kirk worked to diminish the Democrats' "special-interest" tendencies.

The fund-raising abilities of the Republican Party committees have outstripped those of their Democratic counterparts in recent years. In the 1992 election cycle, the Republican Party raised $254.8 million compared with the Democrats' $162.2 million.[376] The money enabled the Republicans to undertake important party-building activities, including funding congressional and state candidates, supporting advertising campaigns, undertaking get-out-the-vote drives, polling, lobbying state legislatures on matters such as redistricting, making direct-mail

appeals, and hiring consultants. Larry Sabato, however, argues that the Republican wealth has led to wasteful spending.[377]

### Interest Groups

Whatever metaphor is most appropriate—"melting pot" or "mosaic"—the United States is a collection of social and ethnic groups with distinctive identities. Successful candidates must make separate appeals to social groups while tying those discrete interests together with broad appeals. Groups with distinctive political interests and voting habits include Catholics, Jews, African Americans, Hispanics, Asians, Irish, Greeks, women, bankers and insurance company executives, real estate developers, laborers, professionals, farmers, environmentalists, young people, senior citizens, urbanites, southerners, members of "New Right" groups, and the poor.

Candidates are sensitive to the participation rates of the different groups—that is, how many in each group vote. Robert Axelrod has estimated that the proportion of the poor in Democratic vote totals fell from 28 percent to 5 percent between 1952 and 1980.[378] It is probably no accident, therefore, that Democratic appeals to the poor have declined in recent years. Candidates must consider the cost of appealing to different groups. While two-thirds of all unregistered voters are at the bottom of the economic ladder, Democrats have been unwilling to risk the costs of a massive registration program or of antagonizing current supporters.

In recent years, political action committees—organizations designed to promote the concerns of ideological or social groups, business, and labor mainly by funding election campaigns—have played an important role in supplementing the direct-mail and mass-media appeals of the two major presidential candidates, who may spend only the money they receive from the federal government. The number of PACs has grown tremendously since the 1970s, and PAC spending has increased along with that growth. *(See Figure 1-2, p. 51.)* PAC expenditures increased from $19.2 million in 1972 to $385.7 million in 1992.[379] PACs enjoy an advantage over campaign organizations because individuals are permitted to donate $5,000 to a PAC and only $1,000 to a campaign under federal law. PAC spending patterns confer an enormous advantage on the Republican Party. In 1980, for example, independent expenditures for Republican Reagan totaled $12.5 million; independent expenditures for Democratic president Carter totaled $1.2 million. *(See "The Campaign Finance System," p. 35.)* The effect of these diverse political action committees is an increase in the number of narrow or single-issue appeals at the expense of the broader concerns of candidates and parties.

## ROLE OF THE MEDIA

The mass media (television, newspapers, magazines, and radio) are playing an increasingly important role in presidential elections largely because they serve as the dominant source of information about candidates and elections for most Americans—more than family, friends, associates, and direct contacts with political parties and candidate organizations.[380] The media also have taken over many of the "intermediary" functions of party organizations, linking voters with the larger political system.[381] News sources appear to be the most influential early in the nominating process when "horse-race" coverage of the primaries helps to winnow the candidates.[382] At that time the media help the public to form impressions of the large field of candidates, many of whom may be unfamiliar. By the time of the general election, voters are more likely to have set feelings about the candidates—making it more difficult for media coverage to influence them.

The pervasive influence of the media dominance has given rise to a new kind of campaign and candidate. Style and image, and an ability to speak pithily and warmly before cameras, have taken on greater importance. A candidate with a colorless, low-key personality, such as Calvin "Silent Cal" Coolidge, or one with a controversial past, such as Grover Cleveland, who fathered a child out of wedlock, probably could not get elected today. "Wholesale" campaigns—those based on mass appeals—focus on the matters that diverse groups can all understand. Careful debate and deliberation of complex issues tend to be foreclosed by mass politics.

News values influence the campaign. News is drama, and drama thrives on conflict.[383] As a result, the media often emphasize the game-like characteristics of presidential campaigns. Strategy, momentum, competition, and error are often treated at the expense of candidates' records and policy pronouncements. Journalists covering presidential debates, for example, are more concerned with who "won" than with the issues articulated. In the process, news coverage is personalized—that is, issues are subordinated to personalities, and electoral outcomes focus on the individual's personal victory or defeat rather than on the process (the implications of that outcome for the American political system as a whole).[384] Thus the media can impinge on the ability of candidates to set the agenda and articulate their positions.

By exposing a flaw in the person's history the media can derail a candidacy long before the election, as happened to Thomas Eagleton in 1972 (forced to give up the Democratic vice-presidential nomination after his past treatment for depression was disclosed), and Gary Hart and Joseph Biden, who in 1987 abandoned fledgling presidential bids for 1988 after receiving adverse publicity (Hart was caught in an extramarital relationship; Biden had engaged in plagiarism).

This being said, the modern media also provide candidates with an unprecedented ability to take their message directly to the people. Television, in particular, is often said to have transformed electoral politics. Cutting across all socioeconomic divisions, television reaches nearly 98 percent of all households in the continental United States.[385] One study shows that as recently as 1982, more Americans had televisions than refrigerators or indoor plumbing.[386]

In analyzing the media content of candidate appeals, politi-

cal scientists David Paletz and Robert Entman have identified three types of content: unmediated messages, partially mediated messages, and mostly mediated messages.[387]

### Advertisements and Other Unmediated Messages

*Unmediated messages* are those in which the candidate's message is passed to the people unfettered by commentary or criticism—those over which the candidates exercise total control, such as paid political advertisements. Since they were first used by Dwight Eisenhower in 1952, television advertisements have played an ever more sophisticated role in presidential elections. Among them, George Bush, Bill Clinton, and Ross Perot spent $92 million on television advertising in 1992.[388]

The precise effects of such commercials are difficult to determine.[389] In trying to assess the influence of the media on public attitudes in this and other areas, many analysts have echoed the wry sentiments of sociologist Bernard Berelson, who concluded some years ago that "some kinds of communications on some kinds of issues, brought to the attention of some kinds of people under some kinds of conditions, have some kinds of effects."[390] The relatively few studies undertaken to determine the effects of televised commercials seem to indicate that they have little influence on the outcome of presidential general election campaigns (a finding that does not appear to be true for lower political offices, where commercials can be instrumental in building name recognition and securing victory).[391]

Paletz and Entman have argued that unmediated messages such as televised ad campaigns are the most difficult for candidates to use to sway voters because many people realize that they are self-serving. In addition, such messages are "vulnerable to the Gorgons of selective exposure, selective perception, and selective retention."[392] As political scientist Doris Graber has concluded: "Commercials are perceiver-determined. People see in them pretty much what they want to see—attractive images for their favorite candidate and unattractive ones for the opponent."[393]

Perot's talk show appearances, along with his half-hour television "infomercials," videos, and books, provided one of the least-mediated campaigns in modern history. Perot never hesitated to express his disdain for the working press. Thus rather than talk to voters through the print and broadcast reports, he set up his own information system. Perot dropped out of the presidential race in July when reporters began investigating his past business and political activities. After he reentered the race in early October, the media at first did not take him seriously, giving him a grace period to offer his candidacy the way he liked. Ultimately, his credibility was damaged when he told the CBS news program *60 Minutes* that he had been driven out of the race by Republican "dirty tricks," which included plans to disrupt his daughter's wedding.

Even newer and more direct than talk shows as a way to reach the voters is by computer. In 1996 the two major parties and most presidential candidates provided sites on the Inter-

In 1960 Vice President Richard Nixon speaks during the first televised presidential debate while his opponent, Sen. John F. Kennedy, takes notes. Since 1976 televised debates have become a regular part of each presidential campaign.

net's World Wide Web where online users could obtain schedules, speech texts, and other handouts from the various campaigns. *(See box, "Political Campaigns on the Internet," p. 113.)*

### Debates, Interviews, and Other Partially Mediated Messages

*Partially mediated messages* are those passed along through such vehicles as televised press conferences, debates, talk shows, and interviews. Here candidates have an opportunity to air their views and repeat well-worn phrases, but these messages are constrained by the questioning of media representatives (and, in debates, the responses of opposing candidates).

First aired in 1960, televised debates have been part of every presidential campaign since 1976. Although they are a vehicle for the transmission of policy positions, viewers often seem to be more impressed by the style of the debaters than by their stands on specific issues. Richard Nixon was widely considered to have lost his first debate with John Kennedy in 1960 because of his style and personal appearance, not because of the substance of his arguments. Likewise, Ronald Reagan succeeded against Jimmy Carter in the 1980 debates largely because of his style: the warm image he conveyed through his folksy anecdotes, his rejoinders to the president ("There you go again . . ."), and the fact that he structured his answers in simple rhetorical terms.

The 1992 campaign debates, involving three candidates apiece, added a new format. The first and third debates used the traditional format in which moderator and reporters ask questions, although candidates were given unusual leeway to respond to each other's points. But the second debate used a television talk-show format, with a moderator eliciting questions from a studio audience. This format best suited Clinton, the candidate of empathetic face-to-face encounters. The vice-presidential debate used the traditional format. It was most no-

table for the confused appearance of Perot's running mate, Adm. James Stockdale.

The effect of debates is hard to measure, especially because they are quickly followed by a barrage of media commentary and speculation over who won. Surveys taken immediately after the second debate between Ford and Carter in 1976, for example, indicated that viewers, by almost two to one, felt that Ford had won. But media attention to Ford's "gaffe"—his statement that Eastern Europe was not dominated by the Soviet Union—dramatically reversed that opinion within three days.[394] Debates have the greatest potential to change votes when the voters are "soft" or undecided in their support for candidates and when "the electorate learned something about the candidates." Nevertheless, as a rule, debates do not appear to alter voter perceptions of the candidates significantly.[395]

Talk shows provided the best setting for partially unmediated messages in 1992. In 1984 and 1988, talk-show host Phil Donahue had tried in vain to get presidential candidates to appear on his program. In 1992 Democratic candidates appeared on *Donahue* twice in one week. On April 6, the day before the New York primary, Clinton and Jerry Brown debated for an hour without interference from Donahue. The program reached eight million viewers. By the end of the campaign, the three major candidates had appeared ninety-seven times on talk shows such as *Larry King Live* and *Today*—Clinton forty-eight times, Perot thirty-three times, and Bush sixteen times. Bush rejected the format early in the year as unpresidential but sought invitations later in the year.[396] For all this, the 1992 election became known as the campaign of the talk shows.

Even though appearances by the three major candidates on programs such as *Donahue, Nightline, Larry King Live,* and *The Arsenio Hall Show* were guided by a host, the candidates exerted great control over style and content. The campaign organizations negotiated what questions would be asked on the programs. Clinton campaign strategist George Stephanopoulos even called into the programs to ask questions as a citizen. In general, questions from talk show audiences were easier than the drilling candidates got from reporters. "Questions from the public are far less confrontational, and an overwhelming number of people ask candidates how they would solve problems that would affect the questioner. . . ."[397] Thus the talk-show format had the appearance of an open-ended, democratic format but was manipulated like other forms of media.

### News Stories and Other Mostly Mediated Messages

*Mostly mediated messages* are those that the candidates control the least, such as news stories that are constructed by the media about the candidate. Paletz and Entman contend that mostly mediated messages have the greatest effect on public opinion precisely because the candidates do not appear to control their content. Candidates' campaign staffs therefore use a wide variety of techniques to try to influence such coverage, including timing and staging events, restricting reporters' access to the candidate, and controlling the flow of information from the campaign organization.[398] Incumbents are particularly able to attract coverage through such activities. Only an incumbent, for example, can schedule an event in the Rose Garden or the East Room of the White House, or participate in foreign "summit meetings" as did Nixon in 1972. Reagan also was able to combine the backdrop of the presidency with precisely coordinated campaign appearances before ecstatic crowds to remarkable effect. Vice President Bush's 1988 campaign was skilled at providing vivid backdrops for television news operations. Even an event as trivial as throwing out the first pitch at a Houston Astros baseball game was subjected to weeks of planning. News organizations were so distressed at how they had been manipulated by the Bush campaign that they vowed to avoid using every backdrop provided by the campaigns in 1992.

### Media "Bias"

Candidates from all points on the ideological spectrum have complained about the "bias" of the media. In complaining about liberal bias, Republicans cite surveys that show reporters to vote regularly for Democrats. Democrats complain about the subtle pressure from conservative editorial boards on reporters in the field. Media bias depends on the circumstances of the race. In 1980, for example, reporters appeared to slant coverage toward the conservative Reagan.[399] In 1992 the media produced more negative reports about Republican Bush than Democrat Clinton.[400]

### THE VICE-PRESIDENTIAL CAMPAIGN

In the Republic's early years, before the Twelfth Amendment was enacted in 1804, the vice presidency went to the candidate who finished second in the voting of the electoral college. Thus early vice presidents such as Thomas Jefferson actually were defeated presidential candidates. With ratification of the Twelfth Amendment in 1804, presidential and vice-presidential candidates were expected to run on the same national ticket.

Since Jimmy Carter's tenure in the White House (1977–1981), vice presidents have played important policy roles in administrations, but traditionally the vice presidency has served mostly to help the president get elected in the first place. The second spot is often used to "balance" the national ticket.

The vice presidency's importance was likened to "a pitcher of warm spit" by Vice President John Nance Garner and "a cow's fifth teat" by Vice President Harry Truman. Until George Bush won the presidency in 1988, the last sitting vice president to be elected president was Martin Van Buren in 1836. Both presidents, handicapped by the lingering image of being "second fiddle," lost their races for reelection.[401] Former vice presidents Harry Truman, Lyndon Johnson, and Richard Nixon won presidential elections on their own.

Despite its indignities, the vice presidency is just "a heartbeat away" from the presidency. The assassination or resignation of two recent presidents—John Kennedy and Richard Nixon—increased the public's awareness that the vice president could someday become president. Nine vice presidents have become president after the president died in office or resigned the position: John Tyler (1841), Millard Fillmore (1850), Andrew Johnson (1865), Chester A. Arthur (1881), Theodore Roosevelt (1901), Calvin Coolidge (1923), Harry Truman (1945), Lyndon Johnson (1963), and Gerald Ford (1974).

Presidential nominees insist that their running mates be "perfectly compatible" with their approaches to government. But especially in tight elections, the vice-presidential candidate is selected to balance the national ticket in terms of geography, religion, ideology, government experience, and political style.

Defying traditional ticket balancing, Bill Clinton of Arkansas selected Al Gore of Tennessee as his running mate in 1992. It was the only major party ticket in American history with candidates from contiguous states. But what the Clinton-Gore ticket lacked in geographic balance it made up with a balance of the candidates' other attributes. Clinton, who had state-level experience as a governor, lacked foreign policy experience and had a mixed environmental record. Gore had a strong foreign policy and environmental record in Congress. Clinton, who had avoided military service in the Vietnam War, also was strengthened by Gore's status as a veteran of the war.

Republican Bob Dole's choice of Jack Kemp as his running mate in 1996, although surprising, was along the lines of traditional ticket balancing. Kemp had ties to New York and California—two important electoral states and a good balance to Dole's Kansas roots. The anti-abortion Kemp also pleased the GOP conservatives who may have been uneasy with Dole's more moderate positions. Kemp was also a "big tent" Republican who had championed efforts to reach out to minorities.

Republican Abraham Lincoln of Illinois was an adept ticket-balancer. In 1860 he picked Hannibal Hamlin of Kentucky, a southern or border state. Four years later he selected Andrew

Johnson of Tennessee, a former Democrat, for the ticket, by then renamed the National Union Party.

One of the most famous ticket-balancing maneuvers was Massachusetts senator John Kennedy's selection of Senate Majority Leader Lyndon Johnson as a running mate. Kennedy's Catholicism, support for civil rights, and northern urban appeal required some sort of gesture to conservative southern Democrats. Kennedy and his top aide, brother Robert Kennedy, reportedly were afraid that Johnson might actually accept the second spot, which was offered as a conciliatory gesture. But as the candidate's father, former ambassador Joseph P. Kennedy, remarked, it was the shrewdest move of the campaign.

The 1988 Democratic nominee, Michael Dukakis, tried to duplicate Kennedy's "Boston-to-Austin" combination. The Massachusetts governor selected Texas senator Lloyd Bentsen as his running mate. But the gambit failed to lure Texas or the rest of the South to the Democratic fold. Texans voted in overwhelming numbers for Republican Bush, a New Englander who had long made Texas his home.

The Republican Party's "southern strategy"—the effort to lure long-term Democrats to the GOP with rhetoric against civil rights and federal power—began with Nixon's 1968 selection of Maryland governor Spiro T. Agnew as his running mate. Agnew was once considered an urban liberal, but he attracted conservative support nationwide by publicly blaming black leaders for not doing enough to end the urban riots that rocked Baltimore in 1968.

Carter picked Sen. Walter Mondale of Minnesota as his running mate in 1976 to counteract his inexperience in national politics and to appeal to some of the traditional Democratic constituencies such as urbanites, African Americans, and organized labor. The same year, the conservative Reagan selected moderate senator Richard Schweiker of Pennsylvania to broaden his appeal before the party's national convention; the ploy failed to win Reagan the nomination, however. President Ford in 1975 abandoned his vice president, Nelson Rockefeller, when he came under criticism from party conservatives suspicious of the New York moderate. From the time of his battle with Barry Goldwater for the 1964 Republican nomination, Rockefeller was treated like a pariah in his party. Ford later admitted he had treated Rockefeller badly.

At other times, running mates are selected to bind party wounds opened during nomination struggles. Kennedy's selection of Johnson and Reagan's 1980 selection of Bush fit that description. Still, some nominees have refused to accept the ticket-balancing wisdom. In 1964 Goldwater picked an obscure New York member of the House of Representatives, William Miller, whose conservative credentials were as consistent as his own. In 1984 Mondale's selection of Rep. Geraldine Ferraro of New York as his Democratic running mate created a ticket of two northern liberals. In 1976 President Ford selected a fellow midwesterner, Sen. Bob Dole of Kansas, as his running mate.

The vice-presidential nomination provides a point of entry to groups traditionally excluded from the political process. Ferraro's selection as Mondale's Democratic running mate in 1984—the first woman to run on a major party national ticket—is perhaps the most notable example of the breakthrough phenomenon. Some Republicans urged President Bush to drop Dan Quayle from the 1992 ticket in favor of Gen. Colin Powell. Powell, the highest-ranking African American in the military, probably would have improved the GOP's appeal to minorities.

How vice-presidential candidates fashion their pitch depends on the party ticket's overall strategy. As a rule, presidential candidates appeal to the broad electorate while their running mates appeal to specific groups. In 1968, for example, Republican Nixon took the "high road" by campaigning for a negotiated end to the Vietnam War while his running mate, Agnew, appealed to southern resistance to the civil rights and antiwar movements. In 1976 GOP standard-bearer Ford ran a campaign stressing his role as a national conciliator after the Watergate scandal and Vietnam while Dole, his vice-presidential candidate, took "the lead in implementing the Attack Carter plan."[402]

Vice-presidential candidates must take part in the televised debates that have become a mainstay of campaigns. Experts closely watch the debates not only because the vice president could be president if anything happened to the chief executive, but also because he or she could be a future party leader regardless of the election outcome. Many experts believed that Dole's debate performance damaged the 1976 GOP ticket—perhaps enough to lose the close election. He alienated Democratic voters by calling U.S. wars since World War I "all Democrat wars." Reports on Ferraro's debate with Vice President Bush in 1984 were mixed.

The 1988 vice-presidential debate reinforced Republican Quayle's poor image. Quayle, trying to rebut critics who questioned his suitability for national office, argued that his government experience was greater than Kennedy's when Kennedy sought the presidency in 1960. The grandfatherly Bentsen scolded Quayle: "Senator, I served with Jack Kennedy. I knew Jack Kennedy. Jack Kennedy was a friend of mine. Senator, you are no Jack Kennedy."[403] The moment undermined Quayle's search for respect but ultimately did not change the dynamics of the campaign. In the three-way 1992 vice-presidential debate, both Vice President Quayle and Democratic challenger Gore showed a command of the subject unmatched by James Stockdale, Ross Perot's running mate. In 1996 Gore reprised his strong command of the issues against Jack Kemp, who seemed unprepared at times.

In general, the vice-presidential candidate serves to reinforce or break down the electorate's attitudes toward the presidential candidate. If a presidential candidate has little foreign policy or Washington experience, as was true of Reagan and Carter, a running mate with that experience can reassure voters. A vice-presidential candidate whose character or issue stances bother voters can turn away undecided voters.

The family of the vice-presidential candidate often plays an active role in campaigning. Likely unknown before the party nominating convention, family members become instant cele-

In the 1896 election William Jennings Bryan, left, traveled over eighteen thousand miles and delivered more than six hundred speeches.

brities. Their personal appearance at campaign events can lend excitement to the campaign. Tipper Gore, the wife of the 1992 vice-presidential candidate, was an effective speaker. She had gained national attention years before as the organizer of a movement to regulate the sale of popular music with offensive lyrics.

The families of the vice-presidential candidates also can be liabilities. Ferraro's husband caused the Democratic ticket embarrassment when the media reported his questionable real estate, trusteeship, and tax activities.

## PERSONAL CAMPAIGNING BY PRESIDENTIAL CANDIDATES

It now is taken for granted that presidential candidates will actively campaign in their own behalf. But for many years candidates avoided personal appearances, claiming it was unsavory to ask voters for the opportunity to serve. As Stephen Wayne has written: "Personal solicitation was [once] viewed as demeaning and unbecoming of the dignity and status of the Presidency."[404] Thus, while their supporters engaged in propaganda, public relations, mass rallies, and other sorts of hoopla, the candidates themselves sat quietly on the sidelines.

The first major party candidate to break that tradition was Stephen A. Douglas in his 1860 race against Abraham Lincoln. The two had held public debates in 1858 when they were running for the same Senate seat from Illinois, but in the presidential race Lincoln made a vow not to "write or speak anything upon doctrinal points."[405] Instead, he remained in Springfield, Illinois, receiving visitors and shunning rallies and political meetings.

Douglas, in contrast, set out on a personal campaign to try to mend the splits in the Democratic Party caused by the slavery issue. Southern Democrats had nominated their own candidate, John C. Breckinridge, on a proslavery platform. Douglas soon realized that he would not win the election, but he ardently fought to save the Union. The speaking tour took him from New England to the South, and then to the Midwest where he heard some initial electoral vote returns. Aware that Lincoln would be the next president, Douglas returned to the South in a last-ditch effort "to lift the voice of reason in behalf of Union."[406]

The circumstances of 1860, however, were unique. Thus it was thirty-six years before another candidate actively campaigned in his own behalf. In the election of 1896, William Jennings Bryan—whose stunning "Cross of Gold" speech at the Democratic convention had secured his nomination—traveled over eighteen thousand miles and delivered more than six hundred speeches.[407] His opponent, William McKinley, followed a more traditional approach. Although he was an excellent public speaker who had engaged in a speaking tour in his own behalf when seeking the Republican nomination, McKinley felt that pleading his own cause once he was his party's nominee was unbecoming to his position. Nevertheless, he did not want to stay completely out of the picture and therefore made a compromise: he stayed home and waged a "front porch" campaign. Instead of going to the people, the people came to him; and they came in droves. Historian Eugene H. Roseboom has referred to these excursions as "mass pilgrimages."[408] From his front porch, McKinley greeted his visitors and—when appropriate—delivered a formal speech. McKinley won the election.

In 1900 McKinley and Bryan were again pitted against each other. As in 1896, Bryan engaged in a lengthy speaking tour. Although McKinley stayed in the White House, he sent his running mate, Theodore Roosevelt, to campaign on his behalf. Outspoken in his views, flamboyant on the podium, and vigorous in his rhetoric, Roosevelt was an immediate success with his audiences. "Buffalo Bill" Cody referred to him as the "American cyclone."[409] Roosevelt appeared in many of the same places as Bryan, and the campaign quickly emerged as a contest between the two orators. Indeed, it often seemed that it was Roosevelt rather than McKinley who was running for president.[410]

In the 1896 campaign Bryan's opponent, William McKinley, took a more traditional approach by staying at home and waging a "front porch" campaign. People traveled to McKinley's home to hear him speak.

With the election of 1904, the candidates reverted to a more traditional approach. Roosevelt (who had been elevated to the presidency with the assassination of McKinley) did not engage in a speaking tour, although his running mate, Charles Fairbanks, campaigned for the Republican ticket. Their Democratic opponent, Alton B. Parker—cautious, colorless, largely unknown, and politically conservative—stayed out of the fray. So did his running mate, the eighty-one-year-old West Virginia millionaire Henry G. Davis. Democrats had hoped that Davis would use his millions to help fund the campaign. He did not. The Republicans won.[411]

Although Republican candidates remained less likely to campaign actively than their counterparts in the Democratic Party, it was clear that traditions were changing. Bryan, nominated yet again in 1908, hit the campaign trail, as did his Republican opponent, Taft. Both Democratic candidate Woodrow Wilson and "Bull Moose" candidate Roosevelt campaigned strenuously in 1912. (Taft, recognizing that his cause was hopeless, did little.) *(See Chapter 3, Chronology of Presidential Elections.)* By 1932 personal campaigning had become the norm. In that year, Herbert Hoover became the first incumbent to campaign actively for his own reelection.[412]

### Campaigning in the Jet and Electronic Ages

Today, direct appeals to the people are an integral part of a campaign-centered selection process—a process that may begin years before the election takes place. With the development of jet travel, candidates are now able to crisscross the country extensively. At the height of the campaign, it is common for candidates to visit several states in one day. In the last days of the 1988 campaign, Democrat Michael Dukakis campaigned around the clock. In the last two days, Dukakis traveled 8,500 miles to make

appearances in eleven cities. In the last thirty-six hours, he crossed all four time zones three times. In 1996 Bob Dole campaigned "non-stop" for 96 hours, flying 10,500 miles and touching down in twenty states.

Personal campaigning has been revolutionized by developments in communications, which have made new forms of direct mass appeals available. Televised debates, campaign commercials, cybernetic bulletin boards and conferences, talk shows, and direct-mail operations are all relatively new ways of taking candidates' messages directly to the people. Even personal campaign appearances are now designed more for the media than for those actually in attendance at the event. Enthusiastic crowds, colorful backdrops, and telegenic symbols are carefully coordinated at every campaign stop. When colorful backdrops are not possible, candidates are content simply to appear in a city to gain local media attention. The 1988 Dukakis campaign hopscotched from airport to airport, often not venturing beyond the tarmac, to appear in as many media markets as possible.

Personal campaigning, then, has become an elaborate enterprise, dependent on the advice of pollsters, media consultants, advertising experts, and speechwriters. Present-day campaigns are a far cry from those of the past.

### Family Appearances

As with vice-presidential candidates, personal appearances by family members of presidential candidates—especially the spouses—have gained in importance since the advent of television and jet travel. Where candidate wives were once seldom seen until the election was won, many today accompany the candidates and share in the shaking of hands and making of speeches.

## POLITICAL CAMPAIGNS ON THE INTERNET

The advent of the Internet gave political parties and candidates a new way to reach voters, and most wasted no time in exploiting the computer technology.

While some parties and candidates jumped on the Internet early, much of the rush online occurred in 1995, when the Democratic National Committee, the Republican National Committee, and most of the major presidential candidates set up sites on the World Wide Web, which is part of the Internet.

The sites offered a variety of information. Typically, the national political party sites provided campaign updates, press releases, party platforms, and links to other Internet sites operated by the party's candidates and its state and local affiliates. Most also offered newsletters. For example, in 1995 the Democratic National Committee site offered a weekly newsletter titled "The Newtgram," which provided updates about the activities of Speaker of the House Newt Gingrich. On a more sober note, the Republican National Committee offered the "Monday Briefing," a weekly eight-page newsletter with news from the previous week, a calendar of upcoming political events, and results from public opinion surveys.

Both parties also offer electronic mailing lists that provide press releases, calendars of events, and related information. Subscribers to the free lists automatically receive the information in their e-mail mailboxes.

In 1995–1996 the presidential campaign sites varied widely in what they offered. Frequently, they had the text of speeches, information about upcoming campaign events, details about how to contribute time or money to the campaign, contact information for the campaign, biographies of the candidate and key campaign staff members, press releases, and audio and video clips from speeches and television ads.

Internet surfers needed to be a bit wary when accessing sites purporting to be operated by a presidential campaign because there were three kinds of campaign sites: *official, unofficial,* and *spoof.* Official sites were run by the campaign, unofficial sites were run by the candidate's supporters without formal campaign backing, and spoof sites were usually run by the candidate's detractors. Telling the sites apart could sometimes be tricky.

For example, in 1995 a World Wide Web site looked like an official campaign site for Bob Dole. When users connected, they were greeted with a message: "Dole '96: An Official World Wide Web Internet Site." The message continued: "Welcome to the Bob Dole for President page. This page is here to offer information about Dole's candidacy, his views, and what you can do to help." But then came the tipoff that this was a spoof site: "Bob Dole is often mixed up with the Dole fruit company."

Here are addresses for the main World Wide Web sites operated by the two major political parties:

Democratic National Committee
*http://www.democrats.org*
Republican National Committee
*http://www.rnc.org*

The 1996 election saw an unusually strong and outspoken career woman at the side of each major party nominee. Hillary Rodham Clinton and Elizabeth Dole were also similar in their high visibility and active participation in their spouse's campaigns. Hillary, a successful lawyer, by most accounts had a rough four years as first lady. In charge of the Clinton administration's ill-fated health care reform plan, she was also tied to various White House ethical problems. Criticized for having too much influence over White House social policy, she took a lower profile in 1995 and 1996, focusing on women and children issues. Elizabeth Dole, who previously had served under Reagan as transportation secretary and under Bush as labor secretary, had taken leave of her job as president of the American Red Cross to campaign. She was a compelling speaker, as she demonstrated at the GOP convention, and her warmth and bright demeanor softened her husband's often stiff and dour temperament.

The personal life of a presidential candidate's spouse can be a sensitive issue for the campaign. In 1988 Kitty Dukakis won praise for admitting that she was fighting a sometimes losing battle against alcohol addiction. Another candidate's wife, Betty Ford, had won that battle and established a clinic for victims of alcohol and drug addiction.

### THE JOURNEY TOWARD THE GENERAL ELECTION

The traditional "opening day" for the presidential election campaign was the first Monday in September, Labor Day, when most Americans had returned to work and school from summer vacations and the election was just two months away. The period before Labor Day was reserved at least partly for the candidates to develop strategy with close aides.

In recent years, candidates have been unwilling to refrain from campaigning before Labor Day. In 1980, for example, Republican Ronald Reagan gave a number of speeches to groups such as the Veterans of Foreign Wars to develop campaign themes. In fact, Reagan used the month before Labor Day as a learning period. He was able to test campaign themes and make the major mistakes of his campaign—such as suggesting that the United States adopt a "two-China" policy, recognizing the governments of both Taiwan and the People's Republic of China—during the period when the media and public were least attentive. In 1992 the candidates took to the campaign trail right after their parties' national conventions. Bill Clinton and running mate Al Gore boarded a bus for a trip through the northeastern states rich in electoral votes. After the GOP convention in August, George Bush headed for campaign stops in Florida.

The issues that the nominees consider as they head into the fall campaign include whether to concentrate their appeals on certain sections of the country, how many issues to stress throughout the campaign, how many and what kind of broadcast commercials to buy, what kind of collaboration to undertake with groups interested in helping the campaign, and how to organize state and local campaign efforts. The candidates also try to anticipate the opposition's style of attack.

The party nominees often must undertake "fence-mending" efforts with rivals of their own party. In 1984 Democratic nominee Walter Mondale made overtures to his nomination rivals, Gary Hart and Jesse Jackson, who represented distinctly different party blocs whose support he would need to run a competitive race in the fall.

The campaign organization for the general election in the fall is usually an extension of the nomination organization, and it is separate from the national and state party organizations. Nominees have the prerogative of naming their party's national committee chair, who will help to coordinate the campaign.

The national campaign committee, usually based in Washington, receives its funding from the Federal Election Commission. The campaign must agree to limit spending to the amount received from the FEC in exchange for federal funding. Since 1976, when federal funding of elections began, all major party candidates have chosen to accept the government funds rather than raise their own money. In 1988 each major party candidate received $46.1 million from the FEC. In 1992 Clinton and Bush each received $55.2 million. Independent candidate Ross Perot financed his campaign.

Although presidential campaigns accepting federal funding are limited in their expenditures, allied organizations can supplement the campaigns with more or less independent efforts. State and local party organizations, political action committees, independent committees established to help specific candidates, and labor unions contribute time, money, and volunteers to assist the candidate of their choice.

Once the campaign begins, the media scrutiny of candidates becomes intense. The candidates must attempt to steer the campaign coverage to the issues that they would like to address. Reagan in 1980 and Mondale in 1984 designated whole weeks for concentrating on major themes such as military preparedness and budget deficits.

Even though the candidates and their advisers map out a campaign strategy before Labor Day, the campaign inevitably shifts its tactics according to polls, political events, and each candidate's instincts about which approaches will be successful. The Nixon-McGovern race in 1972 shifted with developments in the Vietnam War; the Reagan-Carter race in 1980 shifted with developments in the Iran hostage crisis. It is often difficult for a challenger to highlight events, however. In 1972, for example, George McGovern neglected to make the Nixon campaign's burglary of Democratic National Committee headquarters a major issue.

One element of campaign strategy that usually remains intact is the decision about where to campaign. The winner-take-all electoral college system, in which the leading vote-getter in a state wins all of that state's electoral votes, encourages candidates to win as many large states as possible rather than build up strength in states in which they are weak. Thus candidates generally spend most of their time in large, closely contested states, and just enough time in "likely win" states to ensure victory. Appearances in unfavorable states are usually symbolic efforts to show that the candidate is not conceding anything.

Most candidates try to determine the states in which they are strongest and then build on that base. A Democrat, for example, might solidify a northeastern industrial base by making appeals in border states such as Minnesota, Wisconsin, Kentucky, and Maryland. A Republican with southern appeal will also try to build strength in Kentucky and the neighboring border state of Tennessee, as well as in more western states such as Texas and Oklahoma.

The 1992 Clinton campaign used a sophisticated computer program to guide decisions on where to focus the candidates' time and other resources. The program identified the major media markets on an electronic map and each week assessed which markets had the most persuadable voters. A color-coded system based on eight sets of data helped to decide the best way to use the candidates and other major party speakers, media advertising, voter canvassing, and get-out-the-vote operations. Clinton won all but one of the thirty-two states targeted with the data. The campaign put significant resources in two other states that Clinton had little chance of winning—Texas and Florida—in order to force the Bush campaign to spend resources there.

Competing in all regions of the country can be difficult. In 1960 Richard Nixon gave some 212 speeches in fifty states but lost the election to John Kennedy. Had he spent less time in states that heavily favored Kennedy or had few electoral votes and more time in close states such as Illinois and Missouri, he might have won the election. In 1984 Democrat Mondale and his running mate, Geraldine Ferraro, missed the opportunity to solidify their support in northeastern states when they campaigned in the solid Republican South and West.

The ideological tone of the presidential campaign usually moderates once the parties have determined their nominees. After appealing to the more extreme wings of their parties, the nominees must try to attract independents and voters from the other party. The candidates usually can depend on the support of the most ideological members of their own party, so they are able to shift their sights in the fall.

The exception to this rule occurs when a candidate has suffered a bruising nominating battle and must persuade the backers of the defeated candidates to go to the polls. In 1980, after President Carter defeated Sen. Edward Kennedy for the Democratic nomination, Carter continued to make liberal appeals to satisfy the disappointed Kennedy supporters.

Whether to highlight specific issue stances or provide a "fuzzy" ideological stance is a major question facing every campaign. Campaign consultants often advise against being too specific. Mondale's pledge in 1984 to raise taxes showed both the opportunity and the risk of being specific. For a while, the proposal put President Reagan, who presided over historic budget deficits, on the defensive, but the proposal backfired when Reagan regained the offensive and charged Democrats with fiscal and taxing irresponsibility.

Candidates also must bear in mind the effects of promises on their ability to govern if they win. During the 1992 campaign,

Clinton vowed to end the ban on gays serving in the military, to allow Haitian refugees into the United States, to act to end genocide in Bosnia, to cut taxes for the middle class, and to hold China responsible for human rights violations. Those promises helped Clinton to get elected, but as president he found a more complex political environment—and he reversed or modified his position on all of them.

Daily campaign activities are geared to getting impressive visual "bites" on the national and local television news programs. The ill fortunes of the 1984 Mondale campaign were underscored on Labor Day, when the television networks stressed the poor turnout at a rainy parade Mondale attended in New York City while President Reagan's campaign opener was a sunny, balloon-filled rally in southern California.

Bush's campaign in 1988 was masterful at getting attractive visuals on television news programs. Most of the visuals served the double purpose of showing Bush in a picturesque setting and bashing Democrat Michael Dukakis. For example, Bush appeared in a sea of uniformed police officers to criticize Dukakis's record on crime, in flag factories to criticize Dukakis's veto of a bill that would direct schoolchildren to recite the Pledge of Allegiance, on a boat in Boston Harbor to criticize Dukakis's failure to clean up the harbor, and on the shore of Lake Erie to identify himself as an environmentalist. Some of Bush's appearances even used backdrops designed to reinforce the color schemes of his television advertisements.

Depending on their standing in the polls, and on whether they are running for or against the party in power, the candidates switch back and forth between appeals to bolster their own image and appeals to undermine their opponent's credibility. In 1984 Mondale had a dual task: first, to break down the positive image of the popular President Reagan, and, second, to portray himself as a worthy replacement. But it was too great a task. If a candidate already has an unfavorable image, as President Carter did in 1980, the opponent only needs to persuade voters that he or she is a trustworthy alternative. Reagan succeeded at that task.

In 1992 Clinton got an assist from independent candidate Ross Perot in this double task of taking on President Bush. While Perot was persistently attacking Bush's record, Clinton was able to present himself as above the fray. Eventually, Perot's attacks on Bush's economic record and foreign policy record "softened up" Bush to the point that voters began to consider an alternative. Perot also attacked Clinton, but not so frequently or so personally.

The candidates use television and radio throughout the fall to advertise their campaigns, but the pace quickens at the end of October when many voters are just beginning to pay close attention to the race. Whether the broadcast spots address specific issues or confine themselves to images of the candidate depends on the target audience, the salience of the issues, the stage of the campaign, and the closeness of the race. In 1984 the Reagan campaign used "feel-good" commercials with vague images of Americana because it needed to reinforce a positive mood in the nation rather than sway many voters. Mondale used issue-oriented spots that year in an attempt to loosen Reagan's coalition of support. In 1988 Bush used the "good cop–bad cop" approach. Some of his commercials presented warm images of Bush in family and patriotic settings. Others hammered relentlessly at Dukakis as an unreliable and elitist liberal. The "Willie Horton" spots, which criticized Dukakis for a Massachusetts program that allowed prisoners to get weekend releases from prison for good behavior, were especially effective. Horton was a convicted murderer who allegedly raped a woman while out on a weekend furlough.

Televised debates by presidential and vice-presidential candidates have become a fixture of campaigns. Before 1976 candidates leading in the polls resisted debates because they had little reason to give their opponents a boost in stature by appearing on the same stage. Front-runners also feared "gaffes" that might undermine their advantages in the polls or give opponents ammunition for the campaign trail.

In recent years, front-runners have been obliged to take part in debates to avoid the charge that they were "hiding" from the opponent. Candidates reluctant to debate try to put off encounters with complaints about the proposed debates' timing and formats. In 1980, for example, Democratic president Carter avoided a debate that included both his Republican and independent opponents. He later faced Republican Reagan one-on-one. President Reagan agreed to debate Mondale in 1984 despite Reagan's huge leads in the polls. In 1992 President Bush agreed to debate Clinton and Perot only after hectoring from his two opponents. In 1996 President Clinton and Bob Dole met in two debates that excluded Perot, who was lagging in the polls.

The impact of debates goes far beyond words—voters also can be swayed by nonverbal messages. The 1960 televised debates between Kennedy and Nixon gained Kennedy support because of his forceful, mature presentation of himself, especially in contrast to the tired-looking Nixon. A study of the 1984 presidential campaign found that the "facial displays" of Reagan and Mondale strengthened Reagan's emotional appeal. Physical appearances in public settings can help a candidate produce "momentum." Such "cues" can be especially important when people do not identify with parties and ideological differences are not compelling. An office like the presidency, which is unique in the system, evokes more such signals than lower offices.[413]

Presidential candidates display different attitudes toward the campaigns of fellow party members in state and congressional elections. Republican Nixon and Democrat Carter were not willing to use their campaigns to help other candidates. In 1980 Republican Reagan, determined to spur a "realignment" of party loyalties in the United States, devoted much time and attention to campaigning for other candidates.[414] Clinton proved a popular attraction for Democratic candidates for congressional and state elections in 1992. Two years later, in an election that saw the Republicans take over both houses of Congress, many Democrats preferred to have Clinton stay away from their state or district campaigns.

TABLE 1-9  Top Vote-Winning Third Parties, 1832–1996

| Party | Election year | Candidate | Popular vote (percent) | No. electoral votes |
|---|---|---|---|---|
| Anti-Masonic | 1832 | William Wirt | 7.8 | 7 |
| Free Soil | 1848 | Martin Van Buren | 10.1 | 0 |
| American ("Know-Nothing") | 1856 | Millard Fillmore | 21.5 | 8 |
| Southern Democrats | 1860 | John C. Breckinridge | 18.1 | 72 |
| Constitutional Union | 1860 | John Bell | 12.6 | 39 |
| Populist | 1892 | James B. Weaver | 8.5 | 22 |
| Socialist | 1912 | Eugene V. Debs | 6.0 | 0 |
| Progressive (Bull Moose) | 1912 | Theodore Roosevelt | 27.4 | 88 |
| Progressive | 1924 | Robert M. La Follette | 16.6 | 13 |
| American Independent | 1968 | George C. Wallace | 13.5 | 46 |
| Independent | 1980 | John B. Anderson | 6.6 | 0 |
| Independent | 1992 | H. Ross Perot | 18.9 | 0 |
| Reform | 1996 | H. Ross Perot | 8.4 | 0 |

SOURCES: *Guide to U.S. Elections* (Washington, D.C.: Congressional Quarterly, 1994), 26; Rhodes Cook, "Even with Higher Vote, Clinton Remains Minority President," *Congressional Quarterly Weekly Report,* January 18, 1997, 188.

NOTE: These parties (or independents) received more than 5.6 percent of the popular vote, the average third party vote historically cast for president. Daniel A. Mazmanian, *Third Parties in Presidential Elections* (Washington, D.C.: Brookings, 1974), 4–5.

## THIRD PARTIES

The American political system favors a two-party competition for national offices. The electoral college system, the first-past-the-post system of congressional elections, election finance laws, and state rules governing parties and campaigns all give a distinct advantage to the two major parties.

But the party system is not static; third parties often enter the electoral fray. Such parties, however, usually garner little support and die quickly. Since 1832, third parties have received more than 10 percent of the popular vote in only eight presidential elections, and more than 20 percent in only two elections. *(See Table 1-9.)*

Most third parties arise in times of intense conflict[415] and depend on regional rather than national support. But whenever and wherever they evolve, they are a sign of dissatisfaction with the two major parties.

### What Makes Third Parties "Significant"?

Since 1832, over forty-three parties have set out in more than 150 races for the presidency.[416] Some commentators have suggested that "significant" third parties are those that have received more than 5.6 percent of the total popular vote—the average third party vote historically cast for president.[417] By that criterion, twelve parties or independents qualify as significant.[418] *(See Table 1-9.)*

Popular support does not tell all, however. The States' Rights Democratic (Dixiecrat) Party, for example, received 7.3 percent of the electoral vote in 1948 even though its candidate, Strom Thurmond, received only 2.4 percent of the popular vote. Conversely, John Anderson and Ross Perot—whose 1980 and 1992 campaigns are deemed significant if judged by popular vote—did not receive a single electoral vote.[419]

Even candidacies with only a small share of the popular or electoral vote can influence an election significantly. For example, the Liberty Party—a movement dedicated to the abolition of slavery—received only 2.3 percent of the popular vote and no electoral votes in 1844, yet it is widely assumed that Liberty candidate James G. Birney drained enough votes from the Whig Party to guarantee the election of the Democratic candidate, James K. Polk. The thirty-six electoral votes that Polk narrowly won in New York were particularly important. As political scientist James L. Sundquist has written: "The New York *Tribune* estimated that 90 percent of the Liberty party vote in New York came from Whigs. Secretary of War John C. Spencer put his estimate at 75 percent."[420] Thus the outcome of the election might well have been different had the Liberty Party not run.

Third parties that ultimately do not garner much support in the general election also may have significant influence by publicizing important issues or options that the major parties have ignored.[421] Since major parties do not want third parties to siphon away their votes, the major parties may even adopt positions they otherwise would not have adopted in an effort to lessen the effect of (or "co-opt") their third party rivals.

Some third parties are most notable for the long periods of time they have survived, even if they may have never captured a significant portion of the popular or electoral vote. The Prohibition Party is an example.

In the nineteenth century, third parties—even when they were primarily issue oriented—tended to mirror the organization of majority parties. They ran a slate of candidates for offices other than president, held nominating conventions, drew up platforms, and existed for at least two elections. The American, or "Know-Nothing," Party elected seven governors, five senators, and forty-three members of the House of Representatives and controlled several state legislatures.

In contrast, third parties of the twentieth century usually have been associated with the candidacy of one person. The Bull Moose Party of 1912 was more a platform for the candidacy of Theodore Roosevelt than an enduring minority party. Once Roosevelt ceased to be a candidate, the party died. The candidacies of George Wallace, Minnesota senator Eugene McCarthy (who ran against Gerald Ford and Jimmy Carter in 1976), and

When Minnesota senator Eugene J. McCarthy waged his independent campaign in 1976, he chose no running mate and purposely refrained from establishing any party machinery.

John Anderson operated with little or no party organization. Perot's personality and business background attracted followers to his 1992 campaign. As the Reform Party nominee in 1996, Perot's following had dropped off.

Each of these men sought the presidency more as independent candidates than as a part of a broader-based third party effort. To a large extent, the later candidates found that technological innovations in transportation and communication were reducing the need for an established party organization to rally voter support.[422]

When McCarthy waged his independent candidacy in 1976, he chose no running mate and purposely refrained from establishing any party machinery.[423] Running simply as an independent candidate, he successfully challenged many states' ballot access laws. That, rather than his 0.93 percent of the popular vote, was the most significant aspect of his candidacy.[424]

### Varieties of Third Parties

Political scientist James Q. Wilson has identified four types of third parties: ideological parties, one-issue parties, economic protest parties, and factional parties.

*Ideological Parties.* Ideological parties, which include parties at both ends of the political spectrum, such as the Socialist and Libertarian parties, possess a "comprehensive view of American society and government that is radically different from that of the established parties."[425] Although ideological parties appeal to a narrow base of support, they have proven to be the most enduring type of third party, largely because of the ideological commitment of their members.

The longest established type of ideological parties are those that have embraced Marxism. The Socialist Labor Party, for example, was established in 1888 and ran its first presidential candidate in 1892. Although the party still exists (and has continued to run presidential candidates), its doctrinal rigidity and increasingly militant stance caused moderate members to bolt in

1901 and form the Socialist Party with Eugene V. Debs as its leader. In 1912, running with vice-presidential candidate Emil Seidel, Debs received 6.0 percent of the popular vote for president. During World War I, Debs was convicted of sedition for making a speech espousing the Socialist Party's antiwar stance. In 1920 he ran for president from the federal penitentiary in Atlanta, Georgia, and won 3.4 percent of the popular vote. (Seymour Stedman was his running mate that year.) The party has run national candidates in most presidential elections since then. The most recent variant of the socialist movement is the Socialist Workers Party, formed in 1938 by the followers of Soviet communist Leon Trotsky who were expelled from the U.S. Communist Party. The Socialist Workers have run candidates for president in every election since 1938. The Communist Party, from which the Socialist Workers split, formed in the early 1920s and ran presidential candidates from 1924 through 1940. Throughout the 1950s, the party was outlawed by restrictive legislation passed by the U.S. Congress. In the late 1960s, however, the party was reconstituted and it ran a presidential candidate (Gus Hall) from 1972 to 1984.

At the opposite end of the political spectrum is the Libertarian Party, formed in 1971. Libertarians are dedicated to the concept of individual freedom, and they oppose government intervention in both the personal and economic spheres. They have

Gus Hall, U.S. presidential candidate on the Communist Party ticket, takes questions at a 1976 press conference at the party's national headquarters in New York.

run candidates in every presidential election since 1972 when Roger MacBride, as a "faithless" Republican elector, cast the only electoral vote the Libertarians have ever received. In 1976 the Libertarians chose MacBride as their presidential candidate and David Bergland as his running mate. They appeared on the ballot in thirty-two states—more states than independent Eugene McCarthy or any other third party candidate. They may have won only 173,000 popular votes—just 0.2 percent of the national vote and far fewer votes than McCarthy— but they won more than any other minor party candidate received that year.

In 1980 the Libertarian Party was on the ballot in all fifty states and the District of Columbia. Presidential nominee Edward E. Clark of California and vice-presidential nominee David Koch of New York garnered 921,000 votes, or 1.1 percent of the vote nationwide. In 1984 the Libertarians appeared on the ballots of thirty-eight states and the District of Columbia— more states than achieved by any other minor party presidential candidate. Bergland and vice-presidential nominee Jim Lewis won 228,000 votes, or 0.3 percent of the popular vote.

The Libertarians' 1994 experience in New York underscores the difficulty that fringe parties face in gaining respectability. The party awarded the gubernatorial nomination in 1994 to Howard Stern, a radio talk-show host whose programs often degenerated into vulgarity. Stern's followers flocked to the party's state convention so that he would win the nomination. Although Libertarian officials were dismayed, they also were intrigued at the possibility of Stern's getting enough votes to improve the party's ballot position for future years. Stern, however, dropped out to avoid a state requirement that candidates disclose information about their financial holdings.

*One-Issue Parties.* Dissatisfaction with the major parties often centers on their stances toward controversial issues. Many third parties have arisen to address a single policy concern, such as slavery, states' rights, currency, opposition to immigration ("nativism"), abortion, and even hostility to lawyers.[426] But once such an issue ceased to be salient, the basis for the party's existence disappeared. Since most issues provoke intense feelings for a relatively short period—or, if they persist, eventually get attention from the major parties—one-issue parties tend to be short-lived.

Many of the earliest third parties evolved out of the slavery issue. The best known of these was the Free Soil Party, formed in 1848 as a coalition of three antislavery movements: the Liberty Party, the Barnburners, and the Conscience Whigs. At its convention in Buffalo, New York, in 1848, the Free Soil Party nominated former Democratic president Martin Van Buren as its presidential candidate and Charles F. Adams (son of former president John Quincy Adams) as his running mate. Although it lost the election, the Free Soil Party succeeded in winning thirteen congressional seats.[427]

The American Party—better known as the "Know-Nothings" because its members told outsiders they knew nothing of its secret rituals and greetings—was another notable single-issue party of the 1800s. The Know-Nothings emerged in the 1850s in opposition to European immigration (which was at a pre–Civil War peak because of severe economic conditions abroad). The party was particularly hostile to Catholics. In 1854 and 1855 the Know-Nothings were extremely successful. They elected five senators, forty-three members of the House of Representatives, and seven governors and won control of the state legislatures in six states (and came close to doing so in many others). In 1856 the Know-Nothings held a national convention in Philadelphia, nominating former Whig president Millard Fillmore for president and Andrew Jackson Donelson for vice president. The party was split, however, over slavery. Most Northern Know-Nothings turned to the Republican Party; Southern and border factions later joined with former Whigs to form the Constitutional Union Party.

One party that persists despite the apparently final resolution of its issue is the Prohibition Party. Dedicated to banning the sale of liquor, the Prohibition Party has run a presidential candidate in every election since 1872 (although the party's name was temporarily changed to the National Statesman Party in 1980). The Prohibitionists are the longest-running third party in U.S. history. Although primarily dedicated to the temperance issue, the Prohibition Party was closely linked to the early feminist movement. It was the first party to endorse women's suffrage.

*Economic Protest Parties.* Economic protest parties evolve in opposition to depressed economic conditions. The Greenback Party, for example, was an outgrowth of the Panic of 1873 (a post–Civil War economic depression). Farmers who called for the issuance of "greenbacks" (paper money) to stem the shortage of capital organized the party. Because paper money was inflationary, farmers also hoped that the use of greenbacks would lead to an increase in the price of their goods.

The Greenback Party held its first national convention in 1876. With Peter Cooper—an eighty-five-year-old New York philanthropist—as their presidential candidate and Samuel F. Cary as the vice-presidential nominee, the Greenbacks won less than 1 percent of the popular vote. But as hard times continued, they mobilized more support. Most important, they joined forces with labor groups. In 1877 and 1878 they won fourteen House seats and showed strength in state and local elections. By 1880, however, economic conditions were improving. Although they held conventions and nominated candidates for the presidential elections of 1880 and 1884, the Greenbacks saw their support dwindle. By 1888 the party was effectively dead. Supporters of the movement later turned to the People's Party (better known as the "Populists").

Prompted by the return of bad economic conditions, the Populists held a national convention in Cincinnati, Ohio, in 1891. Currency was again a prime concern, although the issue now hinged on the free coinage of silver. The Populists, with James B. Weaver as their presidential candidate and James G. Field as his running mate, won 8.5 percent of the popular vote in the 1892 presidential election. Four years later, however, the Democrats embraced the Populists' issue and nominated William Jennings Bryan on a free-silver platform. The Populists ran candidates in presidential elections through 1908 but with no appreciable accumulation of support.

*Factional Parties.* Factional parties evolve from splits in one of the major parties. They usually form to protest "the identity and philosophy of the major party's presidential candidate."[428] In the twentieth century, they have been the most successful at winning votes. Examples include three twentieth-century candidacies that have used the Progressive Party label (although the party itself was not a continuous organization).

The Progressive Party was first formed to support the candidacy of former president Theodore Roosevelt after the raucous Republican convention of 1912 in which President William Howard Taft defeated Roosevelt for the nomination. Dubbed the "Bull Moose" Party, it held a convention in Chicago where it nominated Roosevelt for president and Hiram Johnson for vice president and drew up a party platform. Although defeated by Woodrow Wilson, Roosevelt on the Bull Moose ticket proved more successful than Taft on the Republican ticket, winning 27.4 percent of the popular vote to Taft's 23.2 percent and eighty-eight electoral votes to Taft's eight. (*See "Wilson and the Divided Republicans: 1912 and 1916," p. 181, in Chapter 3.*) In 1912 the Bull Moose, or Progressive, Party also ran candidates in state and local races and even won thirteen House seats. But the Progressives' appeal was generated by Roosevelt, and when he later defected the party disintegrated. Wilson's Democratic administration incorporated many of the Progressives' reform proposals and therefore drew away much of the Progressives' support.

Like Theodore Roosevelt, Sen. Robert M. La Follette of Wisconsin represented the liberal wing of the Republican Party. In 1924 he split off from the Republicans and revived the Progressive Party label. The Progressives then held a convention in Cleveland where they nominated La Follette for president and Burton K. Wheeler for vice president. La Follette went on to receive an impressive 16.6 percent of the popular vote but only thirteen electoral votes. Again, the party relied primarily on La Follette's personal appeal. When he died in 1925, the party collapsed.

In 1948 the Progressive Party label was revived yet again. This time, however, it split off from the liberal wing of the Democratic Party. At a convention in Philadelphia, Henry A. Wallace (former vice president under Franklin Roosevelt) was nominated as the Progressives' presidential candidate and Glen H. Taylor as the vice-presidential candidate. That same year, southerners also split off from the Democratic Party over a dispute about President Truman's civil rights program. They walked out of the Democratic convention, formed the States' Rights Democratic ("Dixiecrat") Party, and convened in Birmingham, Alabama, where they nominated South Carolina governor Strom Thurmond for president and Mississippi governor Fielding Wright for vice president.

Although both the Progressives and the Dixiecrats received close to the same popular vote nationwide (Wallace received 1.157 million votes to Thurmond's 1.169 million), the Dixiecrats received more than 22 percent of the vote in the South, captur-

In 1948 southerners split off from the Democratic Party over Truman's civil rights program. They formed the "Dixiecrat" Party and nominated South Carolina governor J. Strom Thurmond, left, for president and Mississippi governor Fielding H. Wright, right, for vice president.

ing four states and thirty-nine electoral votes while the Progressives captured none. The Dixiecrats' success illustrates the system's bias toward third parties with a regional base. Despite the fracturing of his party, Harry Truman managed to win the election over his Republican challenger, Thomas Dewey.

There were more defections from the Democratic Party twenty years later when Alabama governor George Wallace bolted and formed the American Independent Party in 1968. He did not hold a convention and chose as his running mate the retired Air Force general Curtis E. LeMay. Wallace had come to national attention in 1963 when he stood in the doorway of the University of Alabama to block the entrance of two black students. The next year he ran in three Democratic presidential primaries in opposition to the 1964 Civil Rights Act.

Wallace's third party candidacy in 1968 gained support from whites and blue-collar workers who were fed up with civil rights activism, antiwar demonstrations, urban riots, and the perceived liberal ideology of incumbent president Lyndon Johnson and Democratic presidential candidate Hubert Humphrey. In the general election Wallace received 13.5 percent of the popular vote and forty-six electoral votes. There was fear at the time that he would stalemate the election and throw it to the House of Representatives, but the Republican candidate, Richard Nixon, managed to outpoll Wallace in many southern states.

Wallace returned to the Democratic Party after 1968, but candidates continued to run under the American Independent Party's label. By 1976 two splinter groups had formed—the American Party and the American Independent Party—each of which ran candidates in the 1976 election. Since the defection of Wallace, however, support for these parties has been virtually unnoticeable.

Illinois representative John Anderson formed the National Unity Campaign as the vehicle for his candidacy as an independent in 1980 when he failed to win the Republican nomination. He chose former Wisconsin governor Patrick J. Lucey, a Democrat, as his running mate. In a year when many citizens were dissatisfied with the candidates of the two major parties, Anderson received widespread publicity for his acumen and his oratory, as well as for his willingness to take often-controversial stands on issues. Despite considerable support in early polls, he ultimately captured only 6.6 percent of the popular vote and no electoral votes.

### The Perot Phenomenon

A billionaire business executive with no experience in government might seem a peculiar vehicle for populist anger against elites. Yet H. Ross Perot, who made a $4 billion fortune in the computer industry, became one of the most successful third party candidates in history when he tapped citizen rage against government in the 1992 presidential race. His run under the Reform Party banner in 1996 was less successful.

Perot had had a long association with Republican presidents and causes, but he had never contemplated a political career until GOP incumbent George Bush fell in the public opinion surveys and the Democrats in the race failed to capture the nation's imagination. At the prodding of a television talk-show host, Perot said he would consider a race for the presidency.

Perot's campaign unofficially began when he appeared on the cable talk show *Larry King Live* on February 20, 1992. When King asked Perot whether he would run for president, Perot at first demurred but then said he would run if supporters from all fifty states could get his name on the ballot. Within weeks, volunteers has gotten his name on the ballot in dozens of states. By June, a Harris poll showed Perot topping all prospective candidates with support from 37 percent of those surveyed. Bush had 33 percent and Clinton 25 percent.

In response to these developments, Perot vowed to spend $100 million or more of his own money to run a "world-class campaign." He hired two of the leading campaign strategists of recent years—Hamilton Jordan, who ran Carter's 1976 and 1980 campaigns, and Ed Rollins, who ran Reagan's 1984 campaign—but they complained that he undermined their advice and quit.

Perot's appeal stemmed not from a strong ideology, stance on a major issue, or past political alliances; instead, voters seemed attracted to his business background and folksy personality. Perot had amassed his fortune by starting his own company, Electronic Data Systems. His pithy statements—he vowed to "take back the country" and "clean out the barn"—contrasted with other candidates' measured and sometimes convoluted pronouncements.

But as volunteers circulated petitions to put him on the ballot, Perot came under growing scrutiny from the media. Re-

Business executive Ross Perot spent millions of his own money on his 1992 presidential bid. He received 18.9 percent of the vote—the strongest third party finish since 1912.

porters investigated Perot's business practices and personal foibles. Analysts—and more voters—criticized his authoritarian management style.

In response, just as the Democrats concluded their July convention Perot stunned followers by announcing that he would not run. Perot's stated reason for dropping out was that his campaign might deadlock the election and send it to the House of Representatives. After a brief hiatus—during which Perot's book *United We Stand: How We Can Take Back Our Country* climbed into paperback bestseller lists—Perot announced on October 1 that he would run after all. He appeared at several rallies but mostly delivered his message in television advertisements. The half-hour "infomercials" that aired in prime-time provided straightforward explanations of the economic and social ills facing the nation. Perot also appeared in three presidential debates with Bush and Clinton, where he hit Bush the hardest.

Except for the brief period when he was advised by Jordan and Rollins, Perot did not employ any high-priced political talent. He used his money to air television and radio commercials, print and distribute campaign literature and other materials, and maintain a Dallas headquarters where volunteers ran telephone banks. Perot traveled little.

Perot's running mate, retired Navy vice-admiral James Stockdale, was a renowned scholar and decorated former prisoner of war in Vietnam, but he had no experience in politics. In the televised vice-presidential debate, Stockdale looked befuddled and performed poorly. As a result, he became an object of parody and undermined Perot's claims to be a serious candidate.

Like many third party candidates, Perot forced the major party candidates to deal with important issues such as the budget deficit, social programs, taxes, military spending, and corruption in politics. But in the end, he could not attract enough support to win any states. Perot ended up with 19 percent of the popular vote and no electoral votes.

Unlike many third party candidates, Perot won support from a broad demographic following. "Perot ran best among self-described independents, men under 30, and voters who viewed their family's financial situation as getting worse."[429]

Perot's impact on the election was a matter of dispute. On the one hand he seemed to draw more voters from Bush than Clinton because of his more conservative stances on economic and military issues. On the other hand, Perot attracted most of his support from voters who expressed a desire for "change" in the national government—the same theme that attracted Clinton supporters. Exit polls showed that if Perot had not been in the race, Clinton still would have won.[430]

After the election Perot formed United We Stand America, a nonpartisan educational organization devoted to promoting his ideas on balancing the budget and reforming government. In 1993 Perot was one of the most vocal opponents of the Clinton administration's North American Free Trade Agreement. Perot met Vice President Al Gore in nationally televised debate on the issue, with most observers saying Gore outperformed him.

In the fall of 1995 Perot announced the formation of a third party, the Reform Party, to appeal to disaffected voters. The party was to have an open presidential nominating process, yet Perot's heavy handed maneuvering to be the party's candidate rankled many supporters. Throughout the campaign, polls placed Perot's support in the single digits. His television infomercials drew smaller audiences than in 1992. The widespread anger with government that had earlier sustained Perot as an independent political force was missing in 1996. Because of this low support, he was not invited to the two debates between President Clinton and Bob Dole. In the November he received 8.4 percent of the vote, less than half of his 1992 total.

## Obstacles to Success

Third parties face considerable legal, political, cultural, and psychological barriers. Often voters do not cast their ballots for third parties because of their loyalties to one of the two major parties. The greater their loyalty to a party, the less likely they are to vote for a third party movement. Instead, loyal members tend to work within their party for change and leave it only as a last resort.[431] This was particularly the case in the nineteenth century, when voters established third parties with the expectation that they would endure. Now a vote for a one-time, independent candidacy (such as Anderson's) may be considered more a "boycott" of the major parties than a real "exit."

Often when there is disillusionment with the major parties, people simply do not vote. Indeed, when third parties prosper, voter participation nationwide often declines.[432] People with weak party allegiances (such as new voters) are most likely to vote for third parties.

The fact that third parties have little chance of winning further diminishes their support. People often feel that a vote for a third party is a "wasted" vote. Many people also have the sense that third parties are somehow illegitimate, that they disrupt the "normal" two-party system.[433] Of particular concern is the fear that third parties will lead to a deadlock in the electoral college, thereby throwing the election to the House of Representatives. Major parties benefit from (and therefore encourage) the feeling that third parties are illegitimate.

Even more potent than these psychological barriers are the legal ones. Most notable are statutory obstacles. Since the 1890s, states have used the so-called Australian ballot, which means that states prepare official ballots listing party slates. These are provided to voters, who then mark them in secret. Before that time, parties prepared the ballots themselves. Voters then chose the ballot of the party they wished to vote for and simply dropped it in the ballot box.[434]

Most states that adopted the Australian ballot also adopted some sort of ballot access laws to keep their official ballots from being too long. The two major parties automatically appeared on the ballot, but minor parties had to pass a series of hurdles that were different in each state, including petition requirements, filing deadlines, fees, and even loyalty oaths. Meeting these requirements was time-consuming, costly, and complicated. At times it was purposely exclusionary. Since the late 1960s, a series of court cases has eased ballot access laws to prevent rules that are blatantly unfair to third parties. Nevertheless, such laws (which continue to differ from state to state) still serve as a considerable hurdle for third parties.

The 1974 Federal Election Campaign Act (FECA) also has served as a barrier to third parties. The act allows major party candidates to receive some $62 million each (in 1996) in public funds during the campaign, but third parties are allowed public funds only after the election is over *and* only if they appear on the ballot in at least ten states and receive at least 5 percent of the popular vote.[435] (Five percent of the popular vote guarantees a third party candidate funding in the next election as well.) Receiving public funds after the fact (rather than during the campaign when they are needed) puts third parties at a significant comparative disadvantage to the major parties. Not only is the money not in hand, but valuable time must be spent on fund raising rather than on other campaign activities. Fund raising itself is more difficult because third parties do not have the organizational structure or expertise of the major parties.

Initially, FECA discriminated against "independent" candidates as opposed to "real" third parties. Eugene McCarthy would not have been eligible to receive public funding in 1976 even if he had received more than 5 percent of the popular vote because he was technically an independent candidate, not a "minor party" nominee. The rule was changed for Anderson's benefit in 1980. In making the change, the Federal Election Commission said that Anderson was the functional equivalent of a third party.[436]

The electoral college itself is sometimes seen as a barrier to third parties, largely because of the "general ticket" system. *(See "Early Experience, 1789–1828," p. 3.)* Under that system, the candidate with the most votes in any given state—whether a plurality or a majority—wins all of that state's electors. This "winner-take-all" approach, it is argued, hurts third parties because it overrepresents the power of the majority parties. The electoral college, however, can magnify the support of minority parties as well. Thurmond, for example, won a disproportionate share of electoral votes in 1948 by carrying four southern states. In such cases, the existing system can help third parties that have a geographical base.

An alternative to the existing system would be a direct popular election (or a proportional system of election). It is often said that such a system would benefit third parties because every candidate would receive his or her percentage of the popular vote. But many fear that such a system would lead to a proliferation of small parties seeking a share of the vote.

Under a direct, or proportional, system, third parties would be most influential if runoff elections were held. To gain strength, they could then form coalitions in the period between the general election and the runoff. Their influence would be the most significant if runoffs were required when no candidate received a majority (that is, more than 50 percent) of the votes. If the winner could be elected by a 40 percent plurality (another common proposal), third parties would gain little. The reasoning: the greater the proportion of votes needed to win, the less likely it will be that any one party will receive that proportion, thereby forcing a runoff election (and thereby increasing the influence of third parties).[437] Third parties can still play an important role under the electoral college system by winning a large enough share of the vote to send the election to the House of Representatives. If the third party were represented in the House, its influence could be significant.

The rise of direct party primaries also has helped to maintain the two-party system. Through primaries, dissident groups within parties have an opportunity to air their views, vent their frustrations, and resolve their differences within the party itself. Without this opportunity, such groups might be more inclined to leave the party.[438]

In addition to psychological and legal barriers, third parties also face political barriers. Because third parties tend to be short-lived, they lack the base of voter support that major parties enjoy. Furthermore, their party organizations tend to be weaker and less experienced, their candidates often are less experienced and less known than those of the major parties, and they have less money to publicize their causes.

Likewise, third parties usually receive less free media coverage. They often are excluded from televised debates between the two major party candidates; their nominating conventions (if they hold any) are not beamed into American homes by television; and—with rare exceptions—they are ignored or given slight attention in news coverage and commentary. Even in 1980, when Anderson received considerable media attention, the two major party candidates received ten times more coverage than he and all ten of the other candidates combined.[439]

Finally, the U.S. political culture, with its politics of moderation, may help to reinforce the two-party system. Both of the major parties are—relatively speaking—centrist and ideologically similar. And, since the political spectrum does not run the gamut of those of some European countries, fewer irreconcilable differences are evident, with the result that political factions in this country "coalesce around pragmatic issues within the two major parties" rather than fragmenting over fundamentals.[440] This spirit of moderation, consensus, and compromise is not conducive to vigorous and persistent third parties.

Whether a two-party system is good or bad is open to debate. Some see third parties as a threat to the stability of the democratic system in the United States. Others see them as a vital element in expressing minority sentiments and as a breeding ground of issue-awareness and innovation.[441] Whatever their merits, and despite obstacles to their success, third parties persist. In so doing they often perform important functions. They focus attention on issues or ideas that might otherwise be ignored; they provide a testing ground for the presentation of new ideas or policies; and they serve as a vehicle for the free expression of opposition sentiments. As a result, they may force major parties to respond in important and beneficial ways.

## The Election

The presidential election in the fall does not present so complex a process as the nominating process in the first half of the year. Not only has the field been limited to two or three "serious" nominees, but the rules of balloting are virtually identical throughout the nation (with some exceptions for third party candidates). The fall election, however, has the potential to become complicated: once the people vote, the selection of the president could move from the electoral college to the House of Representatives and the Senate. Although this has happened only twice, there have been sixteen instances of presidents being elected with less than a majority of the popular vote. *(See box, "Minority" Presidents, p. 127)*

### ELECTION DAY

When the more than 100 million people go to the polls across the United States on a presidential election day, the first Tuesday after the first Monday in November, the great American political and media machines go into gear for the last time in the quadrennial election cycle. It is a day of parties for the frazzled campaign staffs and a day of aggressive competition for the media.

In recent years, the media have been criticized for approaching their election-day competition too aggressively. Some observers have suggested that broadcasters have undermined the democratic process in their eagerness to report the winners early. The major television networks have developed a variety of ways to make their own counts of the elections in all states and of reporting the results as soon as they come in. The networks project winners in a state on the basis of their analyses of as few as 5 percent of the state's precincts. The precincts chosen for analysis are considered to be representative of the state's overall voting patterns. Through "exit polls"—surveys of voters as they leave the voting places—the networks are able to make projections even before the polls close.

The networks' practice of declaring winners on the basis of incomplete information caused a major controversy in 1980. All three networks declared Republican Ronald Reagan the winner over President Jimmy Carter before the polls closed in the western states, and Carter conceded the election at 8:45 in the evening eastern standard time (EST). Media critics argued that the early projection discouraged western voters from going to the polls since the national election was apparently a foregone conclusion. Although the scholarly evidence is mixed, it is known that a higher turnout in the West could have changed the outcome of close state and congressional races there.[442] Four years later, in 1984, CBS projected a Reagan victory at 8:01 in the evening (EST), followed by ABC and NBC by 8:30. The precise effect of such projections has not been determined.[443] Nonetheless, since 1985 ABC, CBS, NBC, and CNN have refrained voluntarily from election-night forecasting until after 9:00 (EST).

Although Congress has considered action to restrict network pronouncements on election day, and the networks have pledged to withhold results until the polls close, the basic problem of news outracing events is likely to remain. Only a longer balloting period—a full twenty-four hours or a full weekend, as was the case in some states in the nineteenth century—would be likely to control the media's imperative to report news instantly.

Whether the presidential election is close or not, CNN, and to a lesser extent the other networks, stay on the air with special election coverage into the wee hours of the next day. The candidates watch the returns on television in their homes or hotel suites before going to their election headquarters either to celebrate or to commiserate with supporters.

The controversy that once swirled around the tampering of paper ballots has declined since today ballots are tallied electronically in most parts of the United States. Ballot counting now consists of collecting and reporting the electronically recorded results from voting booths. Although few elections have aroused counting controversies in recent years, the 1960, 1968, and 1976 elections were close enough that a change of five thousand votes in four or five states would have changed the results. In 1960 Richard Nixon considered declaring a recount of his losing contest with John Kennedy after ballot tampering was reported in Texas, Illinois, and other closely contested states. But almost two weeks after the election, Nixon decided against the call for a recount. He later wrote in his memoir *Six Crises* that he made that decision because of the constitutional crisis in presidential succession that a recount might have provoked.

Scholars disagree about the effect of "coattails" during presidential election years. The *coattails effect* is the positive or negative influence that a presidential candidate has on the fortunes of other party members running for office. Strong presidential candidates such as Franklin Roosevelt and Reagan helped other candidates get elected. In 1980 the Republican Party gained con-

trol of the U.S. Senate for the first time since 1955 as Reagan not only ran a strong national race but also campaigned personally for other Republicans.

In 1992 Democratic candidates eagerly campaigned alongside Bill Clinton, while Republicans often avoided their own president, George Bush. Clinton's claim to be a "new kind of Democrat"—and his chance to win the election—prompted those candidates to seek his financial and hortatory support. Just two years later, during the midterm elections, many Democrats openly repudiated President Clinton's programs and did not want his campaign help. However, by 1996 Clinton's public support had rebounded, and most congressional candidates were enthusiastic to have the president campaign with them.

Because the kinds of issues that voters consider important are usually different for presidential and congressional campaigns, the coattails effect is considered to be of minor importance. Most congressional candidates stress local concerns and their role as a liaison between citizens and the federal government; presidential candidates, in contrast, stress broad themes. Political scientist James MacGregor Burns has argued that American politics is best understood not as a single system but as an uneasy marriage of separate presidential and congressional systems. While presidents set broad themes for the national political system, Congress tends to the parochial concerns of constituents. Voters therefore have different standards for presidential and congressional selection.

## THE ELECTORAL VOTE

The Founders intended that a group of the nation's most learned and public-spirited citizens—"the electoral college"—would select the president. The electors were to be chosen by the states as the states saw fit. Some time after their selection the electors would then meet in their separate states to pick the next president.

The Constitutional Convention included advocates of direct presidential elections, but most delegates were as concerned about the dangers of "mob rule" as they were concerned about excessive government power. As George Mason of Virginia stated: "It would be as unnatural to refer the choice of a proper magistrate to the people as it would to refer the choice of colors to a blind man."[444]

As the electoral system operates today, electors meet in their respective state capitals on the first Monday after the second Wednesday in December and prepare a statement of their vote to send to Washington. Congress counts the votes on January 6. States receive one elector for each representative and senator in Congress.

The electoral college system favors the very small and very large states. The smallest states are favored because they have, regardless of their population, at least two electors representing the state's two Senate seats plus at least one elector for the delegation to the House of Representatives. (The Twenty-third Amendment allotted three electoral votes to the District of Columbia.) Large states are favored because their large blocs of electoral votes ensure that the candidates will pay close attention to their demands.

Since 1836, all the states except Maine have allocated delegates to candidates on a "winner-take-all" basis. (Maine allocates delegates by special presidential-elector districts.) The winner-take-all system is a moderating influence on U.S. politics. Political strategies depend on attracting as many diverse groups as possible under the same political banner in order to win the whole state rather than only part of it. Systems of proportional representation (in which parties or candidates receive representation according to their percentage of the popular vote) tend to complicate bargaining and to fragment coalitions by giving representation to minority parties. The state-by-state system of allocating electors encourages candidates to identify a base of strength and attempt to build slowly on that base. Candidates typically make appeals to groups in states just outside their strong base of support in order to lure these voters into their camps. Modern Democrats, for example, usually can count on the industrial regions in the Northeast and Midwest to serve as a strong base of support; their job is to appeal to groups with common concerns in other states with geographic and ideological proximity. Modern Republicans appear to have a strong hold on the West and many states of the South.

Democrat Carter's winning 1976 campaign won over not only the solid South but also border states from Maryland to Ohio and Illinois. The "across-the-board" strategy of Walter Mondale's losing 1984 campaign prevented him from building on his natural strength in traditionally liberal areas. In 1992 Clinton focused on the big states and won eight of the twelve states having the largest number of electoral votes, including California and New York. (See Figure 1-4, p. 99.)

The Framers expected a plethora of state "favorite-son" candidates to produce regular electoral college deadlocks, sending the elections to the House. Such a situation would create a variant of a parliamentary system. If no candidate wins an electoral majority, the House of Representatives decides the election, with each state casting one vote. Each state's delegation of House members votes on which candidate to support. If a precedent set in 1825 were followed, a state could cast a House vote only if a majority of its whole delegation supported a candidate (as opposed to a majority of House members present for the vote). This requirement could disenfranchise a state with strong two-party competition if some of its House members missed the vote. The Senate selects the vice president by a simple majority vote. (See "When the Electoral College Is Deadlocked," p. 125.) This system was part of the web of compromises between large and small states during the constitutional convention.

Critics of the electoral college system point out several possible sources of an electoral crisis. For one thing, should a candidate with a popular vote lead lose the electoral vote, the nation must face a problem of legitimacy. John Quincy Adams in 1824, Rutherford B. Hayes in 1876, and Benjamin Harrison in 1888 won the presidency with smaller popular votes than those of their opponents. The election of Adams was decided in the House. Hayes was chosen when a congressionally appointed commission gave him the disputed electoral votes of three states. The legitimacy of both elections was seriously questioned, with allegations made that corrupt deals thwarted the will of the people in both cases. In the case of Benjamin Harrison, he attracted about 100,000 fewer votes (of almost 12 million cast) than President Grover Cleveland, but he won the electoral college vote by 233–168.

More concern has been expressed about a possible deadlock in the electoral college if the election involves more than two candidates. As noted, if no candidate wins a majority of all elec-

Despite losing the popular vote by 100,000 ballots, Benjamin Harrison, left, won the 1888 presidential election with 233 electoral votes to 168 for Grover Cleveland.

toral votes, the election is to be decided by the House. If a third party candidate wins one or two states in a close race, he or she could play an important "broker" role either in the electoral college or (less likely) in the House. The legitimacy of a race decided by backroom deals would be in serious question.

A related controversy surrounds the instructions that electors have when they meet to vote. About a third of the states require electors to cast their ballots for the candidate who won the popular vote in the state. The Constitution does not require electors to adhere to the party line, and in theory they may vote however they like, but electors who do so—known as "faithless electors"—are rare. Still, in 1960 Sen. Harry Byrd of Virginia, who was not listed on any ballot, won fifteen electoral votes from unpledged electors and one faithless elector. In 1988 a Dukakis elector in West Virginia voted for Dukakis's running mate, then-senator Lloyd Bentsen of Texas. An organized movement could produce even more electoral vote defections—and a constitutional crisis. The outcome of an election could depend on the willingness of a candidate with only minority or regional support to cooperate with a major candidate.

Numerous reforms have been proposed to alter both the fundamental concept of the electoral college and some of its obsolete and odder aspects. One reform would eliminate faithless electors by automatically casting a state's electoral votes for the candidate receiving the most popular votes. A second reform would allocate electoral votes by congressional district rather than by state and would give the state's two electors who represent its senators to the top presidential candidate as a bonus. A third proposal would provide for proportional allocation of a state's electoral votes—which could lead to more deadlocks and congressional selection of presidents because there would be more opportunity for third and fourth parties to garner electors. A fourth proposal would do away with the electoral college altogether through direct election of the president, with a runoff if no candidate achieved 40 percent of the popular vote. Another reform would give the popular vote victor "bonus" electors for each state. And a final proposal would alter the way Congress voted in the event of an electoral college deadlock by allowing House members to vote individually rather than having one vote for each state.

Congress has never passed a constitutional reform of presidential elections for submission to the states, although the Senate passed a direct election proposal in the 1970s. Any of these changes would require a constitutional amendment, and amending the Constitution is a long and arduous process. Even when Congress submits a proposed amendment to the states for ratification, three-fourths of all state legislatures must approve the amendment for it to become law. Thus in the absence of a major crisis, an overhaul of the electoral college is unlikely. The way in which the electoral college highlights state identity has many supporters. Perhaps that is why the most serious efforts to reform the electoral college failed in 1950, 1969, and 1977.

## WHEN THE ELECTORAL COLLEGE IS DEADLOCKED

When no presidential candidate receives a majority of the electoral vote, the Constitution directs that the election be decided by the House of Representatives. Originally, the House also selected the vice president in such a situation (as it did in 1800) because there was then no separate ballot for presidential and vice-presidential candidates. Under that system, the second-place candidate became vice president. That changed in 1804 with the ratification of the Twelfth Amendment, which directs that electors vote for president and vice president on separate ballots. Since then, the House has been directed to select the president and the Senate the vice president when there is a deadlocked election.

The Framers of the Constitution originally thought that most presidential elections would be deadlocked. George Mason, for one, predicted that nineteen out of twenty elections would be decided by the House.[445] In fact, only two presidential elections—those of 1800 and 1824—have been so decided.

### Procedure

If an election is thrown into the House, the newly elected representatives, rather than the "lame-duck" House, select the president from among the three candidates with the most electoral votes. This procedure is provided for by statute. Before ratification of the Twentieth Amendment to the Constitution in 1933, both the new Congress and the new presidential term began on March 4. Thus the old lame-duck Congress was forced to select the president. Now the new Congress convenes on January 3 and the president's inauguration takes place on January 20.

The changes brought about by the Twentieth Amendment mean that, if the electoral college were deadlocked, Congress would have considerably less time than before to choose a president. Originally, the Twelfth Amendment gave the House until March 4 to select the president. If the House did not make a decision by that date, the amendment called for the vice president-elect (chosen, if necessary, by the Senate) to "act as president as in the case of the death or other constitutional disability of the president."[446] Under the current system, the House has only about two weeks to make a choice before the inaugural date of January 20. If the House is deadlocked and cannot make a choice by that date, the Twentieth Amendment directs that the vice president-elect "shall act as president *until a president shall have qualified.*"[447]

The language surrounding that provision can be read in different ways. For example, legal scholars Laurence H. Tribe and Thomas M. Rollins of Harvard have argued that the House, if deadlocked, "could go on voting, with interruptions for other business and indeed with an infusion of members in midterm, for four full years." They pointed out that this would transform the government into a "quasi-parliamentary system," since the acting president would be "subject to termination at any time until the House deadlock is finally broken."[448] Political scientist Allan P. Sindler has argued, however, that the deadline of March

4 imposed by the Twelfth Amendment was not superseded by the Twentieth Amendment. As such, the House can replace the acting president only *until* that time. If the House acts before March 4, the acting president becomes vice president.[449]

When selecting the president, each state delegation in the House has one vote, and no vote is cast if the delegation is evenly divided. Members of the delegation vote by secret ballot, and an absolute majority of the delegations (twenty-six of the fifty states) is necessary for election.[450]

If no vice-presidential candidate receives a majority of votes in the electoral college, the selection is made by the Senate between the two candidates with the most electoral votes. Unlike the House procedure, each senator has one vote. Again, an absolute majority—fifty-one votes—is needed for the election. Since the Senate chooses among only the top two candidates and is not beset with the potential problems of split delegations, the vice-presidential selection process is somewhat less complicated than the presidential selection process. By statute, the new Senate (as convened on January 3) makes the decision.

The selection process is further complicated if neither a president nor a vice president can be decided on by the date set for inauguration. In such an event, the Twentieth Amendment empowers Congress to decide by law "who shall then act as President, or the manner in which one who is to act shall be selected, and such person shall act accordingly until a President or Vice President shall have qualified."[451]

The Presidential Succession Act of 1947 now covers such a circumstance. The act calls for the Speaker of the House and the president pro tempore of the Senate, in that order, to serve as acting president until a candidate qualifies. To so serve, they must resign their seat in Congress.[452] If they refuse, the line of succession reverts to members of the cabinet of the incumbent (previous) administration in the order the cabinet offices were established (starting with secretary of state). Although there were two earlier presidential succession acts (in 1792 and 1886), the 1947 act—in conformity with the Twentieth Amendment—

was the first to deal with vacancies caused by the failure of candidates to qualify.[453]

Neither the constitutional provisions nor the succession act specify what criteria legislators should use in choosing among the designated candidates. As many commentators have pointed out, this raises several problems. Should legislators vote for the candidate with the most electoral votes or the most popular votes? If they base their decision on the popular vote, should they look at the popular vote in their district, or in their state, or in the nation as a whole? Or should they simply vote for the candidate of their party or of their conscience? Could they bargain away their votes to the "highest bidder," so to speak?[454] Although there is little to guide legislators in making such decisions, there no doubt would be considerable pressure to act in a fashion that would foster an orderly and legitimate transfer of power.

### Precedents: 1800 and 1824

Presidential elections have been thrown into the House of Representatives only twice in U.S. history: in 1800 and 1824. In the first case, the deadlock was brought on by the old method of electors voting for the president and vice president on the same ballot. Each elector had two votes, and when all the votes were tallied the second-place candidate became vice president. The Federalist ticket consisted of John Adams for president and Charles Cotesworth Pinckney for vice president; the Republican ticket consisted of Thomas Jefferson for president, with Aaron Burr as his running mate. When the electors voted in December 1800, the two Republican candidates tied for first place.

This example illustrates some of the pitfalls of the legislative selection process. Under the provisions then in effect, the lame-duck House (which had a Federalist majority) selected the president. Many Federalists considered Aaron Burr less repugnant than Thomas Jefferson and therefore plotted to elect him president (even though it was clear that Jefferson was the presidential candidate and Burr was the vice-presidential candidate).

Although Federalist leader Alexander Hamilton strongly dis-

Only two presidential elections—those of 1800 and 1824—have been decided by the House of Representatives. In 1800 Thomas Jefferson, left, and the intended vice-presidential candidate, Aaron Burr, right, tied in the electoral college vote.

## "MINORITY" PRESIDENTS

In seventeen presidential elections the victor has been elected, either by the electoral college itself or by the House of Representatives, with less than a majority of the popular vote cast in the election. Three of them—John Quincy Adams, Rutherford B. Hayes, and Benjamin Harrison—actually trailed their opponents in the popular vote.

The following table shows the percentage of the popular vote received by candidates in the elections in which a "minority" president (designated by **boldface** type) was elected:

| Year/<br>candidate | Percentage of<br>popular vote | Year/<br>candidate | Percentage of<br>popular vote |
|---|---|---|---|
| **1824** | | **1892** | |
| Jackson | 41.34 | **Cleveland** | **46.05** |
| **Adams** | **30.92** | Harrison | 42.96 |
| Clay | 12.99 | Weaver | 8.50 |
| Crawford | 11.17 | Others | 2.25 |
| **1844** | | **1912** | |
| **Polk** | **49.54** | **Wilson** | **41.84** |
| Clay | 48.08 | T. Roosevelt | 27.39 |
| Birney | 2.30 | Taft | 23.18 |
| | | Debs | 5.99 |
| **1848** | | | |
| **Taylor** | **47.28** | **1916** | |
| Cass | 42.49 | **Wilson** | **49.24** |
| Van Buren | 10.12 | Hughes | 46.11 |
| | | Benson | 3.18 |
| **1856** | | Others | 1.46 |
| **Buchanan** | **45.28** | | |
| Fremont | 33.11 | **1948** | |
| Fillmore | 21.53 | **Truman** | **49.52** |
| | | Dewey | 45.12 |
| **1860** | | Thurmond | 2.40 |
| **Lincoln** | **39.82** | Wallace | 2.38 |
| Douglas | 29.46 | | |
| Breckinridge | 18.09 | **1960** | |
| Bell | 12.61 | **Kennedy** | **49.72** |
| | | Nixon | 49.55 |
| **1876** | | Others | 0.72 |
| Tilden | 50.97 | | |
| **Hayes** | **47.95** | **1968** | |
| Cooper | 0.97 | **Nixon** | **43.42** |
| | | Humphrey | 42.72 |
| **1880** | | Wallace | 13.53 |
| **Garfield** | **48.27** | Others | 0.33 |
| Hancock | 48.25 | | |
| Weaver | 3.32 | **1992** | |
| Others | 0.15 | **Clinton** | **43.01** |
| | | Bush | 37.45 |
| **1884** | | Perot | 18.91 |
| **Cleveland** | **48.50** | Others | 0.64 |
| Blaine | 48.25 | | |
| Butler | 1.74 | **1996** | |
| St. John | 1.47 | **Clinton** | **49.23** |
| | | Dole | 40.71 |
| **1888** | | Perot | 8.40 |
| Cleveland | 48.62 | Others | 1.65 |
| **Harrison** | **47.82** | | |
| Fisk | 2.19 | | |
| Streeter | 1.29 | | |

couraged the idea, the majority of Federalists in the House backed Burr. If the Constitution had allowed the decision to be made by the vote of individual members (rather than by the bloc votes of state delegations), Burr would have won. But as it stood, the situation remained deadlocked. Balloting began on February 11, 1801, but no candidate received a majority. It quickly became apparent that the House deadlock would not be broken soon. As one observer recalled: "Many [congressmen] sent home for night caps and pillows, and wrapped in shawls and great-coats, lay about the floor of the committee rooms or sat sleeping in their seats. At one, two, and half-past two, the tellers roused the members from their slumbers, and took the same ballot as before."[455]

Seven days and thirty-six ballots later, the tide turned. The day before, Federalist representative James Bayard of Delaware had told a party caucus that the balloting had gone on long enough. To delay the process any longer would endanger the Constitution. After receiving word from Maryland Republican boss Samuel Smith that Jefferson would preserve the Hamiltonian financial system, respect the integrity of the navy, and refrain from dismissing Federalists in subordinate government jobs simply on the grounds of politics, Bayard was convinced that the Federalists must relent. Thus on the thirty-sixth ballot, Bayard and the Burr supporters from Maryland, South Carolina, and Vermont cast blank ballots, giving the presidency to Jefferson and the vice presidency to Burr.[456]

The election of 1824 is the only one thrown into the House since the adoption of the Twelfth Amendment. The fact that no candidate received a majority of the electoral vote count that year was largely a result of the crowded field of candidates. By 1824 the Federalist Party was dead. It appeared that whoever was nominated by the Democrat-Republicans' "King Caucus" would surely be elected president. The congressional caucus, however, was subject to increasing criticism. The caucus system was a holdover from an age that distrusted mass democratic sentiments, and that age was coming to an end.

As it turned out, attendance at the caucus was meager. The caucus nominated William H. Crawford (who had served as secretary of the Treasury under President James Monroe), but others balked at the choice for two reasons. First, Crawford had suffered a paralytic stroke the year before that had left him greatly impaired. Second, populist sentiment was rising, and Crawford's selection by a small group of legislators smacked of political manipulation. State legislatures promptly nominated John Quincy Adams, John C. Calhoun, Henry Clay, and Andrew Jackson for president.

Attempts were made to limit the field of candidates, but they were to little avail. Crawford's men dropped his running mate, Albert Gallatin, in the hopes that they could persuade Clay to take his place. Their plan was that Clay supporters, recognizing that Crawford might not live out his term, would push Crawford to victory. Clay, preferring to gamble on the possibility of winning on his own merits, refused.[457] Among the candidates, only Calhoun withdrew from the presidential race.

In the election of 1824, none of the candidates won an electoral majority. Although Andrew Jackson, right, outpolled his competitors, John Quincy Adams, left, was chosen by the House of Representatives.

When the votes of the electoral college were tallied, no candidate had a majority. Jackson stood in front with ninety-nine electoral votes, followed by Adams with eighty-four, Crawford with forty-one, and Clay with thirty-seven. In accord with the Twelfth Amendment, the names of Jackson, Adams, and Crawford were placed before the House. It was immediately evident that the support of Clay would tip the balance between the two front-runners.

Clay was not fond of either candidate, but he clearly felt that Adams was the lesser of two evils. In early January, Clay and Adams conferred, and Clay let it be known that he would support Adams in the House election. Soon thereafter, a letter in a Philadelphia newspaper alleged that Adams had offered Clay the post of secretary of state in return for his support. Jackson was furious, and his rage was all the greater when Adams won the House election with a bare majority of thirteen out of twenty-

After finishing last in the election of 1824, Henry Clay threw his support to John Quincy Adams, making him president. Adams subsequently appointed Clay secretary of state.

four state delegations and proceeded to name Clay secretary of state. Thus Jackson, who had more popular and electoral votes than any of the other candidates in the general election, did not become president.

The Senate has chosen a vice president only once, in 1837. Martin Van Buren was elected president that year with 170 of 294 electoral votes. But his running mate—Richard M. Johnson of Kentucky—received only 147 electoral votes (one less than a majority). A group of twenty-three Virginia electors who supported Van Buren had boycotted Johnson because of his long-term romantic entanglement with a black woman.[458] The remainder of the electoral votes were split among three other candidates: Francis Granger of New York, who received seventy-seven electoral votes; John Tyler of Virginia, who received forty-seven; and William Smith of Alabama, who received twenty-three.

The names of the top two candidates were sent to the Senate. In making the selection, the Senate adopted a resolution that called for the senators to vote by voice vote in alphabetical order.[459] The Senate confirmed Johnson's election by a vote of 33–16.

### Threats

Although no presidential election has been thrown to the House since 1824, several have come close. The elections of Abraham Lincoln in 1860 and John Kennedy in 1960, for example, would have gone to the House with a shift of only thirty thousand popular votes.[460] A relatively small shift of votes also could have sent the elections of 1836, 1856, 1892, 1948, 1968, and 1976 to the House. (See Chapter 3, Chronology of Presidential Elections.)

In 1968 Alabama governor George Wallace ran as a strong third party candidate on the American Independent Party ticket. There was widespread fear that year that Wallace would deadlock the election and throw it to the House. Republican Richard Nixon and Democrat Hubert Humphrey ran one of the closest races in history. Despite earlier hopes of winning the whole South, Wallace won only five states and forty-six electoral votes. If Nixon had lost just California or two or three smaller states that were close, he would have been denied an electoral majority. Well aware of his strategic position, Wallace elicited written affidavits from his electors promising that they would vote as he instructed them. Wallace took a hard stance on the terms he required for delivering those votes to another candidate. Among other things, he called for the repeal of all civil rights legislation, the repeal of the federal antipoverty program, and the criminal indictment of anyone advocating a North Vietnamese victory in the Vietnam War.[461]

Although the independent candidacy of John Anderson failed to win any electoral votes in 1980, and Ronald Reagan won the race by a wide margin, there was fear early in the campaign that Anderson's presence would deadlock the election. At the 1980 Republican convention, former president Gerald Ford predicted precisely such an outcome.[462] Similar fears were expressed about the third party candidacies of Theodore Roosevelt in 1912 and Robert La Follette in 1924. *(See Chapter 3, Chronology of Presidential Elections.)*

In 1992 independent Ross Perot dropped out of the race in July, claiming that his presence in the race threatened to throw the race into the House of Representatives. If Perot had attracted a more viable running mate and conducted a stronger campaign, he might have won some western states and been in a position to broker the final election result. After reentering the race, he won 18.9 percent of the popular vote, but no electoral votes. Perot ran again for president in 1996 under the Reform Party's banner. The freshness of his candidacy had worn off, however, and he received less than half of his 1992 vote total.

To an extent, such fears are fanned by party regulars in an attempt to discount the influence of a third party candidate. A vote for such a candidate is worse than just a wasted vote, they argue; it is one that could lead to a "constitutional crisis." But it is not just the presence of third party candidates that threatens to deadlock presidential elections. Neck-and-neck races between Kennedy and Nixon in 1960 and between Carter and Ford in 1976 came close to such a deadlock.

Ironically, the Constitution's Framers took great pride in the same system of House election that is now viewed with great trepidation. Whether that trepidation is justified is a matter of debate. Nonetheless, it is a fear that periodically haunts the U.S. political landscape.

## DEATH OR RESIGNATION AFTER ELECTION DAY

If a president-elect or vice president-elect dies or resigns after election day but before the date in December when the electors cast their ballots, the national party committee would likely choose a replacement in an effort to guide the vote of the electors. Although Republican vice president James S. Sherman died October 30, 1912, just before the election, his name remained on the ballot. After the election, the Republican National Committee nominated a replacement and awarded him Sherman's electoral votes.

If the death or resignation takes place after the electoral votes are counted and announced by Congress but before the inauguration, the selection process is governed by the Twentieth Amendment to the Constitution. That amendment specifies that if the president-elect dies or resigns, the vice president-elect will become president. If both were to die or resign during that period, the Presidential Succession Act would take effect.

The procedure is less clear if the death or resignation takes place between the time when the electors cast their votes and the time when the votes are counted by Congress. Since the electoral votes are technically not valid until counted by Congress, no president-elect or vice president-elect would exist, and the Presidential Succession Act could not be used. If the candidate who died or resigned during that period did not have a majority of the electoral votes, the majority candidate simply would win. If, however, the candidate who died or resigned did have a majority of the electoral votes, the choice of a president would be thrown to the House of Representatives, and the choice of a vice president to the Senate.[463]

## NOTES

1. *Guide to U.S. Elections,* 3d ed. (Washington, D.C.: Congressional Quarterly, 1994), 415–416.
2. Richard M. Pious, *The American Presidency* (New York: Basic Books, 1979), 22.
3. Ibid., 25–29.
4. The term *electoral college* does not appear in the text of the Constitution. Citing Andrew C. McLaughlin, Edward Corwin wrote that the term "was used by Abraham Baldwin in 1800 and by John Randolph in 1809, and 'officially' in 1845" (Edward S. Corwin, *The President: Office and Powers,* 5th ed. [New York: New York University Press, 1984], 385 n. 21).
5. The original compromise called for the Senate to make the final decision in such circumstances.
6. Richard Hofstadter, *The Idea of a Party System* (Berkeley: University of California Press, 1969), 16–39.
7. John F. Hoadley, *Origins of American Political Parties* (Lexington: University Press of Kentucky, 1986), 34.
8. Ibid.; A. E. Dick Howard, *Commentaries on the Constitution of Virginia,* vol. 1 (Charlottesville: University Press of Virginia, 1974), 318–319.
9. Howard, *Commentaries,* 320.
10. Quoted in ibid., 323.
11. Ibid., 325–326.
12. See, for example, Hoadley, *Origins,* 34–35; Robert E. Brown, *Charles Beard and the Constitution* (Princeton, N.J.: Princeton University Press, 1956), 61–72.
13. *McPherson v. Blacker,* 146 U.S. 1 (1892) at 29; Eugene H. Roseboom, *A History of Presidential Elections,* 2d ed. (New York: Macmillan, 1964), 15.
14. Corwin, *The President,* 45.
15. Edward Stanwood, *A History of the Presidency from 1788 to 1897,* revised by Charles Knowles Bolton (Boston: Houghton Mifflin, 1928), 21–22.
16. Ibid., 38–39.
17. Roseboom, *History of Presidential Elections,* 28.
18. Stanwood, *History of the Presidency,* 38–39.
19. Ibid., 136.
20. Corwin, *The President,* 45–46.
21. Nelson W. Polsby and Aaron Wildavsky, *Presidential Elections,* 6th ed. (New York: Scribner's, 1984), 298 n.94.
22. *Ray v. Blair,* 343 U.S. 214 (1952), quoted in Harold W. Chase and Craig R. Ducat, *Edward S. Corwin's The Constitution and What It Means To-*

*day,* 13th ed. (Princeton, N.J.: Princeton University Press, 1973), 380.

23. Stanwood, *History of the Presidency,* 78.

24. *McPherson v. Blacker,* 146 U.S. 1 (1892).

25. Roseboom, *History of Presidential Elections,* 17.

26. Margaret Horsnell, "Who Was Who in the Constitutional Convention," *This Constitution* 15 (summer 1987): 38.

27. Stanwood, *History of the Presidency,* 27. According to Stanwood: "Although in all the newspaper references to the coming election . . . Mr. Adams was spoken of as a candidate for Vice-President, that gentleman did not so regard himself, but rather as a candidate for the presidency. If he received more votes than Washington, he would be President; if the votes were equal, the House of Representatives would choose one of the two. He showed plainly that he regarded his own merits as equal to those of Washington" (p. 26).

28. Roseboom, *History of Presidential Elections,* 33.

29. James S. Chase, *Emergence of the Presidential Nominating Convention: 1789–1832* (Urbana: University of Illinois Press, 1973), 8.

30. Richard L. Rubin, *Press, Party, and Presidency* (New York: Norton, 1981), 11.

31. Culver H. Smith, *The Press, Politics, and Patronage* (Athens: University of Georgia Press, 1977), 13.

32. John Tebbel, *The Compact History of the American Newspaper* (New York: Hawthorn Books, 1963), 64, 65.

33. From the December 23, 1796, issue of the *Aurora,* quoted in Willard Grosvenor Bleyer, *Main Currents in the History of American Journalism* (Boston: Houghton Mifflin, 1927), 116.

34. James MacGregor Burns, *The Deadlock of Democracy: Four-Party Politics in America* (Englewood Cliffs, N.J.: Prentice-Hall, 1963), 29.

35. Chase, *Presidential Nominating Convention,* 11. But see others who say that the caucus did meet: *Guide to U.S. Elections,* 9; Noble E. Cunningham Jr., *The Jeffersonian Republicans: The Formation of Party Organization, 1798–1801* (Chapel Hill: University of North Carolina Press, 1957), 91. Austin Ranney, in *Curing the Mischiefs of Faction* (Berkeley: University of California Press, 1975), notes that it is not clear when the first caucuses were, but that most historians agree that both parties held caucuses in 1800 (p. 64).

36. Noble E. Cunningham Jr., ed., *The Making of the American Party System: 1789–1809* (Englewood Cliffs, N.J.: Prentice-Hall, 1965), 14.

37. From text of the speech in ibid., 16–17.

38. Stanwood, *History of the Presidency,* 45–46.

39. Chase, *Presidential Nominating Convention,* 12.

40. Quoted in Stanwood, *History of the Presidency,* 70.

41. The history of the amendment is covered in some detail in ibid., 77–82.

42. Ibid., 111.

43. Quoted in ibid., 90.

44. William J. Crotty, *Political Reform and the American Experiment* (New York: Crowell, 1977), 11.

45. Thomas Byrne Edsall and Mary D. Edsall, *Chain Reaction: The Impact of Race, Rights, and Taxes on American Politics* (New York: Norton, 1991).

46. See ibid.

47. By the mid-1970s Republicans were becoming competitive for the first time in the South, but the Democrats still held most legislatures. In 1954 only 86 of 1,559 state legislators, or 5.5 percent, were Republicans; by 1972 the figure had climbed to 280 out of 1,516 (18.5 percent). See Everett Carll Ladd Jr. and Charles D. Hadley, *Transformation of the American Party System* (New York: Norton, 1975), 150.

48. F. Clifton White with William J. Gill, *Suite 3505: The Story of the Draft Goldwater Movement* (Ashland, Ohio: Ashbrook Press, 1992).

49. Richard Fenno, *Home Style: House Members in Their Districts* (Boston: Little, Brown, 1978), 160–162.

50. Woodrow Wilson also called for national primaries in his first message to Congress as president in 1913, but the initiative died because of neglect. Polls since World War II have found steady majorities favoring national primaries, but there has never been a serious effort to bring about such a system.

51. Rhodes Cook, *Congressional Quarterly Weekly Report,* August 19, 1995, 2484.

52. Nine amendments affect the way citizens participate in elections: Twelfth (1804), placing the presidential and vice-presidential candidates on a single ticket; Fourteenth (1868), providing for equal protection under the law and for a decrease in the number of House members of any state that denied citizens the vote; Fifteenth (1870), specifying that the right to vote cannot be denied because of race; Seventeenth (1913), providing for direct election of senators; Nineteenth (1920), giving women the right to vote; Twenty-second (1951), limiting presidents to two terms; Twenty-third (1961), giving the District of Columbia electoral votes; Twenty-fourth (1964), eliminating the poll tax; and Twenty-sixth (1971), giving eighteen-year-olds the right to vote.

53. *Smith v. Allwright,* 321 U.S. 649 (1944); *Harman v. Forssenius,* 380 U.S. 528 (1965); *Harper v. Virginia State Board of Elections,* 383 U.S. 663 (1966).

54. Some jurisdictions below the state level retained tax-paying requirements into the twentieth century.

55. E. E. Schattschneider, *The Semisovereign People* (Hinsdale, Ill.: Dryden, 1975), 82.

56. *Guinn v. United States,* 238 U.S. 347 (1915); *Smith v. Allwright,* 321 U.S. 649 (1944); *Harper v. Virginia State Board of Elections,* 383 U.S. 663 (1966).

57. Charlotte Perkins Gilman's *Moving the Mountain,* for example, pictures the utopian state that might exist if there were true equality of the sexes. Gilman's study, *Women and Economics,* analyzed the way gender discrimination and repression deformed the economy. See *Charlotte Perkins Gilman Reader* (New York: Pantheon, 1980). Gilman and other feminists of the late nineteenth century designed schemes for cooperative cooking and housekeeping that they hoped would release women for full participation in the world of work and politics. See Delores Hayden, *The Grand Domestic Revolution* (Cambridge, Mass.: MIT Press, 1981).

58. *Marston v. Lewis,* 410 U.S. 679 (1973).

59. *Shaw v. Reno, Attorney General,* 509 U.S. 630 (1993).

60. Jasper B. Shannon, *Money and Politics* (New York: Random House, 1959), 19–20.

61. Robert Merton, *Social Theory and Social Structure* (New York: Free Press, 1957), 71–82.

62. Herbert E. Alexander and Anthony Corrado, *Financing the 1992 Election* (Armonk, N.Y.: M. E. Sharpe, 1995), 6.

63. Professor Hadley Cantril's department of psychology at Princeton University conducted a wide variety of polls both about domestic production and consumption during the war and about the attitudes and needs of troops on the front. See James R. Beniger and Robert J. Giuffra Jr., "Public Opinion Polling: Command and Control in Presidential Campaigns," in *Presidential Selection,* ed. Alexander E. Heard and Michael Nelson (Durham, N.C.: Duke University Press, 1987), 190.

64. This account draws on William J. Crotty, *Party Reform* (New York: Longman, 1983); Nelson W. Polsby, *Consequences of Party Reform* (New York: Oxford University Press, 1983); and David E. Price, *Bringing Back the Parties* (Washington, D.C.: CQ Press, 1984), chap. 6.

65. From the McGovern-Fraser Commission Report, quoted in Crotty, *Party Reform,* 25.

66. Ibid., 26.

67. Quoted in Price, *Bringing Back the Parties,* 146.

68. Crotty, *Party Reform,* 62.

69. For an overview of the literature on this point, see Austin Ranney, "The Political Parties: Reform and Decline," in *The New American Political System,* ed. Anthony King (Washington, D.C.: American Enterprise Institute, 1978), 214–215.

70. Polsby, *Consequences of Party Reform,* 34–35, quoting Byron Shafer.

71. Crotty, *Political Reform,* 245.

72. Terry Sanford, *A Danger of Democracy: The Presidential Nominating Process* (Boulder, Colo.: Westview, 1981), 20–21.

73. For examples of those who take issue with these critics, see Robert T. Nakamura, "The Reformed Nominating System: Its Critics and Uses," *PS*

16, no. 4 (fall 1983): 667–672; and Kenneth A. Bode and Carol F. Casey, "Party Reform: Revisionism Revised," in *Political Parties in the Eighties,* ed. Robert A. Goldwin (Washington, D.C.: American Enterprise Institute, 1980), 3–19.

74.  James W. Ceaser, *Presidential Selection: Theory and Development* (Princeton, N.J.: Princeton University Press, 1979), 284.

75.  Price, *Bringing Back the Parties,* 151.

76.  Crotty, *Political Reform,* 246.

77.  Austin Ranney, "Changing the Rules of the Nominating Game," in *Choosing the President,* ed. James David Barber (Englewood Cliffs, N.J.: Prentice-Hall, 1974), 73–74.

78.  While it is generally accepted that the reforms led to the proliferation of presidential primaries, Kenneth Bode and Carol Casey (both members of the McGovern-Fraser Commission) have suggested that other factors played a role as well. See Bode and Casey, "Party Reform," 16–17. For a refutation of their position, see Polsby, *Consequences of Party Reform,* 57–58.

79.  Crotty, *Party Reform,* 76–77.

80.  Price, *Bringing Back the Parties,* 154.

81.  Ibid., 151; and James W. Davis, *Presidential Primaries: Road to the White House* (Westport, Conn.: Greenwood Press, 1980), 66.

82.  Price, *Bringing Back the Parties,* 170.

83.  Michael Oreskes, "Jackson Still Irked by Delegate Vote Tally," *New York Times,* July 22, 1988, A11.

84.  This account of the Republican Party's reform efforts is based on Crotty, *Party Reform,* chaps. 17 and 18; Robert J. Huckshorn and John F. Bibby, "National Party Rules and Delegate Selection in the Republican Party," *PS* 16, no. 4 (fall 1983): 656–666; and Price, *Bringing Back the Parties,* 156–159.

85.  For a discussion of this, see Ceaser, *Presidential Selection,* 265–271.

86.  Price, *Bringing Back the Parties,* 156.

87.  Jean Bethke Elshtain, "Issues and Themes in the 1988 Campaign," in *The Elections of 1988,* ed. Michael Nelson (Washington, D.C.: CQ Press, 1989), 111–126.

88.  Howard L. Reiter, *Parties and Elections in Corporate America* (New York: Longman, 1993), 163.

89.  Robert L. Heilbroner, *The Nature and Logic of Capitalism* (New York: Norton, 1985), 55.

90.  Elizabeth Drew, *Politics and Money: The New Road to Corruption* (New York: Macmillan, 1983), 2, 4.

91.  Robert J. Samuelson, "The Campaign Reform Fraud," *Newsweek,* July 13, 1987, 43.

92.  Jeffrey Berry, *The Interest Group Society* (Boston: Little, Brown, 1984), 168.

93.  Herbert E. Alexander, *Financing Politics: Money, Elections, and Political Reform,* 3d ed. (Washington, D.C.: CQ Press, 1984), 7, 123.

94.  Drew, *Politics and Money,* 96.

95.  John Kenneth Galbraith, *American Capitalism: The Concept of Countervailing Power* (Boston: Houghton Mifflin, 1952), esp. chap. 2.

96.  A number of academic debates fall within the demand-side school of electoral behavior. The debate whether voters address issues "prospectively" (by estimating how the candidates' issue stances will affect their own fortunes in the future) or "retrospectively" (by judging the effects of candidates' past policy positions) emphasizes the voters' ability to shape the system (see Morris P. Fiorina, *Retrospective Voting in American National Elections* [New Haven, Conn.: Yale University Press, 1981]). Debates whether a winning candidate has a "mandate" for particular policies assume that the system operates according to the signals that voters send (see Walter Dean Burnham, "The 1980 Earthquake: Realignment, Reaction, or What?" in *The Hidden Election: Politics and Economics in the 1980 Campaign,* ed. Thomas Ferguson and Joel Rogers [New York: Pantheon, 1981], 98–140). The debate about the winning candidate's differing roles as "delegate" or "trustee" also falls into this school of U.S. election studies (see Fenno, *Home Style: House Members in their Disctricts.*)

97.  Thomas Ferguson and Joel Rogers, *Right Turn: The Decline of the*

*Democrats and the Future of American Politics* (New York: Hill and Wang, 1986), 45.

98.  Ira Katznelson, "A Radical Departure: Social Welfare and the Election," in Ferguson and Rogers, *Hidden Election,* 332–334.

99.  Mancur Olson, *The Logic of Collective Action* (Cambridge, Mass.: Harvard University Press, 1965).

100.  Jack L. Walker Jr., *Mobilizing Interest Groups in America: Patrons, Professions, and Social Movements* (Ann Arbor: University of Michigan Press, 1991), 83.

101.  Thomas Geoghegan, *Which Side Are You On? Trying to Be for Labor When It's Flat on Its Back* (New York: Farrar, Straus, and Giroux, 1991).

102.  Shannon, *Money and Politics,* 15.

103.  Ibid., 17–18.

104.  Ibid., 25.

105.  Ibid., 31.

106.  By the time of McKinley's reelection drive in 1900, Hanna had refined his fund-raising system to the point where it was "unofficial taxation." Corporations were expected to contribute "according to [their] stake in the general prosperity of the country." Hanna returned $50,000 of the Standard Oil Company's $250,000 donation because it was considered more than the company's fair "share" for the campaign. See Michael E. McGerr, *The Decline of Popular Politics: The American North, 1865–1928* (New York: Oxford University Press, 1986), 44–45; and Shannon, *Money and Politics,* 33.

107.  Shannon, *Money and Politics,* 37.

108.  Michael Nelson, "A Short, Ironic History of American Bureaucracy," *Journal of Politics* 44 (winter 1982): 767.

109.  Samuel Kernell, *Going Public: New Strategies of Presidential Leadership,* 2d ed.(Washington, D.C.: CQ Press, 1993), 109, 118.

110.  Shannon, *Money and Politics,* 60–61.

111.  Herbert E. Alexander, *Money in Politics* (Washington, D.C.: Public Affairs Press, 1972), 10.

112.  David W. Adamany and George E. Agree, *Political Money: A Strategy for Campaign Financing in America* (Baltimore: Johns Hopkins University Press, 1975), 113–114.

113.  *Congressional Quarterly Weekly Report,* August 19, 1995, 2488.

114.  Ibid., 32. Of the money raised before the disclosure requirement took effect, eighty-seven contributors of $50,000 or more gave a total of $12.4 million. Some $4.4 million of the $43.3 million raised after that point came from thirty-seven contributors of $50,000 or more.

115.  Adamany and Agree, *Political Money,* 39.

116.  Polsby and Wildavsky, *Presidential Elections,* 66. As might be expected, the sequence of events is as disputed as it is crucial. From 1969 to 1971, the Nixon administration negotiated with International Telephone and Telegraph (ITT) over the suit. President Nixon was involved personally. Tapes revealed that, at the same time, administrative officials knew of ITT's offers for campaign and convention assistance. See Herbert E. Alexander, *Financing the 1972 Elections* (Lexington, Mass.: Lexington Books, 1976), 263–268.

117.  Stephen Hess, *The Presidential Campaign* (Washington, D.C.: Brookings, 1974), 82. Long after the 1972 election, the public continued to associate John Connally, the administration's Treasury secretary, with influence peddling. During his losing presidential campaign in 1980, Connally faced persistent questions about the dairy scandal, for which he was indicted and acquitted. Connally tried to defuse the issue by saying, "I'm the only certified non-guilty political figure in the country," a posture that seemed to betray a certain cynicism about the nonlegal, moral standards of politics. See Richard Harwood, ed., *The Pursuit of the Presidency 1980* (New York: Berkley, 1980), 145.

118.  Adamany and Agree, *Political Money,* 41.

119.  Ibid., 48.

120.  *Buckley v. Valeo,* 424 U.S. 1 (1976).

121.  From *Buckley v. Valeo.* Cited in *Guide to Congress,* 4th ed. (Washington, D.C.: Congressional Quarterly, 1991), 729.

122.  Ibid.

123. The delays in revamping the FEC had an immediate effect on the 1976 presidential nomination contests. Arizona representative Morris Udall and former California governor Ronald Reagan did not receive federal funds they had planned to use, and they had to trim their primary efforts in several states. It is conceivable that both candidates could have won their party nominations if they had had the money at the critical periods. See Jules Witcover, *Marathon: The Pursuit of the Presidency, 1972–1976* (New York: Viking Press, 1977), 219–221.

124. Dan Clawson, Alan Neustadt, and Denise Scott, *Money Talks: Corporate PACs and Political Influence* (New York: Basic Books, 1992), 213.

125. Richard L. Berke, "Why Nothing Ever Changes," *New York Times*, July 17, 1994.

126. Quoted in Reiter, *Parties and Elections in Corporate America*, 171.

127. Herbert E. Alexander, "American Presidential Elections since Public Funding, 1976–84," in *Comparative Political Finance in the 1980s*, ed. Herbert E. Alexander (New York: Cambridge University Press, 1989), 121.

128. Davis, *Presidential Primaries*, 217–218; Alexander, *Financing the 1972 Election*, 110–159.

129. Figures on the 1992 election, unless otherwise noted, were supplied by the Citizens Research Foundation, from figures gathered by the Federal Election Commission. Comprehensive figures on the 1992 election are included in Alexander and Corrado, *Financing the 1992 Election*; and in Harold W. Stanley and Richard G. Niemi, *Vital Statistics on American Politics*, 5th ed. (Washington, D.C.: CQ Press, 1995).

130. Federal Election Commission press releases, March 8, 1989, and March 31, 1993.

131. Michael J. Malbin, "You Get What You Pay for, but Is That What You Want?" in *Before Nomination: Our Primary Problems*, ed. George Grassmuck (Washington, D.C.: American Enterprise Institute, 1985), 86.

132. Davis, *Presidential Primaries*, 206. Committees to draft reluctant candidates are not automatically subject to campaign spending limits. The money spent by the 1979 draft committees for Massachusetts senator Edward Kennedy did not count against Kennedy's overall spending limits.

133. Glenn R. Simpson, "Coughing It Up for Campaign Coffers: Checks from 10021 Are in the Mail," *New York Observer*, June 13, 1994.

134. Davis, *Presidential Primaries*, 207.

135. Xandra Kayden, "Regulating Campaign Finance: Consequences for Interests and Institutions," in *Presidential Selection*, ed. Alexander Heard and Michael Nelson (Durham, N.C.: Duke University Press, 1987), 261.

136. Paul-Henri Gurian, "The Influence of Nomination Rules on the Financial Allocations of Presidential Candidates," *Western Political Quarterly* 43 (September 1990): 668.

137. "Campaign Finance Bills Compared," *Congressional Quarterly Weekly Report*, February 5, 1994, 268.

138. Davis, *Presidential Primaries*, 206–207.

139. Harwood, *Pursuit of the Presidency*, 102–103.

140. "Manufacturing the Next President," *Harper's*, December 1987, 49.

141. Reducing the party's role can have enormous repercussions for the political system. It is wrong to assign complete responsibility for the separation of presidential politics and the party system to the finance system. A variety of other developments—such as the increasing dominance of media and campaign professionals in the process—are just as important. Furthermore, the split between the campaign organization and the rest of the system was evident before federal financing. Perhaps the best example of a campaign cut off from the rest of the system was Richard Nixon's 1972 reelection campaign, which operated completely on privately raised funds. That campaign illustrated the perils involved in an isolated presidential campaign—whether it is publicly or privately financed. The independence of the Committee to Re-elect the President was probably a major reason behind the committee's illegal activities, from influence-peddling to dirty tricks to espionage activities. When the so-called Watergate affair reached its climax in the summer of 1974, Nixon could not count on the loyalties of Republican members of Congress he had declined to support vigorously in 1972.

142. F. Christopher Arterton, "Campaign '92: Strategies and Tactics of the Candidates," in *The Election of 1992*, ed. Gerald M. Pomper (Chatham,

N.J.: Chatham House, 1993), 84; Thomas Byrne Edsall, *The New Politics of Inequality* (New York: Norton, 1984), 91–92.

143. Anthony Corrado, *Creative Campaigning: PACs and the Presidential Selection Process* (Boulder, Colo.: Westview, 1992), 35.

144. Edsall, *New Politics of Inequality*, 91–92.

145. Quoted in Kayden, "Regulating Campaign Finance," 276.

146. Quoted in Herbert Asher, *Presidential Elections and American Politics* (Homewood, Ill.: Dorsey Press, 1980), 279–280.

147. John W. Mashek, "Democratic Candidates Seek Funding Amid a Donor Drought," *Boston Globe*, February 8, 1992.

148. John W. Mashek, "Brown Wins a Race," *Boston Globe*, May 2, 1992.

149. Ferguson and Rogers, *Right Turn*, 47.

150. Peter W. Bernstein, "Fritz's Fat Cats Shake the Money Tree," *Fortune*, August 20, 1984, 153.

151. Ferguson and Rogers, *Right Turn*, 73–83.

152. Stanley and Niemi, *Vital Statistics on American Politics*, 5th ed., 176.

153. Ibid., 169.

154. Ferguson and Rogers, 53.

155. Edsall, *New Politics of Inequality*, 99.

156. Ibid., 100.

157. Ibid., 98.

158. Ibid., 98.

159. Herbert E. Alexander, "Political Parties and the Dollar," *Society*, January/February 1985, 55.

160. Ibid.

161. Harold W. Stanley and Richard G. Niemi, *Vital Statistics on American Politics*, 4th ed. (Washington, D.C.: CQ Press, 1994), 180–181.

162. Herbert E. Alexander and Brian A. Haggerty, *Financing the 1984 Election* (Lexington, Mass.: Lexington Books, 1987), 109, 110, 359, 381.

163. See Edsall, *New Politics of Inequality*, 252.

164. Charles Babcock, "Top 1995–96 'Soft Money' contributors to the National Party Committees," *Washington Post*, February 17, 1997, A23.

165. The most notable PACs were run by the AFL-CIO, the American Medical Association, and the National Association of Manufacturers.

166. Berry, *Interest Group Society*, 159.

167. Corrado, *Creative Campaigning*, 185.

168. The following discussion relies on David Corn, "Inside Gephardt's PACscam," *The Nation*, May 2, 1987.

169. Telephone calls to the PAC were answered: "Gephardt for President." Queries about the PAC were referred to Gephardt's formal campaign staff. PAC donors—who also gave to the formal presidential campaign—acknowledged that the PAC, ostensibly formed to help other Democrats, really operated to promote Gephardt: "I gave under the assumption that I was giving to Gephardt" (Corn, "Inside Gephardt's PACscam," 575).

170. Ibid., 577. The Federal Election Commission has been lenient in interpreting the role of multicandidate PACs. In a 1986 case the FEC ruled 4–2 that George Bush's Fund for America's Future was not acting as part of Bush's campaign when it recruited, assisted, and donated money to Republican Party members in Michigan who were attempting to become delegates to the 1988 national convention. As long as the PAC helps a variety of candidates it can also promote Bush's presidential bid, the FEC held. Thomas Harris, an FEC member, issued a dissenting opinion in the decision. "Only persons just alighting from a U.F.O.," he wrote, "can doubt that activities of these sorts will promote the candidacy of the [PAC's] founding father. That, of course, is why so many would-be presidents, of both parties, have created and utilized PACs of this sort in recent years. The commission, however, is willing to turn a blind eye to the realities."

171. Ferguson and Rogers, *Right Turn*, 181–182.

172. Drew, *Politics and Money*, 96.

173. Quoted in D. M. Alpern, "Reforming the Reforms," *Newsweek*, September 3, 1984, 25.

174. Alexander and Corrado, *Financing the 1992 Election*; and Stanley and Niemi, *Vital Statistics on American Politics*, 4th ed., 180.

175. "The Gold Mine Is Playing Out," *Forbes*, April 6, 1987, 146.

176. *Congressional Quarterly Weekly Report*, June 3, 1995, 1595.

177. The estimates for campaign spending vary, depending on what ele-

ments are included. The Federal Election Commission uses only figures that fit within its official limits and campaign reports, such as money raised for primaries, the nominating process, matching funds, official convention budgets, and the federal government's equal allotments for the fall campaign organizations. Herbert Alexander and his associates at the Citizens' Research Foundation, however, include figures that fall outside the official reports, such as third party candidates; labor, corporate, and association spending; the costs of complying with federal laws; spending by "independent" organizations formed to back or oppose presidential candidates; spending by party organizations; and total spending on conventions.

178.  "Behind All the Fuss over Election Money," *U.S. News & World Report*, October 8, 1984, 74.

179.  Marjorie Pritchard, "On the Bus," *Boston Globe*, August 7, 1992.

180.  American advertisers spend more than even the most lavish political campaigns. The industry spent $19 billion in 1985. Procter and Gamble alone spent some $652 million—more than double the total amount spent by all organizations in the 1984 presidential campaign (Kayden, "Regulating Campaign Finance," 276). Elections logically should cost more than promotion of other public and private activities because they are so intermittent and fragmented. Campaign organizations must start afresh every two or four years, preventing any continuity in the delivery of the message.

181.  Corrado, *Creative Campaigning*, 35.

182.  Adamany and Agree, *Political Money*, 113–114.

183.  Joseph Nocera, "Why American Voters Should Watch French Television," *Washington Monthly*, September 1981, 40–42.

184.  See charts in Edsall, *New Politics of Inequality*, 86, 91, 133.

185.  Ibid., 91. Democratic money as a percentage of Republican money fell from 30.1 percent to 21.9 percent to 18.1 percent during those cycles.

186.  Federal Election Commission press release, March 19, 1997.

187.  Kayden, "Regulating Campaign Finance," 262–263.

188.  Quoted in Alpern, "Reforming the Reforms," 25–26.

189.  William M. Lunch, *The Nationalization of American Politics* (Berkeley: University of California Press, 1987), 112–114.

190.  "Behind All the Fuss over Election Money," 75.

191.  The explosion in campaign spending in state and congressional races has mirrored that of presidential races. In the 1994 congressional elections, candidates spent a record $724 million, an average of more than $304,000 per candidate.

Higher election costs have been most apparent in the Senate races. In 1980 the most expensive Senate races were five close elections that each cost between $2.1 million and $2.7 million. In 1994 the 333 Senate candidates spent $318.4 million for an average of almost $1 million apiece. Some races cost more than $10 million and one, Republican challenger Michael Huffington's losing campaign against Democratic senator Dianne Feinstein in California, cost almost $30 million. Feinstein herself spent $14.4 million to keep her seat.

The costs for congressional races vary widely. Differences in spending depend on the costs of commercial media blitzes, the density of population, the strengths of state and local party organizations, the competitiveness of the two-party system, and the importance of primary contests.

Congressional elections were under few enforceable regulations before the passage of the Federal Election Campaign Act in 1971. The law and its subsequent amendments and regulatory rulings have redirected spending patterns instead of limiting them. The most important element of the FECA turned out to be disclosure requirements. The law required quarterly financial statements from all candidates or political committees taking part in a federal election. The effectiveness of the requirements is difficult to gauge. It is hard for local newspapers to examine the candidates' reports critically before the campaign.

In 1974 Congress passed a number of amendments to the FECA that affected congressional elections. The major provision was a $1,000 limit on donations to federal candidates in each of the major stages of the campaign—the primary, runoff, and general election. Donors could not spend more than $25,000 for all federal candidates. Political action committees, however, could spend up to $5,000 per candidate per election, with no overall national limitation. Congress moved slowly on further reform. De-

spite the support of President Jimmy Carter, proposals for public financing of congressional elections failed in 1977, 1978, and 1979. A bill to limit PAC contributions in House races failed in 1980.

192.  E. E. Schattschneider, *Party Movement* (New York: Holt, Rinehart, and Winston, 1942), 52.

193.  Schattschneider, *Semisovereign People*, 1–3.

194.  The continuous-residency requirement has not been followed to the letter. Herbert Hoover lived overseas for several years before his election in 1928, and Gen. Dwight D. Eisenhower was commander of the North Atlantic Treaty Organization (NATO) in Europe before his successful 1952 candidacy. Other prospective candidates—such as Ambassador Anne Armstrong in 1976 and NATO commander Alexander Haig in 1980—also lived overseas. A person born of American parents on foreign soil would presumably be permitted to seek the presidency. See Charles Gordon, "Who Can Be President of the United States," *Maryland Law Review* 28 (winter 1968): 1–32.

195.  For recent examinations of the president's need to make public appeals for support of policy initiatives, see Jeffrey K. Tulis, *The Rhetorical Presidency* (Princeton, N.J.: Princeton University Press, 1987); and Kernell, *Going Public*.

196.  Rossiter's portrait of the president reads in part:

He must be, according to unwritten law: a man, a white, a Christian. He almost certainly must be: a Northerner or Westerner, less than 65 years old, of Northern European stock, experienced in politics and public service, healthy. He ought to be: from a state larger than Kentucky, more than forty-five years old, a family man, of British stock, a veteran, a Protestant, a lawyer, a state governor, a Mason, a Legionaire, or Rotarian—preferably all three, a small-town boy, self-made man, especially if a Republican, experienced in international affairs, a cultural middle-brow who likes baseball, detective stories, fishing, pop concerts, picnics, and seascapes. It really makes no difference whether he is: a college graduate, a small businessman, a member of Congress, a member of the Cabinet, a defeated candidate for the Presidency, providing that he emerged from his defeat the very image of the happy warrior. . . . He almost certainly cannot be: a Southerner. . . , of Polish, Italian, or Slavic stock, a union official, an ordained minister. He cannot be, according to unwritten law: a Negro, a Jew, an Oriental, a woman, an atheist, a freak. . . .

See Clinton Rossiter, *The American Presidency* (New York: Harcourt Brace, 1960), 193–194.

197.  David Canon, *Actors, Athletes, and Astronauts* (Chicago: University of Chicago Press, 1990).

198.  Alan Ehrenhalt, *The United States of Ambition: Politicians, Power, and the Pursuit of Office* (New York: Times Books, 1992), 256.

199.  Polling data before the 1984 campaign showed that women differed greatly from men in both their level of support of the Reagan administration and opinions on several major issues. A number of state and congressional races also appeared to turn on women's support. See Eleanor Smeal, *Why and How Women Will Elect the Next President* (New York: Harper and Row, 1984), 1–16. On the basis of that evidence, several organizations including the National Organization for Women lobbied the Democratic Party to nominate a woman for vice president.

200.  In 1983, 13 percent of state legislators were women—still far below their share of the population at large but three times their share in 1969. See Erwin D. Hargrove and Michael Nelson, *Presidents, Politics, and Policy* (Baltimore: Johns Hopkins University Press, 1984), 142.

201.  The ambivalence of white voters toward a black candidacy is suggested in Andrew Kopkind, "A Populist Message Hits Home," *The Nation*, July 18/25, 1987, 55. One Iowa voter, asked whether she might vote for an African American such as Jackson, said farm issues were more important than race: "The presidency is so far away. Now if he was going to marry my daughter, that might be a different story."

202.  Hargrove and Nelson, *Presidents, Politics, and Policy*, 20–24.

203.  David S. Broder, "The Story That Still Nags at Me," *Washington Monthly*, February 1987, 29–32.

204.  David S. Broder and T. R. Reid, "Schroeder Garners Encouragement, Money," *Washington Post*, August 22, 1987, A5.

205.  A variety of psychological studies of political leadership have ar-

gued that a candidate's insecurities can be an important part of his or her energy but also an unhealthy distraction from rational political behavior. See James David Barber, *The Presidential Character* (Englewood Cliffs, N.J.: Prentice-Hall, 1972), for portraits of Wilson, Johnson, and Nixon. Among the most prominent "psychobiographies" are those by Alexander George and Juliette George, *Woodrow Wilson and Colonel House* (New York: John Day, 1956); and Bruce Mazlish, *In Search of Nixon* (New York: Basic Books, 1972).

206. Jimmy Carter, *Why Not the Best?* (New York: Bantam Books, 1976), 158–159.

207. Allen D. Hertzke, *Echoes of Discontent: Jesse Jackson, Pat Robertson, and the Resurgence of Populism* (Washington, D.C.: CQ Press, 1993).

208. Howard L. Reiter, *Selecting the President: The Nominating Process in Transition* (Philadelphia: University of Pennsylvania Press, 1985), 49, 165.

209. Davis, *Presidential Primaries,* 159.

210. Polsby and Wildavsky, *Presidential Elections,* 95.

211. See Corn, "Inside Gephardt's PACscam."

212. Elaine Ciulla Kamarck, "Structure as Strategy: Presidential Nominating Politics since Reform" (Ph.D. diss., University of California, Berkeley, 1986), 46–47.

213. Ryan J. Barilleaux and Randall E. Adkins, "The Nominations: Process and Patterns," in *The Elections of 1992* (Washington, D.C.: CQ Press, 1993), ed. Michael Nelson, 46, 48–49, 50; Federal Elections Commission.

214. William G. Mayer, "The New Hampshire Primary: A Historical Overview," in *Media and Momentum: The New Hampshire Primary and Nomination Politics,* ed. Gary Orren and Nelson W. Polsby (Chatham, N.J.: Chatham House, 1987), 24.

215. Two others, Jerry Brown and Frank Church, entered the campaign late.

216. William C. Adams, "As New Hampshire Goes . . . ," in Orren and Polsby, *Media and Momentum,* 45.

217. Ibid., 49.

218. Quoted in Theodore J. Lowi, "Constitution, Government, and Politics," in *Before Nomination: Our Primary Problems,* ed. George Grassamuck (Washington, D.C.: American Enterprise Institute, 1985), 7.

219. David S. Broder, "Listening Carefully in Iowa," *Washington Post,* August 12, 1987, A23. Gore, struggling in the Iowa polls, later attacked the prominence of Iowa in the nominating process and pulled all but a few campaign workers out of the state.

220. Alan I. Abramowitz, "Viability, Electability, and Candidate Choice in a Presidential Primary Election: A Test of Competing Models," *Journal of Politics* 51 (November 1989): 989.

221. Witcover, *Marathon: The Pursuit of the Presidency,* 327–354.

222. Jack Germond and Jules Witcover, *Wake Us When It's Over: Presidential Politics of 1984* (New York: Macmillan, 1985).

223. Martin Schram, *Running for President: A Journal of the Carter Campaign* (New York: Pocket Books, 1976), 64.

224. Davis, *Presidential Primaries,* 185.

225. Gurian, "The Influence of Nomination Rules," 668.

226. A television call-in show in Iowa included the following exchange between Connally and a Connally supporter who could not persuade his wife to vote for the former Texas governor:

"What's the problem?" asked Connally. "She thinks you're a crook."
"I'm the only certified non-guilty political figure in the country," Connally answered after an explanation of his acquittal in a federal bribery case.
"I told my wife all of that."
"What did she say?"
"She still thinks you're a crook."

See Richard Harwood, *The Pursuit of the Presidency 1980* (New York: Berkley, 1980), 145.

227. New York governor Mario Cuomo argued that the "stature problem" of the 1988 Democratic candidates would fade as soon as one or two candidates emerged from the field in the Iowa caucuses and New Hampshire primary.

228. Norman H. Nie, Sidney Verba, and John R. Petrocik, *The Changing American Voter* (Cambridge, Mass.: Harvard University Press, 1979), 210–242.

229. The stress that political pundits place on appearance was underscored by the reaction of two observers of the first debate of Democratic candidates in 1987. One said of Sen. Paul Simon: "He may have the highest IQ, but he's never going to photograph well. . . . His earlobes are unbelievable." Another said Simon "does not project the vigor and youthfulness" of other candidates (David S. Broder, "Gephardt, Simon, Dukakis Score Well Among Viewers," *Washington Post,* July 3, 1987, A16).

230. Stephen Hess, "Why Great Men Are Not Chosen Presidents: Lord Bryce Revisited," in *Elections American Style,* ed. A. James Reichley (Washington, D.C.: Brookings, 1987), 81.

231. Davis, *Presidential Primaries,* 213–219, 224–239.

232. Polsby and Wildavsky, *Presidential Elections,* 149.

233. On the nexus of parties and issues in voting, see Nie et al., *Changing American Voter,* 47–73, 156–73. For a discussion of the different vote orientations toward presidential politics and congressional politics, see Burns, *The Deadlock of Democracy,* esp. 241–264.

234. The effect of presidential coattails should not be overstated. More important may be the "drag" effect that an unpopular president may have on the party's candidates. See Warren E. Miller, "A Study in Political Myth and Mythology," *Public Opinion Quarterly* 19 (winter 1955–1956): 26–39.

235. Polsby and Wildavsky, *Presidential Elections,* 49.

236. See Berry, *Interest Group Society.*

237. The organizations backing Mondale included the American Federation of Labor-Congress of Industrial Organizations, the United Auto Workers, the National Education Association, the National Organization for Women, and a number of members of Congress and other politicians such as Atlanta mayor Andrew Young.

238. William G. Thiemann, "President Hoover's Efforts on Behalf of FDR's 1932 Nomination," *Presidential Studies Quarterly,* 24 (winter 1994): 87–91.

239. Maureen Dowd, "New Model Iowa for '88: Less Corn, More Silk," *New York Times,* November 25, 1987, B12.

240. Stephen Skowronek, *The Politics Presidents Make: Leadership from John Adams to George Bush* (Cambridge, Mass.: Harvard University Press, 1993).

241. Arthur M. Schlesinger Jr., *The Cycles of American History* (Boston: Houghton Mifflin, 1986).

242. Fred Barnes, "Earthquake," *New Republic,* October 17, 1994, 18.

243. Erwin C. Hargrove and Michael Nelson, "The Presidency: Reagan and the Cycle of Politics and Policy," in *The Elections of 1984,* ed. Michael Nelson (Washington, D.C.: CQ Press, 1985), 189–213.

244. James MacGregor Burns, *The Power To Lead* (New York: Simon and Schuster, 1984), 163.

245. Davis, *Presidential Primaries,* 65.

246. Ibid., 71.

247. Ibid., 67–68.

248. Paul R. Abramson, John H. Aldrich, and David W. Rohde, *Change and Continuity in the 1984 Elections,* rev. ed. (Washington, D.C.: CQ Press, 1986), 25.

249. For a classic account of the widening scope of conflict, see Samuel H. Beer, "Liberalism and the National Interest," *Public Interest,* no. 1 (fall 1966): 70–82.

250. Davis, *Presidential Primaries,* 139.

251. Ibid., 139–142.

252. On the "plugged-in" hypothesis, see Sidney W. Verba and Norman H. Nie, *Participation in America* (New York: Harper and Row, 1972), 125–137; Angus Campbell, Philip E. Converse, Warren E. Miller, and Donald E. Stokes, *The American Voter* (New York: Wiley, 1960), 475–481. On the effect of registration laws on voter turnout, see Raymond Wolfinger and Stephen Rosenstone, *Who Votes?* (New Haven, Conn.: Yale University Press, 1980), 61–88. Also see Stanley Kelley Jr., Richard E. Ayres, and William G. Bowen, "Registration and Voting: Putting First Things First," *American Political Science Review* 61 (June 1967). Useful overviews are contained in Walter Dean Burnham, "The Turnout Problem," and Eddie N. Williams and Milton D.

Morris, "Is the Electoral Process Stacked against Minorities?" in Reichley, *Elections American Style*.

253. *Guide to U.S. Elections*, 422.

254. James Q. Wilson, *The Amateur Democrat* (Chicago: University of Chicago Press, 1962).

255. Kay Lawson, "How State Laws Undermine Parties," in *Elections American Style*, 247.

256. See Anthony Downs, *An Economic Theory of Democracy* (New York: Harper and Row, 1957).

257. Theodore H. White, *America in Search of Itself: The Making of the President, 1956–1980* (New York: Harper and Row, 1982), 318–319.

258. Ceaser, *Presidential Selection*, 325, 343, 345. Ceaser writes:

Polarization is a necessary component of building constituencies anew.... [T]here are certain values, such as restraint on the pursuit and exercise of power, that are more important than adhering to the formulae of full democracy. If the existence of parties with intermediary power brokers—modern bosses if you like—can provide an informal check on the presidency and discourage candidates from going to the roots in quadrennial crusades, then the cost in terms of deviation from some abstract notion of 'democratic ethic' is well worth bearing.... The 'leverage' that parties possess enables them to withstand, at least temporarily, undesirable currents of opinion and extreme movements.

259. Polsby and Wildavsky, *Presidential Elections*, 45.

260. See Kathleen Hall Jamieson, *Eloquence in an Electronic Age* (New York: Oxford University Press, 1988).

261. James W. Davis, *National Conventions in an Age of Party Reform* (Westport, Conn.: Greenwood Press, 1983), 45.

262. Ibid., 77–78; Polsby and Wildavsky, *Presidential Elections*, 66.

263. Maureen Dowd, "Democrats Confront 'The Thing That Ate the Hall,' " *New York Times,* July 14, 1988, A21.

264. Morton Krondracke, quoted in Davis, *National Conventions*, 47; see also Polsby and Wildavsky, *Presidential Elections*, 115–116.

265. Paul T. David, Ralph M. Goldman, and Richard C. Bain, *The Politics of National Party Conventions* (Washington, D.C.: Brookings, 1960), 165.

266. Ibid., 166–168.

267. Davis, *National Conventions*, 58–59.

268. Ibid., 54.

269. Andrew Rosenthal, "Poll Finds Atlanta Delegates More Liberal than the Public," *New York Times,* July 17, 1988, A17.

270. Democratic National Committee.

271. Davis, *National Conventions*, 42–44.

272. Richard Reeves, *Convention* (New York: Harcourt Brace Jovanovich, 1977), 39–40.

273. Roseboom, *History of Presidential Elections*, 361.

274. Davis, *National Conventions*, 93.

275. David et al., *Politics of National Party Conventions*, 203–208.

276. Terri Susan Fine, "Interest Groups and the Framing of the 1988 Democratic and Republican Party Platforms," *Polity* 26 (spring 1994): 517–530.

277. Davis, *National Conventions*, 49–50.

278. Ibid., 87.

279. David et al., *Politics of National Party Conventions*, 66.

280. Quoted in Malcolm Moos and Stephen Hess, *Hats in the Ring* (New York: Random House, 1960), 119.

281. Jack W. Germond and Jules Witcover, *Whose Broad Stripes and Bright Stars? The Trivial Pursuit of the Presidency 1988* (New York: Warner Books, 1989), 352.

282. Quoted in Roseboom, *History of Presidential Elections*, 309.

283. Quoted in Stefan Lorant, *The Glorious Burden* (New York: Harper and Row, 1968), 440.

284. Text of keynote address by Gov. Mario Cuomo, *New York Times,* July 17, 1984, A16.

285. Theodore H. White, *The Making of the President 1972* (New York: Atheneum, 1973), 244.

286. Reeves, *Convention*, 207.

287. Davis, *National Conventions*, 201.

288. "Rift Over Campaign Films," *New York Times,* August 11, 1988, D19; Maureen Dowd, "A Man Is Chosen, but a Verb Is Born," *New York Times,* August 18, 1988, A23.

289. Witcover, *Marathon: The Pursuit of the Presidency*, 487.

290. Reeves, *Convention*, 19.

291. Sanford, *Danger of Democracy*, 31.

292. Moos and Hess, *Hats in the Ring*, 124.

293. "We Point with Pride," *New York Times,* August 10, 1988, A14.

294. *Congressional Quarterly Weekly Report*, July 18, 1992, 2125.

295. Moos and Hess, *Hats in the Ring*, 130–131.

296. Warren Weaver Jr., "A Choice Seat Is More Luck than Politics," *New York Times,* July 20, 1988, A19.

297. Andrew Rosenthal, "For Delegate Trackers, Timing Is Everything," *New York Times,* July 22, 1988, A12.

298. Quoted in Lorant, *Glorious Burden*, 638.

299. Ibid., 302–304; see also Roseboom, *History of Presidential Elections*, 215.

300. Davis, *National Conventions*, 203.

301. Joel K. Goldstein, *The Modern American Vice Presidency* (Princeton, N.J.: Princeton University Press, 1982), 47.

302. Moos and Hess, *Hats in the Ring*, 144–158.

303. Harold F. Bass, "The President and the National Party Organization," in *Presidents and Their Parties*, ed. Robert Harmel (New York: Praeger, 1984), 73–81.

304. Quoted in Lorant, *Glorious Burden*, 592–594.

305. Schram, *Running for President*, 254–255.

306. H. L. Mencken, quoted in Moos and Hess, *Hats in the Ring*, 15.

307. Irwin Ross, *The Loneliest Campaign: The Truman Victory of 1948* (New York: New American Library, 1968), 93–94.

308. Kurt Lang and Gladys Engel Lang, *Politics and Television* (Chicago: Quadrangle, 1968), 78–79.

309. Quoted in ibid., 24.

310. Reeves, *Convention*, 35–36.

311. Ibid., 68.

312. Davis, *National Conventions*, 202–203; Moos and Hess, *Hats in the Ring*, 131.

313. Reeves, *Convention*, 108–109.

314. David L. Paletz and Martha Elson, "Television Coverage of Presidential Conventions: Now You See It, Now You Don't," *Political Science Quarterly* 91 (spring 1976), discussed in Davis, *National Conventions*, 206–207.

315. Theodore H. White, *The Making of the President 1960* (New York: Atheneum, 1961), 151–152.

316. Davis, *National Conventions*, 204.

317. Walter Goodman, "Desultory Coverage of Convention," *New York Times,* July 21, 1988, A20.

318. Michael Oreskes, "Convention Message Is Garbled by Quayle Static," *New York Times,* August 19, 1988, A16.

319. This section is based on Davis, *National Conventions*, 5–11, 150–156.

320. James E. Campbell, Lynna L. Cherry, and Kenneth A. Wink, "The Convention Bump," *American Politics Quarterly* 20 (July 1992): 287–307.

321. For an overview, see William Crotty and John S. Jackson, *Presidential Primaries and Nominations* (Washington, D.C.: CQ Press, 1985), 213–220.

322. Michael Nelson, "The Case for the Current Presidential Nominating Process," in *Before Nomination*, 24.

323. Ibid., 217 (citing Robert T. Nakamura and Denis G. Sullivan, "Party Democracy and Democratic Control," in *American Politics and Public Policy*, ed. Walter Dean Burnham and Martha Wagner Weinberg [Cambridge, Mass.: MIT Press, 1978], 26–40).

324. Thomas E. Mann, "Should the Presidential Nominating System Be Changed (Again)?" in *Before Nomination*, 39.

325. Ibid., 40–41.

326. Michael Nelson, "Two Cheers for the National Primary," in *Re-*

*thinking the Presidency,* ed. Thomas E. Cronin (Boston: Little, Brown, 1982), 55.

327. Mann, "Should the Presidential Nominating System Be Changed (Again)?" 44–45.

328. Gerald Pomper, *Passions and Interests* (Lawrence: University Press of Kansas, 1992).

329. Nelson, "Two Cheers," 55–58.

330. Crotty and Jackson, *Presidential Primaries and Nominations,* 222.

331. Mann, "Should the Presidential Nominating System Be Changed (Again)?" 43. For a further discussion of the costs and benefits of such a system, see Austin Ranney, *The Federalization of Presidential Primaries* (Washington, D.C.: American Enterprise Institute, 1978), chap. 5.

332. Crotty and Jackson, *Presidential Primaries and Nominations,* 223.

333. Ibid., 225–227.

334. Mann, "Should the Presidential Nominating System Be Changed (Again)?" 42.

335. Crotty and Jackson, *Presidential Primaries and Nominations,* 227.

336. Ibid., 227–228; Mann, "Should the Presidential Nominating System Be Changed (Again)?" 42.

337. Nelson, "Case for the Current Process," 33.

338. Abramson et al., *Change and Continuity in the 1984 Elections,* 49.

339. Ibid., 51.

340. Lewis Chester, Godfrey Hodgson, and Bruce Page, *The American Melodrama: The Presidential Campaign of 1968* (New York: Viking, 1969), 620.

341. Polsby and Wildavsky, *Presidential Elections,* 148.

342. Pious, *American Presidency,* 104.

343. Richard M. Pious and Robert C. Weaver, "Presidential Campaigns: Strategies and Tactics," in *Selection/Election: A Forum on the American Presidency,* ed. Robert S. Hirschfield (New York: Aldine, 1982), 121.

344. Stephen J. Wayne, *The Road to the White House,* 3d ed. (New York: St. Martin's Press, 1988), 182.

345. Polsby and Wildavsky, *Presidential Elections,* 149.

346. Pious and Weaver, "Presidential Campaigns," 118.

347. Polsby and Wildavsky, *Presidential Elections,* 170, 182.

348. Wayne, *Road to the White House,* 194–199.

349. Ibid., 188–191; Polsby and Wildavsky, *Presidential Elections,* 82–85.

350. The complete text of the memorandum, prepared by Mike Duval and Foster Channock of the White House staff and dated June 11, 1976, is included in: Martin Schram, *Running for President: A Journal of the Carter Campaign,* expanded edition (New York: Pocket Books, 1978), 320–324.

351. Richard B. Cheney, "The 1976 Presidential Debates: A Republican Perspective," in *The Past and Future of Presidential Debates,* ed. Austin Ranney (Washington, D.C.: American Enterprise Institute, 1979), 110.

352. Schram, *Running for President,* 326.

353. John R. Cranford, "Economy Will Be Wild Card in Presidential Election," *Congressional Quarterly Weekly Report,* July 25, 1992, 2153–2157.

354. Richard Joslyn, *Mass Media and Elections* (Reading, Mass.: Addison-Wesley, 1984), 32.

355. Larry J. Sabato, *The Rise of Political Consultants* (New York: Basic Books, 1981), 69.

356. Howard L. Reiter, *Parties and Elections in Corporate America* (New York: St. Martin's Press, 1987), 159–160 (based on a 1984 memorandum from Stuart Spencer to Ronald Reagan).

357. Beniger and Giuffra, "Public Opinion Polling," 189–215.

358. Bruce E. Altschuler, *Keeping a Finger on the Public Pulse: Private Polling and Presidential Elections* (Westport, Conn.: Greenwood Press, 1982), 7.

359. Sabato, *Political Consultants,* 70.

360. Joslyn, *Mass Media and Elections,* 21.

361. See Sabato, *Political Consultants,* 92–104.

362. Wayne, *Road to the White House,* 243–244.

363. Beniger and Giuffra, "Public Opinion Polling," 194–196.

364. Altschuler, *Public Pulse,* 3.

365. Sabato, *Political Consultants,* 113–115. For an account of Nixon's 1968 campaign, see Joe McGinniss, *The Selling of the President: 1968* (New York: Trident Press, 1969).

366. Beniger and Giuffra, "Public Opinion Polling," 192; Wayne, *Road to the White House,* 215–216.

367. Sabato, *Political Consultants,* 224–229.

368. Ibid., 238.

369. Dom Bonafede, "Part Science, Part Art, Part Hokum, Direct Mail Now a Key Campaign Tool," *National Journal,* July 31, 1982, 1334–1335.

370. Reiter, *Parties and Elections,* 189 n. 13.

371. Sabato, *Political Consultants,* 201.

372. Ibid., 254.

373. Reiter, *Parties and Elections,* 162–168.

374. Sabato, *Political Consultants,* 337.

375. Lawson, "How State Laws Undermine Parties."

376. Stanley and Niemi, *Vital Statistics on American Politics,* 5th ed., 141.

377. Larry J. Sabato, *The Party's Just Begun* (Glenview, Ill.: Scott, Foresman, 1988), 75–90.

378. Robert Axelrod, "Where the Votes Come from: An Analysis of Electoral Coalitions, 1952–1968," *American Political Science Review* 66 (March 1972).

379. Alexander and Corrado, *Financing the 1992 Election,* 204.

380. F. Christopher Arterton, *Media Politics: The News Strategies of Presidential Campaigns* (Lexington, Mass.: Lexington Books, 1984), 1.

381. See, for example: Nelson W. Polsby, "The News Media as an Alternative to Party in the Presidential Selection Process," in *Political Parties in the Eighties,* ed. Robert A. Goldwin (Washington, D.C.: American Enterprise Institute, 1980), 50ff; and Donald R. Matthews, "Winnowing," in *Race for the Presidency,* ed. James David Barber (Englewood Cliffs, N.J.: Prentice-Hall, 1978), 55ff.

382. Wayne, *Road to the White House,* 231.

383. David L. Paletz and Robert M. Entman, *Media Power Politics* (New York: Free Press, 1981), 16.

384. W. Lance Bennett, *News: The Politics of Illusion* (New York: Longman, 1983), 7–8; Paletz and Entman, *Media Power Politics,* 52.

385. Barry Cole, ed., *Television Today: A Close-Up View* (New York: Oxford University Press, 1981), 183.

386. National Institute of Mental Health, *Television and Behavior,* vol. 1 (Washington, D.C.: Government Printing Office, 1982), 1.

387. Paletz and Entman, *Media Power Politics,* 45–49.

388. Alexander and Corrado, *Financing the 1992 Election,* 237.

389. See Joslyn, *Mass Media and Elections,* chap. 7, for an overview of this question.

390. Bernard Berelson, quoted in Joseph T. Klapper, *The Effects of Mass Communication* (Glencoe, Ill.: Free Press, 1960), 4.

391. Doris A. Graber, *Mass Media and American Politics* (Washington, D.C.: CQ Press, 1993), 248–249.

392. Paletz and Entman, *Media Power Politics,* 45.

393. Graber, *Mass Media,* 248–249.

394. Wayne, *Road to the White House,* 223.

395. Joslyn, *Mass Media and Elections,* 210 (see 203–214 generally for a discussion of the effects of presidential debates).

396. Paul J. Quirk and Jon K. Dalager, "The Election: A 'New Democrat' and a New Kind of Presidential Campaign," in *Elections of 1992,* 62.

397. Richard L. Berke, "Why Candidates Like Public's Questions," *New York Times,* August 15, 1992, 7.

398. Wayne, *Road to the White House,* 227.

399. Graber, *Mass Media,* 256, 264.

400. Ibid., 267.

401. Joseph Ernest Kallenbach, *The American Chief Executive* (New York: Harper and Row, 1966), 232–233.

402. Witcover, *Marathon: Pursuit of the Presidency,* 535.

403. "Quayle and Bentsen, Running Mates Under Fire," *Congressional Quarterly Weekly Report,* October 8, 1988, 2838–2839.

404. Wayne, *Road to the White House,* 171.

405. Quoted in Lorant, *Glorious Burden,* 246.

406. Ibid., 249.

407. Wayne, *Road to the White House,* 172.

408. Roseboom, *History of Presidential Elections,* 313–314.

409. Lorant, *Glorious Burden,* 466.

410. Roseboom, *History of Presidential Elections,* 331.

411. Lorant, *Glorious Burden,* 486.

412. Wayne, *Road to the White House,* 173.

413. Denis G. Sullivan and Roger D. Masters, "'Happy Warriors': Leaders' Facial Displays, Viewers' Emotions, and Public Support," *American Journal of Political Science* 32 (May 1988): 345–368.

414. Sabato, *Party's Just Begun,* 59–61.

415. Daniel A. Mazmanian, *Third Parties in Presidential Elections* (Washington, D.C.: Brookings, 1974), 27–28.

416. This number, based on Appendix A in Steven J. Rosenstone, Roy L. Behr, and Edward H. Lazarus, *Third Parties in America* (Princeton, N.J.: Princeton University Press, 1984), includes only those parties and candidates that received popular votes in more than one state in any given election.

417. Mazmanian, *Third Parties in Presidential Elections,* 4–5 (drawing on William Nisbet Chambers).

418. Some would discount the Anti-Masons in 1832 since two-party competition was not yet firmly established throughout the country. See Rosenstone, Behr, and Lazarus, *Third Parties in America,* 10–11.

419. Ibid., 17.

420. James L. Sundquist, *Dynamics of the Party System,* 58 (notes omitted). Sundquist notes that analysis of the election returns also supports this view (p. 58 n. 23).

421. Rosenstone, Behr, Lazarus, *Third Parties in America,* 8.

422. Ibid., chaps. 3 and 4 (esp. pp. 78–79, 119–121).

423. Eugene McCarthy had no national running mate because he favored eliminating the office of vice president. But because laws in various states required a running mate, McCarthy chose different ones in different states—amounting to nearly two dozen—all political unknowns.

424. Rosenstone, Behr, and Lazarus, *Third Parties in America,* 115.

425. James Q. Wilson, *American Government: Institutions and Policies* (Lexington, Mass.: D.C. Heath, 1980), 155.

426. Rosenstone, Behr, Lazarus, *Third Parties in America,* 5.

427. Sundquist, *Dynamics of the Party System,* 60–65.

428. Wilson, *American Government,* 155.

429. Rhodes Cook, "Clinton Picks the GOP Lock on the Electoral College," *Congressional Quarterly Weekly Report,* November 7, 1992, 3553.

430. Voter Research and Surveys, General Election, November 3, 1992.

431. For a full discussion of the dynamics of the use of "exit" versus "voice" by members of organizations, see Albert O. Hirschman, *Exit, Voice, and Loyalty: Responses to Decline in Firms, Organizations, and States* (Cambridge, Mass.: Harvard University Press, 1970).

432. Mazmanian, *Third Parties in Presidential Elections,* 77.

433. Rosenstone, Behr, Lazarus, *Third Parties in America,* 40.

434. This discussion of legal constraints is based on ibid., 19–27.

435. The major candidates may forgo public funds if they prefer private financing. Candidates are not eager to take that option, however; although acceptance of the public funds precludes them from raising funds privately, it does not preclude independent organizations (such as political action committees—PACs) from spending an unlimited amount on their behalf, nor does it preclude state and local parties from raising money for voter registration and other volunteer activities. The amount of public funding, originally set at $20 million for each major party candidate, has increased annually in response to cost-of-living adjustments calculated by the Department of Labor (Polsby and Wildavsky, *Presidential Elections,* 64 and 302 n. 27).

436. Rosenstone, Behr, and Lazarus, *Third Parties in America,* 26.

437. Ibid., 17–18.

438. Mazmanian, *Third Parties in Presidential Elections,* 3.

439. Rosenstone, Behr, and Lazarus, *Third Parties in America,* 33.

440. Mazmanian, *Third Parties in Presidential Elections,* 1.

441. Ibid., 67.

442. John E. Jackson, "Election Night Reporting and Voter Turnout," *American Journal of Political Science* 27 (November 1983): 615–635.

443. Graber, *Mass Media,* 280.

444. Richard A. Watson and Norman C. Thomas, *The Politics of the Presidency* (Washington, D.C.: CQ Press, 1988), 68.

445. Laurence H. Tribe and Thomas M. Rollins, "Deadlock: What Happens if Nobody Wins," *Atlantic Monthly,* October 1980, 49.

446. U.S. Constitution, Amendment XII, Section 1.

447. U.S. Constitution, Amendment XX, Section 3.

448. Tribe and Rollins, "Deadlock," 60–61.

449. Allan P. Sindler, "Presidential Selection and Succession in Special Situations," in *Presidential Selection,* ed. Alexander Heard and Michael Nelson (Durham, N.C.: Duke University Press, 1987), 355.

450. Ibid.

451. U.S. Constitution, Amendment XX, Section 3.

452. Sindler, "Presidential Selection," 356.

453. Corwin, *The President: Office and Powers,* 61–62.

454. Sindler, "Presidential Selection," 355; Tribe and Rollins, "Deadlock," 58–60.

455. Quoted in Tribe and Rollins, "Deadlock," 60.

456. Milton Lomask, *Aaron Burr: The Years from Princeton to Vice President (1756–1805)* (New York: Farrar, Straus, Giroux, 1979), 291–294.

457. Eugene H. Roseboom and Alfred E. Eckes Jr., *A History of Presidential Elections,* 4th ed. (New York: Macmillan, 1979), 38.

458. Tribe and Rollins, "Deadlock," 60.

459. Stanwood, *History of the Presidency,* 187.

460. Tribe and Rollins, "Deadlock," 50.

461. Ibid., 56. Wallace's terms were delivered in a press conference on February 19, 1968.

462. Ibid., 50.

463. Walter Berns, ed., *After the People Vote: Steps in Choosing the President* (Washington, D.C.: American Enterprise Institute, 1983), 18–20.

## SELECTED BIBLIOGRAPHY

Abramson, Paul R., John H. Aldrich, and David W. Rohde. *Change and Continuity in the 1984 Elections.* Rev. ed. Washington, D.C.: CQ Press, 1987.

———. *Change and Continuity in the 1992 Elections.* Rev. ed. Washington, D.C.: CQ Press, 1995.

Alexander, Herbert E., and Monica Bauer. *Financing the 1988 Election.* Boulder, Colo.: Westview, 1991.

Alexander, Herbert E., and Anthony Corrado. *Financing the 1992 Election.* New York: Sharpe, 1995.

Alexander, Herbert E., and Brian A. Haggerty. *Financing the 1984 Election.* Lexington, Mass.: Lexington Books, 1987.

Arterton, F. Christopher. *Media Politics: The News Strategies of Presidential Campaigns.* Lexington, Mass.: Lexington Books, 1984.

Barber, James David, ed. *Choosing the President.* Englewood Cliffs, N.J.: Prentice-Hall, 1974.

———. *The Presidential Character.* Englewood Cliffs, N.J.: Prentice Hall, 1972.

Bennett, W. Lance. *News: The Politics of Illusion.* 3d ed. White Plains, N.Y.: Longman, 1996.

Berkman, Ronald, and Laura W. Kitch. *Politics in the Media Age.* New York: McGraw-Hill, 1986.

Ceaser, James W. *Presidential Selection: Theory and Development.* Princeton, N.J.: Princeton University Press, 1979.

———. *Reforming the Reforms.* Cambridge, Mass.: Ballinger, 1982.

Chambers, William Nisbet, and Walter Dean Burnham, eds. *The American Party Systems: Stages of Development.* New York: Oxford University Press, 1967.

Chase, James S. *Emergence of the Presidential Nominating Convention: 1789–1832.* Urbana: University of Illinois Press, 1973.

Cole, Barry, ed. *Television Today: A Close-Up View.* New York: Oxford University Press, 1981.

Congressional Quarterly. *Guide to U.S. Elections.* 3d ed. Washington, D.C.: Congressional Quarterly, 1994.

Corwin, Edward S. *The President: Office and Powers.* 5th ed. New York: New York University Press, 1984.

Crotty, William J. *Political Reform and the American Experiment.* New York: Crowell, 1977.

Crotty, William J., and John S. Jackson III. *Presidential Primaries and Nominations.* Washington, D.C.: CQ Press, 1985.

Cunningham, Noble E., Jr., ed. *The Making of the American Party System: 1789–1809.* Englewood Cliffs, N.J.: Prentice-Hall, 1965.

Davis, James W. *National Conventions in an Age of Party Reform.* Westport, Conn.: Greenwood Press, 1983.

——. *Presidential Primaries: Road to the White House.* Westport, Conn.: Greenwood Press, 1980.

Drew, Elizabeth. *Politics and Money: The New Road to Corruption.* New York: Macmillan, 1983.

Edsall, Thomas Byrne. *The New Politics of Inequality.* New York: Norton, 1984.

Ferguson, Thomas, and Joel Rogers, eds. *The Hidden Election: Politics and Economics in the 1980 Presidential Campaign.* New York: Random House, 1981.

——. *Right Turn: The Decline of the Democrats and the Future of American Politics.* New York: Hill and Wang, 1986.

Fiorina, Morris P. *Retrospective Voting in American National Elections.* New Haven, Conn.: Yale University Press, 1981.

Graber, Doris A. *Mass Media and American Politics.* 4th ed. Washington, D.C.: CQ Press, 1993.

Germond, Jack W., and Jules Witcover. *Mad as Hell: Revolt at the Ballot Box, 1992.* New York: Warner, 1993.

——. *Wake Us When It's Over: Presidential Politics of 1984.* New York: Macmillan, 1985.

——. *Whose Broad Stripes and Bright Stars: The Trivial Pursuit of the Presidency 1988.* New York: Warner, 1989.

Hanson, Russell L. *The Democratic Imagination in America: Conversations with Our Past.* Princeton, N.J.: Princeton University Press, 1985.

Harmel, Robert, ed. *Presidents and Their Parties.* New York: Praeger, 1984.

Heard, Alexander, and Michael Nelson, eds. *Presidential Selection.* Durham, N.C.: Duke University Press, 1987.

Hirschman, Albert O. *Exit, Voice, and Loyalty: Responses to Decline in Firms, Organizations, and States.* Cambridge, Mass.: Harvard University Press, 1970.

Hofstadter, Richard. *The Idea of a Party System.* Berkeley: University of California Press, 1969.

Jackson, John S., and William Crotty. *The Politics of Presidential Selection.* New York: HarperCollins, 1996.

Joslyn, Richard. *Mass Media and Elections.* Reading, Mass.: Addison-Wesley, 1984.

Ladd, Everett Carll, Jr., and Charles D. Hadley. *Transformations of the American Party System.* New York: Norton, 1978.

Lang, Kurt, and Gladys Engel Lang. *Politics and Television.* Chicago: Quadrangle, 1968.

Lowi, Theodore J. *The Personal President.* Ithaca, N.Y.: Cornell University Press, 1985.

McGinniss, Joe. *The Selling of the President: 1968.* New York: Trident Press, 1969.

Mann, Thomas E. "Should the Presidential Nominating System Be Changed (Again)?" In *Before Nomination: Our Primary Problems,* ed. George Grassmuck. Washington, D.C.: American Enterprise Institute, 1985.

Marshall, Thomas R. *Presidential Nominations in a Reform Age.* New York: Praeger, 1981.

Matthews, Donald R. "Winnowing." In *Race for the Presidency,* ed. James David Barber. Englewood Cliffs, N.J.: Prentice-Hall, 1978.

Mazmanian, Daniel A. *Third Parties in Presidential Elections.* Washington, D.C.: Brookings, 1974.

Moos, Malcolm, and Stephen Hess. *Hats in the Ring.* New York: Random House, 1960.

Nelson, Michael. "Two Cheers for the National Primary." In *Rethinking the Presidency,* ed. Thomas E. Cronin. Boston: Little, Brown, 1982.

Orren, Gary R., and Nelson W. Polsby. *Media and Momentum: The New Hampshire Primary and Nomination Politics.* Chatham, N.J.: Chatham House, 1987.

Paletz, David L., and Martha Elson. "Television Coverage of Presidential Conventions: Now You See It, Now You Don't." *Political Science Quarterly* 91 (spring 1976).

Paletz, David L., and Robert M. Entman. *Media Power Politics.* New York: Free Press, 1981.

Patterson, Thomas E. *The Mass Media Election.* New York: Praeger, 1980.

Pika, Joseph A., and Richard A. Watson. *The Presidential Contest.* 5th ed. Washington, D.C.: Congressional Quarterly, 1995.

Pious, Richard M. *The American Presidency.* New York: Basic Books, 1979.

Pious, Richard M., and Robert C. Weaver. "Presidential Campaigns: Strategies and Tactics." In *Selection/Election: A Forum on the American Presidency,* ed. Robert S. Hirschfield. New York: Aldine, 1982.

Piven, Frances Fox, and Richard A. Cloward. *Why Americans Don't Vote.* New York: Pantheon, 1988.

Polsby, Nelson W. "The News Media as an Alternative to Party in the Presidential Selection Process." In *Political Parties in the Eighties,* ed. Robert A. Goldwin. Washington, D.C.: American Enterprise Institute, 1980.

Polsby, Nelson W., and Aaron Wildavsky. *Presidential Elections: Strategies of American Electoral Politics.* 9th ed. Chatham, N.J.: Chatham House, 1995.

Ranney, Austin. *The Federalization of Presidential Primaries.* Washington, D.C.: American Enterprise Institute, 1978.

Reeves, Richard. *Convention.* New York: Harcourt Brace Jovanovich, 1977.

Roseboom, Eugene H. *A History of Presidential Elections.* 2d ed. New York: Macmillan, 1964.

Rosenstone, Steven J., Roy L. Behr, and Edward H. Lazarus. *Third Parties in America.* Princeton, N.J.: Princeton University Press, 1984.

Sabato, Larry J. *The Party's Just Begun.* Glenview, Ill.: Scott, Foresman, 1988.

——. *The Rise of Political Consultants.* New York: Basic Books, 1981.

Sanford, Terry. *A Danger of Democracy.* Boulder, Colo.: Westview, 1981.

Schlesinger, Arthur M., Jr., ed. *The Cycles of American History.* Boston: Houghton Mifflin, 1986.

Schram, Martin. *Running for President: A Journal of the Carter Campaign.* Exp. ed. New York: Pocket Books, 1978.

Stanley, Harold W., and Richard G. Niemi. *Vital Statistics on American Politics.* 5th ed. Washington, D.C.: CQ Press, 1995.

Sundquist, James L. *Dynamics of the Party System.* Rev. ed. Washington, D.C.: Brookings, 1983.

Wayne, Stephen J. *The Road to the White House: The Politics of Presidential Elections.* 4th ed. New York: St. Martin's Press, 1992.

White, Theodore H. *The Making of the President 1960.* New York: Atheneum, 1961.

——. *The Making of the President 1972.* New York: Atheneum, 1973.

Witcover, Jules. *Marathon—The Pursuit of the Presidency: 1972–1976.* New York: Viking, 1977.

Wolfinger, Raymond, and Stephen Rosenstone. *Who Votes?* New Haven, Conn.: Yale University Press, 1980.

# CHAPTER 2

# Taking Office

CHARLES C. EUCHNER AND JOHN ANTHONY MALTESE

SOME OF THE president's most fateful decisions are made before the administration takes the reins of power. In filling appointments, developing budget priorities, and taking command of foreign policy leadership, the president-elect goes a long way toward determining the possibilities and limits of the new administration.

## The Transition Period

In the time between the election and the inauguration of a president, the nation's capital bustles with speculation and intrigue. To ensure a smooth transition, the incumbent invites the president-elect to the White House, and the new chief executive and incoming staff receive a battery of briefings on matters ranging from budget deficits to U.S. military alliances. All the while, the new president's transition team pores over resumes and considers legislative strategy.

Media and academic accounts stress the cooperative nature of the transition period. Only in the United States, the analysts say, can the government be turned over to political opponents with such good cheer and cooperation. Transitions rarely involve active recrimination, and almost never is there a struggle over the legitimacy of the electoral outcome. The transition is a rare celebration of a stable democracy based on parties that differ on specific policies but achieve consensus on the most important matters of state.

In recent years, Congress has appropriated $3.5 million for the incoming president to organize the new administration. Bill Clinton's 1992–1993 transition spent a total of $8.3 million, $4.8 million from private sources. *(See Table 2-1.)* The money is used for staff salaries, travel expenses, talent searches, policy deliberation, and public relations activities. Separate federal funds are used for the inaugural ceremonies.

In many ways, the presidential transition is the most important phase of the new president's term. The transition period offers incoming presidents a chance to consolidate political strategy, aided by an overview of national security and economic issues. The incoming administration of Bill Clinton was especially active during the transition period. For example, the president-elect convened an economic conference in Little Rock, Arkansas, in December 1992 to address the economic and budgetary problems facing the nation.

New presidents, in fact, often are so confident in the wake of their success at winning the election that they pay little attention

TABLE 2-1 Growth of Transition Teams and Expenditures, 1952–1993

| President | Size of transition team | Expenditure dollars (in millions) | | |
|---|---|---|---|---|
| | | Public funds | Private funds | Total funds |
| Eisenhower (1952–1953) | 100 | 0 | 0.4 | 0.4 |
| Kennedy (1960–1961) | 50[a] | 0 | 1.3 | 1.3 |
| Nixon (1968–1969) | 125–150 | 0.5 | 1.0 | 1.5 |
| Carter (1976–1977) | 300 | 1.7 | 0.2 | 1.9 |
| Reagan (1980–1981) | 1,550 | 2.0 | 1.0 | 3.0 |
| Bush (1988–1989) | 150[b] | 3.5 | 0 | 3.5 |
| Clinton (1992–1993) | 450 | 3.5 | 4.8 | 8.3 |

SOURCES: Laurin L. Henry, *Presidential Transitions* (Washington, D.C.: Brookings, 1960); Frederick C. Mosher, W. David Clinton, and Daniel G. Lang, *Presidential Transitions and Foreign Affairs* (Baton Rouge, Louisiana State University Press, 1987); Herbert E. Alexander, *Financing the 1968 Election* (Lexington, Mass.: Lexington Books, 1971); *Financing the 1976 Election* (Washington, D.C.: CQ Press, 1979); *Financing the 1980 Election* (Lexington, Mass.: Lexington Books, 1983); Herbert E. Alexander and Monica Bauer, *Financing the 1988 Election* (Boulder, Colo.: Westview, 1991); Herbert E. Alexander and Anthony Corrado, *Financing the 1992 Election* (New York: Sharpe, 1995); General Services Administration.

NOTES: a. Estimate based on statement by Richard Neustadt that Carter's transition staff was six times the size of Kennedy's (Richard Neustadt, *Presidential Power* [New York: Macmillan, 1980], 218).   b. Plus 100–150 volunteers.

to the perils awaiting them at the White House. Presidents-elect have their own agendas and sometimes are unwilling to listen to the counsel of political adversaries. Historian Carl M. Brauer, in one of the few academic studies of presidential transitions, wrote:

Transitions are filled with peril and opportunity. . . . Newly elected presidents have ended wars or prolonged them. They have demonstrated acumen or ineptitude on national security and foreign policy issues. They have maximized their mandates and led Congress, or squandered their mandates and failed to lead Congress. They have inspired or failed to inspire the public through their statements and actions. They have established economic and social policies with widely varying results. They have wisely or imprudently adopted or discarded inherited policies. They have appointed people who helped them achieve their goals and who graced public service and others whom they came to regard as liabilities and mistakes.[1]

The question of an electoral "mandate" is central to the transition period. Yet John F. Kennedy's slim victory in 1960 did not stop him from taking an aggressive approach to leading the nation. Kennedy stated after the election: "The margin is narrow, but the responsibility is clear. There may be difficulties with

Congress, but a margin of only one vote would still be a mandate."[2] And, as foreseen, Kennedy had many problems with Congress. Reagan's 1980 landslide election led to more policy victories than a slimmer electoral triumph would have allowed.

Sometimes the most important transition moves are made behind the scenes. In 1992 President-elect Clinton met with Alan Greenspan, the chairman of the Federal Reserve Board, to confer about what policies would reassure markets enough to justify keeping interest rates low—a key condition for economic growth. Indeed, Clinton and his wife, Hillary Rodham Clinton, nurtured a relationship with Greenspan, a Republican, to help push the president's economic plans through Congress. At the same time, Vice President-elect Albert Gore Jr. sounded out key Republicans on Capitol Hill about various deficit-cutting measures. Gore learned from these meetings that the GOP would not provide a cushion of support on budgetary and tax issues. That moved the Clinton White House toward a partisan approach to congressional relations.

As transition officials scramble around the capital, the media complicate the situation with their search for exclusive stories on the new administration. One transition official remembers dining in a group that included a *Newsweek* reporter eager for information about who would be appointed secretary of state. The reporter asked a table of transition officials for information in several different ways. Using a standard reporter's trick, he asked that the officials reveal the appointment not by talking but by signaling. The officials refused. He offered to buy dinner for everyone at the table. They refused again. Finally, the reporter asked about a candidate who was never seriously in the running. The transition officials told him that the candidate was not the appointee and only then accepted the free dinner.

Finally, the transition period can be crucial in determining what kind of "honeymoon" the new president is likely to have with Congress and the public. The length of the honeymoon, in turn, has a great effect on whether the new president can be a decisive and strong leader in the first term.

## APPOINTMENTS

Perhaps the most important matter facing the president-elect is staffing. The men and women chosen to fill the upper levels of the bureaucracy and the White House staff, and the "management style" of the new administration, will determine the administration's success or failure. In the 1990s the president controls the appointment of slightly more than five thousand people in a federal bureaucracy of two million civilian employees. The major sources of staff for the new president are:

• Close associates. Most presidents fill the White House staff with close political associates, many of whom have little experience in government. The new president's trust of former campaign strategists is the key factor in filling such positions as chief of staff, press secretary, congressional liaison, and various presidential assistants. Clinton chose his best friend from kindergarten, Thomas F. "Mack" McLarty III, as his first chief of staff.

Kennedy chose his brother Robert as his attorney general and confidant.

• Business men and women. The private sector has been a rich recruiting ground for all presidents, but Republicans have been the most enthusiastic about applying business techniques to government. Dwight D. Eisenhower preferred business and financial leaders for his cabinet, especially for the Treasury and Defense posts. Kennedy's most fateful appointment probably was Robert S. McNamara, the head of Ford Motor Company, as secretary of defense. McNamara became a key figure in Lyndon B. Johnson's unsuccessful Vietnam War policy.

• Academic figures. During the campaign, academics from universities and think tanks may be enlisted to provide the presidential candidate with briefings, position papers, and "instant advice" as different issues develop. If their candidate wins, some are recruited for posts in the new administration. In fact, such consultants frequently move in and out of academe according to which party holds the White House. The most notable academic in recent years to hold a position of influence was Henry Kissinger, a Harvard University professor who became Richard Nixon's top foreign policy adviser. Other academics to join administrations have included Arthur M. Schlesinger Jr. and John Kenneth Galbraith under Kennedy; Daniel P. Moynihan under Nixon and Gerald R. Ford; Zbigniew Brzezinski and Ray Marshall under Jimmy Carter; Jeane J. Kirkpatrick, Terrel H. Bell, and Martin Feldstein under Reagan; and Robert B. Reich and Alice M. Rivlin under Clinton.

• Constituency representatives. The new president faces a tension between the desire to control the executive bureaucracy and the desire to reach out to constituencies served by the various departments. Many departments—such as Agriculture, Commerce, Labor, Education, Veterans Affairs, and Housing and Urban Development—were created to represent constituent groups. Those groups, then, expect one of their own to head the department. A president who wants to limit that group's influence, however, might appoint someone from outside the interest group's community, such as James G. Watt, the first secretary of interior in the Reagan administration. Watt, a lawyer for the development-oriented Mountain States Legal Foundation, worked against many environmental groups that had dominated the department in previous administrations.

• Party leaders and elected officials. Many presidential appointments serve to reward the efforts of party leaders and workers. George Bush, a one-time GOP national chair, received several appointments in the Nixon and Ford administrations. Although many party officials do receive lesser appointments in the White House and in government agencies, the possibility of rewarding party faithful on a large scale has diminished with the professionalization of the civil service. Less than 1 percent of federal workers are appointed by the president.

The postal service was the traditional government agency for rewarding party faithful because of its geographic scale, relatively straightforward tasks, and large number of employees. It was

President Bill Clinton and Vice President Al Gore applaud Janet Reno, Clinton's nominee in February 1993 to be the first woman attorney general of the United States.

a good place for a president to build a party machine. Franklin D. Roosevelt's postmaster general, James A. Farley, was the consummate party builder with a federal post. Other positions also have gone to party faithful, but with less of a patronage-minded strategy.

In more recent years, party leaders and elected officials have been appointed to bring different kinds of managerial and policy expertise into the administration. President Carter's appointment of former Democratic Party chair Robert Strauss as a special negotiator for the Middle East was intended to take advantage of Strauss's mediation skills. And Carter appointed former Florida governor Reubin Askew as his special trade representative on the strength of Askew's foreign investment efforts in state government. In 1993 Clinton appointed Democratic Party chair Ronald Brown as commerce secretary because of Brown's extensive ties to business. Each of these appointments was a payment of a political debt, but more important in each case was the recipient's expertise.

• Opposition figures. Especially after a close election, a president-elect might feel the need to "reach out" to the opposition party to build a consensus for policies. In 1968 Nixon asked Democratic senator Henry M. Jackson to be secretary of defense; Jackson declined. Reagan appointed then-Democrat Jeane Kirkpatrick ambassador to the United Nations.

Staff turf battles can have an important effect on appointments and the whole style of the new presidency. In the Carter administration, a struggle took place between White House staffers Jack Watson and Hamilton Jordan, in which Jordan won control over key personnel decisions. Watson and Jordan had markedly different approaches to management, as well as different sets of political contacts. Nixon staffer John Ehrlichman's role as referee in the struggle between White House policy advisers Daniel Patrick Moynihan and Arthur F. Burns over domestic policy was pivotal in shaping the Nixon White House.

Clinton vowed to appoint a cabinet that "looks like America" in his 1992 campaign, but he experienced difficulties finding people who met his demands for diversity and high ethical standards. Although Clinton's first term cabinet was most racially diverse in history, it had more lawyers and millionaires than the cabinets of previous administrations. Clinton came under criticism form past allies for not appointing enough women and minorities, and from opponents for trying too hard to meet minority targets.[3] His search for a woman to be attorney general was especially difficult. His first two choices—Zöe Baird and Kimba Wood—withdrew after reports that they had hired illegal immigrants as nannies.[4] Clinton finally settled on Miami prosecutor Janet Reno. His cabinet also included three other women (Donna E. Shalala at Health and Human Services, Hazel R. O'Leary at Energy, Madeleine K. Albright as ambassador to the United Nations) and five men who were members of minority groups: Ronald H. Brown at Commerce (later Mickey Kantor), Federico Peña at Transportation, Henry G. Cisneros at Housing and Urban Development, Mike Espy at Agriculture (later Dan Glickman), and Jesse Brown at Veterans Affairs. But the leading figures in the cabinet were white men: Secretary of State Warren M. Christopher, Secretary of Defense Les Aspin (later William J. Perry), Treasury secretary Lloyd M. Bentsen Jr. (later Robert E. Rubin), Interior secretary Bruce E. Babbitt, Labor secretary Robert B. Reich, and Education secretary Richard W. Riley.

In reorganizing his cabinet for his second term, Clinton asked Reno, Shalala, Glickman, Brown, Rubin, Babbitt, and Riley to stay on and moved Peña over to Energy. Since the Democrats had been running the executive branch for four years, Clinton had a more experienced pool of talent for to draw on in filling vacant slots than he had in 1992. He appointed William Daley to Commerce; Andrew M. Cuomo to Housing and Urban Development, Rodney Slater to Transportation, and Alexis Herman to Labor. In composing his second term cabinet, Clinton also labored to maintain the diversity of his first four years. His cabinet contained three blacks, one Hispanic, four women, and, in the spirit of bipartisanship, one Republican (William S. Cohen at Defense). In addition he appointed another Hispanic, representative Bill Richardson, to be U.S. ambassador to the UN. Clinton's most notable choice was elevating Madeleine Albright to be secretary of state—the highest cabinet office held by a woman in U.S. history.

## MANAGEMENT STYLE

Transition-watchers pay especially close attention to the incoming president's management style. Although presidents-elect usually promise to involve cabinet members in the decision-making process, a strong White House staff can reduce the influence of the cabinet on that process. Eisenhower was the last president to have anything approaching a true "cabinet government." Recent presidents, determined to control the bureaucracy, have relied more on a White House staff with a strong chief of staff. Nixon found the hundreds of cabinet meetings under Eisenhower "unnecessary and boring."[5] Much like Franklin Roosevelt and Eisenhower before him, Kennedy insisted on playing advisers off one another. "I can't afford to confine myself to one set of advisers," he said. "If I did that I would be on their leading strings."[6]

Largely because of the important roles that Nixon White House staff members played in the Watergate scandal, Carter was reluctant to appoint a chief of staff; he maintained that the position encouraged overzealous aides to insulate the president. Instead, he acted at first as his own chief of staff (Hamilton Jordan later filled this role), providing direct access to a number of competing advisers. Reagan, who always espoused delegation of authority on a wide range of issues, appointed a chief of staff at the beginning of his administration.

At the risk of losing control of initiatives in the bureaucracy, presidents usually allow their cabinet secretaries to choose their own assistant secretaries. For that reason, the loyalty of subordinates is perhaps more important than the loyalty of the cabinet officers. Nixon in his first term and Carter did not exert control over midlevel appointments, as many other presidents have done; both found that the departments were "captured" by career bureaucrats and the interest groups connected with the agencies. Recognizing that the lack of central coordination of appointments reduced Carter's ability to effectively control his administration, Clinton insisted on his right to make subcabinet appointments. By placing loyal supporters in key departmental posts, he hoped to ensure the policies carried out within the bureaucracy were those of his administration. Although Clinton was criticized for slowness in filling policy-making positions,

this strategy effectively centralized political power within the White House.

The administration's congressional liaison—though not a household name outside Washington—is an important member of the administration. Carter's liaison, Frank Moore, lacked experience on Capitol Hill and was ineffective as the president's lobbyist. Reagan's liaisons, Max Friedersdorf and Kenneth Duberstein, won high marks, especially for their efforts in behalf of the administration's tax- and budget-cutting initiatives.

## EARLY ADVICE

Incoming presidents have outside allies who offer advice on appointments and policy options. For example, the Democratic Leadership Council, a moderate think tank which Clinton had chaired, prepared a set of proposals for President-elect Clinton in 1992. Earlier, in 1980, the Heritage Foundation had provided Reagan's transition team with a three-thousand-page report urging a quick selection of top aides and several policy initiatives.

The outgoing administration's briefings of the president-elect and the incoming team could be important, but the different styles of the two sides often block meaningful exchanges. The most important briefing deals with the nuclear capacities of other nations—a briefing that never fails to shake the new president from the intoxication of the recent electoral success.

The meeting between the incoming and outgoing president is usually cordial, but the new executive is reluctant to take much advice. In 1952, after providing President-elect Eisenhower with advice on staff operations, Harry S. Truman remarked, "I think all this went into one ear and out the other."[7] Carter reported that Reagan was inattentive during their Oval Office meeting. The Reagan transition team's cooperation with other

### BOWING OUT

From John Adams's "midnight" judge appointments to Jimmy Carter's unsuccessful efforts to free American hostages from Iran, the outgoing president's last days have been fateful moments. The outgoing administration prepares a budget for the next fiscal year and issues administrative regulations. President George Bush pardoned key figures in the Iran-contra scandal before leaving office. And, one month after he lost reelection, he ordered U.S. troops to strife-torn Somalia to ensure famine relief, initiating what became a controversial fifteen-month mission for the Clinton administration.

The outgoing president often delivers a "farewell address" to draw attention to the major problems of the nation. George Washington's call for limited foreign engagements remains the most famous farewell address. Recent prominent addresses include Eisenhower's warning about the "military-industrial complex" and Carter's plea for recognition of environmental and economic limits.

agencies such as the Office of Management and Budget was more sustained.

## EARLY CONSIDERATIONS

A president's early signals to the bureaucracy can be a decisive factor in relations between the White House and the rest of the executive branch. Nixon encouraged bureaucratic resistance with his repeated statements about the Democratic and liberal bias of civil servants.[8] Reagan appointed lower-level administrators only after a thorough screening by his transition team to ensure ideological purity and loyalty to the administration.

The size of the legislative agenda is another important consideration for the new administration. Clinton's initiatives—the reduction of the federal budget deficit, economic stimulus, health care reform, free trade, "reinventing government," campaign finance reform, relations with Russia—were so wide-ranging that the president was not able to muster the forces and concentration needed to succeed in all areas. Even when his efforts succeeded, Clinton did not receive much credit because of the failures along the way. Carter had had the same difficulty. Reagan, by contrast, had emphasized issues directly pertaining to the budget—taxes, cuts in domestic spending, and increases in military spending. The work of budget director David Stockman was crucial to Reagan's ability to "hit the ground running."

# The Inauguration

Ritual acts pervade politics in recognition of the fact that the symbolism of public rites reassures and binds together diverse peoples and that the rituals themselves legitimize existing power relationships. In keeping with this notion, each presidential election is capped by a ceremony of grand proportions: the inauguration of the new president. This ceremony is an overt political ritual intended to instill patriotism, unite the nation behind its leader, and provide for an orderly transfer of power. It does so through a combination of symbolism, pageantry, and rhetoric.[9] Yet almost none of that ceremony is formally required. Most of it has evolved by way of tradition.

The four-year presidential and vice-presidential terms expire at noon on January 20 following an election year. Before the 1933 passage of the Twentieth Amendment to the Constitution, presidential inaugurations were held on March 4 as required by a 1792 act of Congress.

## OATH OF OFFICE

The only part of the inaugural ceremony that is required by the Constitution is the taking of the oath of office. Article II, section 1, clause 8, sets out the words that every president has repeated: "I do solemnly swear (or affirm) that I will faithfully execute the Office of President of the United States, and will to the best of my Ability, preserve, protect, and defend the Constitution of the United States." Only Franklin Pierce in 1853 affirmed (rather than swore) to faithfully execute the office that he was

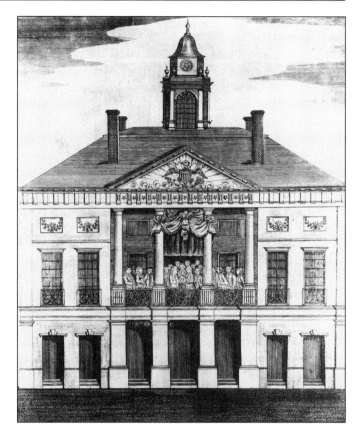

On April 30, 1789, at Federal Hall in New York City, George Washington took the oath of office. The practice of adding the words "so help me God" at the end of the oath was begun by Washington at this first inaugural ceremony.

about to enter. The practice of adding the words "so help me God" at the conclusion of the oath was begun by George Washington at the first inaugural ceremony. The vice president recites the same oath taken by all other federal officers except the president. It is prescribed by Congress in the *United States Code.*

Washington also was the first president to take the oath of office with his left hand placed on the Bible and his right hand raised toward heaven. Although not required by the Constitution, the practice of taking an oath on a Bible was deeply ingrained in English and American colonial history. For centuries, the kings and queens of Britain had taken their coronation oaths on Bibles, and the use of a Bible was an established practice in the administration of oaths in civil and ecclesiastical courts.[10]

Nevertheless, no one thought to secure a Bible for Washington's inauguration until shortly before the general's arrival at Federal Hall in New York City for his swearing in. The chief justice of the New York state judiciary, Chancellor Robert R. Livingston, who was to administer the oath, feared that the oath would lack legitimacy without a Bible, but none could be found in the building. One was finally borrowed, however, from St. John's Masonic Lodge No. 1, a few blocks away on Wall Street.[11]

There is no definite record of a Bible being used again at a swearing-in ceremony until James K. Polk's inauguration in 1845 (although it is believed that Andrew Jackson used one in 1829 and again in 1833). Since James Buchanan in 1857, every president has taken the oath on a Bible except for Theodore Roosevelt in 1901, when he was hastily sworn in after the assassination of William McKinley. The oldest inaugural Bible was the one used by Franklin Roosevelt in all four of his inaugurations. It was printed in Amsterdam around 1686 (in Dutch) and contained the Roosevelt family records—the earliest of which was the birth of Jacob Roosevelt in "1691/92."[12]

The page that the Bible is opened to during the administration of the oath is sometimes a random choice and sometimes a deliberate one. During Washington's first inauguration, it was randomly opened to Genesis 49–50. Rutherford B. Hayes placed his hand on Psalm 118:11–13, which reads, in part, "Thou hast thrust sore at me that I might fall: but the Lord helped me." These words were significant, given the circumstances of Hayes's fiercely contested election. Franklin Roosevelt's Bible was opened to I Corinthians 13 for all four of his inaugurals ("Though I speak with the tongues of men and of angels, and have not charity, I am become as sounding brass . . ."). Nixon, entering office in the midst of the Vietnam War in 1969, placed his hand on Isaiah 2:4—". . . and they shall beat their swords into plowshares, and their spears into pruning hooks: nation shall not lift up sword against nation, neither shall they learn war any more."[13]

After Washington's first inauguration, the oath of office was administered indoors until 1817. Washington's second inauguration, as well as that of John Adams, was held in Philadelphia in the Senate chamber of Independence Hall. Thomas Jefferson was the first president to be inaugurated in the District of Columbia, where in 1801 he took his oath in the new Senate chamber. In later years, the ceremony was moved to the House chamber. It was not until James Monroe's inauguration in 1817 that the ceremony was moved outdoors—to a platform erected in front of the east portico of the Capitol. In 1981 Reagan moved the site of the ceremony from the East to the West Front of the Capitol.

With rare exceptions, the presidential oath of office has been administered by the chief justice of the United States, although the Constitution makes no provision for this. An associate justice of the Supreme Court usually swears in the vice president. The first vice president sworn in by a woman was James Danforth "Dan" Quayle, who took the oath in 1989 from the first female justice, Sandra Day O'Connor.

At Washington's first inauguration, the Supreme Court had not yet been appointed, and at his second inauguration Associate Justice William Cushing filled in for Chief Justice John Jay, who was out of the country on official business. Thus John Adams was the first president to take the oath of office from the chief justice (who was then Oliver Ellsworth).

Other judges have administered the oath in times of unexpected presidential succession. But such times raise questions.

For example, can a person assume the presidency without having taken the oath of office? The first president to die in office was William Henry Harrison in 1841. His vice president, John Tyler, initially thought that he need not take the presidential oath. In his mind, the vice-presidential oath sufficed. Nevertheless, Tyler took the presidential oath on April 6, 1841 (two days after Harrison's death) for "greater caution"—a practice that has been followed since then in similar circumstances.[14]

Still, the period between the death of a president and the swearing in of the successor to that office remains a gray area. As recently as the assassination of Kennedy in 1963, there was some question whether Lyndon Johnson should take the oath immediately in Dallas or wait until his return to Washington. Attorney General Robert F. Kennedy advised that the oath should be administered immediately, and it was, by federal district judge Sarah T. Hughes aboard *Air Force One*.[15]

## CEREMONY AND CELEBRATION

From the beginning, inaugurations have included far more than just the swearing in. When Washington set out from his home at Mount Vernon on his journey to New York City (then the seat of government) for his swearing in, he hoped to have a quiet trip. He only recently had recovered from a severe bout of rheumatism, and he was depressed about leaving the home he loved. On April 16, 1789, he wrote in his diary: "About ten o'clock I bade adieu to Mt. Vernon, to private life, to domestic felicity, and with a mind oppressed with more anxious and painful sensations than I have words to express, set out for New York. . . ."[16]

But along the way, Washington was met by crowds, celebrations, speeches, ringing bells, cavalry troops, and cannon fire. In Philadelphia, thousands turned out to watch him ride down Market and Second Streets. By the time he finally reached New York, the crowds had worked themselves into a frenzy. Indeed, they were so loud when Washington stepped off the barge at Murray's Wharf that even the ringing church bells were drowned out.

On April 30, 1789—the morning of his inauguration—Washington traveled from his quarters at Franklin House to Federal Hall in an ornate horse-drawn carriage. Upon his arrival at Federal Hall, he was escorted to the balcony where he took the oath of office in front of a huge crowd. After yet more pandemonium, he moved inside the Senate chamber to deliver a brief speech—thus establishing the precedent for inaugural addresses. That night the celebration was capped by a fireworks display. Since then, inaugurations have usually been a time for much pomp and circumstance.

Customarily, when the office changes hands, the president-elect and the incumbent president ride together from the White House to the Capitol for the inauguration ceremony. On occasion, however, this has been an awkward journey. In 1869 President-elect Ulysses S. Grant refused to ride in the same carriage with Andrew Johnson, prompting President Johnson to boycott the inauguration, as had John Adams in 1801, John Quincy

Adams in 1829, and Martin Van Buren in 1841 (although Van Buren had made a point of meeting President-elect William Henry Harrison during the interregnum). Herbert Hoover and Franklin Roosevelt barely exchanged glances during the trip in 1933. Most presidents, however, have made the trip. Even Woodrow Wilson, partially paralyzed and on the verge of death, drove with Warren G. Harding to the Capitol in 1921, although the bitter cold prevented him from witnessing the ceremony.[17]

In the early days, inaugural parades were held before the swearing in and proceeded *to* the Capitol. Initially, these were relatively simple events with small presidential escorts and spontaneous crowds. James Madison was the first president to wrap the parade in military formality when he was escorted by cavalry in 1809. With the exception of Andrew Jackson—who vetoed the idea of any kind of parade and simply walked to the Capitol on the sidewalk—successive presidents saw larger and larger parades.

With William Henry Harrison in 1841 came a parade filled with bands, loyal supporters, and militia units, and Buchanan's parade in 1857 added a huge float representing the goddess of liberty. It was not until Benjamin Harrison's inauguration in 1889 that parades came *from* the Capitol after the swearing in. Harrison also was the first president to watch the parade from a reviewing stand rather than participate in it.[18]

Today, inaugural parades are elaborate events that are broadcast live on television with presidents watching the proceedings from behind bullet-proof glass. President Reagan's 1985 inaugural parade—canceled because of extremely cold weather—was scheduled to include 12,000 people, 730 horses, 66 floats, and 57 marching bands. Just the cost of building the reviewing stand and bleachers and housing the horses reached nearly $1 million. All told, the estimated cost of the 1985 inauguration was $12 million, with some $800,000 to have been raised from the selling of 25,000 parade tickets (ranging in price from $12.50 to $100 each).[19]

Only eight years later, the total cost of a presidential inauguration had grown tremendously. The direct costs of the inauguration of Bill Clinton and Al Gore were estimated to have been more than $25 million with additional governmental costs—such as police and public safety expenses—bumping the figure to more than $36 million. However, the government was able to recoup two-thirds of the cost through ticket and souvenir sales ($17 million) and television broadcast rights to the inaugural events ($7 million).[20]

The 1993 inauguration also demonstrated how much the spectacle of Americans embracing their new president had grown. Beginning with a preinaugural bus ride for the presidential party from Jefferson's home at Monticello, Virginia, to Washington, D.C., festivities crowded an entire week in January. One highlight was at the inaugural ceremony itself when Maya Angelou read a special poem written for the occasion. Angelou was the first poet to read at a presidential inauguration since Robert Frost read at Kennedy's 1961 inauguration.

The total cost of Clinton's second inauguration in 1996—

From the West Front of the Capitol on January 20, 1993, poet Maya Angelou reads from "On the Pulse of Morning," a poem she wrote for the inauguration of Bill Clinton.

which was spread over a three-day weekend—was estimated at $30 million. Once again the presidential inaugural committee paid for the event with ticket and souvenir sales and broadcast rights. Clinton chose Arkansas native Miller Williams to compose and recite the inaugural poem, "Of History and Hope."

Gestures during inaugural ceremonies range from the mundane to the highly symbolic. To the horror of Secret Service agents, President Carter—in an act reminiscent of Jackson—walked back to the White House from his swearing in at the Capitol in 1977 with his wife and children at his side. The Bushes and the Clintons walked part of the way as well. Yet the ease with which presidents can mingle with the public has changed markedly over the years. In 1789 Washington thought nothing of walking home through crowds of people in New York after watching the evening fireworks display with friends. In 1829 Jackson's swearing in was followed by an open reception at the White House for anyone who cared to attend. Refreshments were prepared for twenty thousand people, but organizers did not anticipate the full force of a hungry throng of people anxious to greet "Old Hickory." The crowd soon became an unruly mob—surging toward Jackson and the food, destroying furniture, tracking in mud, breaking windows, and ultimately forcing the president to flee.[21] After Abraham Lincoln's second inauguration in 1865, the crowd also became unruly, romping through the White House, stealing food, silver, and even parts of draperies.[22] Yet despite the mayhem of those inaugural festivities, many presidents continued to greet virtually anyone who stood in line to meet them at the White House after the inauguration. Presidents Bush and Clinton carried on the tradition in 1989 and 1993.

Extremely cold weather forced the swearing-in ceremony for the second term of President Ronald Reagan and Vice President George Bush to be held indoors underneath the Capitol Rotunda.

In the evening, the festivities traditionally have ended with an inaugural ball. The first such ball was held by James and Dolley Madison in 1809, and, with a few exceptions, the tradition has continued. There was no ball after Jackson's first inauguration because of the recent death of his wife. Wilson—appalled at the idea of being paraded around in front of hundreds of gawking people—scuttled plans for balls in 1913 and 1917. Harding wanted a ball in 1921, but after complaints that his plans were too extravagant, he reluctantly canceled all postinaugural festivities. Calvin Coolidge simply went to bed in 1925 (even though there was an unofficial ball held at the Mayflower Hotel), and Franklin Roosevelt suspended the practice of balls after his first inauguration because of the crises of the Great Depression and World War II.[23]

Since then, however, balls have been a prominent part of the inaugural day landscape. In recent years, to accommodate the throngs of people who have wanted to attend, several balls have taken place throughout the city with the president and his wife making appearances at all the official ones. In 1977 Carter had inaugural "parties" rather than "balls" to symbolize a new era of simplicity in government. In 1985 Ronald and Nancy Reagan visited nine balls attended by some fifty thousand people who had paid $125 each.[24] Bill and Hillary Clinton attended eleven inaugural balls in 1993. In 1997 the Clintons celebrated their second inauguration at a record fourteen official balls.

## INAUGURAL ADDRESSES

When Washington entered Federal Hall after taking the oath of office in New York City on April 30, 1789, he proceeded to the Senate chamber and gave a brief speech. That was the first inaugural address, and every inaugural ceremony since then has included one—even though a speech is not a constitutional requirement.

Initially, such speeches were made to a joint session of Congress and were held in either the House or Senate chamber. But beginning with Monroe in 1817, inaugural addresses were delivered outdoors to the general public. Inclement weather sometimes has made this tradition uncomfortable. The most tragic example was the inauguration of 1841. Although the day was damp and extremely cold, Gen. William Henry Harrison insisted on delivering his inaugural address—the longest in history, taking over an hour and forty minutes to read—without an overcoat or hat. To make matters worse, he had traveled to the Capitol on horseback (again with no coat or hat) in a very slow procession, even though he was sixty-eight years old and exhausted from the campaign and a long journey to Washington. The exposure brought on pneumonia, and Harrison died exactly one month after his inauguration. In 1985, when the wind chill factor sent temperatures plummeting well below zero, seventy-three-year-old Reagan (the oldest president to be sworn in) moved the ceremony indoors to the Capitol Rotunda and canceled the parade. Four years earlier, Reagan had enjoyed one of the warmest January inaugurations, when temperatures soared close to sixty degrees. The average high temperature for a January 20 in Washington is forty-four degrees.

Every inaugural address since Truman's in 1949 has been carried live on television. Today such instant communication is taken for granted, but early in the nation's history the distribution of the president's remarks to all parts of the country took a long time. In 1841 a record was set when the text of President Harrison's address was rushed by train from Washington to New York in only ten hours.[25] Four years later, Samuel Morse stood on the inaugural platform and transmitted an account of the proceedings to Baltimore via his telegraph machine as Polk was sworn in.[26] Coolidge's 1925 inaugural address was the first to be broadcast by radio. The earliest known photograph of an inauguration was taken at Buchanan's swearing in on March 4, 1857.

After the divisiveness of a presidential election, inaugural addresses usually stress unity and nonpartisanship. Carter—having beaten incumbent president Ford in the 1976 election—opened his inaugural address with conciliatory words: "For myself and for our nation, I want to thank my predecessor for all he has done to heal our land." Jefferson reminded the joint session of Congress that listened to his inaugural address that "every difference of opinion is not a difference of principle. We have called by different names brethren of the same principle. We are all Republicans, we are all Federalists." And when Wilson entered the White House in 1913, he said: "This is not a day of triumph; it is a day of dedication. Here muster, not the forces of party, but the forces of humanity."

In troubled times, an inaugural address is an opportunity for reassurance and supplication. Franklin Roosevelt, entering office in the midst of economic crisis, recognized that "only a foolish optimist can deny the dark realities of the moment." But he preached the gospel of restoration and entreated his audience with memorable words: ". . . the only thing we have to fear is fear itself—nameless, unreasoning, unjustified terror which paralyzes needed efforts to convert retreat into advance."

Lincoln—beginning his second term in 1865 as the Civil War, which had ravaged the nation, was winding to a close—told a hushed crowd: "Fondly do we hope, fervently do we pray, that this mighty scourge of war may speedily pass away. . . . With malice toward none, with charity for all, with firmness in the right as God gives us to see the right, let us strive on to . . . bind up the nation's wounds. . . ."

One hundred years later, the nation was once again faced with civil unrest. On that occasion, Lyndon Johnson reminded his audience: "We are one nation and people." Those, he said

who seek to reopen old wounds and to rekindle old hatreds . . . stand in the way of a seeking nation. . . . For the hour and the day and the time are here to achieve progress without strife, to achieve change without hatred—not without difference of opinion, but without the deep and abiding divisions which scar the union for generations.

When Ford became the first unelected president after Nixon resigned in 1974, he addressed a crowd in the East Room of the White House, saying:

This is the earliest known photograph of an inauguration, taken at James Buchanan's swearing in on March 4, 1857.

. . . I assume the Presidency under extraordinary circumstances never before experienced by Americans. This is an hour of history that troubles our minds and hurts our hearts. . . . We must go forward now together. . . . Our long national nightmare is over. Our Constitution works; our great Republic is a Government of laws and not of men. Here, the people rule. . . .

Such optimism is probably the most common theme of inaugural addresses. That theme was perhaps best represented by Kennedy's inauguration in 1961. As the nation's youngest elected president, he set the tone for change:

Let the word go forth from this time and place to friend and foe alike, that the torch has been passed to a new generation of Americans—born in this century, tempered by war, disciplined by a hard and bitter peace, proud of our ancient heritage—and unwilling to witness or permit the slow undoing of those human rights to which this nation has always been committed. . . . Let us begin. . . .

Most new presidents echo the theme of new challenges and old responsibilities. As Bush remarked in 1989: "The new breeze blows, a page turns, the story unfolds—and so today a chapter begins: a small and stately story of unity, diversity and generosity—shared and written together."

Clinton's 1993 inauguration was billed as a "people's" celebration. In his address, Clinton asked the American public to restore their faith in government.

And so I say to all of you here, let us resolve to reform our politics so that power and privilege no longer shout down the voice of the people. Let us put aside personal advantage so that we can feel the pain and see the promise of America. Let us resolve to make our government a place for what Franklin Roosevelt called bold, persistent experimentation, a government for our tomorrows, not our yesterdays.

For his second inaugural address Clinton took up the theme of the "new promise" being offered to Americans as the dawn of the twentieth-first century approached. "It is our great good fortune that time and change have put us at the edge of a new century in a new millennium, but on the edge of a bright new prospect in human affairs: a moment that will define our course and our character for decades to come."

The "poetry" of politics, as New York governor Mario Cuomo called rhetoric, is difficult yet important. But it is simple compared to the "prose" of governing. Every president discovers that when finally seated in the Oval Office for the first day of business.

## NOTES

1. Carl M. Brauer, *Presidential Transitions: Eisenhower Through Reagan.* (New York: Oxford University Press, 1986), xiv.

2. Quoted in Brauer, 62.

3. Kirk Victor, "Asleep at the Switch?" *National Journal* January 16, 1993, 132.

4. Baird withdrew from consideration after being formally nominated for attorney general. Wood, the Clinton administration's near-certain sec-ond choice, withdrew at the conclusion of her background check and was not formally nominated for the post.

5. Brauer, *Presidential Transitions,* 127.

6. Ibid., 65.

7. Quoted in Brauer, 16.

8. Ibid., 177.

9. For a more thorough discussion of rituals and symbols in politics, see Murray Edelman, *The Symbolic Uses of Politics* (Urbana: University of Illinois Press, 1985).

10. *Presidential Inaugural Bibles: Catalogue of an Exhibition (November 17, 1968–February 23, 1969)* (Washington, D.C.: Washington Cathedral, 1969), 6–7.

11. Ibid., 12.

12. Ibid., 43.

13. Ibid., 12, 29, 43; 1969 Inaugural Committee, *The Inaugural Story: 1789–1969* (New York: American Heritage, 1969), 67.

14. Edward S. Corwin, *The President: Office and Powers, 1787–1957,* 4th rev. ed. (New York: New York University Press, 1957), 54.

15. Harold W. Chase and Craig R. Ducat, *Edward S. Corwin's The Constitution and What It Means Today,* 13th ed. (Princeton, N.J.: Princeton University Press, 1973), 119.

16. Quoted in Edna M. Colman, *Seventy-five Years of White House Gossip: From Washington to Lincoln* (Garden City, N.J.: Doubleday, Page, 1925), 4.

17. *Inaugural Story,* 42–45.

18. Ibid., 86–87.

19. Phil Gailey, "The Cold Bottom Line: No Parade and No Profit," *New York Times,* January 22, 1985, A19. Ticket holders could receive a refund if they made their request before February 10, 1985.

20. Herbert E. Alexander and Anthony Corrado, *Financing the 1992 Election* (New York: Sharpe, 1995), 290–291.

21. Colman, *Seventy-five Years,* 155.

22. *Inaugural Story,* 103.

23. Ibid., 97–107.

24. Irvin Molotsky, "Nine Grand Balls: The Reagans and Thousands of Well-Wishers Go Dancing," *New York Times,* January 22, 1985, A19.

25. Colman, *Seventy-five Years,* 186.

26. *Inaugural Story,* 56.

## SELECTED BIBLIOGRAPHY

Brauer, Carl M. *Presidential Transitions: Eisenhower Through Reagan.* New York: Oxford University Press, 1988.

Clinton, W. David, ed. *Presidential Transitions: The Reagan to Bush Experience.* Lanham, Md.: University Press of America, 1992.

Clinton, W. David, and Daniel G. Lang. *What Makes a Successful Transition?* Lanham, Md.: University Press of America, 1993.

Colman, Edna M. *Seventy-five Years of White House Gossip: From Washington to Lincoln.* Garden City, N.J.: Doubleday, Page, 1925.

Edelman, Murray. *The Symbolic Uses of Politics.* Urbana: University of Illinois Press, 1985.

Hess, Stephen. *Organizing the Presidency.* Washington, D.C.: Brookings, 1988.

Macy, John W., Bruce Adams, and J. Jackson Walter. *America's Unelected Government: Appointing the President's Team.* Cambridge, Mass.: Ballinger, 1983.

Mosher, Frederick C., W. David Clinton, and Daniel G. Lang. *Presidential Transitions and Foreign Affairs.* Baton Rouge: Louisiana State University Press, 1987.

Pfiffner, James P. *The Strategic Presidency: Hitting the Ground Running.* Chicago: Dorsey Press, 1988.

# CHAPTER 3

# Chronology of Presidential Elections

BY CHARLES C. EUCHNER

I N THE EARLY YEARS of the Republic, the American people and their leaders were ambivalent about the concept of democracy. On the one hand, Americans searched for ways to prevent the kind of tyranny they had experienced at the hand of such elite rulers as King George. On the other hand, political elites feared the instability that might result from mass participation in politics. This ambivalence was evident in the compromise for presidential selection worked out at the Constitutional Convention in 1787 and in the halting steps the nation took toward party competition.

The presidential selection process has changed significantly since George Washington was elected to his first term in 1789. The electoral college is still the center of the system, but all of the related institutions and processes are dramatically different, in part because the constitutional provisions for presidential selection are so vague.

The major features of the electoral system have developed over time as a process of trial and error. The Constitution includes no provisions for organizing political parties, nominating candidates, or campaigning for office. The Framers assumed, incorrectly, that the selection process would be a reasoned one that would transcend petty partisanship. The original provision for balloting by the electoral college was flawed and had to be superseded by the Twelfth Amendment in 1804. *(See "The Twelfth Amendment," p. 8, in Chapter 1.)*

Until the eighteenth century, contested elections were rare. The nation's first legislative body, the Virginia House of Burgesses, had largely uncontested elections until the 1700s, and later, even when the elections for state legislatures attracted more than one candidate, there was little active campaigning. It was only with the decline of homogeneous communities and the end of elite control over politics that contested elections began to occur.

The very concept of the political party—a way to organize electoral coalitions—was viewed with distrust by the nation's earliest leaders. As George Washington described the dangers of parties in a letter: "A fire not to be quenched; it demands a uniform vigilance to prevent its bursting into a flame, lest instead of warming it should consume."[1] Only after the experience of factional debate in Congress, where bitter strife developed over such issues as banking, tariffs, and slavery, did the idea of parties seem necessary and capable of control.

## The Emergence of the Electoral Process

The method of choosing presidential and vice-presidential candidates has moved through four distinct phases, according to political scientist Richard P. McCormick.[2] The first phase was a period marked by uncertain and hazardous rules that lasted until the Twelfth Amendment was ratified in 1804. The second phase, continuing through 1820, saw the decline of the Federalists as a national force and the dominance of the Democratic-Republicans. This phase is associated with "King Caucus"—the nomination of candidates by congressional caucuses. In the third phase, King Caucus was replaced by factional politics and unsettled rules for selecting candidates. The fourth phase—still in effect today—evolved between 1832 and 1844. It is characterized by a two-party system that nominates candidates by national conventions. In recent years, however, the conventions have been rendered obsolete by mass politics, which takes the form of mass media presentations of candidates to the public and mass participation of party members in primary elections.

### WASHINGTON'S FIRST ELECTION: 1789

Establishment of the rules for democratic decision making in the United States occurred inauspiciously. The states completed their separate ratifications of the Constitution in July 1788—nearly nine months after the close of the Constitutional Convention in Philadelphia. The Continental Congress then decided that New York City would serve as the seat of government. There, on September 13, 1788, Congress passed a resolution requiring the states to appoint electors on the first Wednesday in January, the electors to assemble and vote in their respective states on the first Wednesday in February, and the new government to convene on the first Wednesday in March.

Under the Constitution, the method of choosing electors was left up to the individual state legislatures. *(See "Role of the Electoral College and the Selection of Electors," p. 3, in Chapter 1.)* The requirement that all electors be chosen on the same day proved to be troublesome for the states. Some did not have time to call elections. In New York, for example, where electors were to have been chosen by the legislature, dissension between the two houses led to a stalemate and prevented the state from participating in the election.

No formal nomination of candidates took place in 1788. Nevertheless, it had been widely anticipated since the Constitutional Convention the previous year that George Washington of Vir-

149

ginia, the reluctant hero of the Revolutionary War, would be president. The only real question was who would be the vice president. Leaders of the Federalist Party, organized in the fall of 1787 to achieve ratification of the Constitution, ultimately decided to support longtime statesman John Adams of Massachusetts.

The inherent flaws of the electoral system became evident quickly. Under the Constitution, each elector was to cast two votes for president. The two votes had to be for different persons, and the two candidates could not both receive votes from a common home state. The individual receiving the votes of a majority of the electors was to be named president, and the person receiving the second highest total was to be named vice president. Since no distinction was made between balloting for president and vice president, it was possible for more than one candidate to receive an equal number of votes, thus throwing the election into the House of Representatives. It also was possible that a candidate for vice president—through fluke or machination—actually could end up with the most votes and become president.

The Federalist leader Alexander Hamilton recognized the danger, and his personal animosity toward Adams aggravated his concern. In response, he plotted to siphon away votes from Adams. In a letter to James Wilson of Pennsylvania, Hamilton wrote: "Everybody is aware of that defect in the constitution which renders it possible that the man intended for vice president may in fact turn up president." To prevent such a crisis, Hamilton recommended that several votes that would otherwise have gone to Adams be thrown away on other candidates: "I have proposed to friends in Connecticut to throw away 2 [votes], to others in New Jersey to throw away an equal number and I submit to you whether it would not be well to lose three or four in Pennsylvania. . . ."[3]

Hamilton's efforts were successful. Washington was unanimously elected president with sixty-nine electoral votes. Adams, however, won the vice presidency with only thirty-four electoral votes. Just two states—New Hampshire and his own Massachu-

setts—voted solidly for him. Because in other states Federalist leaders withheld support from Adams and sometimes worked against him, he did not receive *any* votes from Delaware, Georgia, Maryland, and South Carolina, and he received only one vote from New Jersey. The remaining votes were spread among ten other candidates, including John Jay, John Hancock, Robert Harrison, John Rutledge, and George Clinton.

Although the new government was supposed to open its doors on March 4, 1789, not enough members of Congress had arrived in New York City by that date to achieve a quorum. When the Senate finally convened on April 6 and counted the electoral votes, a messenger was dispatched on horseback to deliver the news to President-elect Washington at his home in Mount Vernon, Virginia. He received the news on April 14. Washington then set out for New York where he was sworn in on April 30. (See "The Inauguration," p. 143, in Chapter 2.)

Before the end of Washington's first term as president, political divisions developed that would lead to a party system. James Madison emerged as the de facto opposition leader in Congress. Seventeen members of the House of Representatives regularly sided with Madison, and a bloc of fifteen supported the administration. The other dozen or so members of the House switched back and forth between the administration's and Madison's faction.[4]

The election of 1789 demonstrated the potential for partisanship and intrigue in presidential contests. It also revealed the weaknesses of the existing election calendar (which had made it difficult for New York to participate in the election) and reminded participants of the danger of the constitutional "defect" in the selection process that made it possible for the person intended to be vice president to become president.

### WASHINGTON'S REELECTION: 1792

George Washington remained first in the hearts of his countrymen when his first term as president drew to a close in 1792. But the facade of national unity was showing signs of crumbling as bitter oppositional factions began to develop. From this arose a system of electoral competition.

President Washington won a second unanimous term as president in 1792, but the election did produce competition for vice president. An overtly partisan contest broke out when the Democratic-Republicans, as one faction was now known, decided to challenge the Federalist John Adams. Some of Adams's approving statements about the British angered populists, who campaigned behind the scenes against him. He managed to win, but not before bitter partisan identities had developed in response to the nation's only unanimous administration.

The election was different from the 1789 one in another way as well. The election calendar was changed and made more flexible by an act of Congress that allowed states to choose electors within a thirty-four-day span before the first Wednesday in December when the electors met to vote. The new law remained in effect until 1845.

Thomas Jefferson, the leader of the Democratic-Republicans,

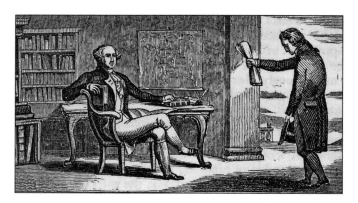

After riding his horse for a full week, Charles Thomson, secretary of the Continental Congress, arrived at Mt. Vernon on April 14, 1789, with the official news of George Washington's election as the first president of the United States.

chose not to run for vice president in 1792, in part because he came from the same state as President Washington. Since electors could vote for only one candidate from their own state, Jefferson was tacitly precluded from receiving the large electoral vote of Virginia. Besides, a "balanced ticket" required regional diversity. Instead, Democratic-Republican leaders from New York, Pennsylvania, Virginia, and South Carolina chose New York governor George Clinton as their candidate at a meeting in Philadelphia in October 1792. The endorsement of Clinton was a milestone in the evolution of the presidential nominating process and a step away from the Framers' original understanding of the selection process.

Both Washington and Adams were reelected, but Clinton scored well in the electoral college. Adams received 77 electoral votes to Clinton's 50 (with 4 votes going to Jefferson and 1 to Sen. Aaron Burr of New York), and Washington was reelected president by a unanimous electoral vote of 132.

The political tensions brought out by the Adams-Clinton contest became even tauter as policy controversies arose. Thomas Jefferson resigned as secretary of state in 1793 in protest over Secretary of the Treasury Alexander Hamilton's growing influence in foreign affairs. Jefferson complained: "In place of that noble love of liberty and Republican government which carried us triumphantly through the war, an Anglican, Monarchical, and Aristocratical party has sprung up, whose avowed subject is to draw over us the substance as they have already done the forms of the British government." Even George Washington was subject to attacks. A Pennsylvania politician wondered aloud if Washington had not "become the tyrant instead of the saviour of his country."[5]

News of the French Revolution's period of terror divided the nation's political leaders. Federalists recoiled in horror with the news of a democratic revolution gone awry, while democrats like Thomas Jefferson expressed sympathy for France's struggle. The U.S. government's use of troops to suppress the Whiskey Rebellion of 1794, approval of the Jay Treaty of 1794, and maneuvering between the warring French and British also polarized the young nation into factions. State-level Democratic and Republican societies formed during this period in opposition to the Federalists.

## THE FIRST SUCCESSION: 1796

George Washington decided not to run for president again in 1796, even though the Constitution did not bar a third term and public sentiment supported it. With Washington out of the race, the United States witnessed its first partisan contest for president. Washington's Farewell Address, published in the summer of 1796, was "a signal, like dropping a hat, for the party racers to start."[6]

On the Democratic-Republican side, Thomas Jefferson faced no opposition as the presidential candidate; a consensus of party leaders selected him to run in 1796. But a caucus of Democratic-Republican senators was unable to agree on a running mate, producing a tie vote for Sen. Aaron Burr of New York and

Thomas Pinckney, the Federalist choice for vice president, was not elected in 1796, although Federalist presidential candidate John Adams won the election. Democratic-Republican Thomas Jefferson won the vice presidency. The Twelfth Amendment (1804) precluded future split-ticket administrations.

Sen. Pierce Butler of South Carolina that ended with a walk-out by Butler's supporters. As a result, there was no formal Democratic-Republican candidate to run with Jefferson.

The Federalists, by contrast, held what historian Roy F. Nichols has described as a "quasi caucus" of the party's members of Congress in Philadelphia in May 1796.[7] The gathering chose Vice President Adams and Minister to Great Britain Thomas Pinckney of South Carolina as the Federalist presidential and vice-presidential candidates. The choice of Adams was not surprising since he was Washington's vice president. Nevertheless, Adams was unpopular in the South, and he continued to be disliked by Hamilton. As a result, Hamilton tried to use the "defect" in the Constitution to make Pinckney president instead of Adams. He urged northern electors to give equal support to Adams and Pinckney in the hopes that the South would not vote for Adams and that Pinckney would therefore win the most votes.

Had the northern electors followed Hamilton's advice, Pinckney might have won the presidency. Instead, eighteen votes were thrown to other Federalists (thereby preventing a Pinckney claim to the presidency), giving Adams the presidency with seventy-one electoral votes. Pinckney—with fifty-nine votes—was not even able to win the vice presidency. Jefferson—the candidate of the opposing Democratic-Republican ticket—came in second with sixty-eight votes and became Adams's vice president. Although the results again played up the defects in the constitutional procedure for electing presidents, Federalists and Democratic-Republicans did not seem unduly concerned that the president and vice president were of opposing parties. Both sides felt that they had prevented the opposition from gaining total victory.

For the first and last time, a foreign figure played an active and public role in the election. French Ambassador Pierre Adet promoted Jefferson's campaign in appearances and in written statements. Whether the Adet effort helped or hurt Jefferson is uncertain. The effort aroused supporters of France but angered others who favored Great Britain or resented outside interference.

## JEFFERSON'S REVENGE: 1800

The election of 1800 was the first in which both parties used congressional caucuses to nominate candidates for their tickets. Such caucuses were an important innovation in the presidential selection process because they formalized partisan alignments in Congress and demonstrated the emergence of organized political parties.

President Adams was hated bitterly by farmers, populists, and states' rights advocates. In one of the nation's first professionally run smear campaigns, Adams was denounced as a "hideous hermaphroditical character which has neither the force and firmness of a man, nor the gentleness and sensibility of a woman."[8]

Federalist members of Congress met in the Senate chamber in Philadelphia on May 3, 1800, to choose their candidates. As in previous presidential election years, Federalists were divided in their support of Adams, yet they felt they had to nominate him because he was the incumbent president. Their ambivalence toward Adams was revealed, however, when they nominated both Adams and Maj. Gen. Charles Cotesworth Pinckney of South Carolina without giving preference to one or the other for president. Pinckney was the elder brother of the Federalist vice-presidential candidate in 1796.

The choice of Pinckney was made at Hamilton's insistence. Once again Hamilton was plotting to use the constitutional defect against Adams. In 1796, South Carolina had voted for an all-southern ticket—Jefferson and Thomas Pinckney—even though the two were of opposing parties. Hamilton hoped that South Carolina would vote the same way in 1800, and that all other Federalist electors could be persuaded to vote for Adams and Charles Pinckney. That would give Pinckney more votes than Adams, thus making him president.

Although the deliberations of the Federalist caucus were secret, the existence of the meeting was not. It was described by the local Democratic-Republican paper, the Philadelphia *Aurora,* as a "Jacobinical conclave." Further denunciations by the paper's editor, Benjamin F. Bache, earned him a personal rebuke from the U.S. Senate.

The Democratic-Republicans once again chose Jefferson as the presidential candidate by consensus. On May 11 a caucus of Democratic-Republican members of Congress met at Marache's boarding house in Philadelphia to choose a running mate. Their unanimous choice was Aaron Burr.

Although there was no such thing as a formal party platform in 1800, Jefferson wrote fairly detailed statements of principle in letters to various correspondents. Among other things, the Democratic-Republicans believed in states' rights, a small national government, and a relatively weak executive. They opposed standing armies in peacetime, a large naval force, and alliances with other countries. And they denounced the Alien and Sedition Acts, which had been passed by the Federalists in 1798, ostensibly to protect the nation from subversives given the threat of war with France.

The election in 1800 witnessed other signs of formal public campaigning. Tickets listing the names of Democratic-Republican electors were printed and distributed in a number of states, including New York, Massachusetts, Pennsylvania, and Delaware. Speeches in behalf of the candidates increased markedly. Partisan newspapers also helped to spread the party positions—the number of newspapers in the United States had grown dramatically in the last decade of the century, from 91 to 234.[9] Despite attempts by the Federalist Party to muzzle the opposition press with the passage of the Sedition Act of 1798, partisan newspapers on both sides actively defamed the opposition. Ultimately, the Sedition Act worked against the Federalists by turning the Democratic-Republicans into public champions of a free press.

Increased partisan activity spurred voter participation. Since electors still were chosen indirectly in twelve of the sixteen states, voters often expressed themselves through state legislative elections as a means of influencing future presidential elections.[10] The seeds were being sown for a new phase in the development of the presidential election process.

A harbinger of Democratic-Republican success came in May when the New York state party won state legislative elections. Burr managed the campaign in the state, building a machine with ward and precinct organizations. Burr's efforts showed the importance of large-scale mobilization—a lesson that would not be lost on the party in future years.

When the electors voted in December, the constitutional defect did not work as Hamilton had hoped. Instead of resulting in a Pinckney victory, the defect produced an unexpected tie vote between the two Democratic-Republican candidates, Jefferson and Burr—each of whom had seventy-three electoral votes. Adams came in third with sixty-five, and Pinckney followed with sixty-four. In accord with the Constitution, the election was thrown into the Federalist-controlled House of Representatives.

Some Federalists felt that Burr was the lesser of the two evils and plotted to elect him president instead of Jefferson, even though Jefferson was clearly the presidential candidate. Hamilton helped to squelch the idea. After thirty-six ballots, Jefferson carried a majority in the House of Representatives. The crisis—which could have fatally wounded the nation by calling into

LOOK ON THIS PICTURE,    AND ON THIS.

This 1807 anti-Jefferson cartoon compares Washington and Jefferson in contrasting images of good and evil.

question the legitimacy of the new president—was over. Jefferson was elected president and Burr vice president.

The near disaster brought about by the constitutional defect led to the passage of the Twelfth Amendment to the Constitution in September 1804. It called for electors to vote for president and vice president on separate ballots, thereby clarifying who was the presidential candidate and eliminating the possibility of a tie between the principal candidate and the running mate.

## JEFFERSON'S REELECTION: 1804

By the 1804 election, President Thomas Jefferson had grudgingly accepted the emergence of a party system. Indeed, the president wrote that year: "The party division in this country is certainly not among its pleasant features. To a certain degree it will always exist."[11]

Jefferson's record—lower taxes, a reduced national debt, repeal of the Alien and Sedition Acts, and purchase of the Louisiana Territory from France—assured him of a second term. Particularly important was Jefferson's willingness to expand the nation's reach and power with the Louisiana Purchase, which compromised his philosophical preference for a small republic. The opposition's case against Jefferson was personal, but the voters were not convinced of the need to make a change.

The 1804 election was the first one held after the Twelfth Amendment went into effect, requiring electors to cast separate votes for president and vice president. Thus as of that election, parties always specifically designated their presidential and vice-presidential candidates.

The Democratic-Republicans retained the caucus system of nomination in 1804, as they did for the next two decades, and for the first time they publicly reported their deliberations. When the party caucus met on February 25, 1804, it attracted 108 of the party's senators and representatives.

President Jefferson was renominated by acclamation, but Vice President Burr, who had fallen out with his party, was not considered for a second term. On the first nominating roll call publicly reported in U.S. political history, New York governor George Clinton was chosen by the caucus to run for vice president. He received sixty-seven votes and easily defeated Sen. John Breckinridge of Kentucky, who collected twenty votes. To "avoid unpleasant discussions" no names were placed in nomination, and the vote was conducted by secret ballot.

Before adjourning, the caucus appointed a thirteen-member committee to conduct the campaign and promote the success of Democratic-Republican candidates. A forerunner of party national committees, the new campaign group included members of both the House and Senate, but with no two persons from the same state. Because the Twelfth Amendment had not yet been passed when the caucus met, the committee was designed to "manage" the vote of Democratic-Republican electors to make sure that the events of 1800 were not repeated. In fact, that precaution was not necessary because the Twelfth Amendment was ratified in September—well before the electors voted.

By 1804 the Federalist Party had deteriorated badly. The new era of dominance by the Virginia-led Democratic-Republicans had begun. The Federalists did not even hold a congressional caucus to select their nominees. Instead, Federalist leaders informally chose Charles Cotesworth Pinckney for president and Rufus King of New York for vice president. How the Federalists formulated this ticket is not clear. There is no record in 1804 of any formal meeting to nominate Federalist candidates.

The Federalists then mounted a disorganized and dispirited national campaign. Despite concerted efforts to win at least the votes of New England, the Federalists failed miserably. Pinckney received only 14 electoral votes—those of Connecticut and Delaware, plus 2 from Maryland. Jefferson, the Democratic-Republican candidate, was the overwhelming victor with 162 electoral votes.

## MADISON'S 1808 VICTORY

Following George Washington's precedent, Thomas Jefferson refused to seek a third term of office. The nation was bitterly divided over Jefferson's policy toward France and Britain. In an attempt to stay out of their war, Jefferson had supported a trade embargo so that neither country would seize American ships. But the embargo only undermined American business interests. Under attack, Jefferson decided to return to his beloved home of Monticello near Charlottesville, Virginia.

Despite the unpopularity of the administration's European policy, Jefferson's secretary of state and chosen successor, James Madison, won the presidency in 1808. Jefferson's retirement provided a serious test to the authority of the Democratic-Republican congressional caucus to select presidential candidates. The caucus met on January 23, 1808 after, for the first time, a formal call was issued. Sen. Stephen R. Bradley of Vermont, chairman of the 1804 caucus, issued the call to all 146 Democratic-Republicans in Congress and several Federalists sympathetic to the Democratic-Republican cause. A few party leaders questioned Bradley's authority to call the caucus, but various reports indicate that between eighty-nine and ninety-four members of Congress attended.

As in 1804, the balloting took place without names being formally placed in nomination. Madison easily won the presidential nomination with eighty-three votes. Despite earlier support for Secretary of State James Monroe among Democratic-Republicans in Virginia, and Vice President Clinton's own desire to be president, each won only three votes at the caucus. But the caucus overwhelmingly renominated Clinton as vice president, giving him seventy-nine votes; runner-up John Langdon of New Hampshire collected five votes.

The Democratic-Republican caucus also repeated its practice of appointing a committee to conduct the campaign. Membership was expanded from thirteen to fifteen House and Senate members, and it was formally called the "committee of correspondence and arrangement." The committee was authorized to fill vacancies on the national ticket, should any occur. Before the caucus adjourned, it passed a resolution defending the caucus system as "the most practicable mode of consulting and respecting the interest and wishes of all." Later caucuses adopted similar resolutions throughout the history of the system.

Still, the Democratic-Republicans suffered divisions. Forty percent of the Democratic-Republican members of Congress had refused to attend the nominating caucus. Monroe refused to withdraw from the presidential race even after his defeat in the caucus. And Clinton, although he was nominated for vice president, was angry at not being nominated for president—so much so that he publicly denounced the caucus, as did Monroe's supporters. Pro-Clinton newspapers in New York launched harsh attacks on Madison and even suggested a Clinton-Monroe ticket. Some Clinton supporters went so far as to hope that the Federalists would nominate Clinton for president later in the year. But such a thought was unpalatable to the Federalists, who ultimately nominated Charles Cotesworth Pinckney.

The Federalists chose their ticket at a secret meeting of party leaders in New York City in August 1808. Initially, the meeting was called by the Federalist members of the Massachusetts legislature. Twenty-five to thirty party leaders from seven states, all north of the Potomac River except South Carolina, attended the national meeting. Despite the suggestion from Massachusetts representatives that Clinton be nominated, the gathering decided to run the same ticket they had chosen in 1804: Pinckney and King.

The Federalists did not actively publicize their ticket. The party itself was divided and devoid of leadership. Indeed, many Virginia Federalists formally endorsed Monroe, even though he was a Democratic-Republican. Others preferred to align themselves with Clinton.

In the end, Madison achieved a wide margin of victory with 122 electoral votes; Pinckney came in second with 47 votes. Monroe received no electoral votes. For the sake of future party unity, Democratic-Republicans had retained Clinton as their vice-presidential nominee even though he had tried to subvert Madison's candidacy. And he won that office, receiving 113 electoral votes for vice president. He even received 6 electoral votes from New York for president.

## MADISON'S REELECTION: 1812

The winds of war were sweeping through presidential politics when James Madison sought a second term in 1812. In response to constant agitation by "war hawks," the president asked Congress on June 1 for a declaration of war against Great Britain. Madison, benefiting from the public's willingness to rally in times of national emergency, swept to a second term. The Federalists did not field a candidate but supported a dissident from Madison's own party.

The possibility of war had long hung over the United States. Great Britain had taken American ships captive for years—boarding the vessels, taking cargo, and intimidating seamen. Anti-British political forces also charged that the British had encouraged Indians in their attacks against Americans in the North and West.

The Democratic-Republican Party held its quadrennial nominating caucus on May 18, 1812. Only 83 of the 178 Democratic-Republicans in Congress participated. The New England and New York delegations in particular were poorly represented. Many of the New Yorkers supported the candidacy of their state's lieutenant governor, DeWitt Clinton (George Clinton's nephew), who also was maneuvering for the Federalist nomination. New England was noticeably upset with Madison's foreign policy, which was leading to war with England. Others did not attend the caucus because they opposed the system in principle.

Madison won a near-unanimous renomination in the caucus, receiving eighty-two votes. John Langdon of New Hampshire got the vice-presidential nomination by a wide margin, collecting sixty-four votes to sixteen for Gov. Elbridge Gerry of Massachusetts. But Langdon declined the nomination, citing his age (seventy) as the reason. The Democratic-Republicans held a second caucus on June 8 to select another vice-presidential candidate. Gerry was the clear winner with seventy-four votes, and he responded with a formal letter of acceptance. Ten members of Congress who had not been present at the first caucus also took the opportunity to endorse Madison's presidential candidacy.

Democratic-Republicans from New York were unwilling to accept the choice of Madison. They held their own caucus, composed of nearly all party members from the New York state legislature, where they unanimously nominated Clinton, who responded with a written "Address" that was a precursor to party platforms. Clinton won the endorsement of the Federalists as well.

As they had four years earlier, the Federalists convened a three-day secret meeting in New York City. The September meeting was more than twice the size of the 1808 gathering, with seventy representatives from eleven states attending. Delegates were sent to the conference by Federalist general committees, with all but nine of the delegates coming from the New England and Middle Atlantic states.

Debate centered on whether to run a separate Federalist ticket or to endorse Clinton. After much debate, they decided to endorse Clinton, and they nominated Jared Ingersoll of Pennsylvania for vice president. Originally, the caucus's decision was meant to be kept a secret, but leaks eventually were reported by Democratic-Republican newspapers.

The presidential election of 1812 was the first wartime contest for power in the United States. The Federalists, calling Madison a dupe of French emperor Napoleon Bonaparte, aligned themselves with the cause of peace and unimpeded commerce. In some northern states the Federalists even adopted the Peace Party label.

Despite all the opposition to President Madison, he beat Clinton by an electoral vote count of 128–89. The vote reflected the growing split between southern agricultural states, which supported Madison, and northern commercial states, which

supported Clinton. Indeed, the common bond that held the Clinton coalition together was a hatred of Virginia—the kingmaker of the Democratic-Republican Party.

The 1812 race was the last real campaign by the Federalists. Disgraced by their obstructionist tactics during the war, isolated by their talk of succession from the Union, and unable to coordinate a national campaign, the Federalists faded from a system increasingly marked by permanent party competition.

## MONROE'S 1816 VICTORY

James Monroe, President Madison's old foe who had left the Democratic-Republican Party in 1808, seemed an unlikely presidential candidate for the party in 1820. But not only did James Monroe return to the Democratic-Republican fold, he also won the White House without any opposition.

The inconclusive War of 1812 colored American politics for years. The United States and Great Britain fought to a stalemate, and then both sides offered conditions for ending the war that the other would not accept. The British, for example, demanded control over the Great Lakes and Mississippi River for commerce, as well as the creation of an Indian state in the Northwest. In the end, both parties simply accepted the end of hostilities. An American representative said the treaty was "a truce rather than a peace."[12] Inconclusive or not, the war sparked a generation of nationalism. Rufus King revived the Federalist Party in 1816 with his race for the governorship of New York. But he lost the race and afterward found the job of maintaining the party a "fruitless struggle." Efforts were made to convene another secret meeting in Philadelphia to nominate candidates for president and vice president, yet the party held no such meeting. With the Federalists not running candidates, nomination by the Democratic-Republican caucus was tantamount to election.

Despite his opposition to Madison in 1808, Monroe had been accepted back into the Democratic-Republican fold in the years that followed. In 1811 Madison had named him secretary of state; by 1816 he was Madison's heir apparent. But many states were increasingly jealous of the Virginia dynasty that had held a grip on the presidency since 1804. Democratic-Republicans in such states opposed Monroe (himself a Virginian) and favored Secretary of War William H. Crawford of Georgia.

A Democratic-Republican caucus met in the House chamber on March 12, 1816, but only 58 members of Congress—mostly Crawford supporters—attended. With the expectation of better attendance, a second caucus was held on March 16. It drew 119 of the 141 Democratic-Republicans in Congress. There, Monroe narrowly defeated Crawford by a vote of 65–54. Forty of Crawford's votes came from five states: Georgia, Kentucky, New Jersey, New York, and North Carolina. The vice-presidential nomination went to New York governor Daniel D. Tompkins, who easily outdistanced Pennsylvania governor Simon Snyder, 85–30.

The nominations of Monroe and Tompkins revived a Virginia-New York alliance that extended back to the late eighteenth century. With the lone exception of 1812, every Democratic-Republican ticket from 1800 to 1824 was composed of a presidential candidate from Virginia and a vice-presidential candidate from New York.

With the Federalist Party still in disarray, the Democratic-Republican ticket won easily. Monroe received 183 electoral votes. The three states—Connecticut, Delaware, and Massachusetts—that had chosen Federalist electors cast their 34 electoral votes for Rufus King.

Although the collapse of the Federalists ensured Democratic-Republican rule, it also increased intraparty friction and spurred further attacks on the caucus system. Twenty-two Democratic-Republican members of Congress had not attended the second party caucus, and at least fifteen were known to be opposed to the system. Mass meetings around the country protested the caucus system.[13] Opponents asserted that the writers of the Constitution did not envision the caucus, that presidential nominating should not be a function of Congress, and that the caucus system encouraged candidates to curry the favor of Congress.

## MONROE'S REELECTION: 1820

The 1820 election took place during the "Era of Good Feeling," a phrase coined by a Boston publication, the *Columbian Centinel,* to describe a brief period of virtual one-party rule in the United States. But that phrase glosses over serious sectional divisions that were growing during Monroe's presidency. The divisions did not prevent Monroe from winning another term, however.

Sectional strife was on the brink of eruption during Monroe's first term over the admission of Missouri as a new state. Tensions between northern and southern states had simmered for years. The emotional core of the struggle was slavery. Thus whichever region controlled Congress might decide whether slavery was extended into new territories—and the shape of the nation's economy and culture—for years to come.

In the Senate, there was a tenuous balance between the two regions—eleven free states and eleven slave states—but the admission of Missouri threatened that balance. The two sides finally agreed to a compromise in which both Missouri and Maine would apply for statehood at the same time, Maine as a free state and Missouri as a slave state. Monroe remained neutral in the debate leading up to the compromise. Despite a financial panic in 1819, he retained overwhelming popular support, bolstered by peace and a wave of nationalistic feeling that overshadowed any partisan divisions.

While the United States struggled over the slavery issue, President Monroe embarked on a bold new foreign policy. Still smarting over the British presence in North America that had resulted in the War of 1812, the president declared that the United States would view any European attempts to colonize the Western Hemisphere as acts of hostility. The Monroe Doctrine claimed the hemisphere as the preserve of the United States. It was the boldest venture yet of the nation into foreign policy and permanently defined America's role in world affairs.

Although several rival Democratic-Republican candidates aspired to win the presidency when Monroe retired in 1824, none wanted to challenge his reelection in 1820. A nominating caucus was called for early March, but fewer than fifty of the Democratic-Republican Party's 191 members of Congress showed up. The caucus voted unanimously to make no nominations and passed a resolution explaining that it was inexpedient to do so since so few of the party's members were in attendance. Although Monroe and Tompkins were not formally renominated, electoral slates were filed on their behalf.

Because the Federalist Party was finally dead, Monroe ran virtually unopposed. Even John Adams, the last Federalist president, voted for Monroe as an elector from Massachusetts. Only one elector, a Democratic-Republican from New Hampshire, cast a vote against Monroe, supporting instead the young John Quincy Adams, son of the former president.

## LAST OF THE OLD ORDER: 1824

The 1824 election, in an odd way, represented everything that the Framers of the Constitution had hoped to see. Without a permanent party system, a number of candidates vied for the presidency. Unable to win an electoral majority, the top three finishers saw their names submitted to the House of Representatives for a final decision. The candidate representative of elite interests and sensibilities and who had House ties won.

But if the 1824 election of John Quincy Adams represented something old, it also represented something new. The popular winner and House loser, Andrew Jackson, protested loudly that the election had been stolen from the people. In fact, soon he would mobilize the Democratic Party around a populist rallying cry. American politics would never be the same.

In 1824, as in 1820, only one working party existed in the United States: the Democratic-Republican. But that party had an abundance of candidates competing for the presidency: Secretary of State John Quincy Adams of Massachusetts, Sen. Andrew Jackson of Tennessee, Secretary of War John C. Calhoun of South Carolina, House Speaker Henry Clay of Kentucky, and Secretary of the Treasury William H. Crawford. The number of candidates, coupled with the growing democratization of the U.S. political system, led to the demise of King Caucus in 1824.

Early on, Crawford was the leading candidate. He had strong southern support and appeared likely to win the support of New York's Democratic-Republicans. Since it was assumed that he would win a caucus if one were held, Crawford's opponents joined the growing list of caucus opponents. But Crawford's apparent invincibility suddenly ended in September 1823 when he suffered a paralytic stroke. Nearly blind and unable even to sign his name, he was incapacitated and stayed in seclusion for months.

In early February 1824, eleven Democratic-Republican members of Congress issued a call for a caucus to be held in the middle of the month. Their call was countered by twenty-four other members of Congress from fifteen states who deemed it "inexpedient under existing circumstances" to hold a caucus. They claimed that 181 members of Congress were resolved not to attend if a caucus were held.

The caucus convened in mid-February, but only 66 members of Congress showed up. Three-quarters of those attending came from just four states—Georgia, New York, North Carolina, and Virginia. Despite his illness, Crawford won the caucus nomination with sixty-four votes. Albert Gallatin of Pennsylvania was selected for vice president with fifty-seven votes. The caucus adopted a resolution defending its actions as "the best means of collecting and concentrating the feelings and wishes of the people of the Union upon this important subject." The caucus also appointed a committee to write an address to the people. As written, the text of the address viewed with alarm the "dismemberment" of the Democratic-Republican Party.

In fact, the action of the caucus just aggravated splits in the party. Since so few members of Congress attended the caucus—almost all of them Crawford supporters—opponents could argue that the choice was not even representative of the Democratic-Republicans serving in Congress. Crawford was roundly criticized as being an illegitimate candidate. His opponents derided King Caucus, and his physical condition made it even easier for them to reject his nomination. As it stood, other candidates simply refused to follow the caucus's decision. Never again were candidates chosen by the caucus system.

With the caucus devoid of power and the party lacking unity or leadership, there was no chance of rallying behind a single ticket. In addition, many political issues proved to be divisive. Western expansion and protective tariffs, for example, benefited some parts of the country but hurt others. Thus the various candidates came to represent sectional interests.

The candidates themselves recognized that such a crowded field was dangerous. The election would be thrown into the House of Representatives if no candidate received a majority. The candidates therefore made efforts to join forces. Adams tried to lure Jackson as his running mate. Adams was a short, stocky, aloof, well-educated New Englander who came from a family of Federalists, while Jackson was a tall, thin, hot-tempered war hero with little formal education who came to epitomize a new brand of populist democracy. In trying to lure Jackson onto their team, Adams supporters envisaged a ticket of "the writer and the fighter." Jackson would have nothing of it.

In the meantime, Crawford dropped Gallatin as his vice-presidential running mate. His supporters then tried to convince Clay to drop his own quest for the presidency and join the Crawford team. They hinted that Crawford's physical condition was such that he would probably not finish out a term of office if elected (in fact, he lived ten more years). But Clay was not swayed. Calhoun then dropped his race for the presidency and joined efforts with Jackson.

Four candidates remained in the field and each collected electoral votes. None, however, received a majority. Jackson received the most with ninety-nine, followed by Adams with

eighty-four, Crawford with forty-one, and Clay with thirty-seven. Thus the election was thrown into the House of Representatives.

In accordance with the Twelfth Amendment, the names of the top three candidates—Jackson, Adams, and Crawford—were placed before the House. Clay, who had come in fourth place and was Speaker of the House, would play a major role in tipping the balance in favor of one of the candidates.

In contrast to Jackson, Adams actively lobbied for support, and Washington rocked with rumors of corruption. Clay informed Adams in January that he would support Adams in the House election—a major blow to Jackson. Shortly thereafter, a letter in a Philadelphia newspaper alleged that Adams had offered Clay the post of secretary of state in return for his support. Adams went on to win the House election narrowly by carrying thirteen out of twenty-four state delegations. Jackson came in second with seven, and Crawford third with the remaining four *(See "When the Electoral College Is Deadlocked," p. 125, in Chapter 1.)* Thus the candidate who won the most electoral votes and the most popular votes did not win the presidency.

Jackson was furious at what he considered to be unfair bargaining between Adams and Clay. He felt that the will of the people had been thwarted, and he seethed when President Adams proceeded to name Clay secretary of state as rumor had indicated he would. In this way, the events of 1824 kindled the flame of popular democracy. The stage was set for a rematch between Adams and Jackson in 1828.

## The Age of Jackson

Andrew Jackson was in many ways the perfect man to usher in an age of popular politics, although his rhetoric was more populist than his style of governing. The textbook version of U.S. history depicts Jackson as a coarse man of the frontier, a war hero, a battler of banks and moneyed interests, and a leader of the unschooled and exploited men who built a mass party on patronage and charismatic leadership. Jackson was the first politician to break the Virginia dynasty that had governed the country since the Revolution. After his bitter defeat in the 1824 election, Jackson fought back and grabbed the reins of government in the turbulent election of 1828. These two elections signaled the passing of elite politics and the rise of popular politics. In 1828 Jackson roused the people to turn Adams and his aristocratic clique out of office.

But the Jacksonian folklore has serious flaws. Jackson traveled in elite business circles, for example, and one of his greatest contributions as president was the creation of a more rationally organized bureaucracy.[14] Still, the textbook depiction of Jackson suffices to show some trends in U.S. politics, including the development of a stable mass party system, sectionalism, urbanization, and shifts in the debate about U.S. expansionism.

While President Adams was struggling with warring factions

This 1836 cartoon depicts Jackson attacking the Bank of the United States with his veto stick. Vice President Van Buren, center, helps to kill the monster, whose heads represent Nicholas Biddle, president of the bank, and directors of the state branches.

in Washington, an opposition force was gathering strength, and, in fact, was able to deal the president a number of humiliating defeats. Adams's desire for a national program of roads and canals, education, and research in the arts and sciences antagonized even the most nationalistic groups in the country. U.S. participation in a conference of countries from the Western Hemisphere and the imposition of a tariff (a tax on imported goods designed either to raise revenues or to protect domestic industries from foreign competition) also were divisive issues. But even though Adams was under constant personal attack, the opposition was divided on the same issues. The opposition was united, however, behind "Old Hickory."[15]

Jackson, hero of the Battle of New Orleans in the War of 1812, had a strong appeal to the common man even though he traveled in the circles of southern gentlemen. People who met with Jackson talked of his unerring "intuition" about people and politics. Jackson's decision to push for reforms of the punishment of debtors was an important gesture to small businessmen and workers who were held to a kind of indentured servitude to their creditors. Sen. Martin Van Buren of New York, Jackson's strongest supporter in the Northeast, said the people "were his blood relations—the only blood relations he had."[16]

### THE 1828 ELECTION

Jackson and his running mate, John C. Calhoun, easily beat Adams in their 1828 rematch; Jackson won 178 electoral votes, and Adams won 83. (Calhoun also had been vice president under John Quincy Adams.) Of the popular vote, Jackson received 643,000 votes (56.0 percent) to Adams's 501,000 (43.6 percent).

Sectional splits showed in the vote distribution. Adams held all but 1 of New England's electoral votes, all of Delaware's and New Jersey's, 16 of New York's 36 votes, and 6 of Maryland's 11 votes. Jackson took all the rest—the South and the West. The election, then, was decided by the newly enfranchised voters in the burgeoning regions of the country. The U.S. electorate, however, was expanding not only in the West but also in the original states. Between 1824 and 1856 voter participation grew from 3.8 percent to 16.7 percent of the total population.[17]

Jackson had only begun to exert electoral influence with his revenge victory over Adams. The expanded pool of politically involved citizens that had brought Jackson victory also brought him demands for patronage jobs with the federal government. Van Buren, a master machine politician from New York State, tutored the beleaguered new president in dealing with the office seekers. Jackson replaced fewer than one-fifth of the government's employees, which he defended as a perfectly reasonable "rotation in office" that would keep the ranks of the bureaucracy fresh. But the effect of his system was greater. Appointees of previous administrations were able to retain their jobs only when they expressed loyalty to Jackson and his party. Far more important than any government turnover, Jackson's spoils system inaugurated an age in which mass party loyalty was a paramount concern in politics.

The increased importance of loyalty, to the president and to the party, became clear with Jackson's dispute with Vice President Calhoun and the subsequent purging of the cabinet. A growing feud between Jackson and Calhoun came to a head when a personal letter in which Calhoun criticized Jackson's conduct of the Seminole Indian campaign and the 1818 invasion of Florida became public. In a letter to Calhoun during the cabinet crisis, Jackson wrote: "Et tu, Brute." A purge of Calhoun men in the cabinet followed the incident. Secretary of State Van Buren enabled the president to make the purge when he and Secretary of War John Eaton, both Jackson allies, resigned their posts; the president then called on the whole cabinet to quit.

The central element of the Jacksonian program was expansion. Much like twentieth-century politicians who would talk about economic growth as the key to opportunity, Jackson maintained that movement West "enlarg[ed] the area of freedom."[18] The administration fought to decentralize the management of expansion. Jackson railed against the "corrupt bargain" between the government and banks, joint-stock companies, and monopolies, which, he said, were squeezing out the average person seeking opportunity.

Indeed, Jackson opposed the Bank of the United States and promoted state banks because of his desire to free finance capital from central control. In his first term, the president carried on a long-running battle with Nicholas Biddle, the head of the Bank of the United States, and with Congress over the status of the bank. Alexander Hamilton had created the bank to manage the nation's monetary policy and investment, but Jackson opposed it as a tool of the eastern financial establishment. Jackson may have failed to close the bank, but he did manage to strip it of much of its basic authority and functions by placing its deposits in a number of regional institutions.

Jackson's presidency was activist from the beginning. His administration negotiated treaties with France, the Ottoman Empire, Russia, and Mexico. Jackson himself established a distinctive interpretation of federalism when he vetoed a number of public improvements bills as unconstitutional infringements of local affairs. He also called for a tariff that would yield revenues for dispersal to the states for their own public projects—an early form of "revenue sharing." And Jackson signed the Indian Removal Act of 1830, which provided for settlement of the territory west of the Mississippi River. Late in his first term, Jackson's strong stand defeated the South Carolina legislature's claim that it could "nullify," or declare "null and void," federal tariff legislation that the state disliked.

## JACKSON'S 1832 REELECTION

There was never any doubt that Jackson would be renominated in 1832; in fact, several state legislatures endorsed him before the convention. Jackson's political strength was further underscored with the introduction of a quintessentially party-oriented institution: the national party convention. *(See "The Development of the Party Nominating Convention," p. 13, in Chapter 1.)* Jacksonians from New Hampshire proposed the Democratic convention of 1832, and the president and his advisers jumped at the opportunity. The only previous national convention had been held by the Anti-Masonic Party in 1831. Conventions had been the principal means of selecting candidates for local offices since the early part of the century. Especially when compared with the caucus system that preceded it, the convention system was a democratic leap forward.

The convention system enabled the parties to gather partisans from all geographic areas, and it welded them together as a cohesive unit that ultimately was accountable to the electorate, if only in a plebiscitary way. Voters had the opportunity to give approval or disapproval to a party program with one vote. Historian Eugene H. Roseboom has written: "It was representative in character; it divorced nominations from congressional control and added to the independence of the executive; it permitted an authoritative formulation of a party program; and it concentrated the party's strength behind a single ticket, the product of compromise of personal rivalries and group or sectional interests."[19]

Given Jackson's popularity in 1832, the purpose of the convention was to rally behind the president and select a new vice-presidential candidate. Van Buren got the nomination, despite lingering resistance from Calhoun supporters and various "favorite sons" (prominent state and local leaders of state party organizations).

As in 1828, Jackson's political opposition was fragmented. The Whigs—the opposition party that had developed from grassroots protests in the North and West against Jackson's tariff and development policies—held their national convention in Baltimore in December 1831 and unanimously nominated Henry Clay of Kentucky for president. Eighteen states used a variety of selection procedures to determine who would be their convention delegates. The party's platform sharply criticized the Jackson administration's patronage practices, relations with Great Britain, and ill-tempered congressional relations, as well as Supreme Court decisions.

In the election, the incumbent easily dispatched the opposition. "The news from the voting states blows over us like a great cold storm," wrote Rufus Choate, a prominent lawyer, to a friend.[20] Despite last-minute maneuvering to unite the opposition to Jackson and a well-financed campaign by the Bank of the United States, the president won 219 electoral votes to Clay's 49, Independent John Floyd's 11, and Anti-Mason William Wirt's 7. Jackson won all but seven states. Clay won Kentucky, Massachusetts, Rhode Island, Connecticut, and Delaware, plus five electors from Maryland. Jackson won 702,000 popular votes to Clay's 484,000 and Wirt's 101,000.[21]

Jackson, who finally left the political stage in 1837, changed the face of U.S. politics. Even if his pretensions to being an everyman were overstated, he did open up the system to mass participation, and he forced politicians to listen to popular demands. He developed the notion of a strong party organization. He fought, and eventually defeated, the national bank by withdrawing its funds and placing them in state banks. He strongly opposed two forces that could have torn the nation apart—the nullification principle of state sovereignty and the Supreme Court's bid for broader discretion over political issues (that is, to review legislation and state actions)—by simply proclaiming the law to be "unauthorized by the Constitution" and "therefore null and void."

## VAN BUREN'S 1836 WIN

Many historians consider the election of 1836 to be the most important event in the development of the party system. Van Buren, a Democratic follower of Jackson and a theorist on the role of political parties in a democratic system, easily won the election against an uncoordinated Whig Party. The defeat eventually convinced Whig leaders of the need for a permanent organization for political competition. The emergence of two permanent parties extinguished the American suspicion of the morality of a party system based on unabashed competition for the levers of power.

Van Buren, who had allied with Jackson during the cabinet controversies and promoted his philosophy of parties and patronage, received the Democratic nomination in 1836 at a convention packed with Jackson administration appointees. The vice-presidential nomination of Richard M. Johnson of Kentucky, whose earlier relationship with a mulatto woman caused controversy, damaged the ticket in the South, but the Democrats won anyway.

The Whigs' campaign strategy was to run several favorite sons to prevent any candidate from getting a majority of the electoral votes, thereby throwing the election into the House of Representatives. As one Whig put it: "The disease [Democratic rule] is to be treated as a local disorder—apply local remedies."[22] The Whig expectation was that one of two favorite sons—Gen. William Henry Harrison of Ohio or Hugh Lawson White of Tennessee—would be selected by the House after the electoral college vote proved inconclusive.

Van Buren, however, had Jackson's machine and his personal backing and was able to overcome the Whigs' local strategy. Thus in this race, the last for the White House before presidential elections became dominated by two national parties, Van Buren took 170 electoral votes—22 more than he needed for election. Of the Whig candidates, Harrison received 73 electoral votes; White, 26; and Daniel Webster of Massachusetts, 14. Willie Mangum, an Independent Democrat from North Carolina, received 11 electoral votes from the South Carolina legislature, which was hostile to White because of his role in nullification politics. Van Buren won 764,000 popular votes (50.8 percent); Harrison, 551,000 (36.6 percent); White, 146,000 (9.7 percent); and Webster, 41,000 (2.7 percent). For the only time in history, the Senate selected the vice president, Richard Johnson, who had fallen one vote shy of election by the electoral college. In the Senate, Johnson defeated Francis Granger by a 33–16 vote.

Van Buren was besieged with problems practically from the minute he took the oath of office in March 1837. About midway through his term, the economy crashed after years of feverish business growth, overspeculation in land and business, huge private debt accumulation, and unregulated financial and trade practices. Van Buren's approach to the economic crisis alternated between stubborn refusal to fix a mess that he had not created and action that was guaranteed to antagonize key interest groups.

When Van Buren moved to create an independent treasury in order to insulate the federal government from state financial institutions, he was opposed by conservative Democrats who were supporters of the state financial institutions that Jackson had promoted in his legendary national bank battles. When Van Buren was not hit from the right, he was hit from the left. The nascent labor movement called for protection of jobs and wages and made protests against monopoly and privilege.

# The Idea of a Party System

Whatever problems Van Buren had in governing, he should receive credit at least for helping to establish the principle of party government in the United States. That principle, much derided in the early days of the nation's history, now enjoys widespread allegiance.

Van Buren's arguments on behalf of a party system—contained in his book, *An Inquiry into the Origin and Course of Political Parties in the United States*—were similar to the economic principle of Adam Smith, which had held that the pursuit of selfish ends redounded to the good of the entire community. American leaders from George Washington through John Quincy Adams had believed that self-interested factions endangered the functioning and virtue of the Republic. These leaders also had warned against the dangers of democracy, which they often called "mob rule." In the worst possible scenario, permanent parties with strong ideological stances appealed to the mass public for support, undermining the ability of national leaders to guide public virtue.[23]

The basic tension that Van Buren had to resolve was the system's need for stability and responsible leadership and the parties' imperative to gain office. How could a party's selfish desire to run the government and award patronage and contracts to political allies benefit the whole system?

Van Buren argued that the absence of parties—that is, collections of people from disparate backgrounds—resulted in a system of personal politics that fueled demagogy, perpetual campaigns, and a lack of accountability. Personal presidential politics was more polarizing than the politics of consensus or of coalition building. Presidents should be able to do their job without constant carping from outsiders who fancied themselves prospective presidents. Mass parties with certain partisan principles would enable presidents to get the backing they needed to do their work.

Moreover, the existence of two parties would enable the nation to move beyond its many cleavages—that is, toward the general interest and away from simple clashes of particular interests. Competition among parties, like competition among economic enterprises, would bring about a situation in which disparate demands would be promoted by a party. The key was to achieve a balance of competing forces. Summarizing Van Buren, political scientist James W. Ceaser has written:

Established parties . . . may stand 'over' the raw electoral cleavages, possessing some leeway or discretion about which potential issues and electoral divisions will be emphasized and which will be suppressed or kept at the fringes. This discretion is exercised according to the interests of the organizations and the judgement of their leaders. But it is important to keep in mind that the degree of this discretion is limited. . . . Their discretion is always threatened or held in check by the possibility that they might be displaced by a new party having as its goal the advancement of a certain policy. . . . When a sufficiently powerful and enduring issue exists, an impartial reading of American party history suggests that the party system in the end will have to respond to it, regardless of how the established parties initially react.[24]

The Age of Jackson brought a fundamental shift from republican to democratic values as the nation's territory and activities expanded. Republicanism was the product of a variety of strains of thought—from the Romans Cicero and Tacitus and the Greek Polybius to the Frenchman Montesquieu—that stressed the need for a balancing of interests to produce public virtue. Republicans worried about excess in any single form of governance, particularly "mob rule." For them, *democracy* was a term of derision. That is why the Constitution contained many buffers against this and other forms of excess.

Republicanism declined in many stages. A greater stress on the individual's role in society, embodied in the work of Adam Smith and David Hume, restricted the kinds of issues open to public deliberation. At the same time, the pace of economic change undermined established patterns. As the nation demanded large-scale projects (such as canals and railways), and as rival factions looked to the mobilization of larger and larger parts of the electorate to augment their strength, democratic rhetoric gained respectability. Mass party participation became a vehicle for pursuing civic virtue and balance, and the notion of a constant opposition party gained strength. If the democratic process had enough constitutional "checks," political thinkers now reasoned, the harmful "mob" aspects of democracy could be tempered. The development of the Jacksonian party as a way of arbitrating interests was the final stage in republican decline and democratic ascendance.

Political scientist Russell Hanson has noted that the new democratic ethos sprang from one of the same goals as the old republican ethos: development of a public spirit by rising above particular restraints. "Support for popular sovereignty became the lowest common denominator for a Democratic Party composed of interests seeking liberation from a variety of sectionally specific restraints on the 'will of the people.'"[25]

A two-party system persisted as the nation drifted toward civil war, but it was not a simple two-party system. The Democrats and Whigs competed for the presidency and other political offices until 1856, when the Republican Party fielded its first national ticket and made the Whigs obsolete. But the parties were so unstable that their many elements were constantly forming and breaking up coalitions—and threatening to bolt from the system itself. Moreover, a series of third parties entered the national electoral arena for short periods, applying or relieving pressures on the two major parties.[26]

Only by examining the parties and their various factions and struggles can one understand the presidential contests in the two decades before the Civil War, and the way that the Civil War revealed the basic fault lines of U.S. politics.

## THE WHIGS' 1840 VICTORY

The Whigs developed to fill the role of their British namesake, which had been to mount a republican opposition to the royal ruling power. When the rise of Andrew Jackson and his supposedly imperial presidency threatened the "balance" of the United States, the Whigs rose to restore that balance. The Whigs saw Jackson's Democrats as a faction of the most dangerous variety—a majority faction that had the ability to trample liberties in its mad scramble for spoils.

The key to Whiggery was the notion of balanced development. The Whigs opposed the war with Mexico and other expansionist programs because they feared the perils of overextending the nation's abilities and getting entangled with foreign powers. They favored internal improvements, but only as a way of maintaining balance and staving off the corruption of the Jackson era. The protective tariff was central to the Whigs' program of internal development and protection from outsiders. According to Hanson,

even in America, which was uniquely blessed by an abundance of natural resources and a citizenry of hardy stock, there was need for informed guidance and direction of progress. For the Whigs, government was the primary agent of this progress. Government represented a strong and positive force to be used in calling forth a richer society from the unsettled possibilities of America. In the economic realm this meant that government was responsible for providing the essential conditions for a sound economy, namely, a reliable currency, ample credit, and the impetus for internal improvements. And in the social realm, the government was responsible for promoting virtue in its citizenry through education and exhortation.[27]

The Whigs' desire for balance and compromise was intended to give the party a national rather than a sectional identity. Moreover, their tendency to nominate widely popular military heroes helped to create at least the illusion of a party of national dimensions. A series of Senate battles with President Jackson, especially the tariff battles of 1833, which resulted in an unsatisfying compromise, gave impetus to grassroots organizations in the North and West and to southern Democratic opponents. In fact, the Whigs developed first in the South where voters were dissatisfied with Jackson's selection of Van Buren as his running mate. There, loose coalitions elected candidates in the 1834 and 1835 state and congressional elections. Westerners also organized to oppose the Democratic Party, which was headed by a New Yorker.

The first serious Whig presidential contest was a loss, but an encouraging one. In 1836 the Whig tickets headed by Harrison and others had shown surprising appeal in the loss to the Democrat Van Buren. The Whigs had won Jackson's home state of Tennessee and neighboring Georgia, as well as three border slave states, and were strong competitors elsewhere. Harrison had carried the old Northwest (now the Midwest) and had come close in such northern states as Pennsylvania.

Because of the rise of the antislavery "conscience Whigs," the Whigs eventually moved to a completely different base of support—the North rather than the South and West—but their early organizing at least broke the Democratic stranglehold on the latter two regions. The Whigs nominated Harrison in 1840 after a nomination struggle with Henry Clay. A Clay supporter, John Tyler of Virginia, was the vice-presidential nominee. This time, the popular if politically inexperienced hero of the War of 1812 won his ticket to the White House. Harrison defeated the incumbent Van Buren in an electoral vote landslide, receiving 234 of the 294 electoral votes—all the states except Alabama, Arkansas, Illinois, Missouri, New Hampshire, South Carolina, and Virginia. For the popular vote, Harrison won 1.3 million (52.9 percent) to Van Buren's 1.1 million (46.8 percent).

According to political scientist Richard P. McCormick,

The campaign of 1840 brought the American party system at last to fruition. In every region of the country, and indeed in every state, politics was conducted within the framework of a two party system, and in all but a handful of states the parties were so closely balanced as to be competitive. In broad terms, it was the contest for the presidency that shaped this party system and defined its essential purpose.[28]

Harrison's campaign was as vague as his government experience was unimpressive. The image of Harrison as a sort of frontier everyman—which received its popular expression when a Baltimore newspaper mocked him as a sedentary man who would sit in a log cabin and drink cider rather than perform great deeds of leadership—was the theme of numerous parades and mass meetings. On issues from banking and currency to slavery, Harrison spoke in generalities. Harrison's strategist acknowledged that he advised the candidate to "say not a single word about his principles or creed. Let him say nothing—promise nothing."[29]

As it happened, Harrison did not have an opportunity to do much as president besides discipline the aggressive Clay. Clay had assumed that he and the rest of the congressional leadership would play the leading role in the government, but Harrison quickly dispelled that notion in a note rebuking him. But one month after his inauguration, the sixty-eight-year-old Harrison developed pneumonia and died. On April 6, 1841, the burdens of the presidency fell on Vice President John Tyler.

The rift between the White House and Congress widened under Tyler. Clay acted as if he were prime minister during a special session of Congress, pushing through a legislative program that included a recharter of the long-controversial Bank of the United States, higher import taxes, and distribution of proceeds from land sales to the states. Tyler, a lifetime states' rights advocate, vetoed two bills for a national bank, and the Whigs in Congress and his cabinet began a bitter feud with the president. In 1842 Clay left the Senate to promote his presidential aspirations, and everyone in the cabinet except Secretary of State Daniel Webster quit. Tyler was all alone, but he did manage to defeat the Whig program in his four years as president.

## POLK'S DARK-HORSE VICTORY IN 1844

The Democrats were transformed into a well-organized mass by Andrew Jackson and Martin Van Buren between 1828 and 1836. But, like the Whigs, the Democratic Party became vulnerable because of the irreconcilable differences among many of its parts.

From the beginning, the Democratic Party had contained contradictory elements. According to political scientist James L. Sundquist: "The party had been formed originally as an alliance between Southern planters and New Yorkers and had always spanned both regions. Northern men of abolitionist sympathies were accustomed to sitting with slaveholders in presidential cabinets and collaborating with them in the halls of Congress."[30] But northern Democrats went so far as to organize antiabolitionist rallies in their cities and towns, and newspapers and churches also defended slavery.

The deepest Democratic divisions—which eventually would lead to the failure not only of the party but also of the nation—were the regional differences based on slavery. But other, more complex divisions also affected the operation of the Democratic Party. When the party was able to reconcile or even delay action on the divisive issues, it won. When the divisions burst into the open, the party was in trouble.

James K. Polk of Tennessee, the first "dark-horse" candidate in history, defeated the Whig Henry Clay in 1844 by supporting an expansionist program and winning the support of the solid South. One of the key issues in the campaign was whether Texas should be admitted to the Union and, if so, whether it should be slave or free. President Van Buren in 1840 had opposed annexation—opposition that may have cost him the presidency—and the Democrats and Whigs hedged on the issue for the next eight years. In 1844 Polk endorsed the annexation of Texas as a slave state; that was enough for him to lock up the South.

During the 1844 nominating convention, the Democrats finessed the sectional dangers of the Texas issue by combining it with a call for occupying Oregon and eventually bringing that state into the Union. The Democrats also appealed to Pennsylvania and the rest of the Northeast by supporting a high tariff. Both parties spoke out against the growing foreign elements in the cities, but the Whigs were more effective because of the Democrats' swelling immigrant ranks.

In the election, the Democrat Polk defeated the Whig Clay, winning 1.34 million votes (49.5 percent) to Clay's 1.30 million (48.1 percent) and 170 electoral votes to Clay's 105. Clay received his strongest support from five northeastern states and five border slave states. Of the expansionist Northwest, only Ohio fell in the Clay column.

The Liberty Party—an abolitionist party formed out of more than two hundred antislavery societies in time for the 1840 election—may have been the deciding factor in the 1844 race. Although the party received only 2.3 percent of the popular vote and no electoral votes, it was strong enough in New York to prevent the Whigs from winning that state's crucial thirty-six electoral votes. Those votes went to the Democrat Polk rather than to the Whig Clay.

The depth of the Democrats' divisions were agonizingly evident even when the party won elections and started to pass out spoils and make policy. Like Harrison, the Whig who had won the presidency four years before, President Polk faced the antagonisms of party factions when he began making appointments after his 1844 win. Westerners were angry when they were shut out of the cabinet and Polk vetoed a rivers and harbors bill. Supporters of both Van Buren and John Calhoun were angry that their faction did not win more prominent positions. Northeasterners were upset at tariff cuts. The New York split between the reformist "Barnburners" and the party-regular "Hunkers"—who disagreed on every issue, including banks, currency, internal improvements, and political reforms—also disrupted the administration.

Creating still more dissension was the war with Mexico (1846–1848), fought because of the dispute over the Texas border and the possible annexation of California. Northerners resented the country's fighting Mexico over a slave state.

## WHIG SUCCESS UNDER TAYLOR IN 1848

In 1848 the Whigs recaptured the White House behind another military hero, Gen. Zachary Taylor, who was vague on most political issues. Hailing from Louisiana, where he was a slave owner, Taylor defeated the irrepressible Clay and Gen. Winfield Scott for the nomination on the fourth convention ballot. His running mate was New Yorker Millard Fillmore. Clay mounted an impressive public campaign that drew large crowds, but the Whigs had lost too many times with Clay.

The Whigs were so determined to avoid sectional and other splits that they not only nominated the popular Taylor but also eschewed writing a platform. Despite such extreme measures to maintain unity, the convention was disturbed by squabbles between pro- and antislavery forces on the question of the Wilmot Proviso, which would ban slavery in any territory the United States obtained from Mexico.

At the Democratic national convention, Sen. Lewis Cass of Michigan defeated Sen. James Buchanan of Pennsylvania and Supreme Court Justice Levi Woodbury for the presidential nomination, and Gen. William Butler was picked as his running mate. (The Democratic incumbent Polk had declared upon entering office that he would not seek a second term.) But the convention experienced splits between two New York factions: the Barnburners, who were part of the antislavery movement, and the more conservative Hunkers, who had ties to southerners. The Barnburners finally defected from the party to become part of the Free Soil Party. *(See "Third Parties," p. 116, in Chapter 1.)*

The Democrats behind Cass praised the administration of the beleaguered Polk, defended the war with Mexico, congratulated the French Republic that emerged from the wave of revolution in Europe, and did everything it could to avoid the nasty slavery issue. The nomination of Cass—a "doughface," or northerner with southern principles—was expected to appeal to both sides of the simmering issue.

But Taylor defeated Cass, winning 1.4 million popular votes (47.3 percent) to Cass's 1.2 million (42.5 percent). New York Democrat Martin Van Buren, the former president, running on the Free Soil ticket, won 291,500 votes (10 percent) but no electoral votes. Taylor received 163 electoral votes to Cass's 127, with a strong showing in the North. Taylor won Connecticut, Massachusetts, New Jersey, New York, Pennsylvania, Rhode Island, and Vermont in the North; Delaware, Kentucky, Maryland, North Carolina, and Tennessee in the border states; and Florida, Georgia, and Louisiana in the Deep South. This combination was enough to beat Cass's coalition of seven slave states, six northwestern states, and two New England states.

On July 10, 1850, Fillmore succeeded to the presidency when Taylor died suddenly. After consuming too many refreshments at a Fourth of July celebration, Taylor had developed cramps and then a fatal illness, probably typhoid fever.

Despite this turn of events, Fillmore was unable to secure the party nomination two years later, in 1852, although he had an early lead in convention polling. Gen. Winfield Scott won the nomination, and the Whigs entered into permanent decline.

## Slavery Divides the Nation

Try as they might by selecting military heroes as candidates and taking vague stances on issues, the Whigs could not delay facing the nation's disagreements forever. When divisive issues erupted, the party suffered.

The tariff issue and their mildly probusiness stance gave the Whigs strength in the North. But, like the Democrats, they also needed to attract support in the South—a goal they sought by trying to keep the slavery question out of their rhetoric. The Whigs could count on being competitive in the border slave states but not in the rest of Dixie. In 1844 Clay had won only the northern rim of slave states (Delaware, Kentucky, Maryland, North Carolina, and Tennessee).

The abolitionist movement, which may be dated to the founding of William Lloyd Garrison's newspaper, the *Liberator*, in 1831, posed problems for the Whigs that eventually proved fatal. The antislavery belt developed in the Whigs' strongest territory—New England—and westward into the modern-day Midwest. Abolitionism was largely an upper- or middle-class and religious cause. But it also became a partisan issue: the Whigs, the party out of power for years, needed an issue with which to confront the Democrats, and slavery was a useful one, even if the Whigs' antislavery stance in the North contradicted their accommodating stance in the South.

As Sundquist has noted, both the Whig and Democratic Parties in the pre–Civil War era attempted to ignore the slavery issue, but the Whigs had less room to maneuver. The Democrats' agrarian and populist position gave them the solid South as a foundation, and they could make a variety of antiabolitionist appeals to the rest of the electorate. Democrats could argue that their support for slavery in the South was compatible with their many "moderate" positions. The appeal of Senators Stephen A. Douglas of Illinois and Buchanan rested on such a coalition-building strategy. The Whigs, however, included vociferous opponents of slavery who could not be reconciled easily with "moderate" positions. Abolitionism had upper-class and religious roots that were difficult to use as a foundation. The support the Whigs were able to retain in the South was based on their positions on local issues. In sum, the Whigs did not have the same potential to build a national party organization as the Democrats.

Because both parties contained slavery sympathizers and opponents, neither was willing to take a principled stand against the institution, particularly where it already existed. This was not the case, however, for such issues as westward expansion, banking questions, public improvements, the tariff, and foreign relations, where their differences were more evident. But third parties such as the Liberty and Free Soil Parties had no such hesitations about pressing the slavery issue. In fact, sectional cleavages were so strong that in 1836 Congress passed a "gag rule" that forbade the reading of antislavery statements in Congress. Such attempts to silence abolitionist fervor were in vain, however, because politics was entering an age of mass communication and organization. The slavery issue would become irrepressible.

The slavery issue split the Whigs badly with the controversy over the admission of Texas to the Union in 1845. A splinter group of young party members calling themselves the "Conscience Whigs" argued for a straightforward statement of principle against slavery. An opposition group, "Cotton Whigs," wanted to defuse the slavery issue by ignoring moral arguments and simply calling for a halt to annexation. The party split became complete with Clay's Compromise of 1850, which admitted California as a free state, ended slave trade in the District of Columbia, and admitted Texas but reduced its size by splitting off the New Mexico territory. After agitation from Conscience Whigs and General Scott's nomination in 1852, the party was irreparably rent by the slavery issue.

The 1852 Whig convention platform contained several statements supporting states' rights and the principles behind Clay's compromise[31]—concessions made by Northern Whigs to win southern support for their presidential favorite, General Scott. But when no Whigs voted for the Kansas-Nebraska Act in 1854, which permitted new states to determine individually the slavery question, the Whigs' remaining ties to Dixie were severed.

The Whigs' strength in the Northwest was almost nonexistent. Only Ohio, in 1844, went for the Whigs even once over the course of the 1844, 1848, and 1852 presidential elections. Previously strong ties between the "lake region" and the South deteriorated as immigrants and others moved from the Northeast to the Northwest and, after the completion of railroad links, the two regions developed strong economic ties.

The Whigs' last gasp came in 1852, when Scott was demolished by Democrat Franklin Pierce who won all thirty-one states except two in New England (Massachusetts and Vermont) and two border states (Kentucky and Tennessee). In 1856 the Whigs split their votes among Democrat Buchanan, former Whig Millard Fillmore, and Republican John C. Fremont. At that time, not all Whigs were ready yet to join the nascent Republican Party because of the extremism of some of the party's abolitionists. But the majority of Whigs folded into the Republicans in 1860 when Republican presidential candidate Abraham Lincoln avoided a white "backlash" by insisting that he supported slavery where it existed and opposed its spread only because of how it would affect the economic fortunes of poor northern whites.

The Democrats suffered a North-South cleavage that Abraham Lincoln exploited in the 1860 election against Stephen Douglas. Southern Democrats were intent on protecting slavery, and control of Congress was necessary to their strategy. They believed that extension of slavery to the new states joining the Union was needed to maintain their congressional strength. In short, the extension of slavery was the issue that most divided the Democratic Party.

Northern Democrats were willing to allow Dixie to maintain its peculiar institution but were scared about their own electoral prospects if slavery should expand. At first they rallied to Douglas's doctrine of "popular sovereignty" (under which the people of new states could decide whether to adopt slavery), but they became nervous when Lincoln hammered away at his argument that any unchecked slavery threatened the freedom of whites as well as blacks. Lincoln argued that Democrats such as Douglas wanted to make slavery a national, rather than an individual state, institution.

Lincoln planted seeds of doubt about partial solutions to the slavery extension question by asserting that slavery could extend to whites if it were nationalized: "If free negroes should be made *things,* how long, think you, before they will begin to make *things* out of poor white men?"[32] Lincoln also maintained that the extension of slavery into new territories would close off those areas for whites seeking upward mobility: "The whole nation is interested that the best use be made of these Territories. We want them for homes of free white people. This they cannot be, to any considerable extent, if slavery shall be planted within them."[33]

Following Lincoln's lead, the growing movement against the extension of slavery was based on a concern for the upward mobility of labor. Rather than stressing the common interests of blacks and poor, northern, white laborers, the antiextension movement played up the competition between the two groups. Horace Greeley's vision of the frontier as "the great regulator of the relations of Labor and Capital, the safety valve of our industrial and social engine" left little room for the extension of slavery into the new territories.[34]

## DEMOCRAT PIERCE'S VICTORY: 1852

Clay's congressional compromise on slavery in the territories, known as the Compromise of 1850, turned out to be the major reason for the Democrats' 1852 victory. The compromise addressed the slavery question in all of the new U.S. territories by making concessions to both sides of the struggle. For the North, California would be admitted as a free state, and the slave trade (but not slavery itself) would be abolished in the District of Columbia. For the South, fugitive slave laws would be strengthened, and the New Mexico territory would be divided into two states where the voters, exercising popular sovereignty, would decide the slave issue.

The compromise was designed to settle the issue of slavery in new territories once and for all. But the slavery issue could not be contained by region; it had an increasingly important "spillover" effect. Because of concerns about the congressional balance of power and the difficulties of enforcing slavery provisions such as the fugitive slave law in states that opposed slavery, it was impossible to isolate the slavery question into particular regions as Clay intended.

President Taylor had stalled action on the compromise for months and even suggested that California and New Mexico might become independent nations. But his successor, Millard Fillmore, had thrown his support behind the compromise. The Whigs were divided on the proposal.

General Scott won the Whig nomination in 1852 after platform concessions to the party's southern delegation. Scott's appeal was always limited to the North, while Fillmore appealed to the South and Daniel Webster appealed to New England. Scott won on the fifty-third ballot.

Gov. Franklin Pierce of New Hampshire, a dark horse candidate who gained fame with his Mexican War record, won the Democratic nomination in 1852. His vice-presidential running mate was Sen. William Rufus de Vane King of Alabama. The party held together a coalition of groups with contradictory positions on the slavery issue and regional affairs. The convention, meeting in Baltimore, pledged to "abide by, and adhere to" Clay's compromise and to do what it could to smother the slavery issue.

Attempts to inject issues of economics and foreign affairs into the election failed, and the campaign degenerated into squabbles over personalities. Pierce easily won with 1.6 million popular votes (50.8 percent) to Scott's 1.4 million (43.9 percent). Pierce carried twenty-seven states and 254 electoral votes to Scott's four states and 42 electoral votes.

## THE DEMOCRATS' BRUISING 1856 VICTORY

By 1856 the North-South split had eliminated the Whigs as a national party and fatally damaged the Democrats' chances for winning national elections in the decades ahead.

Congress opened the slavery issue by passing the Kansas-Nebraska Act of 1854. The act declared "null and void" the Missouri Compromise of 1820, which had prohibited slavery in new territories north of the 36"30' parallel except in Missouri. The 1854 legislation created two territories (Kansas and Nebraska) from the original Nebraska territory and left the slavery issue to be determined by popular sovereignty there and in the Utah and New Mexico territories.

The Kansas-Nebraska Act was a vehicle to spur the development of the West. Such development was part of a long-standing American approach to creating opportunity and freedom via growth. Sen. Stephen Douglas of Illinois—the promoter of the law and the main advocate of popular sovereignty—held that the law was necessary if the country was to be bound together by rail and telegraph lines and was to drive Great Britain from the continent. The latter goal was based on the widely held suspicion that Britain was exploiting the slavery issue to distract American politics and stunt American growth.

Whatever the economic motives for unification, the Kansas-Nebraska Act was bitterly divisive. Northern state legislatures passed resolutions denouncing the law. The development of sectional parties continued.

A flood of new settlers into Kansas, and the violence that accompanied balloting over whether Kansas was to be a free or a slave state, further inflamed passions. Neighboring Missourians took part in the controversy, arguing that their status as slave owners would be undermined if Kansas voted to be free. Especially in view of the Supreme Court's infamous 1857 *Dred Scott* decision, which denied Congress the power to ban slavery in the territories and barred blacks from citizenship, and the Lincoln-Douglas debates in Illinois in 1858, the slavery question was becoming decisive in American politics.

The Democrats won the White House in 1856 when the party endorsed the Kansas-Nebraska Act and nominated the pro-South James Buchanan as its presidential candidate. John Breckinridge of Kentucky, who later served as a Confederate general, was Buchanan's running mate. The Democrats, who were becoming mainly a southern party, benefited from close wins in Buchanan's home state of Pennsylvania and in New Jersey, and in such western states as Illinois, Indiana, and California. But the only strong region for the Democrats was the South. Buchanan won all the slave states except Maryland. Overall, Buchanan won 1.8 million popular votes (45.3 percent) to Fremont's 1.3 million (33.1 percent). The electoral college gave Buchanan a 174–114 victory.

The nativist American Party—or the "Know-Nothings," as they were called—nominated former Whig president Millard Fillmore, but the party was never able to move beyond an urban strength based on parochial resistance to immigration and Catholicism. Fillmore won only the state of Maryland; overall, he got 873,000 popular votes (21.5 percent) and 8 electoral votes. (See "Third Parties," p. 116, in Chapter 1.)

Col. John Charles Fremont was named the Republicans' first presidential candidate. Former Whig senator William Dayton of New Jersey received the vice-presidential nomination. After an 1854 meeting in Ripon, Wisconsin, where a new national party

Stephen Douglas, at five feet and four inches, was the 1860 Democratic candidate for president.

was first proposed, the Republican Party developed quickly. The Republicans had developed a strong grassroots organization in the Northwest after the Kansas-Nebraska Act passed in 1854 and attracted disgruntled abolitionists, Whigs, Know-Nothings, Northern Democrats, and members of the Liberty and Free Soil Parties who were troubled by the possible extension of slavery. Uncertainty about how the extension of slavery would affect laborers who sought opportunity in the territories also helped to unite the new coalition.

The first Republican nominating convention met in Philadelphia in 1856 with delegates from all of the free states, four border states, three territories, and the District of Columbia. The party's opposition to slavery was far from unanimous, but its willingness to address rather than suppress the issue enabled it to redefine the political dialogue. Besides strong antislavery statements, the party platform contained proposals for several internal improvements advantageous to the North. The party did not offer anything to the solidly Democratic South. To win a national election, it would have to sweep the North.

## THE FATEFUL ELECTION OF 1860

In 1860 the Democratic split was complete when the party's southern elements supported Vice President Breckinridge and Northerners backed Stephen Douglas. The Buchanan administration earlier had waged war on Douglas by ousting his allies from the federal bureaucracy for opposing the administration's prosouthern stance on the Kansas issue.

When the time came for the 1860 presidential campaign, the Democrats were hopelessly split over slavery. The biggest sticking point was the *Dred Scott* decision, which, by decreeing that Congress had no power to prohibit slavery in a territory, was just what southerners favoring popular sovereignty wanted. Yet it also created uncertainty about any legislature's authority over slavery. If Congress could not regulate slavery, could state legislatures? The Republicans were able to use the decision as a rallying point for popular control of government; the Democrats were in the uncustomary position of defending the Supreme Court, which since Thomas Jefferson they had pictured as elitist. Douglas, the eventual Democratic nominee and architect of the platform, insisted on state resolution of the slavery issue. Jefferson Davis of Mississippi, who later became president of the Confederate States of America, fought in Congress for the right of Congress to promote and protect slavery in new territories.

Eventually, the Davis Democrats held their own convention and nominated Vice President Breckinridge for the presidency. Although the Davis Democrats insisted that they were the backbone of the party and had been strong enough to elect Buchanan four years before, the party divided would not be able to win a national election.

And that was the outcome; Democratic Party splits enabled Lincoln to win the 1860 election, resulting in the secession of seven Southern states from the Union even before his inauguration. (The remaining four states forming the Confederacy seceded after the fall of Fort Sumter, on April 13, 1861.)

Because the regional splits that had been tearing the nation apart for decades reached their peak in 1860, none of the four major candidates who were seeking the presidency could compete seriously throughout the nation. The winner was likely to be a candidate from the North, the region with the most electoral votes—that is, either former U.S. representative Abraham Lincoln of Illinois, a Republican, or Stephen Douglas, a Democrat, who defeated Lincoln for the Illinois Senate seat in 1858. Moderate Constitutional Union nominee John Bell of Tennessee and Democrat John Breckinridge of Kentucky were the candidates competing in the South.

The Republicans succeeded in 1860 because they were able to pull together a variety of potentially warring factions. But above all else the Republicans stood against the extension of slavery into new territories. By accepting slavery where it already existed but warning against the spread of the system, the Republicans divided the Democrats and picked up support from a diverse array of otherwise contentious factions—abolitionists, moderate abolitionists, and whites who feared for their position in the economy. Moreover, the *Dred Scott* decision enabled the Republicans to rail publicly against the high court in the tradition of Jefferson and Jackson. While opposing the Democratic doctrine of popular sovereignty, the Republicans picked up some states' rights sympathizers by having a middle-ground slavery stance.

At a frenzied Republican convention in Chicago, which blocked several radical candidates, Lincoln emerged as the consensus compromise choice. The fact that Lincoln was known widely throughout Illinois had improved his chances at the Chicago convention.

Douglas, Lincoln's principal rival, managed several moderate platform victories at the Democratic convention in Charleston, South Carolina, defeating resolutions that called for acceptance of the *Dred Scott* decision and protection of slavery in the territories. But Douglas's success prompted delegates from ten southern states to bolt the convention. After disputes over quorum rules and fifty-seven ballots, the Democrats were unable to muster the necessary two-thirds majority for Douglas. Thus the convention adjourned, reassembled in Baltimore, and faced disputes about the seating of delegates that caused further defections from the South. With southern radicals effectively eliminated from the convention, Douglas swept to a unanimous nomination victory.

The Democratic defectors named Vice President Breckinridge to run for president in the South. The Constitutional Union Party, which developed as a futile attempt to repair the nation's geographic divisions, nominated Bell to oppose Breckinridge. *(See "Third Parties," p. 116, in Chapter 1.)* These two candidates were doomed from the start, however, since the South's electoral vote total was significantly below that of the North.

Thanks to the wide-ranging Republican coalition—one that eluded the Whigs in their last years of existence—Lincoln was able to count on strength in the areas that Fremont had won in

Republican presidential candidate Abraham Lincoln stood tall at six feet and four inches.

1856: New England and the upper Northwest, as well as New York and Ohio. Lincoln's political ties to Illinois, where he practiced law and began his public career, would help in Illinois and Indiana, and his background as a former Whig was a plus in the Ohio valley. The coal and iron regions of Pennsylvania and Ohio were attracted to the party's high-tariff policy. Urban immigrants, particularly Germans, were attracted by the Republican support of homestead (frontier settlement) legislation and the Lincoln campaign's "Vote Yourself a Farm" appeal.[35] The vice-presidential selection of Hannibal Hamlin of Maine, a former Democrat, broadened the coalition beyond partisan lines. Lincoln's oft-stated desire not to challenge slavery where it then existed was an appeal to border states.

Lincoln won easily with a total of 180 electoral votes to Breckinridge's 72, Bell's 39, and Douglas's 12. Lincoln's closest competitor in the popular vote was Douglas. Lincoln had 1.9 million northern popular votes (40.0 percent); Douglas had 1.4 million (29.5 percent) spread out geographically. The two other principal candidates received much less support, which was concentrated in the South: Breckinridge won 848,000 popular votes (18.1 percent); Bell, 591,000 (12.6 percent).

Because some southerners had vowed to secede from the Union if Lincoln won the election, in the period before Lincoln's inauguration congressional committees sought to put together a compromise that would save the nation from civil war. They failed, however, because of Lincoln's refusal to abandon his policy of containing slavery. He rejected proposals for popular sovereignty or a slave-free geographic division of western states, and he would not comment on proposals for constitutional amendments or popular referenda on the issue.

After Lincoln was elected, South Carolina, Louisiana, Mississippi, Alabama, Georgia, Texas, and Florida seceded from the Union and on February 7, 1861, adopted a constitution forming the Confederate States of America. After a protracted standoff between Union soldiers who held Fort Sumter and the Confederate soldiers who controlled South Carolina, the Confederates fired on the fort. Virginia, Arkansas, North Carolina, and Tennessee then joined the Confederacy, and the Civil War was under way.

## THE CIVIL WAR ELECTION: 1864

The Union's military difficulties in 1861 and 1862 created resentment against and impatience with President Lincoln. The splits that developed in the Republican Party seemed to imperil his chances for renomination and reelection.

From the very beginning of his administration, Lincoln suffered because of the difficulty he had finding a general who could successfully prosecute the war. Repeated military setbacks and stalemates—such as the Battles of Fredericksburg and Chancellorsville, Confederate general Robert E. Lee's escape after the battle of Antietam (Sharpsburg), and heavy casualties in the drive to Richmond—hurt the Republicans. Publicized conflicts with such Union generals as George McClellan caused further damage. In addition to the military problems, the presi-

dent's announcement in September 1862 of the emancipation of slaves in rebellious states (the Emancipation Proclamation) created legal and political controversy.

In the 1862 midterm elections, the Republicans experienced widespread losses in congressional and state elections. Among the more bitter defeats for Lincoln was Democrat John Stuart's victory in the president's old congressional district in Illinois. By the time of the presidential election, Stuart, a former law partner of the president, was an ardent political foe.

The military frustrations gave rise to deep divisions within Lincoln's own cabinet. Treasury Secretary Salmon P. Chase was a constant critic of Lincoln's capacity to serve as commander in chief, and the Philadelphia banker Jay Gould briefly led a movement for Chase's nomination for president in 1864. Chase withdrew only after the Lincoln forces dealt him a severe blow at the party caucus in his home state of Ohio. Other radicals met in Cleveland in May 1864 and named John Fremont to run against Lincoln in the fall. Fremont withdrew only after a series of Union military victories strengthened Lincoln's political standing.

The president manipulated the Republican convention in Baltimore brilliantly, ensuring not only his own renomination but also the selection of pro-Union governor Andrew Johnson of Union-occupied Tennessee—a lifelong Democrat—as the vice-presidential candidate. Lincoln professed indifference about a possible running mate. "Wish not to interfere about V.P. Cannot interfere about platform," he said in a letter. "Convention must judge for itself."[36] Nevertheless, he maneuvered to build support for Johnson. Johnson's selection was in accord with the desire of the party, which also called itself the Union Party as a way to attract Democrats and to develop nationwide unity. Yet Lincoln's reelection drive was so uncertain that he obliged his cabinet in August 1864 to sign a statement pledging an orderly transition of power if he lost. The statement read: "This morning, as for some days past, it seems exceedingly probable that this Administration will not be reelected. Then it will be my duty to so cooperate with the President-elect, as to save the Union between the election and the inauguration; as he will have secured his election on such ground that he cannot possibly save it afterwards."[37]

The man for whom Lincoln anticipated arranging a wartime transition was Democratic nominee George McClellan, whom Lincoln had fired as general in January 1863. McClellan had won the Democratic nomination with the strong backing of "peace Democrats" such as Clement L. Vallandigham of Ohio, who was arrested by Union general Ambrose E. Burnside after making a series of antiwar speeches. (Vallandigham later took up exile in Canada.) McClellan's running mate was Rep. George Pendleton of Ohio, who after the war would sponsor landmark civil service reform legislation.

Although popular with his soldiers, General McClellan had not won a single major battle of the war despite many infusions of extra troops. Yet he blamed Lincoln for the losses. Indeed, he was a vocal critic of the administration. McClellan's presidential

## PRESIDENT OF THE CONFEDERACY

*Jefferson Davis*

In 1861, two weeks before Abraham Lincoln was inaugurated in Washington, D.C., as the sixteenth president of the United States, another president was inaugurated in Montgomery, Alabama. On February 18, 1861, Jefferson Davis became the first and only president of the Confederate States of America.

Davis was born in Christian (now Todd) County, Kentucky, on June 3, 1808. He was the youngest of the ten children of Samuel and Jane Davis, who moved their family to a small Mississippi plantation when Jefferson was a boy. He attended private schools and Transylvania University in Lexington, Kentucky, before his oldest brother, Joseph, secured his appointment to West Point in 1824.

After graduating from the academy, Davis was stationed in Wisconsin under Col. Zachary Taylor. There he saw action in the Black Hawk War during the early 1830s and fell in love with Taylor's daughter, Sarah Knox. In 1835 he left the army, married Sarah, and settled on a one-thousand-acre plantation in Mississippi, which was given to him by his brother Joseph. Tragically, Sarah died from malaria three months after the wedding, and for several years Davis devoted himself to developing his land and wealth.

In 1845 Davis married Varina Howell, a member of the Mississippi aristocracy, and was elected to the U.S. House of Representatives. He served in Washington less than a year before the Mexican War began, and he gave up his seat to accept a commission as a colonel. He became a national hero when his company made a stand at the Battle of Buena Vista that was said to have saved Gen. Zachary Taylor's army from defeat.

In 1847 he left the army and was elected to the Senate. He served there until 1851, when he ran unsuccessfully for governor of Mississippi. He returned to Washington in 1853 after being appointed secretary of war by President Franklin Pierce. Davis was credited with strengthening the armed forces during his time in office. He also was influential in bringing about the Gadsden Purchase from Mexico in 1853, which added areas of present-day Arizona and New Mexico to the United States.

In 1857 Davis was reelected to the Senate. Although he became a leading spokesperson for the South, he did not advocate secession until 1860 when it had become inevitable. Davis hoped to be appointed commanding general of the South's army, but instead he was chosen as president by a convention of the seceding states.

Davis believed his first priority as president was to preserve Southern independence. He tried to secure French and British assistance for the Confederacy, but he was largely unsuccessful. Like Lincoln he helped develop military strategy and on occasion interfered with the plans of his generals. In managing the war effort, Davis was hampered by his paradoxical position. The South could fight most effectively as a unified nation run by the central government in Richmond, but the Southern states had succeeded in part to preserve their rights as independent states. Davis took actions, including the suspension of *habeas corpus* and the establishment of conscription, that were regarded as despotic by many Southerners.

When the Union's victory appeared imminent in early 1865, Davis fled south from Richmond and was captured by federal troops. He was indicted for treason and imprisoned for two years, but he never stood trial. He lived in Canada and Europe for several years before retiring to Mississippi. There he wrote his *Rise and Fall of the Confederate States,* which was published in 1881. He died in New Orleans on December 6, 1889.

campaign was built around a call for a cease-fire and a convention to restore the Union. He and his fellow peace Democrats also criticized the administration's violation of civil liberties and other unconstitutional actions.

Lincoln's fortunes improved in the two months before the election. When Gen. William Tecumseh Sherman took Atlanta after a scorched-earth march through the South, the Confederacy was left badly divided geographically. The military victory cut off the Gulf states from the Confederate capital of Richmond. Gen. Philip Sheridan had had important successes in the Shenandoah Valley, and Gen. Ulysses S. Grant had fared well in Virginia.

Not only did the Democrats face a Republican Party reconstituted for the war election as the Union Party and united by recent military victories, but McClellan also had a difficult time developing consistent campaign themes. He was at various times conciliatory toward the Confederacy and solicitous of the soldiers who fought for the Union. The balancing problem was underscored by the inclusion of both war and peace songs in the *McClellan Campaign Songster,* a piece of campaign literature.[38] McClellan also had a difficult time selling his message to Northern industrialists who were profiting from munitions procurement.

Not until the arrival of election results from three state elections on October 11 were Lincoln and the Unionists confident that they would win the national election in November. Republican victories in Indiana, Ohio, and Pennsylvania were the first concrete indications that Lincoln's fortunes had turned around.

Lincoln overwhelmed McClellan by winning all of the loyal states except Delaware, Kentucky, and New Jersey for a 212–21 electoral vote victory. Lincoln garnered 2.2 million popular votes (55.0 percent) to McClellan's 1.8 million (45.0 percent). The electoral votes of Louisiana and Tennessee, the first Confederate states to return to the Union, were not accepted by Congress.

## Postwar Radicalism

The end of the Civil War left the nation almost as divided as it had been in the antebellum years. Concerns about punishment of the rebel states, the status of the freedmen, and economic development replaced slavery as the principal sources of disagreement.

The nation undoubtedly would have experienced bitter splits no matter who had served as chief executive, but the assassination of President Lincoln on April 14, 1865, shortly after the Confederate surrender, created a crisis of leadership. Lincoln's vice president, Andrew Johnson, ascended to the presidency and quickly came into conflict with the radical Northern Republicans who controlled Congress. Johnson, a Democrat from Tennessee, was stubborn, which only aggravated the troubles that were inevitable anyway because of his party and regional background.

Johnson intended to continue Lincoln's plans for the reconstruction of the North and South "with malice toward none"; he chafed at the notion of the South as a conquered territory. A states' rights politician, Johnson attempted to put together a coalition of moderates from all parts of the country that would bring about a quick reconciliation between his administration and Congress.

But Congress was intent on establishing political institutions that would respect the rights of former slaves and promote economic growth and vowed to use military occupation to destroy the South's old political elite.[39] Thus Johnson and Congress fought over bills that would extend the life of the Freedmen's Bureau (an agency established to help blacks make the transition from slavery to citizenship) and guarantee the franchise and equal protection to blacks, with the result that Johnson vetoed both bills. Johnson also opposed the Fourteenth Amendment, which guaranteed equal protection, as well as the stipulation that Confederate states approve the amendment as a condition of their readmission to the Union.

When the Radical Republicans took over Congress in the 1866 midterm elections, the war with Johnson began in earnest. In March 1867 Congress established limited military rule in recalcitrant Southern states and in May passed the Tenure of Office Act limiting the president's right to dismiss his appointees. Johnson contemptuously disregarded the tenure act and fired Edwin Stanton, his secretary of war. For this action Johnson was impeached by the House and tried by the Senate. When the Senate voted in May 1868, he avoided conviction by a single vote (35–19).

### THE GRANT VICTORIES: 1868 AND 1872

Ulysses S. Grant was more than a concerned citizen during the dispute between Johnson and Congress. Despite its portrayal in many history books as a clear instance of congressional abuse of power, the affair was more complicated. All of the players in the drama negotiated their way with care, and almost none of them escaped without major scars. Grant was a central figure, and his style of maneuvering was dictated by his ambition to succeed Johnson as president.

Radical Republicans in Congress achieved a lasting victory when they secured passage of the Civil Rights Act of 1866 over President Johnson's veto, but they were increasingly disturbed by reports that the statute was not being enforced. A congressional investigation of violence against blacks in Memphis concluded that the Freedmen's Bureau could not enforce civil rights without help. Radicals began to look to Secretary of War Stanton to enforce the law that the president clearly disliked and repeatedly subverted. When Stanton indicated that he would carry out the law in the Confederacy as Congress intended, Johnson began to think about replacing him. At this point Congress passed the Tenure of Office Act over Johnson's veto in May 1867, reasoning that its constitutional "advise and consent" powers over appointments could be extended to removal as well. Johnson, however, decided to test the law's constitutionality.

In replacing Stanton, Johnson's concern—and indeed the concern of all involved—was who could assume the secretary of war post with minimal threat to Johnson's own position. Johnson first considered General Sherman but decided to appoint Grant on a temporary basis. Originally a Democrat and supporter of moderate Southern policies, Grant worried about appearing too close to the unpopular president. As a result, after vaguely assuring Johnson that he would accept a temporary appointment, Grant hedged. He increasingly expressed support for the notion that appointees should interpret and obey laws according to congressional intent. Eventually Grant told the president in a letter that he could not accept the appointment.

After the drama of Johnson's impeachment in 1868, Grant was in a good position to seek the White House. He had avoided allying himself with controversy during both Johnson's search for a replacement for Stanton and the ensuing impeachment battle. In fact, he and Chief Justice Salmon Chase were the only ones not tainted by the affair. Grant even managed to maintain his public posture of disinterested duty. Thus during one of the nation's ugliest political episodes, Grant looked clean. He was ready for a presidential campaign.

As Johnson endured his Senate impeachment trial in March, Grant won his first electoral victory. A New Hampshire congressional campaign, which normally would favor the Democrat, became an early Grant referendum when Republican candidate Donald Sickles told voters that a vote for a Republican was a vote for Grant; Sickles won. Just before the Republican convention in May, a Soldiers and Sailors Convention "nominated" Grant. Yet he avoided an excessively military image when he vowed to reduce the size of the standing army. Grant was on his way.

Grant won the presidential nomination without opposition. The real battle at the 1868 Republican convention was for the vice-presidential nomination. Schuyler Colfax of Indiana, the Speaker of the House, won on the sixth ballot; eleven candidates received votes on the initial roll call.

The Democrats had a difficult time finding a nominee. Johnson sought the Democratic nomination, but his appeal was to the South. (Because many Southern states were still outside the Union, Northern politicians were selecting the nominee.) Chief Justice Chase, highly regarded for his fairness during Johnson's Senate trial, was a possibility, but his strong stand for black suffrage was a barrier. Sen. Thomas A. Hendricks of Indiana was strong in the East, and George Pendleton of Ohio, the party's vice-presidential candidate four years earlier, was strong in the West. Gen. Winfield Scott Hancock of Pennsylvania presented the opportunity of running one military hero against another.

After twenty-three bitter ballots in a sweltering New York City, Horatio Seymour, the national party chair and popular war governor of New York, accepted the Democratic nomination against his will. Gen. Francis P. Blair Jr. of Missouri was the vice-presidential nominee. The party platform called for the rapid reentry of Confederate states to the Union, state authority over suffrage questions, and the "Ohio Idea," which promised an inflationary money supply that would help the indebted South.

Both sides were well financed in the election, but the Republicans had the edge. The Republican Party's probusiness positions on the tariff, railroad grants, and the currency attracted millions of dollars. Newspapers and magazines tended to be pro-Republican because of their urban business orientations.

Grant, who ran his campaign from his home in Galena, Illinois, was vague about issues ranging from the currency to voting rights. Appearances in Colorado with fellow generals Sherman and Sheridan were taken to be endorsements. Everything seemed to go Grant's way. Even the traditional campaign gossip about the sexual activities of candidates did not hurt him. Charges that Grant was excessively problack—"I am Captain Grant of the Black Marines, the stupidest man that was ever seen" were the lyrics of one ditty[40]—helped him with the recently enfranchised citizens. Without the black vote, Grant probably would have lost the popular vote and perhaps the electoral vote. Results from October state elections that favored the Republicans created a brief movement for Seymour and Blair to quit the contest so that the Democrats could name a new ticket. Instead Seymour took the October results as an incentive to get to the campaign stump. Seymour was a good speaker, but nothing he could do could help the Democrats.

Grant defeated Seymour by 3.0 million (52.7 percent) to 2.7 million votes (47.3 percent). The electoral vote tally was 214 for Grant and 80 for Seymour. Finally, Grant won all but eight of the thirty-four states taking part in the election. He benefited from Radical Republican reconstructionist sentiment in the North and newly enfranchised blacks in the South.

With Grant's ascension to the presidency in 1869, the Republican Party entered a new era—what the German sociologist Max Weber would have called a shift from "charismatic" to "rational" institutional authority. In other words, the party shifted

its devotion from a great moral cause to its own survival as an organization. It had begun as a coalition of activists fervently opposed to the expansion of slavery (many opposed slavery itself) and to the rebellion of Southern states from the Union. The Republicans' 1868 victory under Grant was the first not dominated wholly by crisis conditions.

The Republicans had a strong base of support: eastern bankers, manufacturers, railroads, and land speculators. With the old Confederacy under the control of military governments and with blacks given the franchise, the Republicans had strength in the South. The West was restive, however, because of depressed farm prices, high taxes, and debt. The industrial-agrarian split between North and South before the Civil War would be resumed as an East-West split in the years after the war.

The Republican leadership itself was changing. Age was claiming a number of the early Republican leaders, such as Thaddeus Stevens, William Seward, Benjamin Wade, Charles Sumner, James Grimes, Edwin Stanton, and Salmon Chase. New party leaders included Senators Roscoe Conkling of New York, Oliver Morton of Indiana, Simon Cameron of Pennsylvania, and Zachariah Chandler of Michigan, and Representatives Benjamin Butler of Massachusetts, John Logan of Illinois, James Garfield of Ohio, and James G. Blaine of Maine.

As for the new Grant administration, it was undistinguished. The new president's inaugural address—spoken without the traditional company of the outgoing president since Grant had neglected to respond to Johnson's polite letters—was decent but uninspiring. Grant vowed that "all laws will be faithfully executed, whether they meet my approval or not," that debtors would not be tolerated, and that blacks should get the vote throughout the country and Indians should be offered "civilization and ultimate citizenship."[41] With a few important exceptions, cabinet positions went to old Grant cronies.

In 1869 the nation experienced a financial panic when financiers Jay Gould and Jim Fisk attempted to corner the world's gold market. Their scheme led to "Black Friday," September 24, 1869. Gould and Fisk had met with President Grant and had urged him not to sell government gold, therefore keeping the price of gold high. At the last minute, however, Grant decided to reject their advice and dumped $4 million worth of gold on the market. That dumping caused a severe drop in gold prices, breaking up the Gould-Fisk conspiracy but also causing tremendous losses for thousands of speculators. It was the worst disaster on Wall Street up to that time. Although it did not cause a depression, the South and West were hard hit by the financial retrenchment program that followed. Tariff rates remained high on most manufactured goods, despite tentative efforts to reform the system.

The spoils system was in full swing during the Grant years. Grant himself was not involved in the scramble for booty, but his family and aides were often shameless in their greed. When Grant learned that liberal Republicans were planning an independent presidential campaign against him in 1872, he took the

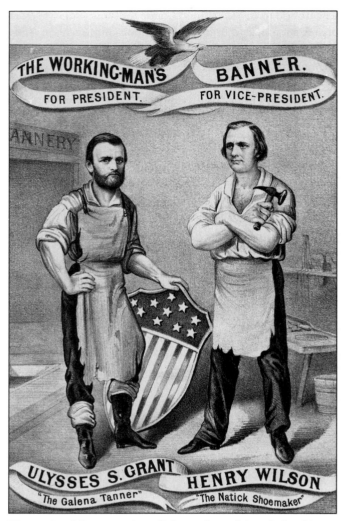

THE WORKING-MAN'S BANNER.
FOR PRESIDENT. FOR VICE-PRESIDENT.

ULYSSES S. GRANT
"The Galena Tanner"

HENRY WILSON
"The Natick Shoemaker"

The 1872 Republican campaign called voters' attention to the humble backgrounds of presidential candidate Ulysses S. Grant and his running mate, Henry Wilson.

edge off the spoils issue by creating the Civil Service Reform Commission, but his neglect of the commission made it ineffective.

Before the 1872 election, the *New York Sun* exposed the Crédit Mobilier scandal. The newspaper reported that the firm's board of directors had many of the same members as the Union Pacific Railroad Company, which hired it to build a transcontinental route, and that Crédit Mobilier had paid its board exorbitant profits. To avoid a public investigation, Crédit Mobilier offered stock to Vice President Colfax and Representative (later president) James Garfield. Colfax lost his place on the Republican ticket for his role in the scandal; Sen. Henry Wilson of New Hampshire took his position as the vice-presidential candidate in 1872.

Liberal Republicans, unhappy with protective tariffs, spoils, and the uneven administration of the Southern states, bolted the party in 1872. The group was interested in policies such as civil service and free trade that would promote individual virtue in a laissez-faire economic system. The reformers thought they had a chance to win. The German-born senator Carl Schurz of

Missouri wrote to a friend that "the administration with its train of offices and officemongers [is] the great incubus pressing upon the party. . . . The superstition that Grant is the necessary man is rapidly giving way. The spell is broken, and we have only to push through the breach."[42]

Candidates for the nomination from this group of Republicans included former ambassador to Great Britain Charles Francis Adams, son of President John Quincy Adams and grandson of President John Adams; Supreme Court Justice David Davis; Chief Justice Salmon Chase; Sen. Lyman Trumbull of Illinois; and Horace Greeley, editor of the *New York Tribune*. Greeley won the nomination on the sixth ballot and ran as a Democrat and Liberal Republican. The Democrats were so weak that they did not field a candidate of their own. They endorsed the Greeley ticket. (Charles O'Conor of New York was nominated by a group of "Noncoalition Democrats" for president. He did not accept the nomination.)

Since his early days as a newspaper reporter, when he described President Van Buren as an effeminate failure, Greeley had won fame as a pungent social critic. He was a crusading, abolitionist editor and a dedicated reformer, but his rumpled appearance and unpolished speaking style made him appear "unpresidential." Greeley was unable to parlay an amalgam of promises to various interest groups—blacks, soldiers, immigrants, and laborers—into a victory over Grant. Groups that Greeley actively courted found him wanting for a variety of reasons, and even though Greeley advocated the tariff favored by the North, he could not cut into Grant's northeastern strength. One Republican cartoon that revealed Greeley's difficult task showed a fence on which sat a laborer, skeptical because of Greeley's stand against strikes, and a black, concerned because of Greeley's advocacy of amnesty for Confederates. Sitting on the sidelines was a German, upset with Greeley's prohibitionist stance: "Oh! Yaw! You would take my Lager away, den you must get widout me along!"[43]

Even though he went on the stump and delivered a series of impressive speeches, Greeley never had a chance. Republican gubernatorial victories in North Carolina in August and in Pennsylvania, Ohio, and Indiana in October were clear harbingers that the Republican Party would do well in November. Grant took the entire North and the newly admitted South with 3.6 million popular votes (55.6 percent). Greeley won three border states, as well as Tennessee, Texas, and Georgia, with 2.8 million popular votes (43.9 percent). Less than a month after the election, Greeley died. Of the electoral votes, which were cast after Greeley's death, Grant received 286; the Democrats' 63 electoral votes were scattered among various candidates, and 17 Democratic electoral votes were not cast.

## THE COMPROMISE OF 1876

The pattern of Republican, northern, and business domination of presidential politics was institutionalized in the 1876 election. Republican Rutherford B. Hayes, the three-time governor of Ohio, lost the popular vote and had a questionable hold on the electoral college vote, but he managed to beat Democrat Samuel J. Tilden for the presidency when the election was settled by a special commission created by Congress. (Hayes won 4.0 million votes to Tilden's 4.3 million—48 and 51 percent of the popular vote, respectively.) Perhaps the most controversial election outcome in history, some feared it would set off a second civil war.

The problem arose when the vote tallies in Florida, South Carolina, and Louisiana were called into question. Violence had accompanied the voting in all three states, but President Grant had not sent in federal troops to ensure fair balloting. On those states hung the electoral outcome. There was good reason to be suspicious of any vote count in those and other southern states. While the Republicans had controlled the balloting places and mounted vigorous drives to get blacks to the polls, the Democrats had used physical intimidation and bribery to keep blacks away. The bitterness between northern interests and southern whites was apparent in the violence that often took place at polls.

When state election board recounts and investigations did not settle the question of the vote tallies, Congress took up the matter. An electoral commission made up of five senators (three majority party Republicans, two minority Democrats), five representatives (three majority party Democrats, two minority Republicans), and five Supreme Court justices (two from each party, one independent) assembled to hear complaints about the disputed states. At the last minute the independent justice disqualified himself, and his place was taken by a Republican who was accepted by Democrats because they considered him to be the most independent of the Republican justices. Weeks of bargaining followed, during which the Republican vote totals of the disputed states were confirmed and the southern Democrats extracted promises of financial aid and political independence from the federal government.

When the validity of the Florida vote count for Hayes was challenged, the commission responded that it did not have the capacity to judge the actual conduct of the balloting, only the validity of the certificates presented to Congress. That decision gave the state to Hayes. Challenges to the vote counts of Louisiana, South Carolina, and Oregon were dismissed in a similar way, so Hayes was awarded the presidency.

The compromise not only settled the partisan dispute between Hayes and Tilden, but also established a rigid alignment of political interests that would dominate U.S. politics for the next half-century. Although Democrats won occasional victories, the Republican, eastern, conservative, business-oriented establishment held sway over the system until Franklin Roosevelt's election in 1932.

The institutional form of the regional splits created by the compromise remained much longer. Historian C. Vann Woodward has argued that secret wheeling and dealing among congressional and party leaders institutionally divided the political system by party, region, economic interest, and governmental branches. Northern Republican industrial interests were given control of the presidential election process, and southern Democratic agricultural interests were given autonomy over their regional politics, which led to domination of Congress.[44] This alignment was not completely dislodged until the passage of important civil rights legislation in the 1960s.

To reward southern Democrats for throwing the 1876 election to the Republican Hayes, northern politicians agreed to pull federal troops out of the South and to allow southern whites to take over the system. Thus within months southern states were erecting a powerful edifice of racial discrimination that would last until the 1960s. Former South Carolina governor Daniel H. Chamberlain, a Republican, later summed up the deal:

What is the president's Southern policy? [I]t consists in the abandonment of Southern Republicans and especially the colored race, to the control and rule not only of the Democratic Party, but of that class of the South which regarded slavery as a Divine Institution, which waged four years of destructive war for its perpetuation, which steadily opposed citizenship and suffrage for the negro—in a word, a class whose traditions, principles, and history are opposed to every step and feature of what Republicans call our national progress since 1860.[45]

## The Age of Republicanism

From 1860 to 1908, the Republicans won nine elections; the Democrats won only two. Only Grover Cleveland could put together a Democratic win, and he was as conservative on most issues as the Republicans of the period. Presidential election winners after the Great Compromise were Hayes (1876), James Garfield (1880), Cleveland (1884), Benjamin Harrison (1888), Cleveland (1892), William McKinley (1896 and 1900), Theodore Roosevelt (1904), and William Howard Taft (1908).

The political aspirants of the day were required to adhere to the creed of high tariffs, laissez-faire economics, and tight money. Tight money policies—the restricted issuance of currency, which favored bankers and other established interests but hurt debtors and those seeking more rapid expansion of some kinds of investment and spending—provided rare openings for effective Democratic resistance to Republican hegemony. Resistance did develop, however, when the scramble for tariff protections created obvious inequities among businesses and hardships for the consumer.

Yet populist uprisings, such as Democrat William Jennings Bryan's 1896 campaign, faltered because of strong mobilization by the Republicans and divisions within the Democratic ranks. Bryan failed to bring a likely Democratic constituency—the worker—into the fold. Eastern businessmen were able to portray their interest in industrial growth as a common concern with labor and Bryan's western agrarian alliance as a danger to that growth.

While the Republican Party dominated presidential politics, the parties were well balanced in Congress and in state governments until the class and sectional cleavages of the 1890s. The Senate was split evenly in 1881, 37–37, and two years later the Republicans had a 38–36 edge. The Democrats had made gains in northern congressional races, and Republicans were making smaller gains in the South. The House tended to provide a majority for whichever party held the White House.

## GARFIELD CARRIES THE REPUBLICAN BANNER: 1880

Hayes honored his pledge to serve only one term, setting off a scramble for both parties' nominations in 1880. When the early momentum for a third term for Grant faltered, the Republican contest became a battle among Grant, Sen. James G. Blaine of Maine, and Treasury Secretary John Sherman of Ohio. Grant was able to muster a first-ballot plurality but could not attract new supporters as the balloting proceeded. A stalemate between Blaine and Sherman ensued.

Rep. James Garfield of Ohio, a former preacher who was impressive in his oratory and organization for Sherman, was the compromise choice for the nomination. He selected as his running mate Chester A. Arthur, the collector of the Port of New York, an important patronage job.

The Democrats named Gen. Winfield Hancock of Pennsylvania and former Indiana representative William English to head their ticket. The Democratic platform advocated the gold standard, a low tariff designed to raise revenue, civil service reform, restrictions on Chinese immigration, and a belated criticism of the 1876 deal that gave the presidency to Hayes. Except for the tariff and 1876 questions, the Democrats' platform was close to the Republicans' statement of principles.

The regional breakdown of support, with most of the North and West falling in Garfield's camp and the South lining up behind Hancock, gave the presidency to Garfield. The popular vote was close—4.45 million (48.27 percent) to 4.44 million (48.25 percent)—but Garfield won a 214–155 electoral vote victory.

The festering issue of patronage and civil service came to a head shortly after Garfield's inauguration. On July 2, 1881, Charles Guiteau, a man later described as a "disappointed office-seeker," shot Garfield while he was en route to Williams College to deliver a commencement address. Garfield died in September, and Arthur became president.

The outstanding feature of Arthur's presidency was the easy passage of the Pendleton Act—legislation that set up a commission to regulate the provision of federal jobs and the behavior of civil servants. The number of federal workers removed from the patronage system was at first small, but successive presidents widened the coverage of nonpartisan workers so that today less than 1 percent of all federal workers are appointed by the president.[46]

The tariff question also emerged as crucial during the Arthur presidency. The Tariff Act of 1883 "gave little or no relief to the consumer and took care of every important industrial interest."[47] The Democrats opposed the bill and later worked for the gradual lowering of rates, but they failed. The tariff would be a major issue in later elections.

## DEMOCRAT CLEVELAND WINS: 1884

Arthur wanted the Republican nomination in 1884, and his record as stand-in for the assassinated Garfield arguably should have earned him the nod—even though no successor president during the nineteenth century had been nominated by his party. Not only was he an important player in civil service reform and the tariff issue, but he initiated modernization of the navy and vetoed the Chinese Exclusion Act of 1882, which prohibited Chinese laborers from entering the United States for ten years. His veto of the $19 million rivers and harbors bill was a model of fiscal probity.

James Blaine of Maine—secretary of state in Arthur's own administration—stood in Arthur's way. After months of public appeals by old-line Republicans interested in stronger leadership and more generous patronage from their party, Blaine quit his administration position and opposed Arthur for the nomination.

Blaine was the most charismatic figure of the period. A former teacher, editor, state legislator, and member of Congress, Blaine's fiery oratory captured the imagination of the political establishment. He had made a national name for himself when he opposed an 1876 congressional resolution expressing forgiveness to Civil War rebels including the Confederate president, Jefferson Davis. Col. Robert G. Ingersoll, a rising political figure in the Republican Party, said of Blaine: "Like an armed warrior, like a plumed knight, James G. Blaine marched down the halls of the American Congress and threw his shining lance full and fair against the brazen forehead of every traitor to his country."[48] The sobriquet "Plumed Knight" caught on.

The Republican convention in Chicago praised Arthur's administration and fudged the tariff issue. The tariff that passed in 1883 was the product of the efforts of swarms of lobbyists for private interests. The Republican platform promised better protection for raw wool interests, angered by their treatment in 1883, and a generally protective stance for domestic industry. The platform also called for an international currency conference, railway regulation, a national agency for labor affairs, and further improvements in the navy.

At a frenzied convention, Blaine took the lead over Arthur on the first ballot. Old-line party leaders quickly united behind Blaine, while Arthur was unable to consolidate the support of reform Republicans still skeptical of his leadership abilities from his days as a patronage politician and collector of the Port of New York. Blaine won the nomination on the fourth ballot. Gen. John Logan of Illinois received the vice-presidential nomination.

The Democrats nominated Grover Cleveland after skirmishes with Sen. Thomas F. Bayard Jr. of Delaware and Sen. Thomas A. Hendricks of Indiana. Hendricks, whose liberal expansionist currency stance would balance the more conservative stance of Cleveland, was named the vice-presidential candidate. The Democratic platform vaguely promised reform of the tariff laws to make them fairer and, even more vaguely, promised a more honest and efficient administration.

The fiery oratory of 1884 Republican candidate James G. Blaine captured the imagination of the political establishment, but it was not enough to win him the election over Democrat Grover Cleveland.

Cleveland was a former teacher, lawyer, assistant district attorney, and reform mayor of Buffalo who had won the governorship of New York only two years before. Members of both parties consistently underestimated Cleveland's intellect and resolve. As governor, he had made enemies through his vetoes of low public transit fares and aid to sectarian schools. He also had defied Tammany Hall, the Democratic Party organization that dominated New York politics, especially in New York City.

Cleveland's nomination signaled a triumph for the "educational politics" characteristic of urban progressivism. (Progressives took a patriarchal view of politics in which elites assumed an obligation to better their social underlings through education and various social services.) In a move away from the highly partisan and vitriolic campaigns of the post–Civil War era, Cleveland and other disciples of former New York governor Samuel Tilden promoted their program through a "literary bu-

reau" that distributed pamphlets describing the party's policy positions. Campaign themes were developed at the national level and disseminated via the mails and meetings with the many professional and community organizations. The educational style was adopted by Republican candidate Benjamin Harrison in 1888.[49]

In contrast, Blaine's campaign was one of the dirtiest in U.S. history. He first attempted to spark sectional antagonisms with his "bloody shirt" warnings that the South was trying to reassert its rebel ways through Cleveland. Blaine also tried to rouse the fears of business with claims that Cleveland would institute free trade policies damaging to domestic industries. But that appeal failed because the Democratic platform's plank on the tariff laws specifically supported protection of those interests. Finally, Blaine tried to make a scandal of Cleveland's admission that he had fathered a child out of wedlock years before. Cleveland was charged, among other things, of kidnapping and immuring both the mother and child to cover up the story.

The campaign eventually turned on Cleveland's victory in New York, which resulted from a number of blunders by Blaine. One blunder had occurred years before, when Blaine mocked New York party boss Roscoe Conkling: "The contempt of that large-minded gentleman is so wilted, his haughty disdain, his grandiloquent swell, his majestic, supereminent, overpowering, turkey-gobbler strut, has been so crushing to myself that I know it was an act of the greatest temerity to venture upon a controversy with him."[50] Conkling was so peeved by the turkey image that he spent his whole career battling Blaine, including the presidential campaign of 1884. Blaine's own running mate, Logan, sympathized with Conkling in the dispute.

The other Blaine faux pas occurred a week before the election when a Protestant minister praised Blaine and proclaimed, "We are Republicans, and do not propose to leave our party and identify ourselves with the party whose antecedents have been rum, Romanism, and rebellion." Blaine did not divorce himself from the remark, which angered New York Democrats—and ethnic voters everywhere—and cost him many votes. Later the same day Blaine attended a formal dinner with a number of wealthy persons that became known as "the millionaires dinner." That event belied Blaine's claim to speak for ordinary people.

Of Irish background, Blaine appealed to Irish immigrants in New York for their votes. But Cleveland countered Blaine's Irish tactic by obtaining the last-minute endorsement of the powerful Tammany leader Edward Kelly. On the Saturday before the election, he attended a parade in New York City that attracted forty thousand people chanting: "Blaine, Blaine, James G. Blaine, the Monumental Liar from the State of Maine!" With the help of an economic downturn and the "Mugwumps"—independents and liberal Republicans offended by Blaine—Cleveland won the presidency.

The race, however, was close. Cleveland received 4.9 million votes (48.5 percent) to Blaine's 4.8 million (48.3 percent). He won the solid South, Indiana, Connecticut, New Jersey, and, most important, New York (although by only 1,047 out of 1.13 million votes cast). Still, the election controversy did not end with the balloting. The *New York Tribune* reported that Blaine had won the race, fueling fears about an election deadlock similar to the Hayes-Tilden contest of 1876. But Cleveland received 219 electoral votes to Blaine's 182, making the Democrat the clear winner.

Cleveland's first two years in the White House were productive. His inaugural address and cabinet selections elicited wide praise. And his style of leadership—examined closely in the newspapers—appeared refreshingly unassuming. The Cleveland agenda included such issues as tariff reform (cutting rates on the "necessaries of life"), modernization of the navy, civil service, expansion, and land law reform. The president oversaw passage of the Presidential Succession Act and the Electoral Count Act, changes in currency policy, and labor controversies.

Just as he had done during his terms as mayor of Buffalo and governor of New York, Cleveland icily refused to compromise his values. This steadfastness proved to be a problem, however, for *President* Cleveland. Thousands of Democratic Party workers went to Washington seeking jobs in the new administration only to be disappointed. "Ah, I suppose you mean that I should appoint two horse thieves a day instead of one," Cleveland said in response to one party leader.[51] In vetoing pension bills, Cleveland called their sponsors "blood-suckers," "coffee-boilers," "pension leeches," and "bums."[52] The president appeared just as aloof to labor when a record number of strikes and disturbances swept the nation in 1886; the federal troops that Cleveland sent to the Haymarket riot in Chicago killed thirty people.

When Cleveland did bend to political realities, his timing was off. After standing firm against patronage when party enthusiasm for reform was at its height, Cleveland disappointed reformers when he allowed lieutenants such as First Assistant Postmaster Adlai E. Stevenson to distribute favors.

The biggest controversy of the Cleveland administration involved tariffs. Concerned about federal budget surpluses that threatened to stall economic activity, Cleveland prodded the House of Representatives to pass tariff reductions. The Senate responded with a protective (high) tariff measure.

## THE 1888 REPUBLICAN RECOVERY

The tariff issue propelled the two parties into the 1888 election. At their national convention the Democrats nominated Cleveland by acclamation and chose seventy-five-year-old judge Allen G. Thurman of Ohio for the vice presidency. The Democrats tried to soften their low-tariff image by promising that open trade would open world markets to domestic industries. Lower tariffs were said to be necessary for avoiding disastrous federal budget surpluses, preventing the development of monopolies, and ensuring consumers reasonable prices for basic goods.

As for the Republicans, a politics-weary James Blaine sent word from Florence and Paris that he would not be a candidate in 1888, leaving the race open to some lesser political lights, in-

Captioned "Another Voice for Cleveland," this 1884 cartoon played on Cleveland's admission that he had fathered an illegitimate son.

cluding Sen. John Sherman of Ohio, Gov. Russell Alger of Michigan, Sen. William Allison of Iowa, and Sen. Benjamin Harrison of Indiana. At the Republican national convention Sherman led the early balloting but quickly lost ground to Alger and Harrison. After extensive backroom maneuvering, including a last-minute plea by party members to Blaine to accept the nomination, Harrison, who had the backing of state party bosses, won on the ninth ballot. Levi Morton, a banker, got the vice-presidential nomination.

Harrison, a senator from Indiana, was a former Civil War brigadier and the grandson of President William Henry Harrison. Characterized by a scandal-free if colorless demeanor, Harrison was a good speaker, but he often appeared aloof. One historian wrote: "Those who talked with him were met with a frigid look from two expressionless steel grey eyes; and their remarks were sometimes answered in a few chill monosyllables devoid of the slightest note of interest."[53] Harrison pledged a modernized navy, civil service reforms, and the traditional Republican policies to protect trusts and restrict U.S. markets.

The election turned, as in 1884, on New York and Indiana—both states with extensive evidence of voter intimidation and manipulation of vote counts. Harrison won the two states narrowly—New York by only 14,373 votes out of the 1.3 million cast—and captured the White House. Except for Connecticut and New Jersey, Harrison swept the North and West. Cleveland won the South. Overall, Harrison won 5.4 million popular votes (47.8 percent) and 233 electoral votes; Cleveland won 5.5 million popular votes (48.6 percent) and 168 electoral votes.

Cleveland left the White House with an unusual amount of good will among the public because of his honest tariff campaign. His popularity increased during the next four years as the economy hit slumps and as the former president, while practicing law, delivered speeches calling for a more egalitarian brand of politics. Cleveland would be back in 1892 for vindication.

With a majority in Congress and a president in the White House—the first time the party had accomplished such a feat in a dozen years—the Republicans went about their business briskly after the election. Postmaster General John Wanamaker dispensed patronage with zeal. President Harrison signed into law the McKinley Tariff Act and the Sherman Silver Purchase Act. The former raised duties on manufactured goods to their highest level ever but also included provisions for negotiating with other countries to bring the rates down. The silver act loosened the money supply, which stimulated economic activity but angered creditors and bankers (money, when it is more readily available, is worth less).

## CLEVELAND'S COMEBACK: 1892

The 1890 midterm elections brought huge Democratic gains. Voters all over the country—but especially in the depressed farm belt—rebelled against the inflation that high tariffs brought. The Republicans held on to the Senate, but the new House of Representatives had 235 Democrats, 88 Republicans, and 9 Farmers' Alliance members. The brief experiment with party government ended with two years of stalemate.

President Harrison evoked widespread discontent in 1892 for both his demeanor and his policies, but no Republican could mount an effective challenge. Through their strong party government, Republicans had cast their lot with Harrison and had few places to turn for an alternative. Political wizard Mark Hanna, a wealthy coal magnate who had become a powerful behind-the-scenes Republican strategist, promoted Ohio governor William McKinley, and Secretary of State James Blaine became an alternative when he abruptly quit the administration just before the Republican convention. But Harrison received a first-ballot nomination. Former minister to France Whitelaw Reid of New York got the vice-presidential nomination.

In the battle for the Democratic nomination, Cleveland enjoyed widespread backing among rank-and-file voters, but party leaders were suspicious. New York governor David B. Hall got a head start when he called a "snap" state convention and won the delegation. An "anti-snapper" convention from New York sent a rival delegation to the national party convention. Democrats across the country rebelled at Hall's move and rapidly switched their support to Cleveland.

Another problem for Cleveland was the rising sentiment in agrarian states for free and unlimited coinage of silver—a way of boosting sagging farm prices by inducing inflation in the overall economy. Cleveland always had opposed this solution. The former president's consistent, principled stance on the issue not only added to his reputation for integrity but also kept business- and finance-dominated northeastern states in the Democratic camp. Cleveland defeated Hall for the nomination on the

Grover Cleveland is welcomed back on board the "Ship of State" in this 1893 cartoon. Having served as president from 1885 to 1889, he lost the 1888 election but regained the White House in the 1892 contest. Cleveland remains the only president to serve two nonconsecutive terms.

first ballot and selected his former first assistant postmaster Adlai Stevenson of Illinois as his running mate.

The fall campaign was uneventful. Historian Eugene Roseboom wrote: "Honest bearded Benjamin Harrison confronting honest mustached Grover Cleveland in a tariff debate was a repeat performance that did not inspire parades with torches or the chanting of campaign ditties. . . . Democrats, out of power, could assail Republican tariff policy without clarifying their own position."[54]

Cleveland won easily. He received 5.6 million popular votes (46.1 percent) to Harrison's 5.2 million (43.0 percent) and 277 electoral votes to Harrison's 145. Populist general James B. Weaver, advocating expansion of currency and limits on interest rates, won 1.0 million popular votes (8.5 percent) and 32 electoral votes.

## The Age of Reform

Throughout the period dominated by Republican conservatism—from Grant's election in 1868 to William McKinley's 1896 win—movements for the reform of political and economic institutions gathered strength at all levels of the American political system. The so-called populists and progressives did not overturn the system, as their rhetoric sometimes suggested, but over time they made major changes in the operation and discourse of U.S. politics.

Depending on the time and place, people who called themselves "populists" and "progressives" promoted such contradictory notions as strict morals and free spirits, tight money and loose money, redistribution to the masses and control of the economy by elites, federal intervention and local control of politics, the opening and closing of electoral participation, technological progress and a return to a long-gone pastoral ideal, individualism and community action, ethnic celebration and immigration barriers, scientific investigation and religion, and internationalism and isolationism.

Reformism was the response to the pressures of national expansion, urban development, and growth. Both major parties had adopted probusiness, laissez-faire policies in the latter part of the nineteenth century; indeed, the parties seemed to exist mainly to make sure the terrain was suitable for economic expansion. But the lack of any program to deal with the undesired consequences of explosive growth led to an accumulation of problems that demanded attention. The most obvious problems evolved on the opposite ends of the rural-urban continuum: on the farms and in the cities.

The farm problem developed as the United States became a major economic power in the world. Agriculture expanded on a vast scale to feed the booming cities and, with international trade, to bring foreign capital to the United States. By 1880, the value of U.S. wheat and flour exports nearly equaled that of cotton exports.[55] As agriculture became part of the international market, farmers became dependent not only on the vagaries of the weather but also on the fluctuations of currency in the larger economy.

In the thirty years after the Civil War, prices for farm staples fell steadily. A debt that could have been paid by producing one thousand bushels of grain immediately after the war required three thousand bushels in 1895. The more farmers produced to meet their obligations, the more prices fell to exacerbate their problems. A solution to the problem required confronting a wide array of issues, including tight money, bankers who charged 20 percent interest for loans, monopolies among farm equipment producers, high tariffs, railroad price gouging, shipping inflation, warehouse monopolies, and land speculation. Throughout the farm belt, particularly in the West, tens of thousands of farmers developed an "intense class consciousness."[56]

All these issues received attention from a variety of third parties and independent organizations, but the two major parties usually were inattentive. The Granger Movement of the 1870s, for example, took hold in several farm states and elected new legislatures and high state officials. The Greenback Party attempted to merge a labor-farmer alliance with a doctrine of silver use for public debts. Later, the Farmers' Alliance politicized the same issues. In 1892 the Populist Party had won 8.5 percent of the vote on a platform calling for free coinage of silver. *(See "Third Parties," p. 116, in Chapter 1.)*

Another site of growing reformist strength was the city. The dominance of machines of both parties in the cities established an electoral system based on patronage but stubbornly opposed to any coherent program for addressing such urban ills as poverty, poor housing, unsanitary conditions, transportation, education, and unfair workplace practices. Electoral fraud spurred mostly middle-class reformers to devise new electoral and city government machinery, while social problems incited some insurgent class politics.[57] The labor movement developed strength during this period.[58]

Other parts of the progressive agenda developed with a greater understanding of the nationalization of the economic and political systems. The wider sphere of economic activities created calls for regulation of corporations, railroads, and banks, as well as attention to health and environmental concerns and product safety.

Until the ascendance of William Jennings Bryan, the Democratic presidential nominee in 1896, 1900, and 1908, the reformers had been unable to capture a major party. Partly because political activism was based at the state and local level, neither national party had adopted the reformers' widely variegated program as its own. But the depression of 1888 caused the populist forces to pull together more than they had during previous economic downturns, probably because of the accumulated effects of inaction. The earlier panic of 1873 had created a sectional rather than a party split, with the Democrats eventually adopting a more conservative stance on the debate over whether the currency should be expanded to spur economic activity and redistribute social burdens.[59]

The Republican presidential candidates in the post–Civil War years steadfastly opposed the class-oriented proposals of the progressive movement, especially the loose-money demands. The only Democrat to win the presidency since the Civil War was Cleveland, a stubborn advocate of hard money and other conservative economic policies, in 1884 and 1892. President Cleveland vetoed dozens of private pension bills, only grudgingly accepted railroad regulation, and did not address domestic problems in any comprehensive way. Cleveland's public statements on the currency question were especially strong. He called the use of silver "a dangerous and reckless experiment" that was "unpatriotic."[60] On the question of labor, Cleveland was just as conservative: he called out federal troops to put down the Pullman strike of 1894 and regularly preached about the evils of disorder that the labor movement seemed to foster.

Despite the complexity of the agriculture issue, the most concerted populist action concentrated on the currency question. The drive to overturn the prevailing conventional economic thought by moving from a gold (tight) to a gold and silver (loose) money standard captured the imagination of the entire farm belt stretching from the Southeast to the prairie and silver-producing states of the West. The silver standard was a very simple answer to the problem of farm prices: "If money was scarce, the farmer reasoned, then the logical thing was to increase the money supply."[61]

## REPUBLICANS AND MCKINLEY TRIUMPH: 1896 AND 1900

Gold runs on banks, manipulation of the gold crisis by J. P. Morgan and other leading financiers, procorporation Supreme Court decisions, and antilabor actions all stirred up resentment in the South and West. The silver sentiment escalated. The Democratic convention in 1896 called for the issuance of silver and rejected a resolution praising President Cleveland.[62] The movement for a silver currency found an eloquent advocate in Bryan, a member of the House of Representatives from Nebraska, who defeated Richard P. Bland of Missouri for the 1896 Democratic presidential nomination on the strength of his fiery "Cross of Gold" speech.

The speech was one of the most emotional and successful in U.S. history. Bryan attacked eastern financiers and businessmen who exploited farmers. Using a theme to which his fall campaign would return, Bryan sought to expand the traditional Democratic conception of the independent working man to include farmers and factory workers.[63] In his speech's fortissimo, Bryan declared: "You shall not press down upon the brow of labor this crown of thorns, you shall not crucify mankind upon a cross of gold."[64]

In 1896 the Republicans nominated Ohio governor William McKinley after brilliant maneuvering by his manager, Mark Hanna. Hanna's chief strengths were fund raising and his mastery over state party organizations.

McKinley had little difficulty defeating Bryan. McKinley outspent the prairie populist by as much as ten-to-one, and he attracted the disaffected progold wing of the Democratic Party.[65] The Grand Old Party (or GOP as it was by then called) platform called for retention of the gold standard unless international negotiations could produce a bimetallic (silver and gold) currency system. The platform also called for restored tariff protections and an aggressive foreign policy in the Western Hemisphere.

Bryan's campaign was a political hurricane. He spent just $650,000, most of it donated by silver interests, compared with the millions McKinley spent. But Bryan traveled eighteen thousand miles and gave some six hundred speeches, and his campaign staffers put out an impressive quantity of literature. Several million copies of *Coin's Financial School,* a prosilver pamphlet, were distributed during the fall of 1896. Other silverites also maintained busy speaking schedules in the fall.

Bryan's appeal to industrial workers to join his coalition of independent businessmen failed, largely because they depended for their livelihoods on the very eastern interests that Bryan attacked. McKinley won not only the East but also the small cities and towns in Bryan's southern and western belt of support. Bryan was unable to win rural areas in the East. McKinley won the popular vote 7.1 million (51.0 percent) to 6.5 million (46.7 percent) and the electoral vote 271–176.

The effect of the 1896 presidential election was lasting. James Sundquist wrote: "For 20 years the two-party system had been based on dead issues of the past. It had offered the voters no means of expressing a choice on the crucial issues of domestic policy around which the country had been polarizing. . . . Then suddenly, with the nomination of Bryan in 1896, the party system took on meaning once again."[66]

The new Republican coalition included residents of cities, where capital and labor were both reasonably content with the economic growth that the GOP tariff policy promoted; farmers in the East and Midwest, who had strong ties to the "party of Lincoln" and who had come to favor high tariffs; Catholic, German Lutheran, and other liturgical Christian denominations; and some border states. Sundquist noted: "It was the persistence of the Civil War attachments that made the realignment of the North so largely a one-way movement—pro-Republican."[67]

After 1896, the competitive party balance that had prevailed for years gave way to lopsided party strength according to region—Democrats in the South, Republicans in the North. Strong opposition parties disappeared in all regions of the country, vesting political power in the hands of those already part of the system.

As political scientist E. E. Schattschneider has observed:

The 1896 party cleavage resulted from the tremendous reaction of conservatives in both major parties to the Populist movement. . . . [S]outhern conservatives reacted so strongly that they were willing to revive the tensions and animosities of the Civil War and the Reconstruction in order to set up a one-party sectional southern political monopoly in which nearly all Negroes and many poor whites were disenfranchised. One of the most important consequences of the creation of the Solid South was that it severed permanently the connection between the western and the southern wings of the Populist movement.[68]

Conservative Republicans won the White House in all but two (1912 and 1916) of the nine elections from 1896 to 1928. During this period the country experienced economic prosperity that blunted the possible activism of workers and the previous activism of farmers. With good harvests and rising commodity prices, the agrarian revolt fizzled. The development of new ore extraction methods and discovery of new gold deposits made calls for silver to expand the currency supply superfluous. The Spanish-American War in 1898, which McKinley reluctantly entered and the burgeoning mass media publicized, created a patriotic fervor.

McKinley's reelection in 1900 was even stronger than his 1896 election. He won 7.2 million popular votes (51.7 percent) to Bryan's 6.4 million (45.5 percent), and 292 electoral votes to Bryan's 155. McKinley swept to victory with all states except the silver states of the West (Colorado, Montana, Idaho, and Nevada).

## THE RISE OF THEODORE ROOSEVELT: 1904

Because Vice President Garret A. Hobart died in office in 1899, the Republicans selected New York's progressive governor, Theodore Roosevelt, to share the ticket with McKinley in the 1900 election. Roosevelt, an independent-minded environmentalist and trust-buster, was promoted for vice president by New

The Democrats selected sober-visaged judge Alton B. Parker to run against the outgoing Theodore Roosevelt in the 1904 election. Roosevelt won by a wide margin.

York GOP boss Thomas Platt, who wanted to rid the state of him and his progressive politics. Roosevelt was reluctant to take the job: "I am a comparatively young man yet and I like to work. . . . It would not entertain me to preside in the Senate."[69] He accepted, however, when a convention movement and McKinley prevailed on him.

When McKinley was assassinated in 1901 and Roosevelt became president, presidential politics came under the influence of a variant of the progressive movement. As Gabriel Kolko and other historians have demonstrated, Roosevelt's administration was friendly to many of the GOP's traditional conservative allies. But Roosevelt's rhetoric and his legacy of regulation and conservation had strong progressive or reformist elements.[70]

Roosevelt's leadership of the progressives was an example of generational politics. (As each generation assumes control over political and social structures, it stamps those institutions with its distinctive style and ethos.) The new president grew up in an era in which economic expansion was straining the nation's fabric, causing political figures to seek idealistic but pragmatic solutions to a wide variety of problems. The previous generation had grown up in a simpler age when "politics were devoid of substance, built around appeals to tradition and old loyalties and aimed at patronage."[71]

Roosevelt steered his party toward conservation of natural resources, enforcement of antitrust laws, promotion of the concerns of labor, and railroad regulation. The government's suit to dissolve the Northern Securities Company under the Sherman Anti-Trust Act and Roosevelt's intervention in the anthracite coal miners' strike, both in 1902, established the tenor for an activist presidency. T R (the first president identified by his initials) also used his office as a "bully pulpit" to promote his progressive ideology.

Roosevelt had no trouble winning the nomination for election as president in his own right in 1904. The Republican convention, arranged in advance at the White House, unanimously voted for Roosevelt and his platform of trust-busting, tariffs, labor relations, and activist foreign policy. Sen. Charles W. Fairbanks of Indiana was the GOP vice-presidential nominee.

To oppose the rambunctious Roosevelt, the Democrats selected a sober-visaged judge. Alton Parker, the chief justice of the New York State Court of Appeals, received the backing of the Democratic Party's conservative establishment when former president Cleveland turned down entreaties to make a fourth presidential run. Parker was opposed by William Randolph Hearst, a member of Congress and newspaper magnate. Bryan forced the party to adopt a liberal platform, as a balance to the conservative judge.

The Roosevelt victory was a landslide. He won 7.6 million votes (56.4 percent) to Parker's 5.1 million (37.6 percent) and carried all but the southern states. Roosevelt won 336 electoral votes to Parker's 140. Both houses of Congress were overwhelmingly Republican. President Roosevelt pledged not to seek a second term of his own because he had served most of McKinley's second term. He occupied himself with his progressive agenda and groomed his secretary of war, William Howard Taft, as his successor.

### ROOSEVELT PICKS TAFT: 1908

Roosevelt appeared to be genuinely dismayed by talk in 1907 of a possible third term, so he made public shows of his support for Taft. Because he also was able to line up state delegations for Taft, the nomination was never in doubt. Taft, through Roosevelt, was particularly strong among Republicans in the South. Attempts to restrict southern representation and pass a more liberal party platform were defeated.

Taft had impressive governmental experience. Before joining Roosevelt's cabinet, he had been a Cincinnati judge, U.S. solicitor general, federal circuit judge, head of the U.S. Commission on the Philippines, and the first civil governor of the Philippines.

Roosevelt's only problem in pushing Taft at the convention was avoiding a stampede in his own favor. Despite a highly disciplined convention, the galleries demonstrated wildly for Roosevelt. But Taft—a newcomer to electoral politics—easily won the nomination on the first ballot. He had 702 votes to the runner-up Philander C. Knox's 68. Rep. James S. Sherman of New York was selected as his running mate.

The Democrats nominated William Jennings Bryan for the third time. The electoral disaster that befell Judge Parker in 1904 was said to be evidence that the party needed an aggressive challenger to the Republicans rather than another conservative candidate. The Democrats were bereft of new talent, especially in competitive states in the East and Midwest, and turned to Bryan despite his disastrous campaign record and the warnings of former president Cleveland.

Taft campaigned on the Roosevelt record. Bryan called for government ownership of railroads and other liberal measures—such as a lower tariff, campaign finance reform, a graduated income tax, labor reforms, and greater enforcement of antitrust and other business regulations.

With Roosevelt and Taft promoting much of the progressive agenda, Bryan's message was no longer distinctive, and Taft won easily. He gathered 7.7 million popular votes (51.6 percent) to Bryan's 6.4 million (43.1 percent), and 321 electoral votes to Bryan's 162. The North, most of the West, and the border states went into the Republican column.

## WILSON AND THE DIVIDED REPUBLICANS: 1912 AND 1916

Taft was not, by temperament, an ideal executive. His lifelong ambition had been to serve on the Supreme Court, and his disciplined legal mind and collegial nature eventually would enable him to become one of the high court's most able chief justices. (He was appointed to the Court by President Warren G. Harding in 1921.) But Taft foundered in the presidency. He carried out Roosevelt's program of business regulation and conservation, yet Roosevelt responded not with gratitude but with a series of nasty statements and plans for a campaign against Taft.

The tariff issue proved to be Taft's early trouble spot. Taft was committed to reducing tariffs, but he was less cautious than Roosevelt, who had fudged the divisive issue. As a result, Taft quickly became embroiled in a fight with Congress, which wanted to raise tariffs. The Senate remolded House legislation to push up various duties, and Taft publicly promoted the legislation after he managed to secure new corporate taxes and tariff reductions for raw materials. Overall, then, Taft proved ineffective and indecisive on the tariff issue and, as a consequence, began losing his party.

The Glavis-Ballinger affair further muddied the image of the administration. The scandal broke when the chief forester of the Interior Department, Gifford Pinchot, charged that Secretary Richard A. Ballinger had betrayed the cause of conservation and

had even engaged in corrupt practices regarding minerals and water power. Pinchot also charged that Ballinger had wrongly fired another Interior official, Louis Glavis, for trying to expose the scandal. Pinchot took his complaints directly to Taft, but Taft sided with Ballinger and urged Pinchot to drop the matter. After an indignant Pinchot went public with the issue, Taft fired him, fueling suspicion of a cover-up at Interior. The incident was a major embarrassment to Taft because of the priority that conservation had received under Roosevelt and because of the inevitable complaints that Taft was betraying his mentor on the issue.[72]

Divisions within the Republican Party eventually created rival Taft and Roosevelt factions. Tariffs, Arizona's new state constitution (which included a provision for recall of the governor, which Taft opposed), treaties, and antitrust issues split the former president and the sitting president. In many ways, the dispute was over personalities. Taft carried out Roosevelt's program but lacked his fervor and decisiveness. In a still conservative age, progressives felt they needed more aggressive leadership than the judicially tempered Taft would ever give them.

Roosevelt spent more than a year of Taft's term hunting in Africa, but he was an active speaker and campaigner when he returned to the United States. He gave a detailed accounting of his philosophy of government in a 1912 speech in Columbus, Ohio, calling for binding votes on public issues, recall of elected officials, and curbs on judicial power. When a dump-Taft movement decided in 1911 that Wisconsin senator Robert La Follette had no chance to defeat the president for the GOP nomination, party discontents turned to the energetic and still young (fifty years) Roosevelt.

Roosevelt made an all-out effort for the Republican nomination, entering twelve primaries and winning all but three. More specifically, Roosevelt won 278 delegates in states with primaries to Taft's 48 and La Follette's 36. In today's system, Roosevelt probably would have marched to a first-ballot nomination. (Today, more delegates are allocated by popular votes than by the party organizations, which then dominated the process.) Three crucial Republican states—Pennsylvania, Illinois, and Ohio—went for Roosevelt. He clearly, then, had great popular appeal and vote-getting ability—perhaps more than ever.

But Taft won the nomination. The president controlled the party machinery, and most of the convention's delegates were sent by the state machines. Roosevelt challenged the credentials of Taft delegates at the Chicago convention, and the nomination's outcome turned on battles over almost one-fourth of the delegates. The fight went to the floor of the convention, but Taft's smooth operation defeated Roosevelt. Roosevelt appeared at the convention to buoy his forces and cry foul.

After the defeat, Roosevelt urged his supporters to continue their fight, which motivated some bolting progressive delegates to organize a convention in August to mount a third-party effort. The bolters formed the Progressive Party. When Roosevelt remarked to a reporter during the GOP convention, "I'm feeling like a bull moose," his vigorous campaign had a symbol.

Woodrow Wilson traveled widely in the 1912 election campaign. His dynamic presence and reformist rhetoric appealed to the crowds who came to hear.

With the Republicans divided, the Democrats saw their first opportunity to win the presidency since Cleveland in 1892. As the 1912 Democratic convention in Baltimore neared, several national candidates and favorite sons were vying for the nomination. The front-runner was House Speaker James Beauchamp "Champ" Clark of Missouri, a party regular who had party organization support and years of experience to recommend him.

Gov. Woodrow Wilson of New Jersey—who held a doctorate in political science and who had moved into politics after a distinguished career as professor and president at Princeton University—was another strong candidate. Wilson's virtues were the opposite of Clark's. He did not have an extensive political record for opponents to attack, and he was supported enthusiastically because of his dynamic presence and reformist rhetoric. Although the New Jersey machine had brought Wilson into politics, he quickly asserted his independence and became something of a crusader.

As a newcomer to national politics, Wilson both refreshed and alienated Democratic crowds in speeches before the convention. He came out strongly for the "radical" platform of referendum, initiative, and recall, prompting a newspaper to report: "The boldness, the directness, the incisiveness, the fearlessness, and the force of the 'Virginian-Jerseyan's' words crashed at times through the throng like a series of thunderbolt jolts."[73] But Wilson's embrace of the progressive agenda and attacks on

business alienated many southerners; even the delegates from Wilson's home state of Virginia opposed him at the convention.

Other Democratic candidates were the conservative representative Oscar Underwood of Alabama, author of a historic tariff act; another conservative, Gov. Judson Harmon of Ohio; and four favorite-son governors. Clark appeared to have won the nomination when a Tammany bloc of delegates moved to support him after he won a tenth-ballot majority. The requirement for a two-thirds majority, however, gave other candidates time to maneuver. Wilson almost dropped out of the race, but Bryan's late transfer of his support from Clark to Wilson created a bandwagon effect for Wilson. On the forty-sixth ballot, Wilson accumulated the necessary two-thirds of delegates for the nomination. Gov. Thomas Marshall of Indiana, one of the favorite-son candidates, was picked to be the vice-presidential nominee because Underwood, Wilson's choice, would not accept.

The Democratic platform was progressive. It called for tariff reduction, utility regulation, banking reforms, legislation to curb monopolies, a national income tax, direct election of senators, campaign finance reforms, and a national presidential primary. Theodore Roosevelt actually praised Wilson as "an able man" in the early fall and said he might not have started a third-party effort if he had known Wilson would be the Democrats' candidate. But Wilson and Roosevelt eventually criticized each other's approach to government, especially after Wilson expressed reservations about government activism.[74]

Wilson easily won the election, receiving 435 electoral votes to Roosevelt's 88 and Taft's 8. The Republican split obviously helped Wilson; if Roosevelt and Taft had combined their totals of 4.1 million votes (27.4 percent) and 3.5 million votes (23.2 percent), they would have topped Wilson's 6.3 million (41.8 percent). Yet even though Wilson was a minority president, there was a clear Democratic trend since the Democrats had taken over the House and replaced several Republican governors in the 1910 midterm elections. It was the worst showing ever for an incumbent president—third place with only two states.

Whatever the strength of Wilson's "mandate," he acted as though he had won by a landslide. His first term was one of the most productive in U.S. history. With the Democrats in control of Congress, and with a shrewd political adviser in Col. Edward M. House, Wilson adopted a reform agenda that had been percolating at various levels of government for years. He broke precedent by delivering his first State of the Union message to Congress in person. At the center of the message was a call for reductions in tariff rates. After a bitter fight that raged for a month, Wilson went public with a demand that members of Congress reveal their property holdings. The revelations, in response to public pressure, showed close links between their holdings and the kinds of tariff protections on the books. Congress soon was shamed into passing tariff cuts of 15 percent. Some one hundred items were placed on a free-trade list for the first time.

Wilson also addressed other areas successfully: taxes (institution of a graduated income tax in 1913, which replaced reliance on tariffs and various excise and user taxes); banking regulation (the Glass-Owen Act of 1913, which created the Federal Reserve system); antitrust legislation (the Clayton Anti-Trust Act of 1914, creation of the Federal Trade Commission in 1914); labor relations (Section 6 of the Sherman Anti-Trust Act, which exempted unions from antitrust strictures); agriculture (the Smith-Lever Act of 1914, the Federal Farm Loan Act of 1916); conservation (creation of the National Park Service in 1916); and the judiciary (the appointment of Louis Brandeis to the Supreme Court).

Despite his strong leadership—highlighted by his stirring oratory—Wilson still faced the prospect in 1916 of a tough reelection. He had won the presidency in 1912 with only 41.8 percent of the popular vote, and the escalating war in Europe was beginning to disturb the American process of steady economic growth.

Public opinion on the Great War was volatile, largely because more than a third of the U.S. population was either foreign born or the offspring of foreign-born parents. Some eleven million Americans surveyed in the 1910 census were of direct German or Austrian descent, and another five million were from Ireland. Many other immigrants were Russian, Italian, Hungarian, British, and French. Wilson sought to diffuse feelings for the immigrants' native lands when he denounced "hyphenism"—the tendency of many citizens to identify themselves with appellations that linked their ethnic origins and American status—but politicians at lower levels tailored their campaigns to specific nationality voting blocs.[75]

Wilson and Vice President Marshall won renomination without any opposition. The most significant event of the Democratic convention was the passage of the platform, which indicated the party's main campaign theme. By calling for national universal suffrage, Wilson helped himself in the eleven western states where women already had won the vote. The platform praised "the splendid diplomatic victories of our great president, who has preserved the vital interests of our government and its citizens, and kept us out of war." The latter phrase would be repeated endlessly during the fall.[76]

The Republicans gave the presidential nomination to Supreme Court Justice Charles Evans Hughes. Hughes was silent in the months before the convention, but a number of party leaders lined up enough delegates for him to win a third-ballot nomination. Other potential candidates in 1916 included former president Roosevelt, former senator Elihu Root of New York, former vice president Fairbanks, and Senators John Weeks, Albert Cummins, and Lawrence Sherman. Fairbanks won the vice-presidential nomination.

Prosperity and reformism limited the campaign themes available to the Republicans. The GOP railed against Wilson's foreign policy as "shifty expedients" and "phrasemaking" that put the United States in danger of entering the war. Hughes turned out to be a bad campaigner, but he bridged the gap between conservative and progressive Republicans that had cost the party the 1912 election. Wilson was occupied with Congress

throughout the summer of 1916, but he emerged to give a series of speeches in the fall. Democratic strategists, meanwhile, conceived and executed a masterful strategy to return Wilson to the White House. The Democrats concentrated all their resources on "swing states" and ignored states they thought Wilson was sure to lose. Illinois, for example, was ignored since it was a certain Republican state. Bryan, Wilson's secretary of state, toured the West.

Wilson won one of the closest elections in history. California, an uncertain state, ensured Wilson's victory when, because of the urban vote, it went the president's way late in the campaign. The margin of victory was 3,420 votes in that state. The president defeated Hughes by a margin of 9.1 million (49.2 percent) to 8.5 million popular votes (46.1 percent). The electoral college gave Wilson 277 votes and Hughes 254.

Even though Wilson's campaign in 1916 was based on his determination to stay out of the Great War, the United States was in the war by 1917. Wilson's conduct of the war won him the status of war hero, but his diplomatic efforts after the war failed. Wilson was the architect of the Treaty of Versailles, which created a League of Nations to prevent future wars. But Wilson was unable to induce the Senate to approve the treaty, and he left office in 1921 a broken and dispirited man.

## The "Return to Normalcy" and the Roaring Twenties

After the tumult of Woodrow Wilson's domestic reforms, the First World War, and the divisive battle over the Versailles treaty, the time was ripe for a period of conservatism and Republican government. Deep resentments had developed toward Wilson and the Democratic Party, and the Democrats themselves were divided over many issues, including economic regulation, Prohibition, and race relations.

Blessed with good luck, substantial financial backing, and a strong trend toward split-ticket voting, beginning in the 1920s the Republicans were able to resume their dominance over national politics with three successful presidential campaigns: Warren G. Harding in 1920, Calvin Coolidge in 1924, and Herbert C. Hoover in 1928.

The 1920s are usually pictured as a time of steady, unexciting politics. The conservatives dominated the federal government, and occupying the White House were men who spoke of "normalcy" and a noninterventionist brand of politics in both domestic and foreign affairs. One of the symbols of the age was President Coolidge's program of tax cuts, which reduced the rates on the wealthy. The wartime Revenue Act of 1918 had driven tax rates to the highest point in U.S. history—77 percent in the highest brackets. In 1921, 1923, and 1926, Secretary of the Treasury Andrew Mellon presented to Congress proposals to cut taxes, the most controversial being the reduction in the maximum surtax from 77 to 25 percent. Congress eventually cut the surtax to 40 percent in 1924 and 20 percent in 1926.[77]

But the three sober men who filled the presidency in the

Democratic presidential candidate James M. Cox of Ohio, left, and vice-presidential candidate Franklin D. Roosevelt (one year before he was stricken with polio), campaign in the 1920 election. They lost to Republican presidential candidate Warren G. Harding and his running mate, Gov. Calvin Coolidge of Massachusetts.

twenties met challenges from progressives of both parties in Congress and in the state governments. On a wide range of issues—including relief of the poor, subsidies for the depressed farm sector, regulation of utilities, immigration, race relations, states' rights, tax cuts, and Prohibition—the conservative presidents encountered strong challenges. They frequently responded by vetoing legislation, but such an expedient would not prevent the pressures for a more activist government from developing.

## HARDING AND "NORMALCY": 1920

Sen. Warren Harding, a product of the GOP machine of Ohio, emerged from a crowded and largely unknown pack to win the Republican nomination in 1920 at a convention dominated by economic interests such as oil, railroads, and steel. The early candidates were Gen. Leonard Wood, an old Roosevelt ally; Gov. Frank Lowden of Illinois, who married into the Pullman family and therefore had ample financing for a campaign; and Sen. Hiram Johnson of California, whose progressive and isolationist stances put him in good stead with voters in many states. A dozen favorite sons hoped that a deadlocked convention might bring the nomination their way. All of the candidates were on hand in Chicago to maneuver for the nomination.

While Wood, Johnson, and Lowden performed reasonably well in the primaries, Harding won only his home state of Ohio and did not arouse much popular enthusiasm. But under the direction of a shrewd campaign manager, Harry Daugherty, Harding gained the support of the party's bosses and won the nomination on the tenth ballot after a brief interview with them in the "smoke-filled room" that was synonymous with boss control. Gov. Calvin Coolidge of Massachusetts, a favorite-son contender for president, became Harding's vice-presidential candidate.

The Democrats selected Gov. James Cox, also from Ohio, after lengthy platform battles and balloting for the nomination. Early ballots put former Treasury secretary William G. McAdoo and Attorney General Mitchell Palmer in the lead, but Cox gained steadily and had the nomination by the forty-fourth roll call. Franklin D. Roosevelt of New York, the assistant secretary of the navy, was rapidly selected to be Cox's running mate.

The image of Woodrow Wilson hung over the convention and would hang over the fall campaign. The Democratic platform praised Wilson's conduct of the war and his domestic reform program. But the results in the November election indicated deep unease over the Democratic administration.

Harding amassed 16.1 million popular votes (60.3 percent) to Cox's 9.1 million (34.2 percent), and 404 electoral votes to Cox's 127. Harding carried the North and West including Oklahoma and all of the southern and border states except Tennessee and Kentucky.

Harding's landslide victory was termed "election by disgust" by political analysts. The wartime sacrifices demanded under Wilson were widely perceived as the cause of Harding's victory rather than a desire for the ideology or policy proposals that Harding was offering. The *New York Post* editorialized: "We are in the backwash from the mighty spiritual and physical effort to which America girded herself when she won the war for the Allies. . . . The war has not been repudiated, though the administration that fought it has been overwhelmed. We are now in the chill that comes with the doctor's bills."[78]

The electorate's ability to shift allegiances from the Republicans to the Democrats and back again—from one period to the next, and from one level of government to the next—suggested a dissolution of partisan alignments. The addition of women to the electorate after passage of the Nineteenth Amendment in 1920 and the increasing independence among all voters induced uncertainty. National exhaustion from the war and the lack of sharp ideological differences between the candidates produced apathy. The electorate's instability was suggested by the divisions within both parties on such high-profile issues as Prohibition, the League of Nations, agricultural policies, and other social and economic issues—among them, technical assistance and trust busting. The appearance of numerous "blocs" in both parties represented "little if anything more than a transitory alignment upon a particular vote or issue."[79]

The shifts in control of congressional and state offices also indicated electoral instability. The Democrats had had comfortable control of Congress under Wilson, but in 1920 the Republicans gained a majority of 301 to 131 in the House and 59 to 37 in the Senate. Impressive liberal gains in congressional and state elections in the midterm election of 1922 appeared to be a slap at the Harding administration. The high turnover of votes also indicated unstable party affiliations: the 14.2 percentage point increase in the Republican vote between the 1916 and 1920 presidential elections was the largest since the Civil War, another time of turmoil.[80]

President Harding died on August 2, 1923, of a heart attack, just as revelations of kickbacks and favoritism in the administration began to surface and several members of the administration quit and two committed suicide. The investigation into the so-called Teapot Dome scandal—so named after the site of naval oil reserves that were transferred to private hands in exchange for bribes—would last five years. The Democrats hoped to make the scandal a major issue in the 1924 election, but Democratic complicity in the wrongdoing and the personal integrity of Harding's successor, Calvin Coolidge, defused the issue.

## COOLIDGE CLEANS UP: 1924

President Coolidge fired Attorney General Harry M. Daugherty and other members of Harding's clique and projected an image of puritan cleanliness. Coolidge—a taciturn man who had slowly climbed the political ladder in Massachusetts from city council member to city solicitor, mayor, state legislator, lieutenant governor, and governor before he became vice president—expounded a deeply individualistic Yankee philosophy that helped to separate him from the corrupt men in the Harding White House.

Except for appointing as attorney general Harlan Fiske Stone, former dean of the Columbia University School of Law, Coolidge allowed others to finish cleaning up the mess left behind by Harding. The new president was concerned about unnecessarily alienating himself from party leaders.

"Keep Cool with Coolidge" was the Republican incumbent's 1924 campaign slogan, used on posters, banners, buttons, and decorative stamps such as this one from Wisconsin.

By the time Coolidge sought the presidency in his own right in 1924, the economy had rebounded. One of the most conservative presidents ever, Coolidge's platform called for additional tax cuts but said nothing substantive about increasingly salient agriculture and labor issues. Coolidge also pushed an isolationist foreign policy plank. He won the nomination on the first ballot.

While the Republicans were able to "Keep Cool with Coolidge," the Democrats spent sixteen days in a seemingly endless attempt to pick a nominee in New York's sweltering Madison Square Garden. A fight developed because the party was badly split between its northeastern urban bloc and its more conservative southern and western rural bloc. New York governor Alfred E. Smith and former Treasury secretary William McAdoo of California were the key combatants at the convention until the delegates were freed from the instructions of party bosses on the one-hundredth ballot.

Suspicions between the two regional blocs were intense. A platform plank denouncing the Ku Klux Klan created the most controversy. Northerners wanted an explicit repudiation of the society that preached hatred of blacks, Catholics, and Jews; in the end, southerners would settle only for a vaguely worded rebuke. (The Klan had infiltrated the party in many rural areas.) Another divisive issue was Prohibition, with northerners attacking the initiative and southerners supporting it. These sectional splits would cripple the Democrats in the 1924 and 1928 elections.

After the delegates were freed from instructions, a stampede developed for John W. Davis of West Virginia, a lawyer with Wall Street connections. The ticket was balanced with the vice-presidential selection of Charles W. Bryan of Nebraska, the younger brother of three-time presidential candidate William Jennings Bryan.

The Progressive candidacy of Robert La Follette complicated the calculations of voters, particularly those on the liberal end of the political spectrum. Since the Democrats had a nearly impenetrable hold on the South, La Follette was not given a reasonable chance of winning. But the conservatism of both Coolidge and Davis meant that La Follette was the only liberal in the race. Still, many liberals voted for Davis or even Coolidge because of the fear of an inconclusive election that would have to be resolved in the House of Representatives.

Coolidge won the election easily, with the Democrats polling their smallest percentage ever. Coolidge won 54.1 percent of the vote, Davis won 28.8 percent, and La Follette won 16.6 percent. Coolidge attracted 15.7 million popular votes and 382 electoral votes; Davis 8.4 million and 136; and La Follette 4.8 million and 13.

On August 2, 1927, when Coolidge announced his decision not to seek reelection by passing out a brief note to reporters and then refusing further comment, the Republicans began jockeying for the nomination for the 1928 election.

## THE HOOVER SUCCESSION: 1928

Secretary of Commerce Herbert Hoover was the obvious choice to replace Coolidge at the head of the GOP ticket. A native of Iowa who learned mining engineering at Stanford University, Hoover was immensely popular with most of the party. Hoover's administration of Belgian relief and food distribution programs during World War I had earned him the status of statesman and humanitarian.

Hoover began working for the nomination soon after Coolidge dropped out, spending $400,000 in the nominating phase of the election. He won the nomination on the first ballot over Governors Frank Lowden of Illinois and Charles Curtis of Kansas. Curtis was named Hoover's running mate.

Hoover was religious in his zeal for what he called "the American system" of free enterprise and individualism. He did not see any inconsistency in having the government vigorously support businesses with tax breaks, tariffs, public provision of infrastructures, and police protection, while at the same time denying relief to people in need. Hoover appeared to be less rigid than Coolidge, however. He proposed creation of a special farm board and said he would consider legislation to protect labor unions from abuses in the use of court injunctions.

Al Smith, the Tammany-schooled governor of New York, was the Democratic nominee. Smith had the support of all the party's northern states, and he won a first-ballot nomination. Sen. Joseph T. Robinson of Arkansas was the vice-presidential candidate.

Smith's candidacy polarized the electorate, particularly the South. He was the first Catholic to be nominated for president by a major party, and he endured religious slurs throughout the fall. Moreover, he favored repeal of Prohibition, still a divisive issue, and he was an urbanite, a problem for a nation that had nurtured a rural ideal since Thomas Jefferson. Because he also was a machine politician, he presented a problem for anyone outside (and many people inside) the nation's great cities. He also was a strong opponent of the Klan, which put him in trouble in the South. Finally, he was an unabashed liberal who proposed public works, farm relief programs, stronger protection of workers, and regulation of banking and industry.

During the fall campaign, Hoover acted like the incumbent and Smith barnstormed the country, trying in vain to pick up support in the South and West. The 1928 campaign was the first with extensive radio coverage, and Hoover generally fared better than Smith on the airwaves. Hoover, the small-town boy who made good, represented fulfillment of the American Dream; Smith, the inner-city boy who made good, also embodied that ideal, but he had too many ethnic traits for much of the nation to realize it.

The November election produced another Republican landslide. Hoover carried forty states with 21.4 million popular votes (58.2 percent) and 444 electoral votes, while Smith carried only eight states with 15.0 million popular votes (40.8 percent) and 87 electoral votes. As disastrous as the election appeared to be for the Democrats, it put them in position to build a wide-ranging coalition in future years.

Smith carried only six southern states, but the defection of the others was temporary. More important to the Democrats' long-range fortunes was the movement of cities into the Democratic column, probably for the rest of the century. Immigrants in cities were expanding their vision from local politics to the national stage for the first time. In all, Smith diverted 122 northern counties from the GOP to the Democratic Party. Catholics, whose turnout previously had been low, turned out in record numbers. Smith also seemed to pick up some of the Progressive farm vote that La Follette had tapped before; in Wisconsin, for example, the Democratic vote jumped from 68,000 to 450,000 from 1924 to 1928. Finally, Smith's candidacy put the Democrats solidly in the "wet" column, just as the national temper began to resent Prohibition.

President Hoover impressed political observers with his managerial skills and "coordinating mind." With passage of the Agricultural Marketing Act in June 1929, the administration appeared to address the most pressing economic problem for the business-minded president. He met some legislative setbacks, but, overall, the Great Engineer appeared to be in good political condition as the nation looked back over his record when Congress began its recess in the summer of 1929.

The national economic and social fiesta that had begun at the close of World War I came to an abrupt end on October 29, 1929. After climbing to dizzying new heights for months, the stock market crashed. First described by economists and politicians as a temporary interruption of the good times, the crash quickly led to a wave of business and bank failures, mortgage foreclosures, wage cuts, layoffs, and a crisis of political leadership. By the end of Hoover's term in 1932, more than twelve million workers had lost their jobs; the unemployment rate was approximately 25 percent. An October 1931 advertisement for 6,000 jobs in the Soviet Union brought 100,000 American applications.[81]

President Hoover, who had celebrated his inauguration with a prediction that poverty and hunger were near an end, did not know how to cope with the crisis. In a special session that Hoover called, Congress created the Federal Farm Board to co-

In 1932, World War I veterans, seeking early receipt of their service bonuses, staged a protest by setting up camps near the Capitol. On July 28, President Herbert C. Hoover ordered federal troops, headed by Gen. Douglas MacArthur, to disperse the veterans with tear gas.

ordinate marketing of agricultural products, but Hoover steadfastly opposed further moves, especially subsidies. In 1930 Hoover signed the Smoot-Hawley Tariff Act to protect manufacturers, but, true to the predictions of economists and bankers, the tariff only aggravated economic conditions by hurting foreign trade.

Hoover later approved agricultural relief and public works programs and established the Reconstruction Finance Corporation. The president refused to approve direct relief to the unemployed and businesses, but he did approve some loans and aid to specific sectors of the economy.

Despite his earnest and tireless efforts, Hoover became a figure of widespread enmity. The low point of his distinguished career came when World War I veterans petitioned for early receipt of their service bonuses, which, by contract, were not to be paid until 1945. They set up camp in Washington, singing old war songs and carrying placards that bore their pleas. The "Bonus Army" numbered twenty thousand at its height. When Hoover feared a protracted protest, he ordered federal troops to take over buildings where some veterans were camping. In two skirmishes, two veterans were killed. The president then sent in Gen. Douglas MacArthur with tanks, infantry, and calvary soldiers. (MacArthur's junior officers included Dwight D. Eisenhower and George Patton.) After successfully removing the veterans, the military forces overran nearby veterans' camps in a rain of fire and tear gas. Thousands of veterans and their families fled the burning district.

The administration's tough stance against a defeated, ragtag band of former war heroes shocked and embittered the nation. The barricaded White House and administration statements about "insurrectionists" symbolized a dangerous gulf between the government and the people.

Partly because of the economic crisis he did not create, but also because of his dour and unimaginative demeanor, Hoover

probably never had a chance to win reelection. The 1930 midterm elections indicated a loss of confidence in the administration. The House went Democratic, 219 to 214, and the Senate came within a seat of going Democratic as well.

Those election results did not convey the bitterness and despair that the depression would aggravate before the next presidential campaign. Hoover was mercilessly ridiculed in newspapers and in Democratic speeches. The Democratic Party coordinated a comprehensive anti-Hoover campaign that made the president politically impotent.

### THE ELECTION OF 1932

Franklin D. Roosevelt, fifth cousin to Theodore Roosevelt, was the perfect candidate to oppose Hoover. The New York governor had been an activist in state politics, first opposing the state's Tammany machine and then pioneering many relief and reconstruction programs that Hoover refused to expand to the national scale. Roosevelt had been the party's vice-presidential candidate twelve years earlier, and he had served in the federal government as assistant secretary of the navy.

Perhaps more important than any of his political accomplishments were FDR's image of strength and optimism and his deft handling of hot issues and disparate members of the potential Democratic coalition. Although he was a polio victim, Roosevelt often smiled—a devastating contrast to Hoover. (Gutzon Borglum, the sculptor, wrote: "If you put a rose in Hoover's hand, it would wilt."[82]) Roosevelt was able to campaign for the presidency without putting forth a comprehensive program: the simple promise of a change in leadership was enough.

Some observers found the man from Hyde Park wanting. Journalist Walter Lippmann, for example, complained that Roosevelt was "a pleasant man who, without any important qualifications for the office, would like very much to be president."[83] But those detractors and a large field of Democratic nominees

Franklin D. Roosevelt campaigns by car in West Virginia, October 19, 1932.

were not able to keep Roosevelt from his "rendezvous with destiny."[84]

The Democratic field included the 1928 Democratic standard-bearer, Al Smith; John Nance Garner, the Speaker of the House; Gov. Albert Ritchie of Maryland; Gov. George White of Ohio; Gov. Harry Byrd of Virginia; and Sen. James Reed of Mississippi. Most considered Smith more of a "stalking horse" for the anti-FDR forces than a serious candidate in his own right. Garner had impressive backing from the newspaper magnate William Randolph Hearst and former Democratic candidate William McAdoo.

The many favorite sons in the race threatened to deadlock the convention and deny the nomination to the front-runner, as they had done so often in the past. Roosevelt had difficulty with his own region of the country because of his opposition to the Tammany machine in New York. Acquiring the required two-thirds vote of delegates for the nomination was difficult for Roosevelt or any other candidate, but FDR eventually won on the fourth ballot when he promised the vice-presidential slot to Garner.

In U.S. political history, Franklin Roosevelt was the first candidate to appear before the convention that nominated him. *(See "National Party Conventions," p. 82, in Chapter 1.)* In an acceptance speech to the conventioneers who had staged wild rallies in his support, Roosevelt made passing reference to the "new deal" that his administration would offer Americans. That phrase, picked up in a newspaper cartoon the next day, came to symbolize the renewal for which Americans yearned as riots and radicalism seemed to threaten the nation's spirit and the legitimacy of its institutions.

Roosevelt conducted an active fall campaign, traveling twen-

ty-three thousand miles in forty-one states to quell suspicions that his physical handicaps would deter him from performing his job. Besides barnstorming the nation, Roosevelt took to the radio airwaves—he was the first sophisticated electronic media candidate—where he conveyed a sense of warmth and confidence. He also showed an intellectual bent and an open mind when he called on academics and professionals—the famed "brain trust"—for their expert advice on the issues.

Roosevelt won 22.8 million votes (57.4 percent) to Hoover's 15.8 million (39.6 percent). Forty-two of the forty-eight states and 472 of the 531 electoral votes went for Roosevelt. The election was a landslide and a realignment of the major forces in U.S. politics.

## The New Deal Coalition

The profound effect of Roosevelt's victory on U.S. politics can hardly be overstated. The New Deal coalition that Roosevelt assembled shaped the political discourse and electoral competition of the United States until the late 1960s. In many respects, that coalition is a central element of politics today.

The new Democratic coalition brought together a disparate group of interests: southerners, African Americans, immigrants, farmers, capital-intensive producers, international businessmen, financiers, urbanites, trade unions, intellectuals, Catholics, and Jews. Rexford Tugwell called it "the most miscellaneous coalition in history."[85] These blocs were not always in perfect harmony—for example, the Democrats juggled the demands of blacks and white southerners with great difficulty—but they were solid building blocks for national political dominance.

The dominance was impressive. Between 1932 and 1964, the

Democrats won seven of nine presidential elections. The only successful Republican, Dwight Eisenhower, could just as easily have run as a Democrat. Party leaders in fact asked him to run as a Democrat in 1948 and 1952, and his name was entered in some Democratic primaries in 1952.

The strength of Roosevelt's rule was attributable partly to the president's personality. He could be soothing. When he gave his first "fireside chat" about the banking crisis, the nation responded with cooperation; the raids and violence at banks ended in a matter of weeks. More important than his soothing nature was his ability to experiment and shift gears. Professor James David Barber described Roosevelt's many public postures:

Founder of the New Deal, modern American democracy's closest approximation to a common political philosophy, Roosevelt came on the scene as the least philosophical of men—"a chameleon in plaid," Hoover called him. Firm fighter of yet another Great War, Roosevelt appeared to H. L. Mencken in 1932 as "far too feeble and wishy-washy a fellow to make a really effective fight." Architect of world organization, he introduced himself as totally concerned with America's domestic drama. His name is inseparable from his generation's great social revolution; in 1932, nearly all the heavy thinkers scoffed at him as just another placebo politician—a "pill to cure an earthquake," said Professor [Harold] Laski.[86]

More important than personality was what Roosevelt had to offer the many groups in his coalition. As historian Richard Hofstadter has noted, the New Deal was "a series of improvisations, many adopted very suddenly, many contradictory."[87] The Roosevelt credo was: "Save the people and the nation, and if we have to change our minds twice a day to accomplish that end, we should do it."[88]

Until the vast expenditures of World War II, there was not enough pump-priming to end the depression, but Roosevelt's initiatives touched almost everyone affected by the slump.[89] For the jobless, there were unemployment insurance and public works programs such as the Works Progress Administration and the Civilian Conservation Corps. For the poor, there were categorical aid programs. For westerners, there were conservation measures. For the banks, there was the famous holiday that stopped runs on holdings, and there were currency and securities reforms. For farmers, there were incentives and price supports and cooperatives. For the aged, there was Social Security. For southeasterners, there was the Tennessee Valley Authority. For southern whites, there was a hands-off policy on race matters. For blacks, there were sympathy and jobs programs. For those living in rural areas, there was electrification. For families, there were home loans. For the weary worker eager for a few rounds at the local tavern, there was the repeal of Prohibition. For laborers, there was acknowledgment of the right to negotiate for their share of the national wealth. For business, there were the Federal Emergency Relief Act and the National Industrial Recovery Act, as well as diplomatic negotiation to reduce trade barriers.

The remarkably divergent interests in the coalition were underscored by the politics of race. Blacks moved en masse to the Democratic Party from their traditional position in the "Party of Lincoln," partly because of Hoover's failure but also because of the inclusive rhetoric of the New Deal. Yet Roosevelt was too concerned about his bloc of southern support to accept even antilynching legislation.

Scholars have argued that the New Deal coalition did not indicate a wholesale shift in existing political loyalties, but rather that new groups such as urbanites and blacks had joined an already stable alliance to tip the competitive balance of U.S. parties. The political discourse in the United States changed not because all or even most groups changed their behavior but because new groups and issues became involved.[90]

The core of Roosevelt's winning coalition was easy to describe: "Southern white Protestants, Catholics, and non-Southern white Protestants of the lowest socioeconomic stratum together accounted for roughly three-fourths of all Americans of voting age in 1940 who thought of themselves as Democrats. By way of contrast, these three groups provided only about 40 percent of the smaller cadre of Republican identifiers."[91] Within the Democratic coalition, there were both new and old elements.

Although the Democratic Party encompassed new constituencies and addressed new issues, it retained many of its traditional supporters. The segregated "Jim Crow" South had consistently been in the Democratic column; in 1896, for example, the South's percentage support for Democrat William Jennings Bryan exceeded that of the rest of the nation by 15.3 points. Even in 1928, when Al Smith's Catholicism reduced support for the Democrats to under 50 percent for the first time, the Deep South supported the Democrats more than the border South did.[92] To the South, the Democrats were reliably the party of white supremacy and agricultural interests, while Republicans favored the industrial interests of the North.

Outside the South, the Democratic Party was the party of immigrants and Catholics. Since Andrew Jackson's day, the overwhelmingly Democratic voting patterns of Catholics had contrasted with the split vote of Protestants in the United States. The Catholic-Protestant divisions represented "not so much religious as more general ethnocultural traditions."[93] The Democratic hold on the Catholic vote was reinforced by the heavy immigration into northern cities in the last half of the nineteenth century. While the anti-Catholic Ku Klux Klan received Democratic backing in the South, it received Republican backing in the North, pushing northern Catholics decisively into the Democratic Party.

A steady base in the Democratic Party consisted of laborers and the poor. From the first party machines in the early nineteenth century to William Jennings Bryan's campaign on behalf of the depressed farm belt in 1896 to Woodrow Wilson's acceptance of labor bargaining in 1914, the Democrats had shown sympathy for the less-privileged classes. Such sympathies often were constricted by prejudice or conservatism, but the Democrats offered more hope of representation than the business-oriented Republicans. Roosevelt solidified the support of the poor and laboring classes.[94] Sundquist has written: "The party system undoubtedly reflected some degree of class before the re-alignment, but there can be little doubt that it was accentuated by the event. It was in the New Deal era that tight bonds were formed between organized labor and the Democratic Party, that ties equally close if less formal and overt were formed between business and the GOP, and that politics for the first time since 1896 sharply accented class issues."[95] Roosevelt consistently received the support of more than two-thirds of the voters of low socio-economic status.[96]

New converts to the Democratic Party included blacks and Jews. The inclusion of blacks into the New Deal coalition underscored a "multiplier effect" at work within thriving interest group politics. The Republicans received the black vote in the seventeen elections from Reconstruction to 1932. That year, Roosevelt received 35 percent of the black vote, but his black support was as low as 23 percent in Chicago and 29 percent in Cincinnati.[97] Even though Roosevelt did little to promote black interests in the South, where most blacks lived but could not vote, the black vote for him increased to 70 percent in 1936 and 1940. Migration of blacks to the North and the spillover effects of Roosevelt's many domestic programs brought blacks to the Democratic Party.

Jews, who had voted Republican since their numbers swelled during immigration around the turn of the century, turned to the Democrats as they became the more liberal party. Roosevelt got 85 percent of the Jewish vote in 1936 and 84 percent in 1940. New Deal assistance programs and Roosevelt's efforts to fight Nazism appealed to Jews, but perhaps more important was "the historic pattern of discrimination which forced or disposed Jews to oppose conservative parties."[98] The class division that split other social groups was absent in the Jewish population.

In many ways, the whole of the New Deal was greater than the sum of its parts. Political scientist Samuel Beer has argued that two long-competing visions of U.S. politics—the national idea and the democratic idea—at last came together during Roosevelt's administration. With the New Deal, the Democratic Party was able to combine its traditional concern for local, individualistic interests with a national vision. By bringing "locked-out" groups into the system, the Democrats enhanced both nation building and individual freedoms. The parts, put together, created a stronger whole. Beer quotes the French sociologist Emile Durkheim: "The image of the one who completes us becomes inseparable from ours. . . . It thus becomes an integral and permanent part of our conscience. . . ."[99]

The political genius of "interest-group liberalism"[100] was not just that it offered something to everyone, but that it created a new age of consumerism in which everyone's interest was in economic growth rather than structural change. The general good was defined as growth. The potentially divisive competition over restricted and unequally distributed resources was avoided with a general acceptance of growth as the common goal. When there was growth, everyone could get a little more. That public philosophy became a permanent part of American political discourse.

## ROOSEVELT'S FIRST REELECTION: 1936

Roosevelt's coalition and leadership were so strong that he became the only president to win more than two elections. He won four elections and served a little more than twelve years in the White House before dying in office.

Roosevelt's four electoral triumphs caused Republicans to fume about his "imperial" presidency; all they could do in response to FDR was to promote a constitutional amendment to limit presidents to two terms. But more important than this perception was the way Roosevelt shaped the American political agenda. For many people of the time, it was difficult to imagine the United States under any other leader.

It is possible that Roosevelt could have forged an even stronger liberal coalition than he did. But Roosevelt was a pragmatist above all else and alternately angered and wooed such groups as business, labor, farmers, and the military. For example, Roosevelt kept his distance from Upton Sinclair's populist campaign for governor of California in 1934. Because he threatened business interests, Sinclair was the target of a sustained personal attack by business and other conservative forces in the state in what one authority has called the first media campaign in American history. Sinclair's losing effort, the historian Greg Mitchell argued, undermined the power of reformers nationally.[101]

Roosevelt's three successful reelection drives evoked a changing response from Republicans. Roosevelt's first reelection opponent, in 1936, was Gov. Alfred M. Landon of Kansas, who strongly criticized every aspect of the New Deal. After 1936, Republican candidates did not criticize federal intervention in economic and social affairs but rather the speed and the skill of Democratic intervention. In the third election the Republicans argued that Roosevelt was a "warmonger" because he tilted toward Great Britain in World War II. The GOP argued in the third and fourth elections that Roosevelt threatened to become a "dictator" by exceeding the traditional two-term limit.

Landon was the early favorite for the Republican nomination in 1936. Sen. Charles McNary of Oregon, Sen. Arthur Vandenberg of Michigan, and *Chicago Daily News* publisher Frank Knox provided weak opposition. A Republican bolter for Theodore Roosevelt's "Bull Moose" candidacy in 1912, Landon was consistently to the left of the GOP. Historian James MacGregor Burns observed: "Landon had just the qualities of common sense, homely competence, cautious liberalism and rocklike 'soundness' that the Republicans hoped would appeal to a people tiring, it was hoped, of the antics and heroics in the White House."[102]

In 1936 the Republicans could not have stated their opposition to the popular New Deal in any stronger terms. The platform read: "America is in peril. The welfare of American men and women and the future of our youth are at stake. We dedicate ourselves to the preservation of their political liberty, their individual opportunity, and their character as free citizens, which today for the first time are threatened by government itself."[103]

The Republicans called for ending a wide range of government regulations, returning relief to state and local governments, replacing Social Security, balancing the budget, and changing tariff and currency policies. Landon's only innovation was to call for a constitutional amendment allowing the states to regulate the labor of women and children; the Supreme Court had struck down a New York minimum wage law in 1935. After Landon won the nomination on the first ballot, he selected Knox as his running mate.

The only time the two presidential candidates met was at a meeting Roosevelt called with state governors in Des Moines to discuss farm relief and a recent drought. FDR hoped to put Landon on the spot about farm relief. But Landon turned out to be the aggressor, demanding that FDR say what to tell 100,000 starving farmers in Oklahoma. FDR responded that he had some federal agencies working on programs "just as fast as the Lord will let them." When Landon said that such an answer was small consolation, Roosevelt retorted: "What more can you say to the hungry farmer, governor? The machinery will be put in gear just as fast as the Lord will let *you*."[104]

Landon's campaign possessed a lavish war chest of $9 million, benefited from the defections of Democratic stalwarts such as John Davis and Al Smith (the party's presidential nominees in 1924 and 1928) and well-coordinated campaign work by business lobbies, and engaged in smear campaigns that portrayed Social Security as a simple "pay reduction" measure and Roosevelt as physically and mentally ill. Landon also argued that New Deal spending was just another form of spoils politics, a charge Roosevelt addressed by folding postmasters into the civil service system.

The only important innovation at the Democratic convention was the repeal of the party's requirement that a candidate receive two-thirds of the delegates to win the nomination. After some arm twisting, southern delegates backed the change, but the governor of Texas wondered aloud if the change was designed for a third Roosevelt run in 1940. Roosevelt was renominated without opposition. He asked Garner to run with him a second time.

In response to Landon's GOP nomination and agitation by leaders of the left and right—including Huey Long of Louisiana, Father Charles E. Coughlin of Detroit, Dr. Francis Townsend of California (who espoused a federal pension plan for senior citizens), and the Socialist Norman Thomas of New York—President Roosevelt in his acceptance speech launched a rhetorical war against "economic royalists" who opposed his programs. He dropped the idea of a "unity" campaign in favor of a partisan ideological attack intended to gain a mandate for a variety of stalled programs rather than a personal vote of confidence.[105]

At first, Roosevelt had planned a low-key campaign of "conciliation," but when Landon got the GOP nomination he decided to wage the more aggressive campaign. After all, Landon had run an impressive nominating campaign and was thought to appeal to American pinings for governmental stability. In the early stages of the fall campaign, Roosevelt pretended not to be a partisan politician. He crisscrossed the country making "official" inspections of drought states and public works programs and delivering speeches on electrical power, conservation, and social welfare programs, among other topics. Roosevelt assigned Postmaster General James Farley the task of addressing party rifts and Republican charges of spoils.

At the end of September, Roosevelt assumed the role of partisan leader. The president answered Republican charges point by point, then lashed out at the Republicans in biting, sarcastic terms. As the campaign progressed and Roosevelt sensed a strong response from the large crowds to his attacks, the attacks became stronger. At the close of the campaign, he said:

We have not come this far without a struggle and I assure you that we cannot go further without a struggle. For 12 years, our nation was afflicted with a hear-nothing, see-nothing, do-nothing government. The nation looked to the government but the government looked away. Nine mocking years with the golden calf and three long years of the scourge! Nine crazy years at the ticker and three long years at the breadlines! Nine mad years of mirage and three long years of despair! And, my friends, powerful influences strive today to restore that kind of government with its doctrine that that government is best which is most indifferent to mankind. . . . Never before in all of our history have these forces been so united against one candidate as they stand today. They are unanimous in their hate for me—and I welcome their hatred.[106]

Especially to sophisticated campaign technicians of the modern age, a poll that predicted a big Landon victory provides some amusement. The *Literary Digest*, which had predicted past elections with accuracy, conducted a postcard poll of its readers that pointed toward a Landon landslide. But the heavy middle- and upper-class bias of the magazine's readership meant that the views of the voters on the lower rungs of the economic ladder were left out of the sample. To this day, the poll is cited as the prime example of bad survey group selection.

The failure of the *Literary Digest*'s survey pointed to the most salient aspect of the election results: the heavy class divisions among the voters. Polls showed that class divisions widened starting around the midpoint of Roosevelt's first term. The broad support Roosevelt had enjoyed because of a common economic disaster had hardened along class lines by the time of the 1936 election.

In the 1936 election, Roosevelt won 27.7 million popular votes (60.8 percent) to Landon's 16.7 million (36.5 percent). Roosevelt carried all but two of the forty-eight states, and he took 523 of the 531 electoral votes. In addition, the Senate's Democratic majority increased to 75 of 96 seats, and the House majority increased to 333 of 435 seats. Roosevelt even ran ahead of candidates—such as gubernatorial candidate Herbert Lehman of New York—who had been recruited to boost his vote totals in various states. In fact, the Democratic victory was almost too overwhelming, Roosevelt suggested, because it would encourage Democrats to fight among themselves rather than with Republicans.

President Franklin D. Roosevelt's Republican opponents during his three reelection campaigns were, from left: Gov. Alfred M. Landon of Kansas in 1936; former Democrat and business executive Wendell L. Willkie in 1940; and Gov. Thomas E. Dewey of New York in 1944.

## ROOSEVELT'S THIRD TERM: 1940

Soon after his 1936 landslide, Roosevelt tempted fate with a proposal that would have increased the size of the Supreme Court from nine to fifteen members in order to "pack" the Court with justices closer to the president's political philosophy. In 1935 and 1936, the high court had struck down important New Deal initiatives such as the Agriculture Adjustment Act, the National Recovery Administration, and the tax on food processing.

Roosevelt shrouded his proposal in statements of concern about the capacities of some of the Court's older justices. In a fireside speech, Roosevelt said the Court's failure to keep pace with the other "horses" in the "three-horse team" of the federal government constituted a "quiet crisis."[107] The elderly chief justice, Charles Evans Hughes, belied that charge with the energy he brought to the tribunal. But Roosevelt refused to compromise on the bill, and it became an executive-legislative dispute. The proposal was widely seen as a brazen power play, and by summer 1937 Congress had defeated it.

Nevertheless, President Roosevelt eventually got the judicial approval he wanted for his initiatives—what wags called "the switch in time that saved nine." The Court appeared to shift its philosophy during the court-packing affair, and, before long, enough justices had retired so that Roosevelt could put his own stamp on the Court.

Other problems awaited Roosevelt in the second term. Splits in the labor movement gave rise to violence during organizing drives, and the president responded haltingly. After his rift with business over the full range of New Deal policies, Roosevelt appeared to be drifting. Conservatives in Congress were more assertive than ever in opposing the "socialist" measures of the Roosevelt years. The only major New Deal legislation in the second term was the Fair Labor Standards Act of 1938, which abol-

ished child labor and set a minimum wage and an official rate of time-and-a-half for overtime.

As Roosevelt looked toward a third term in 1940, the widening war in Europe posed a difficult problem. Nazi Germany had invaded the Rhineland, Poland, France, Norway, Denmark, Holland, Belgium, and Luxembourg and had made alliances with Italy and the Soviet Union. Japan had invaded China. Adolf Hitler launched the Battle of Britain in the summer of 1940; all-night air raids of London came soon afterward.

British prime minister Winston Churchill desperately petitioned President Roosevelt to provide fifty naval destroyers. Britain's need for the destroyers was so great that Roosevelt balked at asking Congress for help. He reasoned that congressional action probably would take three months, and isolationists might even block action, dealing a crippling blow to Britain. After lengthy debate within the administration, Roosevelt agreed to send Churchill the destroyers as part of a "lend-lease" agreement. The United States would receive British bases in the Caribbean as part of the deal.

A favorite parlor game as the 1940 election approached was guessing whom Roosevelt might tap as his successor. Roosevelt publicly maintained that he did not want another term, but he refused to issue a definitive statement begging off the race. Despite the historic precedent against third terms, Roosevelt wanted to remain president. And to avoid the appearance of overzealousness, Roosevelt wanted the Democrats to draft him in 1940.

While the nation waited for Roosevelt to act, Vice President Garner announced his candidacy. Postmaster General Farley and Secretary of State Cordell Hull also wanted to be president, and Roosevelt gave both vague assurances of support. Roosevelt, whose relations with Garner had been soured since the court-packing episode (which Garner opposed), simply watched the vice president struggle to gain a respectable public profile. The Farley and Hull prospects withered without the help of the old master.

From a distance, Roosevelt watched state Democratic delegations declare their support. Polls showed Roosevelt's fortunes rising with the deepening European crisis. Just before the GOP convention, Roosevelt appointed Republicans Henry Stimson and Frank Knox to his cabinet. But Roosevelt did not reveal his plans for 1940, even to his closest aides. The president did not forbid aides such as Harry Hopkins to work on a draft, but he did not get involved because he wanted the Democrats to call on him and not the other way around.

At the Chicago convention, Sen. Alben Barkley told the delegates: "The president has never had, and has not today, any desire or purpose to continue in the office of president. . . . He wishes in all earnestness and sincerity to make it clear that all the delegates of this convention are free to vote for any candidate."[108] The statement was followed by an hour-long demonstration and Roosevelt's first-ballot nomination.

The convention mood turned sour, however, when Roosevelt announced that he wanted the liberal secretary of agriculture, Henry Wallace, as his running mate. The announcement disgruntled delegates who already had lined up behind other candidates. But Wallace eventually beat Alabama representative William Bankhead, his strongest opponent for the nomination.

The Republicans mounted their strongest challenge to Roosevelt in 1940, largely based on the charge that Roosevelt was moving the United States toward involvement in the world war. Several moves toward military preparedness had failed at the hands of isolationists in Congress. When Roosevelt asked for increases in defense spending after Gen. Francisco Franco's victory in Spain and Hitler's invasion of Austria in 1938, critics asserted that the president was attempting to cover up domestic failures with foreign adventures. Roosevelt pressed on, however, and Congress passed the Selective Service Act and increases in military spending in 1940.

The Republican field in 1940 included several fresh faces: Sen. Robert A. Taft of Ohio, son of the former president; District Attorney Thomas E. Dewey of New York City; and Sen. Charles L. McNary of Oregon and Sen. Arthur H. Vandenberg of Michigan who had been considered long shots for the Republican nomination in 1936. The freshest face of all was Wendell L. Willkie, a utility executive who had never run for political office. A large, affable man, former Democrat Willkie had barnstormed the country for seven years speaking in opposition to the New Deal.[109] Hundreds of "Willkie clubs" sprang up in the summer of 1940, and a number of publications, including Henry Luce's *Time* magazine, chronicled Willkie's career and encouraged the Willkie groundswell. Despite concern about Willkie's lack of political experience, which led to a "stop Willkie" movement, the Indianan won a sixth-ballot nomination by acclamation. Senator McNary, the Republicans' Senate floor leader, reluctantly accepted the vice-presidential nomination.

Traveling thirty thousand miles in thirty-four states, Willkie gave some 540 speeches. By the time his campaign ended, his already husky voice had turned hoarse. The Republicans spent lavishly and organized grassroots clubs for Willkie across the country. Charges against Roosevelt of managerial incompetence, "warmongering," and imperial ambitions punctuated the Willkie effort. A dramatic moment came when labor leader John L. Lewis called on workers to back Willkie.

After a period of strictly "presidential" behavior, Roosevelt took to the campaign trail with partisan vigor. He answered Willkie's warmongering charges with a promise never to involve the United States in "foreign wars" (which left Roosevelt free to respond to a direct attack).

The alienation of some Democratic and independent voters was symbolized by Vice President Garner, who did not even vote. Roosevelt won, but by the slimmest popular vote margin of any race since 1912. He received 27.3 million popular votes (54.7 percent) to Willkie's 22.3 million (44.8 percent). The electoral vote tally was 449–82.

## THE WAR AND ITS LEGACY: 1944

Roosevelt's third term and fourth election were dominated by the Second World War. Japan attacked U.S. bases at Pearl Harbor, Hawaii, on December 7, 1941. The president, speaking before Congress, declared the date of the surprise attack "a day that will live in infamy." Congress shook off its isolationist inclinations and declared war. A few days after Pearl Harbor, Germany and Italy declared war on the United States, confronting the nation with a two-front war.

The war did for the economy what the New Deal, by itself, could not: it brought economic prosperity. The number of unemployed workers fell from eight million to one million between 1940 and 1944. The boom brought seven million more people, half of them women, into the job market. Inflation, worker shortages, and occasional shortages in raw materials posed problems for wartime agencies. The number of U.S. families paying taxes quadrupled, and by 1945 tax revenues were twenty times their 1940 level. Budget deficits reached new heights.[110]

The fighting in Europe and Asia was grim for the first two years of the president's new term. Isolationist sentiment again built up in Congress, with the Midwest proving the region most resistant to Roosevelt's foreign policy. Criticism of how the Roosevelt administration was managing U.S. participation in the wars on both fronts was rampant. The administration won key congressional votes on the war but faced stubborn resistance on domestic measures. In the 1942 midterm elections, the Republicans gained ten seats in the Senate and forty-seven seats in the House—a major repudiation of Roosevelt.

After several setbacks, the Allied forces won impressive victories. Roosevelt and Churchill worked together closely. Allied forces, led by Gen. Dwight Eisenhower, routed the Axis powers in North Africa in 1942. The Soviet Union beat back a Nazi assault on Stalingrad in the winter of 1942–1943. The Allies took over Italy in 1943 and struggled with the Nazis in France. In September 1944, British and American troops entered Germany. In the Pacific war, American offensives secured Australia in 1942 and the Philippines in 1944.

Despite the bitter opposition that prevailed through much of his third term, Roosevelt had no trouble winning a fourth term in 1944. The Allies found greater success on the battlefield and on the sea, and the nation did not appear willing to risk untested leadership to prosecute the war. The Republicans turned to the governor of New York, Thomas Dewey. Willkie wanted another shot at the White House, and his best-selling book *One World* put him in the public eye, but old-line conservatives blamed him for the 1940 election defeat. Governors John Bricker of Ohio and Harold Stassen of Minnesota and Gen. Douglas MacArthur were the other hopefuls.

Dewey's primary victories over Willkie in the Wisconsin, Nebraska, and Oregon primaries ended Willkie's public career. Dewey was too far in front to stop. At the convention he won a nearly unanimous first-ballot nomination after Bricker and Stassen dropped out. After Gov. Earl Warren of California refused the vice-presidential nomination, Bricker accepted it.

The party platform extolled the virtues of free enterprise but did not criticize the concept of the New Deal and even made bids for the votes of blacks and women. In his acceptance speech Dewey criticized "stubborn men grown old and tired and quarrelsome in office."[111]

The 1944 election marked the early resistance of the South to the modern Democratic Party. Roosevelt was a shoo-in for the nomination, but southerners wanted a replacement for Wallace as vice president, restoration of the two-thirds nominating rule, and a platform declaration of white supremacy. Dissatisfied southerners threatened to bolt the party in November, but when the party adopted only a vague civil rights plank in its platform, southern discontent dissipated. The rest of the platform called for an internationalist thrust in foreign policy and further New Deal-style reforms domestically.

Roosevelt expressed support for Wallace but said he would allow the convention to pick his running mate. Wallace gave a stirring convention speech but disturbed conservatives with his stand against the poll tax and for equal opportunity for all "regardless of race or sex." Sen. Harry S. Truman of Missouri, who had won fame as a critic of defense spending, beat Wallace for the vice-presidential nomination on the second ballot.

The Democratic campaign was dominated by references to the need for wartime unity and reminders of the Republican rule under Hoover. One leaflet bore the words "Lest We Forget" and a photograph of an unemployed man selling apples in front of a "Hoover Club"; an inset photograph showed Dewey conferring with former president Hoover. The Republicans spent nearly as much money in 1944 as they had in the record-setting 1936 election.

Roosevelt won with 25.6 million popular votes (53.4 percent) to Dewey's 22.0 million (45.9 percent). The electoral vote was 432-99. But President Roosevelt, who reshaped U.S. politics at all levels, did not have the opportunity to see the end of the war or to participate in the making of the postwar world. On April 12, 1945, less than two months after his fourth inauguration, he collapsed while sitting for a portrait in Warm Springs, Georgia, and died a few hours later.

## THE TRUMAN PRESIDENCY: 1948

The shock of President Roosevelt's death was perhaps greatest for the former haberdasher and machine politician who succeeded him. Truman had been a last-minute choice as FDR's running mate the previous year, and he never became a part of Roosevelt's inner circle. Truman did not know about the most important military program of the age—the Manhattan Project, which, in a race with the Nazis, was developing a nuclear bomb in the secrecy of the brand-new town of Oak Ridge, Tennessee.

Truman also faced a problem of stature. Roosevelt had done nothing less than redefine the presidency in his twelve years in office. He not only effected a partisan realignment in U.S. politics, but he changed the very scope of government activity. As would become clear during the Eisenhower presidency, even Republicans had come to accept, grudgingly, the notion that the government ought to play an active role in stimulating the economy and addressing the needs of specific constituency groups.

Another problem facing Truman: many people could not fathom a presidency without Roosevelt. One member of the White House staff said later: "It was all so sudden, I had completely forgotten about Mr. Truman. Stunned, I realized that I simply couldn't comprehend the presidency as something separate from Roosevelt. The presidency, the White House, the war, our lives—they were all Roosevelt."[112] Other aides could not bring themselves to call Truman "Mr. President," as if so doing would dishonor the late president.

Truman's personality could not have presented a greater contrast to that of Roosevelt. Plain-speaking, blunt, middle-class, midwestern, high school educated, wheeling-and-dealing, and surrounded by old pals from the Pendergast machine of Missouri (the Democratic organization that dominated politics in the state), Truman offended people who had been accustomed to the charisma of Roosevelt. Truman's wife, Bess, also paled in comparison to the dynamic, more public Eleanor Roosevelt as first lady. Nevertheless, Truman showed absolute loyalty to the New Deal, but that would never be enough for many old Roosevelt hands and a nation entering a difficult period of postwar readjustment.

By the time the 1948 election neared, Truman was in grave political shape. He brought former president Hoover back from exile for special projects—one of the many ways he rankled the sensibilities of former Roosevelt aides and Mrs. Roosevelt. Truman also professed a desire to "keep my feet on the ground" and avoid the "crackpots and lunatic fringe" that had surrounded FDR.[113] Toward that end he got rid of Commerce Secretary Henry Wallace and others. The independent journalist I. F. Stone wrote of Truman's personnel moves: "The little nameplates outside the little doors . . . began to change. In Justice,

Treasury, Commerce and elsewhere, the New Dealers began to be replaced by the kind of men one was accustomed to meeting in county court-houses."[114]

The politics of postwar adjustment was difficult. The Republican Eightieth Congress, elected in 1946, sought to dismantle many New Deal programs, and it frustrated anti-inflation efforts. Truman, then, had to duel with Congress, vetoing 250 bills (eleven vetoes were overridden). Tentative civil rights initiatives disgruntled the South. Labor unrest was on the rise. Truman's efforts to "contain" Soviet geopolitical ambitions not only created splits among Democrats but also brought attacks from Republican isolationists. And to make matters worse, Truman was said to have performed inadequately at Potsdam, the conference of World War II victors held in the summer of 1945 that established many geographic borders in Europe.

The situation was so bad that Roosevelt's own son promoted General Eisenhower and Supreme Court Justice William O. Douglas for a 1948 run for the Democratic nomination against Truman. Truman, in other words, was doing a good job antagonizing both the left and the right. In August 1948 the Democratic convention appeared to reflect a dangerously polarized nation. The convention began with a feeling of desperation when Eisenhower and Douglas refused to run. Then a "states' rights" plank offered by southern delegates was defeated, and, after strong speeches by Minneapolis mayor Hubert H. Humphrey and others, a strong northern civil rights plank passed. The party's New Deal and northern machine elements decided that southern defection would be less damaging than northern defection.

Defect is just what some southerners did. The "Dixiecrats," under the leadership of South Carolina's governor J. Strom Thurmond, left the convention to conduct their own fall campaign. Thurmond's candidacy ran under the Democratic Party label in four states (Alabama, Louisiana, Mississippi, and South Carolina) and under the States' Rights Democratic Party elsewhere in the South. Meanwhile, the party's left wing, behind Henry Wallace, protested Truman's Marshall Plan (a multi-million-dollar program to rebuild the economies of western Europe), military buildup, and confrontational stance toward the Soviet Union. It, too, ran its own fall campaign under the banner of the Progressive Citizens of America (the Progressive Party).

The seeds of Dixie defection were planted long before the convention. In 1947 the President's Committee on Civil Rights issued a report calling for the protection of the rights of all minorities. It was just the kind of spark southern segregationists needed to begin a dump-Truman drive and to organize their own campaign in 1948. The Southern Governors Conference in March 1948 recommended that southern states send delegates to the Democratic convention and electors to the electoral college who would refuse to back a pro–civil rights candidate.

As political scientist V. O. Key Jr. has shown, the degree of resistance to civil rights in southern states depended on two basic factors: the proportion of blacks in the population and the strength of the two-party system. Key argued that the existence of a large black population led to stronger Democratic measures against black enfranchisement and led whites to support the Democratic Party in greater numbers. "To them [the whites in such districts], a single Negro vote threatened the whole caste system."[115] Alabama, Louisiana, Mississippi, and South Carolina ended up voting for the Thurmond ticket. Other southern states found broader economic and political issues more compelling than race and voted for Truman.[116]

Many of FDR's old political allies eventually got behind the new man, but Truman's election prospects looked bleak. Some support was grudging—Mrs. Roosevelt offered a straightforward endorsement only to rebut newspaper reports that she favored the Republicans. While the Democratic Party was badly fractured, the Republican Party united behind Dewey.

Dewey, who had been the 1944 GOP candidate, survived a large field in 1948 to become the nominee once again. Senator Taft of Ohio was the main threat, but his isolationism and dull public demeanor were liabilities. The most spirited opposition came from Governor Stassen of Minnesota, who appealed to the more liberal and internationalist wing of the party. An anathema to party bosses, Stassen proved his strength in a series of primary victories. Other candidates or potential convention contenders included Generals Eisenhower and MacArthur, Governor Warren, and Senator Vandenberg. Polls showed all of the Republicans but Taft beating Truman.[117]

Dewey gained the preconvention momentum he needed with an impressive primary victory over Stassen in Oregon. He spent three weeks in the state, while Stassen frittered away his time and resources with a hopeless challenge to Taft in the Ohio primary. Dewey was especially tough in a primary debate with Stassen about communism. With these successes, as well as his impressive organizational strength and mastery over convention mechanics, Dewey won the presidential nomination on the third ballot. Warren was selected the vice-presidential nominee.

Dewey was part of a new breed of Republican leaders—pragmatic and accepting of the New Deal and the international role that the United States would play in the postwar era. He expressed support for the basic tenets of postwar liberalism, including Social Security, civil rights, and the United Nations. In the 1948 campaign, Dewey planned to put himself above the slashing attack style of President Truman. His constant calls for national unity—spoken in a baritone voice and perfect English—expressed broad public acceptance of the vast changes in U.S. politics over the previous twenty years.

From the beginning of the campaign, the media and professional politicians gave Truman little chance of retaining the White House. Early polls showed Dewey with such a strong lead that pollsters simply stopped surveying voters. But the polls failed because of a bias in the way the questions were asked and a presumption that the large undecided vote would cast their ballots in the same way as the rest of the population, when it in fact heavily favored Truman.[118]

Dewey was so certain of victory that he ran as if he were the

In 1948 pollsters and the media fed Republican candidate Thomas E. Dewey's overconfidence in his campaign to unseat President Harry S. Truman. Truman had the last laugh on the press and his opponent.

incumbent. He made a series of bland, almost diplomatic statements rather than energetic campaign speeches. Dewey appeared confident that his advice to one audience—"Vote your own interests"—would attract an amalgam of disaffected groups. Never even mentioning the president's name, Dewey calmly canvassed the country and just smiled when people called him "President Dewey." Dewey was careful to avoid the overaggressive posture that he thought had ruined his 1944 campaign against Roosevelt. He even made some initial cabinet and policy decisions.

Truman's strategy from the beginning was simply to mobilize the New Deal coalition. The biggest danger was apathy, he and campaign aide Clark Clifford reasoned, so the best strategy was to give the voters a reason to go to the polling booths. Since the Democrats were the majority party, they had to concentrate mainly on getting their longtime supporters to the polls.

Truman ran a scrappy and blunt underdog campaign that could have been mistaken for an outsider's effort. Truman was the president, but he ran against the Washington establishment. Crisscrossing the nation on a whistle-stop train tour, Truman traveled some 31,000 miles and spoke before six million people. He turned his record of vetoes into an asset, claiming that the "do-nothing" Republican Eightieth Congress made him do it. He assailed the conservative Republican record on inflation, housing, labor, farm issues, and foreign affairs. The president drew large crowds—sometimes many times the size of Dewey's crowds—but he was virtually the only political professional who thought he would win.

Truman himself predicted in October that he had 229 solid electoral votes to Dewey's 109 and Thurmond's 9; 189 votes, he

said, could go either way. The best anyone would say about the Truman campaign was that its fighting spirit improved the Democrats' chances to win the Senate. Truman answered the Republicans' claims of liberalism and reformism by criticizing the GOP for obstructing his policies. Truman's outsider taunt was constant: "that no-account, do-nothing, Republican 80th Congress!"[119]

Despite the *Chicago Tribune*'s now-famous headline— "Dewey Defeats Truman"—President Truman prevailed. Early returns put Truman in front, but it was expected that the later-reporting western states would give Dewey the win. When California and Ohio went into the Truman column mid-morning on Wednesday, Dewey conceded defeat.

Considering the Democratic defections, Truman's appeal was widespread. He won twenty-eight states with 24.11 million votes (49.51 percent) and might have won more in the South and North with a united party—as it was, Thurmond won 22 percent of the vote in the South. Dewey won 21.97 million votes (45.12 percent), and Thurmond polled 1.17 million votes (2.40 percent). Henry Wallace won some 1.16 million votes (2.38 percent) but no electoral votes. Wallace's candidacy may have cost Truman New York, Michigan, and Maryland. Yet Wallace may have done Truman a favor by freeing him from the taint of being the most liberal candidate in a time when the electorate was weary of liberalism. Particularly because the Republicans did not have a midwesterner on their ticket and talked about cutting back agricultural subsidies, farmers felt safer with Truman. In all, Truman won 303 electoral votes, Dewey 189, and Thurmond 39.

The Democratic defections may have helped Truman by

making him the candidate of the center. The Wallace campaign freed the president from suspicions on the right, and the Thurmond defection strengthened Truman's more liberal northern constituency. In addition, the defections may have inspired Democratic voters to turn out in larger numbers than they would have had victory seemed certain.

In the end the election mostly confirmed long-held partisan allegiances. In the words of political scientist Angus Campbell and his colleagues, it was a "maintaining" election: "The electorate responded to current elements in politics very much in terms of its existing partisan loyalties. Apparently very little of the political landscape attracted strong feeling in that year. But what feeling there was seemed to be governed largely by antecedent attachments to one of the two major parties."[120]

## "I LIKE IKE": 1952

Truman's political fortunes worsened during his second term to the extent that he decided belatedly against making a bid for the Democratic nomination. In 1952, for the first time in twenty-four years, neither party had an incumbent president as its nominee.

The Democrats suffered from a weariness that is bound to affect any party that has been in power for twenty years. Problems and opponents' frustrated ambitions were piling up, and in Dwight Eisenhower the Republicans were able to recruit a candidate with universal appeal who was coveted by both parties. The national mood in the years before the 1952 election was sour. The nation was tiring of price controls, recurring scandals among members of the White House staff, and the Korean War, which the Truman administration had begun in 1950 but did not appear interested in either winning or pulling out U.S. troops. The Republicans asked for a chance to "clean up the mess" in Washington and punctuated their appeals with the question: "Had enough?"

The Truman administration had met with repeated frustration in dealing with Congress. On civil rights, tariffs, taxes, labor reform, and the sensationalized question of communist sympathizers in the government, Truman had had to cope with a stubborn Democratic Congress, which, in turn, became more stubborn after Republican gains in the 1950 midterm elections. When Truman seized control of the steel mills because he said the steelworkers' strike threatened the nation's security, he was rebuffed by the Supreme Court.[121]

Truman's biggest problems, however, had concerned cronyism and war. Republicans in congressional investigations and on the stump had hammered away at conflict-of-interest scandals in Truman's administration, creating nationwide sentiment to "clean up" Washington with a new administration. Meanwhile, the United States was mired in a stalemate in Korea—a distant war that was being fought inconclusively under the aegis of the United Nations, with uncertain goals (was it to protect South Korea or to defeat North Korea as well?) and uncertain enemies (was the People's Republic of China an opponent as well as North Korea?). Truman evoked ire with his firing of General

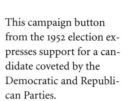

This campaign button from the 1952 election expresses support for a candidate coveted by the Democratic and Republican Parties.

MacArthur, who wanted to take the war into China, and with the slow movement toward a settlement. Just as the nation had tired of sacrifices in World War I under Woodrow Wilson, it had tired of sacrifices under Truman.

General Eisenhower—who had just left the presidency of Columbia University to take charge of the forces of the North Atlantic Treaty Organization (NATO)—was recruited by Republicans to run when it appeared that other GOP candidates lacked the national appeal to win the White House. Senator Taft was running again, but his isolationism was considered a liability in the postwar age of internationalism. Stassen, MacArthur, and Warren were other likely Republican candidates.

Eisenhower's popular appeal was revealed when he attracted 50.4 percent of the vote in the New Hampshire primary to Taft's 38.7 percent and Stassen's 7.1 percent. Eisenhower performed well in the northeast area primaries, and Taft generally performed well in the Midwest. A write-in campaign for Eisenhower almost upset Stassen in his home state of Minnesota.

When the GOP convention finally met in Chicago, Taft had the lead in convention delegates. In crucial delegate-seating contests, many of them played out on national television, Eisenhower defeated Taft and won the right to seat pro-Eisenhower insurgents from the South. Taft had relied on the old strategy of mobilizing state machines, but such tactics looked unsavory on television. Eisenhower had undisputed popular appeal, and he won on the first ballot after his early lead turned into a stampede.

Eisenhower selected Sen. Richard Nixon of California as his running mate. The thirty-nine-year-old conservative had won national recognition with his activities on the controversial House Committee on Un-American Activities, which investigated the alleged Soviet ties of Alger Hiss, a former State Department official. Hiss served time for a perjury conviction.

The Democrats moved haltingly toward putting together a ticket. Truman did not announce his decision to stay out of the race until April, after two primary losses. Sen. Estes Kefauver of Tennessee, who had gained fame with his televised hearings on organized crime, ran an aggressive primary campaign and entered the convention with the lead in delegates. Other candidates included Gov. Averell Harriman of New York, Vice President Alben Barkley, Sen. Robert Kerr of Oklahoma, and Sen. Richard Russell of Georgia.

The eventual nominee was Gov. Adlai Stevenson of Illinois, grandson of Grover Cleveland's second vice president. Stevenson had had experience in the Navy and State departments before running for governor. President Truman had privately recruited Stevenson for the race—at first unsuccessfully. Then Truman and Illinois backers set up a draft movement for Stevenson, which the governor disavowed until the last minute. Kefauver was the early leader in convention balloting, but Stevenson, always close, pulled into the lead on the third ballot.

Stevenson's campaign was an eloquent call to arms for liberals and reformers. Years later Democrats would recall that the campaign had inspired the generation that would take the reins of power under John F. Kennedy in 1960. Democratic politics at all levels in the 1950s and 1960s would revolve around battles between party regulars and reformers.

Stevenson did not have a chance, however, against the popular Eisenhower. Some southern states bolted the Democratic Party, and the Republicans hammered away at the misdeeds of the Democratic administration under Truman. Such issues as the 1949 communist revolution in China ("Who lost China?"), the protracted Korean War, administration corruption, and the alleged communist infiltration of the government captured the nation's attention more than Stevenson's oratory.

More than anything, however, the desire for party change rather than policy change determined the election. The Republican evocation of the theme of "Corruption, Korea, and Communism" did not challenge the policies that the Democrats offered the nation as much as the way they executed those policies. Eisenhower was a proven administrator and was free of the taint of everyday U.S. politics. Stevenson was a reformer himself, but his campaign had the conspicuous backing of President Truman. Stevenson's divorce and his public support of Hiss were constant if only vaguely stated issues.

The campaign's biggest controversy developed when newspaper reports alleged that Nixon had used a "secret fund" provided by California millionaires to pay for travel and other expenses. To a Democratic Party weary of charges of impropriety, the revelation offered an opportunity to accuse Nixon of being beholden to special interests. Nixon admitted the existence of the fund but maintained that he used the money solely for travel and that his family did not accept personal gifts.

Nixon originally reacted to the story by asserting that it was a communist smear. When Eisenhower would not publicly back his running mate, speculation developed that Ike would ask Nixon to leave the ticket—and the Republican *New York Herald Tribune* openly called for him to drop out. When Nixon decided to confront his accusers with a television speech, campaign aides told him he would be dropped if the public reaction was not favorable.

Nixon's speech was remarkable. He denied any impropriety and stated that the Stevenson campaign was hypocritical in its criticisms because it had similar funds. More specifically, Nixon

denied that he had accepted such gifts as a mink coat for his wife, Pat; he said that his wife wore a "Republican cloth coat." He acknowledged, however, receiving a pet dog named Checkers from a Texas admirer: "And you know, the kids love that dog, and I just want to say this right now, that regardless of what they say about it, we're going to keep it."[122] His folksy message and appeal for telegrams created a wave of sympathy, which Eisenhower rewarded with a pledge of support. The crisis was over.

In a personal victory—surveys showed that the nation still favored the programs of the New Deal but simply wanted to put the cronyism, sacrifices, and Korean War behind it—Eisenhower swept to the White House. Ike won the entire North and West, parts of the South, and some border states—a total of thirty-nine states to Stevenson's nine. His 442 electoral votes and 33.9 million popular votes (55.1 percent) overwhelmed Stevenson's 89 electoral votes and 27.3 million popular votes (44.4 percent). The election of 1956 would bring more of the same.

## EISENHOWER'S REELECTION: 1956

Despite his age (sixty-six) and having had a heart attack in 1955, Eisenhower was the strong favorite to be the GOP nominee for another term. Close cooperation with the Democratic congressional leadership and a "hidden-hand" leadership style seemed to comport with the electorate's wishes for normalcy.[123] The White House staff was ably run by the chief of staff, Sherman Adams, and foreign policy was supervised by Secretary of State John Foster Dulles. The genius of Eisenhower's management style was his use of aides as "lightning rods" for unpopular policies.

Even without lightning rods, Eisenhower probably would have fared well. The economy was booming, and Eisenhower had quickly brought the Korean War to a close. His nuclear policy gave the nation a "bigger bang for the buck" in defense spending and kept the troop requirements low. Federal housing and highway programs gave impetus to suburbanization, now considered part of the middle-class American Dream. Issues that would in the future become divisive, such as civil rights, were muffled.

The only unsettled Republican issue was whether Nixon would again be the vice-presidential candidate. Eisenhower offered him a cabinet post, and Stassen mounted a campaign to replace Nixon with Massachusetts governor Christian Herter. After some hesitation, however, Eisenhower stood by his controversial running mate.

In the Democratic camp, Kefauver challenged Stevenson for the right to face Eisenhower in the fall. After impressive primary victories in New Hampshire and Minnesota for Kefauver, the Stevenson campaign fought back with a string of primary wins in states as varied as California, Florida, and Oregon.

Former president Truman endorsed New York governor Harriman—not Stevenson—at the opening of the Democratic convention. A variety of other favorite sons entered the race. But with the help of Eleanor Roosevelt, Stevenson was able to win the nomination for a second time. Stevenson won on the first ballot.

Stevenson left the vice-presidential slot open to the convention delegates. Kefauver, after battling Senators John Kennedy, Albert A. Gore of Tennessee, and Hubert Humphrey and New York mayor Robert Wagner, eventually won. The open contest highlighted the future national political potential of Kennedy, who, according to later accounts, mainly intended not to win the second spot on the ticket but to gain visibility for a 1960 presidential run.

The campaign was bereft of real issues. Eisenhower's campaigning was a tempered appeal to American values and bipartisan consensus. Nixon was left the job of hacking away at the opposition; he called Stevenson "Adlai the Appeaser" and a "Ph.D. graduate of Dean Acheson's cowardly College of Communist Containment."[124] Overall, however, the campaign was an example of what James David Barber has called "the politics of conciliation," with little conflict or desire for change.

Whether or not the electorate was "asleep," as frustrated critics charged, Eisenhower nailed down another strong victory. He won forty-two states, 457 electoral votes, and 35.6 million popular votes (57.4 percent), compared with Stevenson's six states, 73 electoral votes, and 26.0 million popular votes (42.0 percent). In an unprecedented development, however, both houses of Congress went to the opposition.

## KENNEDY AND THE POLITICS OF CHANGE: 1960

The periodic national desire for change came at the expense of the Republicans in 1960, when Sen. John F. Kennedy of Massachusetts became the youngest person ever elected president by defeating Vice President Richard Nixon.

The presidential election was foreshadowed by the 1958 midterm election, when the Democrats made impressive gains in Congress. An economic recession and generational politics created the first major shift toward liberalism since the administration of Franklin Roosevelt. The "Class of '58" decisively changed the discourse of U.S. politics. After the election the Democrats held 64 of 98 Senate seats and 283 of 435 House seats, and thirty-five states had Democratic governors. The time appeared ripe for reopening issues that had long been stifled such as civil rights, urban problems, and education.[125]

The 1960 Democratic field was dominated by senators—Kennedy, Lyndon B. Johnson of Texas, Hubert Humphrey of Minnesota, and Stuart Symington of Missouri. Each had important advantages and disadvantages. Kennedy was from a wealthy and politically minded family, but his Catholicism and undistinguished Senate record were liabilities. Johnson was a masterful majority leader, but no southerner had won the White House since James K. Polk in 1844. Humphrey was popular in the Midwest, but he lacked financial backing and was considered too loquacious and liberal. Symington had a strong Senate record and Harry Truman's backing, but he was considered colorless, and Truman's backing carried liabilities.

In the 1960 presidential campaign John F. Kennedy worked hard to win the West Virginia primary. His victory in this overwhelmingly Protestant state blunted the issue of his Catholicism and set him on the way to a first-ballot nomination.

Former Illinois governor Adlai Stevenson, the party's nominee in 1952 and 1956, stood on the sidelines, hoping that a convention deadlock or draft movement would finally bring him a ticket to the White House. Early speculation was that the convention would be deadlocked and a compromise candidate would have to emerge. It appeared likely that the nomination would go to Symington, Johnson, Humphrey, or to one of the two senior candidates, Stevenson and Kefauver; the other candidates were good bets for the vice-presidential slot.

Kennedy presented the most intriguing candidacy. He was the son of Joseph P. Kennedy, the millionaire who had been Franklin Roosevelt's ambassador to Britain before their bitter break over U.S. involvement in World War II. John Kennedy also was an Ivy League graduate (of Harvard University), a war hero (described in the book *P.T. 109*), and a Pulitzer Prize winner (for *Profiles in Courage*). With an experienced campaign staff, he had won an overwhelming reelection to the Senate in 1958. Moreover, he had been planning a run for the White House for years.

There were Kennedy skeptics, however. No Catholic except Alfred Smith had been a major-party nominee, and Smith's bitter loss and the anti-Catholic sentiments he aroused in 1928 made political professionals wary of naming another Catholic. Some considered Kennedy, at age forty-three, to be too young.

Others focused on the influence of Joseph Kennedy, who had bankrolled his son's political career.[126] Truman's comment captured the crux of Kennedy's liabilities: "It's not the Pope I'm afraid of, it's the Pop."[127]

To address the doubts, Kennedy entered political primaries that would enable him to demonstrate vote-getting ability and to confront the religion problem. The two key primaries were Wisconsin and West Virginia. In Wisconsin, Kennedy would answer the charge that he was too conservative. But the Kennedy strategists were divided about whether he should oppose Senator Humphrey of neighboring Minnesota. Wisconsin's growing independence in party politics eventually convinced them, however, that it would present a low risk in return for the possibility of beating Humphrey in his native region. In West Virginia, Kennedy would attempt to blunt the religion issue by attracting the votes of an overwhelmingly Protestant electorate.

In the end, Kennedy defeated Humphrey in Wisconsin. Kennedy's impressive campaign treasury enabled him to staff offices in eight of the ten congressional districts in the state; Humphrey had only two offices. Humphrey maintained that the defeat stemmed from crossover Republican Catholic votes and was therefore illegitimate. (Most of the state's Catholics, who made up 31 percent of the population, belonged to the GOP.) But to Kennedy and many political observers, it was still an important victory.

Humphrey wanted to even the score in West Virginia. If Humphrey had quit the campaign and left Kennedy with no opponents, as many advised him to do, a Kennedy victory would have attracted little attention.[128] But Kennedy was able to use the Appalachian state as a way to deflect the religion issue as well as the "can't win" problem. Kennedy had a thorough organization in West Virginia, and he worked hard. He had commissioned polls in the state as far back as 1958 in anticipation of the presidential race.

Kennedy's handling of the religion question in the primaries was shrewd and would be repeated in the fall campaign. He framed the question as one of tolerance—which put Humphrey on the defensive since he had never tried to exploit the religion issue. Kennedy had his campaign workers plant questions about how his religious beliefs would affect his loyalty to the nation, to which the candidate replied with a stock answer: "When any man stands on the steps of the Capitol and takes the oath of office as president, he is swearing to uphold the separation of church and state; he puts one hand on the Bible and raises the other hand to God as he takes the oath. And if he breaks the oath, he is not only committing a crime against the Constitution, for which the Congress can impeach him—but he is committing a sin against God."[129]

Kennedy's direct confrontation of the religion issue worked to his benefit. Kennedy had the money to get his message across: his television expenditures alone in the state totaled $34,000, while Humphrey had only $25,000 for the whole primary campaign in West Virginia.[130] Early polls gave Humphrey wide leads, and interviews elicited strong reservations about Kennedy's

Catholicism. As the commercials aired and the primary neared, the lead became smaller, and voters privately said they would vote for Kennedy.

JFK, as he asked headline writers to call him instead of the youthful-sounding "Jack," easily won the primary. He was on his way to a first-ballot nomination.

The Kennedy campaign staffers managed the Democratic convention with consummate skill. Had they failed to gain a majority on the first ballot, pressure might have developed for another candidate. But the Kennedy team efficiently lobbied delegations to augment support; the vice-presidential slot was vaguely offered to several politicians. In the end, Lyndon Johnson was the surprise choice for running mate. Even Kennedy supporters had doubts about Johnson, but the selection of the southerner was a classic ticket-balancing move.[131]

Central to Kennedy's winning campaign was his younger brother Robert F. Kennedy. A former counsel to Republican senator Joseph McCarthy, Robert developed into the consummate political operative. He was JFK's confidant, chief strategist, delegate counter, fund-raiser, taskmaster, and persuader. Biographer Arthur M. Schlesinger Jr. wrote that Robert Kennedy's strength "lay in his capacity to address a specific situation, to assemble an able staff, to inspire and flog them into exceptional deeds, and to prevail through sheer force of momentum."[132]

Vice President Richard Nixon was the overwhelming choice for the Republican nomination. Nelson A. Rockefeller, elected governor of New York in 1958, was a liberal alternative, but he announced in 1959 that he would not run. There was a brief surge for Rockefeller when he criticized the party and its "leading candidate," but meetings with Nixon settled the differences. Some conservatives were disgruntled with Nixon, but their efforts for Sen. Barry Goldwater of Arizona would have to wait until 1964.

Nixon selected United Nations Ambassador Henry Cabot Lodge as his running mate, and the party platform and rhetoric stressed the need for experience in a dangerous world. Nixon promised to continue President Dwight Eisenhower's policies. He attempted to portray Kennedy as an inexperienced upstart, even though he was Kennedy's senior by only four years and the two had entered Congress the same year. Nixon led in the polls at the traditional Labor Day start of the fall campaign.

Kennedy's campaign was based on a promise to "get the nation moving again" after eight years of calm Republican rule. Specifically, he assured voters that he would lead the nation out of a recession. The gross national product increased at a rate of only 2.25 percent annually between 1955 and 1959. Economists puzzled over the simultaneously high unemployment and high inflation rates.[133] Kennedy repeatedly called for two related changes in national policy: pump up the economy and increase defense spending dramatically.

The Democrat faced up to the religion issue again with an eloquent speech before the Greater Houston Ministerial Association, and he attracted attention from civil rights leaders when he offered moral and legal support to the Reverend Martin

Luther King Jr. after King was arrested for taking part in a sit-in at an Atlanta restaurant. While Kennedy appealed to the party's more liberal and moderate wing, Johnson toured the South to appeal to regional pride and to assuage fears about an activist government.

The high point of the campaign came on September 26, 1960, when the candidates debated on national television before seventy million viewers. Kennedy was well rested and tanned; he had spent the week before the debate with friends and associates. Nixon was tired from two solid weeks of campaigning; he had spent the preparation period by himself. Their appearances alone greatly influenced the outcome of the debates.

Kennedy's main objective had been simply to look relaxed and "up to" the presidency. He had little to lose. Nixon was always confident of his debating skills, and he performed well in the give-and-take of the debate. But the rules of debating—the way "points" are allocated—are not the same for formal debating and televised encounters. Kennedy's managers prepared their candidate better for the staging of the debate. Nixon's five-o'clock shadow reinforced the cartoon image of him as darkly sinister. As a result of all these factors, polls of radio listeners found that Nixon had "won" the debate, but polls of the more numerous television viewers found that Kennedy had "won." Historian Theodore H. White wrote: "It was the picture image that had done it—and in 1960 it was television that had won the nation away from sound to images, and that was that."[134]

While Kennedy called for a more activist and imaginative approach to world problems, Nixon stressed the candidates' similarities so much that their differences paled into insignificance. Kennedy called for a crusade to eliminate want and to confront tyranny. Nixon responded: "I can subscribe completely to the spirit that Sen. Kennedy has expressed tonight."[135] With ideology an unimportant part of the debate, the images of personal character the candidates were able to project gained in importance.

The candidates held three more debates, addressing such issues as Fidel Castro's Cuba, whether the United States should defend the Chinese offshore islands of Quemoy and Matsu in the event of a military strike by China, and relations with Nikita Khrushchev's Soviet Union. None of the debates had the effect of the first, which neutralized Nixon's quasi-incumbency advantage. Nor was Nixon greatly helped by President Eisenhower, who did not campaign for his protégé until late in the campaign.

The election results were so close that Nixon did not concede his defeat until the afternoon of the day after the election. After a vacation in Florida and Nassau, Nixon returned to Washington on November 19 to consider a series of charges that voter fraud had cost him the election. A shift of between eleven thousand and thirteen thousand votes in a total of five or six states could have given Nixon the electoral vote triumph. Nixon said he decided against demanding a recount because it would take "at least a year and a half" and would throw the federal government into turmoil.[136]

When the electoral college voted, Kennedy won 303 electoral votes to Nixon's 219. Democratic senator Harry F. Byrd of Virginia attracted 15 electoral votes. Kennedy won twenty-three states to Nixon's twenty-six. (Six Alabama electors and all eight Mississippi electors, elected as "unpledged Democrats," as well as one Republican elector from Oklahoma, cast their votes for Byrd.) The overall popular vote went 34.2 million for Kennedy and 34.1 million for Nixon. The margin was about one-tenth of 1 percent, or 115,000 votes. Moreover, the margins in many states were very close. Kennedy won Illinois by 8,858 votes and Texas by 46,242 votes. Despite statements that the religion question would hurt Kennedy, it probably helped him by mobilizing Catholics on his behalf. Gallup polls showed that 78 percent of Catholics voted for JFK. Although Catholics were a traditional Democratic constituent group—supporting the party by margins of three or four to one—they had shown support for Republicans Eisenhower and Sen. Joseph McCarthy.[137] In addition, Kennedy put together a predictable coalition: he won the support of voters in the Northeast, in most of the South, and in cities, plus blacks and union workers. Upper New England, the Midwest, and the West went primarily to Nixon.

After the election, Kennedy and Goldwater discussed, in an informal way, how they would conduct their campaigns for the presidency in 1964. The two expected to win their parties' nominations easily, and they talked about crisscrossing the nation in head-to-head debates, which would set a new standard for national campaigns.[138]

The Kennedy-Goldwater campaign never came to be, however. On November 22, 1963, while riding in a motorcade in Dallas, Texas, President Kennedy was assassinated by a gunman named Lee Harvey Oswald.[139] Vice President Johnson assumed the presidency.[140]

In his brief administration, Kennedy had compiled a record disappointing even to many of his supporters. The Bay of Pigs fiasco in which a Central Intelligence Agency plan to overthrow the Cuban government failed miserably, the inability to obtain passage of landmark civil rights legislation, budget deficits and a drain of gold supplies from the United States, confrontations with the Soviet Union in Cuba, Hungary, and Berlin, and the nascent U.S. involvement in the Vietnam War created doubts about the young president's control of the government.

Kennedy had, however, made a start on many important issues. Arms control initiatives such as the test ban treaty, economic growth through tax cuts, modernization of the military, the successful management of the Cuban Missile Crisis, civil rights and other domestic initiatives, the Peace Corps and Alliance for Progress, and growing world stature all offered hope for the second term. It would fall to Johnson, the legendary former Senate majority leader, to bring the Kennedy plans to fruition. First acting as the loyal servant of the slain president, then as his own man, Johnson was able to bring to legislative enactment many of the initiatives long-cherished by liberals—most notably the Civil Rights Act of 1964, which was considerably stronger than the Kennedy bill that had stalled in Congress.

## "ALL THE WAY WITH LBJ": 1964

From the time of his sad but graceful ascension to the White House, Johnson was never in doubt as the Democrats' 1964 nominee. He was expected to select an eastern or midwestern liberal as his running mate, and he did so when he tapped Senator Humphrey of Minnesota at the convention, which his campaign organization stage-managed down to the last detail. The only dissent from Democratic unity was provided by Gov. George C. Wallace of Alabama, whose segregationist campaign took advantage of a backlash against the civil rights movement. Wallace entered three primaries against Johnson-allied favorite sons, and he polled 43 percent of the vote in Maryland. Wallace talked about mounting a third-party bid in the fall, but he backed off.

The Republicans were divided into two bitter camps led by Senator Goldwater of Arizona, the eventual nominee, and by Governor Rockefeller of New York. The nomination contest was a struggle for the soul of the party. Other active and inactive candidates included Ambassador to Vietnam Henry Cabot Lodge, former vice president Nixon, and Gov. William Scranton of Pennsylvania. After a New Hampshire primary victory by Lodge, achieved through a well-organized write-in drive while he was still ambassador to Vietnam, Goldwater and Rockefeller scrapped through a series of primaries. The moderate Lodge later helped Scranton in a late effort to recruit uncommitted delegates to stop Goldwater, but by then it was too late. Goldwater lined up strong delegate support to get the nomination before the primary season even began, but he needed to use the primaries to show that he had vote-getting ability. And the state organizations that backed him needed evidence that his conservative message would find popular acceptance.

In the "mixed" nominating system then in place, candidates were able to pick and choose the primaries that best suited their strategies. Front-runners avoided risks, and long shots entered high-visibility and often risky contests as a way to attract the attention of party professionals. As expected, Goldwater won widespread support in the southern state conventions and had strong primary showings in Illinois and Indiana. Rockefeller beat Lodge in Oregon, but the decisive test came when Goldwater narrowly upset Rockefeller in California.

More important than the confusing preconvention contests was the rhetoric. Both the conservative Goldwater and the liberal Rockefeller vowed to save the party from the other's ideology. Goldwater, who rode the bestseller success of his *Conscience of a Conservative* to hero worship among conservatives, made a vigorous case against New Deal politics and for American sway in world politics: "I don't give a tinker's damn what the rest of the world thinks about the United States, as long as we keep strong militarily."[141] Rockefeller implied that Goldwater would risk nuclear war and would recklessly dismantle basic social programs.

The nominating contest was a regional as well as an ideological struggle. The westerner Goldwater—backed by labor-intensive manufacturers, small business and agricultural enterprises, and domestic oil producers—opposed internationalist

In accepting the 1964 Republican nomination, Sen. Barry Goldwater called for a moral crusade, declaring "Extremism in defense of liberty is no vice; moderation in pursuit of justice is no virtue."

banking and commercial interests.[142] Goldwater made eastern media the objects of scorn. Rockefeller and his family, of course, represented the apex of the eastern establishment. Because of his strategy, Goldwater isolated his campaign from the manufacturing and financial interests that were at the center of American economic growth for a generation.

Bitter battles over the party platform and unseemly heckling of Rockefeller displayed the party's divisions at the convention. When the conservatives won the nomination and the platform, there was no reconciliation. Goldwater selected Rep. William Miller of New York, another conservative, as his running mate and vowed to purge the party of liberal and moderate elements.

In a defiant acceptance speech, Goldwater painted a picture of the United States as inept in international affairs and morally corrupt in domestic pursuits, and he vowed an all-out crusade to change the situation: "Tonight there is violence in our streets, corruption in our highest offices, aimlessness among our youth, anxiety among our elderly, and there's a virtual despair among the many who look beyond the material successes toward the inner meaning of their lives. . . . Extremism in defense of liberty is no vice; moderation in pursuit of justice is no virtue."[143]

To a nation experiencing prosperity and unaware of the true proportions of its involvement in Vietnam, the "choice, not an echo" that Goldwater offered was a moral crusade. But the American consensus was built on material, consumer foundations, and an "outsider" appeal would have to wait until the system's foundations became unstable.

The divided GOP made for easy pickings for Johnson. The fall campaign was dominated by Goldwater's gaffes, which started long before the campaign began. He said, for example, that troops committed to the North Atlantic Treaty Organization (NATO) in Europe probably could be cut by at least one-third if NATO "commanders" had the authority to use tactical nuclear weapons in an emergency.[144] Goldwater also proposed a number of changes in the Social Security system, called for selling off the Tennessee Valley Authority, criticized the civil rights movement, and denounced the Supreme Court, the National Labor Relations Board, and the federal bureaucracy. Except for the use of nuclear weapons and changes in Social Security, most of Goldwater's proposals when taken alone were not shocking. But the sum of his proposals—and his sometimes halting explanations—scared many voters.

President Johnson campaigned very actively to win a mandate for an activist new term. He traveled throughout the country making speeches to build a consensus for his domestic programs as well as his reelection. Johnson resisted Goldwater's frequent calls for televised debates. The nation's prosperity was probably enough to keep the president in the White House.[145]

Johnson desperately wanted a personal mandate to pursue a variety of domestic programs that fell under the rubric of the "Great Society"—a term that Johnson used in a 1964 commencement address (borrowed from a book of the same title by British socialist Graham Wallas). The desired landslide—underscored by his campaign slogan, "All the Way with LBJ"—was essential to initiatives in civil rights, health care, community action, education, welfare, housing, and jobs creation. Central to the landslide was not only economic prosperity but also peace in the world's trouble spots. Johnson therefore ran as a "peace" candidate.

But while he was trying to build a coalition that would sustain his domestic initiatives, Johnson faced an increasingly difficult dilemma about the U.S. role in Vietnam. The United States had been involved in opposing Ho Chi Minh's revolution against French colonial rule in the 1940s and 1950s, and under Presidents Eisenhower and Kennedy the United States had made a commitment to the leaders of South Vietnam (created after the failure of the 1954 Geneva accord) as a bastion against communist expansion in Asia. But talk of war would likely imperil the domestic initiatives of the Great Society.

So while Johnson was campaigning as the peace candidate in 1964, he also was preparing for a major increase in U.S. involvement in Vietnam. As early as February 1964, the administration began elaborate covert operations in Southeast Asia and prepared a resolution to give the president a "blank check" in Vietnam.[146] By June, the resolution was ready, and the Pentagon had chosen ninety-four bombing targets in North Vietnam and made provisions for bombing support systems on the ground. But on June 15, Johnson decided to delay major offensives until after the election.[147] In August, Johnson sent to Congress what would be known as the Tonkin Gulf resolution, which granted the president broad authority to wage war in Vietnam. The res-

olution passed quickly and nearly unanimously—after all, the president had instructed congressional leaders to get an overwhelming majority so his policy would be bipartisan.

Johnson also seized on Rockefeller's use of the peace issue during the Republican primaries against Goldwater. He alluded to some of Goldwater's scarier statements about war, and he pledged that "we are not about to send American boys nine or ten thousand miles away from home to do what Asian boys ought to be doing for themselves."[148] A week before the election Johnson said: "The only real issue in this campaign, the only one you ought to get concerned about, is who can best keep the peace."[149]

Johnson's popular vote landslide was the largest in U.S. history. He won 61 percent of the popular vote to Goldwater's 38 percent (or 43.1 million to 27.2 million votes). In the electoral college Johnson received 486 votes to Goldwater's 52, and he carried forty-four states—all but Goldwater's home state of Arizona and five deep South states. In addition, the Democratic Party amassed huge majorities in both the Senate (67–33) and the House of Representatives (295–140).

On election day, Johnson created a working group to study "immediately and intensively" the U.S. options in Southeast Asia.[150] The war was increasing far beyond what most supporters of the Tonkin Gulf resolution or "peace" supporters of the president imagined. In 1965 alone the number of U.S. troops in Vietnam increased from 15,000 to nearly 200,000.[151]

## The Breakup of Consensus

A long period of uncertainty in American politics began sometime after Johnson's landslide victory over Goldwater in 1964.

By 1968, some thirty thousand Americans had been killed in action in Vietnam, and television was bringing the war into the living rooms of American families. Despite repeated assertions that the United States was defeating the North Vietnamese enemy, U.S. bombing efforts and ground troops did not break the resolve of the communists in the North or their sympathizers who had infiltrated the South. The corrupt South Vietnamese government and army appeared to lack the will to fight the war on their own.

In the United States, the opposition to the war developed as the casualties mounted, and the administration experienced a "credibility gap" because of its statements about the war. Before the United States left Vietnam in 1975, fifty-five thousand Americans had died in combat. Perhaps more important than the number of casualties—about the same as in the Korean War—was the long-term commitment that the United States appeared to have made with little evidence of progress. The "quagmire," as New York Times reporter David Halberstam called the war, was perhaps typified by the program of intense U.S. bombing raids that were judged by many experts to be ineffectual against the North's guerrilla warfare strategy.[152]

As opposition to the war grew among an increasingly vocal

and well-organized minority, strains developed in Johnson's economic and domestic programs. Starting with the riots in the Watts section of Los Angeles in 1965, urban areas sizzled with resentment of the mainstream liberal establishment. Detroit, Newark, and many major U.S. cities erupted in other riots that burned miles of city streets and caused millions of dollars in damage. The assassination of civil rights leader Martin Luther King Jr. in Memphis on April 4, 1968, led to riots throughout the nation. Even before the riots, however, a conservative reaction against the Great Society had developed.

The activities of the Great Society were many and varied: the Civil Rights Act of 1964, the Voting Rights Act of 1965, Head Start, Model Cities, mass transit legislation, food stamps, Medicaid, the Elementary and Secondary Education Act, college loans, and housing programs that included subsidies for poor, to name just the most prominent programs.

The conservative backlash was apparent before many programs had time to do their work. Efforts such as the Model Cities program and the Community Action Program, which mandated that poverty programs promote "maximum feasible participation" by the poor themselves, often were badly organized. They also created new struggles over jurisdiction in cities that already were notorious for divisive politics. Liberal efforts that predated the Great Society, such as school desegregation, only added to the tensions in cities.

One of the greatest sources of backlash in the late 1960s was an alarming increase in street crime. Even though blacks and the poor were the chief victims of the increase, the issue was most salient for conservative whites. Many tied the breakdown in order to the growth of the welfare state caused by the Great Society. The crime rate seemed to many to be nothing less than ingratitude on the part of the poor. James Sundquist wrote: "While increasing millions were supported by welfare, rising state and local taxes made the citizen more and more aware of who paid the bill. And while he armed himself for protection against thieves or militants, the liberals were trying to pass legislation to take away his guns."[153]

The crime problem was an important element in both national and metropolitan politics. Polls taken in the late 1960s showed that half the women and a fifth of the men in the country were afraid to walk alone in their own neighborhoods at night.[154] In Alabama, Gov. George Wallace was whipping up his supporters in a frenzy of prejudice and resentment. The fear of crime also would be an important element in Richard Nixon's 1968 campaign.

## "NIXON NOW": 1968

With the nation divided over the war and domestic policy, the Democrats entered the 1968 campaign in an increasingly perilous state. In December 1967 Sen. Eugene McCarthy of Minnesota challenged President Johnson for the Democratic nomination, a move based almost entirely on McCarthy's antiwar stance. McCarthy did unexpectedly well against Johnson's write-in candidacy in the New Hampshire primary on March 12, 1968,

Former vice president Richard Nixon tapped into widespread discontent over the Vietnam War and domestic turmoil to win the 1968 presidential election, one of the closest in U.S. history.

drawing 42.4 percent of the vote to Johnson's 49.5 percent. Anticipating a devastating defeat in the Wisconsin primary on April 2, Johnson dramatically announced his withdrawal from the campaign in a televised address March 31.

After the New Hampshire primary, New York senator Robert F. Kennedy declared his antiwar candidacy, which put in place all the elements for a Democratic fight of historic proportions. Vice President Humphrey took Johnson's place as the administration's candidate.

McCarthy and Kennedy fought each other in the primaries, and Kennedy appeared to have the upper hand when he closed the primary season with a victory in California on June 5. But after making his acceptance speech, he was assassinated, and the party was in greater turmoil than ever.

At the party convention in Chicago, a site Johnson had chosen for what he thought would be his own nomination, Humphrey became the Democratic Party's candidate. He had eschewed the primaries; he won the nomination on the strength of endorsements from state party organizations. The vice president took the nomination on the first ballot after Mayor Richard Daley of Chicago committed the Illinois delegation to his effort. Humphrey won with support from the traditional elements of the Democratic coalition—labor, African Americans, urban voters—plus the backers of President Johnson. Humphrey appealed to many of the party's "moderates" on the issue of the Vietnam War.

Preliminary battles over rules and delegate seating, the representativeness of the party, and the Vietnam War caused ugly skirmishes on the convention floor. The party's platform eventually endorsed the administration's war policy, including bombing, but strong opposition to this plank left the Democrats divided.[155]

Outside the convention halls, demonstrations for civil rights and an end to the war met brutal rejection from the police. After three days of sometimes harsh verbal and physical battles with antiwar demonstrators in city parks, the police charged a group of protesters who planned a march on the convention. Theodore H. White described the scene that played on national television:

Like a fist jolting, like a piston exploding from its chamber, comes a hurtling column of police from off Balbo into the intersection, and all things happen too fast: first the charge as the police wedge cleaves through the mob; then screams, whistles, confusion, people running off into Grant Park, across bridges, into hotel lobbies. And as the scene clears, there are little knots in the open clearing—police clubbing youngsters, police dragging youngsters, police rushing them by their elbows, their heels dragging, to patrol wagons, prodding recalcitrants who refuse to enter quietly.[156]

Humphrey and his running mate, Sen. Edmund S. Muskie of Maine, faced an uphill fight.

The Republicans united behind Richard Nixon, the 1960 nominee whose political career had seemed at an end after he lost in the 1962 California gubernatorial election. The GOP did not have to deal with any of the divisiveness of the 1964 Goldwater-Rockefeller battle.

Nixon outspent Humphrey two-to-one. He also followed a carefully devised script that avoided the exhausting schedule of his 1960 campaign and capitalized on the national discontent created by the Vietnam War, urban riots, political assassinations, and general concern about the speed of change wrought by the Great Society. Nixon traveled the high road in his own campaign by calling for the nation to unite and heal its wounds. Promising an "open administration," Nixon's main offer was change. "I must say the man who helped us get into trouble is not the man to get us out."[157] To avoid scrutiny by the national media, Nixon gave few major addresses, preferring instead a series of interviews with local newspapers and broadcasters.

As President Johnson resisted calls for a halt in the bombing of North Vietnam, Nixon said he had a "secret plan" to end the war. He appealed to weary Democrats with his pledge of an activist administration and alternative approaches to dealing with some of the problems the Great Society addressed. Nixon promised to give blacks, in his words, "a piece of the action with a program to encourage entrepreneurial activity in cities." The "new Nixon" appeared willing to deal with the Soviet Union, which he had scorned earlier in his career. Meanwhile, his vice-presidential nominee, Gov. Spiro T. Agnew of Maryland, offered a slashing critique of the Democrats to middle-class and blue-collar Americans who resented the civil rights laws, government

bureaucracy, Vietnam War protesters, and the young protest generation.

Gov. Wallace of Alabama, heading up one of the strongest third party campaigns in U.S. history, ran as an antiestablishment conservative, railing away at desegregation, crime, taxes, opponents of the war in Vietnam, social programs, and "pointy-head" bureaucrats and "intellectual morons." His American Independent Party was the strongest effort since Theodore Roosevelt's Bull Moose campaign in 1912 and Robert La Follette's Progressive run in 1924. Like the earlier third-party campaigns, the Wallace run caused concern about the soundness of the electoral college system. Because the race was so close, it was conceivable that no candidate would win an electoral college victory. In that event, Wallace could have held the balance of power.[158]

Despite his early disadvantage, Humphrey made steady inroads into Nixon's support by disassociating himself from Johnson's Vietnam policies. When Johnson on November 1 ordered a halt to all bombing of North Vietnam, Humphrey appeared to be free at last from the stigma of the administration. But this change in policy was not enough to win the election for Humphrey.

The 1968 election was one of the closest in U.S. history. Nixon's victory was not confirmed until the day after the election when California, Ohio, and Illinois—each with very close counts—finally went into the Nixon column. Nixon attracted 31.8 million votes (43.4 percent of all votes cast); Humphrey, 31.3 million votes (42.7 percent); and Wallace, 9.9 million votes (13.5 percent). Nixon won thirty-two states and 301 electoral votes, compared with Humphrey's thirteen states and 191 electoral votes. Nixon won six southern states (Wallace won five others), all of the West except Texas, Washington, and Hawaii, and all the midwestern states except Michigan and Minnesota. Humphrey won all of the East except New Hampshire, Vermont, New Jersey, and Delaware, plus West Virginia, Maryland, and the District of Columbia.

One long-lasting effect of 1968 was a transformation of the nominating process. In response to the bitter complaints about their 1968 convention, the Democratic Party adopted rules that would make the primaries the center of the nominating process. The Chicago convention, dominated by party professionals at the expense of many important constituencies—African Americans, women, youth—had nominated a candidate who did not compete in any primaries. The key reform was a limit on the number of delegates that state committees could choose—after 1968, no more than 10 percent of the delegation. (See "Rules Changes in the Democratic Party," p. 26, in Chapter 1.)

## NIXON'S REELECTION: 1972

Sen. George S. McGovern of South Dakota was the miracle candidate of 1972, but his miracle did not last long enough. Edmund Muskie, a veteran of the U.S. Senate and the vice-presidential nominee in 1968, was the early favorite to win the Democratic nomination. But because of party reforms enacted in response to the disastrous 1968 convention, the nominating process was bound to create surprises and confusion.

No fewer than fifteen contenders announced their candidacy, twelve with serious hopes of winning or influencing the final selection. Some twenty-two primaries to choose 60 percent of the party's delegates—a third more than in 1968—were to take place over four months. The marathon would be decided by accidents, media strategy, and a confusing array of voter choices that changed with each new development.

Muskie was badly damaged before the New Hampshire primary when he appeared to cry while lashing back at the *Manchester Union Leader*'s vicious and unrelenting attacks on his campaign and on his outspoken wife, Jane. The *Union Leader* had printed a series of attacks on Jane and then falsely reported that Muskie had laughed at a derogatory joke about French Canadians. Muskie later said of the incident: "It changed people's minds about me, of what kind of a guy I was. They were looking for a strong, steady man, and here I was weak."[159]

Muskie won the first-in-the-nation New Hampshire primary, but his 46.4 percent of the vote was considered a "disappointing" showing. Senator McGovern, the antiwar candidate who won 37.1 percent of the vote, was pronounced the real winner by media and pundits. His strong showing—engineered by such imaginative young political operatives as Gary Hart and Patrick Caddell and a corps of youthful volunteers—was a surprise.

After New Hampshire, the Democrats battled through the summer. Wallace parlayed his antibusing rhetoric into an impressive victory in the Florida primary (41.6 percent). Better organized than the others, McGovern won the Wisconsin delegation by winning 29.6 percent of the state vote. McGovern then won an easy Massachusetts victory with 52.7 percent of the vote to Muskie's 21.3 percent. Humphrey edged McGovern in Ohio by 41.2 to 39.6 percent, but McGovern claimed a moral victory.

In the popular primary vote before the late summer California primary, McGovern actually stood in third place behind Wallace and Humphrey. But the delegate allocation rules gave the edge to the candidate who could squeeze out narrow victories in congressional districts, and that was McGovern. McGovern had 560 delegates to Humphrey's 311. Wallace had 324 delegates, but he was paralyzed after being shot in a Maryland shopping center on May 15, 1972, and therefore no longer appeared to have a chance at the nomination.

The big McGovern-Humphrey showdown was California, which offered 271 delegates to the winner. It was a spirited campaign that included a head-to-head debate and strong Humphrey assaults on McGovern's positions on welfare and defense spending. McGovern went on to beat Humphrey by five percentage points in the winner-take-all primary. McGovern also won a majority of the delegates in New Jersey, South Dakota, and New Mexico on the last day of the primary season.[160]

After platform battles over welfare, busing, and the Vietnam War, McGovern won the nomination handily. He then selected Sen. Thomas Eagleton of Missouri as his running mate after several others declined. McGovern did not get to deliver his acceptance speech—perhaps the best speech of his career—until almost three o'clock in the morning, when most television viewers already were in bed.

President Nixon and Vice President Agnew were renominated with barely a peep out of other Republicans. Rep. Paul N. "Pete" McCloskey Jr. of California opposed Nixon in the primaries but won only one delegate (from New Mexico). Rep. John M. Ashbrook of Ohio also ran in the primaries.

McGovern would have been an underdog in the best of circumstances, but his chances were badly damaged by what came to be known as the "Eagleton affair." As the McGovernites celebrated their hard-won nomination, rumors circulated that Eagleton had been hospitalized for exhaustion in the early 1960s. Eagleton finally told McGovern operatives that he had been hospitalized three times for nervous exhaustion and fatigue, and his treatment included electroshock therapy. Despite McGovern's public statement that he was "1,000 percent for Tom Eagleton, and I have no intention of dropping him," Eagleton left the ticket less than two weeks after his nomination.

McGovern eventually replaced Eagleton with his sixth choice, R. Sargent Shriver, former executive of the Peace Corps and Office of Economic Opportunity. But the aura of confusion that surrounded the Eagleton affair and the search for a new vice-presidential candidate hurt the campaign badly. The columnist Tom Braden likened it to a school teacher who could not control the class: "Nice people, too. One looks back with sympathy and a sense of shame. But at the time—was it that they were too nice?—their classes were a shambles. The erasers flew when they turned their backs."[161]

Nixon was in command of the fall campaign. He paraded a litany of accomplishments—the Paris peace talks over the Vietnam War, the diplomatic opening to China, the arms limitation treaty with the Soviet Union, and a number of domestic initiatives. Most of all, he was a strong figure. And if he still aroused suspicion, he was at least a known commodity.

Nixon won all but Massachusetts and the District of Columbia in the fall election. His popular vote margin was 47.2 million to McGovern's 29.2 million; the electoral college cast 521 votes for Nixon and only 17 for McGovern. Nixon's 60.7 percent share of the popular vote stood second only to Johnson's 61.1 percent in 1964.

On the surface, it appeared in 1972 that American politics was entering an age of calm consensus. At the time of the election, the economy was temporarily strong. Moreover, opposition to the Vietnam War had faded as the two sides negotiated in Paris for an end to the war, and the United States had signed an important nuclear arms treaty with the Soviet Union and had made important diplomatic moves with that country and the People's Republic of China. Nixon's landslide victory appeared to be a mandate and a vote of confidence.

But trouble loomed behind the apparent stability and consensus. The war in Vietnam continued, as did the antiwar protests, and generational cleavages remained. The economy experienced the first of many "shocks" in 1973 when the Organization of Petroleum Exporting Countries agreed to increase the world price of oil. The economic turmoil that resulted in the United States was topped off with a wage and price freeze. In addition, a warlike atmosphere between the White House and the media (as well as other perceived enemies of the administration who appeared on Nixon's "enemies list") and the mushrooming Watergate scandal combined to create a dark side to U.S. politics in the 1970s.[162]

The Watergate affair was perhaps the greatest political scandal in U.S. history. For the first time, a president was forced to leave office before his term expired. President Nixon resigned on August 9, 1974, when it became apparent that the House of Representatives would impeach him for "high crimes and misdemeanors" and the Senate would convict him. In addition, a number of Nixon aides, including his first attorney general and campaign manager, John Mitchell, would spend time in jail because of the scandal.

At its simplest, the Watergate affair was "a third-rate burglary," followed by a cover-up by President Nixon and his aides. In the summer of 1972, several employees of the Committee to Re-elect the President (dubbed "CREEP") were arrested after they were discovered breaking into and bugging the Democratic National Committee's offices at the posh Watergate complex in Washington. The break-in was not a major issue in the 1972 election, but the next year a Senate committee began an investigation of the entire affair.

During the investigation, a presidential aide revealed that Nixon had secretly taped Oval Office conversations with aides. When the Watergate special prosecutor, Archibald Cox, ordered Nixon to surrender the tapes in October 1973, Nixon ordered Cox fired. But because Nixon's attorney general, Elliot Richardson, and assistant attorney general, William D. Ruckelshaus, refused to fire Cox, the task was carried out by Solicitor General Robert Bork, igniting a constitutional crisis dubbed the "Saturday night massacre."

Nixon soon handed over the tapes Cox had sought. In the summer of 1974, the Supreme Court ruled that Nixon had to surrender even more tapes, which indicated that he had played an active role in covering up the Watergate scandal. Nixon resigned the presidency when his impeachment and conviction appeared certain. The impeachment articles charged him with obstruction of justice, abuse of presidential powers, and contempt of Congress.

Many students of the Watergate affair maintain that the illegal campaign activities were just part of a tapestry of illegal activities in the Nixon administration—including secretly bombing Cambodia, accepting millions of dollars in illegal campaign contributions, offering government favors in return for contributions, "laundering" money through third parties, wiretapping and burglarizing a wide variety of people thought to be unsup-

portive of the president, offering executive clemency to convicted campaign workers, engaging in "dirty tricks" to discredit other political figures, compromising criminal investigations by giving information to the people under scrutiny, and using government funds to renovate the president's private residence.[163]

In 1973 Nixon's vice president, Spiro Agnew, resigned after pleading "no contest" to charges of taking bribes while he was governor of Maryland. After Agnew's resignation on October 10, 1973, Nixon named House Minority Leader Gerald Ford, a longtime GOP stalwart, to become vice president under the Twenty-fifth Amendment. Ford, who had never entered a national election, then became president upon Nixon's resignation and quickly attracted the support of the American public with his modest, earnest disposition. He responded to the widespread feeling that Nixon's isolation in the Oval Office had contributed to his downfall by promising to work closely with Congress and to meet with the press regularly.

One month after becoming president, however, Ford ignited a firestorm of criticism with his full pardon of Nixon for all crimes he may have committed while president. Ford testified before Congress that he believed Nixon had suffered enough and that the nation would have been badly torn if a former president were brought to court to face criminal charges. Critics asserted that Ford had made a "deal" in which Nixon resigned the presidency in exchange for the pardon.[164]

Ford selected former New York governor Nelson Rockefeller to be his vice president. Rockefeller received Senate and House confirmation on December 10 and 19, respectively, after long, difficult hearings that centered on his financial dealings.

## THE ELECTION OF 1976: JIMMY WHO?

With the benefit of the Watergate scandal and Ford's pardon of Nixon, the Democrats won resounding victories in the 1974 midterm elections. The Democrats' gains of fifty-two House seats and four Senate seats not only created stronger majorities but also reduced the number of members with allegiance to the old system of organizing congressional business.

The moralistic zeal of the "Watergate class" forced major changes on Congress as well as on the presidency and the nation's process of pluralistic political bargaining. The new crop of legislators was so large that it was able to undermine the seniority system that had ordered the way Congress had operated for years. The new system of committee assignments led to a proliferation of subcommittees on which most members had prominent roles. That, in turn, created a fragmented policy-making process—less susceptible to coercion by presidents and party leaders but more susceptible to interest group politics.[165]

The 1976 campaign was the first governed by campaign finance reform legislation enacted in 1971 and 1974. The Federal Election Campaign Act (FECA) of 1971 limited campaign expenditures and required disclosure of campaign receipts and expenditures. The Revenue Act of 1971 created a tax check-off that enabled taxpayers to allocate $1.00 of their taxes for public fi-

Virtually unknown to the country at the outset of the campaign, former Georgia governor Jimmy Carter emerged from a field of candidates to win the Democratic nomination and the presidency. His casual and honest approach appealed to many voters.

nancing of elections. The FECA amendments of 1974 limited spending and donations for both primary and general election campaigns, established a system of partial public funding of elections, and created the Federal Election Commission to monitor campaign activities.

The Democrats and their eventual nominee, Jimmy Carter, continued to exploit the nation's discontent through the 1976 election. Ronald Reagan, a former movie actor and California governor, added to the Republican Party's vulnerability by waging a stubborn primary campaign against President Ford.

The Democrats appeared headed for a long and bitter nomination struggle for the third time in a row. A few candidates—such as Senators Henry Jackson of Washington and Birch Bayh of Indiana and Governor Wallace of Alabama—had greater stature than others, but their appeal was limited to specific factions of the Democratic coalition. Other candidates included Rep. Morris Udall of Arizona, Sen. Fred Harris of Oklahoma, Sen. Frank Church of Idaho, and Gov. Edmund G. "Jerry" Brown Jr. of California. Church and Brown entered the race late, and Senators Humphrey of Minnesota and Edward M. Kennedy

of Massachusetts awaited a draft in the event of a deadlocked convention.

The moderate Carter, whose name recognition in polls stood in single figures when the campaign began, executed a brilliant campaign strategy to win the nomination on the first ballot. Constructing strong organizations for the Iowa caucuses and the New Hampshire primary, Carter won both contests by slim margins. Although liberal candidates Udall and Bayh together polled more votes than Carter, it was Carter who received cover billings on national magazines and live interviews on morning television talk shows.[166] Within a matter of days, Carter went from long shot to front-runner.

Udall performed well in the primaries but never won a single state; he and other liberals were splitting the liberal vote. Udall's chance for a Wisconsin primary win fizzled when Harris refused to back out to create a one-on-one matchup of a liberal with Carter.[167] Carter ran into strong challenges from Church and Brown in later primaries, but he had the delegates and endorsements by the time of the Democratic convention in New York for a first-ballot nomination. The convention itself was a "love fest" with the Democrats united behind Carter and his running mate, Sen. Walter F. Mondale of Minnesota.

The GOP was divided between Ford and Reagan. Ford won the early contests, but Reagan scored big wins in the North Carolina and Texas primaries. Reagan was put on the defensive with his proposals for transferring welfare obligations to the states, but when he focused on foreign policy he had success. For example, he attacked Ford for his policy of détente with the Soviet Union and his negotiation of a treaty that would forfeit U.S. control of the Panama Canal.

In the late summer, with Ford and Reagan locked in a close contest for delegates, Reagan tried to gain the advantage by breaking precedent and naming his vice-presidential candidate before the convention. Reagan's choice—Sen. Richard S. Schweicker of Pennsylvania, a moderate—widened Reagan's ideological appeal but angered many of his conservative supporters. When Reagan tried to force Ford to name a vice-presidential candidate in advance as well, the convention vote on the issue became a crucial test of the candidates' delegate strength. But Ford won that test and the nomination. He selected the acerbic senator Robert Dole of Kansas as his running mate as a consolation prize for disappointed conservatives.

Carter emerged from the Democratic convention with a wide lead over Ford, but the race was too close to call by election day. A number of gaffes—such as Carter's interview with *Playboy* magazine, his ambiguous statements about abortion, and his confused observations on tax reform—hurt the Democratic contender.[168] Ford also gained in the polls when he began to use the patronage powers of the presidency and effectively contrasted his twenty-seven years of Washington experience to Carter's four years as governor of Georgia.

For the first time since 1960, the major candidates took part in televised debates. As the outsider, Carter helped himself by demonstrating a good grasp of national issues and by appealing to Democrats to vote the party line. Ford hurt himself with a claim that Eastern European nations did not consider themselves to be under the control of the Soviet Union.[169] The remark was intended to be testimony to the Europeans' sense of national identity, but it was interpreted as evidence of the president's naiveté.

Carter's main advantage was regional pride. The Democrats had long since lost their hold over the South, but Carter gained widespread support as the first candidate nominated from the region on his own in more than a century. The Democratic Party's many factions—including such big-city mayors as Richard Daley of Chicago and Abraham Beame of New York, civil rights activists, and organized labor—put on a rare display of unity.

Carter defeated Ford by a slim margin, winning 40.8 million votes (50.1 percent) to Ford's 39.1 million (48.0 percent). In the electoral college, 297 votes went to Carter, 240 to Ford. Carter won by pulling together the frazzled New Deal coalition of industrial and urban voters, African Americans, Jews, and southerners. Ford won the West, and Carter won the South, except Virginia. Ford won all the states from the Mississippi River westward except Texas and Hawaii, plus states in his native Midwest like Iowa, Illinois, Michigan, and Indiana. Ford also won Connecticut and the three northernmost New England states—New Hampshire, Vermont, and Maine.

## CARTER'S UNCERTAIN LEADERSHIP: 1980

After his election, President Carter's ability to hold the coalition together was limited. The growing influence of the mass media, the fragmenting effects of interest groups, poor relations with Congress, and difficult issues that cut across many different sectors—inflation and unemployment, oil shocks and the more general energy crisis, the Iran hostage crisis, relations with the Soviet Union, and budget austerity moves such as proposed cutbacks in water projects and social welfare—all damaged Carter's governing ability.

As the 1980 election approached, Carter appeared to have lost all but his institutional strength and the reluctance of voters to reject a president for the fourth time in a row. Carter controlled party processes, such as the primary schedule; he had access to key financial support and skilled political operatives; and he shaped much of the political agenda. But Kennedy was hitting him hard from the left, and Reagan and others were hitting him hard from the right. As a result, Carter was unable to forge a lasting consensus on important issues. Kennedy was leading Carter in the polls by a two-to-one margin when he announced his challenge to the incumbent president in November 1979. But Carter overcame that lead by the start of the nominating season when the seizure of American hostages in Iran rallied the nation around the president and Kennedy made a series of political mistakes. Kennedy was unable to develop campaign themes or answer questions about his personal conduct in the 1969 Chappaquiddick incident in which a woman died after a car he was driving went off a bridge. Other "character" issues, such as Kennedy's alleged "womanizing," and more substantive issues,

such as his liberal voting record, also hurt him in a year dominated by conservative themes. Finally, Kennedy's campaign was in financial jeopardy early because of lavish spending on transportation, headquarters, and other expenses.

The campaign of Gov. Jerry Brown of California was unable to find much support for his appeal for recognition of economic and environmental limits. He dropped out of the race on April 1, 1980.

The president was able to manipulate the primary and caucus schedule to bunch together states favorable to him and to match pro-Kennedy states with pro-Carter states. The result was an early, strong Carter lead in delegates. Kennedy came back with some solid primary wins in New York and Pennsylvania, but his campaign by then had been reduced to a vehicle for anti-Carter expressions. Many Kennedy voters hoped for a deadlocked convention at which a third candidate would win the nomination.

Carter won the nomination on the first ballot despite a variety of stop-Carter efforts and Kennedy's attempt to free delegates to vote for any candidate. When Carter won the crucial floor vote on the "open convention" question, Kennedy did not have a chance. The Carter-Mondale ticket entered the fall campaign as a wounded army unable to generate much enthusiasm from the troops.

The Republicans united early behind Reagan. By April 22, 1980, less than two months after the New Hampshire primary, six candidates had dropped out of the race, and George Bush, Reagan's only surviving competitor, was desperately behind in the delegate count. Reagan's campaign experienced an early scare when Bush beat Reagan in the Iowa caucus, but Reagan rebounded, changed campaign managers and tactics, and won a string of primaries and caucuses. By the time of the convention, Reagan was the consensus candidate, and he improved party unity by adding Bush to the fall ticket.

Reagan called on the electorate to replace politics that he said was marked by "pastels," or compromising and uncertain policies, with "bold colors." Reagan's proposed bold strokes included a 30 percent reduction in marginal income tax rates based on a "supply-side" economic theory—which even Bush had said was a dangerous kind of "voodoo economics"—and massive increases in military expenditures. At the same time Reagan criticized Carter's alleged vacillation and his commitment to liberal policies.

President Carter, who was vulnerable as the hostage crisis neared its first anniversary (on November 4, election day) and high inflation and unemployment rates persisted, attempted to portray Reagan as a dangerous, heartless, and inexperienced amateur. Reagan managed to use Carter's attacks to his own advantage by assuming a posture of hurt feelings at the unfair criticism. When in a televised debate Carter attacked Reagan's previous opposition to social welfare programs, Reagan cut him off with a line, "There you go again," that suggested Carter was unfairly and relentlessly distorting Reagan's record.

The greatest controversy of the campaign did not emerge

until years later. Books published after the Reagan years charged that the Reagan-Bush campaign negotiated a deal with Iran to delay release of the hostages until after the campaign to embarrass President Carter. Gary Sick, a national security aide for Carter, charged that Reagan campaign officials met with Iranian officials in Europe in the summer of 1980 to arrange weapons sales in exchange for holding the hostages. If true—and many disputed the charges—the deal could have cost Carter the presidency.[170]

Carter strategists also were concerned about the independent candidacy of Rep. John B. Anderson of Illinois, a moderate who dropped out of the Republican race when it became clear that conservatives would dominate that party. After some stronger support in the polls, Anderson stood at about 10 percent for the final two months of the campaign. Carter was concerned that Anderson would take more votes from him than from Reagan, even though analysis of Anderson support suggested otherwise.[171]

Private money almost doubled the amount that Reagan was legally entitled to spend under the federal campaign financing system. Well-organized groups from the "new right," which opposed abortion, gun control, détente, and many social welfare programs, spent lavishly on television commercials and efforts to register like-minded voters. These groups also made a "hit list" of leading liberals in Congress. These candidates were so weakened by the new right's attacks that they put a local and regional drag on an already dragging Democratic ticket.[172]

Polls before election day predicted a close race. Reagan, however, won all but six states and took the White House in an electoral landslide, 489 electoral votes to 49. Reagan won 51 percent of the vote, while Carter managed 41 percent and Anderson 7 percent. Carter ran tight races in ten additional states that could have gone his way with a shift of less than one and a half percentage points. In twenty-one states, Anderson's vote totals made up most or all of the difference between Reagan and Carter. Despite these factors and polls that regularly showed preference for Carter's policy positions, Reagan's victory was impressive. He beat Carter by a better than two-to-one margin in nine states.

Even more surprising than Reagan's electoral landslide was the Republican takeover of the Senate. The new right's targeting of several Senate liberals—such as McGovern, Bayh, Gaylord Nelson of Wisconsin, John Tunney of California, and John Culver of Iowa—created the biggest Senate turnover since 1958. The Republicans now held the Senate by a 53–46 margin.

President Reagan was able to parlay his claims of an electoral mandate into wide-ranging changes in tax, budget, and military policies. Among other things, he won passage of a three-year, 25 percent cut in tax rates that would reduce federal revenues by $196 billion annually by the time the three-stage program was in place. He also secured omnibus legislation that cut the domestic budget by $140 billion over four years and increased defense spending by $181 billion over the same period. The media hailed

Reagan as the most successful handler of Congress since Lyndon Johnson.

## The New Conservative Discourse

Reagan's rise ushered in a new age of conservatism in the American political discourse. The vigorous conservative campaigns for the presidency and Congress were accompanied by a host of new "think tanks" and publications with a restyled set of philosophical and policy pronouncements.

The most celebrated event of the conservative revival was the publication in 1980 of George Gilder's *Wealth and Poverty,* a far-reaching attack on welfare state policies that rested on supply-side economic theory. Gilder argued that free markets and low taxes promoted not only economic efficiency and growth but also other benefits such as family strength and artistic creativity. Gilder's book was a central element of Reagan's campaign for major tax cuts.[173] But the supply-side tracts of Gilder and others were only the most visible signs of the conservative movement. Reagan's criticism of the Supreme Court decisions on abortion and school prayer helped to bring evangelical Christians into the political process. Businesses and conservative philanthropists, meanwhile, sponsored an unprecedented level of public policy research that shaped the debate of elections and government policy.[174]

Reagan's political appeal, according to scholar Garry Wills, turned on his ability to blend contradictory elements of American culture such as capitalism, conservatism, and individualism. While Reagan decried the decline of "traditional American values," for example, he extolled the dynamic economic system that demanded constant change. Wills wrote: "There are so many contradictions in this larger construct that one cannot risk entertaining serious challenge to any of its details. In Reagan, luckily, all these clashes are resolved. He is the ideal past, the successful present, the hopeful future all in one."[175]

Using the "bully pulpit" of the presidency, Reagan was able to overwhelm his opponents with his vision. When Democrats criticized specific Reagan policies, Reagan deflated them with expressions of disdain for "little men with loud voices [that] cry doom."[176] Jeane Kirkpatrick's depiction of Democrats as the "blame America first crowd" neatly expressed the way the Reagan rhetoric foreclosed debate on major policy issues such as the budget and trade deficits, military spending, the U.S. role in the third world, and U.S.-Soviet relations.

By the time the 1984 campaign took place, much of the nation had adopted Reagan's terms of debate. Mondale's strongest performance, in fact, was in the first debate when he congratulated Reagan for restoring national pride and suggested not that Reagan should be ousted but rather that he be given a graceful retirement. Mondale's campaign was basically conservative: he did not propose a single new social program and called the federal budget deficit the nation's top problem.

## REAGAN'S 1984 LANDSLIDE

Reagan's popularity dipped to 44 percent in 1983—about the average for modern presidents—but it rebounded when the economy later picked up.[177] As the 1984 election approached, Reagan faced no opposition from Republicans, but a large field of Democrats sought the right to oppose him in the fall.

The Democrats' early front-runner was former vice president Mondale, who had accumulated a wide range of endorsements (AFL-CIO, National Education Association, United Mine Workers, and the National Organization for Women) and an impressive campaign treasury. The more conservative senator John Glenn of Ohio, the first American to orbit the earth, was considered a strong challenger. Other candidates included Senators Gary Hart of Colorado, Alan Cranston of California, and Ernest Hollings of South Carolina, civil rights leader Jesse Jackson, former presidential candidate George McGovern, and former governor Reubin Askew of Florida.

The early results eliminated all but Mondale, Hart, and Jackson just sixteen days after the New Hampshire primary. Hart became the serious challenger to Mondale when he finished second in Iowa and first in New Hampshire, creating an explosion of media coverage. After Mondale recovered, the two fought head-to-head until the convention. Jackson, the second black to run for the presidency, stayed in the race to promote his liberal party agenda.[178]

After interviewing a wide range of candidates, Mondale selected Rep. Geraldine A. Ferraro of New York as his running mate—the first woman ever to receive a major-party nomination for national office. Representative Ferraro's vice-presidential candidacy probably was a drag on the ticket, not so much because she was a woman but because of the controversy created by her husband's finances and her stand on the abortion question. The controversies hindered the Democratic campaign's effort to articulate its own vision for the nation.[179]

Ferraro appeared knowledgeable and strong in her debate with Vice President Bush, and she often drew large and enthusiastic crowds. But she was stuck in controversy when details of her husband's questionable real estate, trusteeship, and tax practices became public. Opponents of abortion held prominent and often loud protests at the sites of her speeches, and she got involved in a lengthy public dispute over abortion with Catholic archbishop John O'Connor. Ferraro also did not help the ticket in regions where the Democrats were weak, such as the South and West.

Mondale ran a generally conservative campaign, concentrating on a proposed tax increase to address the unprecedented budget deficit of more than $200 billion and proposing no new social programs. Mondale criticized Reagan's record on the arms race, but he did not outline basic disagreements on other foreign affairs issues. He charged that Reagan, the oldest president in history, was lazy and out of touch. Only late in the campaign, when his speeches became unabashedly liberal and combative, did Mondale create any excitement.

Just once—in the period after the first presidential debate—did Mondale appear to have a chance to defeat President Reagan. Political pundits had marked Mondale as a poor television

Democratic presidential candidate Walter F. Mondale and his running mate, Geraldine Ferraro, the first woman to receive a major party nomination for national office, campaign in the 1984 presidential race.

performer, but the challenger outfoxed Reagan in the debate and afterward appeared to be gaining ground for a few days. Before the debate, Mondale aides had leaked erroneous information that suggested he would make a slashing attack. But Mondale surprised Reagan. At the advice of strategist Patrick Caddell, Mondale adopted a "gold-watch approach" suitable to a family business retiring an oldtimer—"sort of embracing a grandfather, and gently pushing him aside."[180] Mondale gave the president credit for helping to restore national patriotism and beginning a national debate on education reform, but he said it was time for new leadership. Reagan appeared confused and, in the rush to demonstrate statistical knowledge of policies, he failed to outline broad themes.

Although the first debate boosted the Mondale campaign's morale, it never brought Mondale within striking range of Reagan—he never came within ten percentage points of Reagan in the polls. Reagan's campaign was a series of rallies with masses of colorful balloons and confident talk about the United States "standing tall" in domestic and world affairs. Reagan was so sure of victory that he made a last-minute trip to Mondale's home state of Minnesota with the hope of completing a fifty-state sweep of the nation.

As it was, Reagan won forty-nine states, with 2-to-1 margins in eight states. Idaho, Nebraska, and Utah each gave Reagan more than 70 percent of the vote. Mondale won only the District of Columbia and his home state of Minnesota, where he beat Reagan by only two-tenths of a percentage point. As for the popular vote, Reagan won 54.5 million votes (58.8 percent) to Mondale's 37.6 million (40.6 percent). In the electoral college, he received 525 votes to Mondale's 13 votes.

Reagan's two landslides and the conservative discourse of his administration led many experts to wonder if they were witnessing a "realignment"—a major shift in political alliances among a variety of social, economic, and ethnic groups.[181] The trend during the 1970s and 1980s appeared to be one of a Democratic hold on congressional and state elections and Republican dominance of presidential elections. Some experts pointed to the electorate's ticket-splitting tendencies as evidence of "dealignment"—a breakdown of the old system without development of an entirely new system.[182]

Perhaps the most noteworthy development of recent years, which fits the dealignment thesis, has been the convergence of the appeal of the two parties. Michael Barone, in *The Almanac of American Politics*, wrote:

Political preferences in the America of the 1940's correlated to a fair degree with income. Republican strength was greater than average in high income states . . . , while Roosevelt and Truman carried virtually every state with incomes below the national average. But today there is virtually no correlation between income level and political preference. Utah, with one of the lowest per capita incomes, was one of the nation's most Republican states in 1980. . . . In the Midwest, high income Illinois is more Democratic than low income Indiana.[183]

## BUSH'S ASCENDANCY: 1988

The election of 1988 was the first after 1968 in which an incumbent president did not run. With no major figure and no major issues, the campaign was a tumultuous affair. Fourteen candidates struggled to develop an identity with the voters, and the campaign lurched from one symbolic issue to the next, never developing the overarching themes of previous campaigns.

In the absence of any major new issues, and in a time of general peace and prosperity, Republican vice president George Bush won the presidency. Bush defeated Democratic Massachusetts governor Michael S. Dukakis by a margin of 54 percent to 46 percent—47.9 million votes to 41.0 million votes. Bush's electoral vote margin was more impressive, 426–111. A negative campaign and limited voter registration efforts resulted in the lowest voter turnout rate since the 1920 and 1924 race percentages of 49 percent of all eligible voters. Just a little more than 50 percent of all eligible citizens voted for president in 1988.

Bush, benefiting from the Nixon-Reagan presidential coalition, won all the states of the old Confederacy, the entire West except Oregon and Washington, and several northern industrial states. Dukakis originally had hoped to crack the South by selecting a favorite son, Sen. Lloyd M. Bentsen Jr. of Texas, as his running mate, but that tactic failed. Dukakis lost crucial states that he had fought for to the end, such as California, Pennsylvania, Illinois, Ohio, and Missouri. He won New York, Massachusetts, Wisconsin, Minnesota, Oregon, Washington, West Virginia, Iowa, Rhode Island, Hawaii, and the District of Columbia.

President Ronald Reagan's retirement after two full terms created a political void. By most accounts, Reagan was the most popular president since Dwight Eisenhower. His dominance of national politics left little room for other figures to establish presidential stature.

Reagan's fiscal and social policies reduced the possibility for candidates to offer ambitious new programs. The national government's huge budget deficits—which exceeded $200 billion, compared with about $73 billion in the last year of the Carter administration—checked any grandiose new spending plans. The Reagan debt had exceeded the debt of the previous thirty-eight presidents.

President Reagan also had reshaped the dialogue on foreign affairs. He maintained strong opposition to the Soviet Union and other "Marxist" nations with his policies in Nicaragua, Afghanistan, and Angola. He also had projected an image of strength with military action in Libya and Grenada. At the same time, however, he had co-opted his critics by meeting with Soviet leader Mikhail Gorbachev several times and signing a nuclear arms control agreement. Reagan even asserted that the Gorbachev regime was fundamentally different from previous Soviet regimes, which he had called the "evil empire."

The early Republican front-runners were Bush and Sen. Robert J. Dole of Kansas; former senator Gary Hart of Colorado was considered the early Democratic leader. The campaign got scrambled before it began, however. Hart left the race in 1987

After two popular terms as president, Ronald Reagan and wife Nancy pass leadership of the "Reagan Revolution" to newly inaugurated President George Bush and wife Barbara in 1989.

when the Miami *Herald* augmented rumors of Hart's infidelity with a report that he had spent the night with a young model. The newspaper had staked out Hart's Washington townhouse with two reporters, two editors, and a photographer. The investigators sat in a rental car, loitered nearby, and jogged down the street. Hart, considered by many to be the brightest and most issue-oriented candidate, had long faced criticism about his "character."

The Hart story dominated the political news in 1987. Network news programs devoted 132 minutes to Hart, mostly in the first half of the year and, on the GOP side, 32 minutes to the long-shot television evangelist Marion G. "Pat" Robertson. The two front-runners and eventual nominees, Bush and Dukakis, got 28 and 20 minutes, respectively.[184]

Sen. Joseph R. Biden Jr. of Delaware was the next casualty of the media's 1987 concern with character issues.[185] Media reports that he had committed plagiarism on a law school paper and in campaign speeches led to Biden's early exit from the campaign. Biden had been considered a leading candidate because of his experience and strong speaking style.

With Hart and Biden out of the race, the Democrats were in disarray. Dubbed "dwarfs," the remaining candidates—Rev. Jesse Jackson of Illinois, Gov. Dukakis, Rep. Richard A. Gephardt of Missouri, Sen. Albert A. Gore Jr. of Tennessee, Sen. Paul M. Simon of Illinois, and former Arizona governor Bruce Babbitt—lacked the combination of extensive government experience and strong national bases many observers thought necessary to win the presidency.

The Republicans had problems of their own. Vice President Bush was the early favorite, and he benefited from his association with President Reagan. But Bush's public fealty to Reagan also created a problem: he was considered a "wimp," unable to stand on his own. Every major position Bush had held in his political career was the result of an appointment: ambassador to the United Nations, chairman of the Republican National Committee, envoy to China, director of the Central Intelligence Agency, and vice president. Bush had represented Texas for two terms in the House of Representatives and lost two Senate races.

At the outset of the race, Dole was considered a strong contender. As Republican leader in the Senate, he had a high profile in national politics and proven fund-raising abilities. His wife, Elizabeth, was prominent as secretary of transportation. Dole also had an acerbic wit, which gave spark to his campaigning style but irritated some voters. Other GOP candidates were Rep. Jack Kemp of New York, former secretary of state Alexander M. Haig Jr. of Pennsylvania, former Delaware governor Pierre S. "Pete" du Pont IV, and television evangelist Pat Robertson of Virginia.

The marathon campaign for the nomination began with the Iowa caucuses, a significant event only because of intense media attention. Gephardt barely edged Simon in the Democratic contests, and Dole won the Republican race. The big story was how badly Bush performed: he finished third behind Dole and Robertson.

The Iowa loss caused Bush to emerge from his isolation and confront his rivals for the nomination. (Bush had been the most restrained and cautious candidate as he tried to benefit from the prestige of the White House.) Bush also became more animated on the campaign trail. As a result of these changes—and a series of television advertisements charging that Dole would raise taxes—Bush beat Dole in the New Hampshire primary. Dole had failed to respond quickly to the Bush offensive, and when he snapped on national television about Bush's "lying about my record," he reinforced his image as a mean-spirited candidate.

Among the Democrats, Governor Dukakis easily won the New Hampshire primary, capitalizing on his regional popularity. Most of the Democratic fire in that race took place between the two runners-up, Gephardt and Simon. Dukakis escaped without any major criticism, and his already strong fund-raising machine went into high gear.

The decisive stage of the GOP campaign was Super Tuesday—March 8—when twenty-two states held presidential primaries or caucuses. Benefiting from a well-organized campaign and his new aggressiveness on the campaign trail, Bush won seventeen of the eighteen GOP contests. Dole staked his campaign on the ensuing Illinois primary, but he lost badly, and Bush was virtually ensured the Republican nomination.

The one issue that threatened Bush throughout 1988 was the Iran-contra scandal. Revelations that the Reagan administration had traded arms to Iran in exchange for the release of hostages, then used the proceeds illegally to fund the war in Nicaragua, raised questions about Bush's role in the matter. Administration officials admitted lying to Congress, destroying evidence, and operating outside normal government channels; one top official even attempted suicide. The question of Bush's involvement in the affair, however, fizzled after months of inconclusive questioning.

On Super Tuesday, Democratic front-runner Dukakis won Texas and Florida and five northern states, thereby confirming his shaky front-runner status. Civil rights leader Jesse Jackson was the big surprise, however, winning five southern states. Gore won seven states. Even though it was designed to help conservative candidates, Super Tuesday fit Jackson's strengths. Six of the nine states in which Jackson had scored best in 1984 held their contests on Super Tuesday in 1988. Super Tuesday also was supposed to put the South in the national spotlight, but the region received only a few more candidate visits in 1988 (149) than it had in 1976 (145).[186]

The Democratic marathon continued into Illinois, Michigan, and New York. Dukakis took and maintained the lead in delegates with steady wins over Jackson and Gore. Gore finally dropped out after finishing third in a divisive New York primary, and the rest of the campaign was a one-on-one race between Dukakis and Jackson. Only once—after his victory over Dukakis in the Michigan caucuses—did Jackson appear to have a chance to win the Democratic nomination. But in their next encounter, the Wisconsin primary, Dukakis defeated Jackson.

Jackson was a mixed blessing for the party. An energetic campaigner, he attracted support from blacks and from farmers and blue-collar workers who were disgruntled by the uneven rewards of economic growth. But Jackson was considerably to the left of the rest of the party and never had held any government office. Race also was a factor: no political professional believed that a liberal black could be elected president.

Dukakis practically clinched the nomination with his victory over Jackson in the New York primary. The issue of race was at the center of the campaign. New York City mayor Edward I. Koch, a Gore supporter, called Jackson a "radical" and said Jews would be "crazy" to vote for him. Such remarks aggravated tensions between blacks and Jews that had festered since the 1960s. Dukakis avoided the race issue and won the primary.

As the summer conventions approached, Bush and Dukakis each had the full support of his party. The parties' internal divisions were on display as the prospective nominees considered possible vice-presidential candidates. Blacks lobbied for Jackson's selection by Dukakis, while "new right" GOP leaders lobbied against a "moderate" running mate for Bush.

Dukakis selected conservative senator Lloyd Bentsen of Texas as his running mate before the Atlanta Democratic convention. Jackson complained publicly and privately about the decision, but he eventually embraced Bentsen for the sake of party unity. Dukakis hoped Bentsen would be able to help carry Texas: no Democrat had won the presidency without winning Texas since the state became part of the nation in 1845.

The July convention was a success for the Democrats. After a week of Bush-bashing and Democratic conciliation, Dukakis gave an effective acceptance speech peppered with statements in Spanish and Greek. Dukakis left the convention with a double-digit lead over Bush in the polls.

The Republican convention in August did not start out as well. Bush announced his vice-presidential selection, Sen. James Danforth "Dan" Quayle of Indiana, when he arrived in New Orleans. After revelations that Quayle had avoided military service in the Vietnam War by enlisting in the Indiana National Guard, many Republicans criticized Bush's choice. Some even said that Quayle might have to be dropped from the ticket.[187] By the end of the convention, however, the Republicans had weathered the storm. Bush delivered a crisp address, which provided the appealing self-portrait the vice president needed, and moved into the fall campaign for a close battle with Dukakis.

Bush took the offensive immediately after the August GOP convention and hit Dukakis as a "liberal" out of touch with American "values." More specifically, Bush attacked Dukakis for his membership in the American Civil Liberties Union, his veto of a bill requiring Massachusetts teachers to lead children in the Pledge of Allegiance, and a Massachusetts program allowing prisoners time off for weekends. The Bush campaign's "Willie Horton" commercial—which told of a black prisoner raping a woman while out on a weekend release program—was particularly controversial. As Bush pounded away at these symbolic issues (effectively drowning out other major issues such as the national debt, trade deficit, housing, education, U.S.–Soviet relations, the environment, and ethics in government), Dukakis's "negative" ratings with voters soared. Roger Ailes, Bush's media adviser, admitted that the Bush camp knew it would have to define Dukakis. The media themselves had no interest in substance, Ailes pointed out, leaving candidates "three ways to get on the air: pictures, attacks, and mistakes." Thus the Bush campaign spent its time "avoiding mistakes, staying on the attack, and giving them pictures."[188]

Not believing the attacks would affect his standing with undecided voters—and believing they might even hurt Bush—

Dukakis did not respond forcefully to the frontal assault until October. By then, however, Bush had effectively defined Dukakis, a newcomer to national politics. Dukakis's counteroffensive in the last two weeks of the campaign came too late.

As Dukakis fell behind Bush, his campaign pinned its hopes on two nationally televised debates. Dukakis performed well in the first debate, but Bush appeared to "win" the second debate. Dukakis failed to gain on Bush.

The only major problem for Bush was Quayle. Most political professionals considered Quayle a "lightweight." The forty-one-year-old Quayle had been a poor student and was a marginal member of Congress.[189] Dukakis said Bush's selection of Quayle amounted to failure in his "first presidential decision." Dukakis compared Quayle to the more experienced Bentsen, who performed much better in a vice-presidential debate. Indeed, in that debate Bentsen gave the campaign perhaps its most memorable moment. Responding to Quayle's assertion that he had as much congressional experience as Jack Kennedy had when he sought the presidency, Bentsen said, "Senator, I served with Jack Kennedy. I knew Jack Kennedy. Jack Kennedy was a friend of mine. Senator, you're no Jack Kennedy."[190]

Public polls revealed that most voters thought that Quayle was a bad choice. The Bush campaign tried to minimize the damage by limiting Quayle's public exposure and carefully scripting his statements. Quayle rarely spoke in major media markets; many of his campaign stops were accessible only by bus. While Bush delivered speeches in several states each day, Quayle often made just one speech before schoolchildren or partisan audiences.

After months of inconsistent and confusing strategy, Dukakis finally developed a strong appeal in the last two weeks of the campaign. He told voters he was on their side and portrayed Bush as a toady to the wealthy. Dukakis said the middle class had been "squeezed" by the policies of the Reagan administration and that the Democrats would provide good jobs, affordable housing and health care, and tough enforcement of environmental protection laws.

But it was not enough. Bush, who had made a fortune in the oil business before entering politics and was the son of a former U.S. senator, persuaded more voters that his experience and values were what they wanted in the very personal choice of a president.

## Democrats Regain the White House

In March 1991, in the aftermath of the U.S.-led victory over Iraq in the Persian Gulf War, President George Bush received the highest approval ratings since opinion polling began: around 90 percent of respondents said they approved of his performance as president. But just a year later, Bush was struggling to keep his job—and he failed.

Bill Clinton's victory over Bush in 1992 could have been viewed, on the one hand, as a dramatic shift in American politics. Touting his campaign slogan of "change," the forty-six-year-old Arkansas governor repeatedly blasted the Republican White House for its inattention to such domestic problems as the budget deficit, health care, welfare, civil rights, crime, trade, and economic investment. President Bush, Clinton said, was too obsessed with foreign policy and unconcerned with domestic affairs.

On the other hand, Clinton's election could have been viewed as an aberration. Only the second Democrat elected president since 1968, Clinton got only 43 percent of the vote in a three-candidate race. Voters said they voted against Bush, not for Clinton. The independent candidacy of Texas billionaire H. Ross Perot may have cost Bush the election, as much by tarnishing his reputation as taking away the votes of the angry middle class. Even people who supported Clinton expressed reservations about his character. Voters reacted warily to reports of Clinton's avoidance of military service in Vietnam, marital infidelity, and conflicts of interest while governor, and to his evasiveness about smoking marijuana as a student. On policy questions, Clinton was well informed, but sometimes he appeared insincere. A label pinned on Clinton in Arkansas—"Slick Willie"—stuck.

### THE BUSH STRATEGY

President Bush began the election cycle looking unbeatable. Coasting on the apparent success of his leadership during the Gulf War, Bush appeared to have the strength to lead the United States into what he called the "new world order." In 1989 the countries of the so-called Soviet bloc—East Germany, Poland, Czechoslovakia, Romania, Yugoslavia—had broken from communist rule in a series of nonviolent revolutions. In August 1991 an attempted coup against Mikhail Gorbachev's "perestroika" government in the Soviet Union had failed. Afterward, the Soviet regime—Communist Party and all—had collapsed. The Bush presidency had overseen the most remarkable realignment of world politics since World War II.

Indeed, Bush took credit for presiding over the dramatic changes, but those American "victories" also undermined his position. The Republican Party had dominated recent presidential politics at least partly because of its hawkish policies during the cold war. With the end of the Soviet threat, the GOP no longer had a "gut" issue to use against the Democrats. According to journalist Sidney Blumenthal, "The Cold War's end was not a photo opportunity, a sound bite, a revelation of 'character,' a political consultant's tactic, or even a theme. It was a global sea change as profound as the Cold War's beginning."[191] Bush had a hard time adjusting.

For a while, President Bush looked so strong that many Democrats were reluctant to take him on. The party's leading figures—Gov. Mario Cuomo of New York; Senators Bill Bradley of New Jersey, Al Gore of Tennessee, and Jay Rockefeller of West Virginia; and Rep. Richard Gephardt of Missouri—announced they would not run. Only former senator Paul E. Tsongas of Massachusetts, recently recovered from a bout with cancer, announced his candidacy in spring 1991.

Despite high polling numbers, President Bush might have been doomed from the start. Despite three decades in public life, Bush had never conveyed a coherent identity or campaign theme. His advisers planned to "narrowcast" messages to selected groups until the summer, when Bush would deliver his big "what-I-stand-for" speech. But by that time, Bush's opponent had defined him as weak and unprincipled. His attempt to divert attention to Clinton's foibles only intensified Bush's image as uncertain of his own values and goals.[192]

By the spring of 1992 Bush's base had crumbled. The president had decided to "sit" on his high popularity ratings and win reelection by avoiding mistakes. Bush's chief of staff, John Sununu, summed up the strategy: "There's not another single piece of legislation that needs to be passed in the next two years for this president. In fact, if Congress wants to come together, adjourn, and leave, it's all right with us."[193] The results of this strategy were devastating. In May 1992 a poll found that 76 percent of the public disapproved of the way Bush was handling the economy.[194] His overall approval rating dropped an unprecedented 57 percentage points from the end of the Gulf War to the beginning of the 1992 GOP convention.

A bitter anti-incumbent mood dominated the new campaign year. Nationwide, reformers promoted the idea of term limits for elected officials as a way to sweep out career politicians.[195] Perot, who had parlayed his wealth into a number of headline-grabbing exploits over the years, became a viable independent candidate.[196] His pithy statements about how to "fix" government captured the imagination of the public.

Pennsylvania voters sent a warning shot to the White House when they rejected the 1991 Senate candidacy of Bush's friend and first attorney general, Richard Thornburgh. Democrat Harris Wofford, appointed to the seat that had opened with the death of Sen. John Heinz in April 1991, won on a platform of national health care and a return to domestic priorities—themes that Bill Clinton reprised in 1992. Wofford, a former college president and Kennedy administration official, came from 30 points behind in the polls to win with 55 percent of the vote. It was the highest percentage that any Democrat had received in Pennsylvania senatorial elections. Wofford's campaign was run by a young operative named James Carville.

Bush's major domestic initiative—the budget law passed in October 1990—angered the Republican Party's right wing. Conservatives had long distrusted Bush because of his past moderate positions on taxes, abortion, civil rights, and social programs. The budget act, which increased taxes by $150 billion, broke the pledge of "no new taxes" that Bush had taken in the 1988 presidential campaign.

As the recession and other domestic crises deepened, the president seemed increasingly out of touch. Bush's reported confusion over the use of bar codes at a grocery store symbolized his elite background and isolation. After race riots in Los Angeles drew the nation's attention to the severity of poverty, Bush was photographed teaching baffled-looking urban youths how to use a fishing pole. In a political environment couched in symbolism, these images were ruinous.

Bush had begun his term with less party support than any president in history—the Democrats controlled the Senate by ten seats and the House by eighty-five seats. As a result, Bush's legislative initiatives were routinely labeled "dead on arrival." In 1989, for the first time, the Senate rejected an incoming president's cabinet nominee when it voted down former senator John G. Tower's bid to be secretary of defense. In his dealings with Capitol Hill, Bush had vacillated between confrontation and compromise. In fact, Bush regularly tussled with Congress, vetoing forty-four bills between 1989 and 1992.

## THE 1992 PRIMARY SEASON

The Democratic field grew slowly. Besides Clinton and Tsongas, the field included former governor Jerry Brown of California, Senators Thomas Harkin of Iowa and Robert Kerrey of Nebraska, and Gov. L. Douglas Wilder of Virginia. Wilder dropped out, however, before the first contest.

Clinton won the "invisible primaries" before the formal balloting began; he attracted $3.3 million in contributions by the end of 1991. Harkin was second best with a little more than $2 million.[197] The Clinton campaign then organized supporters in most states holding early contests.

By calling himself a "new Democrat," Clinton hoped to separate himself from some of the rejected Democratic candidates of the past: Jimmy Carter, Walter Mondale, and Michael Dukakis. In keeping with this strategy, Clinton promised to move beyond liberal orthodoxy and "reinvent government."[198] His record in Arkansas suggested a willingness to oppose liberal nostrums on such issues as the death penalty, economic growth, and public education.

The centerpiece of Clinton's strategy was to appeal to the "forgotten middle class." Suburbanites, the working class, and southerners and westerners had abandoned the Democratic Party since the late 1960s. Unfortunately for the Democrats, these groups composed a growing part of the electorate. In fact, many pundits argued that these groups gave the Republicans a "lock" on the presidency.[199] Clinton's goal, then, was to forge a new ideological center and "pick" the lock.

As expected, "favorite-son" Harkin won the Iowa caucuses, winning 76.4 percent of the delegates selected on February 10. Early on, Clinton had led the polling in New Hampshire, but he ran into trouble when the media questioned his character. A woman claimed that she and Clinton had had an affair and that Clinton had helped her to get a state job. Meanwhile, Clinton was reported to have misled an Army Reserves recruiter as part of a scheme to avoid service in Vietnam. And, to make matters worse, at one point Clinton's campaign was almost broke.

But Clinton hit back. Appearing on the television news magazine 60 Minutes after the January 1992 Super Bowl game, Clinton admitted he had "caused pain" in his marriage but said he and his wife had solved their problems. Hillary Clinton's appearance with her husband seemed to close the matter. Skeptics should vote against Clinton, she said, but they also should drop the character charges.

Tsongas won the New Hampshire primary on February 18 with 33.2 percent of the vote to Clinton's 24.7 percent. Tsongas offered the policy equivalent of castor oil. He said the nation needed to make difficult economic choices such as higher taxes and program cutbacks. He called Clinton, who spoke in favor of a tax cut and the costly Connecticut-built Polaris Navy submarine, a "pander bear."

Clinton, who fell some 20 points in polls in a month, exuberantly called his second-place finish a victory by noting Tsongas's regional ties and declaring himself the "Comeback Kid." His campaign, however, was out of money and had to be rescued by a $3.5 million line of credit from an Arkansas bank.

Tsongas and Brown won the occasional contest after New Hampshire, but Clinton rolled to the nomination starting with his March 3 victory in the Georgia primary. Kerrey and Harkin dropped out in early March. Clinton's sweep of southern states on "Super Tuesday," March 10, and his decisive wins in Michigan and Illinois on March 17 practically clinched the nomination. But he had a scare when Brown beat him in Connecticut on March 24. He then beat Brown decisively in New York on April 7. Tsongas, by that time an inactive candidate, finished ahead of Brown in New York.

Clinton won thirty-one state primaries with 51.8 percent of the vote; Tsongas, four states with 18.1 percent; and Brown, two states with 20.1 percent.[200] Even as Clinton won state after state and Bush plummeted in the polls, Democratic leaders searched for an alternative; they had grown nervous about Clinton's ability to confront the character issue. In March almost half the Democratic voters in Connecticut's primary said Clinton lacked the "honesty or integrity" to be president.[201] Former governor Brown fed the uncertainty with his relentless attacks on Clinton's ties to special interests. Talk of drafting another candidate continued, but party professionals became resigned to Clinton's nomination.

President Bush faced an unusually pointed challenge from conservative columnist and former White House aide Patrick J. Buchanan, who charged that Bush betrayed the conservative faith. His main point of attack was the 1990 tax increase. But he also criticized Bush's activism in world affairs, federal support of arts projects that he called "blasphemous," and the nationwide recession.

Buchanan's campaign in New Hampshire, run by his sister, was simple. He wrote his own speeches, showed roughly designed television ads in which people mimicked Bush's "no new taxes" pledge, and mocked Bush's superior campaign organization and resources. According to Buchanan, the "Buchanan brigades" would defeat "King George and his armies." Bush, however, ignored Buchanan's campaign. He sent his wife and other administration representatives to campaign in New Hampshire.

Although in the end Bush won New Hampshire, the media

Independent H. Ross Perot mounted his 1992 campaign for the presidency by relying on his own money and appearing on the television talk shows, such as here with Larry King.

focused on the 37 percent of the vote that the underdog Buchanan received. Buchanan then made a vigorous effort to win some of the southern contests in early March, but he never matched his New Hampshire numbers. Buchanan continued his campaign until June, assured of media attention by virtue of his quixotic quest and uncompromising rhetoric. In the final analysis, however, he did not win any states with his 22 percent of the total primary vote.[202]

Ironically, in taking his hard hits at Bush, Buchanan may have helped to neutralize another protest candidate, former Ku Klux Klan leader David Duke, who had finished second in the Louisiana gubernatorial contest in 1991. Republican leaders were embarrassed by Duke's GOP membership, but he disappeared after a poor showing in New Hampshire.

Perot's on-and-off campaign unsettled Republicans' plans to build on their base in the South and West. Perot's folksy antigovernment rhetoric appealed to voters in the suburbs and high-growth areas of the 1980s—the heart of the GOP base since Richard Nixon's 1968 campaign.

Perot's campaign began where much of the 1992 campaign was waged: on the television talk-show circuit. On the cable TV show *Larry King Live*, Perot said in February that he would run for president if volunteers put him on the ballot in all fifty states. He also said he would spend up to $100 million of his own money to fund a "world-class campaign." At one point, Perot appeared to have a chance to win the presidency. Polls in May showed him in second place nationally behind President Bush and winning some southern and western states outright.

As Perot's unofficial campaign progressed, the media raised doubts about his background and grasp of government. For example, Perot had made his fortune by gaining rights to a computer accounting system for government health programs, and it was only his behind-the-scenes lobbying that prompted the Nixon administration to halt a government battle for control of the computer system. On a more personal level, Perot's conspir-

Democratic presidential candidate Bill Clinton talks with young people on a program hosted by the MTV cable channel. The 1992 campaign was revolutionary in the way candidates used nontraditional media to reach voters.

acy theories about such issues as prisoners of war in Vietnam and political opponents led to speculation about possible paranoia. When asked about the details for his plans to address the budget deficit, improve government efficiency, improve U.S. trade, and address foreign affairs, Perot appeared ill-informed and irritable. Thus by summer more people viewed Perot unfavorably than favorably.

Perot dropped out of the campaign before he had a chance to formally announce his entry. He pointed out that Clinton's selection of Sen. Al Gore of Tennessee as his running mate indicated that the Democrats were "getting their act together." He also recognized that his campaign might split the vote badly and send the election into the House of Representatives.

Perot resumed his campaign in the fall, blaming his temporary exit on a Republican "dirty tricks" effort to smear his family. By then the critical reporting had faded. But it was too late for Perot because his erratic behavior had driven away supporters and curious voters alike. Perot also had difficulty finding a credible running mate. His selection of retired admiral James Stockdale became the subject of parody when Stockdale appeared confused and poorly informed at a debate of vice-presidential candidates.

Even though Perot had no real chance to win, his campaign was significant. He spent $60 million of his own money, mostly to purchase half-hour television advertisements. Some of the ads, dubbed "infomercials," won critical acclaim for their plain talk about the dangers of the federal budget deficit. Perot's bluntness lent credibility to his relentless attacks on Bush.

## THE 1992 ELECTION

The communications revolution changed the way the candidates reached voters. For example, candidates appeared in settings once considered undignified for potential presidents. Television talk shows such as *Larry King Live* and *The Arsenio Hall Show,* as well as such radio programs as *Imus in the Morning,* provided a way for candidates to bypass the establishment media. The blurred lines between news and entertainment were perhaps most evident on cable television in the rock music MTV channel's ongoing coverage of the presidential campaign. New outlets were especially important for candidates facing credibility problems in mainstream media (Bill Clinton) and for the insurgents (Ross Perot and Jerry Brown).

Bush's campaign was on the defensive early for using "dirty" campaign tactics. Democrats cited Bush's 1988 "Willie Horton" commercials as evidence of a Republican willingness to appeal to racism and fear. Newspaper citations of the Horton campaign were greater in 1992 than 1988, suggesting that the Democrats eventually got more from the ad's backlash than Republicans got from the original campaign.

Clinton parroted Perot's rhetoric about the evils of special-interest influence in Washington and promised reforms of the campaign finance system. But he also raised money aggressively. The Democrats raised $71 million in 1992, $9 million more than the Republicans.[203] Clinton's selection of moderate senator Al Gore of Tennessee as a running mate was central to his fall strategy. Gore's service in Vietnam and military expertise countered Clinton's suspect status in foreign policy. Moreover, Gore's Washington experience going back to 1976 helped Clinton to compensate for his own lack of experience. Finally, Gore's reputation as an intellectual—he wrote an acclaimed book about the environment in 1992[204]—contrasted with Vice President Quayle's lightweight reputation.

In his campaign, Clinton benefited from the "year of the woman." Women had supported Democratic candidates in greater numbers than men since the Republican Party dropped its support for the Equal Rights Amendment and abortion rights in 1980. But the Democrats were not able to exploit the "gender gap" until 1992. The galvanizing issue was the allegation that Clarence Thomas, a Bush appointee to the Supreme Court, had sexually harassed a former colleague named Anita Hill. Women were outraged with the Senate Judiciary Committee's handling of the matter, and feminist groups mobilized to increase female representation in politics. The issue put President Bush on the defensive, while Clinton rallied liberals and libertarians alike with his calls for equal opportunity and abortion rights.

The Republican convention in Houston was a turning point in the campaign. Strategists decided to shore up Bush's right-wing support and raise doubts about Clinton's character. The party's platform committee was dominated by the right-wing Christian Coalition. Speeches by Patrick Buchanan, Pat Robertson, and Marilyn Quayle, questioning the Democrats' patriotism and arguing for a rollback of civil liberties, played badly. Bush's lost convention opportunity was apparent in the meager 3 percentage point "bounce" in poll support, compared with Clinton's 17 to 20 percent increase after the Democratic convention.[205]

Clinton ran a sophisticated general election campaign, coordinated from the "war room" in Little Rock by strategists, led by James Carville, who choreographed every aspect of the campaign, from television commercials to talk-show appearances to speechwriting to the bus tours of small towns. The campaign professionals were especially adept at answering charges from the opposition. When Bush attacked, Clintonites issued instant, detailed responses. The quick response prevented Bush's charges from dominating the news cycle.

The Bush-Quayle fall campaign was erratic. Early on, it focused on "family values," critiquing the Democrats as elitists out of touch with ordinary people. Then Bush used the powers of incumbency by announcing billions of dollars in grants to different states. All along, Bush criticized Clinton's character and experience. But the personal attacks often appeared shrill; at one point, he called Clinton and Gore "bozos" and said "my dog Millie" would be better at foreign policy than they. Bush criticized Clinton's visit to the Soviet Union as a student and suggested that he wanted to import British-style socialism to the United States.

Bush's own credibility came under fire in the campaign's final days when a special prosecutor indicted former defense secretary Caspar Weinberger and released a memorandum that indicated Bush had participated in the Iran-contra scandal much more actively than he had acknowledged.

The Clinton-Gore ticket gave the Democrats a solid base in the border states to build on. With Arkansas and Tennessee in the Democratic camp, the Democrats could build outward into the old Confederacy (Georgia, Louisiana, Kentucky), north into the industrial states (Illinois, Michigan, Ohio) and west and north into the farm states (Iowa, Minnesota, Wisconsin). The

Democrats had consistently lost those states in presidential elections in the past generation, despite strong support in congressional and statewide races.

The Democrats also built on their core of support in the Northeast (winning all the states from Maine to West Virginia) and capitalized on disgruntlement with Bush in the West (California, Colorado, Hawaii, Montana, Nevada, New Mexico, Oregon, and Washington went for Clinton). That was enough to "pick" the Republican "lock" on the electoral college.

Clinton took only 43 percent of the popular vote but garnered 370 electoral votes. This compared with Bush's 38 percent of the popular vote and 168 electoral votes. Perot's 19 percent share of the vote did not win any states.

The hard anti-incumbent mood of the electorate, stoked by Perot, helped to produce the highest voter turnout rate since 1960. Some 55 percent of eligible voters participated in the election. That participation rate was far below rates of other countries and earlier periods in U.S. history. But it seemed to stem, momentarily, the apathy and resignation of American politics.

## SETTING THE STAGE FOR 1996

In 1994 many voters sent a strong message of disapproval with President Clinton's record by electing a Republican Congress. That dramatic event led many political analysts to conclude that Clinton would be a one-term president. But what many had not anticipated was that the new GOP Congress, led prominently by controversial House Speaker Newt Gingrich (Georgia), would incorrectly interpret the 1994 elections results as a mandate for their conservative ideological agenda and then push for substantial—and unpopular—policy reform. This miscalculation provided President Clinton with a new opportunity to redefine himself and to rehabilitate his political future.

While the Republicans strove hard for conservative policy change, Clinton adopted more moderate positions and portrayed himself as a check against the "extremism" of the GOP agenda. That tack proved successful by the end of 1995. With the president and Republican legislators feuding over spending priorities, Congress failed to pass a budget on time to avoid two temporary government shutdowns. As the impasse persisted, the GOP Congress began to appear unreasonable in the public's eye, and the president benefited from the comparison. This budgetary standoff against Congress was perhaps the single most important event to Clinton's political rehabilitation.

The president entered the 1996 election season with renewed political strength and high approval ratings. In addition to the political miscalculations of the Republican Congress, Clinton benefited from a strengthening economy. A third factor also began to weigh in the president's favor: he lacked an intraparty challenge for renomination, while the GOP nomination contest was an expensive, highly negative, and divisive process.

From the beginning Senate Majority Leader Bob Dole (Kansas) was the clear front-runner for the Republican Party's nomination. He had the broadest party support of any announced candidate, the most prominent endorsements, and the best grassroots campaign organization. Although there never was any serious doubt that he would be the Republican nominee, for several months Dole had to fight off a large group of presidential aspirants including television commentator Pat Buchanan, former Department of Education secretary Lamar Alexander, Texas senator Phil Gramm, Indiana senator Richard Lugar, California representative Robert Dornan, and multimillionaire publisher Malcolm S. "Steve" Forbes Jr.

Of these candidates, initially Gramm appeared to be the most formidable because of his status in the Senate and ability to raise huge sums of money for a campaign. Yet Gramm lacked grassroots support and his campaign faded quickly. Colleague Lugar was highly regarded by party moderates and many opinion leaders, but he ran a bland campaign that dwelt on foreign policy issues that were not driving the Republican electorate. Buchanan had support among many of the dedicated antiabortion conservatives in the party, and he fared surprisingly well in some of the early caucuses and primaries, but most in the GOP considered him too extreme and his campaign too faltered.

The most important opponent to Dole ultimately was the publishing tycoon Forbes, who spent an extraordinary sum of his personal fortune to challenge the front-runner with extensive negative television ads. Although Forbes's campaign failed to dislodge Dole from the front of the pack, it succeeded at raising serious doubts about the senator's ability to beat Clinton. The negative ads also hurt Dole's standing with the wider public and forced him to spend his campaign resources on the nomination battle as Clinton amassed campaign funds for the general election.

Dole's eventual nomination—even after losing the traditionally crucial battleground primary in New Hampshire to Buchanan—did not ensure a united Republican Party to challenge the president. Although Dole had long supported the antiabortion stance of many in his party, social conservatives who made up a crucial bloc of the Republican vote were not convinced of his commitment to their cause. Many considered him too moderate in temperament and too willing to compromise principles. Party moderates worried that Dole would allow the Christian right to force his campaign to adopt positions that would enable the Democrats to once again capitalize on the "extremism" charge.[206]

Even after his nomination was assured, Dole's campaign failed for weeks to capture the public's attention. In part he appeared too much a part of the GOP agenda in Congress that Democrats had successfully defined as harshly conservative. As senate majority leader Dole had found himself in the difficult position of having to manage his official duties while campaigning for president. This involved promoting the GOP agenda in Congress while at the same time trying to distance himself from its less popular elements. Dole made a bold strategic gamble when he decided to resign from the Senate altogether to campaign full time for the presidency. His emotional departure from the Senate on June 11 temporarily energized his campaign.

At his nominating convention in San Diego, Dole performed a tough balancing act in keeping warring moderates and social conservatives from dividing the party. Dole especially sought to avoid the kind of negative publicity that had surrounded "family values night" at the 1992 GOP convention in Houston.[207] The Republicans struck an awkward compromise: although the party platform was very conservative and kept the antiabortion plank, the convention that the country saw on television was moderate in tone and did not feature prime time addresses by such controversial figures as Rev. Pat Robertson and Pat Buchanan.

Dole surprised many with two bold campaign moves. First, he selected former New York representative and secretary of Housing and Urban Development Jack Kemp for vice president—Kemp had earlier endorsed Forbes. Second, Dole proposed an across-the-board 15 percent income tax cut. This proposal was especially surprising because Dole had cultivated a well-deserved reputation as a "deficit hawk" who opposed supply-side economic theory. Yet to energize his lagging campaign, Dole abandoned his lifelong approach to economic policy. Although Dole succeeded in attracting attention with this move, not all of it was positive as many political analysts focused on the contradictions between his tax cut proposal and earlier statements.

## CLINTON'S REELECTION

Although polls throughout 1996 showed Clinton with a commanding lead against Dole, those same polls pointed to voter uneasiness with the president's character. Because of continued poor media coverage resulting from Whitewater-related charges, the poorly handled White House firing of its travel office staff, and a sexual harassment lawsuit against Clinton, most of the public believed that their president was an individual of poor personal character. Yet the polls also indicated that Americans would reelect a flawed president because of their uneasiness with the Republican nominee, their poor opinion of the GOP-led Congress, and their general satisfaction with the state of the economy.

Throughout the campaign season, Clinton often seemed to be running against the very unpopular Gingrich and the Republican Congress more than he was taking on Dole. What made Clinton's campaign so strong, in part, was his governing strategy of one what key aide called "triangulation": that is, separating himself from the unpopular elements of both political parties and establishing a less partisan identity at the center of the political spectrum. To achieve that end, Clinton adopted a number of policy initiatives that were conservative, but also largely popular. He signed a welfare reform bill that liberals in his party detested, pushed for imposition of a V-chip in televisions to allow parents to screen program content for children and for a television program rating system, advocated curfews for teenagers and school uniforms as well as mandatory drug tests for sixteen-year-olds applying for driving licenses, proposed a balanced budget by the year 2002, and extolled his record in reducing the federal budget deficit. Clinton also stayed true to his Demo-

President Bill Clinton and Vice President Al Gore accept their renomination at the Democratic National Convention in August 1996. In the general election Clinton became the first Democratic president reelected to a second term since Franklin Roosevelt in 1936.

cratic roots by opposing congressional efforts to reduce Medicare spending and weaken environmental regulation and by proposing new government programs to make college education more affordable.

Clinton's strategy was brilliant. He effectively took away from Dole's campaign a number of issues that usually help Republican presidential candidates such as welfare reform, deficit reduction, and family values. He kept his Democratic base by positioning himself as the only viable check against the "extremism" of the Republican Congress.

From a stylistic standpoint, the Clinton and Dole campaigns could not have been more different. Admirers and critics alike agree that Clinton was an effective campaigner and a very strong communicator. By contrast, despite protestations by those who know him to be a warm and humorous person, Dole projected the image of a threatening and humorless politician. Despite a vigorous campaign, Dole never overcame the uneasiness that most voters felt about him personally. In past campaigns he had acquired the negative persona of a political "hatchet man" and that image stuck with him throughout the 1996 race. Indeed, Dole tried so hard to change that image that he spent months refusing to attack Clinton's most serious political weakness: his character. When implored by partisan Republicans to attack the president, Dole would reply that he considered Clinton "my opponent, not my enemy." In his two debates with Clinton, Dole did little to improve his public image, as his presentational style was stiff and somewhat harsh—in large contrast to Clinton who projected a much more assuring image.

In the last weeks of the campaign, when it was clear that Dole had no realistic chance of winning, the Republican candidate made a final gamble: he decided finally to attack the president's character and to make it an overriding theme of the campaign. Dole's attacks on the president made a difference in the campaign polls when the news media began to report on questionable fund-raising practices by the Democratic National Committee (DNC) and meetings between foreign lobbyists and Clinton. Stories of unethical and possibly illegal Democratic campaign contributions dovetailed with the Dole message that Clinton lacked good character—and that such a fault was unsuitable for the person serving as president.

Clinton perhaps further hurt himself when he avoided directly confronting the negative stories about the fund-raising practices of his party. Instead, he protested that candidates had no choice but to raise funds and campaign under a flawed system and that, if reelected, he would propose fundamental campaign finance reform. Although this negative publicity and the Dole charges were not enough to deny Clinton's victory, just days before the election one major poll by the Zogby Group for Reuters News Agency placed Clinton's lead at only 7 percent, significantly below the double-digit margins he had maintained throughout the race.[208]

Reform Party candidate, billionaire H. Ross Perot, also benefited somewhat from the negative Clinton press. Although he had never been a serious factor in 1996 as he had been as an independent candidate in 1992—and as a result was excluded from the presidential debates—Perot's support increased by several percentage points in the late polls. But in the end, Perot had little impact on the elections. Because of a perceived strong economy and a substantial reduction in the federal debt, the public frustration with the two major parties that had given growth to Perot's candidacy in 1992 simply did not exist in 1996.

As the Dole campaign emphasized the character issue, his senior staff were aware that the Washington Post was investigating a story about a past marital indiscretion by their candidate. In a controversial decision, the Post decided not to publish the information it had gathered about an extramarital affair Dole had in 1969. The newspaper's decision to not publish even after confirming beyond any doubt all the facts angered Clinton partisans who felt that the Post had displayed a double standard. Clinton, of course, had been subjected to unrelenting coverage of allegations of extramarital affairs, and these stories had always played a key role in the president's reputation for poor character. Had the newspaper published the story late in the campaign there is little doubt that it would have had an adverse impact on Dole's late surge in the polls that had largely been driven by the character issue. The Post's editor concluded that the story had no relevance to the issue of Dole's qualification to be president—a decision that most journalists thought should have been left to an informed electorate.[209]

Clinton easily won reelection with 49.2 percent of the popular vote and 379 electoral votes to Dole's 40.7 percent and 159 electoral votes. Reform Party candidate Ross Perot polled 8.4 percent of the vote, less than half of his 1992 total, and received no electoral votes.[210] Clinton's victory made him the first Democrat to win reelection since Franklin D. Roosevelt won his second term in 1936. He became the first Democrat to be elected to the presidency along with a Republican-controlled Congress. Clinton won every state he had captured in 1992, except for Georgia, Montana, and Colorado. However, he picked up Florida and Arizona—becoming the first Democratic presidential candidate to win Florida since 1976 and first to win Arizona since 1948. The so-called gender gap was key to Clinton's victory: while male vote was evenly split between the two candidates, Clinton won the female vote by 16 percent, the largest margin ever. Clinton also beat Dole among every age group and was the clear choice of minorities: he received 80 percent of the black vote and 70 percent of the Hispanic vote.[211]

Yet three facts remained discouraging for Clinton. First, for the second straight election he had failed to win a majority of the popular vote. Second, voter turnout was less than 50 percent, the lowest since 1924. Third, Democrats failed to regain control of the Congress, despite the unpopularity of Gingrich and many of his Republican colleagues. Given this scenario, it was difficult for the president to credibly claim that he had achieved any kind of mandate from the American people.

Exit polling data suggested that the incumbent Clinton indeed benefited from positive public feelings about the economy. In one voter poll conducted by numerous news organizations about 60 percent of the respondents said that the economy was doing well. Those respondents heavily favored Clinton. In 1992 the exit polls found that less than 20 percent said the economy was doing well, a situation that had benefited the challenger Clinton.[212]

Perhaps what was most remarkable about the 1996 national elections was just how little had actually changed, despite the two major parties having spent about $500 million on campaign activities. Political analysts have aptly referred to the 1996 elections as reaffirming the status-quo, a dramatic difference from both the 1992 and 1994 elections in which voters expressed frustration with the existing political arrangement and sought substantial changes in their government.

**NOTES**

1. A. James Reichley, *The Life of the Parties: A History of American Political Parties* (New York: Free Press, 1992), 17.

2. Richard P. McCormick, *The Presidential Game: The Origins of American Presidential Politics* (New York: Oxford University Press, 1982), chap. 1.

3. Ibid., 33–34.

4. Reichley, *Life of the Parties*, 42.

5. Ibid., 49.

6. Robert J. Dinkin, *Campaigning in America: A History of Election Practices* (New York: Greenwood Press, 1989), 18.

7. Roy F. Nichols, *The Invention of the American Political Parties* (New York: Macmillan, 1967), 192.

8. Bruce L. Felkner, *Political Mischief: Smear, Sabotage, and Reform in U.S. Elections* (New York: Praeger, 1992), 31.

9. Dinkin, *Campaigning in America*, 15, 18.

10. Edward Stanwood, *A History of the Presidency* (Boston: Houghton Mifflin, 1898), 63.

11. John F. Hoadley, *Origins of American Party Politics, 1789–1803* (Lexington: University Press of Kentucky, 1986), 191.

12. T. Harry Williams, *The History of American Wars: From Colonial Times to World War I* (New York: Knopf, 1981), 134.

13. Stanwood, *History of the Presidency*, 110.

14. Matthew A. Crenson, *The Federal Machine* (Baltimore: Johns Hopkins University Press, 1971), 11–30.

15. Jackson biographer Robert V. Remini explains the nickname "Old Hickory." In an arduous five-hundred-mile march, Jackson gave his three horses to wounded soldiers and marched on foot with his troops to give them moral support. The soldiers serving under him agreed that their general was as tough as hickory. "Not much later," Remini writes, "they started calling him 'Hickory' as a sign of their respect and regard; then the affectionate 'Old' was added to give Jackson a nickname . . . that admirably served him thereafter throughout his military and political wars" (Robert V. Remini, *Andrew Jackson* [New York: Harper and Row, 1969], 54).

16. Arthur M. Schlesinger Jr., *The Age of Jackson* (New York: New American Library, 1945), 34.

17. *Guide to Congress*, 2d ed. (Washington, D.C.: Congressional Quarterly, 1982), 613.

18. Russell L. Hanson, *The Democratic Imagination in America: Conversations with Our Past* (Princeton, N.J.: Princeton University Press, 1985), 125.

19. Eugene H. Roseboom, *A History of Presidential Elections* (New York: Macmillan, 1970), 106.

20. Schlesinger, *Age of Jackson*, 55.

21. Estimates of vote totals vary, especially in the years before standardized methods of balloting. Discrepancies developed because of disputes about stuffing ballot boxes, the eligibility of some voters, absentee ballots, and simple counting and reporting difficulties in the pre-media age.

22. Roseboom, *History of Presidential Elections*, 112.

23. Hanson, *Democratic Imagination*, 54–120.

24. Ibid., 140–141.

25. Ibid., 136.

26. See Albert O. Hirschman, *Exit, Voice, and Loyalty* (Cambridge, Mass.: Harvard University Press, 1970).

27. Hanson, *Democratic Imagination*, 138.

28. Richard P. McCormick, "Political Development and the Second Party System," in *The American Party Systems: Stages of Development,* ed. William Nisbet Chambers and Walter Dean Burnham (New York: Oxford University Press, 1967), 102.

29. Paul Taylor, *See How They Run: Electing a President in the Age of Mediaocracy* (New York: Knopf, 1991), 4.

30. James L. Sundquist, *Dynamics of the Party System*, rev. ed. (Washington, D.C.: Brookings, 1983), 51.

31. Roseboom, *Presidential Elections*, 143.

32. Richard Hofstadter, *The American Political Tradition* (New York: Vintage, 1948), 113.

33. Ibid.

34. Hanson, *Democratic Imagination*, 176.

35. Roseboom, *History of Presidential Elections*, 177–181.

36. Paul N. Angle, ed., *The Lincoln Reader* (New York: Pocket Books, 1954), 523.

37. Ibid., 531.

38. Roseboom, *History of Presidential Elections*, 201.

39. Eric Foner, *Reconstruction: America's Unfinished Revolution, 1863–1877* (New York: Harper and Row, 1988).

40. William S. McFeely, *Grant* (New York: Norton, 1981), 283.

41. Ibid., 288–289.

42. Ibid., 381.

43. Bernhard Bailyn et al., *The Great Republic: A History of the American People* (Boston: Little, Brown, 1977), 802.

44. C. Vann Woodward, *Reunion and Reaction* (New York: Doubleday Anchor Books, 1951).

45. Kenneth M. Stampp, *The Era of Reconstruction, 1865–1877* (New York: Vintage, 1965), 210–211.

46. Michael Nelson, "A Short, Ironic History of American National Bureaucracy," *Journal of Politics* 44 (winter 1982): 747–777.

47. Roseboom, *History of Presidential Elections*, 264.

48. Harry Thurston Peck, *Twenty Years of the Republic, 1885–1905* (New York: Dodd, Mead, 1906), 20.

49. Michael E. McGerr, *The Decline of Popular Politics: The American North, 1865–1928* (New York: Oxford University Press), 82–106.

50. Peck, *Twenty Years of the Republic*, 41.

51. Ibid., 78.

52. Ibid., 144.

53. Ibid., 169.

54. Roseboom, *History of Presidential Elections*, 290.

55. Bailyn et al., *Great Republic*, 786.

56. Sundquist, *Dynamics of the Party System*, 107.

57. For a concise account of the machine reform struggle, see Dennis R. Judd, *The Politics of American Cities* (Boston: Little, Brown, 1984), 50–110.

58. See David Montgomery, *The Fall of the House of Labor* (New York: Cambridge University Press, 1987).

59. Sundquist, *Dynamics of the Party System*, 116–118.

60. Ibid., 143, 152.

61. Hofstadter, *American Political Tradition*, 187.

62. Sundquist, *Dynamics of the Party System*, 149–152.

63. Hofstadter, *American Political Tradition*, 192–193.

64. See "William Jennings Bryan, Cross of Gold Speech," in *Great Issues in American History: From Reconstruction to the Present Day, 1864–1969*, ed. Richard Hofstadter (New York: Vintage, 1969), 166–173.

65. Jasper B. Shannon, *Money and Politics* (New York: Random House, 1959), 30–32.

66. Sundquist, *Dynamics of the Party System*, 158.

67. Ibid., 169; for a general discussion of the 1896 election's resulting realignment, see pages 160–169.

68. E. E. Schattschneider, *The Semisovereign People* (Hinsdale, Ill.: Dryden Press, 1975), 76–77.

69. Edmund Morris, *The Rise of Theodore Roosevelt* (New York: Ballantine, 1979), 718.

70. See Gabriel Kolko, *The Triumph of Conservatism* (New York: Free Press, 1963).

71. Sundquist, *Dynamics of the Party System*, 176.

72. See Alpheus I. Mason, *Bureaucracy Convicts Itself* (New York: Viking Press, 1941); and James Penick Jr., *Progressive Politics and Conservation* (Chicago: University of Chicago Press, 1968).

73. August Hecksher, *Woodrow Wilson* (New York: Scribner's, 1991), 231–232.

74. Ibid., 259.

75. J. Leonard Bates, *The United States, 1898–1928* (New York: McGraw-Hill, 1976), 187.

76. Roseboom, *History of Presidential Elections*, 384.

77. John L. Shover, ed., *Politics of the Nineteen Twenties* (Waltham, Mass.: Ginn-Blaisdell, 1970), 148.

78. Ibid., 4.

79. Ibid., 12.

80. Ibid., 10.

81. James David Barber, *The Pulse of Politics: Electing Presidents in the Media Age* (New York: Norton, 1980), 239.

82. William E. Leuchtenberg, *Franklin D. Roosevelt and the New Deal* (New York: Harper and Row, 1963), 13.

83. Frank Friedel, *Franklin D. Roosevelt: The Triumph* (Boston: Little, Brown, 1956), 248–249.

84. Barber, *Pulse of Politics*, 243.

85. Ibid., 244.

86. Ibid., 238.

87. Hofstadter, *American Political Tradition*, 332.

88. Barber, *Pulse of Politics*, 244.

89. See Robert Lekachman, *The Age of Keynes* (New York: Random House, 1966).

90. Schattschneider argues in *The Semisovereign People* that the key element of any conflict is the extent to which the protagonists are able to control how many people get involved. Every "scope of conflict" has a bias. The size of the group involved in the conflict is almost always open to change. Schattschneider writes: "A look at political literature shows that there has indeed been a long-standing struggle between the conflicting tendencies toward the privatization and socialization of conflict" (p. 7). The New Deal was a stage of socialization of conflict.

91. Everett Carll Ladd Jr. and Charles D. Hadley, *Transformations of the American Party System* (New York: Norton, 1978), 86.

92. Ibid., 43.

93. Ibid., 46.

94. Ibid., 64–74, 112; Sundquist, *Dynamics of the Party System*, 214–224.

95. Sundquist, *Dynamics of the Party System*, 217.

96. Ladd and Hadley, *Transformations*, 82.

97. Ibid., 58–59.

98. Ibid., 63.

99. Samuel H. Beer, "Liberalism and the National Interest," *Public Interest*, no. 1 (fall 1966): 81.

100. Theodore J. Lowi, *The End of Liberalism* (New York: Norton, 1969). See also Hanson, *Democratic Imagination*, 257–292.

101. Greg Mitchell, *The Campaign of the Century: Upton Sinclair's Race for Governor of California and the Birth of Modern Media Politics* (New York: Random House, 1992).

102. James MacGregor Burns, *Roosevelt: The Lion and the Fox* (New York: Harcourt Brace and World, 1956), 282–283.

103. Roseboom, *History of Presidential Elections*, 447.

104. Burns, *Roosevelt*, 277–278.

105. Ibid., 269–271.

106. Ibid., 282–283.

107. Ibid., 300.

108. Ibid., 427.

109. Barber, *Pulse of Politics*. This book tells the story behind the Willkie movement and the role played by Henry R. Luce, the founder of Time Inc.

110. See Lekachman, *Age of Keynes*, esp. chaps. 5 and 6.

111. Roseboom, *History of Presidential Elections*, 483.

112. William E. Leuchtenberg, *In the Shadow of F.D.R.: From Harry Truman to Ronald Reagan* (Ithaca, N.Y.: Cornell University Press, 1983), 1–2.

113. Ibid., 15.

114. Ibid., 21.

115. V. O. Key Jr., *Southern Politics in State and Nation* (Knoxville: University of Tennessee Press, 1984), 649.

116. Ibid., 330–344.

117. Barber, *Pulse of Politics*, 50.

118. Nelson W. Polsby and Aaron Wildavsky, *Presidential Elections* (New York: Scribner's, 1984), 205–206.

119. Barber, *Pulse of Politics*, 61.

120. Angus Campbell, Philip E. Convers, Warren E. Miller, and Donald E. Stokes, *The American Voter* (New York: Wiley, 1960), 532.

121. Richard Neustadt, *Presidential Power* (New York: Wiley, 1980), 10, 12–14, 16, 18, 19, 22–25, 43, 67–68, 178.

122. Garry Wills, *Nixon Agonistes* (New York: New American Library, 1969), 91.

123. Fred Greenstein, *The Hidden-Hand Presidency* (New York: Basic Books, 1982).

124. Barber, *Pulse of Politics*, 269.

125. Eric F. Goldman quipped, "The returns, as the gangsters said, made even Alf Landon look good," in *The Crucial Decade* (New York: Vintage, 1960), 326.

126. The elder Kennedy always had planned for his sons to enter national politics. He originally pushed his eldest son, Joseph Jr., but the son died in combat in World War II. John was next; he ran for Congress in 1946. Robert, the third Kennedy son, served as an aide to Sen. Joseph McCarthy before managing John's 1960 presidential campaign and serving as

his attorney general. Edward, the youngest, worked on the 1960 campaign and won a Senate seat in 1962.

127. Merle Miller, *Plain Speaking* (New York: Berkeley, 1974), 199.

128. Theodore H. White, *The Making of the President 1960* (New York: Atheneum, 1961), 114–116.

129. Ibid., 128.

130. Ibid., 130.

131. Ibid., 198–204.

132. Arthur M. Schlesinger Jr., *Robert F. Kennedy and His Times* (Boston: Houghton Mifflin, 1978), 193.

133. Henry Fairlie, *The Kennedy Promise* (New York: Dell, 1972), 30–31.

134. White, *Making of the President 1960*, 329.

135. Ibid., 327.

136. Richard M. Nixon, *Six Crises* (Garden City, N.Y.: Doubleday, 1962), 412.

137. White, *Making of the President 1960*, 397–401.

138. Sen. Barry Goldwater, letter to the author, January 25, 1988.

139. The Warren Commission, appointed by Johnson, concluded that Oswald acted alone, but Oswald himself was killed before he had a chance to give full testimony. Many experts dispute the Warren Commission conclusion.

140. The Kennedy assassination fomented passage of the Twenty-fifth Amendment, which provides for a more orderly system of replacement. Previously, when a vice president ascended to the White House after the death or removal of a president, the vice presidency was left vacant. The amendment provides for presidential appointment of a vice president to fill the vacant spot. It also provides for at least temporary replacement of the president in the case of disability. The latter provision developed out of a concern that the country could have become leaderless had Kennedy been physically or mentally impaired but not killed.

141. Barber, *Pulse of Politics*, 167.

142. Thomas Ferguson and Joel Rogers, *Right Turn: The Decline of the Democrats and the Future of American Politics* (New York: Hill and Wang, 1986), 53.

143. Theodore H. White, *The Making of the President 1964* (New York: New American Library, 1965), 261.

144. Ibid., 353.

145. The central importance of economic conditions to electoral politics is widely documented. See, for example, Stanley Kelley Jr., *Interpreting Elections* (Princeton, N.J.: Princeton University Press, 1983); Edward R. Tufte, *Political Control of the Economy* (Princeton, N.J.: Princeton University Press, 1978); and Campbell, et al., *The American Voter*. On the link between economic conditions and the 1964 election, see Kelley, *Interpreting Elections*, 194.

146. Stanley Karnow, *Vietnam: A History* (New York: Viking, 1983), 358.

147. Ibid., 362.

148. Ibid., 395.

149. James David Barber, *The Presidential Character* (Englewood Cliffs, N.J.: Prentice-Hall, 1972), 34.

150. Karnow, *Vietnam*, 403.

151. Ibid., 479.

152. David Halberstam, *The Best and the Brightest* (New York: Random House, 1969).

153. Sundquist, *Dynamics of the Party System*, 384.

154. Ibid., 383.

155. The administration plank supported a bombing halt only when it "would not endanger the lives of our troops in the field," did not call for a reduction in search-and-destroy missions or a withdrawal of troops until the end of the war, and advocated a new government in Saigon only after the war had ended. The minority plank, drafted by McCarthy and McGovern, called for an immediate halt to the bombing, reduction of offensive operations in the South Vietnamese countryside, a negotiated troop withdrawal, and encouragement of the South Vietnamese government to negotiate with communist insurgents. After nearly three hours of debate, the minority plank was defeated, 1,567¾ to 1,041¼.

156. Theodore H. White, *The Making of the President 1968* (New York, Atheneum, 1969), 371.

157. Roseboom, *History of Presidential Elections*, 603.

158. See Russell Baker, *The Next President* (New York: Dell, 1968).

159. David Broder, "The Story That Still Nags at Me," *Washington Monthly*, February 1987, 29–32. See also Theodore H. White, *Making of the President 1972* (New York: New American Library, 1973), 82.

160. White, *Making of the President 1972*, 129.

161. Ibid., 207.

162. On the politics of the period, see Sundquist, *Dynamics of the Party System*, 393–411; and Theodore H. White, *America in Search of Itself* (New York: Harper and Row, 1981). Good accounts of the Watergate scandal include those by Theodore H. White, *Breach of Faith* (New York: Atheneum, 1975); Jonathan Schell, *The Time of Illusion* (New York: Knopf, 1976); and Lewis Chester et al., *Watergate* (New York: Ballantine, 1973).

163. See Bruce Odes, ed., *From the President: Richard Nixon's Secret Files* (New York: Harper and Row, 1989).

164. Seymour Hersch, "The Pardon," *Atlantic*, August 1983, 55–78.

165. David J. Vogler, *The Politics of Congress* (Boston: Allyn and Bacon, 1977), 15–20, 25–26, 34, 147–155, 243–245.

166. For a good account of Jimmy Carter's 1976 Iowa victory, see Hugh Winebrenner, *The Iowa Precinct Caucuses* (Ames: University of Iowa Press, 1987), 67–93.

167. Jules Witcover, *Marathon* (New York: Viking, 1977), 274–288.

168. Ibid., 545–560.

169. Responding to a question during a debate, Ford said: "There is no Soviet domination of Eastern Europe, and there never will be under a Ford administration. . . . I don't believe . . . that the Yugoslavians consider themselves dominated by the Soviet Union. I don't believe that the Romanians consider themselves dominated by the Soviet Union. I don't believe that the Poles consider themselves dominated by the Soviet Union" (ibid., 597, 598).

170. See Gary Sick, *October Surprise: America's Hostages in Iran and the Election of Ronald Reagan* (New York: Times Books, 1992).

171. Richard Harwood, ed., *The Pursuit of the Presidency 1980* (New York: Berkeley, 1980), 305–307.

172. Thomas Byrne Edsall, *The New Politics of Inequality* (New York: Norton, 1984), 77–78.

173. George Gilder, *Wealth and Poverty* (New York: Basic Books, 1980). Another prominent supply-side tract is that by Jude Wanniski, *The Way the World Works* (New York: Basic Books, 1978). A sympathetic summary of the whole movement can be found in Robert Craig Paul, *The Supply-Side Revolution* (Cambridge, Mass.: Harvard University Press, 1984).

174. Ferguson and Rogers, *Right Turn*, 86–88, n. 245.

175. Garry Wills, *Reagan's America: Innocents at Home* (Garden City, N.Y.: Doubleday, 1987), 387.

176. Ibid., 385.

177. Thomas Ferguson and Joel Rogers, *Right Turn* (New York: Hill and Wang, 1986), 26.

178. Rep. Shirley Chisholm of Brooklyn, New York, was the first black to seek a major-party nomination. Her participation in the 1972 Democratic primaries won 151 delegates.

179. Geraldine Ferraro, with Linda Bird Francke, *Ferraro: My Story* (New York: Bantam, 1985), 164.

180. Paul R. Abramson, John H. Aldrich, and David W. Rohde, *Change and Continuity in the 1984 Elections*, rev. ed. (Washington, D.C.: CQ Press, 1986), 58.

181. V. O. Key Jr., "A Theory of Critical Elections," *Journal of Politics* 17 (February 1955): 3–18.

182. Abramson et al., *Change and Continuity*, 286–287.

183. Michael Barone and Grant Ujifusa, *The Almanac of American Politics: 1984* (Washington, D.C.: National Journal, 1983), xiv. See also Ladd and Hadley, *American Party System*, 237–249.

184. Taylor, *See How They Run*, 76.

185. Also that year, two Supreme Court nominees, Robert H. Bork and Douglas H. Ginsburg, failed to win Senate confirmation. Bork lost because

of his views on a wide variety of social issues, but many criticisms focused on his personality. Ginsburg withdrew from consideration after revelations that he had smoked marijuana as a student and law school professor.

186. Barbara Norrander, *Super Tuesday: Regional Politics and Presidential Primaries* (Lexington: University Press of Kentucky, 1992), 101.

187. In the twelve days after Bush picked Quayle, ABC, CBS, and NBC aired ninety-three stories about him—more than Michael Dukakis received during the whole primary season. Two-thirds of the stories were negative. See Taylor, *See How They Run*, 162.

188. Nelson W. Polsby and Aaron Wildavsky, *Presidential Elections: Contemporary Strategies of American Electoral Politics*, 8th ed. (New York: Basic Books, 1991), 248.

189. Quayle did not meet the requirements set for political science majors and failed the first general examination at DePauw University in Indiana. He also failed to gain admission to law school under the usual application procedure. A study of Quayle's congressional career concludes that Quayle had no policy achievements in the House of Representatives but mastered some policy issues in the Senate. See Anthony Lewis, "The Intimidated Press," *New York Times*, January 19, 1989, 27; and Richard F. Fenno Jr., *The Making of a Senator: Dan Quayle* (Washington, D.C.: CQ Press, 1988).

190. *The Presidency A to Z* (Washington, D.C.: Congressional Quarterly, 1992), 29.

191. Sidney Blumenthal, *Pledging Allegiance: The Last Campaign of the Cold War* (New York: HarperCollins, 1990), 317.

192. Michael Duffy and Dan Goodgame, *Marching in Place: The Status Quo Presidency of George Bush* (New York: Simon and Schuster, 1992), 267–268.

193. Quoted in Michael Nelson, "The Presidency: Clinton and the Cycle of Politics and Policy," in *The Elections of 1992*, ed. Michael Nelson (Washington, D.C.: CQ Press, 1993), 144.

194. Paul J. Quirk and Jon K. Dalager, "The Election: A 'New Democrat' and a New Kind of Presidential Campaign," in Nelson, *Elections of 1992*, 61.

195. The unofficial manifesto of this movement is that by George F. Will, *Restoration: Congress, Term Limits, and the Recovery of Deliberative Democracy* (New York: Free Press, 1993).

196. Perot's rescue of employees from Tehran during the 1979 Iranian revolution, for example, resulted in a bestselling book—Ken Follett's *On Wings of Eagles* (New York: Morrow, 1983)—and a made-for-TV movie. Earlier, he had founded a national organization to support President Nixon's Vietnam policy. Later, his company's merger with General Motors provoked a public dispute that cast him as the problem solver and GM officials as entrenched bureaucrats.

197. Ryan J. Barilleaux and Randall E. Adkins, "The Nominations: Process and Patterns," in Nelson, *Elections of 1992*, 38–39.

198. See David Osborne and Ted Gaebler, *Reinventing Government: How the Entrepreneurial Spirit Is Transforming the Public Sector* (Reading, Mass.: Addison-Wesley, 1992), for a manifesto of Clinton's approach to government reform.

199. For an excellent treatment of the importance of the middle class and suburbanism on modern American politics, see Thomas Byrne Edsall and Mary D. Edsall, *Chain Reaction: The Impact of Race, Rights, and Taxes on American Politics* (New York: Norton, 1991).

200. Barilleaux and Adkins, "The Nominations," 48–49.

201. Duffy and Goodgame, *Marching in Place*.

202. *Congressional Quarterly Weekly Report*, supplements, July 4, 1992, 71, and August 8, 1992, 67.

203. Daniel Hellinger and Dennis R. Judd, *The Democratic Facade* (Belmont, Calif.: Wadsworth, 1994), 180.

204. Al Gore, *Earth in the Balance: Ecology and the Human Spirit* (Boston: Houghton Mifflin, 1992).

205. Ross K. Barker, "Sorting Out and Suiting Up: The Presidential Nominations," in *The Election of 1992*, ed. Gerald M. Pomper (Chatham, N.J.: Chatham House, 1993), 67.

206. See Mark J. Rozell and Clyde Wilcox, "It Isn't the Old Christian Right Anymore," *Los Angeles Times*, April 29, 1996, B5.

207. See Clyde Wilcox and Mark J. Rozell, "Dole's Delicate Balancing Act," *Christian Science Monitor*, June 4, 1996, 20.

208. "Polls and the Election," *The Public Perspective*, December 1996/January 1997, 58.

209. Howard Kurtz, "A Big Story: But Only Behind the Scenes; Media Fretted Over Reporting Dole Affair," *Washington Post*, November 13, 1996, D1.

210. Green Party candidate Ralph Nader polled 0.7 percent and Libertarian Harry Browne polled 0.5 percent. Rhodes Cook, "Even with Higher Vote, Clinton Remains Minority President," *Congressional Quarterly Weekly Report*, January 18, 1997, 185–188.

211. Howard Fineman, "Clinton's Big Win," *Newsweek*, November 18, 1996, 8–13; Rhodes Cook, "Clinton's Easy Second-Term Win Riddles GOP Electoral Map," *Congressional Quarterly Weekly Report*, November 9, 1996, 3189–3194.

212. See Richard L. Berke, "Clinton Wins Second Term by Solid Margin," *New York Times*, November 6, 1996.

## SELECTED BIBLIOGRAPHY

Abramson, Paul R., John H. Aldrich, and David W. Rohde. *Change and Continuity in the 1988 Elections*. Washington, D.C.: CQ Press, 1990.

Barber, James David. *The Pulse of Politics: Electing Presidents in the Media Age*. New York: Norton, 1992.

Blumenthal, Sidney. *Pledging Allegiance: The Last Campaign of the Cold War*. New York: HarperCollins, 1990.

Buell, Emmett H., Jr., and Lee Seligman. *Nominating the President*. Knoxville: University of Tennessee Press, 1991.

Burnham, Walter Dean. *Critical Elections and the Mainsprings of American Politics*. New York: Norton, 1970.

Burns, James MacGregor. *The Deadlock of Democracy*. Englewood Cliffs, N.J.: Prentice-Hall, 1963.

Ceaser, James W. *Presidential Selection: Theory and Development*. Princeton, N.J.: Princeton University Press, 1979.

Chambers, William Nisbet, and Walter Dean Burnham, eds. *The American Party Systems: Stages of Development*. New York: Oxford University Press, 1967.

Chase, James S. *Emergence of the Presidential Nominating Convention: 1789–1832*. Urbana: University of Illinois Press, 1973.

Cunningham, Noble E., Jr., ed. *The Making of the American Party System: 1789–1809*. Englewood Cliffs, N.J.: Prentice-Hall, 1965.

Davis, James W. *National Conventions in an Age of Party Reform*. Westport, Conn.: Greenwood Press, 1983.

Edsall, Thomas Byrne, and Mary D. Edsall. *Chain Reaction: The Impact of Race, Rights, and Taxes on American Politics*. New York: Norton, 1991.

Ferguson, Thomas, and Joel Rogers. *Right Turn: The Decline of the Democrats and the Future of American Politics*. New York: Hill and Wang, 1986.

Heard, Alexander. *Made in America: Improving the Nomination and Election of Presidents*. New York: HarperCollins, 1991.

———, and Michael Nelson, eds. *Presidential Selection*. Durham, N.C.: Duke University Press, 1987.

Hofstadter, Richard. *The Idea of a Party System*. Berkeley: University of California Press, 1969.

Ladd, Everett Carll, Jr., and Charles D. Hadley. *Transformations of the American Party System*. New York: Norton, 1978.

Maisel, L. Sandy. *The Parties Respond: Changes in American Parties and Campaigns*. Boulder, Colo.: Westview, 1994.

Orren, Gary R., and Nelson W. Polsby, eds. *Media and Momentum: The New Hampshire Primary and Nomination Politics*. Chatham, N.J.: Chatham House, 1987.

Polsby, Nelson W., and Aaron Wildavsky. *Presidential Elections: Contemporary Strategies of American Electoral Politics*. 8th ed. New York: Basic Books, 1991.

Pomper, Gerald. *Passions and Interests: Political Party Concepts of American Democracy*. Lawrence: University Press of Kansas, 1992.

Reichley, A. James, ed. *Elections American Style*. Washington, D.C.: Brookings, 1987.

———. *The Life of the Parties: A History of American Political Parties*. New York: Free Press, 1992.

Roseboom, Eugene H., and Alfred E. Eckes Jr. *A History of Presidential Elections*. 4th ed. New York: Macmillan, 1979.

Rosenstone, Steven J., Roy L. Behr, and Edward H. Lazarus. *Third Parties in America*. Princeton, N.J.: Princeton University Press, 1984.

Sabato, Larry J. *The Party's Just Begun*. Glenview, Ill.: Scott, Foresman, 1988.

Sundquist, James L. *The Dynamics of the Party System: Alignment and Realignment of Political Parties in the United States*. Washington, D.C.: Brookings, 1983.

White, Theodore H. *America In Search of Itself: The Making of the President, 1956–1980*. New York: Harper and Row, 1982.

———. *The Making of the President 1960*. New York: Atheneum, 1961.

# Illustration Credits and Acknowledgments

**Chapter 1 The Electoral Process**

4 Library of Congress   5 Library of Congress   9 Library of Congress   10 (both) Library of Congress   12 Moorland-Spingarn Research Center   14 (left) National Portrait Gallery, Smithsonian Institution, (right) Library of Congress   16 Theodore Roosevelt Collection, Harvard College Library   21 (both) Library of Congress   23 Library of Congress   35 no credit   37 Library of Congress   39 UPI/Bettmann Newsphotos   58 (both) no credit   59 (both) Library of Congress   61 The Garrison Studio   67 UPI/Bettmann Newsphotos   68 R. Michael Jenkins   73 AP/Wide World Photos   75 Wide World Photos   79 Jimmy Carter Library   81 UPI/Bettmann Newsphotos   83 Library of Congress   86 no credit   87 R. Michael Jenkins   90 Owen W. H. Blackstar   91 Library of Congress   93 Library of Congress   95 Library of Congress   100 Courtesy of Princeton University Library   101 Gerald R. Ford Library   104 AP/Wide World Photos   106 Courtesy of League of Women Voters   108 UPI/Bettmann Newsphotos   111 Smithsonian Institution   112 Smithsonian Institution   117 (top) Judith Barry Smith, (bottom) UPI/Bettmann Newsphotos   119 UPI/Bettmann   120 no credit   124 (both) Library of Congress   126 (both) Library of Congress   128 (all) Library of Congress

**Chapter 2 Taking Office**

141 R. Michael Jenkins   143 Library of Congress   145 R. Michael Jenkins   146 Ronald Reagan Library   147 Architect of the Capitol

**Chapter 3 Chronology of Presidential Elections**

150 John Frost, *History of the United States, 1836;* The New York Public Library   151 Library of Congress   153 Courtesy of the New-York Historical Society, New York City   158 Library of Congress   166 The Bettmann Archive   167 Library of Congress   169 Library of Congress   172 Library of Congress   175 Library of Congress   176 Library of Congress   177 Library of Congress   180 (left) Library of Congress, (right) Theodore Roosevelt Collection, Harvard College Library   182 Library of Congress   184 Franklin D. Roosevelt Library   185 Smithsonian Institute   187 The Bettmann Archive   188 Franklin D. Roosevelt Library   192 (left) Library of Congress, (center) Library of Congress, (right) Courtesy of the New-York Historical Society, New York City   196 From the collection of the St. Louis Mercantile Library Association   197 Courtesy of the Dwight D. Eisenhower Library   199 Charleston Gazette   202 Library of Congress   204 AP/Wide World Photos   208 Sygma   211 UPI/Bettmann Newsphotos   213 David Valdez, White House   217 Reuters/Bettmann   218 MTV   221 Reuters

# Index